the irish SPOR[TS] ALMANAC 1999

published by
artcam ireland ltd, inishowen, co. donegal
tel: (077) 68686 *fax:* (077) 68687
international code: 00-353-77
e-mail address: editor@artcamil.iol.ie

executive editor *damian dowds*
associate editor *dónal campbell*
sub-editors *helen curley, pat mc art*
chief researcher *anita gallagher*
design-layout *dónal campbell*
sports logos *fergal grant*
printed by *techman ireland ltd.*

ISBN *0 9529596 4 X*

THE NEW *BIBLE* OF IRISH SPORT

EDITOR'S INTRO

by ***damian dowds***

EDITOR, IRISH SPORTS ALMANAC

WELCOME to the **Irish Sports Almanac 1999**, the most complete and comprehensive compendium of statistics relating to Irish sport ever assembled. The genesis of this book lies in the production of **The Irish Almanac and Yearbook of Facts,** the third edition of which has recently been published. The amount of information relating to sport assembled for that publication convinced us that a sports equivalent could be produced.

In the course of the following pages you will find a wealth of information on over 40 Irish sports and a useful Chronology of the Sports Year which sets the sports in context. The sports are arranged alphabetically with each chapter containing results from the past twelve months, an easy to read factfile on the sport and a substantial record section detailing past winners of national competitions. The sporting year in pictures, a comprehensive biographical section on Irish sporting greats, a detailed breakdown of lottery funding to Irish sport since 1987 and a directory of Irish sports bodies are all to be found and much, much more besides

Leading figures from the sports media and the world of Irish sport generously agreed to pen articles which provide interesting and sometimes provocative reading. Rugby internationalist Victor Costello on the new professionalism which has embraced his sport, former Irish international boxer Mick Dowling on boxing, Liam Horan of the *Irish Independent* on Gaelic Games, Steve Beacom of the *Belfast Telegraph* on Irish soccer, journalist and former international swimmer Chalkie White on a turbulent year in swimming, Keith Duggan of *The Irish Times* on his recollections of the sporting year, BLÉ PRO Patsy McGonagle on an outstanding year for Irish Athletics and David Walsh of *The Sunday Times* on the humbling of Tour de France.

This book could not have been completed without the help and expertise of countless officials, secretaries, public relations officers and private individuals across the country who patiently answered our queries, suggested sources, completed questionnaires, looked up dates, times and winners. When one considers many of these people work in a voluntary capacity, their helpfulness is even more praiseworthy. To all those who helped us, we offer our sincerest thanks. While the response was overwhelmingly positive it was not without its difficulties. Some organisations with limited resources and records were unable to help while a few did not respond at all to our repeated requests for information. We hope that this can be rectified in future editions.

It is envisaged that this will become, like its sister publication, an annual publication. So whether you're an avid fan or an armchair enthusiast, enjoy the book. Read, browse or skim as you require, settle that long running sports argument and look out for the next edition.

Damian Dowds

Damian Dowds
EDITOR

ACKNOWLEDGMENTS

The Editors and Researchers would like to thank the following people and organisations for their much valued assistance in compiling information for this publication:

Ita Barry and Patsy McGowan - BLÉ; Marie Scully - Irish Basketball Association; Cora Harris - Golfing Union of Ireland; Pat Turvey, Brigid McCaw, Mary Power, Liz Foley, Helen Sweeney, Netta Colgan - Irish Ladies Golf Union; Irene Johnston - Irish Ladies Hockey Union; Joan Morgan - Irish Hockey Union; Bobby Clinton - Irish Tarmac Championship Registrar; Alex Sinclair - RIAC Motorsport Department; Harry Havelin - Motorcycle Union of Ireland; Eavan Lyons, Paul Byrne, Pat Cawley, John Coleman, Michael Reid and Pat Geraghty - Irish Rugby Football Union; Paula Jordan - Republic of Ireland Billiards and Snooker Association; Brendan McKenna - Football Association of Ireland; Veronica Byrne and Joan Mulcahy - Irish Amateur Swimming Association; Jan Singleton - Tennis Ireland; Seán Crowley - Irish Amateur Boxing Association; John Wright and Gerry Byrne - Irish Cricket Union; Sheila Wallace - Cumann Camógaíochta na nGael; Helen O'Rourke and Finbarr O'Driscoll - Ladies Gaelic Football Association; Eamonn Cusack, Brian Gleeson and Austin Mallon - the Department of Tourism Sport and Recreation; Norman McCloskey and Billy Stickland - INPHO; John Keane - Secretary, North American GAA Board; Tracey Durkin - Secretary, Canadian GAA Board; Denise McLaughlin - Donegal; Gerard McNamara - Galway; Marshall Gillespie - author, Northern Ireland Football Players Directory; Michael Hayes, Dublin; Gerard Callaghan - Donegal; Pearse Callaghan - Donegal; Feargal MacGiolla - Leitrim; Ciarán Doherty - Tuam; Simon Hunter and Patrick Murphy - Northern Ireland Volleyball Association; The Irish Horse Racing Authority; William Campbell - Irish Football Association; Hugh O'Rorke - Irish Federation of Sea Anglers, Dublin; Brendan Coulter - National Coarse Fishing Federation of Ireland, Cavan; Victor Refausse - Ulster Coarse Fishing Federation, Tyrone; John Feeney - Badminton Union of Ireland, Dublin; Lisa Royal - Northern Ireland Blind Sports; Ann Lyster - Irish BlindSports, Dublin; Jack Burke (RIP) - Bowling League of Ireland, Dublin; June Fincher - Ladies Bowling League of Ireland, Dublin; D. Hunter - Irish Indoor Bowling Association, Belfast; Tara Martin - Equestrian Federation of Ireland, Dublin; Shay McDonald - Irish Amateur Gymnastics Association, Dublin; Jim Graves - Northern Ireland Ice Hockey, Belfast; Bertie Nicholson - Taekwondo Association of Northern Ireland, Lisburn; Rosemary McWhinney - Northern Ireland Netball Association, Belfast; Martin Burke - Olympic Council of Ireland, Dublin; Rebecca Middleton & Sal Shield - British Olympic Association, London; Claire Hunt - Special Olympics Ireland, Dublin; Wendy Henderson - The Sports Council for Northern Ireland, Belfast; Tommy Campbell - PRO, Federation of Irish Cyclists, Dublin; John Keane - Darts; Stephen Hannon - Irish Canoe Union; Jane Shorten - Croquet Association of Ireland; John McCullough and Frank Ryan - Irish Orienteering Association; Michael Hayes - Pitch and Putt Union of Ireland; Peadar Casey - Irish Amateur Rowing Union; Moira MacNamara - Irish Squash; David O'Donnell - Sligo; Zoë Lally - Irish Surfing Association, Sligo; Nuala Hubbard - Tug-of-War Association; Michael McAuley - Irish Amateur Wrestling Association; Richard Farrell and Rita - Community Games Head Office; Pauline Murray - Royal Yachting Association; Sophie - Irish Sailing Association, Dublin; Donal Mulligan; Rosie McArt, Burt; Michael Curley - Sligo; Mary McLaughlin - Derry; a special thank you to Philip O'Dwyer - Buncrana; and as always Colm McKenna for his continued support and advice, without which this book would not be possible. ❑

QUICK CONTENTS

FREQUENTLY USED ABBREVIATIONS

"-" Information less than 0.5 of a unit or not available
approx. approximately
assoc. association
avg. Average
b. born
d. died
excl. excluding
incl. including
Ire. Ireland
mth month
no. Number
tba To be announced
v versus

AIL All Ireland League
BLÉ Bord Luthchleas Éireann
BBC British Broadcasting Corporation
CAI Croquet Association of Ireland
DCU Dublin City University
DIT Dublin Institute of Technology
GAA Gaelic Athletic Association
FAI Football Association of Ireland
FAI PD Football Association of Ireland Premier Division
FINA Federation Internationale de Natation Amateur
GUI Golfing Union of Ireland
IAAF International Amateur Athletics Federation
IABA Irish Amateur Boxing Assoc.
IARU Irish Amateur Rowing Union
IASA Irish Amateur Swimming Association
IAWA Irish Amateur Wrestling Association
IBA Irish Basketball Association
ICU Irish Cricket Union
IFA Irish Football Association.
IFA PD Irish Football Association Premier Division
IHA Irish Horseracing Authority
ILGU Irish Ladies Golf Union
ILHU Irish Ladies Hockey Union
IOA Irish Orienteering Association.
IRFU Irish Rugby Football Union
ISA The Irish Sailing Association
ISA Irish Surfing Association.
IT Institute(s) of Technology
NI Northern Ireland
MHC Minor Hurling Championship
NFL National Football League
NHL National Hurling League
NUI National University of Ireland
OCI Olympic Council of Ireland
PGA Professional Golfing Association
QUB Queen's University Belfast
RIAC Royal Irish Automobile Club
ROI Republic of Ireland
RTÉ Radio Telefís Éireann
RYA Royal Yachting Association
SFC Senior Footballing Championship
SHC Senior Hurling Championship
TT Tourist Trophy *Motor cycling*
UCC University College Cork *(NUI, Cork)*
UCD University College Dublin *(NUI, Dublin)*
UCG University College Galway *(NUI, Galway)*
UEFA European Union of Football Associations
UK United Kingdom
UL University of Limerick
US / USA United States of America
UTV Ulster Television
WAA World Athletic Association
WBO World Boxing Organisation
WBA World Boxing Association
WBC World Boxing Council

MEASUREMENTS:
Metric units are used in most cases throughout this book.
cm centimetre
g grams
kg Kilogram
km Kilometre
m metre
s / secs seconds
mins minutes
feet ft or '
inches ins. or "
st. stone

INTRODUCTION

of success, sonia and seedy sports stars

by **keith duggan**

THE IRISH TIMES

WHAT goes around comes around. Just over 12 months ago, Maurice Fitzgerald, lithe and tanned, could be found ghosting and dancing his way to 1-10 on a crisp afternoon in New York. Kerry were All-Ireland football champions and Fitzgerald, The Man, was at his most enigmatic. There was talk of him packing his bags permanently and going off to conversions for the new England Patriots. Maurice stayed in Cahirciveen. "There'll be little that will stop the Kingdom next year", we declared. So Kildare ran them ragged, Maurice flickered and fretted in the corner and Paidí O'Shea embraced the loss with that gap-toothed smile.

"Nothing there to stop now", we asserted. Kildare listened. Galway arrived in Croke Park in September, spun a beguiling plan based on speed and the traditional long game and stole our hearts.

Thus, the gaelic football sporting year orbits around itself, seamlessly drifting into the new winter season of frostbitten games and running in the shadows, thought all the time turning to next summer. September's All-Ireland football Final was, deservedly or not, the most eagerly devoured sporting fixture on this island. In Croke Park, on television, on the Internet, we witnessed some of the prettiest football played in over a decade of Septembers and already the final has been hailed as a classic. But what of the year itself?

How will 1998, as it prepares to cocoon itself in English soccer and European rugby, how will it be viewed in retrospect? Sadly, it is not unlikely that by 2008, the untimely death of Florence Griffith Joyner will be the abiding memory of this 12 months of sport. For some reason, the relevance of the athlete's passing has been glossed over by the majority of American commentators and received token coverage in Ireland and Britain. Although East European athletes have suffered unnoticed and premature death through drug abuse long before Joyner, she, through her life and death, seems to embody the barren, dead zone of substance abuse. While she persistently denied an impropriety, Flo-Jo had always been eyed with suspicion and was all but of accused by her fellow American Evelyn Ashford in Seoul. The images of those games, Joyner's blistering speed in the 100m final, her hard appeal and shiny smile, all carry poignancy now.

And the spectre of substance abuse has impinged upon the Irish consciousness like never before. Michelle de Bruin is preparing for court in an effort to ward off ignominy. We argued her case on phone-in radio shows and said it couldn't be so. The Tour de France briefly seduced us with glorious colour and magnitude, but no sooner had it departed our shores than the fetid stench of a sport in the throes in decay drifted back across the channel. Now come the revelations that Irish rugby is tainted.

There is no escaping the sourness. Just last month, tales of a modern-day Babe Ruth were made known here via smoke-signal and random sports columns. Mark McGwire had spent the summer slugging baseballs out of American ball parks. Notched up 70 and is now mentionable in the same breath as the Babe and Roger Maris. That a chemical substance which would have left him hung in many sports was found in his locker was over looked by the vast majority of Americans, who crave home-spun heroes like no other nation.

Against this seedy backdrop, the sporting year was played out. There were moments to celebrate all right, frozen moments of sublime and simple athletic brilliance, some of which were set in these lands, others in distant arenas.

Television marketing for the World cup went into over-drive around New Year's Day last. By the time the happy event came around, the public had been bludgeoned by saturation coverage alone into watching the games. it was, overall, a much more memorable affair than USA '94 (and nobody got shot).

What stands out? Denis Bergkamp's clinical poise as he stunned Argentina with a last-minute goal in the quarter final. The speed and exuberance of Michael Owen, also against the Argentinians. Lilian Thuram. A bloated Michel Platini in the stands. And there were other memories. The maiming of Daniel Nivel by German hooligans. The character assassination of David Beckham on the same pages which deified him a week previous to his sending-off. Ronaldo, who crumbled on the eve of the final, finally wilting under the glare of an expectant world, mesmerised a combination of his talent and the hype which has buoyed him. Against that, the blossoming of Zinedane Zidane. The French elevated mass celebration into a sophisticated expression of their culture. If only they hosted it all the time.

The year divided itself around that colossal event.

In April, Mark O'Meara showed magnificent poise in taking the US Masters title, birdying the last two holes to defeat David Duval by a single shot.

On the same Sunday afternoon, one DJ Carey returned from retirement against Laois in Nowlan Park. Two weeks later we bade farewell to Paul McGrath. He accepted the sustained applause of 39,000 with that same shy unassuming grace. Lengthy evenings provided a clarion call to the championship. Mayo fell, Offaly, new champions, were scythed, Limerick were wiped off the hurling board. The weeks passed and steadily they dropped. Summer events paraded their wares in the shadow of the World Cup. Pete Sampras took his fifth Wimbledon title in a row. Jana Novotna took her first, to everyone's delight. Early July in Croke Park and Kilkenny scalped Offaly in a much maligned Leinster Hurling Final. The Mardi Gras stuff was going on in Munster.

Brian Kerr inspired one of the more memorable occasions of the year, when Ireland defeated Germany 4-3 on penalties to win the European Youth Soccer Championships, following hot on the heels of his U-16 squad.

In August, the domestic summer turned on an unprecedented sequence of events climaxing with refer Jimmy Cooney's time-keeping error as Clare went on to defeat Offaly. A pitch protest and debate gave way to a replay. Offaly, their morale in tatters just weeks earlier, played their way back to the Final. Clare folk were left bewildered.

The month closed with the gladdening, once familiar sight of Sonia O'Sullivan rejoicing again. She captured the European 5,000m Championship with a breath-taking sprint on the home straight, leaving Romania's Gabriela Szabo for dead. Kildare's fantasy days continued as they beat Kerry for a place in the All-Ireland final. That same afternoon, Irishman Eddie Jordan watched on as his cars took first and second place in the Belgian Grand Prix. Relief gave way to tears but days later, it became apparent that he would lose the services of precocious young German starlet, Ralf Schumacher.

Onwards the year trundled, with moments good and bad. Offaly took the All-Ireland hurling title with pure, blinding skill, a fortnight before Galway finished the football season. Word broke that Sky was to buy Manchester United. Ireland's soccer team raised hopes with a win over Croatia. A youngster from Sligo went to Holland and won himself the world junior cycling championship. Mark Scanlon, a name for the future, just like Emily Maher and the kids who make up Brian Kerr's team sheets.

In short, the year left Ireland with much to celebrate. But for this fan, sport in 1998 belonged to an unforgettable moment on a hard-wood floor in far off Utah. In the NBA Championship, the Chicago Bulls returned to the home of Jazz for the penultimate game in the Series. Utah, led by the legendary combination of Karl Malone and John Stockton had them licked too. Just forgot about Michael Jordan. With Chicago down three in the final minute, Jordan drove for a lay-up. On the next play, he stripped the ball from Malone, dribbled up court, let the clock run and drained a jump-shot for the Championship. Although played out before a worldwide TV audience, this wonderful sequence encapsulated the very essence of sport; simplicity combined with poise and athleticism. No-one will ever come closer to perfecting a sport than Jordan has with basket ball.

It was a late-night moment which passed largely unnoticed in this country, except in isolated quarters. Minutes after the result, a good friend called from Sean Ferguson's bar in Ballyshannon. It was late and he and the proprietor had supped a fair few in isolation as they watched events unfold in Utah.

"That F****n' Jordan" he drawled down the phone. "Can you believe him?"

Not a bad way to remember 1998.

TOP SPORTS STORIES

THE BIG STORIES IN SPORT: October 1997 to September 1998

SONIA'S BIG BIG YEAR

This past year marked a watershed in the career of Sonia O'Sullivan, emerging from the debris of the previous two seasons she won two World and two European titles. Never had she enjoyed such a successful season in terms of major championships won, in previous years O'Sullivan proved all but unbeatable on the Grand Prix Circuit but did not always deliver in the major championships. Realising that few remember Grand Prix winners and the success of an athlete's career will ultimately be judged on their record at major championships she focused solely on these. Success came in the World Cross Country Championship in March where she won both the long course (7.6km) and short course (4 km) titles within 24 hours. A summer of fourths, fifths and sixths on the Grand Prix circuit dovetailed into an unprecedented 5,000m/10,000m double victory in the European Championships. The ghosts of championships past were well and truly exorcised in 1998.

TROUBLES FOR MICHELLE DE BRUIN

It was an awful year for Irish swimming star, Michelle de Bruin. Since her glory days of Olympic success in Atlanta in 1996, there had been allegations and whispers about the reasons for that success. De Bruin eventually issued legal proceedings against a number of media outlets. However, it all reached a climax this year when she was banned by the international swimming body, FINA, for allegedly manipulating a urine sample. De Bruin has steadfastly rejected this finding, stating that she "will not go away" just to please the critics who want to believe her guilt. She is issuing proceedings against FINA to clear her name.

WORLD CUP GOLF TRIUMPH

Padraig Harrington and Paul McGinley joined an illustrious club when they won the 43rd Golf World Cup at Kiawah Island, South Carolina, scene of the 1991 Ryder Cup. Emulating the achievement of Harry Bradshaw and Christy O'Connor Senior, who won the then Canada Cup in 1958, Harrington and McGinley set a new tournament record of an aggregate 31 under par to claim the title. Five shots clear of second placed Scotland and a further shot ahead of the United States McGinley finished fourth overall and Harrington finished joint fifth. The pair moved from joint sixth after the first round, to joint second after the second round to outright second after the third round. Parallels with Ireland's 1958 victory are obvious but recompense in the intervening years has changed considerably. In 1958 Bradshaw and O'Connor Senior won £357 each with Bradshaw picking up a further £187 for finishing second overall in the individual competition. In 1997 McGinley and Harrington won $200,000 each, McGinley won a further $15,000 for finishing fourth in the individual competition while Harrington won $5,000 for equal fifth.

FEAST OR FAMINE - GALWAY EAT OUT!

For thirty-two years Galway and Connacht waited on Sam Maguire, while Kildare had waited 70. The Lilywhites of Kildare liberated from Leinster for the first time since 1956 defeated Dublin, Meath and Kerry, the 1995, '96, and '97 All-Ireland Champions respectively en route to the All-Ireland final. The Tribesmen defeated the most consistent team in the country in the previous two years, Mayo, in the first round of the Connacht championship in Castlebar, dismissed Leitrim in the semi final but stumbled against Roscommon in the Connacht decider. On final day a whiter-than-white Hill 16 looked like an advertisement for washing powder while the maroon and white on the Canal End were determined to give the old terrace a good send off. Initially Kildare's short passing game troubled Galway but poor shooting left them only a goal ahead at half-time. An unanswered goal and four points in the first ten minutes of the second half all but won the game for Galway. A last minute punched ball which rebounded off the post would have drawn Kildare level and possibly ended their famine, but it was Galway who tasted the sweet fruits of victory. Tens of thousands welcomed the victors back to the West lining the road from Ballinasloe through Moutbellew to Tuam and on to Galway. In Kildare the followers celebrated the achievement of getting there and winning their first Leinster Championship in 42 years but they must have worried about getting out of Leinster in 1999.

THREE STRIKES AND YOU'RE OUT - NOT SO FOR OFFALY HURLERS

Offaly's summer of hurling mediocrity ended with 70 glorious minutes in Offaly v Clare Part I. The resignation of Babs Keating after a Leinster final hurling lesson from Kilkenny and his replacement by little known Galway man Michael Bond turned a summer on its head. Tempers frayed in a Munster final replay in Thurles while New Offaly got to work. A workmanlike victory over Antrim was followed by a 1-13 apiece draw with Clare (Part I). That draw initiated an unparalleled sequence of events. Referee Jimmy Cooney prematurely ended Offaly v Clare Part II, apparently mistaking the length of a championship hurling half for 30 minutes, the game was declared void and a replay ordered for Thurles six days later. A weary Clare prepared for Part III (their third replay of the championship) and were beaten perhaps more convincingly than the 0-16 to 0-13 scoreline suggested. Cue an Offaly rematch with Kilkenny in the All-Ireland title decider. In the final the teamwork acquired in the three game series and the individual brilliance of Brian Whelahan secured victory leading captain Hubert Rigney to proclaim that while they may have entered by the back door, Offaly were leaving by the front.

JOY IN SOLITUDE FOR CLIFTONVILLE

April 18, 1998. Cliftonville won the Irish League for the first time since the 1909/10 season and secured entry to the preliminary round of the European Champions League. The oldest club in Ireland had its 78 year wait extended by an hour hoping the 1-1 draw with Glenavon would deliver the championship and old rivals Linfield (whose match had been delayed for an hour for what were described as 'security reasons') could not secure the result away to Coleraine which would extend the season to the last game. Linfield lost, and the usual Solitude celebrations at the demise of the old foe were dwarfed by the unrestrained outpouring of joy from the Cliftonville faithful. In the presence of former ballboy but now Irish Football Association President Jim Boyce, captain Mickey Donnelly was presented with the Gibson Cup by Irish League Vice President Jim Semple. Solitude had never in its 108 year history witnessed celebrations like it. Fans streamed onto the pitch, and the *Fields of Athenry* were once again sinned against.

CATHERINA - THE MARATHON WOMAN

Cavan woman Catherina McKiernan dominated road racing in the twelve months past. Having set the fastest ever marathon debut time of two hours 23 minutes and 44 seconds in winning the Berlin marathon in September 1997 she remained unbeaten in fourteen races until June 1998. In winning the London marathon in April McKiernan realised her huge potential in the event, London is after all, one of the most lucrative marathons on the international circuit and attracts a strong talented field. Despite her inexperience she beat the 1996 champion, Liz McColgan and the 1997 champion Joyce Chepchumba into second and third respectively and her time of two hours 26 minutes twenty six seconds was the seventh fastest time recorded in London. Success had often eluded McKiernan as evidenced by four consecutive silver medals at the World Cross Country Championships between 1992 and 1995 and under performance at major track championships but the switch to road running has already paid rich dividends. Already she is being touted as a possible Olympic champion in Sydney, but she hasn't turned her back completely on cross country. A clash between her and a certain Sonia O'Sullivan at the 1999 World Championships in Belfast is a mouth watering prospect indeed.

JORDAN'S COMING OF AGE

Eddie Jordan turned 50 somewhere in Brazil on March 30th 1998. The Brazilian Grand Prix on the previous day had seen his team underperform - Ralf Schumacher crashed out, Damon Hill finished but was disqualified for having an underweight car and now here was a cake groaning under the weight of fifty candles. The season was only two races old, Jordan were well off the pace and McLaren were miles ahead of everyone, Ferrari, Williams, Bennetton couldn't live with them, no-one could. Worse lay ahead. The season was half finished before Ralf Schumacher scraped home in sixth at the British Grand Prix in July to score Jordan's first championship point. Reliability had proven elusive all season but the Silverstone sixth proved a turning point. Damon Hill finished fourth in consecutive races, Ralf Schumacher was scoring too. The Belgian Grand Prix on August 30 was Jordan's 126th race since entering Formula 1 in 1991. In heavy rain Hill and Schumacher survived a first corner crash. After the restart the rain caused problems for others, but not the Jordan team. Hill won, Schumacher was second and Eddie Jordan wept and whooped with delight. Jordan Grand Prix had finally come of age and were well on their way to their best season points tally ever.

DOHERTY NARROWLY FAILS IN BRAVE TITLE DEFENCE

In 1998, as in 1997, Ken Doherty saved his best form for the Crucible Theatre in Sheffield, the venue of the Embassy World Championships. Despite a good showing in the 1998 Irish Masters where he was beaten 9-3 by Ronnie O'Sullivan in the final (which he was later awarded when O'Sullivan failed a drugs test) Doherty went into the World Championships in a decidedly low key way. Attention was focused elsewhere on O'Sullivan, John Higgins, Stephen Higgins and the people's champion, Jimmy White. Doherty remained out of the limelight and after defeating Lee Walker, Stephen Lee and Matthew Stephens he faced Mark Williams in the semi-final. After Williams' high profile victories and Doherty's solid but not spectacular ones Doherty found himself in a familiar position. Underdog. Thriving on this Doherty beat Williams and faced John Higgins in the final. No previous first-time champion had successfully defended his title and so it proved for Doherty. He played well, but Higgins' game was flawless. Capitalising on virtually every scoring opportunity and punishing mistakes when they occurred he ran out winner on a scoreline of 18-12. Two world finals in two years, Doherty passed the mantle of champion gracefully, and he could afford to, as runner-up he collected a cool £132,000.

LE TOUR DE FRANCE EN IRLANDE 1998

Men with shaved legs, bright jerseys and high-tech machines. Freshly tarred roads, Wicklow Gap and the peleton. *Le Grande Depart,* the caravan and French tricolours. After many years of lobbying, and then planning, the Tour de France arrived in Ireland in July. The drugs storm which later engulfed the Tour was but a distant cloud when Chris Boardman won the Prologue in Dublin City Centre on July 11th. The first stage proper rolled out of Dundrum, home of 1987 Tour winner Stephen Roche a spectacular trip over Wicklow gap was seen, we were assured, by hundreds of millions of people worldwide. The finish in the Phoenix park provided a spectacular crash. Top sprinter and one of the pre-race favourites Mario Cipollini crashed near the finish, the stage was won by Tom Steels while Cipollini, surrounded by his *domestiques,* trailed in over five minutes down. The second stage covered 200 kilometres from Enniscorthy to Cork travelling through Carrick-on-Suir, the home of Seán Kelly. The stage was won Jan Svorada but race leader Chris Boardman crashed out and failed to finish the stage and a young female spectator was also injured. The Tour and entourage then boarded three ferries and three aeroplanes and arrived in Roscoff for the start of the third stage.

❐

CHRONOLOGY

THE YEAR IN SPORT: October 1997 to September 1998

OCTOBER

02: Boxing WBO Super Middleweight champion, Steve Collins, announced his retirement from boxing. The tearful Celtic Warrior made his shock announcement in London 24 hours after his ninth title defence was cancelled on medical grounds.
Soccer Finn Harps lost 2-0 to Dundalk in the FAI PD.

03: Rugby English side Wasps defeated Ulster 38-21 in the European Cup at Ravenhill.
Snooker Nigel Bond beat Ken Doherty 6-5 in the Regal Masters quarter-final.
Soccer Results from the FAI PD: Drogheda United 2, Sligo Rovers 4; Shelbourne 3, Cork City 1.

04: Greyhound Racing Toms The Best won the £50,000 Irish Derby at Shelbourne Park.
Rugby Five penalties and a conversion by Eric Elwood led Connacht to a 22-15 victory over French side Begles in the European Conference.
Leinster beat Milan 23-6, while Munster lost 21-6 to Bourgoin in the European Cup.
Soccer In the IFA PD Cliftonville and Glenavon recorded victories while the Omagh Town/Crusaders, Portadown/Ballymena and Linfield/Coleraine games all ended with 1-1 scorelines.
In the FAI PD Derry City beat Bohemians 1-0 and Shamrock Rovers beat Kilkenny City 2-1.

05: Basketball The men's Superleague opened with victories for Star of the Sea, Killester, St Vincent's and Notre Dame.
In the women's Superleague Wildcats, Tolka Rovers, Meteors and Blarney all recorded victories.
GAA Limerick beat Galway 1-12 to 1-9 in the National League Hurling final.
Cork easily won the All-Ireland Vocational Schools Hurling final beating Galway by 4-13 to 3-3.
Antrim side, Dunloy, won the Ulster Club Hurling final beating Derry champions Lavey 3-16 to 4-10. The game was marred by a fight eight minutes into injury time which resulted in five sendings off and led to a pitch invasion. Referee, John Anthony Gribben had to be escorted from the pitch.
Golf Defending champion, Darren Clarke, finished joint seventh in the German Masters, ten shots behind winner, Bernard Langer.
Soccer In the FAI PD UCD and St Pat's drew 1-1.

07: Soccer The Republic of Ireland beat Northern Ireland 4-0 in an U18 friendly match at Tolka Park.

09: Soccer Dundalk defeated Kilkenny City 3-0 in the FAI PD.

10: Soccer Romania beat the Republic of Ireland 2-0 in the European U21 qualifying match at Drogheda.
Shamrock Rovers beat Derry City 1-0 in the FAI PD.

11: Boxing Antrim's Mark Winters beat Carl Wright on points to win the vacant British Light Welterweight title.
Cycling Finishing places of Ireland's representatives at the World Junior Championships in San Sebastian were Mark Scanlon (28th), Derek Finnegan (29th) and David McQuaid (102nd).
Rugby Toulouse beat Leinster 38-19 in the European Cup.
Connacht's good form in the European Conference continued when they beat Northampton 20-15 and qualified for the quarter-finals.
Soccer The Republic of Ireland finished second in group eight of the European World Cup qualifiers following their 1-1 draw with group winners, Romania. The Republic's qualification for the World Cup finals will be decided in a two-leg play-off.
Northern Ireland finished their qualifying group with a 1-0 defeat in Portugal.
Ballymena United, Cliftonville, Coleraine, Glentoran and Linfield all recorded victories in the IFA PD.

12: Formula 1 Ferrari's Eddie Irvine finished third in the Japanese Grand Prix at Suzuka. The Jordans of Giancarlo Fisichella and Ralf Schumacher finished outside the points in eighth and tenth places respectively.
GAA Monaghan retained their All-Ireland Women's football title beating Waterford 2-15 to 1-16 in front of 15,501 spectators in Croke Park. Longford won the women's Junior football title beating Tyrone 2-12 to 1-11 in the Croke Park curtain raiser.
Golf Paul McGinley won the Smurfit Irish PGA Championship at Fota Island by one shot from David Higgins, John McHenry and Stephen Hamill.
Rugby Munster beat Harlequins 23-16 but Ulster were beaten 30-15 by Glasgow in the European Cup.
Sailing Ballyholme Yacht Club held off hosts Royal St George Yacht Club to win the Irish Sailing Association Dinghy Team Racing National Championship.
Soccer In the FAI PD there were victories for Finn Harps, UCD and St Pat's, Bohemians drew 1-1 with Drogheda.

13: Golf Husband and wife team Eddie and Eileen Rose Power won the East of Ireland mixed foursomes.
Soccer In the FAI League Cup quarter final, Dundalk beat Cork City 2-1 after extra time.

14: GAA Eamon Cregan took over from Tom Ryan as Limerick senior hurling manager.

15: Rugby The French Barbarians beat a Lansdowne President's XV 31-24 at Lansdowne Road
Soccer Home Farm/Everton beat Cobh Ramblers 3-2 after extra time in the League Cup quarter final.

16: Golf South Africa beat the Irish team of Paul McGinley, Darren Clarke and Padraig Harrington 2-1 in the opening round of the Dunhill Cup.
Horse Racing Istabraq won his debut race of the season at Tipperary by seven lengths; Cockney Lad was second.

17: Golf Ireland lost 2-1 to Scotland in their second group match in the Dunhill Cup.
Soccer Shamrock Rovers beat Drogheda United 3-1 and Shelbourne beat Sligo Rovers 3-0 in the PD.

18: Athletics Sonia O'Sullivan won the Commonwealth

festival 5,000m road race in Edinburgh.

Basketball Ballina beat Neptune 99-89 and Dungannon beat Killester 83-78 in the men's Superleague.

GAA Maurice Fitzgerald once again led Kerry to victory when he scored 1-10 of Kerry's 1-12 to beat Cavan in the National Football League. The game was held in front of 10,000 spectators at Downing Stadium, New York. At home there were victories for Louth, Kildare and Meath in the opening games of the League.

Golf Ireland won their final match of the Dunhill Cup by defeating Germany 2-1.

Horse Racing Mick Kinnane partnered Pilsudski to victory in the Dubai Stakes at Newmarket.

Skiing S. Von Bloemandall from Holland won the Irish Open Men's Slalom at Kilternan, D. Von Bloemandall won the women's Slalom.

Soccer Linfield, Ballymena, Coleraine and Portadown all recorded victories in the Irish League while Glenavon drew 2-2 with Omagh Town.

Dundalk and Finn Harps won their FAI PD ties while the St Pat's/Bohemians tie ended scoreless.

19: Basketball There were victories for St Vincent's, Star of the Sea and Notre Dame in the men's Superleague.

In the women's Superleague, Naomh Mhuire, Limerick, Wildcats and Tolka Rovers all won their matches.

Boxing Brian Magee (Middleweight) and Damian McKenna (Bantamweight) were eliminated on points from the World Amateur Championships in Budapest. Welterweight Neil Gough and light heavyweight Steven Kirk both won their bouts.

G.A.A. Laois, Mayo, Galway, Donegal, Armagh, Tyrone, Sligo, Offaly, Cork and Wicklow all won their National Football League games. The Derry / Westmeath and Roscommon/Clare games were drawn.

Golf Derry beat Donegal in the Ulster Inter-county Championship final.

Rugby Connacht won the Ladies Interprovincial series remaining unbeaten in their four games. The Irish Exiles finished second.

Soccer Cork City beat UCD 1-0 in the FAI PD.

Sligo Rovers beat Bray Wanderers 1-0 in the League Cup quarter-final.

21: Boxing Neil Gough qualified for the World Championship quarter-finals.

Horse Racing Kieren Fallon had four winners at Folkestone with cumulative odds of 561-1.

Soccer Shelbourne beat Limerick 2-1 in the League Cup quarter-final.

22: Boxing Belfast's Steven Kirk won his quarter-final bout with Bulgarian Tamer Erolov on points. Waterford's Neil Gough lost 6-2 on points in his quarter-final.

Soccer The Republic of Ireland U18s beat Azerbaijan 4-2 in Moldova.

23: Horse Racing Champion Chaser Klairon Davis won the Dunstown Wood Chase at Fairyhouse by eleven lengths from Fiftysevenchannels.

Soccer Northern Ireland manager, Bryan Hamilton, was sacked by the IFA.

In the FAI PD the Dundalk-Drogheda United derby game ended in a 1-1 draw.

24: Boxing Steven Kirk won a bronze medal in the light heavyweight division at the World Championships when he was stopped in the second round of his semi-final by Russian Alexandr Lebziakin.

Soccer St Patrick's Athletic beat Shamrock Rovers 1-0 in the FAI PD.

The Republic of Ireland U18s beat their Moldovan counterparts 1-0 in their European qualifying group.

25: Hockey In the women's senior interprovincial, Ulster beat Connacht 5-0 before losing to Munster 2-1, Connacht lost 6-0 to Leinster and Munster drew 3-3 with Leinster.

Soccer Finn Harps, Derry City and Cork City all won their FAI PD ties.

In the IFA PD there were victories for Cliftonville, Crusaders, Glenavon, Omagh Town and Coleraine.

26: Basketball In the men's Superleague there were victories for Ballina, Star of the Sea, Notre Dame, St Paul's Killarney and UCD Marian.

In the women's Superleague Naomh Mhuire, Limerick, Meteors and Wildcats all recorded victories.

Formula 1 Eddie Irvine finished fifth in the final Grand Prix of the season, the European Grand Prix at Jerez, Spain. The Drivers' Championship was headed by Canadian Jacques Villeneuve with Irvine in eighth place overall. The Constructors' Championship was won by Williams, the Jordan team finished fifth overall.

Golf Paul McGinley recorded his second ever European PGA Tour victory in winning the Oki Pro-Am in Madrid by four shots. His four round total of 266 was 22 shots under par.

Hockey On the final day of the women's Interprovincial Championship, Munster beat Connacht 3-0 and Leinster beat Ulster 4-0. Leinster claimed the title by virtue of their superior goal difference.

Soccer Roy Keane (Senior Player), David Connolly (Young Player), Peter Hutton (National League) and Franz Beckenbauer (International Celebrity) were among the major winners at the 1997 FAI Opel Awards ceremony.

In the FAI PD Bohemians beat Shelbourne 1-0.

27: Hockey Avoca beat Pembroke 5-4 on penalty strokes to win the Stephen Doyle Trophy final.

29: Soccer The Republic of Ireland were held to a 1-1 draw by Belgium in the World Cup play-off first leg match at Lansdowne Road. Denis Irwin scored the Republic's goal from a free kick in the eighth minute, Luc Nilis equalised for Belgium on 30 minutes.

30: Hockey Bangor Grammar School won the All-Ireland School's Championship beating Ashton 4-2.

31: Soccer Drogheda drew 0-0 with Kilkenny City and Shelbourne drew 1-1 with Shamrock Rovers in the FAI Premeir Division.

Swimming Michelle de Bruin was slightly injured in a car accident in Kilkenny, putting plans to compete in January's World Championships in Australia in doubt.

NOVEMBER

01: Equestrian Sport The Volvo World Cup qualifier

held at Millstreet was won by Cruising and Trevor Coyle.

Soccer Derry City beat Finn Harps 1-0 in the FAI PD. In the IFA PD there were victories for Linfield, Portadown and Ards while Crusaders drew 2-2 with Cliftonville.

02: Basketball In the first round of the Sprite Cup for men there were victories for St Vincent's, Notre Dame, Tralee, Star of the Sea, Ballina, Blue Demons, and Tolka Rovers.

In the women's cup Naomh Mhuire, Tralee, Wildcats, and Tolka Rovers all won their ties.

GAA Mickey Whelan's two-year tenure as Dublin football manager ended when he announced his resignation after Dublin's 1-11 to 1-8 defeat to Offaly in the National League.

Elsewhere in the National League there were victories for Laois, Fermanagh and Leitrim in Section A; for Meath, Armagh, Longford and Donegal in Section B; for Kerry, Tyrone, and Monaghan in Section C; and for Cork, Kildare, and Down in Section D. The Mayo/Galway and Roscommon/Wicklow games ended in draws.

Golf Padraig Harrington finished second in the Volvo Masters at Jerez, Spain. Bad weather limited the tournament to three rounds.

Snooker Ken Doherty beat John Higgins 7-5 in the Malta Grand Prix Trophy final.

At the Ivy Rooms in Carlow Ulster won the Interprovincial Snooker Championship; Dublin finished second and Munster third.

Soccer In the FAI PD St Patrick's Athletic beat Dundalk 1-0 while the Cork City/Bohemians and UCD/Sligo Rovers games both ended with 1-1 scorelines.

Poland beat the Republic of Ireland 1-0 in the women's World Cup qualifying match at Tolka Park.

04: Soccer In the IFA PD Cliftonville beat Coleraine 3-1, Linfield beat Portadown 2-0 and Ballymena drew 0-0 with Glenavon.

05: Horse Racing Tony McCoy broke his record for the fastest 100 winners in a season by 16 days when partnering Sam Rockett to victory at Newton Abbot.

06: Hockey Trinity College ladies won the intervarsity Chilean Cup beating University College Cork in the final 2-1 after extra time.

Horse Racing Dorans Pride beat Imperial Call in the Morris Oil Chase at Clonmel.

Soccer Shelbourne beat Dundalk 1-0 in the FAI PD.

07: Soccer Bohemians drew 0-0 with UCD in the FAI PD.

08: Rugby Connacht's European adventure ended when they lost 40-27 to French side, Agen, in the quarter-finals of the European Conference.

In the semi-finals of the Leinster Senior Championship Lansdowne beat Carlow 24-6 and Terenure beat Clontarf 39-22.

In the Munster Senior Club semi-finals Cork Constitution beat Young Munster 16-14 and Garryowen beat Bohemians 36-10.

Soccer Derry City and St Pat's both won their FAI PD matches while Sligo Rovers drew 2-2 with Finn Harps. Portadown and Coleraine won their IFA PD games while the Ards/Glentoran, Glenavon/Cliftonville and Ballymena/Linfield matches ended in draws.

09: Basketball Tralee, St Vincent's, Ballina, Notre Dame and Star of the Sea all won their Men's Superleague matches.

In the women's Superleague there were victories for Wildcats, Naomh Mhuire, Meteors and Killester.

GAA Munster beat Leinster by 0-14 to 0-10 in the Railway Cup hurling final at Ballinasloe.

Louth won the All-Ireland B Football championship defeating Clare 1-11 to 1-8.

Dungiven became Ulster Club football champions defeating Errigal Ciaran 0-14 to 1-8.

Soccer Cork City beat Shamrock Rovers 3-1 in the PD.

11: Rugby Clontarf beat Old Belvedere 29-14 in the semi-final of the Old Belvedere floodlit cup.

Soccer In the first leg of the FAI League Cup semi-final Home Farm Everton drew 0-0 with Sligo Rovers.

12: Rugby Lansdowne beat Wanderers 43-17 in the semi-final of the Old Belvedere floodlit cup.

14: Soccer There were victories for Shelbourne, St Patrick's Athletic and Derry City in the FAI PD while Finn Harps drew 1-1 with Sligo Rovers.

15: Basketball St Vincent's beat Killarney 109-95 in the Men's Superleague.

Bowls Ireland, who led the six nation European Indoor team championship for much of the week long competition were pushed into second place by England. After 20 rounds of competition England had 61 points, Ireland 58.

GAA Meath beat Antrim 2-18 to 1-8 in the National Football League.

Hockey Leinster beat Munster 5-3 in the men's U21 Interprovincial championship.

Rugby Ireland conceded seven tries (with five conversions) and six penalties in the 63-15 defeat by New Zealand at Lansdowne Road.

Soccer The Republic of Ireland failed to qualify for the 1998 World Cup finals when they lost 2-1 to Belgium in the second leg play-off in Brussels. The Republic lost 3-2 on aggregate.

In the IFA PD Cliftonville beat Linfield 2-1, Portadown beat Glentoran 3-2, Crusaders beat Glenavon 3-2, Ballymena beat Omagh 4-2 and Coleraine beat Ards 2-1.

Squash The Irish team of Chris Collins, Maurice Collins, Patrick Foster and Derek Ryan finished 16th overall in the World Team Championships which were held in Kuala Lumpur, Malaysia. In the week long competition Ireland beat Austria, Brazil and Hong Kong before finally losing 2-1 to Scotland in the 15th/16th place play-off.

16: Athletics Catherina McKiernan won the 15km Seven Hills event in Amsterdam in a time of 48 minutes 30 seconds.

Basketball Notre Dame, UCD Marian, Dungannon, and Killester all won their men's Superleague ties. In the women's Superleague Wildcats, Naomh Mhuire, Tolka Rovers and Blarney won their matches.

GAA In the NFL Section A there were victories for Louth, Mayo and Leitrim while Galway drew with Laois 0-10 to 1-7. In Section B there were victories for Donegal, Derry and Longford. In Section C there were victories for Tyrone, Offaly (over All-Ireland

Champions Kerry), and Dublin, Sligo drew with Monaghan 1-11 each. In Section D there were victories for Cork, Roscommon, Kildare and Down.

Soccer In the FAI PD Cork City beat Shamrock Rovers 2-1, UCD beat Bohemians on the same scoreline.

18: Soccer Shelbourne beat Dundalk 1-0 in the first leg of the League Cup semi-final.

19: Rugby Lansdowne beat Old Belvedere 35-20 in the opening game of the AIB All Ireland League.

Snooker Ken Doherty lost 9-4 to Neal Foulds in the UK Championship.

Joe Canny was beaten 4-3 by former professional Kirk Stevens at the World Amateur Championships in Zimbabwe.

21: Soccer Shamrock Rovers beat UCD 2-0, Finn Harps beat Drogheda United 2-0 and Bohemians drew 1-1 with Sligo Rovers in the FAI PD.

22: Basketball St Paul's Killarney beat reigning champions Neptune 89-83 in the men's Superleague. Elsewhere there were victories for Notre Dame, Star of the Sea, Ballina and Killester. In the women's Superleague there were victories for Naomh Mhuire, Wild Cats, Limerick and Tolka Rovers.

Hockey Ulster retained the women's U21 Interprovincial crown.

Rugby In the All-Ireland League Division One, Clontarf beat Old Crescent 11-8, Ballymena beat Dolphin 45-16, St Mary's beat Blackrock 41-23, Shannon beat Dungannon 20-13 and Terenure beat Cork Constitution 18-15.

Snooker TJ Dowling and Joe Canny qualified for the last 32 in the World Amateur Championships in Zimbabwe.

Soccer In the IFA PD there were victories for Cliftonville and Ballymena. The Ards / Portadown, Glenavon /Coleraine and Linfield/Crusaders games all ended in draws.

In the FAI PD Stephen Geoghegan scored his 99th and 100th goals in helping Shelbourne beat Kilkenny City 3-1 and Derry City drew 1-1 with St. Patrick's Athletic.

23: Golf The Irish team of Padraig Harrington and Paul McGinley won the World Cup at Kiawah Island, South Carolina by five shots, they finished with a record 31 under par aggregate. McGinley finished fourth on the individual leaderboard with Harrington in fifth.

Rugby Garryowen drew 3-3 with Young Munster in the All-Ireland League first division clash at Dooradoyle.

Soccer Dundalk beat Cork City 1-0 in the FAI PD.

25: Golf Four new Irish golfers qualified to take part in the 1998 European PGA Tour at the qualifying school in Spain. They are: David Higgins, Cameron Grant, Richard Coughlan and Francis Howley.

Horse Racing One Man beat Viking Flagship into second place in the Peterborough Chase at Huntingdon.

Soccer Results from the IFA PD: Ards 1, Crusaders 1; Linfield 0, Portadown 0; and Glentoran 1, Omagh Town 0.

26: Rugby Ireland A beat Canada A 26-10 in a friendly at Ravenhill.

Snooker TJ Dowling progressed to the last 16 of the World Amateur Championships but Joe Canny was eliminated 5-4 by Johan Johanesson of Iceland.

27: Rugby Clontarf beat Lansdowne 15-10 in the final of the Smithwicks Old Belvedere Floodlit Cup.

Snooker TJ Dowling was knocked out of the World Amateur Championships by Englishman Stewart Bingham on a scoreline of 5-2.

Soccer George Best was voted the second best footballer of all time behind Pele in International Hall of Fame. Half a million fans recorded their votes via the Internet, Best was ahead of luminaries such as Bobby Charlton (3rd), Johan Cruyff (4th) and Franz Beckenbauer (8th)

28: Soccer Results from the FAI PD: Shelbourne 1, Derry City 0; St Patrick's Athletic 2, Drogheda United 0.

29: Hockey In the first round of the men's Irish Senior Cup, there were victories for: Civil Service, Cliftonville, Cookstown, Instonians, Lisnagarvey, North Down, Parkview, Down, Pembroke Wanderers, Raphoe, Three Rock Rovers, Down and Railway Union.

Trinity beat Harlequins 2-0 in the women's Irish Senior Cup.

Horse Racing Suny Bay, the mount of Graham Bradley, won the Hennessy Gold Cup by 13 lengths from Barton Bank.

Rugby Cork Constitution beat Garryowen 16-10 in the inaugural Munster Club Championship final.

Connacht beat Munster 15-10 in the U20 Interprovincial Championship.

Soccer Results from the IFA PD: Ballymena 1, Portadown 2; Cliftonville 0, Glentoran 2; Coleraine 1, Linfield 0; Crusaders 1, Omagh Town 0; Glenavon 1, Ards 2. The Coleraine/Linfield game was abandoned after 83 minutes due to crowd trouble.

Results from the FAI PD: Finn Harps 3, Bohemians 2; Sligo 0, Shamrock Rovers 1.

Tennis Israel beat the Irish women's team 3-0 in the European Team Championships in Malta.

30: Athletics Seamus Power retained his senior men's National Intercounties Cross-Country title with the team title going to Dublin. In the women's event Teresa Duffy emerged victorious with Donegal winning the team title.

Boxing Ireland were beaten by six bouts to four by France in an International Amateur match.

GAA There were victories for Galway, Leitrim, and Laois in Section A of the NFL, in Section B Donegal drew with Meath while Armagh, Longford and Derry all recorded victories. In Section C there were victories for Offaly, Dublin, Monaghan and Sligo and in Section D there were victories for Roscommon, Down, Clare and Kildare.

Rugby Ireland beat Canada 33-11 at Lansdowne Road, Kevin Nowlan from St Mary's College scored two of Ireland's five tries.

Soccer Results from the FAI PD: Cork City 1, Kilkenny City 0; UCD 1, Dundalk 3.

DECEMBER

02: Soccer Glenavon beat Coleraine 4-1 in the final of the Ulster Gold Cup.

03: GAA In his first budget the Minister for Finance,

Charlie McCreevy, announced the allocation of £20 million to the GAA towards the redevelopment of Croke Park.

The 1997 Hurling All-Stars were announced. Clare have six representatives, Tipperary four, Kilkenny three (including DJ Carey's sixth in seven years), while Galway and Wexford have one apiece.

Squash Derek Ryan had a walk over in the last 16 of the Madhrina tournament in Bombay.

04: Soccer Dundalk beat Sligo Rovers 5-0 in the FAI PD.

Squash World number one, Jansher Khan, beat Ireland's Derek Ryan in the quarter-final of the Madhrina Squash International tournament.

05: Basketball Notre Dame beat St Vincent's 99-85 in the men's Superleague.

GAA The 1997 Gaelic Football All-Stars were announced. All-Ireland champions Kerry received five, Kildare three, Meath and Mayo two each and Derry, Cavan and Offaly one each.

Rugby Shannon hammered Old Crescent 50-0 in Division One of the All Ireland league.

Soccer Results from the FAI PD: Drogheda 0, Shelbourne 1; St Patrick's Athletic 1, Finn Harps 0; Shamrock Rovers 2, Bohemians 1.

06: GAA Sarsfields of Galway won the Connacht Club hurling title beating Tooreen of Mayo by 5-15 to 1-5.

Hockey Church of Ireland beat Avoca 3-1 in their Irish Senior Cup replay.

Rugby Results from Division One of the All-Ireland League: Blackrock 54, Lansdowne 32; Dolphin 25, Garryowen 24; Dungannon 18, Cork Constitution 9; Old Belvedere 12, Ballymena 26; Terenure 18, St Mary's 12; Young Munster 25, Clontarf 19.

Soccer Results from IFA PD: Ards 2, Ballymena 1; Glentoran 1, Crusaders 1; Linfield 1, Glenavon 1; Omagh Town 1, Coleraine 3; Portadown 0, Cliftonville 2.

Kilkenny City drew 1-1 with UCD in the FAI PD.

07: Basketball In the men's Superleague Notre Dame, Neptune, Killarney, Dungannon and Star of the Sea all recorded victories. In the women's Superleague Blarney, Killester, Meteors and Naomh Mhuire all recorded victories.

Rallying Dessie Nutt and Elkin Robinson won the Killarney Historic Car Rally in a Porsche 911.

GAA Erin's Isle from Dublin won the AIB Leinster Club football championship while Clarecastle won the Munster Club hurling championship.

In Section D of the NFL there were victories for Cork, Tipperary and Clare.

Soccer Derry City drew 1-1 with Cork City in the FAI PD.

The Republic of Ireland beat Wales 3-0 in the women's UEFA Championship qualifiers.

08: GAA Tommy Carr was formally appointed as Dublin senior football manager.

Golf Keith Nolan and Richard Coghlan both qualified for the USA PGA Tour in 1998 when they finished 9th and 20th respectively in the qualifying school in Florida.

Rugby Leinster clinched the schools interprovincial series on a superior points difference when they beat Munster 29-5 at Anglesea Road.

Soccer Omagh Town beat Dundalk 4-2 in the Irish News Cup.

10: Soccer Padraig Horan's tenth minute goal gave Sligo Rovers a 1-0 victory over Home Farm/Everton in the League Cup semi-final second leg.

12: Cricket Ireland's women beat their Danish counterparts in the World Cup in Madras.

Soccer St Patrick's Athletic beat Shelbourne 2-0 at Tolka Park in front of 6,500 spectators.

13: Rugby Ballymena, Young Munster, Garryowen, Shannon and St. Mary's College all won their matches in the AIL Division One.

Soccer Results from the FAI PD: Finn Harps 2, Shamrock Rovers 1; Sligo Rovers 2, Kilkenny City 0.

14: Athletics Catherina McKiernan won a 6km road race in Palermo, Italy.

Cricket South Africa beat Ireland by nine wickets in the women's World Cup in India.

GAA Castlehaven won the Munster Club football championship beating Fethard 1-14 to 1-8.

Clarecastle comfortably beat St. Gabriel's in the All-Ireland Club hurling championship semi final in London.

Down beat Kildare 0-12 to 1-8 in Section D of the NFL.

Horse Racing Mick Kinane recorded another notable victory when he partnered Luso to victory in the Group Two International Vase in Hong Kong.

Rugby Lansdowne drew with Terenure College while Old Crescent lost to Cork Constitution in the AIL.

Soccer Results from the FAI PD: UCD 1, Derry City 2; Cork City 1, Drogheda 1; Bohemians 2, Dundalk 0.

16: Cricket England beat Ireland by 208 runs in their women's World Cup match in Pune, India.

Horse Racing Tony McCoy set a new record for the fastest 150 winners in a season when winning on Deano's Beep at Bangor.

18: Cricket Ireland beat Pakistan by 182 runs to advance to the quarter finals of the women's World Cup.

Soccer Dundalk and Shamrock Rovers played out a scoreless draw in the FAI PD.

19: Soccer Results from the FAI PD: St Patrick's Athletic 3, Cork City 3; Shelbourne 3, Finn Harps 2; the Drogheda-UCD match was 1-1 when it was abandoned due to fog after 47 minutes.

20: Basketball In the men's Superleague there were victories for Marian UCD, Star of the Sea, St Vincent's and Tralee. In the women's Superleague there were victories for Meteors, Wildcats, Tolka Rovers and Blarney.

Boxing Darren Corbett won the Commonwealth Cruiserweight title when he beat England's Rab Norton on points.

Hockey Old Alexandra beat Ards 2-1 in their second round replay in the women's Irish Senior Cup.

Horse Racing Cockney Lad beat a brave Imperial Call by one length in the Navan Hurdle.

Rugby Italy inflicted the third consecutive defeat on Ireland when they won 37-22 in Bologna.

Soccer Results from the IFA PD: Cliftonville 2, Ards 2; Coleraine 2, Portadown 0, Crusaders 3, Ballymena 4; Glenavon 1, Glentoran 0; Linfield 0, Omagh Town

0.
In the FAI PD Derry City drew 0-0 with Sligo Rovers while the Kilkenny City/Bohemians game was at 1-1 when it was abandoned after 54 minutes because of fog.

21: Basketball St Paul's Killarney shocked men's Superleague leaders Notre Dame with a 85-83 victory at the National Arena.
GAA Former Kerry star, Jack O'Shea, announced his retirement from Gaelic football. The 41-year-old saw his club side Leixlip lose to Clane in the Leinster Leader Kildare Cup final.
Rugby Lansdowne beat Terenure College 31-13 in the Leinster Championship final at Donnybrook.
Squash Derek Ryan won the National Championship when he beat Willie Hosey in straight sets. Madeline Perry won the women's Championship beating Anna McGeever 3-1 in sets.

22: Horse Racing Jockey Mark Dwyer announced his retirement from racing. Dwyer did not fully recover from an arm injury sustained in 1996.
Soccer Shelbourne qualified for the final of the League Cup when they beat Dundalk 3-0 (4-0 on aggregate).
Swimming Michelle de Bruin announced her withdrawal from the World Championships in Perth in January.

23: Cricket Ireland lost to tournament favourites New Zealand in the quarter-final of the women's World Cup.

26: Horse Racing Kieran Gaule on Dardjini won the Denny Gold Medal Novice Chase at Leopardstown.
Soccer Results from the IFA PD: Ballymena 2, Coleraine 2; Glentoran 1, Linfield 1; Portadown 2, Glenavon 0.
Bohemians beat Derry City 1-0 in the FAI PD.

27: Horse Racing Time For a Run, the mount of Philip Fenton, won the Paddy Power Chase at Leopardstown.
Soccer Omagh Town beat Ards 2-1 in the IFA PD.
Results from the FAI PD: Finn Harps 0, Dundalk 1; Sligo Rovers 2, Drogheda 1.

28: Horse Racing Conor O'Dwyer and Imperial Call won the Ericcson Chase at Leopardstown.
Soccer Results from the FAI PD: Cork City 4, Shelbourne 4; Shamrock Rovers 1, Kilkenny City 0; UCD 1, St Patrick's Athletic 1.

31: Soccer Results from the IFA PD: Coleraine 0, Cliftonville 2; Glenavon 3, Ballymena 3; Linfield 1, Portadown 1; Omagh Town 0, Glentoran 5.

JANUARY

02: Soccer Results from the FAI PD: Drogheda United 0, Bohemians 1; St Patrick's Athletic 1, Sligo Rovers 2; Shelbourne 3, UCD 1.

03: Athletics Catherina McKiernan won the 5.2 kms senior women's race in the IAAF Cross Country International in Durham. Other good performances came from Seamus Power who finished fifth in the Senior Men's 9.2 km race, Gareth Turnbull won the Senior Men's 4 km race and Enda Johnson won the Men's Under 20 5.4 km race.
Basketball In the men's Superleague there were victories for Marian, Ballina and Killester.
In the women's Superleague there were victories for Wildcats, Tolka Rovers, Meteors and Tralee.
Rugby Results from the All-Ireland League Division One: Blackrock 8, Garryowen 29; Clontarf 3, Cork Constitution 11; Dungannon 28, Lansdowne 8; Old Belvedere 15, Dolphin 23; Terenure 5, Ballymena 25.
Soccer Shamrock Rovers beat Derry City 1-0 in the FAI PD.
Results from the IFA PD: Ballymena 0, Linfield 2; Cliftonville 1, Glenavon 1 (game abandoned after 58 minutes due to worsening weather); Crusaders 3, Coleraine 0; Portadown 1, Omagh Town 1.

04: Basketball Star of the Sea beat St Vincent's 90-62 in the men's Superleague.
Hockey Avoca won the National Indoor League, beating Railway union 2-0 in the final which was held at the National Basketball Arena in Tallaght.
Snooker The Republic of Ireland beat Northern Ireland 14-4 in the B International held in Belfast.
Tennis Owen Casey won the men's Irish Indoor Open Championship beating John Doran in three sets. Gina Niland won the women's title beating Laura McCracken by two sets to love.

09: Basketball Neptune beat Tralee 95-88 in the men's Superleague.
Soccer Results from the first round of the FAI Cup: Bohemians 0, Cork City 1; Drogheda United 1, Shamrock Rovers 1; Waterford United 2, St Patrick's Athletic 2.

10: Basketball In the men's Superleague there were victories for Notre Dame and Star of the Sea. Limerick, Naomh Mhuire, Wildcats and Blarney all recorded victories in their women's Superleague.
Hockey UCC beat Collegians 2-1, Randalstown beat Glenanne 3-0, Old Alexandra beat Loreto 1-0 and Pegasus beat Belvedere 7-0 in the quarter-finals of the women's Irish Senior Cup.
In the second round of the men's Irish Senior Cup there were victories for Annadale, Belvedere, Cliftonville, Corinthians, Cookstown, Dublin University, Instonians, Harlequins, Monkstown, North Down, Parkview, Pembroke Wanderers, Raphoe, RUC and Three Rock Rovers. The Railway Union/Bangor match finished 2-2 after extra time.
Horse Racing Race favourite Graphic Equaliser won the Ladbroke Handicap Hurdle at Leopardstown by four lengths.
Rugby Results from the All-Ireland League Division One: Ballymena 27, Dungannon 12; Cork Constitution 11, Shannon 12; Dolphin 13, Blackrock 13; Lansdowne 51, Old Crescent 6; St Mary's College 12, Clontarf 23; Young Munster 26, Old Belvedere 12.
Soccer Results from the first round of the FAI Cup: Athlone Town 3, College Corinthians 0; Cobh Wanderers 0, Galway United 2; Derry City 7, Rockmount 0; Home Farm/Everton 3, Home Farm FC 1; Kilkenny City 0, UCD 4.
Results from the IFA PD: Ards 1, Coleraine 0; Glenavon 2, Crusaders 2; Glentoran 2, Portadown 1; Linfield 0, Cliftonville 1; Omagh Town 3, Ballymena 0.

11: Basketball In the men's Superleague Neptune beat Ballina 103-86 and St Vincent's beat Tralee 97-

87.

Soccer Results from the first round of the FAI Cup: Dundalk 5, Swilly Rovers 0; Fanad United 0, Whitehall Rangers 3; Finn Harps 2, Bray Wanderers 0; Monaghan 0, Cobh Ramblers 3; St Francis 1, Cherry Orchard 0; Shelbourne 4, Limerick FC 1; Sligo Rovers 1, Mervue United 1; Wayside Celtic 0, Longford Town 0.

12: Soccer St Patrick's Athletic beat Waterford United 3-0 in the FAI Cup first round replay.

Swimming Adrian O'Connor and Colin Lowth finished 43rd and 45th, respectively, in the 200m Freestyle at the World Championships in Perth.

14: Soccer In the FAI Cup first round replays Shamrock Rovers beat Drogheda United 2-0, Sligo Rovers beat Mervue United 2-0 while Longford Town drew 1-1 with Wayside Celtic after extra time.

Swimming At the World Championships Colin Lowth set a new Irish record of 2:03.05 in the 200m Butterfly, he also won his heat and was 26th overall. Nick O'Hare and Hugh O'Connor finished in 51st and 55th overall in the 100m Freestyle.

15: Soccer Derry City beat Dundalk 1-0 in the FAI PD.

16: Soccer Bohemians drew 0-0 with St Pat's in the FAI PD.

Swimming Colin Lowth set a personal best of 57.56 and finished 49th overall in the 100m Butterfly in Perth.

17: Basketball In the men's Superleague there were victories for Killester, Ballina and Notre Dame. In the women's Superleague there were victories for Wildcats, Killester, Naomh Mhuire and Meteors.

Rugby Results from the All-Ireland League Division One: Blackrock 44, Old Belvedere 19; Clontarf 42, Lansdowne 10; Cork Constitution 16, Young Munster 9; Dungannon 10, Garryowen 37; Old Crescent 9, Ballymena 6; Shannon 32, St Mary's 11; Terenure 23, Dolphin 10.

Soccer Results from the IFA PD: Ballymena 1, Glentoran 2; Cliftonville 1, Omagh Town 0; Coleraine 3, Glenavon 3; Crusaders 1, Linfield 2; Portadown 1, Ards 0.

Results from the FAI PD: Finn Harps 2, Kilkenny City 1; Sligo Rovers 1, Shelbourne 1.

18: Athletics Catherina McKiernan won the Oeust-France cross country race in Le Mans.

Basketball Neptune beat St Vincent's 88-78 and Star of the Sea beat Marian 124-88 in the men's Superleague.

Hockey Ulster won the U18 boys Interprovincial championship held over two days, while Munster won the U16 boys championship. Leinster won the girls U18 Interprovincial championship.

Soccer In the European Championship 2000 draw, the Republic of Ireland was drawn in Group Eight with Croatia, FYR Macedonia, Malta and Yugoslavia. Northern Ireland was drawn in Group Three with Finland, Germany, Moldova and Turkey.

Squash Derek Ryan was beaten in the semi-final of the Greenwich Open in New York.

Swimming At the World Championships in Perth, brothers Adrian and Hugh O'Connor finished in 24th and 26th overall in the 200m Backstroke. Nick O'Hare finished 38th overall in the 50m Freestyle.

21: Soccer Longford Town finally beat Wayside Celtic with an extra time goal from Damian Gannon in the second replay of their FAI Cup first round tie.

23: Basketball Notre Dame beat Star of the Sea 77-74 in the National Cup semi-final at the National Arena. In the first of the women's Cup semi-finals, Naomh Mhuire beat Tolka Rovers 64-62.

Boxing The National Finals were held in the National Stadium. Winners and their weights were: Light fly - James Rooney; Fly - Martin Murphy; Bantam - Bernard Dunne; Feather - Pat O'Donnell; Light - Eugene McEneaney; Light welter - Mark Wickam; Welter - Neil Gough; Light middle - Michael Roche; Middle - Brian Magee; Light heavy - Alan Sheerin; Heavy - John Kiely; Super heavy - Stephen Reynolds.

Soccer Bohemians beat Shelbourne 1-0 and Drogheda United beat Dundalk 1-0 in the FAI PD.

24: Athletics Peter Matthews, in fourth place, was the top Irish finisher at the International Cross Country meeting held in Belfast, the race was won by Laban Chege of Kenya. In the women's event, Maureen Harrington, in fourteenth, was best of the Irish and the race was won by Romanian Marianna Chirila.

Rugby Results from the All-Ireland League Division One: Ballymena 46, Clontarf 18; Dolphin 18, Dungannon 10; Garryowen 34, Old Crescent 13; Lansdowne 18, Shannon 14; Old Belvedere 12, Terenure 10; St Mary's 38, Cork Constitution 23; Young Munster 26, Blackrock 16.

Soccer Results from the first round of the IFA Irish Cup: Ards 0, Institute 2; Ballyclare 5, Ballymoney United 1; Ballymena 1, Glentoran 1; Carrick 2, Armagh City 3; Cliftonville 0, Glenavon 2; Coleraine 3, Chimney Corner 1; Crusaders 1, Bangor 0; Distillery 2, RUC 0; Drumaness 0, Killyleagh 0; Dungannon Swifts 6, Ballinamallard 2; Dunmurry 0, Ards Rangers 4; Larne 1, Portadown 2; Linfield 1, Tobermore United 0; Loughgall United 4, Crumlin United 0; Newry 1, Dundela 0; Omagh Town 3, Limavady United 0.

In the FAI PD Derry City drew 1-1 with Kilkenny City.

Ten Pin Bowling P Delany won the Irish Open Championship at Stillorgan with a score of 1835, N Thienpondt was second on 1769. M Goldwater won the women's event with a score of 1689 with I Oien second on 1643.

25: Athletics Irish athletes enjoyed considerable success at the Scottish Indoor championships, David Matthews (800m), James Nolan (1,500m), Gary Ryan (200m), Sean Lonergan (Triple Jump) Lena Barry (200m) and Sharon Foley (High Jump) all won their respective events.

Basketball Notre Dame beat Neptune 79-73 in the men's Sprite National Cup final while in the women's final Wildcats beat Naomh Mhuire 72-58.

Bowls Margaret Johnston beat Phillis Nolan in the National Indoor singles final.

GAA In the semi-finals of football's Railway Cup Leinster beat Munster 2-8 to 0-12 while Connacht drew with Ulster 0-15 apiece after extra time.

Golf Padraig Harrington finished in joint eighth position in the Johnnie Walker Classic in Thailand.

Soccer Results from the FAI PD: Cotk City 1, Sligo

Rovers 1; St. Patrick's Athletic 2, Shamrock Rovers 0; UCD 0, Finn Harps 0.

27: Squash Derek Ryan beat Dan Jenson in four sets to win the Hartford Cup in Conneticut, his first ranking tournament victory.

28: Soccer Drogheda drew 0-0 with UCD in the FAI PD. The Republic of Ireland beat Scotland 2-0 in an U16 friendly at Richmond Park.

29: Soccer Dundalk and St Pat's drew 0-0 in the FAI PD.

30: Soccer Shamrock Rovers lost 2-0 to Shelbourne in the FAI PD.

31: Rugby Results from the All-Ireland League Division One: Clontarf 14, Garryowen 16; Cork Constitution 26, Lansdowne 19; Dungannon 16, Old Belvedere 12; Old Crescent 24, Dolphin 9; Shannon 19, Ballymena 13; St Mary's 13, Young Munster 7; Terenure College 13, Blackrock 20.

Soccer Results from the IFA PD: Ards 1, Glenavon 1; Glentoran 1, Cliftonville 0; Linfield 1, Coleraine 0; Omagh Town 1, Crusaders 2; Portadown 4, Ballymena 0.

Results from the FAI PD: Kilkenny City 2, Drogheda 1; Sligo Rovers 2, UCD 1.

Hockey In the semi-finals of the women's Irish Senior Cup, Old Alexandra beat UCC 1-0 and Pegasus beat Randalstown 3-1.

In the third round of the men's Irish Senior Cup there were victories for Three Rock Rovers, Corinthians, Harlequins, Annadale, Instonians, Pembroke Wanderers and Raphoe. The Parkview/Dublin University game ended in a 2-2 draw.

FEBRUARY

01: Athletics Catherina McKiernan won the 6,000m Rás na hÉireann at Dunleer, Seamus Power won the men's 10,000m event.

Badminton Title winners from the National Championships at Lisburn: M. Watt (men's singles), S. McGinn (women's singles), B. Topping & M. O'Meara (men's doubles), C. Henderson & J. Plunkett (women's doubles) and G. Henderson & J. Plunkett (mixed doubles).

GAA Ulster beat Connacht 0-20 to 1-14 after extra time in the Railway Cup semi-final replay.

In Section D of the NFL there were victories for Clare, Cork, Limerick and Tipperary.

Golf Padraig Harrington finished equal third in the Perth Classic, two shots behind winner Thomas Bjorn.

Soccer Results from the FAI PD: Bohemians 4, Cork City 2; Finn Harps 1, Derry City 0.

03: Awards The 1997 Texaco Awards were announced with Maurice Fitzgerald, Keith Wood, Ken Doherty and Michelle Smith among the winners.

04: GAA D.J. Carey shocked the sporting nation when he announced his retirement from hurling at the age of 27.

05: Soccer Dundalk drew 0-0 with Shelbourne in the second round of the FAI Cup.

06: Boxing Ireland recorded a seven bouts to two victory in the annual Kuttner Shield Match with Scotland. Terry Carlyle, Paul McCloskey, Francie Barret, Brian Magee, Sean O'Grady, Stephen Reynolds and John Kinsella all won their bouts.

Rugby Ireland U21 beat Scotland U21 23-7, the Irish Students team beat their Scottish counterparts 25-11 but Ireland A lost 11-9 to Scotland A.

Snooker Ken Doherty beat James Wattana by six frames to one in the quarter finals of the British Masters at Wembley.

Squash Derek Ryan qualified for the final of the European Champion of Champions in Norway by beating Paul Gregory by three sets to one.

07: Hockey Parkview beat Dublin University 4-0 in their Irish Senior Cup third round replay.

Rugby Ireland lost the opening game of the Five Nations Championship when Scotland beat them 17-16 at Lansdowne Road. Ireland led for most of the match but a 70th minute penalty gave the Scots a one point victory.

Soccer Results from the second round of the FAI Cup: Athlone Town 2, Shamrock Rovers 1; Cobh Ramblers 1, St Patrick's Athletic 3; Galway United 2, Finn Harps 2; Longford Town 1, Whitehall Rangers 0; Sligo Rovers 2, St Francis' 0.

Kilkenny City drew 1-1 with Bohemians in the FAI PD. Results from the IFA PD: Ballymena 1, Ards 1; Cliftonville 1, Portadown 0; Coleraine 1, Omagh Town 1; Crusaders 0, Glentoran 3; Glenavon 2, Linfield 4.

Snooker Stephen Hendry beat Ken Doherty 6-5 in the semi-final of the British Masters.

Volleyball Sligo Institute of Technology won the men's Intervarsity title while University College Cork won the women's competition.

08: GAA Ulster beat Leinster 0-20 to 0-17 after extra time in the final of the football Railway Cup.

In Section A of the NFL Mayo beat Carlow 0-14 to 0-4.

Hockey Glennane won the Leinster U21 men's hockey title with a 1-0 win over Three Rock Rovers.

Horse Racing Dorans Pride comfortably won the Hennessy Gold Cup at Leopardstown beating Dun Belle by 15 lengths.

Soccer Results from the second round of the FAI Cup: Cork City 1, Derry City 1; UCD 1, Home Farm/Everton 1; and Shelbourne 2, Dundalk 0 (a replay).

Squash Derek Ryan won the European Champion of Champions tournament in Oslo.

10: Basketball Winners from the Schools Cup finals held at the National Arena in Tallaght: Girls' A Cup, St Vincent's Cork; Boys' B Cup, St Mary's Moyderwell; Girls' C Cup, Presentation, Bandon.

Skiing Pauli Patrick Schwarzacher-Joyce, Ireland's only skier at the Winter Olympics, finished 21st in the slalom section of the men's combined competition.

Soccer Cork City beat Derry City 1-0 and UCD beat Home Farm/Everton 1-0 in the FAI Cup second round replays.

Crusaders beat Cliftonville 1-0 and Glentoran beat Ards 2-0 in the IFA PD.

11: Boxing Mark Wickham and Adrian Sheerin recorded victories in the light welterweight and light heavyweight divisions respectively at the European Amateur Championships in Istanbul.

Soccer A 44th minute goal from George O'Boyle gave Northern Ireland a 1-0 victory over the Republic of

Ireland in the 'B' International at Tolka Park.

12: Boxing At the European qualifying tournament in Istanbul, featherweight Pat O'Donnell and light heavyweight Adrian Sheerin won their bouts on points. Light welterweight Mark Wickham (points), heavyweight Michael Roche (retired fifth round) and super heavyweight Stephen Reynolds (level on points but beaten because of a public warning for holding) all suffered defeats.

Soccer Shelbourne beat Kilkenny City 3-0 in the FAI PD.

13: Athletics Marcus O'Sullivan became the third athlete in history to run 100 sub four minute miles. The Cork man finished third, in a time of 3:58.10, in the Wannamaker Mile at the Melrose Games in New York. (Prior to Roger Bannister's sub-four minute mile in 1954 the time was judged to be outside human capability. For O'Sullivan to complete 100 of them is a truly magnificent achievement). Elsewhere Shane Healy finished eighth in the race and Mark Carroll won his third consecutive Melrose Games 3,000m title in a time of 7:49.37.

Skiing At the Winter Olympics in Nagano, Japan, Pauli Patrick Schwarzacher-Joyce finished 27th in the Downhill section of the men's combined which earned him 16th position overall.

Soccer St Patrick's Athletic beat Derry City 1-0 in the FAI PD.

14: Athletics Ireland's men finished eighth overall at the European Cross Country Championships at Lisbon, the leading Irish finisher was Peter Matthews in 16th. The Irish women's team finished 10th overall with Valerie Vaughan in 42nd as their top finisher.

Badminton In the Thomas Cup for men in Norway Ireland beat Estonia 5-0. In the Uber Cup for women Ireland beat Azerbaijan 5-0.

Basketball In the men's Superleague there were victories for Ballina, Neptune and Tralee. Notre Dame's 117-110 defeat to Tralee meant Star of the Sea could not be caught in the race for the Superleague title.

In the women's Superleague there were victories for Naomh Mhuire, Tolka Rovers, Wildcats and Limerick.

Hockey A scoreless draw with Old Alexandra was enough to elect Hermes as the 1997/98 women's Leinster Senior League champions.

Rugby Results from the All-Ireland League Division One: Ballymena 6, Cork Constitution 19; Blackrock 23, Dungannon 9; Dolphin 21, Clontarf 46; Old Belvedere 27, Old Crescent 23; and Young Munster 22, Terenure College 16.

Ireland U19 beat Italy U19 26-19.

Soccer Results from the IFA PD: Cliftonville 5, Ballymena 2; Coleraine 1, Glentoran 5; Crusaders 2, Portadown 1; Glenavon 2, Omagh Town 4; Linfield 2, Ards 0.

In the FAI PD Finn Harps beat Drogheda United 1-0 and Sligo Rovers beat Bohemians 2-1.

15: Athletics Some of the major winners in the men's competition from the National Indoor Championships (held in Nenagh) were Neil Ryan, 60m; Gary Ryan, 200m; S Fleming, 400m; James Nolan, 800m ; E O'Neill, 1,500m; J Daly, 3,000m; Mark Mandy, high jump; S Finnie, long jump; Dylan McDermott, pole vault; and Jason Flynn, shot putt.

Major winners in the women's competition include Lena Barry, 60m and 200m; Karen Shinkins, 400m; Freda Davoren, 800m and 1,500m; A Cuddihy, long jump; Sharon Foley, high jump; E Murphy, pole vault; and Bridie Lynch, shot putt.

Haile Gebrselassie (Ethiopia) broke Eamon Coghlan's indoor 1987 2,000m world record by over a second.

Badminton The Irish men's team beat Brazil 5-0 while the women beat Spain, also on a 5-0 scoreline in the international competition in Norway.

Basketball Champions in waiting Star of the Sea recorded a 110-90 victory over Dungannon.

GAA The All-Ireland Club hurling semi finals both ended drawn, Dunloy (Antrim) drew 4-11 to 3-14 with Sarsfields (Galway) and Birr (Offaly) drew 1-15 to 3-9 with Clarecastle (Clare).

In the National Football League there were victories for Laois, Mayo, Carlow and Galway in Section A; for Antrim, Armagh, Derry and Donegal in Section B; for Cavan, Monaghan and Tyrone in Section C; and for Cork, Kildare, Tipperary and Wicklow in Section D. The Section C match between Sligo and Offaly ended in a draw, 0-12 to 1-9.

Waterford beat Cork 1-11 to 1-9 in the South East League senior hurling final.

Rugby Shannon beat Limerick rivals Young Munster 17-14 in the All-Ireland League Division One clash at Dooradoyle.

Soccer In the FAI PD, the Cork City/Dundalk and UCD/Shamrock Rovers ties both ended scoreless.

16: Badminton Ireland's women beat Portugal 5-0 in the Uber Cup qualifying tournament in Norway.

17: Badminton Sweden beat Ireland 5-0 in the women's Uber Cup European Zone semi final.

Snooker Fergal O'Brien won his Scottish Open third round match with John Perry 5-3.

Soccer Neil Ogden's 64th minute goal separated the sides as Sligo Rovers beat Shelbourne 1-0 in the League Cup final first leg at the Showgrounds.

In the FAI PD Shamrock Rovers drew 0-0 with Drogheda United.

Linfield beat Crusaders 1-0 in the final of the County Antrim Shield.

19: Badminton Ireland beat the United States 3-2 in the women's Uber Cup European Zone semi-finals series.

Rugby Willie Anderson was sacked as London Irish Director of Rugby and replaced by former England coach, Dick Best.

Snooker Ken Doherty beat Steve Davis 5-2 to set up a Scottish Open quarter-final with fellow Dubliner Fergal O'Brien.

Soccer UCD beat Dundalk 2-1 in the FAI PD.

Finn Harps beat Galway United 3-1 in the FAI Cup second round replay.

Surfing Wild card entries Terence and Joe McNulty finished third and fourth overall in the Big Wave World Championships in Mexico to give Ireland an astounding second place overall. The quality of the result can be judged by the positions of other 'recognised' surfing nations, Brazil were first, the United States third and Australia fourth.

20: Bobsleigh Ireland 1 (Terry McHugh, G Power,

Simon Linscheid and J Pamplin) finished 29th overall in the four man heats at the Nagano Winter Olympics.

Snooker Fergal O'Brien beat Ken Doherty 5-4 in the quarter-final of the Scottish Open in Aberdeen.

Soccer St Pats beat Drogheda 2-1 and Shamrock Rovers drew 0-0 with Sligo Rovers in the FAI PD.

St Mary's College, Belfast beat the University of Limerick 2-0 in the Collingwood Cup final.

21: Athletics Sonia O'Sullivan won the 3,000m at the Robin Tait Classic in Auckland, New Zealand. Marcus O'Sullivan finished second in the men's 1,500m.

Basketball In the men's Superleague there were victories for Star of the Sea, Killester, Ballina, Marian and St Vincent's.

In the women's Superleague Killester, Meteors, Tolka Rovers and Blarney all recorded victories.

Hockey In the quarter-finals of the men's Irish Senior Cup, Pembroke Wanderers beat Corinthians 3-1, Three Rock Rovers beat Harlequins 3-2 after extra time, Instonians beat Raphoe 1-0 and Annadale beat Parkview 6-0.

Rugby Results from the All-Ireland League Division One: Clontarf 17, Old Belvedere 10; Cork Constitution 15, Garryowen 23; Dungannon 22, Terenure 28; Lansdowne 9, Young Munster 16; Old Crescent 5, Blackrock 3; Shannon 30, Dolphin 3; and St Mary's 64, Ballymena 33.

Snooker John Higgins beat Fergal O'Brien 6-2 in the semi-final of the Scottish Open.

Soccer In the sixth round of the IFA Irish Cup, there were victories for Glentoran, Institute, Crusaders, Linfield, Distillery and Portadown. The Armagh City/Ards Rangers and Glenavon/Ballyclare ties ended scoreless.

Results from the FAI PD: Derry City 1, Shelbourne 2, Kilkenny City 1, Cork City 2.

22: Boxing British light welterweight champion Mark Winters successfully defended his title when beating Englishman Bernard Paul on points in Belfast.

GAA In the semi-finals of the All-Ireland Club football championship Corofin (Galway) beat Dungiven (Derry) by 0-11 to 0-9 and Erin's Isle (Dublin) beat Castlehaven (Cork) by 2-12 to 0-17.

Motor Sport Austin McHale and Brian Murphy won the Galway International Rally by over a minute from Bertie Fisher and Rory Kennedy.

23: Hockey Riet Kuper was appointed as the national ladies team new coach. Ms Kuper is a former Dutch international.

24: Rugby Brian Ashton resigned as the Irish national coach, within hours the IRFU announced that Connacht's New Zealand born coach, Warren Gatland, would take over coaching responsibilities for the remaining three games of the Five Nations Championship.

Soccer Sligo Rovers claimed the League Cup when they held Shelbourne scoreless in the second leg at Tolka Park. They won 1-0 on aggregate.

25: Athletics Sonia O'Sullivan won the 5,000m in the IAAF Grand Prix meeting in Melbourne. Marcus O'Sullivan finished third in the men's mile in another sub four minute time of 3:56.35

Horse Racing Two times Irish Grand National winner, Francis Woods, announced his retirement from racing due to shoulder injury.

Soccer The Republic of Ireland beat Belgium 2-1 in the U16 European Championship qualifiers.

St Joseph's CBS Fairview, Dublin beat St Kieran's College, Kilkenny 2-0 in the final of the Leinster Senior Schools Cup.

27: Athletics James Nolan and David Matthews qualified for the final of the 800m in the European Indoor Championships in Spain when they finished second in their respective heats. Freda Davoren recorded a personal best of 4:18.21 in qualifying for the 1,500m final for women but Lena Barry who equalled her personal best of 7.48 failed to advance to the final of the 60m.

Snooker World Champion Ken Doherty qualified for the semi-final of the Liverpool Victoria Charity Challenge by beating Steve Davis 5-4.

Soccer A scoreless draw with Northern Ireland was enough to help the Republic qualify for the U16 European Championship finals.

Shamrock Rovers beat Bohemians 1-0 in the FAI PD.

Swimming Irish winners from the Leisureland International meet included Nick O'Hare (whose time of 22.76 was a new Irish record) in the 50m Freestyle, Hugh O'Connor in the 50m backstroke. In the women's events Lee Kelleher won the 200m Butterfly, and Niamh Cawley set a national junior record of 1.03.66 in winning the 100m backstroke.

28: Athletics Sonia O'Sullivan won the 1,500m in the IAAF Grand Prix in Sydney. Marcus O'Sullivan came third in the men's 1,500m.

Basketball In the final round of the men's Superleague there were victories for Killester, Dungannon, Notre Dame, St Vincent's and Star of the Sea. In the final round of the women's Superleague there were victories for Wildcats, Naomh Mhuire, Tolka Rovers and Killester.

GAA Birr beat Clarecastle 0-12 to 0-11 in the All-Ireland Club hurling semi final replay at Thurles.

Galway won the Oireachtas hurling final; when they beat Cork 0-14 to 0-8 in Ballinasloe.

Wexford beat Kilkenny in the Walsh Cup (hurling) final.

Westmeath beat London 3-19 to 1-6 in Section B of the National Football League.

Hockey Pegasus won the the women's Irish Senior Cup beating Old Alexandra 5-0 at Belfield.

Harlequins won the Munster Senior League for women when they beat Belvedere 5-1.

Horse Racing Tony McCoy broke the record for the fastest 200 winners in a single National Hunt season.

Rugby Results from the All-Ireland League Division One: Blackrock College 13, Clontarf 29; Dolphin 29, Cork Constitution 35; Garryowen 13, St Mary's College 12; Old Belvedere 20, Shannon 70; Terenure 41, Old Crescent 23; Young Munster 29, Dungannon 13.

Ireland beat Wales 15-0 in a friendly Youth International.

Snooker Ken Doherty was beaten 6-5 in the semi-final of the Liverpool Victoria Charity Challenge by Scotland's John Higgins.

Soccer Results from the IFA PD: Ards 1, Cliftonville 1; Ballymena United 1, Crusaders 0; Glentoran 1, Glenavon 0; Omagh Town 0, Linfield 3; Portadown 1,

Coleraine 1.
Results from the FAI PD: Shelbourne 1, Drogheda United 0; Sligo Rovers 3, Dundalk 0.
Swimming Irish winners in men's competition at the first day of the Leisureland International Meet in Galway were Hugh O'Connor (200m backstroke) and Colin Lowth (200m butterfly). Winners in women's events were C O'Keefe (800m freestyle), N Cawley (200m backstroke) and Michelle de Bruin (400m individual medley).

MARCH

01: Athletics UCD athletes, James Nolan and David Matthews, finished fourth and fifth, respectively, in the 800m final at the European Indoor Championships. Freda Davoren finished ninth in the 1,500m final and Antoine Burke finished 13th overall in the high jump.
Basketball In the last round of the men's Division One Championship Sligo beat Limerick 98-81 to win the title.
Cycling Ireland's Ciaran Power finished 87th and Raymond Clarke finished 96th in the Tour of Langkawi in Malaysia.
GAA Sarsfields beat Dunloy by 1-15 to 1-11 in the All-Ireland Hurling Club Championship semi-final replay but it took extra time for Birr to beat Clarecastle on a scoreline of 0-12 to 0-11.
University College Cork beat the Waterford Institute of Technology 2-17 to 0-13 in the Fitzgibbon Cup final.
In the NFL Section A there were victories for Fermanagh, Galway and Meath while Leitrim drew with Laois. In Section B there were victories for Armagh, Derry and Donegal. In Section C there were victories for Dublin, Kerry, Offaly and Sligo, while Clare, Down, Kildare and Wicklow all recorded victories in Section D.
Soccer Results from the FAI PD: Cork City 0, Derry City 1; UCD 1, Kilkenny City 0.
Swimming Michelle de Bruin set a new Irish record of 4:14.02 when winning the 400m freestyle at Galway. Other Irish winners in women's events were Niamh Cawley (50m backstroke) and M Corless (200m breaststroke). Hugh O'Connor (100m backstroke) G Beegan (200m individual medley) and Colin Lowth (400m freestyle) were the Irish winners in the men's events.
02: Hockey Glynis Taylor was appointed assistant to national women's coach Riet Kuper.
04: Hockey Wesley College beat Mount Anville 2-1 in the Leinster Schoolgirls Senior Cup final at Belfield.
Soccer The Republic of Ireland U18s drew 1-1 with France in Nice.
06: Rugby Ireland A drew 30-30 with France A while the Irish U21 team lost 36-28 to France U21.
Soccer St Patrick's Athletic drew 2-2 with Shelbourne in the quarter-final of the FAI Cup.
Republic of Ireland captain Andy Townsend announced his retirement from international football.
07: GAA Tyrone drew with Donegal in the Ulster Vocational Schools final.
Rugby The much maligned Irish team, under new coach Warren Gatland, restored their reputation with an heroic, if ultimately losing, performance in Paris. With pundits predicting a record defeat, Ireland instead took the game to the French and led 13-3 at half time, a 35th minute try came courtesy of Denis Hickie. However France scored two second half tries, a penalty and a conversion to Ireland's single penalty to secure a narrow 18-16 victory.
Soccer Results from the IFA PD: Coleraine 0, Ballymena 0; Crusaders 0, Cliftonville 2; Glenavon 3, Portadown 0; and Linfield 3, Glentoran 0. Crowd trouble marred the day, riot police clashed with Glentoran supporters at Windsor Park when tempers frayed following a free for all between the players. Riot police also intervened during the Crusaders-Cliftonville match when a fracas on the pitch sparked off trouble on the terraces forcing referee Alan Snoddy to stop the game for five minutes.
Table Tennis Leinster won the senior interprovincial held in Dublin.
08: Formula 1 Eddie Irvine finished fourth in the first Grand Prix of the year in Australia. The Jordan team did not fare well; Damon Hill finished eighth but Ralf Schumacher spun out after one lap.
GAA Tralee Institute of Technology won the Sigerson Cup beating University of Ulster, Jordanstown 0-10 to 0-8 in the final, held at Tralee.
In Division One A of the NHL there were victories for Clare, Dublin and Limerick while Cork, Wexford and Waterford recorded victories in Division One B.
Snooker Fergal O'Brien beat Scotland's John Higgins 5-3 in the opening round of the Thailand Masters in Bangkok.
Soccer In the quarter-finals of the FAI Cup Finn Harps beat UCD 1-0 and Cork City beat Sligo Rovers 2-0. Home Farm/Everton beat Cobh Ramblers 3-1 in the First Division Shield final first leg.
The Republic of Ireland beat Wales 4-0 in the women's World Cup qualifier at Bray.
Squash Leinster won the men's Grade A interprovincial championship while Ulster won the women's Grade A championship.
09: Snooker Ken Doherty beat Mark King 5-0 in only 66 minutes in the Thailand Masters. Thailand's James Wattana beat Joe Swail 5-1, also in the first round.
Soccer St Pat's and Shelbourne drew 1-1 after extra time in their FAI Cup quarter-final replay.
10: Snooker Anthony Hamilton beat Fergal O'Brien 5-0 in the second round of the Thailand Masters.
Soccer Athlone Town drew 1-1 with Longford Town in the FAI Cup quarter-final.
11: Bowls Ireland comfortably defeated Wales in the Home International Championship at Swansea.
Snooker Ken Doherty came back from 4-0 down to beat James Wattana in the second round of the Thailand Masters.
12: Bowls Ireland were beaten by Scotland in the Home Nations International Championship.
Golf Des Smyth equalled the course record when hitting an opening round 64 in the Moroccan Open.
Soccer Dundalk drew 3-3 with Bohemians in the FAI PD.
13: Snooker Ken Doherty beat Alan McManus 5-3 in the quarter-final of the Thailand Masters.
Soccer Results from the FAI PD: St Pat's 0, Shelbourne 0; Shamrock Rovers 2, Finn Harps 2.

14: GAA Galway beat Kilkenny 1-18 to 0-6 in Section A of the NFL.

Hockey In the semi-finals of the men's Irish Senior Cup Three Rock Rovers beat Annadale 3-2 and Instonians beat Pembroke Wanderers 3-2 after extra time.

Rowing Neptune won the men's Open Eights at the Tribesmen Head of the River event on Lough Corrib. The British national squad won the women's event.

Rugby Results from AIL Division One: Ballymena 31, Lansdowne 20; Garryowen 38, Terenure 26; Old Crescent 16, St Mary's College 17. Elsewhere in the AIL Portadown won Division Three after securing a 9-6 victory over North, while Carlow's 23-16 victory over Sligo secured first place in Division Four.

Snooker Stephen Hendry came back from 4-2 down to beat Ken Doherty 5-4 in the semi-final of the Thailand Masters.

Soccer Results from the quarter-finals of the IFA Irish Cup: Armagh City 1, Glentoran 3; Crusaders 4, Institute 0; Distillery 0, Glenavon 2; and Linfield 3, Portadown 0.

Results from the FAI PD: Derry City 0, UCD 3; Drogheda United 1, Cork City 2; and Kilkenny City 2, Sligo Rovers 1.

15: Athletics Catherina McKiernan won the Lisbon half-marathon in a time of 1hr 7mins 50 secs.

Basketball Star of the Sea beat Notre Dame 92-74 in the men's Superleague Championship final while Wildcats beat Tolka Rovers 82-68 in the women's decider.

Cycling Karl Donnelly won the 50 mile Jim McQuaid Memorial Race in the Phoenix Park, M. Reilly won the women's event.

GAA In the NFL Section A there were victories for Mayo and Leitrim while Carlow drew with Fermanagh. In Section B there were victories for Derry, Donegal, Meath and Westmeath. In Section C there were victories for Cavan, Dublin, Monaghan and Offaly. In Section D there were victories for Cork and Down while Waterford drew with Limerick. These were the final games of the 1997/98 league, the league quarter-finalists are Cork, Derry, Donegal, Down, Galway, Monaghan, Mayo and Offaly.

Scotland beat Ireland 0-12 to 0-7 in the annual Shinty International which was held in Kilkenny.

Rugby Shannon beat Young Munster 16-10 in the AIL Division One derby match at Thomond Park.

16: Soccer Shelbourne beat St. Patrick's Athletic 5-3 on penalties in their FAI Cup quarter final replay (the score was 2-2 after extra time).

17: Bowls England beat Ireland in the women's Home International Indoor Championship at Darlington.

GAA Corofin beat Erin's Isle by 0-15 to 0-10 in the All-Ireland football club championship final at Croke Park. In the hurling decider Birr, champions in 1995, proved too strong for Sarsfields, champions in 1993 and 1994, beating them 1-13 to 0-9.

St Colman's of Newry beat St Patrick's, Maghera 2-14 to 2-7 in the Ulster senior school's MacRory Cup football final.

Hockey Pembroke won the Mills Cup final beating Glenanne 2-1.

Muckross beat Loreto 4-2 in the women's Leinster Senior Cup final and UCG won the women's Connacht Senior Cup final beating Yeats County 4-3 on penalty strokes.

Horse Racing The Cheltenham festival got off to a great start for the Irish when the Aidan O'Brien trained Istabraq carried Charlie Swan to a twelve length victory in the Champion Hurdle. Ireland's French Ballerina won the opening race of meeting, the Supreme Novice's Hurdle.

Soccer Cobh Ramblers drew 2-2 with Home Farm/Everton in the First Division Shield final second leg but lost 5-3 on aggregate.

Athlone Town beat Longford Town 2-1 in their FAI Cup quarter-final replay.

In the FAI PD Cork City beat Finn Harps 3-1 and Dundalk beat Kilkenny City 2-1.

18: Bowls Ireland lost to Scotland in the women's Home international indoor championship at Darlington.

Hockey St Andrew's beat St Columba's 10-1 in the boys Leinster Schools Senior Cup final.

Horse Racing Richard Dunwoody guided the Willie Mullins-trained Florida Pearl to victory in the Royal & SunAlliance Chase on the second day of the Cheltenham festival. Alexander Banquet made it double for Ireland and Mullins when he won the Festival Bumper.

Rugby Garbally College, Ballinasloe, beat St Saran's College, Ferbane 18-0 in the Connacht School's Senior Cup final.

19: Bowls Ireland secured their only victory in the women's Home International Indoor Championship when they beat Wales 128-112.

Horse Racing There were no Irish winners on the last day of the Cheltenham. Gold Cup favourite Dorans Pride finished third behind Cool Dawn and Strong Promise. Tony McCoy rode the last three winners of the festival to claim the Jockey's Championship. Adrian Maguire was seriously injured in the Grand Annual Chase.

20: GAA DJ Carey announced his intention to return to hurling barely six weeks after announcing his retirement.

Hockey Leinster beat Ulster 2-1 and Munster beat Ireland U21 2-1 in the first games of the men's interprovincial championship.

Rugby The Irish Universities beat their Welsh counterparts 44-24, the Irish Under 21s beat Wales U21 27-25 but Ireland A lost 27-42 to Wales A.

Soccer In the FAI PD Bohemians beat Kilkenny City 4-3.

21: Athletics Sonia O'Sullivan became the first Irish woman to win the World Cross Country Championship when she completed the eight kilometre course, near Marakesh in Morocco, in a time of 25 minutes 39 seconds.

Hockey In the men's interprovincial championship Leinster beat Munster 1-0 and Ulster beat Ireland U21 2-1.

Rugby Twenty points from man-of-the-match Neil Jenkins led Wales to a 30-21 victory over Ireland in the Five Nations Championship. Despite leading 12-3 after 26 minutes and 15-13 at half-time Ireland, through a number of handling and defensive errors, fell behind early in the second half. An 80th minute Jenkins try put the Welsh on the right side of a somewhat flattering scoreline.

Soccer Results from the IFA PD: Ards 0, Crusaders 1; Ballymena 2, Glenavon 1; Cliftonville 1, Coleraine 0; Glentoran 2, Omagh Town 0; and Portadown 0, Linfield 0.

Results from the FAI PD: Finn Harps 0, Shelbourne 0; Sligo Rovers 1, Derry City 1.

The Republic of Ireland drew 1-1 with Poland in an U15 international held at Newbridge.

22: Athletics Sonia O'Sullivan won the 4,000m short course World Cross Country Championship in Morocco.

GAA In the all Kilkenny Leinster Schools hurling final Colaiste Eamonn Rís beat St. Kierans 1-10 to 0-9. In the Munster Schools football final Colaiste Chriost Rí beat Spioraid Naoimh 3-17 to 3-3 while in Connacht Roscommon CBS beat St Jarlath's of Tuam 1-14 to 1-6.

In Division 1A of the NHL there were victries for Antrim, Galway and Limerick, in Division 1B Kilkenny and Cork won thier matches while Laois and Tipperary drew 1-13 apiece.

Golf Darren Clarke finished ninth in the Portuguese Open four shots behind winner Peter Mitchell.

Hockey Pegasus won the women's Irish league on goal difference following their scoreless draw with Hermes.

Leinster won the men's Interprovincial title.

Rugby Clongowes Wood beat Terenure College 37-18 in the Leinster Schools Senior Cup final while in the Munster Cup final CBC Cork beat PBC Cork 22-17.

Soccer Results from the FAI PD: Cork City 1, St Patrick's Athletic 1; Shamrock Rovers 5, Dundalk 4; UCD 1, Drogheda 1.

24: Horse Racing Tony McCoy equalled Peter Scudamore's record of 221 winners in a season when winning the Court Selling Hurdle at Chepstow.

Snooker In the first round of the Benson & Hedges Irish Masters at Goffs, Fergal O'Brien beat Peter Ebdon 6-2 and John Parrot beat Tony Drago, also on a 6-2 scoreline.

Soccer The Czech Republic beat the Republic of Ireland 3-0 in the U21 international in Drnovice.

25: Snooker Ronnie O'Sullivan beat Jimmy White 6-2 in the first round of the Irish Masters, while Steve Davis beat Nigel Bond.

Soccer The Republic of Ireland were beaten 2-1 by the Czech Republic in the friendly international in Olomouc. Gary Breen was the Republic's goalscorer. Slovakia provided the opposition at Windsor Park but a 51st minute goal from captain Steve Lomas gave Lawrie McMenemy a winning start to his tenure as Northern Ireland manager.

The Republic of Ireland beat Greece 1-0 in the first leg of the UEFA U18 qualifying round play-off.

26: Snooker In the quarter-finals of the Irish Masters John Parrot beat Mark Williams 6-3 while Ken Doherty triumphed in the all Dublin clash beating Fergal O'Brien 6-1.

Soccer Dundalk beat Finn Harps 2-1 in the FAI PD. Republic of Ireland international Mark Kennedy moved from Liverpool to Wimbledon for a fee of £1.75 million.

27: Boxing England beat Ireland 6-5 in the amateur boxing international held at the National Stadium. There were victories for Bernard Dunne (bantamweight), Aodh Carlyle (lightweight), Brian Magee (middleweight) and Sean Collier (middleweight). Ireland also got a walk over in one of the light middleweight bouts.

Snooker Ronnie O'Sullivan beat Stephen Hendry 6-3 and John Higgins beat Steve Davis in the quarter-finals of the Irish Masters.

Soccer Results from the FAI PD: Drogheda United 1, Sligo Rovers 1; St Pat's 1, UCD 0; Shelbourne 1, Cork City 1.

Irish international David Connolly moved from Feyenoord to Wolves on loan.

28: Athletics Catherina McKiernan continued her impeccable sequence of victories (13 in all) when winning a ten kilometre road race in Mobile, Alabama.

Rowing Neptune won the men's Open Eights title in the Head of the River Race on the Liffey. Trinity College won the women's Open Eights race.

Rugby Results from Division One of the AIL: Ballymena 13, Young Munster 21; Clontarf 36, Terenure College 17; Cork Constitution 63, Old Belvedere 12; Lansdowne 30, Garryowen 27; Old Crescent 16, Dungannon 13; Shannon 37, Blackrock College 6; St Mary's College 36, Dolphin 32; .

Snooker Ken Doherty beat John Parrot 6-1 in the semi-final of the Irish Masters while Ronnie O'Sullivan beat John Higgins 6-4.

Soccer Results from the IFA PD: Ards 0, Glentoran 2; Coleraine 0, Crusaders 0; Glenavon 0, Cliftonville 0; Linfield 1, Ballymena 0; and Omagh Town 0, Portadown 2.

Kilkenny City drew 1-1 with Shamrock Rovers in the FAI PD.

Swimming Michelle de Bruin set a new Irish record of 1:59.69 for the 200m freestyle at the Leinster championships.

29: Formula 1 Mika Hakkinen won the Brazilian Grand Prix while Eddie Irvine finished eighth overall, Damon Hill was disqualified for having an underweight car and Ralf Shumacher was not classified.

GAA Results from the NHL Division One A: Offaly 3-13, Antrim 0-9; Galway 1-9, Limerick 1-10; Dublin 2-8, Clare 1-18. Results from Division One B: Tipperary 3-13, Kilkenny 1-13; Laois 1-9, Waterford 4-11; and Wexford 1-11, Cork 1-11.

Hockey Pembroke Wanderers won the men's Leinster Senior League when close rivals Glenanne were held to a draw.

Snooker Ronnie O'Sullivan won the Irish Masters final beating Ken Doherty 9-3 in the final. O'Sullivan picked up the winner's cheque of £75,000, Doherty £34,000 plus £3,000 for the highest tournament break of 129.

Soccer Derry City beat Bohemians 1-0 in the FAI PD.

APRIL

02: Soccer Dundalk beat Kilkenny City 1-0 in the FAI PD.

03: Rugby Ireland claimed two Triple Crowns courtesy of the U21 and Universities teams. Ireland U21 beat England U21 9-7 while the Irish Universities beat their English counterparts 80-30. Ireland A however, were beaten 40-30 by England A.

Soccer Bohemians beat Drogheda United 2-1 and Shamrock Rovers beat Derry City 3-1 in the FAI PD.

04: Golf Dublin won the All-Ireland intercounties final, beating Kerry 4-1 at Lahinch.

Hockey Harlequins beat UCC 4-3 in the women's Munster Senior Cup final, while Pegasus won the women's Ulster Shield final beating Randalstown 4-0. In the final of the women's Irish Junior Cup Pembroke Wanderers seconds beat Old Alexandra's seconds 3-1.

Cork Church of Ireland beat Harlequins 4-3 on penalty strokes in the men's Munster Senior Cup final.

Rugby Ireland finished the Five Nations Championship pointless when they lost 35-17 to England at Twickenham in their last game of the championship. Denis Hickey with two tries and Eric Elwood with two conversions and a penalty were Ireland's scorers.

The Ireland U19 team beat their American opponents 47-13 in the 16 nation World Junior Championships in France.

Soccer Cork City beat Athlone Town 3-1 in the semi-final of the FAI Cup at St Mel's Park. In the other semi-final at Ballybofey, Finn Harps and Shelbourne drew 0-0.

05: Cycling Tommy Evans won the 87 mile Des Hanlon Memorial Race at Carlow.

GAA In the quarter finals of the NFL Derry beat Mayo, Donegal beat Cork, Monaghan beat Down and Offaly beat Galway.

Tralee IT won the women's senior intervarsity beating Sligo IT by 2-16 to 2-13.

Snooker T Gleeson beat J Farrell in the final of the Leinster Masters held at Carlow.

In the second round of the British Open Joe Swail beat Wille Thorne 5-0.

Soccer St Patrick's Athletic drew 1-1 with Sligo Rovers in the FAI PD.

Volleyball In the men's European Championships in Malta the Republic of Ireland were beaten by 3 sets to 1 by Luxembourg and 3-0 by Cyprus.

06: Rugby The Irish U19s lost to South Africa on a penalty shoot out having drawn 17-17 after normal time, they subsequently were awarded the match after a successful appeal.

Snooker Michael Judge and Jason Prince were both knocked out of the British Open at Plymouth.

Soccer The Republic of Ireland U15s beat Portugal 1-0 in a tournament in France.

07: Rugby Ireland beat Scotland 49-0 in the schools' international at Thomond Park.

Snooker Ken Doherty progressed in the British Open but Fergal O'Brien and Joe Swail were knocked out at the second and third rounds respectively.

Soccer Shelbourne beat Finn Harps 1-0 in the replay of their FAI Cup semi-final at Toka Park, their goal came from a controversial second half penalty from Stephen Geoghegan. The game was disrupted for 40 minutes at the end of the first half due to a bomb hoax.

08: Soccer The Republic of Ireland's U18 team beat hosts Portugal 2-0 in the four nation invitational tournament in Lisbon.

09: Hockey Northern Ireland's men and women's teams both won gold at the British Universitites Games at Jordanstown.

Rugby Ireland beat Argentina 18-3 in the World Junior U19 Championship semi-final in France.

Snooker Ken Doherty qualified for the quarter-finals of the British Open by whitewashing England's Karl Burrows 5-0.

Soccer The Republic of Ireland U15s beat Uruguay 5-4 on penalties to advance to the quarter-finals of the Montagiu tournament in France. The Republic's U18 team drew 0-0 with France in the quadrangular tournament in Portugal.

Shamrock Rovers beat Dundalk 1-0 in the FAI PD.

10: Basketball Ireland beat Wales 72-37 in the four countries tournament at Tallaght.

Cycling Michael McNena won the ninth stage of the Tour of Greece.

Tommy Evans won the Tour of the North Prologue time trial.

Motor Rallying Bertie Fisher finished the first day racing in the 1998 Circuit of Ireland 22 seconds ahead of Andrew Nesbitt.

Snooker Ken Doherty beat Neal Foulds 5-1 in the quarter-final of the British Open.

Soccer In the FAI PD Bohemians beat St Pats 2-0 and Finn Harps drew 2-2 with Kilkenny City.

England beat the Republic of Ireland 1-0 in the U15 competition in France.

11: Basketball Ireland beat England 76-57 in the women's Four Countries International tournament in Tallaght.

Cycling Ian Chivers won the 60 miles second stage of the Tour of the North.

GAA Kerry beat Tipperary in the Munster U21 football final.

In Division 1A of the NFL Clare beat Offaly and Galway beat Antrim.

Rugby Results from the AIL Division One: Blackrock College 20, Cork Constitution 29; Dolphin 13, Lansdowne 13; Dungannon 47, Clontarf 12; Garryowen 66, Ballymena 29; Old Belvedere 15, St Mary's College 41; Terenure College 17, Shannon 19; Young Munster 19, Old Crescent 15.

Galwegians gained promotion to Division 1 of the AIL following their victory over Malone.

Ireland beat Wales 13-6 in the schools' international at Galway.

Snooker Stephen Hendry beat Ken Doherty 6-4 in the semi-final of the British Open.

Soccer Results from the IFA PD: Ballymena 2, Omagh 1; Cliftonville 0, Linfield 3; Coleraine 2, Ards 2; Crusaders 4, Glenavon 1; Portadown 2, Glentoran 0.

Results from the FAI PD: Derry City 0, Dundalk 0; Shelbourne 2, Sligo Rovers 0.

The Republic of Ireland beat Austria 2-1 in the final of the Oporto Tournament in Lisbon.

12: Basketball Ireland completed a clean sweep of victories to win the Four Countries International tournament when they beat Scotland 69-38.

Cycling Andy Proffitt moved into the overall lead of the Tour of the North following his victory in the 12 miles time trial at Ballyclare.

Formula One: Ferrari's Eddie Irvine finished third in the Argentinian Grand Prix at Buenos Aries.

Golf With rounds of 76, 73, 67 and 69 Darren Clarke finished in joint eighth in the US Masters at Augusta, Georgia. The tournament was won by Mark O'Meara.

GAA In the semi-finals of the NFL Derry beat Monaghan 1-12 to 0-8 and Offaly beat Donegal 3-10 to 1-14.

In Division 1A of the NHL Limerick beat Dublin. In Division 1B there were victories for Cork and Laois while Waterford drew with Wexford.

Laois won the Leinster U21 Provincial Football title.

Rugby Ireland beat France 18-0 to win the World U19 Championship. Paddy Wallace and Darragh Holt provided Ireland with a try apiece, Wallace also helped himself to a drop goal while Brian O'Driscoll kicked a penalty and a conversion.

Soccer UCD beat Cork City 2-1.

The Republic of Ireland U15 team lost 4-3 to Spain on penalties in the Montaigu tournament in France.

13: Cycling R. Blayney won the 70 miles penultimate stage of the Tour of the North but Andy Proffitt maintained his overall lead.

Ras Mumhan was won by Brian Kenneally.

Hockey Pembroke Wanderers lost 1-0 to French side Montrouge in the Men's European Cup Winners' Cup B Division final.

Motor rallying Bertie Fisher provisionally won the Circuit of Ireland by 19 seconds from Austin McHale. The result was subsequently overturned when McHale had a 20 second penalty, which he incurred on the first day of the rally, quashed. His one second winning margin was the narrowest ever in the Circuit of Ireland.

Soccer St Patrick's Athletic beat Finn Harps 2-0 in the FAI PD.

14: Cycling The final days racing in the Tour of the North was abandoned due to bad weather and leader after four stages, Andy Proffitt, was declared the winner.

Golf Noel Fox won the West of Ireland Amateur Championship in Enniscrone, beating Pat Lyons on a score of 2 and 1.

Soccer Results from the IFA PD: Glenavon 4, Coleraine 0; Glentoran 2, Ballymena 2; Linfield 0, Crusaders 0; Omagh Town 0, Cliftonville 1.

16: Soccer Drogheda United beat Dundalk 2-0 in the FAI PD.

Volleyball The Republic's women's team were beaten by Cyprus (3-0) and Iceland (3-0) in a Small Nations tournament held in Liechtenstein.

17: Soccer Shelbourne beat Bohemians 1-0 in the FAI PD.

18: Badminton The Irish team lost 4-1 to Finland at the European team championships.

GAA Galway won the Connacht U21 football title beating Leitrim 0-13 to 1-7.

Hockey Cork Church of Ireland won their seventh consecutive Munster League title when they beat Harlequins 2-1.

Three Rock Rovers seconds beat Annadale's seconds 4-0 in the men's Irish Junior Cup final.

Rugby Shannon beat St Mary's College 28-21 in the AIL semi-final played at Thomond Park.

Richmond secured promotion to Division 3 of the AIL when they beat Collegians 15-10 (30-18 on aggregate) in their playoff.

England beat Ireland 26-22 in the Schools Triple Crown decider.

Soccer Cliftonville's 1-1 draw with Glentoran was enough to win the Irish League following Linfield's scoreless draw with Coleraine. Cliftonville, which has one less home fixture than other Irish League teams, last won the title in 1910. Other results from the IFA PD: Ballymena 1, Portadown 2; Crusaders 2, Omagh Town 2; Glenavon 0, Ards 0.

Results from the FAI PD: Finn Harps 1, UCD 2; Kilkenny City 1, Derry City 0; Sligo Rovers 4, Cork City 1.

19: Badminton Ireland lost to Switzerland and Poland on 3-2 scorelines at the European team championships.

GAA Armagh beat Derry in the Ulster U21 football final.

In Division 1A of the NHL there were victories for Galway, Limerick and Offaly, while in Division 1B Waterford, Wexford and Cork all enjoyed victories.

Rugby Garryowen beat Limerick rivals Young Munster 24-10 in the second of the AIL semi-finals at Dooradoyle.

Snooker In the first round of the World Championships at Sheffield defending champion Ken Doherty beat Lee Walker 10-8, and fellow Dubliner Fergal O'Brien beat Thailand's James Wattana 10-9.

Soccer In the FAI PD St Patrick's Athletic beat Shamrock Rovers 1-0.

Former Irish international John Aldridge announced his intention to retire on at the end of the English season on May 3.

20: Badminton Ireland lost 3-2 to Portugal in their final match of the European championships, overall the team finished last of the 16 competing nations.

21: Snooker Terry Murphy from Derry was beaten 10-3 by Peter Ebdon in the first round of the World Championships at Sheffield.

Soccer Shelbourne beat UCD 3-2 in the FAI PD.

Northern Ireland beat Switzerland 2-1 in an U21 friendly.

22: GAA Australia beat Ireland 56-51 in the U17 Compromise Rules test match at Croke Park.

Rugby Pat Whelan announced his shock resignation as manager of the national team. In his 20 games in charge Ireland won five, and lost 15.

Snooker Northern Ireland pair Joe Swail and Jason Prince were knocked out of the World Championships by Ronnie O'Sullivan and Darren Morgan respectively.

Soccer In senior international friendlies the Republic of Ireland were beaten 2-0 by Argentina at Lansdowne Road while Northern Ireland recorded their second successive victory under new manager Lawrie McMenemie when they beat Switzerland 1-0 at Windsor Park.

Finn Harps lost 2-1 to Cork City in the FAI PD.

23: Sports Minister Dr Jim McDaid announced the 1998 sports allocation by government of over £3.65 million.

24: Rugby Warren Gatland was confirmed as national coach by the IRFU. His contract will run until the end of the 1999-2000 season. Donal Lenihan was appointed team manager for the summer tour to South Africa following Pat Whelan's resignation.

Dublin side Wanderers were relegated to Division Three of the AIL when the IRFU's AIB working party awarded the points from their postponed match with Buccaneers to Buccaneers.

Soccer Results from the FAI PD: Drogheda United 1, Kilkenny City 1; Shelbourne 2, Shamrock Rovers 1.

25: GAA Laois beat Galway 0-13 to 1-9 in the All-Ireland U21 semi-final.

Hockey Two late goals from Neil Cooke secured a 3-2 victory for Instonians over underdogs Three Rock Rovers in the Irish Senior Cup final.

Rugby Shannon beat Garryowen 15-9 in the final of the AIL held at Lansdowne Road. Four penalties and a dropped goal from man-of-the-match Andrew Thompson helped Shannon to their fourth successive AIL title.

Elsewhere Buccaneers were promoted to Division One of the AIL following their defeat of Dungannon in the Division 1 playoff second leg.

Snooker Ken Doherty beat Stephen Lee 13-8 to qualify for the World Championship quarter finals.

Soccer Results from the final round of the IFA PD: Ards 0, Ballymena 2; Glentoran 1, Crusaders 1; Linfield 2, Glenavon 1; Omagh Town 1, Coleraine 3; Portadown 1, Cliftonville 2.

In the FAI PD Finn Harps drew 0-0 with Derry City.

26: Athletics Catherina McKiernan won the London marathon in a time of two hours 26 minutes and 26 seconds. This was her second marathon victory (from two starts) and fourteenth consecutive victory in road racing.

Formula One Eddie Irvine secured his second consecutive podium finish when he finished third in the San Marino Grand Prix behind David Coulthard and Michael Schumacher.

GAA Offaly won their first ever National Football League title when they beat Derry by 0-9 to 0-7 in heavy rain at Croke Park.

Tyrone won All-Ireland vocational schools title when they beat Offaly by 2-17 to 1-5 at Croke Park.

Down beat Armagh 1-12 to 2-8 in the McKenna Cup final.

Rugby Naas beat Kilkenny 13-3 in the final of the Provincial Towns' Cup held at Enniscorthy.

Bruff and Corinthians shared the All-Ireland U18 club trophy after normal time and a sudden death penalty shoot out failed to separate them.

Soccer Results from the FAI PD: Cork City 2, Bohemians 0; St Pats 4, Dundalk 2; UCD 5, Sligo Rovers 1.

The Republic of Ireland drew 0-0 with Scotland in the UEFA U16 Championship finals in Scotland.

Water Polo Half Moon beat Clonard 10-7 in the men's Irish Senior Cup final. In the women's Cup final Glenalbyn beat Half Moon 8-7 after extra time.

27: Snooker Fergal O'Brien was beaten 13-5 by Peter Ebdon in the second round of the World Championships.

28: GAA Former All-Star and Footballer of the Year , Peter Canavan, sustained a broken jaw in a challenge match in Tyrone.

Soccer The Republic of Ireland beat Finland 2-0 in the U16 UEFA Championships in Scotland.

Swimming Allegations about Michelle de Bruin resurfaced when it emerged that a drugs test taken by her in January allegedly produced some evidence of 'physical manipulation'. De Bruin rejected the claim.

29: Snooker Ken Doherty beat Matthew Stevens 13-10 in their World Championship quarter-final.

30: Soccer A goal from David McMahon gave the Republic of Ireland a 1-0 victory over defending champions Spain in the UEFA U16 Championships.

MAY

01: Cricket Ireland were beaten by 115 runs by Glamorgan in the Benson & Hedges Cup match at Castle Avenue.

Hockey The Irish women's team drew 2-2 with Scotland.

Soccer St Patrick's Athletic won the FAI National League when they beat Kilkenny City 2-1 at Kilkenny. Shelbourne, two points clear at the top before the final round of matches, lost 2-1 away to Dundalk allowing St Pats to claim the title by a single point. Elsewhere Shamrock Rovers drew 2-2 with Cork City.

Tennis Ireland suffered a double defeat to Hungary in the Davis Cup match when John Doran and Scott Baron both lost in the singles.

02: GAA Kerry qualified for the final of the U21 All-Ireland football championship when the beat Armagh 1-14 to 0-9 at Parnell Park.

Hockey The Irish senior women's team drew 1-1 with Scotland while the U21s beat Germany 1-0.

Horse Racing Mick Kinane guided the Aidan O'Brien trained King of Kings to victory in the 2,000 Guineas at Newmarket.

Rugby The Irish women's team were beaten 21-0 by Australia in the Women's World Cup in Holland.

Snooker Ken Doherty beat Mark Williams 17-14 to qualify for the final of the World Championships at Sheffield.

Soccer Glenavon beat Glentoran 1-0 after extra time in the Bass Irish Cup final.

03: GAA in the NHL semi-finals at Semple Stadium Waterford beat Limerick 2-17 to 2-11 and Cork beat Clare 2-15 to 0-10.

In the opening games of the 1998 Leinster SFC Westmeath beat Carlow and Wexford drew with Longford.

Golf Ulster won the Youths' Interprovincial Championship which was held in Connemara.

Soccer The Republic of Ireland beat Denmark 2-0 in the UEFA U16 Championship quarter final.

Results from the FAI PD: Bohemians 2, UCD 0; Derry City 3, Drogheda United 0; Sligo Rovers 2, Finn Harps 0. The results mean UCD play Limerick FC in a promotion/relegation play-off.

Squash Minnies of Dungarvan beat Old Belvedere 3-1 in the final of the All-Ireland men's club championship.

Tennis Ireland lost their Davis Cup tie 4-1 to Hungary in Budapest. The only Irish victory came from Scott Barron in the reverse singles.

04: Athletics Tommy Hughes won the Belfast marathon and England's Jackie Newton won the women's race.

Cricket Essex beat Ireland by 171 runs in the Benson & Hedges Cup at Chelmsford.

Cycling Tommy Evans won the Tour of Ulster by 36 seconds from Nick Salmon.

Hockey Instonians won the men's All-Ireland Club Championship on goal difference from Cork Church of Ireland.

Snooker John Higgins beat Ken Doherty 18-12 in the final of the World Championships in Sheffield. Doherty did however, collect the runner's up cheque of £132,000.

05: Cricket Middlesex beat Ireland by six wickets in their Benson & Hedges Cup match at Lord's.

Soccer The Republic of Ireland beat Portugal 2-0 in the semi-final of the UEFA U16 Championship in Perth, Scotland.

UCD beat Limerick 2-1 in the first leg of the promotion/relegation play-off.

Tennis Bosnia-Herzegovina beat Ireland 2-1 in the Federation Cup in Turkey.

06: Tennis Ireland beat Estonia 2-1 in the Federation Cup with Gina Niland and Lesley O'Halloran winning their singles matches.

07: Tennis Ireland beat Moldova 2-1 in the Federation Cup

08: Hockey Three goals from Kim Mills helped the Irish women's team to a 5-1 victory over Italy in a four nations tournament at Belfield.

Rugby Ireland's tour to South Africa was put in doubt when the South African National Sports Council requested a postponement pending the resolution of the dispute between it and the South African Rugby Football Union and President Louis Luyt.

The IRFU resolved their dispute with Wanderers when the committee announced Wanderers would not be relegated from Division Two. Malone and Ballynahinch will also play in Division Two of the AIL in the 1998/99 season bringing the total number of teams in that division to 16.

Soccer The Republic of Ireland U16 team won the European U16 Championship beating Italy 2-1 in the final in Scotland. The Irish goal scorers were Keith Foy and David McMahon.

UCD won their second leg of their promotion/relegation play off with Limerick by three goals to one.

Tennis Ireland were beaten 3-0 by Georgia in the Federation Cup in Turkey.

09: GAA Kerry beat Laois 2-8 to 0-11 in the All-Ireland U21 football final held in Limerick.

Hockey The Irish women's team beat France 5-0 at the Four Nations tournament at Belfield.

Rugby Skerries and Lansdowne qualified for the final of the Leinster Senior Cup, while in Munster the Senior Cup final will be between Young Munster and Shannon.

Ireland beat Holland 21-18 in the women's World Cup to qualify for the Shield semi-final.

Tennis Ireland beat Iceland 3-0 in their final match in the Federation Cup but failed to progress to the next round.

10: Canoeing Ian Wiley won the K1 class at the Irish Open held on the Liffey near Lucan. Tadhg McIntyre won the C1 class.

Formula 1 Eddie Irvine crashed out of the Spanish Grand Prix as did Damon Hill. Ralf Schumacher finished eleventh in the race which was won by Mika Hakkinen.

GAA Longford beat Wexford 0-16 to 2-7 in the Leinster SFC. In the Munster SFC Tipperary beat Limerick 1-13 to 1-12.

Golf Nineteen-year-old Michael Hoey won the Irish Amateur Open Strokeplay title at Royal Dublin by two shots from Gary Cullen.

Paul McGinley finished third in the Turespana Masters held in Majorca.

Hockey Ireland beat Wales 5-1 to claim top spot in the women's Four Nations tournament at Belfield.

Rugby Corinthians shocked Galwegians to win the Connacht Senior Cup 19-15 at the Galway Sportsground.

Soccer The FAI Cup final at Dalymount Park between Cork City and Shelbourne finished scoreless.

11: Rugby The resignation of South African Rugby Football Union President Louis Luyt meant that Ireland's tour to South Africa in June could go ahead.

12: Rugby Ireland beat Italy 20-5 in the Women's World Cup shield semi-final.

Malone beat Bangor 38-5 in the semi-final of the Ulster Senior Cup.

14: Soccer The Republic of Ireland qualified for the European U18 Championships with a 2-0 victory over Greece (3-0 on aggregate).

15: Snooker It emerged that Benson & Hedges Irish Masters winner Ronnie O'Sullivan failed a random drugs test at Goffs in March when traces of cannabis were found in his sample. O'Sullivan was stripped of his title and prize-money on July 6th.

16: Cycling The first stage of the FBD Milk Rás was won by Estonian Sigvard Kukk.

Rugby In the Munster Senior Cup final Shannon beat Young Munster 19-18 to record their second AIL/Munster Cup double in three years.

In the Leinster Senior Cup Lansdowne beat Skerries 23-17.

Soccer A 73rd minute goal from Derek Coughlan gave Cork City a 1-0 victory over Shelbourne in the FAI Cup final replay at Dalymount Park.

17: Cycling The second stage of the FBD Milk Rás from Mullingar to Tubbercurry was won by England's Jeff Wright.

GAA Cork beat Waterford 2-14 to 0-13 in the NHL final held at Semple Stadium.

Down beat Tyrone 0-15 to 2-7 in the Ulster SFC, in Leinster Westmeath beat Longford 3-14 to 1-13.

Golf Darren Clarke won the Benson & Hedges International at The Oxfordshire course by three shots from Spaniard Santiago Luna.

Joe McDermott, originally from Clare but based in the US for the past 40 years, won the Irish Seniors Open at Woodbrook on the fifth sudden death play-off hole.

Soccer: Thirty nine thousand fans attended Paul

McGrath's testimonial match at Lansdowne road which saw the Republic of Ireland lose to an international selection. McGrath also made his final appearance in an Irish shirt.

18: Cycling Dave Williams of the UK Bentec team won the third stage of the FBD Milk Rás from Tubbercurry to Westport. South Africa continued to lead the team competition from Ireland in second.

Soccer The Republic of Ireland U21s beat Scotland 3-0 in the opening match of their triangular tournament at Ballybofey.

19: Basketball In the opening games of men's European basketball championship preliminary round, Ireland beat Switzerland 88-80 but were beaten 57-56 by Cyprus.

Boxing Brian Magee advanced in the European Amateur Championships in Minsk.

Cycling Belgian Peter Lernout won the fourth stage of the FBD Milk Rás, covering the 116 miles from Westport to Kilrush in 4hrs 19mins 14 seconds.

Rugby Dungannon beat Malone 19-16 in the Ulster Senior Cup final at Ravenhill.

21: Boxing Eugene McEneaney was beaten in the quarter final of the lightweight division at the European Amateur Championship in Minsk

Soccer Northern Ireland drew 1-1 with Scotland in the U21 quadrangular tournament.

22: Boxing Belfast's Brian Magee qualified for the European Championship middleweight final in Belarus by beating Russian Strelchinin Dimitri 5-0.

Cycling Michael Fitzgerald of the Dublin-Usher team won the seventh stage of the Milk Rás.

Soccer Northern Ireland won the quadrangular tournament thanks to a 1-0 victory over the Republic in Castlebar.

23: Cycling Jeff Wright won the 95 miles eighth stage of the FBD Milk Rás which finished in Ballymore-Eustace.

Golf Lillian Behan won the Irish Women's Amateur Close Championship at Clandeboye beating Oonagh Purfield at the nineteenth hole in the final.

Horse Racing Olivier Peslier guided Desert Prince to victory in the 1,000 Guineas at the Curragh leaving red hot favourite Second Empire three lengths back in third.

Soccer The Republic of Ireland drew 0-0 with Mexico in a friendly at Lansdowne Road.

24: Boxing Belfast middleweight Brian Magee claimed a silver medal at the European Championships when he was beaten in the middleweight final 10-2 by Hungarian Zsolt Erdei

Cycling The FBD Milk Rás was won by Waterford man Ciaran Power in a time of 29 hours, 44 minutes and 49 seconds. Tommy Evans from County Down made it a one-two for the Irish team 45 seconds behind Power. The ninth and final stage of the Rás was won by Michael Fitzgerald.

Formula 1 Eddie Irvine finished third in the Monaco Grand Prix.

GAA Offaly hurlers hammered Meath 4-28 to 0-8 in the Leinster SHC quarter-final at Croke Park but the footballers of Meath extracted a quick revenge beating Offaly 3-10 to 0-7 less than two hours later.

In the Connacht SFC Galway beat Mayo 1-13 to 2-6. Waterford beat Kerry 0-20 to 1-9 in the Munster SHC. In the Ulster SFC Donegal beat Antrim 1-11 to 0-11.

Horse Racing Seventeen-year-old Jamie Spencer rode Tarascon to victory in the 2,000 Guineas at the Curragh.

Snooker Ken Doherty beat Jimmy White 10-2 in the final of the Dr. Martens Premier League.

28: Golf Co. Sligo beat Galway 6½ to 3½ in the Connacht final of the Fred Daly Trophy.

30: GAA A special congress convened to discuss the deletion of Rule 21 - the rule which prohibits members of the RUC and British Army from membership of the organisation and members of the GAA from attending functions organised by those forces - agreed to do so when the provisions relating to policing set out in the Good Friday Agreement are implemented.

Rugby Ireland opened their tour of South Africa with a 48-35 victory over provincial side Boland.

31: GAA National League champions Limerick were eliminated at the first hurdle in the Munster SHC beaten 1-20 to 3-11 by Cork at the Gaelic Grounds. Kilkenny had 21 points to spare over Dublin on a scoreline of 4-23 to 0-14 in the Leinster SHC while in the Leinster SFC Louth beat Wicklow, in the Ulster SFC Derry beat Monaghan and in the Connacht SFC Sligo beat London 0-14 to 1-7 at Ruislip.

Horse Racing Charlie Swan brought his ninth successive season at the head of the jockey's championship to a winning conclusion with a winner at Tralee.

Rowing At the World Cup regatta in Munich the Commercial quadruple scullers claimed a silver medal while Gearóid Towey won a bronze in the single sculls.

JUNE

01: Golf Darren Clarke finished second in the Deutsche Bank Open in Hamburg, one shot behind winner Lee Westwood. Philip Walton finished fourth.

Hockey Muckross claimed a bronze medal in the European women's Club Championship when they beat Swansea 3-1 on penalty strokes (3-3 aet).

Snooker TJ Dowling retained his National Snooker Championship title beating Douglas Hyde 8-4 in the final held at the Ivy Rooms in Carlow.

03: Rugby South-West District beat Ireland 27-20 in the second game of the South African tour in George.

Soccer Spain beat Northern Ireland 4-1 in Santander, Gerry Taggart scored for the North.

04: Athletics Sonia O'Sullivan finished third in the 5,000m at the IAAF meeting in Paris. Susan Smith finished sixth in the 400m hurdles.

Cricket Ireland drew with the MCC in their two day match at Lurgan.

05: Cricket Ireland beat Bangladesh by four wickets at Waringstown.

05: Horse Racing Mick Kinane guided the Aidan O'Brien trained Shahtoush to victory in the Oaks at Epsom.

06: Rugby Western Province beat Ireland 12-6 in Cape Town, with David Humphreys scoring two penalties for Ireland.

07: Athletics Catherina McKiernan comfortably won the Women's Mini Marathon in Dublin. Her time of 33

minutes 22.0 seconds was over a minute quicker than that of her nearest rival.

Irish records from Karen Shinkins in the 400m and Susan Smith in the 100m Hurdles were the outstanding results in a strong team performance at the Europa Cup in Lithuania. Eight victories for the men's team and seven for the women's team ensured promotion to Division One of the Cup for the 1999 season.

Canoeing Ian Wiley won a World Cup preliminary Class A international race in Italy.

Formula 1 Ferrari's Eddie Irvine finished third in the Canadian Grand Prix at Montreal while the Jordan team once again failed to have a car finish the race.

GAA Waterford beat Tipperary by 0-21 to 2-13 in the semi-final of the Munster SHC.

Over 60,000 spectators packed Croke Park and saw Dublin and Kildare draw 10 points apiece and Laois beat Westmeath 1-15 to 0-15 in the Leinster SFC.

In the Ulster SFC defending champions, Cavan, survived to beat a spirited Fermanagh by 0-13 to 0-11.

Golf Christy O'Connor Jnr finished joint tenth in the English Open at Hanbury Manor.

Soccer The Republic of Ireland women's team were beaten 3-0 by Poland. The defeat ended their hopes of qualifying for the World Cup.

08: Motor cycling Joey Dunlop won the 250 cc Lightweight Race in heavy rain at the Isle of Man TT races.

09: Athletics Sonia O'Sullivan finished second in the 1,500m at a meeting in Slovakia.

Rugby Ireland were beaten 52-13 by Griqualand West in the fourth game of their South African tour.

10: Motor cycling Robert Dunlop won the Isle of Man TT 125cc Ultra-Lightweight race.

11: Swimming Larne's Andrew Reid set a new Irish long course record of 25.82 seconds for the 50m butterfly at the Scottish national championships.

13: Hockey Scotland beat Ireland 2-1 in the men's international. Julian Stevenson scored the Irish goal.

Rugby Ireland lost the first of their two tests with South Africa by 37 points to 13. Three late unanswered tries gave the South Africans a flattering 24 point margin of victory.

14: Cycling Tommy Evans won the Noel Taggart Memorial race, part of the Classic League, at Banbridge.

GAA A last minute Johnny Dooley goal handed Offaly a 1-15 to 0-17 Leinster SHC semi-final victory over defending champions Wexford. In the other semi-final Kilkenny beat Laois 3-11 to 1-14.

In the Ulster SHC semi-final a controversial last minute point gave Antrim a 0-19 apiece draw with an unfancied London side.

Armagh beat Down by 0-16 to 0-11 in the Ulster SFC.

In the Connacht SFC semi-final Galway hammered Leitrim by 1-16 to 0-5.

15: Cricket Bangladesh beat Ireland A by 107 runs at Cork.

16: Rugby A try from Richard Wallace and seven penalties from David Humphreys helped Ireland beat North West Districts 26-18 in Pootchefstroom.

17: Golf Eddie Power from Kilkenny Golf Club beat Bryan Omelia from Newlands by one hole in the final of the Irish Amateur Close Championship.

19: Athletics Siobhan Hoey set a new national triple jump record of 12.38m at the Five Nations tournament in Estonia.

Horse Racing Royal Anthem, the mount of Kieren Fallon, won the King Edward VII Stakes at Royal Ascot. Mick Kinane on Kilimanjaro finished second.

20: Rugby Ireland lost 33-0 to South Africa in a bad tempered final test in Pretoria.

Soccer Shamrock Rovers lost 3-1 to Altay Spor in the Inter-Toto Cup.

21: Athletics Catherina McKiernan's string of fifteen consecutive victories ended when she finished third in an eleven kilometre race in Portugal.

GAA Donegal deposed defending champions Cavan beating them by 15 points to 13 in the Ulster SFC semi-final at Clones.

In the Leinster SFC quarter-final replay, Kildare beat Dublin 0-12 to 1-8.

In the Munster SHC semi-final, 16 points from play helped Clare to a 0-21 to 0-13 victory over Cork.

In the Ulster SHC semi-final Derry overcame defending champions Down beating them by 2-17 to 0-18 while Antrim hammered London in their semi-final replay winning 6-28 to 1-7.

Rallying Andrew Nesbitt won the Donegal International Rally by one minute seven seconds from Austin McHale.

Rowing The Irish lightweight quadruple scullers (Niall Byrne, Donal McGuinness, Emmet O'Brien and Niall O'Toole) won a bronze medal the World Cup Regatta in Belgium.

23: Sailing The Jeep Cherokee yacht won the Round Ireland Yacht Race in a record time of 76 hours 23 minutes 57 seconds.

25: Cricket Warwickshire beat Ireland by 41 runs in the Nat West Trophy match at Edgbaston.

27: Athletics Sonia O'Sullivan set a new two miles World Record of 9 minutes 19.56 seconds at the Cork City sports. Algerian Noureddine Morceli won the men's 1,500m, while Australian Cathy Freeman won the women's 200m.

28: Cycling R Clarke won the Irish Road Race Championship covering the 110 miles in 4 hours 19 minutes 34 seconds. The junior race was won by Mark Scanlon, the women's race by S. O'Mara and the men's team event was won by Navan.

Formula 1 Eddie Irvine finished second to team mate Michael Schumacher in the French Grand Prix at Magny Cours.

GAA Freescoring Tipperary beat Clare by 1-16 to 0-12 in the Munster SFC semi-final.

In the Connacht SFC semi-final to late Roscommon goals helped the draw with Sligo on a scoreline of 2-12 to 1-15.

Meath narrowly beat Louth by 0-15 to 1-11 in the Leinster SFC semi-final.

In the Ulster SFC semi-final Derry beat Armagh 2-13 to 0-12.

Golf Royal County Down won the Irish Women's Senior Cup defeating Co. Louth 3^1/2 to 1^1/2 in the final.

Horse Racing American jockey Cash Asmussen guided the 2/1 favourite Dream Well to victory in the Budweiser Irish Derby. City Honour was second and

Desert Fox third.

Soccer Shamrock Rovers beat Altay Spor 3-2 in the Inter-Toto Cup but lost 5-4 on aggregate.

30: Cricket Scotland beat Ireland by nine runs in the opening Triple Crow match at Greenock, Scotland.

JULY

01: Cricket Ireland beat the English amateur XI by four runs in the their triple crown match in Scotland.

Soccer Shamrock Rovers beat Cork City 2-1 in the first game of the FAI Super Cup.

02: Soccer St Patrick's Athletic beat Shelbourne 5-4 on penalties in the FAI Super Cup.

04: Cricket Clontarf, YMCA and Strabane all progressed to the semi-finals of the men's Irish Senior Cup.

Cycling Aidan Duff won the Tour of the Mournes from Michael McNena in second and David Peelo in third.

Tennis At the County Dublin Open Championship Owen Casey won the men's singles title and Claire Curran won the women's singles.

05: GAA Kilkenny were crowned Leinster hurling champions when they beat Offaly 3-10 to 1-11.

Antrim beat Derry by 1-19 to 2-13 in the Ulster SHC final.

All-Ireland champions Kerry beat Cork 1-14 to 1-11 in the Munster SFC semi-final.

Roscommon beat Sligo 1-13 to 0-15 in the Connacht SFC semi-final replay.

Golf David Carter beat defending champion Colin Montgomerie at the first extra hole to win the Murphy's Irish Open. Ireland's John McHenry finished in joint third place.

Soccer Shamrock Rovers won the inaugural FAI Super Cup when they beat St Pat's 2-0 in the final at Tolka Park. Cork City won the third/fourth place play-off when they beat Shelbourne 4-1 on penalties (1-1 after extra-time).

07: Hockey Ireland's women team drew 1-1 with Belarus in the European Nation's Cup qualifier in Helsinki.

09: Athletics Sonia O'Sullivan finished fourth in the 1,500m at the Bislett Games in Oslo.

Hockey The Czech Republic beat Ireland 2-1 on penalties strokes in the semi-final of the women's European Cup qualifiers.

10: Cricket Rain caused the abandonment of the Ireland-South Africa match at Downpatrick.

Hockey Ireland beat Belarus 6-1 to qualify for the 1999 Europeans Nations' Cup finals.

11: Cycling - Tour de France: Chris Boardman won the Prologue Time Trial of the Tour de France in Dublin city centre. He covered the 5.6 kilometre course in 6 minutes 12 seconds, Abraham Olano was second while Laurent Jalabert finished third.

GAA Galway easily defeated Roscommon in the Connacht SHC final on a scoreline of 2-27 to 3-13.

Tennis Owen Casey beat David Mullins 6-0, 6-1 in the Irish Close Championship men's singles final. In the women's final Gina Niland beat Claire Curran 4-6,6-4, 61.

12: Cricket South Africa beat Ireland by 63 runs at Castle Avenue.

Cycling - Tour de France: Belgian Tom Steels won the first stage proper of the Tour de France covering the 180 kilometre course from Dublin through Wicklow and back to the Phoenix Park in 4 hours 29 minutes and 58 seconds. Briton Chris Boardman retained the yellow jersey but one of the pre-race favourites Mario Cipollini crashed seven kilometres from the finish.

Formula 1 Ralf Schumacher scored Jordan's first points of the season when finishing sixth at the British Grand Prix. The race was won by his brother Michael while Ireland's Eddie Irvine finished third. Damon Hill spun out of the race on lap 16.

GAA Despite being eight points down at half time Waterford came back to draw 3-10 to 1-16 with defending Munster and All-Ireland champions Clare in the Munster SHC final.

Golf Ireland won the European Boys Team Championship beating Scotland 4-3 in the final which was held at Gullane in Scotland.

Horse Racing Winona and jockey Johnny Murtagh won the Irish Oaks at the Curragh from Kitza in second and Bahr in third.

13: Cycling - Tour de France: Jan Svorada won the 200km Enniscorthy to Cork second stage of the Tour de France in a time of five hours 45 minutes 10 seconds. Overall leader Chris Boardman crashed out of the Tour and was detained in hospital, his yellow jersey was taken Erik Zabel. A young girl was also detained in hospital after she was struck by a member of the peleton. The Tour then moved back to the continent with the third stage starting in Roscoff.

14: Athletics Sonia O'Sullivan finished ninth in the 1,500m at the Golden League meeting in Rome.

15: Athletics Seventeen-year-old Emily Maher won the 100 metres 11.92 seconds at the World Youth Olympics in Moscow.

16: Athletics Emily Maher struck gold again in winning the 200m in 24.16 seconds at the World Youth Olympics.

Sonia O'Sullivan finished second in the 3,000m at a Grand Prix meet in Nice. James McIlroy finished fourth in the 800m in a personal best time of 1 minute 45.32 seconds.

Horse Racing A double at Doncaster gave Kieren Fallon his 100th and 101st winners of the season, making 1998 the third successive season in which he recorded over 100 winners.

17: Tennis Victories from Owen Casey and John Doran gave Ireland a 2-0 lead in the Davis Cup match with Monaco.

18: Cricket Ballymena beat Donemana by three wickets in the quarter final of the Irish Senior Cup.

Rowing Neptune's men enjoyed a successful day at the National Championships winning the Senior Coxed and Coxless Fours, the Senior Pairs and the Senior Double Sculls. The women of Commercial enjoyed a similar hegemony winning the Senior Fours, Senior Pairs and Senior Quads.

Tennis Owen Casey and Tommy Hamilton secured an Irish victory in the Davis Cup match with Monaco, their three sets to love victory gave Ireland an unassailable 3-0 lead in the match.

19: Athletics Catherina McKiernan won a 10km road race in Amsterdam in a time of 32 minutes 53 seconds.

At the BUPA Games at Gateshead James McIlroy won the 800m in a time of 1 minute 46.87 seconds.

Cricket Holland inflicted a five wicket defeat on Ireland at The Hague.

Cycling Brian Kenneally won the 100 mile Matt Corcoran Cup race at Naas, Paul Butler was second with Paul Griffin third.

GAA An injury time goal from corner forward Joe Brolly handed Derry victory over Donegal by 1-7 to 0-8 in the Ulster SFC final.

In the Connacht SFC final unfancied Roscommon held Galway to a draw, 0-11 apiece.

Kildare advanced to the Leinster SFC final beating Laois 2-13 to 0-8.

In a torrid hard hitting Munster SHC replay Clare ran out 2-16 to 0-10 victors over Waterford.

Rowing The men's National Senior Eights title was won by Neptune who beat Trinity by two lengths. The women's title was won by Commercial by one length from UCD.

Soccer In the opening match of the U18 European Championships in Cyprus the Republic of Ireland beat Croatia 5-2.

Tennis George McGill and John Doran completed an Irish whitewash of Monaco in the Davis Cup winning their reverse singles ties.

21: Athletics Sonia O'Sullivan finished fifth overall in the mile at the Goodwill Games in New York.

Cricket Denmark beat Ireland by three wickets in the European Championship.

Swimming On the opening day of the Irish Open Championships Terenure won the men's 4x200m Freestyle relay.

Soccer England beat the Republic of Ireland 1-0 in the U18 European Championships.

22: Soccer In the European Champions League Preliminary round first leg National League champions St Patrick's Athletic held Celtic to a scoreless draw at Parkhead while Irish League champions Cliftonville lost 5-1 to Slovakian side FC Kosice at Solitude.

In the qualifying round first leg of the UEFA Cup Shelbourne raced into a 3-0 lead against Glasgow Rangers before losing 5-3 in a game held in Liverpool due to security considerations. Omonia Nicosia beat Linfield 5-1 in Cyprus.

Swimming Hugh O'Connor captured the men's 200m Backstroke and 100m Individual Medley titles at the National Championships while Niamh Cawley won the women's 200m Backstroke title.

23: Athletics Corkman Mark Carroll finished seventh in the 5,000m at the Goodwill Games in New York.

Cricket Scotland beat Ireland by 20 runs in the European Championships.

Golf Co. Sligo professional Leslie Robinson won the Irish Club Professional Championship at Nuremore Golf Club in Monaghan.

Soccer A 3-0 victory over hosts Cyprus and England's 3-0 defeat to Croatia helped the Republic of Ireland qualify for the European Youth Championships final.

Swimming Lee Kelleher won the women's 100m Butterfly and 200m Individual Medley titles at the National Championships. Hugh O'Connor collected a further two titles in winning the 50m Backstroke and 200m Freestyle.

24: Cricket Australia beat Ireland by 172 runs in the women's match held at College Park.

A four wicket defeat by Scotland saw Ireland finish fourth overall in the European Championships in Holland.

Swimming Lee Kelleher and Hugh O'Connor continued their good form at the National Championships picking up further titles while Colin Lowth set a national record of 2.00.33 in winning the 200m Butterfly.

25: Athletics Winners from the opening day of the National Championships at Santry were, Men: Noel Berkley (10,000m); Pierce O'Callaghan (10km Walk); Joseph Naughton (Long Jump); Terry McHugh (Javelin); and John Dermody (Shot Putt).

Women: Sonia O'Sullivan (5,000m); Gillian O'Sullivan (5km Walk); Orna Donoghue (High Jump); Jacqui Stokes (Long Jump); and Ailish O'Brien (Discus).

Rowing Ireland's won the men's senior eights at the Home International Championships in Scotland. Other victories came in the men's senior coxed fours and the women's quadruple scull.

Swimming Chantal Gibney (women's 100m freestyle) and Nick O'Hare (men's 100m freestyle) were among the winners on the final day of the Irish National Championships.

Tennis Lucie Ahl won the Irish Women's Open Championship beating Petra Mandulla 7-6, 6-3.

26: Athletics Winners from the second day of the National Championships were, Men: Neil Ryan (100m); Gary Ryan (200m); Brian Forbes (400m); James Nolan (800m); James McIlroy (1,500m); Martin McCarthy (5,000m); Eugene O'Neill (3,000m steeplechase); Peter Coghlan (110m Hurdles); Tom McGuirk (400m Hurdles); Mark Mandy (High Jump); Michael McDonald (Triple Jump); Roman Linscheid (Hammer); John Menton (Discus); Neil Young (Pole Vault); and John Menton (56lbs for distance), who set a new Irish record of 9.16 metres.

Women: Lena Barry (100m); Ciara Sheehy (200m); Karen Shinkins (400m); Sinead Delahunty (800m); Una English (1,500m); Susan Smith (100m Hurdles); Orla Power (400m Hurdles); Siobhan Hoey (Triple Jump); Marg O'Halloran (Pole vault); Olivia Kelleher (Hammer); Emma Gavin (Shot Putt); and Alison O'Brien (Javelin). Susan Smith set a new Irish record of 13.31 seconds in winning the 100m Hurdles.

Cycling The Hardings Grand Prix at Cork was won by Brian Kenneally.

Robin Seymour retained the National Mountainbike Championship.

Formula 1 Eddie Irvine finished fourth in the Austrian Grand Prix while Jordan secured valuable championship points when Ralf Schumacher finished fourth.

GAA The All-Ireland SHC quarter-finals held at Croke Park saw Waterford and Offaly overwhelm Galway and Antrim, respectively.

Golf Darren Clarke finished second to Australian Stephen Leaney in the Dutch Open at Hilversum and collected a prize of £88,880.

Suzanne O'Brien won the Irish Women's Amateur Open which rain limited to only 36 holes. O'Brien's

141 total was six shots clear of Lillian Behan in second.

Soccer The Republic of Ireland beat Germany 4-3 on penalties in the final of the European Youth Championships in Cyprus. With the score 1-1 after full time and extra time, a save from keeper Alex O'Reilly and converted penalties from Ryan Casey, Paul Donnolly, Barry Quinn and Liam George secured victory.

27: Cricket Women's World Champions, Australia, secured a 3-0 test series result when they beat Ireland by 95 runs.

29: Horse Racing Amlah, trained by Philip Hobbs and the mount of Brendan Powell won the centrepiece of the Galway Festival, the Compaq Galway Plate.

Soccer In the second leg games of the Champions League preliminary round Celtic beat St Pats 2-0 (2-0 on aggregate) at Tolka Park while Cliftonville were hammered 8-0 (13-1 on aggregate) by FC Kosice.

In the UEFA Cup second-leg games, Rangers beat Shelbourne 2-0 (7-3 on aggregate) at Ibrox while Linfield beat Omonia 5-3 (losing 6-8 on aggregate) at Windsor Park.

30: Horse Racing Black Queen, the mount of Shay Barry and trained by John Kiely, won the Guinness sponsored Galway Handicap Hurdle.

AUGUST

01: Cricket Leinster beat Malahide by seven wickets in the Leinster Senior Cup final. The North West Senior Cup final was won by Brigade who beat Ardmore by 5 wickets.

GAA Galway sneaked past Roscommon in the Connacht SFC final replay. 0-11 apiece after 70 minutes Galway ran out winners 1-17 to 0-17 after extra-time.

02: Athletics Sonia O'Sullivan was beaten into second place by great rival Paula Radcliffe in the 3,000m at the British Grand Prix in Sheffield. In the men's 800m James Nolan and David Matthews finished fifth and sixth respectively.

Cycling Brian Kenneally's good form in the Classic League continued with victory in round nine at Listowel from David Peelo in second and C Bracken in third.

Formula 1 Jordan enjoyed their best day of the 1998 season when drivers Damon Hill and Ralf Schumacher finished fourth and sixth respectively at the German Grand Prix. Eddie Irvine finished eighth.

GAA Defending All-Ireland champions Kerry proved too good for Tipperary in the Munster SFC final at Thurles. The men from te Kingdom won by 0-17 to 1-10.

In the Leinster SFC final perennial under achievers Kildare beat neighbours Meath 1-12 to 0-10.

Golf At the Scandinavian Masters in Stockholm Darren Clarke finished second, three shots behind Sweden's Jesper Parnevik.

04: Grants Minister for Tourism, Sport and Recreation Dr Jim McDaid announced grants for 170 athletes totalling £925,825.

Soccer The Republic of Ireland beat Denmark 4-0 in their opening game of the U16 Nordic Cup in Iceland.

05: Soccer The Republic of Ireland U16s beat hosts Iceland 1-0 in the Nordic Cup.

07: Golf Leinster won the women's golf interprovincial title with Ulster second, and Munster and Connacht joint third.

Rugby Connacht defeated the touring Morocco side by 30 points to 5 at Corinthian Park.

Soccer A 20th minute goal from Robert Doyle gave the Republic of Ireland a 1-0 victory over Norway in the U16 Nordic Cup.

08: Cricket Strabane beat YMCA by three wickets in the Irish Senior Cup semi-final, while Ballymena made it an all-Ulster final with a narrow two run victory over Clontarf.

Hockey Belgium beat Ireland 1-0 in the men's senior international held at Belfield.

09: Athletics Susan Smith lowered her Irish 100m hurdles record to 13.12 seconds at the National League finals in Tullamore.

GAA All-Ireland champions Clare were rocked by a resurgent Offaly side in the All-Ireland SHC semi-final at Croke Park. A Johnny Pilkington goal followed by two points put Offaly in front in the 68th minute but 1997 hurler of the year Jamesie O'Connor equalised from a free on the stroke of full time to keep Clare's championship alive. The final score was 1-13 apiece. In the minor semi-final Cork beat Wexford, 0-12 to 0-10.

Golf Welshman Brian Huggett beat Ireland's Eddie Polland at the first play-off hole in the British Seniors' Open at Royal Portrush. Both men had finished the tournament in a five under par score of 283.

A bogey on the last hole at the German Open in Berlin cost Padraig Harrington victory. His final round of 69 for a total of 281 saw him share second place with three other players.

Horse Racing Fourteen-to-one shot Lavery, ridden by Walter Swinburn won the Group One Heinz 57 Phoenix Stakes at Leopardstown.

Soccer Brian Kerr's remarkable underage success continued when his U16 charges beat England 3-2 in the final of the Nordic Cup in Iceland.

10: Rugby Ulster hammered the visiting Moroccan national side 50-5.

12: Athletics Susan Smith broke her second national record in three days when she lowered her 400m hurdles mark to 54.31 in finishing seventh at the Weltklasse meeting in Zurich.

Sonia O'Sullivan finished seventh in the 1,500m at the same meeting.

13: Soccer In the Cup Winners' Cup qualifying round first leg, Cork City beat CSKA Kiev 2-1 at Turners' Cross while Glentoran were beaten 1-0 by Maccabi Haifa in Belfast.

14: Rugby In the opening game of the Guinness Interprovincial Series, Ulster beat Leinster 34-14 at Donnybrook.

Soccer In the opening game of the 1998/99 IFA PD campaign new boys Newry Town beat Linfield 2-1.

15: Cycling Ciarán Power finished 13th overall in the 180km European U23 road race championships in Sweden.

Cricket Strabane beat Ballymena by 24 runs in the Irish Senior Cup final at Beechgrove. The match, which began the previous day was interrupted by rain.

Rugby Munster beat Connacht 18-13 in the Interprovincial held at the Galway Sportsgrounds. Leinster A beat Morocco 33-14 at Donnybrook.

Soccer In the IFA PD there were victories for Ballymena, Portadown, Coleraine and Glentoran.

Tennis Owen Casey won the men's singles and Gina Niland won the women's singles at the East of Ireland Open Championships held at Londonbridge Road.

16: Formula 1 Team Jordan moved into fifth in the Constructors' Championship by virtue of Damon Hill's fourth place finish in the Hungarian Grand Prix. Ferrari's Eddie Irvine retired early in the race.

GAA Leinster champions Kilkenny beat Munster runners-up Waterford by 1-11 to 1-10 in the Guinness sponsored All-Ireland SHC semi-final at Croke Park. In the curtain raiser Kilkenny qualified for the All-Ireland MHC final beating Galway on a scoreline of 2-10 to 1-12.

18: Athletics At the European Athletics Championships in Budapest Niall Bruton qualified for the final of the 1,500m while Tom McGuirk qualified for the semi-finals of the 400m hurdles.

Rugby Munster outclassed Morocco beating them 49-17 at Musgrave Park.

19: Athletics In her first ever race over the distance Sonia O'Sullivan claimed the European 10,000m title in a time of 31 minutes, 29.33 seconds. On an outstanding day for Irish women's athletics, Susan Smith won her 400m hurdles semi-final and Karen Shinkins set a new national record of 52.13 seconds in qualifying for the 400m semi-final.

20: Athletics Niall Bruton finished twelfth in the final of the men's 1,500m at the European Championships in Hungary. In the men's 200m Gary Ryan ran 20.76 to qualify for the semi-finals while Karen Shinkins missed out by mere hundredths of a second on qualifying for the women's 400m final.

21: Athletics Susan Smith finished a disappointing eighth in the final of the 400m hurdles. Elsewhere Sinead Delahunty qualified for the 1,500m final and in the 800m for men James McIlroy, James Nolan and David Matthews all qualified for the semi-finals.

Rugby Leinster bounced back from their defeat by Ulster by beating Munster 24-18 in the Interprovincial Series.

22: Athletics Mark Carroll won a superb bronze medal in the men's 5,000m at the European Championships, in the semi-finals of the 800m James McIlroy was the only Irish athlete to progress to the finals.

GAA Controversy engulfed the All-Ireland SHC semi-final replay between Clare and Offaly when referee Jimmy Cooney blew the final whistle two minutes before full-time with the score standing at Clare 1-16, Offaly 2-10. A 90-minute protest by Offaly supporters on the pitch caused the U21 B All-Ireland hurling final to be postponed. The Games Administration Committee of the GAA ordered a replay for the following Saturday.

Rugby Connacht beat favourites Ulster 21-18 in the Interprovincial match at the Sportsgrounds.

Soccer Results from the IFA PD: Cliftonville 2, Glentoran 4; Coleraine 1, Portadown 0; Glenavon 3, Crusaders 0; Linfield 1, Balymmena 0.

23: Athletics Sonia O'Sullivan secured an unprecedented double when she beat Romanian rival Gabriella Szabo to win the 5,000m at the European Championships. O'Sullivan is now the reigning European 3,000m, 5,000m and 10,000m champion. In the men's 800m James McIlroy finished outside the medals in fourth place while Sinead Delahunty finished ninth in the women's 1,500m final.

GAA Underlining the rise to prominence of Connacht teams Galway qualified for the All-Ireland SFC final beating a lethargic Derry side by 0-16 to 1-8. In the All-Ireland MFC semi-final Tyrone defeated Leitrim 1-14 to 1-3.

Golf Swede Mathias Gronberg was a runaway ten shot runner winner of the Smurfit European Open at the K Club in Kildare collecting a first prize of £208,300. Darren Clarke was the leading Irish finisher eleven shots back in fourth place.

North of Ireland champion Paddy Gribben became the first Irishman to win the European Amateur Golf Championship finishing two shots clear of the field in Bordeaux.

26: Cricket Australia A beat Ireland by just three wickets in a match curtailed to 35 overs.

27: Cricket Australia A beat Ireland by eight wickets at Waringstown.

Soccer Cork City were beaten 2-0 (3-2 on aggregate) by the Ukranian champions CSKA Kiev in the Cup Winners' Cup. In the same competition Northern Ireland representatives, Glentoran, were beaten 2-1 (3-1 on aggregate) by Maccabi Haifa in Israel.

28: Athletics Mark Carroll set a new Irish record of seven minutes 33.84 seconds for the 3,000m at the IAAF Golden League meeting in Brussels. At the same meeting Sonia O'Sullivan finished fourth and Sinead Delahunty tenth in the 1,500m. Susan Smith finished sixth in the 400m hurdles and James McIlroy was sixth in the 800m.

Cricket Australia A made it three victories in a row when they beat Ireland by 170 runs at Downpatrick.

GAA Tipperary beat Offaly 2-9 to 0-6 in the All-Ireland Junior football final.

Rugby Leinster beat Connacht 29-24 in the Interprovincial Championship.

Soccer Results from the FAI PD: Bohemians 2, Finn Harps 3; Shelbourne 2, Shamrock Rovers 2; Waterford United 1, UCD 0.
Results from the IFA PD: Glenavon 2, Coleraine 1; Newry Town 2, Cliftonville 1.

29: Cricket Australia A completed a series whitewash when they beat Ireland by four wickets in the fourth and final one day international.

GAA In the third installment of the Clare v Offaly All-Ireland SHC semi-final Offaly, led by five points from play by Joe Dooley, beat the reigning All-Ireland Champions by 0-16 to 0-13.
In the All-Ireland U21 hurling championship semi-final Galway hammered Kilkenny on a scoreline of 4-18 to 3-7.

Soccer Linfield beat Crusaders 4-1 in the IFA PD.

30: Cycling Irish Junior champion Sligoman Mark Scanlon won the 490 miles Credit Union Junior Tour by over three minutes from British Junior champion Yanto Barker.

Formula 1 Jordan Grand Prix recorded their first ever victory when Damon Hill won the Belgian Grand Prix at Spa Francorschamps. In wet conditions Hill survived a restart and led team-mate Ralf Schumacher to the chequered flag and a history making one-two.

GAA Leinster champions Kildare dethroned 1997 All-Ireland champions Kerry in the All-Ireland SFC semi-final at Croke Park. Kildare's 0-13 to 1-9 to victory ensured their appearance in their first All-Ireland final since 1935.

In the All-Ireland minor football semi-final defending champions Laois beat Kerry by 1-10 to 2-5.

Kerry beat Kildare by 3-9 to 0-17 in the All-Ireland U21 B final.

Hockey Ireland U21 men's team won the European B Division championship beating France 4-0 in Padova. Earlier victories included an 11-1 trouncing of Denmark and a 3-1 defeat of Italy.

Soccer Results from the FAI PD: Bray Wanderers 0, Cork City 1; Derry City 0, St Patrick's Athletic 1.

SEPTEMBER

01: Athletics Mark Carroll set a new Irish record of 13 minutes 3.93 seconds for the 5,000m in finishing seventh at the IAAF Grand Prix meeting in Berlin. Sonia O'Sullivan finished a distant fourth in the women's 5,000m while Sinead Delahunty was seventh in the 1,500m.

GAA The GAA opened their new state-of-the-art museum at Croke Park. The museum, situated under the Cusack Stand, cost £3.5million and tells the history of the organisation and the games.

Soccer Results from the IFA PD: Cliftonville 0, Ballymena 1; Coleraine 1, Glentoran 3; Linfield 2, Glenavon 0; Omagh 0, Crusaders 0; Portadown 2, Newry 3.

02: Soccer Jackie Blanchflower, former Northern Ireland international and 'Busby Babe', died aged 65.

England beat the Republic of Ireland 5-0 in an U18 international played at Tolka Park.

04: Rugby In the Interprovincial Series Ulster beat Munster 29-12 at Ravenhill.

In friendly matches Connacht lost 13-28 to Glasgow and Leinster defeated Edinburgh Reivers 15-13.

Soccer The Republic of Ireland U21s drew 2-2 with Croatia in their opening European Championship match at Buckley Park, Kilkenny.

In the FAI PD St Patrick's Athletic beat Dundalk 3-1 while Bray Wanderers beat Shamrock Rovers 1-0 at Tolka Park.

05: Athletics Sonia O'Sullivan finished 5th in the 3,000m in the IAAF Golden League final in Moscow.

Canoeing The 39th annual Liffey Descent attracted 1,200 entrants. The men's K1 Class was won by Malcolm Banks and the K2 Class was won by Alan and Ian Tordoff. The women's K1 Class was won by Michelle Barry.

Soccer A penalty from Denis Irwin and a header from Roy Keane gave the Republic of Ireland a 2-0 victory over Croatia in the opening game of the European Championships qualifying campaign. Croatia had two players sent off in the closing stages.

Northern Ireland were beaten 3-0 by Turkey in the opening game of Group Three.

Results from the IFA PD: Ballymena 1, Linfield 2; Cliftonville 1, Glenavon 2; Omagh 0, Coleraine 2; Newry 1, Glentoran 2; Portadown 0, Crusaders 2.

Results from the FAI PD: Finn Harps 1, Waterford 2; Sligo Rovers 2, Bohemians 2.

06: Camogie Cork retained the All-Ireland Senior Camogie Championship beating Galway 2-13 to 0-15 at Croke Park. The Junior All-Ireland final was won by Galway who beat Tipperary 3-11 to 2-10.

Golf Swede Sophie Gustafson won the Irish Women's Open at Ballyliffin. The tournament was curtailed to three rounds as gales buffeted the Inishowen links.

Darren Clark collected £50,070 when he finished third in the European Masters taking his 1998 tournament earnings to £597,847.

Soccer Results from the FAI PD: Cork City 2, Shelbourne 1; Derry City 1, UCD 1.

Tennis Ireland won both the men's and women's Four Nations Senior International held at Cork, winning each of the matches against England, Scotland and Wales.

07: Soccer Shamrock Rovers beat Bohemians 1-0 in the quarter final of the League Cup.

09: Golf Ireland beat Scotland 11-4 in the opening match of the men's Home Internationals in Wales.

The Irish women's team lost 4-5 to England in the opening match of the women's Home Internationals.

Damian Mooney won the Ulster PGA title at Enniskillen.

10: Golf Ireland drew 7$^1/2$-7$^1/2$ with Wales in the men's Home Internationals.

Ireland's women drew 4$^1/2$-4$^1/2$ with Scotland in the Home International in England.

Soccer Dundalk and Shamrock Rovers drew 1-1 in the FAI PD.

11: Golf Ireland lost 7-8 to England in the deciding match of the men's Home Internationals to finish second overall.

Ireland's women also finished second in the Home Internationals when they beat Wales 6-3.

Rugby In the Interprovincial series Leinster crushed Ulster 35-11 at Ravenhill.

Soccer Results from the FAI PD: Bohemians 0, Cork City 2; Shelbourne 0, Finn Harps 0; Waterford 0, St Patrick's Athletic 2.

12: Athletics Sonia O'Sullivan, representing Europe, won the 5,000m in the World Cup Championship in South Africa collecting $50,000.

Rugby Munster beat Connacht 21-7 in the Interprovincial Series.

Soccer Results from the IFA Premier Division: Cliftonville 2, Glenavon 2; Coleraine 2, Newry 2; Glentoran 2, Ballymena 1; Omagh 1, Linfield 3; Portadown 0, Crusaders.

13: Formula 1 Eddie Irvine finished second in the Italian Grand Prix at Monza behind Ferrari team mate Michael Schumacher. Jordan drivers Ralf Schumacher and Damon Hill finished third and sixth respectively to move within striking distance of Williams and Benetton in the Constructors' Championship

GAA Offaly created hurling history when they became the first side to win the All-Ireland title via the 'back-door'. In the final, the experience gained from three matches with Clare and the inspirational switch of Brian Whelahan from defence to attack overwhelmed a bemused Kilkenny side who had five points to spare over them in the Leinster decider only two months earlier. Led by a goal and six points from Whelahan Offaly ran out winners by 2-16 to 1-13.

Cork dismissed the challenge of Kilkenny in the All-Ireland Minor final defeating them by 2-15 to 1-9.

Rowing The Irish lightweight quadruple scullers finished fourth in the World Rowing Championship final at Cologne, Germany.

Soccer Results from the FAI PD: Derry City 5, Bray Wanderers 1; UCD 2, Sligo Rovers 0.

14: Soccer St Patrick's Athletic beat Longford Town 3-2 on penalties to advance to the semi-final of the League Cup.

15: Soccer Galway United beat Shelbourne 2-1 in the League Cup quarter final at Tolka Park.

17: Golf Warrenpoint beat Co. Sligo by one hole in the final of the Barton Shield at Athlone.

18: Golf At the National Cups and Shields finals held at Athlone Old Conna beat Tuam 3-2 to win the Junior Cup and Nenagh beat Woodbrook 3½-1½ to win the Pierce Purcell Shield.

Rugby Ulster drew with Edinburgh Reivers in their opening match of the European Cup. The sides shared seven tries and the match ended 38 points apiece.

Soccer St Patrick's Athletic beat Bohemians 3-0 in the FAI PD.

19: Boxing Michael Carruth overcame Scott Dixon to win the WAA World Welterweight title at the National Basketball Arena.

Golf Cork beat Shandon Park 4-1 in the final of the National Senior Cup at Athlone while Moate beat Portumna 3½-1½ in the final of the Jimmy Bruen Shield.

Rugby Munster beat Padova 20-13 in Pool B of the European Cup while Leinster beat Llanelli 33-27 in Pool A.

Soccer Results from the IFA PD: Ballymena 1, Newry 1; Crusaders 0, Glentoran 0; Glenavon 1, Portadown 0; Linfield 1, Cliftonville 0; Omagh 2, Coleraine 0.

Results from the FAI PD: Bray Wanderers 1, Shelbourne 0; Cork City 4, Dundalk 1; Finn Harps 0, UCD 0; Sligo Rovers 1, Waterford 1.

20: Camogie Down won the All-Ireland Intermediate Championship beating Cork 1-12 to 1-8.

Golf Richard Coughlan recorded his best result of the year in the US PGA Tour finishing ninth overall in the B.C. Open at New York.

Soccer Shamrock Rovers drew 0-0 with Derry City in the FAI PD.

22: Soccer Cork City beat Derry City 3-0 on penalties in the League Cup quarter final.

25: Rugby Stade Francais beat Leinster 28-17 in the European Cup match at Donnybrook.

Soccer Results from the FAI PD: Bohemians 1, Bray Wanderers 2; Dundalk 2, Derry City 2; Shelbourne 1, Sligo Rovers 1; Waterford 1, Shamrock Rovers 1.

26: Rugby Munster beat Neath 34-10 in Pool B of the European Cup, in Pool C Ulster lost 39-3 to Toulouse.

In the European Conference Connacht travelled to Newport and inflicted a 31-12 defeat on their hosts.

Soccer Finn Harps beat St Patrick's Athletic 2-1 in the FAI PD.

Results from the IFA PD: Cliftonville 2, Omagh 1; Coleraine 2, Ballymena 1; Glentoran 5, Glenavon 2; Newry 0, Crusaders 0; Portadown 0, Linfield 2.

27: Formula 1 Eddie Irvine finished fourth in the Luxembourg Grand Prix while the Jordan duo of Damon Hill and Ralf Schumacher failed to register championship points for the first time in six races.

GAA A second half western awakening saw Galway overturn a three point half time deficit to claim the All-Ireland Football Championship with four points to spare over Kildare on a scoreline of 1-14 to 1-10. Match winning displays from Jarlath Fallon, Michael Donnellan and manager John O'Mahony saw Galway bridge a 32 year barren gap between All-Ireland victories and extended Kildare's 70 year wait by at least twelve months.

Tyrone claimed the All-Ireland Minor football Championship beating defending champions Laois by 2-11 to 0-11. In an exceptional act of sportsmanship Laois formed a guard of honour and applauded the new champions off the pitch.

Golf Paul McGinley finished joint sixth in the German Masters at Cologne.

Soccer Cork City beat UCD 1-0 in their FAI PD match at Belfield.

❑

YEAR IN QUOTES

"Well, I was hitting somebody out there, I hope the referee is all right."

Neil Gough, Waterford welterweight after Jimmy Magee suggested that his points total indicated that he hadn't landed a punch.

"This is not a normal win, this is an incredible win."

Padraig Harrington, professional golfer after winning the World Cup with partner Paul McGinley.

"He is a few french fries short of a happy meal. His mind goes on vacation and leaves his mouth in charge. But he's not really a bad guy."

David Feherty, the former Ryder Cup golfer on Colin Montgomerie.

"All I can say to them now is that Elvis had a tremendous game out on the wing for us."

Stephen Napier, Cork City defender, after being told by his team mates that for him to score in a third consecutive game would take a cross from Elvis.

"She's a great filly. I once rode her mother on the Curragh."

Ted Walsh, RTÉ sports commentator.

"I didn't believe there were so many fans out there."

D J Carey, Kilkenny County Hurler, returning to hurling after announcing his retirement in February 1998.

"I miss the things like the camaraderie in the gym. I don't miss being smacked in the mouth everyday."

Barry McGuigan, former WBA World feather-weight champion boxer, reflecting on his retirement from the boxing ring.

"I am innocent."

Michelle de Bruin, triple Olympic swimmer, amid allegations that a urine sample given by her had been tampered with.

"It's special for all the people who have been involved in schoolboy football around Ireland for the last 60 years or so. It's for the people, those who mark pitches, put up nets and wash gear and don't get the glory of a day like this."

Brian Kerr, the Republic of Ireland under-16 soccer manager, after they beat Italy to win the UEFA Youth's Championship in Scotland.

"It's fabulous for us as well as for everyone in football in Ireland. It's the best feeling of my life. I would like to think that I would go on to do better things, but up to now this has been the best feeling."

Barry Quinn, the Republic of Ireland under-18 football captain, on becoming European Champions.

"The 21st was off-side."

Brian Kerr, coach of the Republic of Ireland under-18 team, after they beat a UN squad (which included Irish Soldiers) 22-0 in Cyprus.

"He's so big, he has an arse like a bag of cement. You can't get near him when the ball comes in, yet he has the most delicate skills."

Joe Brolly, Derry Gaelic footballer acknowledging his team mate Geoffrey McGonigle for setting up his goal in the Ulster Final.

"That was the hardest fight of my life."

Steve Collins, former WBO super-middleweight champion boxer, after winning a legal battle with his former manager Barry Hearn.

"Columbo's a must for any trainee barrister ... often in front of a jury, I would try and slip in a Columbo line. Just as they're about to sit down, I'll stand up and say 'Just one more thing ...'."

Joe Brolly, Derry Gaelic footballer and Barrister.

"When I retired from Kerry football I thought I'd seen the last of one man . . . I never thought he'd come back to haunt me!"

Páidí Ó Sé, the Kerry Manager, on his old friend Mick O'Dwyer, the Kildare Manager.

"I wished to God the whole world could open up and take me away altogether."

Jimmy Cooney, Galway referee after he brought a premature end to the Clare-Offaly Replay.

"We may have come in through the back door, but we're going out the front!"

Hubert Rigney, Captain of the Offaly Hurling team after lifting the McCarthy Cup in their All-Ireland success over Kilkenny.

"They thought that the west was asleep. I hope some of them bookies know better next time. They should stick to horses."

A Galway Supporter, after the team's success over Kildare in the All-Ireland Gaelic Football Final.

❑

OBITUARIES

October 1997 to September 1998

BALL, Peter (1943-1997) b. England, sports journalist and author of several sporting books. Soccer correspondent with *The Sunday Tribune*, Northern football correspondent with *The Times* at time of death. Former sports editor of *Time Out* magazine. Also contributed articles to *The Observer*, *The Times* and *Magill*. Collaborated with Eamon Dunphy on *Only a Game*, and with Graeme Fowler on *Fox on the Run* which won the Channel 4 Sports Book of the Year in 1988. Died November, 1997.

BECKETT, Martin (1980-1998) Kerry Under-21 Gaelic footballer. A member of the 1998 winning Kerry All-Ireland Under-21 football team in May. Played his club football with Dr Crokes and had trained on several occasions with the Kerry senior football team. Killed tragically in a car accident in September, 1998.

BLANCHFLOWER, Jackie (1933-1998) b. Belfast, former Northern Ireland International and Manchester United soccer player. Made his Northern Ireland debut in 1954, winning 12 caps. Joined Manchester United in 1949 as an amateur, turning professional in 1950. Survived the Munich Air Crash in 1958 (which killed eight United players) but was badly injured and retired prematurely from football to become an accountant. Brother of Danny, also a Northern Ireland International and Tottenham player. Died September, 1998.

BRENNAN, Charlie (CJ) former tennis player. Former president (twice) and former secretary of the Irish Lawn Tennis Association twice. A member of the Elm Park, Fitzwilliam and Sutton Clubs. A long-term administrator in the game at Leinster and Irish Council levels. Died October, 1997.

CAIRNS, David (1942-1998) Northern Ireland's Schools Football Association Chairman. Former amateur international, he played with Ballymena, Cliftonville and Linfield in the Irish League. Former Principal of Ballycraigy Primary School in Antrim. Manager of the Northern Ireland Schoolboy Team for 18 years. Died July, 1998.

COSTELLO, Paddy (1931-1997) b. Dublin, former rugby player. Played with Bective Rangers, Leinster and Ireland. An international athlete who represented Ireland at shot putt and a former soccer player. Won Leinster Senior Cup medals with Bective Rangers in 1955, 1956 and 1962. Was capped for Leinster seven times in the interprovincial series (1956-60) and capped for Ireland in 1960 against France in an International Championship Match. Died October, 1997.

CRYAN, Tom (1932-1998) former sports journalist. Boxing correspondent and chief sports reporter with the *Irish Independent*, also covered the olympic games and golf. Retired in 1996, his career in journalism spanned over 47 years. Died September, 1998.

DALTON, Mick League of Ireland footballer in the late 1950s and 1960s. Made his debut with Bohemians, then moved to Sligo Rovers, Dundalk and Shelbourne. Died December, 1997.

DAVEY, Shane (1979-1998) Co. Down Minor and under-21 Gaelic footballer. A member of the Newry Shamrocks Gaelic club. Killed in New York. Died September, 1998.

DOLAN, Paul b. Donegal, former olympic athlete. Represented Ireland at the Olympic Games in London (1948), competing in the 4x100m. Died September, 1998.

DUNPHY, Adam b. Dublin, freelance sports journalist. Contributed to the *Irish Independent* and the *Evening Herald*. Nephew of journalist Eamon Dunphy. Died April, 1998.

DURKAN, John (1967-1998) former amateur jockey. Rode 93 winners as a jockey. Son of trainer Bill Durkan. Died January, 1998.

FOSTER, David (1955-1998) Olympic Rider and one of Ireland's best known three-day event riders. Participated in more than 100 three-day events and was the leading Irish rider ten times. Rode seven winners in Hunter Chases. Former Army Captain and member of the Army Equitation School from 1974. Represented Ireland at three Olympic Games: Los Angeles (1984), Seoul (1988) and Atlanta (1996). Won the Spanish three-day event in Madrid (1984), the World Military Showjumping Champion-ships (1984) and the International Horse Trials in Punchestown. Left the Army in 1989 and set up his own yard in Enfield, Co. Meath. Killed in a riding accident, April, 1998.

GANNON, Tom (1899-1998) b. Leitrim, former Gaelic footballer. Captain and sole survivor of the only previous Leitrim team to win a Connacht title in 1927. Celebrated in 1994 when Leitrim won the Connacht title and helped Leitrim's captain, Declan Darcy, lift the Nestor Cup in triumph. Died March, 1998.

GREENE, Christy (1926-1997) b. Wicklow, professional golfer with Milltown club. Won the Irish National Professional Championship Title at Clandeboye (1956) and at Knock (1968). Represented Ireland in the World Cup (1965). Won the Irish Dunlop Title (1964) and the Southern Irish Professional Title (1965, 1974). Served as Captain, Chairman and Director of the Professional Golfers Association (PGA). Died December, 1997.

HOLLYWOOD, Sean (1944-1998) former Down Senior and Ulster

Hurling Player/Manager and member of the Shamrocks Club, Newry. A teacher - was head of English and Drama at St. Colman's, Newry. Involved in amateur dramatics - was responsible for the Newpoint Players, one of the most successful amateur dramatic companies in the country. Died July, 1998.

LAWLOR, Joseph 'Robin' (1925-1998) b. Dublin, international soccer player. Played his club football with Home Farm, Distillery and Fulham (1949). Played eight times for Ireland, winning his first cap against Austria (1953). Died May, 1998.

McCARTHY, Mick (1965-1998) b. Cork, Cork Gaelic footballer. Played senior football for Cork (1987-93), winning All-Ireland medals in 1989 and 1990 and captained the side defeated by Derry in the 1993 All-Ireland Final. Won a Cork County Championship medal with his club O'Donovan Rossa in 1992 and captained them to All-Ireland Club Championship victory in 1993. Killed in a car accident, February, 1998.

McGETTIGAN, Shane (b. 1977-1998) Leitrim Senior Gaelic footballer and a member of the Allen Gael's GAA Club. Son of singer Charlie McGettigan. Killed in a construction site accident in Boston, August, 1998.

McINERNEY, Tom (1905-1998) former Clare Hurling Player. The second last survivor of the Clare Hurling Team which reached the 1932 All-Ireland Hurling Final; this team remained the only Clare team to win a Munster Title up until three years ago. Died May, 1998.

MELLON, Tommy (1918-1998) b. Derry, chairman of the Derry GAA County Board for 17 years and former Secretary of the Derry City GAA Board. Died August, 1998.

O'CONNELL, Jackie (1912-1997) former Limerick hurler. The last surviving member of the Limerick team that won the 1934 All-Ireland Hurling Championship. Winner of a National League Medal in 1935. His playing career ended early when he received a knee injury. Was Limerick County Secretary for 27 years and County Chairman and President of the Limerick County Board. Died October, 1997.

POWER, Jim (1895-1998) b. Galway, former Galway Hurling player. The oldest surviving member of the team which won the 1923 All-Ireland Final (took place in September 1924). Died May, 1998.

ROONEY, Tom (1954-1997) b. Galway, RTÉ sports reporter and commentator. Started his career with the *Connacht Tribune*, becoming sports editor. Joined RTÉ Sports in 1986. Covered three rugby World Cup Championships - New Zealand and Australia (1987), Ireland and Britain (1991) and South Africa (1995). Died October, 1997.

RYDER, Mick (1919-1998) former Galway footballer. Founder member of Ballymun Kickhams GAA Club. Played with Galway in the 1938 All-Ireland Football Final, beating Kerry. Died February, 1998.

SPILLANE, Eddie b. Galway, cross-country runner. Won eight National Titles with Donore Harriers club in Dublin. Elected to the IAAF's Cross-Country and Road Racing Commission in 1976. Died December, 1997.

TOLERTON, Alan international hockey player. Monkstown Hockey Club Coach and former Ireland, Ulster, Lisnagarvey and Friends School forward. Gained 42 International caps (1970-76). Made his debut against Wales at the age of 19. Died February, 1998.

WALSH, Johnny (1911-1998) b. Kerry, former Kerry footballer, teacher and publican. Won five All-Ireland medals with Kerry (1932, 1937 and 1939-41). Made his debut for the Kerry team in the 1932 All-Ireland Final against Mayo. Played rugby with the the Rockwell club, playing and winning in the Munster School Rugby Final and played for Garryowen and Munster. Was also a former Munster boxing champion. Died June, 1998.

❑

a great race humiliated and a story of unexpected achievement

by **david walsh**

THE SUNDAY TIMES

LIFE, said Macbeth to Seyton, "is a tale told by an idiot." A little harsh. Maybe not. If the story of Irish cycling in 1998 had been foretold at the beginning of the year, the prophet would have been locked up. Not just for telling folk what they didn't wish to hear but for forecasting a catalogue of events on the far side of the improbable.

The Tour de France in Ireland - it should have been the sports event of the year. Eleven years after his heroism in the race, the Tour was to start from Stephen Roche's home town. Sixteen years after Sean Kelly claimed his first green jersey in the Tour, the race would pass through Main Street, Carrick-on-Suir. Pay-back time had arrived, the boys were back in town.

Time blurs and it is hard now to appreciate just how good they were. Kelly, the farmer's son, tough in the way that country boys are. "Chary of words when not downright hostile," the American writer Robin Magowan wrote of the young Kelly. Roche was a different kettle of smoked cod; loquacious, affable and "tres mediatique". At one time they were comfortably rated and considered to be two of the top five riders in the sport. Memories? The only question is which to choose. One stands out.

Another hot day in the mountains, high up in the Pyrenees, close to the summit of the Col D'Aubisque, where that morning's stage finished. Roche had decided this was for him, he wanted to show Bernard Hinault and Greg LeMond that he could and would attack. Actually, he counterattacked after the Colombian mountain goat Luis Herrera. No one caught Lucho, not on a bike anyway. That morning Roche did. He flew away from the pack, closed a 100-metre gap and once he got to the Colombian's backwheel, he rested for 20 or 30 seconds and then went again.

Herrera couldn't go with the Irish rider and within a couple of minutes, every rider close to the front was thinking of second place. Maybe it was because of Roche's exploit, but Kelly got it into his head that he would be second and he sprinted through the final 200 metres to make it an Irish one-two. Strange feeling, that day. Something had happened which was a once-in-a-lifetime happening. It was a privilege to have witnessed it.

Of course other Tour days remain. Roche's heroic climb of La Plagne to save his chance of winning in '87, Kelly's irresistible surge to win a big mountain stage into Pau in 1982 and Roche's farewell win at La Bourbelle in 1992.

No one could deny Ireland's place in the Tour's history and because of the country's much improved economy, the two million asking price was met. So where did it all go wrong? Pretty much everywhere. For a start, the timing was awful. As the Tour arrived in ireland, the four-week soccer World Cup was reaching its climax. people weren't interested in sport unless Ronaldo had a starring role. This made things difficult for the Tour in Ireland and it got worse.

To mark the official opening of the race, RTÉ showed a short film celebrating Ireland's involvement with the Tour. By concentrating almost totally on Roche and more or less ignoring Kelly, the national broadcasting service got an important story seriously wrong. This was bad journalism and downright insulting to Kelly and his supporters. Unusually for him, Kelly expressed his deep disappointment at the slight. Normally above these things, his wife Linda could not contain her disgust and she too made her feelings known.

That controversy rumbled on for a couple days and just as it died, Wily Voet entered the Tour. Or to be more precise, the Festina team masseur was stopped while about to enter. Voet had just crossed the Franco-Belge border while en route to Ireland when the French police asked him to open the boot of his car. In the moments it took him to comply, Voet may have sensed that the history of the Tour de France was about to change dramatically.

Inside Voet's boot lay a quantity of illegal and performance-enhancing drugs big enough to supply half of the peloton. Voet first tried to claim the drugs were for his own use which didn't go down with his interrogators. It is easy to imagine how the questions would have become a little more serious after that, and soon Voet admitted the drugs were for the Festina team and so the game was up for the race.

In the beginning, the Tour suggested it was Voet and Festina's problem. But Voet's statement to the police demonstrated the nonsense of that. If the Tour was not prepared to accept responsibility, the police could encourage them. They raided team hotels and took away riders for questioning. Under pressure to be seen to do something, the Tour organisation kicked out Festina, although it was clear their only crime was to have gotten caught.

Seething resentment at the police tactics led to riders' complaints and a refusal to compete on one of the stages. Spanish teams left the race in protest but theirs was a strange kind of logic. Were they opposed to drug-taking within the sport and if they were, what kind of message did their abandonment send out? Each day brought fresh revelations about the extent of the sport's problem with drugs, especially the stamina-aid, EPO, and the race itself seemed not to matter.

For years the Tour de France organisation had been ambivalent on the question of drugs - they wanted tests but not ones that might catch people - and it paid a big price. Leblanc should probably have abandoned the Tour and dedicated himself and his race to the elimination of drug-taking in cycling. But that was never going to happen, the show had to go on and so it limped back to Paris. For what it's worth, the Italian climber Marco Pantani won the Tour but it was tainted success. It wasn't that Pantani was anymore suspicious than the rest, but the Tour itself raced to its conclusion under a cloud. It was the wrong year to win the Tour de France. Wrong year too to host the start. Many people did get to the roadsides to watch but hardly had the race departed Ireland when scathing questions were being asked about the kind of show that had been in town. Sadly, not the kind we expected.

It was with sadness that one watched a great race being humiliated. For even if the Tour's past is too steeped in the culture of performance-enhancing drugs, it remains one of the world's most thrilling events. Maybe the disgrace brought by the police investigation will help to create a better future for the sport. Because now the organisers do not really have a choice. What happens if the police target the Tour as they undoubtedly did in '98?

The act will have to be tidied and the organisation must dedicate itself to regaining the credibility that seeped out of the sport. It will not be easy but then nothing of consequence ever is. As for Ireland, there was no money-back guarantee in the event of something as shocking as the series of drug scandals and the event of the year faded into nothing.

Was it a sort of disastrous year for Irish cycling? Damn right it wasn't. Hardly had the Tour folded its tent and headed for cover but a young Sligo lad, mark Scanlon, was making his way to the World Championships where he won the gold medal in the junior road race. Only those who have been to these championships will appreciate the enormity of Scanlon's achievement. It was terrific.

And so a year that promised so much ended with a story of utterly unexpected achievement. Life, a tale told by an idiot?

So it seems.

85th TOUR DE FRANCE, STAGE RESULTS

Detailed Results from Irish Stages

PROLOGUE TIME TRIAL, DUBLIN 11 July (5.6km): 1. Chris Boardman (GAN) 06:12; 2. Abraham Olano (Banesto) @ 4secs; 3. Laurent Jalabert (ONCE) @ 5secs; 4. Bobby Julich (Cofidis); 5. Christophe Moreau (Festina); 6. Jan Ullrich (Telekom) all same time; 7. Alex Zulle (Festina) @ 7 secs; 8. Laurent Dufaux (Festina); 9. Andrei Tchmil (Lotto); 10. Viatcheslav Ekimov (US Postal) all same time.

STAGE ONE, DUBLIN - DUBLIN 12 July (180km): 1. Tom Steels (Mapei) 4:29:58; 2. Erik Zabel (Telekom); 3. Robbie McEwen (Rabobank); 4. Gian Matteo Fagnini (Saeco); 5. Nicola Minali (Riso Scotti-Aiwa); 6. Frederic Moncassin (GAN); 7. P. Gaumont (Cofidis); 8. Mario Traversoni (Mercatone Uno); 9. François Simon (GAN); 10. Jan Svorada (Mapei) all same time.

Overall Classification: 1. Chris Boardman (GAN) 4:36:10; 2. Abraham Olano (Banesto) @ 4secs; 3. Laurent Jalabert (ONCE) @ 5secs; 4. Bobby Julich (Cofidis); 5. Christophe Moreau (Festina); 6. Jan Ullrich (Telekom) all same time; 7. Alex Zulle (Festina) @ 7 secs; 8. Erik Zabel (Telekom) @ 8secs; 9.Tom Steels (Mapei) @ 9 secs; 10. Laurent Dufaux (Festina) at same time.

Points: 1. Tom Steels (Mapei) 35; 2. Erik Zabel (Telekom) 34; 3. Robbie McEwen (Rabobank) 26.

King of the Mountains: 1. Stefano Zanini (Mapei) 10; 2. Jens Voight (GAN) 7; 3. Fransisco Benitez (Vitalicio) 5.

Teams: 1. Festina 13:48:51; 2. GAN @ 7secs; 3. Cofidis @ 16secs.

STAGE TWO, ENNISCORTHY - CORK 13 July (200km): 1. Jan Svorada (Mapei) 5:45:10; 2. Robbie McEwen (Rabobank); 3. Mario Cipollini (Saeco); 4. Alain Turicchia (Asics); 5. Tom Steels (Mapei); 6. Emmanuel Magnien (La Française des Jeux); 7. Jann Kirsipuu (Casino); 8. Nicola Minali (Riso Scotti-Aiwa); 9. Jeroen Blijlevens (TVM); 10. Silvio Martinello (Polti) all same time.

Overall Classification: 1. Erik Zabel (Telekom) 10:21:16; 2. Tom Steels (Mapei) @ 7secs; 3. Frederic Moncassin (GAN) same time; 4. Abraham Olano (Banesto) @ 8secs; 5. Laurent Jalabert (ONCE) @ 9secs; 6. Bobby Julich (Cofidis); 7. Christophe Moreau (Festina); 8. Jan Ullrich (Telekom) all same times; 9. Jan Svorada (Mapei) @ 10secs; 10. Robbie McEwen (Rabobank) @ 11secs.

Points: 1. Tom Steels (Mapei) 63; 2. Jan Svorada (Mapei) 57; 3. Robbie McEwen (Rabobank) 56.

King of the Mountains: 1. Stefano Zanini (Mapei) 16; 2. Pascal Herve (Festina) 13; 3. Jens Voight (GAN) 10.

Teams: 1. Festina 31:04:21; 2. GAN @ 7secs; 3. Cofidis @ 16secs.

Stage	1st	Time	2nd	3rd	Overall Leader	Time
3 Roscoff-Lorient	**J. Heppner**	3:33:36	**X. Jan**	**G. Hincapie** @2s	**B. Hamburger**	13:55:00
Tue 14 July 171km	Telekom		LFdJ	US Postal	Casino	
4 Plouay-Cholet	**J. Blijlevens**	5:48:32	**N. Minali**	**J. Svorada**	**S. O'Grady**	19:43:29
Wed 15 July 252km	TVM		RIS	Mapei	GAN	
5 Cholet-Chateauroux	**M. Cipollini**	5:18:49	**E. Zabel**	**C. Mengin**	**S. O'Grady**	25:02:18
Thurs 16 July 228.5km	Saeco		Telekom	LFdJ	GAN	
6 Chatre-Brive	**M. Cipollini**	5:05:32	**N. Minali**	**J. Svorada**	**S. O'Grady**	30:07:48
Fri 17 July 210km	Saeco		RIS	Mapei	GAN	
7 Meyrignac-Correze	**J. Ullrich**	1:15:25	**T. Hamilton** @1:10	**B. Julich** @ 1:18	**J. Ullrich**	31:24:37
Sat 18 July 58km	Telekom		US Postal	Cofidis	Telekom	
8 Brive-Montauban	**J. Durand**	4:40:55	**A. Tafi**	**F.Saachi**	**L. Desbiens**	36:09:56
Sun 19 July 190.5km	Casino		Mapei	PLT	Cofidis	
9 Montauban-Pau	**L. Van Bon**	5:21:10	**J. Voight**	**M. Lelli**	**L. Desbiens**	41:31:18
Mon 20 July 224km	Rabobank		GAN	Cofidis	Cofidis	
10 Pau-Luchon	**R. Massi**	5:49:40	**M. Pantani** @0:36	**M. Boogerd** @ 0:59	**J. Ullrich**	47:25:18
Tue 21 July 197km	Casino		M. Uno	Rabobank	Telekom	
11 Luchon-Pla' deBeille	**M. Pantani**	5:15:27	**R. Meier** @1:26	**B. Julich** @1:33	**J. Ullrich**	52:42:25
Wed 22 July 170km	M. Uno		Cofidis	Cofidis	Telekom	
12 Tarascon-Capd'Agde	**T. Steels**	4:12:51	**F. Simon**	**S. Barthe**	**J. Ullrich**	56:55:16
Fri 24 July 221km	Mapei		GAN	Casino	Telekom	
13 Frontigan-Carpentras	**D. Nardello**	4:32:46	**V. Garcia-Acosta**	**A. Tafi**	**J. Ullrich**	61:30:53
Sat 25 July 191km	Mapei		Banesto	Mapei	Telekom	
14 Valreas-Grenoble	**S. O'Grady**	.4:30:53	**G. Calcaterra**	**O. Rodrigues**	**J. Ullrich**	66:11:51
Sun 26 July 186.5km	GAN		SAE	Banesto	Telekom	
15 Grenoble-Deux Alps	**M. Pantani**	5:43:45	**R. Massi** @1:54	**F. Escartin** @ 1:59	**M. Pantani**	71:58:37
Mon 27 July 189km	M. Uno		Casino	Kelme	M. Uno	
16 Vizille-Albertville	**J. Ullrich**	5:39:47	**M. Pantani**	**B. Julich** @ 1:49	**M. Pantani**	77:38:24
Tue 28 July 204km	Telekom		M. Uno	Cofidis	M. Uno	
17 Stage annulled following strikes by the riders. Banesto, ONCE and Vitalicio withdraw from race.						
18 Aix l'Bains-Neuchatel	**T. Steels**	4:53:27	**E. Zabel**	**S. O'Grady**	**M. Pantani**	82:31:51
Thurs 30 July 218km	Mapei		Telekom	GAN	M. Uno	

Continued from previous page

Stage	1st	Time	2nd	3rd	Overall Leader	Time
19 Le Chaux-Autun	**M. Backstedt**	5:10:14	**M. Den Bakker**	**E. Mazzoleni**	**M. Pantani**	87:58:43
Fri 31 July 242km	GAN		RAB	SAE	M. Uno	
20 Montceau-Le Creusot	**J. Ullrich**	1:03:52	**B. Julich** @ 1:01	**M. Pantani** @ 2:35	**M. Pantani**	89:05:10
Sat 1 Aug 52km	Telekom		Cofidis	M. Uno	M. Uno	
21 Melun-Paris	**T. Steels**	3:44:36	**S. Zanini**	**S. O'Grady**	**M. Pantani**	92:49:46
Sun 2 Aug 147km	MAP		MAP	GAN	M. Uno	

Second and third placed riders have same time as leader unless otherwise stated.

FINAL OVERALL STANDINGS

	Individual	Time	Points	Pts	KoM	Pts	Teams	Time
1	**Marco Pantani**	92:49:46	**Erik Zabel**	327	**Christophe Rinero**	200	**Cofidis**	278:29:58
2	**Jan Ullrich**	@ 3:21	**Stuart O'Grady**	230	**Marco Pantani**	175	**Casino**	@ 29:09
3	**Bobby Julich**	@ 4:08	**Tom Steels**	221	**Alberto Elli**	165	**US Postal**	@ 41:40
4	**Christophe Rinero**	@ 9:16	**Robbie McEwen**	196	**Cedric Vasseur**	156	**Telekom**	@ 46:01
5	**Michael Boogerd**	@ 11:26	**George Hincapie**	151	**Stephane Heulot**	152	**Lotto**	@ 1:04:14
6	**Jean-Cyril Robin**	@ 14:57						
7	**R. Meier**	@ 15:13						
8	**Daniele Nardello**	@ 16:07						
9	**Guiseppe DiGrande**	@ 17:35						
10	**Axel Merckx**	@ 17:39						

THE TEAMS

Team	Leader(s)	Final Position	Time	Based	World Rank
Cofidis	F. Casagrande, B. Julich	1	278:29:58	France	10
Casino	A. Elli, B. Hamburger	2	@ 29:09	France	3
US Postal Service	V. Ekimov, J-C. Robin	3	@ 41:40	United States	19
Team Deutsche Telekom	B. Riis, J. Ulrich	4	@ 46:01	Germany	6
Lotto-Mobistar	J. Planckaert, A. Tchmil	5	@ 1:04:14	Belgium	13
Team Polti	L. Leblanc, D. Rebellin	6	@1:06:32	Italy	8
Rabobank	M. Boogerd, P. Luttenberger	7	@1:46:20	Holland	5
Mapei-Bricobi	F. Ballerini, T. Steels, A. Tafi	8	@1:59:53	Italy	2
Big Mat-Auber 93	P. Lino	9	@2:03:32	France	29
Mercatone Uno-Bianchi	M. Pantani	10	@ 2;23:04	Italy	14
La Francaise des Jeux	E. Berzin	11	@2:23:35	France	15
Saeco-Cannondale	M. Cipollini, I. Gotti	12	@ 3:25:23	San Marino	16
Gan	C. Boardman, F. Moncassin	13	@ 3:33:11	France	12
Asics-CGA	A. Shefer	14	@ 4:05:11	Italy	7
Festina Lotus	R. Virenque, A. Zülle			France	1
ONCE	L. Jalabert			Spain	4
TVM-Farm Frites	J. Blijlevens			Holland	9
Banesto	J-M. Jimenez, A. Olano			Spain	11
Kelme-Costa Blanca	F. Escartin			Spain	17
Riso Scotti-Aiwa	N. Miceli, N. Minali			Italy	22
Vitalicio-Seguos	S. Blanco			Spain	20

TOUR DE FRANCE STATISTICS

- 189 riders started the Tour in Dublin on Saturday July 11th, 96 finished the race in Paris on Sunday August 2nd.
- The 1998 Tour covered 3,737.1km, 385.6 kilometres of which were in Ireland. With 20 stages held over 21 racing days the average stage length was 177.95km.
- The longest stage of the Tour was the 248 kilometre fourth stage from Plouay to Cholet.
- The shortest non-time trial stage of the Tour was 147 kilometre final stage from Melun to Paris.
- The highest climb on the Irish leg of the Tour was the 540m Wicklow Gap on stage one.
- Ireland became the first country not on the European mainland to host the opening stage of the Tour de France. Other countries which have hosted the opening stage are: Belgium (1958 and 1975), Germany (1965, 1980 and 1987), Holland (1954, 1973, 1978 and 1996), Luxembourg (1989), Spain (1991) and Switzerland (1982).

IRISH COMPETITORS IN THE TOUR DE FRANCE

Irish Stage Winners in the Tour de France

Shay Elliott	**1** (1963 Roubaix).
Sean Kelly	**5** (1978 Poitiers, 1980 Voreppe-Saint-Etienne and Auxerre-Fontenay-sous-Bois, 1981 Besançon-Thonon, 1982 Fleurance-Pau).
Stephen Roche	**3** (1985 Luz-Saint Sauveur-Pau, 1987 Samur-Futroscope, 1992 La Bourboule).
Martin Earley	**1** (1989 La Bastide d'Armagnac-Pau).

Irish Results from the Tour de France

Year	Shay Elliott	Sean Kelly	Stephen Roche	Martin Earley	Paul Kimmage	Laurence Roche
1956	DNF	-	-	-	-	-
1958	48th	-	-	-	-	-
1959	DNF	-	-	-	-	-
1961	47th	-	-	-	-	-
1963	61st	-	-	-	-	-
1964	DNF	-	-	-	-	-

No Irish cyclist competed in the Tour de France from 1964-78.

Year	Shay Elliott	Sean Kelly	Stephen Roche	Martin Earley	Paul Kimmage	Laurence Roche
1978	-	34th	-	-	-	-
1979	-	38th	-	-	-	-
1980	-	29th	-	-	-	-
1981	-	48th	-	-	-	-
1982	-	15th	-	-	-	-
1983	-	7th	13th	-	-	-
1984	-	5th	25th	-	-	-
1985	-	4th	3rd	60th	-	-
1986	-	-	48th	46th	131st	-
1987	-	DNF	1st	65th	DNF	-
1988	-	46th	-	DNF	-	-
1989	-	9th	DNF	44th	DNF	-
1990	-	30th	44th	DNF	-	-
1991	-	DNF	DNF	DNF	-	153rd
1992	-	43rd	9th	80th	-	-
1993	-	-	13th	-	-	-

No Irish cyclist has competed in the Tour de France since 1993.

MAIN SPORTING CONTACTS

The Irish Sports Council	House of Sport	Sports Council of Northern Ireland
21 Fitzwilliam Square	Long Mile Road	House of Sport
Dublin 2	Walkinstown	Upper Malone Road
Tel. (01) 6763847	Dublin 12	Belfast BT89 5LA
	Tel. (01) 4501633	Tel. (01232) 381222

SPORTING ORGANISATIONS

Badminton Union of Ireland Baldoyle Industrial Estate, Grange Road, Baldoyle, Dublin 13. Tel. (01) 8393028.

Ból Chumann na hÉireann (*Mr. Pat O'Sullivan*), Lower Froe, Rosscarbery, Co. Cork. Tel. (023) 48128.

Bord Lúthchleas na hÉireann (Athletics), 11 Prospect Road, Glasnevin, Dublin 9. Tel. (01) 8309901.

Bord na gCon (Irish Greyhound Board), 104 Henry Street, Limerick. Tel. (061) 316788.

Bowling League of Ireland (*J. B. Duff*), c/o 7 Glendoher Close, Dublin 16.

Canoe Association of Northern Ireland (*Mr. M. Murray*), 143 Oakhurst Avenue, Belfast BT10 0PD.

Cerebral Palsy Sport Ireland (*Ms. Brenda Green*), Sandymount Avenue, Dublin 4. Tel. (01) 2695355

Comhairle Liathróid Láimhe na hÉireann Páirc an Chrócaigh, Baile Átha Cliath 3. Tel. (01) 8741360.

Community Games National Community Games, 5 Lower Abbey Street, Dublin 1. Tel. (01) 8788095.

Croquet Association of Ireland c/o Carrickmines Croquet & Lawn Tennis Club, Glenamuck Road, Carrickmines, Co. Dublin.

Cumann Camógaíochta na nGael Páirc an Chrócaigh, Baile Átha Cliath 3. Tel. (01) 8554257.

Cumann Lúthchleas Gael (GAA) Páirc an Chrócaigh, Baile Átha Cliath 3. Tel. (01) 8363222.

Equestrian Federation of Ireland Ashton House, Castleknock, Dublin 15. Tel. (01) 8387611.

Federation of Irish Cyclists Kelly Roche House, 619 North Circular Road, Dublin 1. Tel. (01) 8551522.

Football Association of Ireland, The 80 Merrion Square, Dublin 2. Tel. (01) 6766864.

Golfing Union of Ireland Glencar House, 81 Eglinton Road, Donnybrook, Dublin 4. Tel. (01) 2694111.

Irish Amateur Archery Association 61 Ashwood Road, Clondalkin, Dublin 22. Tel.(01) 4573186.

Irish Amateur Boxing Association National Boxing Stadium, South Circular Road, Dublin 8. Tel. (01) 4533371.

Irish Amateur Fencing Association Branksome Dene, Frankfort Park, Dundrum, Dublin 14. Tel. (01) 6793888.

Irish Amateur Gymnastics Association House of Sport, Long Mile Road, Walkinstown, Dublin 12. Tel. (01) 4501805.

Irish Amateur Rowing Union House of Sport, Long Mile Road, Walkinstown, Dublin 12. Tel. (01) 4509831.

Irish Amateur Swimming Association House of Sport, Long Mile Road, Walkinstown, Dublin 12. Tel. (01) 4501739.

Irish Amateur Weightlifting Association 27 O'Connell Gardens, Bath Avenue, Dublin 4. Tel. (01) 6601390.

Irish Amateur Wrestling Association c/o 54 Elm Mount Drive, Beaumont, Dublin 9. Tel. (01) 8315522.

Irish Aviation Council c/o 38 Pembroke Road, Dublin 4. Tel. (01) 2874474.

Irish Baseball & Softball Association 14 Innishmaan Road, Whitehall, Dublin 9. Tel. (01) 8378118.

Irish Basketball Association National Basketball Arena, Tymon Park, Dublin 24. Tel. (01) 4590211.

Irish BlindSports c/o 25 Turvey Close, Donabate, Co. Dublin. Tel. (01) 8436501.

Irish Bowling Association (*Mr. J. N. McQuay*), 2 Ashdene Road, Moneyreagh, Co. Down BT23 6DD. Tel. (01232) 448348.

Irish Canoe Union House of Sport, Long Mile Road, Walkinstown, Dublin 12. Tel. (01) 4509838.

Irish Cricket Union 45 Foxrock Park, Foxrock, Dublin 18. Tel. (01) 2893943.

Irish Deaf Sports Association (*Mr. Dermot Saunders*), 8 Dun Emer Drive, Dundrum, Dublin 16. Tel. (01) 2956030.

Irish Federation of Sea Anglers 67 Windsor Drive, Monkstown, Co.

Dublin. Tel. (01) 2806873.

Irish Football Association 20 Windsor Avenue, Belfast BT9 6EG. Tel. (01232) 669458.

Irish Hang Gliding Association House of Sport, Long Mile Road, Walkinstown, Dublin 12. Tel. (01) 4509845.

Irish Hockey Union 6A Woodbine Park, Blackrock, Co. Dublin. Tel. (01) 2600087.

Irish Horseracing Authority Leopardstown Racecourse, Foxrock, Dublin 18. Tel. (01) 2892888.

Irish Indoor Bowling Association (*Mr. D. Hunter*), c/o 204 Kings Road, Knock, Belfast BT5 7HX.

Irish Judo Association 79 Upper Dorset Street, Dublin 1. Tel. (01) 8308233.

Irish Ladies Golf Union 1 Clonskeagh Square, Clonskeagh Road, Dublin 14. Tel. (01) 2696244.

Irish Ladies Hockey Union 95 Sandymount Road, Dublin 4. Tel. (01) 6606780.

Irish Olympic Handball Association Tymon Bawn Community Centre, Firhouse Road West, Old Bawn, Tallaght, Dublin 24. Tel. (01) 4599142.

Irish Orienteering Association c/o AFAS, House of Sport, Long Mile Road, Walkinstown, Dublin 12. Tel. (01) 4501633.

Irish Rugby Football Union 62 Lansdowne Road, Ballsbridge, Dublin 4. Tel. (01) 6684601.

Irish Sailing Association 3 Park Road, Dun Laoghaire, Co. Dublin. Tel. (01) 2800239.

Irish Squash House of Sport, Long Mile Road, Walkinstown, Dublin 12. Tel. (01) 4501564.

Irish Surfing Association Easkey House, Easkey, Co. Sligo. Tel. (096) 49020.

Irish Table-Tennis Association 46 Lorcan Villas, Santry, Dublin 9. Tel. (01) 8421679.

Irish Ten Pin Bowling Association (*Ms. Ros O'Reilly*), 40 Cabinteely Green, Dublin 18. Tel. (01) 2857529.

Irish Triathlon Association 202 St. Donagh's Road, Donaghmede, Dublin 13. Tel. (01) 8470818.

Irish Trout Fly Fishing Association (*Mr. James McNally*), Cullies, Co. Cavan. Tel. (049) 31501.

Irish Tug of War Association (*Mrs. Nuala Hubbard*), c/o Longhouse, Ballymore Eustace, Co. Kildare. Tel. (045) 864222.

Irish Water-Polo Association 3 Strand Mews, Lea Road, Sandymount, Dublin 4. Tel. (01) 2693918.

Irish Waterski Federation 91 South Mall, Cork. Tel. (021) 334605.

Irish Windsurfing Association (*Mr. Chris Sparron*), Boherboy, Dunlavin, Co. Wicklow.

Irish Women's Bowling Association (*Mrs. V. Canning*), 1 Beach Road, Whitehead, Co. Antrim BT38 9QS. Tel. (01960) 378563.

Irish Women's Cricket Union "Woodcroft", 50 St. Alban's Park, Sandymount, Dublin 4.

Irish Women's Indoor Bowling Association (*Mrs. D. Miskelly*), 101 Skyline Drive, Lambeg, Lisburn, Co. Antrim BT27 4HW. Tel. (01846) 663516.

Ladies Football Association of Ireland 80 Merrion Square, Dublin 2. Tel. (01) 6766864.

Ladies Gaelic Football Association, The House of Sport, Long Mile Road, Walkinstown, Dublin 12. Tel. (01) 4569113.

Ladies' Bowling League of Ireland (*Mrs. June Fincher*), c/o Kimmage Road West, Dublin 12. Tel. (01) 4555302.

Motor Cycling Union of Ireland 35 Lambay Road, Glasnevin, Dublin 9. Tel. (01) 8378090.

Mountaineering Council of Ireland c/o AFAS, House of Sport, Long Mile Road, Walkinstown, Dublin 12. Tel. (01) 4509845.

National Chinese and Associated Martial Arts (*Mr. C. Walsh*), 72 Ramoan Gardens, Belfast BT11 8LN.

National Coarse Fishing Federation of Ireland (*Mr. Brendan Coulter*), "Blaithin", Dublin Road, Cavan, Co. Cavan. Tel. (049) 32367.

Northern Ireland Amateur Fencing Association (*Miss. K. Lowry*), 40 Groomsport Road, Bangor, Co. Down BT20 5LR. Tel. (01247) 454000.

Northern Ireland Amateur Gymnastics Association (*Miss. D. Orme*), 31 Palmerstown Road, Belfast BT4 1QB. Tel. (01232) 381414.

Northern Ireland Amateur Weightlifters Association (*Mr. J. Sheppard*), 71 Beechgrove Avenue, Belfast BT6 0ND. Tel. (01232) 798464.

Northern Ireland Archery Association (*Mr. Wellesley McGown*), 17 Bridge Road, Kilmore, Lurgan, Co. Armagh, BT67 9LA. Tel. (01762) 326987.

Northern Ireland Billiards & Snooker Control (*Mr. A. Rainey*), 52 Jonesboro Park, Belfast BT5 5FY.

Northern Ireland Blind Sports (*Ms. L. Royal*), 12 Sandford Avenue, Belfast BT5 5NW. Tel. (01232) 657156.

Northern Ireland Ice Hockey (*Mr. Jim Graves*), c/o 88 Coronation Park, Dundonald, Belfast BT16 0HF. Tel. (01232) 483859.

Northern Ireland Jiu Jitsu Association (*Mr. J. Canning*), 279 Coalisland Road, Dungannon, Co. Tyrone BT71 6ET. Tel. (018687) 40467.

Northern Ireland Judo Federation House of Sport, Upper Malone Road, Belfast BT9 5LA. Tel. (01232) 383814.

Northern Ireland Karate Board (*Mr. M. Leydon*), 33 Corrina Park, Upper Dunmurry Lane, Belfast BT17 0HA. Tel. (01232) 240558.

Northern Ireland Netball Association House of Sport, Upper Malone Road, Belfast BT9 5LA. Tel. (01232) 383806.

Northern Ireland Orienteering Association (*Ms. K. Millinson*), 311 Ballynahinch Road, Hillsborough, Co. Down. Tel. (01846) 638185.

Northern Ireland Sports Association for People with Learning Disabilities (*Ms. A. Shane*), 11b Belsize Road, Lisburn, Co. Antrim BT27 4AL. Tel. (01820) 662357.

Northern Ireland Surfing Association (*Mr. R. Allen*), 'Shague', Tempo Road, Enniskillen, Co. Fermanagh BT74 6HR. Tel. (01365) 322591.

Northern Ireland Tug of War Association (*Mr. P. Doherty*), 56 Belrangh Road, Garvagh, Co. Derry. Tel. (01265) 868697.

Northern Ireland Volleyball Association (*Mr. A. Dudman*), 29a Cranmore Gardens, Belfast BT9 6JL. Tel. (01232) 667011.

Olympic Council of Ireland 27 Mespil Road, Dublin 4. Tel. (01) 6680444.

Parachute Association of Ireland c/o AFAS, House of Sport, Long Mile Road, Walkinstown, Dublin 12. Tel. (01) 4509845.

Pitch and Putt Union of Ireland, The House of Sport, Long Mile Road, Walkinstown, Dublin 12. Tel. (01) 4509299.

Racquetball Association of Ireland (*Mr. John Comerford*), 5 Edenvale Close, Kilkenny.

Republic of Ireland Billiards & Snooker Association House of Sport, Longmile Road, Walkinstown, Dublin 12. Tel. (01) 4509850.

Republic of Ireland Netball Association 10 Barry Avenue, Finglas, Dublin 11. Tel. (01) 8347634.

Royal Irish Automobile Club RIAC, 34 Dawson Street, Dublin 2. Tel. (01) 6775628.

Royal Yachting Association House of Sport, Upper Malone Road, Belfast BT9 5LA. Tel. (01232) 381222.

Ski Club of Ireland, The Kilternan Hotel, Kilternan, Co. Dublin. Tel. (01) 2955658.

Special Olympics Ireland Ormond House, Upper Ormond Quay, Dublin 7. Tel. (01) 8720300.

Speleological Union of Ireland c/o AFAS, House of Sport, Long Mile Road, Walkinstown, Dublin 12. Tel. (01) 4509845.

Taekwondo Association of Northern Ireland (*Mr. B. Nicholson*), 20 Lester Avenue, Lisburn, Co. Antrim BT28 3QD. Tel. (01846) 604293.

Tennis Ireland Argyle Square, Morehampton Road, Donnybrook, Dublin 4. Tel. (01) 6681841.

Ulster Camogie Council (*Ms. M. Leonard*), 27 Lough Road, Ballinderry Upper, Lisburn, Co. Antrim BT28 2JY. Tel. (01849) 452646.

Ulster Deaf Sports Council (*Mr. E. McCaffrey*), 3 Richmond Grove, Glengormley, Co. Antrim.

Ulster Squash House of Sport, 2a Upper Malone Road, Belfast BT9 5LA. Tel. (01232) 381222.

Volleyball Association of Ireland 5 Shanliss Road, Santry, Dublin 9. Tel. (01) 8622038.

ANGLING

Irish Federation of Sea Anglers

c/o 67 Windsor Drive, Monkstown, Co. Dublin. Tel. (01) 2806873

Founded 1953
President .... Capt. Christy O'Toole
Chairman .... Brian Prendergast
Secretary .... Hugh O'Rorke
Press Officer .... Tony Gosnell
Number of Clubs 182
Number of Councils .... 4 (Connacht, Leinster, Munster and Ulster)

Connacht Council:
- **President** .... Seamus Durkan
- **Chairman** .... John Walkin
- **Secretary** .... Josephine Kilroy
- **Number of Clubs** 16

Leinster Council:
- **President** .... Dermot Finnegan
- **Chairman** .... George McCullagh
- **Secretary** .... Frank Baxter
- **Number of Clubs** 64

Munster Council:
- **President** .... Vincent O'Donovan
- **Chairman** .... Matt Kearney
- **Secretary** .... John Martin
- **Number of Clubs** 43

Ulster Council:
- **President** .... Bill McFerran
- **Chairman** .... Joe Mullan
- **Secretary** .... Paul Divito
- **Number of Clubs** 59

DOMESTIC STATISTICS

Irish Federation of Sea Anglers - National Championships

Master Angler Boat - Sligo (August 29th-30th, 1998)

1	L. O'Callaghan	Bray
2	N. Blaney	Post-Irish, Old Bushmills
3	J. Davis	Bray
4	J. Cronin	Dungarvan
5	K. Dunne	Wicklow Bay

Master Angler Shore - Wexford (October 3-4th, 1998)

Won by .... Tim O'Sullivan .... Tralee Bay SAC

National Coarse Fishing Federation of Ireland

c/o "Blaithin", Dublin Road, Cavan, Co. Cavan. Tel. (049) 32367

Founded 1960s
President .... Ned O'Farrell
Chairman .... Dave Egan
Secretary .... Brendan Coulter
Press Officer .... Mark O'Donoghue
Number of Clubs 50-60
Number of Councils .... 4 (Connacht, Leinster, Munster and Ulster)

DOMESTIC STATISTICS

The 39th Smithwicks All Ireland Championships: Lough Muckno, Castleblayney, Co. Monaghan (26th July 1998)

Results		Name	Club	Weight
Seniors:	1st	Philip Jackson	Lurgan CAC	15kg. 320grams

Continued from previous page

Results		Name	Club	Weight
	2nd	Brian Kane	Dublin AC	11kg
	3rd	Rory O'Neill	Carrickmacross MAG	10kg. 780grams
	4th	Fintan Lawlor	Erne Anglers AC	10kg. 560grams
Juniors:	1st	Keith Royal	Portobello A.C	7kg. 950grams
	2nd	Neil Davitt	Leixlip ADS	3kg. 650grams
	3rd	David Armstrong	East Belfast CAC	3kg. 550grams
	4th	Alan McLoughlin	Royal Enfield AC	3kg. 350grams
Ladies:	1st	Anne O'Donoghue	Royal Enfield AC	200grams

All Ireland, Angler of the Year Final: On the Shannon at Portumna (27th September 1998)

Results	Name	Club	Weight
1st:	Niall Mazurick	Carrickmacross	30kg 210 grams
2nd:	Karl Woodhouse		16kgs 920 grams
3rd:	Tony Burke		
Junior:	Robert Payne	Royal Enfield AC	2kg 300 grams

INTERNATIONAL STATISTICS

European Coarse Angling Championships: River Reia, Portugal (26-27th June 1998)

Individual			Team	
Results	Name	Club	Results	County
Gold:	Sean McEvoy	Maynooth (Ireland)	**Gold:**	England
Silver:	Jose Duarte	Portugal	**Silver:**	Italy
Bronze:	Tom Pickering	England	**Bronze:**	Germany

The National Coarse Fishing Federations European team *Trabucco Ireland*, placed in 4th position, consisted of: **Sean McEvoy** (Maynooth), **Niall McKitterick** (Carrickmacross), **Fergal Smith** (Cavan), **Derek Rowley** (Rooskey) and **Michael Black** (Northern Ireland)

Selected Irish Record Weights for Various Specimens

Fish	Weight	Fish	Weight
Angler Fish	42.985 kilos	**Mackerel**	4lbs. 2ozs.
Bass	17lbs. 1.25 ozs.	**Megrim**	1.85 kilos
Bream	12lbs. 3ozs.	**Monkfish**	73lbs.
Brill	9lbs. 8ozs.	**Plaice**	8.23kgs
Carp	27.78lbs.	**Pollack**	19lbs. 3ozs.
Cod	42lbs.	**Ray - Electric**	69lbs.
Conger	72lbs.	**Ray - Sting**	51lbs.
Eel	6lbs. 15ozs.	**Salmon**	57lbs.
Haddock	10lbs. 13.5ozs.	**Sea Trout**	16lbs. 6ozs.
Hake	25lbs. 5.5ozs.	**Shark - Blue**	206lbs.
Halibut	156lbs.	**Skate - Common**	221lbs.
Herring	.425 kilos	**Torsk**	10lbs. 11ozs.
John Dory	7lbs. 8ozs.	**Turbot**	34lbs.
Ling	46lbs. 8ozs.	**Whiting**	4lbs. 14.5ozs.

PAST PRESIDENTS

Year	Name	Club
1987-1994	Jimmy Keaveney	Dublin
1994-to date	Ned O'Farrell	Prosperous

women: leading the way in irish athletics

by **patsy mc gonagle**

PUBLIC RELATIONS OFFICER B.L.E. AND IRISH OLYMPIC TEAM MANAGER

THE IAAF, the World governing body for athletics, designated 1998 as the Year of Women in Athletics, in essence no doubt to highlight the sport in areas of the world where the local culture makes it difficult for women to participate. No such problem exists in the Ireland of 1998, not only in participation as shown by the involvement of 36,000 women in the Dublin 10K held annually in June, but in success - Sonia O'Sullivan - arguably the greatest female athlete in Europe, and Catriona McKiernan, the daughter of a farming family from Co. Cavan, going to 4th on the Marathon all-time list at 2:22.22 winning the Amsterdam Marathon in November.

The development of women's athletics has emerged from an organised basis in the early 60's to what it is today, an integral part of the sport on the island, while the ladies have also embraced the challenge of the 'new' events like pole vault and hammer and await the introduction of the steeplechase for women in 1999. So we approach the year 2000, the year of the Sydney Olympic Games, in very upbeat mood.

As Irish Elite Team Manager, I relish the challenge and view the increased financial input on a criteria basis with great enthusiasm. Opportunities of an international nature are increasing, standards are improving, awareness in the media has been heightened and while there is much development still to be done, the volunteers on the ground continue to ensure new talent emerges - whether it is Community Games, Schools, BLOE or Sportshall, athletics provides an outstanding discipline whether one remains or moves to another sport.

I was introduced to the sport while at St. Columbs College, Derry in the sixties, an introduction that dictated much of what I have achieved since. It's a time of change and athletics should be aware that to survive it must become more professional in the coaching, promotional and administration areas, a challenge which the National Federation BLE is presently considering.

So what began as a year of women in athletics became a success story in the cities around the world as the Irish participated at world level and as Olympic Team Manager I sincerely hope we can continue to 2000 and beyond.

ATHLETICS

Bord Lúthchleas na hÉireann

11 Prospect Road, Glasnevin, Dublin 9. Tel. (01) 8309901

Founded 1967
President .... Nick Davis
Honorary Secretary .... Dermot Nagle
Number of Senior Clubs 144
Number of Junior Clubs 135
Total Membership 16,495
Principal Venues .... Morton Stadium, Dublin (10,000), Mardyke, Cork (8,000), Tullamore Harriers A.C. (5,000)
Biggest Recorded Crowd .... 30,000 (1979. World Cross Country Championships, Limerick)

DOMESTIC RESULTS (TRACK AND FIELD)

National Championship Results (Santry Stadium, Dublin) July 25-26 1998

MEN

Event	1st	Club	Time	2nd	Club	3rd	Club
100m	N. Ryan	Nenagh	10.79	I. Craig	Annadale	D. Power	DCH
200m	G. Ryan	Nenagh	20.88	T. Comyns	Limerick	D. Power	DCH
400m	B. Forbes	Mid Ulster	47.72	E. Farrell	DCH	P. McKee	Cuchulainn
800m	J. Nolan	UCD	1.47.75	D. Matthews	UCD	B. O'Shea	Slaney
1,500m	J. McIlroy	Ballymena	3.49.83	N. Bruton	Clonliffe	A. Walker	UCD
5,000m	M. McCarthy	Leevale	14.02.43	C. Smith	DSD	N. Cullen	Clonliffe
10,000m	N. Berkley	DSD	29.56.65	T. McGrath	Mullingar	G. Ryan	Tuam
3,000m s/chase	E. O'Neill	Crusaders	9.04.87	C. Troy	Tullamore	C. Gallagher	Finn Valley
110m Hurdles	P. Coghlan	Crusaders	14.20	A. Delaney	Castlerea	J. Naughton	Nenagh
400m Hurdles	T. McGuirk	DCH	50.92	B. Liddy	Crusaders	D. Keoghan	DCH
4x100m Relay		DCH	42.05		Leevale		
10,000m Walk	P. O'Callaghan	UCD	42.45.7	M. Casey	Sligo	R. Heffernan	Togher

Event	1st	Club	Perf	2nd	Club	3rd	Club
High Jump	M. Mandy	Birchfield	2.10m	J. Naughton	Nenagh	B. O'Brien	Leevale
Long Jump	J. Naughton	Nenagh	7.23m	D. O'Farrell	Borrisokane	G. Devlin	Ballymena
Triple Jump	M. McDonald	Border	14.62m	S. Lonergan	KCH	R. Galvin	Limerick
Javelin	T. McHugh	DCH	72.94m	M. Allen	Ballymena	B. Haughton	Ballymena
Hammer	R. Linscheid	Donore	72.42	P. McGrath	Raheny	S. Linscheid	Donore
Shot	J. Dermody	DSD	16.85m	P. Quirke	Crusaders	J. Flynn	W. Waterford
Discus	J. Menton	Donore	56.59m	P. Quirke	Crusaders	J. Farrelly	DSD
Pole Vault	N. Young	Lisburn	4.70m	J. Hallissey	Ferrybank	D. McDermott	Borrisokane
56lbs Distance	J. Menton	Donore	9.16m*	S. Fitzpatrick	N. Laois	J. Farrelly	DSD

WOMEN

Event	1st	Club	Time	2nd	Club	3rd	Club
100m	L. Barry	Emerald	11.83	A. Hearne	Waterford	C Sheehy	W. Dublin
200m	C. Sheehy	W. Dublin	24.31	L. Barry	Emerald	K. Shinkins	DCH
400m	K. Shinkins	DCH	53.09	J. McKenna	Metro	M. Smith	Clonliffe
800m	S. Delahunty	KCH	2.05.19	M. Prenderville	UCC	A. Byrne	DSD
1,500m	U. English	DCH	4.14.21	V. Vaughan	Blarney	N. Beirne	Lucan
5,000m	S. O'Sullivan	B ' Cobh	15.20.16	V. Vaughan	Blarney	M. McMahon	Marian
100m Hurdles	S. Smith	Waterford	13.31*	D. O'Rourke	Leevale	O. Power	CoS
400m Hurdles	O. Power	CoS	60.17	M. O'Meara	Nenagh	M. Hynes	Loughrea
4x100m Relay		West Dublin	47.99		DCH		Leevale
5,000m Walk	G. O'Sullivan	UCC	21.57.22	O. Loughnane	Loughrea	S. O'Keefe	KCH

Event	1st	Club	Perf	2nd	Club	3rd	Club
High Jump	O. Donoghoe	CoS	1.73m	D. Ryan	Claremorris	B. Corrigan	DCH
Long Jump	J. Stokes	Ferrybank	5.96m	T. Robinson	Limerick	A. Furlong	DMP
Triple Jump	S. Hoey	DCH	12.26m	A. Furlong	DMP	F. Mullen	Clonliffe
Pole Vault	M. O'Halloran	UCD	2.60m	E. O'Meara	Borrisokane	O. Walsh	W. Waterford
Hammer	O. Kelleher	Limerick	53.68m	N. Coffey	Navan	C. Thompson	Slaney
Shot	E. Gavin	Limerick	13.43m	J. McCorry	Ballymena	E. Massey	N. Down

Continued from previous page

Event	1st	Club	Perf	2nd	Club	3rd	Club
Discus	A. O'Brien	W. Waterford	47.93	A. Wallace	Windsor	E. O'Keefe	KCH
Javelin	A. Moffitt	Windsor	46.48	K. Campbell	Lisburn	E. Kitney	Medway

* Denotes National Record

B ' Cobh - Ballymore Cobh; CoS - Carrick on Suir; DCH - Dublin City Harriers; DSD - Dundrum South Dublin; DMP - ; KCH - KilkennyCity Harriers; Metro - Metro-St Brigids; Perf - Performance; UCC - University College Cork; UCD - University College Dublin.

National Indoor Championship Results (Nenagh) February 14-15 1998

MEN

Event	1st	Club	Time	2nd	Club	3rd	Club
60m	N. Ryan	Nenagh	6.96	J. Carroll	Fingallians	B. Cullinane	Nenagh
200m	G. Ryan	Nenagh	21.54	T. Comyns	Limerick	B. Cullinane	Nenagh
400m	S. Fleming	UCC	49.46	D. Thom	Ballymena	J. McIlroy	Ballymena
800m	J. Nolan	UCD	1.50.20	P. Campbell	Raheny	D. Seward	Kildare
1,500m	E. O'Neill	Crusaders	4.06.70	B. Farren	Sparta	J. Murphy	N. Cork
60m Hurdles	A. Henry	Corran	8.77	S. McCormack	DMP	J. Hallissey	Ferrybank
4x400m Relay		Ballybrack	3.29.5		Borrisokane		Sligo
5km Walk	R. Heffernan	Togher	21.05.14	P. O'Callaghan	UCD	J. Costin	W. Waterford

Event	1st	Club	Perf	2nd	Club	3rd	Club
Shot	J. Flynn	W. Waterford	15.94m	J.P. Leahy	Limerick	S. Breathnach	C. na Mona
Long Jump	S. Finnie	Border	6.96m	D. O'Farrell	Borrisokane	I. Graham	Clonliffe
Weight for Dist.	S. Fitzpatrick	N. Laois	7.61m	A. Kennedy	Crusaders	J. Farrelly	DSD
Pole Vault	D. McDermott	Borrisokane	4.40m	J. Hallissey	Ferrybank	N. Anderson	Annadale
High Jump	M. Mandy	Birchfield	2.23m	A. Burke	UCD	R. Kane	Crusaders

WOMEN

Event	1st	Club	Time	2nd	Club	3rd	Club
60m	L. Barry	Emerald	7.53	E. Maher	KCH	N. McGlynn	W. Dublin
200m	L. Barry	Emerald	24.69	E. Maher	KCH	N. McGlynn	W. Dublin
400m	K. Shinkins	DCH	53.99	S. Hickey	Emerald	K. O'Farrell	Borrisokane
800m	F. Davoren	UCC	2.08.55	P. Quinn	Ballymena	E. O'Shea	St Michael's
1500m	F. Davoren	UCC	4.24.65	N. Menendez	DCH	L. Sheelin	DCH
60m Hurdles	A. Cuddihy	CoS	8.87	S. Foley	Lifford	E. Murphy	Nenagh
3km Walk	G. O'Sullivan	UCC	13.21.2	O. Loughnane	Loughrea	M. Hamilton	Limerick
4x400m Relay		Borrisokane 'A'	4.15.70		Borrisokane 'B'		

Event	1st	Club	Perf	2nd	Club	3rd	Club
Shot	B. Lynch	Tirchonaill	11.85m	E. Meagher	Blarney	D. Murphy	Leevale
Triple Jump	S. Hoey	DCH	11.98m	F. Mullen	Clonliffe	A. Furlong	DMP
High Jump	S. Foley	Lifford	1.75m	B. Corrigan	DCH	F. Kavanagh	St L. O'Toole

DOMESTIC RESULTS (CROSS COUNTRY)

National Inter County C'ships (Tinryland, Carlow) November 30 1997

SENIOR MEN, 10,000m — Individual Results

	Athlete	County	Time
1	Seamus Power	Clare	29.29
2	Peter Matthews	Dublin	29.40
3	Noel Cullen	Dublin	29.56
4	David Burke	Westmeath	30.15
5	Colm De Burca	Dublin	30.16
6	Tom McGrath	Westmeath	30.35
7	Pauric McKinney	Donegal	30.45
8	Cian McLoughlin	Ind	30.49
9	Kieran Carlin	Donegal	30.59
10	Alan Merriman	Dublin	31.10

TEAM RESULTS

	Team	Pts	Positions
1	Dublin 'A'	59	2 .3 ..5 .10 .19 .20
2	Donegal 'A'	133	7 ..9 .15 .28 .32 .42
3	Cork 'A'	143	13 .16 .24 .26 .31 .33

SENIOR WOMEN, 5,000m — Individual Results

	Athlete	County	Time
1	Teresa Duffy	Ind	16.58
2	Maureen Harrington	Kerry	17.16
3	Annette Kealy	Dublin	17.17
4	Ann Carroll	Offaly	17.18
5	Margaret Synnott	Donegal	17.23
6	Pauline Curley	Offaly	17.27
7	Louise Cavanagh	Cork	17.30
8	Kay Byrne	Donegal	17.31
9	Dawn Hargan	Donegal	17.34
10	Beth McCluskey	Dublin	17.40

TEAM RESULTS

	Team	Pts	Positions
1	Donegal 'A'	33	5 ..8 ..9 .11
2	Dublin 'A'	38	3 .10 .12 .13
3	Cork 'A'	69	7 .18 .19 .25

National Inter Club Championships (Bree, Co. Wexford) February 22 1998

Senior Men, 12,000m — Individual Results

	Athlete	Club	Time
1	Peter Matthews	Dundrum South Dublin	37.51
2	Noel Berkeley	Dundrum South Dublin	38.27
3	Tom McGrath	Mullingar Harriers	38.47
4	Cormac Finnerty	Mullingar Harriers	38.59
5	John Burke	Mullingar Harriers	39.01
6	David Burke	Mullingar Harriers	39.03
7	Noel Cullen	Clonliffe Harriers	39.18
8	Cian McLaughlin	Clonliffe Harriers	39.33
9	Colm De Burca	Metro/St Brigid's	39.37
10	Pauric McKinney	Civil Service	40.00

Team Results

	Team	Pts	Positions
1	Mullingar Harriers 'A'	18	3 ...4 ...5 ...6
2	Dundrum South Dublin 'A'	45	1 ...2 .12 .30
3	Clonliffe Harriers 'A'	58	7 ...8 .21 .22

Senior Women, 6,000m — Individual Results

	Athlete	Club	Time
1	Maureen Harrington	Riocht	21.27
2	Louise Cavanagh	UCC	21.35
3	Teresa Duffy	Beechmount Harriers	21.44
4	Anne Keenan-Buckley	North Laois	21.52
5	Pauline Curley	Tullamore Harriers	21.59
6	Margaret Synott	Letterkenny	22.22
7	Ann Carroll	Tullamore Harriers	22.44
8	Helena Crossan	Finn Valley	22.49
9	Rosaleen Campbell	Finn Valley	22.54
10	Annette Kealy	Raheny Shamrock	22.56

Team Results

	Team	Pts	Positions
1	Finn Valley 'A'	50	8 ..9 .15 .18
2	UCC 'A'	76	2 .16 .17 .41
3	Mayo 'A'	82	14 .19 .23 .26

INTERNATIONAL RESULTS (TRACK AND FIELD)

European Athletics C'ships (Budapest, Hungary) August 18-23 1998

Irish Results

MEN

Date	Event	Round	Winner	Time/Perf	Irish Competitor	Time/Perf	Status
18.08.98	1,500m	s/f	F. Cacho (Esp)	3:38.52	7. Niall Bruton	3:39.73	Qual. for final
18.08.98	400m Hurdles	1st Rnd	C. Silva (Por)	49.00	7. Tom McGuirk	49.92	Qual. for s/f
18.08.98	20km Walk	Final	I. Markov (Rus)	1:21:10	25. Michael Casey	1:38:58	25th Overall
18.08.98	20km Walk	Final	I. Markov (Rus)	1:21:10	Pierce O'Callaghan	DNF	Eliminated
18.08.98	Hammer	Pool A	A. Annus (Hun)	79.52m	17. Paddy McGrath	66.25	Eliminated
18.08.98	Hammer	Pool A	A. Annus (Hun)	79.52m	18. Roman Linscheid	63.75	Eliminated
19.08.98	400m	1st Rnd	T. Czubak (Pol)	45:96	8. Eugene Farrell	47:56	Eliminated
19.08.98	400m Hurdles	s/f	P. Januszewski (Pol)	48:90	7. Tom McGuirk	51:12	Eliminated
20.08.98	1,500m	Final	R. Estevez (Esp)	3:41.31	12. Niall Bruton	3:47.48	12th Overall
20.08.98	200m	1st Rnd	D. Turner (Brit)	20.63	3. Gary Ryan	20.76	Qual. for s/f
20.08.98	200m	1st Rnd	R. Nordin (Fra)	20.52	7. Paul Brizzel	21.25	Eliminated
21.08.98	800m	1st Rnd	James McIlroy (Irl)	1:46.81			Qual. for s/f
21.08.98	800m	1st Rnd	N. Cahan (Bel)	1:47.02	6. David Matthews	1:47.39	Qual. for s/f
21.08.98	800m	1st Rnd	L. Vydra (Cze)	1:48.20	2. James Nolan	1:48.36	Qual. for s/f
21.08.98	110m Hurdles	1st Rnd	F. Balzer (Ger)	13.47	5. Peter Coughlan	14.00	Eliminated
21.08.98	Javelin	Pool A	P. Blank (Ger)	83.41m	13. Terry McHugh	72.82m	Eliminated
21.08.98	200m	s/f	D. Walker (Brit)	20.74	8. Gary Ryan	21.28	Eliminated
22.08.98	Discus	Pool A	J. Schult (Ger)	63.63m	8. Nicky Sweeney	60.36	Eliminated
22.08.98	800m	s/f	N. Schumann (Ger)	1:47.28	3. James McIlroy	1:47.66	Qual. for final
22.08.98	800m	s/f	N. Schumann (Ger)	1:47.28	8. David Matthews	1:49.65	Eliminated
22.08.98	800m	s/f	A. Bucher (Swi)	1:47.68	6. James Nolan	1:48.50	Eliminated
22.08.98	5,000m	Final	I. Viciosa (Esp)	13:37.46	3. Mark Carroll	13:38.15	3rd Overall
23.08.98	800m	Final	N. Schumann (Ger)	1:44.89	4. James McIlroy	1:45.46	4th Overall

WOMEN

Date	Event	Round	Winner	Time/Perf	Irish Competitor	Time/Perf	Status
19.08.98	400m	1st Rnd	H. Fuchsova (Cze)	51.61	3. Karen Shinkins	52.13*	Qual. for s/f
19.08.98	400m Hurdles	s/f	Susan Smith (Irl)	55.65			Qual. for final
19.08.98	10,000m	Final	Sonia O'Sullivan (Irl)	31:29.33			Champion
20.08.98	400m	s/f	G. Breuer (Ger)	50.79	5. Karen Shinkins	52.40	Eliminated
21.08.98	1,500m	s/f	S. Masterkova (Rus)	4:08.62	5. Sinead Delahunty	4:09.62	Qual. for final
21.08.98	400m Hurdles	Final	I. Tirlea (Rom)	53.37	8. Susan Smith	55.61	8th Overall
21.08.98	Hammer	Pool A	O. Kuzenkova (Rus)	64.10m	16. Nicola Coffey	52.63	Eliminated
21.08.98	Hammer	Pool B	M. Melinte (Rom)	68.65m	- Olivia Kelleher	No Valid Throw	Eliminated
23.08.98	110m Hurdles	s/f	I. Korotya (Rus)	13.09	5. Susan Smith	13.51	Eliminated
23.08.98	5,000m	Final	Sonia O'Sullivan (Irl)	15:06.50	7. Valerie Vaughan	15:39.99	Champion

Continued from previous page

WOMEN							
Date	Event	Round	Winner	Time/Perf	Irish Competitor	Time/Perf	Status
23.08.98	5,000m	Final	Sonia O'Sullivan (Irl)	15:06.50	14. Una English	16:03.64	14th Overall
23.08.98	1,500m	Final	S. Masterkova (Rus)	4:11.91	9. Sinead Delahunty	4:15.38	9th Overall

*= National Record

European Athletics C'ships - Final Medals Table

	Gold	Silver	Bronze
1. Britain	9	4	3
2. Germany	8	7	8
3. Russia	6	9	7
4. Poland	3	4	1
5. Romania	3	2	2
6. Ukraine	3	2	1
7. Italy	2	4	3
8. Portugal	2	3	1
9. Spain	2	1	4
10. France	2	1	1
11. IRELAND	2	0	1
12. Hungary	1	1	0
13. Bulgaria	1	0	3
14. Greece	1	0	2
15. Estonia	1	0	0
16. Czech Republic	0	2	1
17. Finland	0	2	1
18. Switzerland	0	1	1
19. Latvia	0	1	0
20. Slovenia	0	1	0
21. Sweden	0	1	0
22. Belarus	0	0	2

European Indoor Championships (Valencia, Spain) February 27-28 1998

IRISH FINALISTS

Men			
800m	James Nolan	1:47.81 (pb)	4th
800m	David Matthews	1:48.37	5th
High Jump	Antoine Burke	2.22m	13th

IRISH FINALISTS

Women			
1,500m	Freda Davoren	4:19.79	9th
3,000m	Una English	9:22.98	12th

INTERNATIONAL RESULTS (CROSS COUNTRY)

World Championships (Marrakech, Morocco) March 21-22 1998

WOMEN

World Cross Country Championship, 8km.		
Position	Country	Time
1. Sonia O'Sullivan	Ireland	25:39
2. Paula Radcliffe	Britain	25:42
3. Gete Wami	Ethiopa	25:49
Also		
56. Valerie Vaughan	Ireland	28:13
68. Maureen Harrington	Ireland	28:58
71. Anne Keenan-Buckley	Ireland	29:11
74. Teresa Duffy	Ireland	29:31

World Cross Country Championship, 4km.		
1. Sonia O'Sullivan	Ireland	12:20
2. Zahra Ouaziz	Morocco	12.34
3. Kutre Dulecha	Ethiopia	12.37

MEN

World Cross Country Championship, 12km.		
Position	Country	Time
1. Paul Tergat	Kenya	34:01
2. Paul Koech	Kenya	34:06
3. Assefa Mezegebu	Ethiopa	34:28
Also		
40. Cormac Finnerty	Ireland	36:20
45. Seamus Power	Ireland	36:26
104. Cian McLaughlin	Ireland	38:02
106. Colm deBurca	Ireland	38:04
129. Pauric McKinney	Ireland	39:14

IRISH NATIONAL RECORDS

Outdoor Records

MEN						
Event	Senior Record	Holder	Date	Junior Record	Holder	Date
100m	10.46	Neil Ryan	30.06.97	20.67	Derek O'Connor	13.07.83
200m	20.67	Gary Ryan	26.08.97	20.96	Derek O'Connor	03.07.83
400m	45.73	Derek O'Connor	05.06.86	47.26	Paul O'Regan	24.08.85
800m	1.44.82	David Matthews	05.09.95	1.47.55	James Nolan	22.08.96
1,000m	2.17.58	David Matthews	09.09.96			
1,500m	3.33.5	Ray Flynn	07.07.82	3.41.5	Ray Flynn	08.05.76
Mile	3.49.77	Ray Flynn	07.07.82			
2,000m	4.55.06	Marcus O'Sullivan	10.07.96			
3,000m	7.33.84	Mark Carroll	28.08.98	8.06.3	Brian O'Keefe	14.07.81
5,000m	13.03.93	Mark Carroll	01.09.98	14.04.6	John Treacy	26.06.75

Continued from previous page

MEN						
Event	Senior Record	Holder	Date	Junior Record	Holder	Date
10,000m	27.48.7	John Treacy	22.08.80	30.17.0	Frank Greally	18.08.70
110m Hurdles	13.55	T.J. Kearns	27.07.96	14.24	John Whelan	21.07.94
400m Hurdles	49.73	Tom McGuirk	01.06.96	52.2	Ciaran McDunphy	19.06.81
4x100m	39.46	National Team	09.08.97	41.31	National Team	11.08.90
4x100m	41.70	Dublin City Harriers	07.06.87			
4x400m	3.07.18	National Team	05.09.87	3.13.09	National Team	26.08.89
4x400m	3.13.21	Dublin City Harriers	05.06.88	3.18.64	Leevale	03.07.84
Marathon	2.09.15	John Treacy	18.04.88			
3km Walk	12.06.89	Jimmy McDonald	25.07.87	12.25.5	David Cullinan	25.05.92
10km Walk	41.02.52	Jimmy McDonald	16.06.96	43.20.78	Jamie Costin	23.08.96
20k Walk	1.23.51.12	Bobby O'Leary	14.07.91			
20k Road Walk	1.21.51	Bobby O'Leary	15.03.92	1.28.56	Jamie Costin	31.03.96
50k Walk	4.23.50	Pat Murphy	05.04.92			
High Jump	2.25m	Mark Mandy	25.08.96	2.21m	Antoine Burke	25.06.94
Pole Vault	5.00m	Alan Bourke	13.08.89	4.53m	Frank Evers	08.07.84
Long Jump	7.86m	Ciaran McDonagh	28.06.96	7.73m	Ciaran McDonagh	28.07.95
Triple Jump	15.89m	Colm Cronin	26.06.77	15.56m	Colm Cronin	13.06.76
Shot	20.04m	Paul Quirke	07.07.92	16.59m	Victor Costello	30.07.88
Discus	67.40m	Nick Sweeney	22.05.96	50.42m	Nick Sweeney	26.07.87
Hammer	77.80m	Declan Hegarty	27.04.85	63.98m	Gary Halpin	28.07.85
Javelin	82.14m	Terry McHugh	07.08.94	71.30m	Terry McHugh	24.04.82
56lbs Height	4.93m	Gerry O'Connell	19.07.86			
56lbs Dist.	9.16m	John Menton	26.07.98			
Decathlon	7882pts	Carlos O'Connell	4/5.06.88	7336pts	Barry Walsh	6/7.08.87

WOMEN						
Event	Senior Record	Holder	Date	Junior Record	Holder	Date
100m	11.43	Michelle Carroll	17.06.78	11.43	Michelle Carroll	17.06.78
200m	23.51	Michelle Carroll	18.06.78	23.51	Michelle Carroll	18.06.78
400m	52.13	Karen Shinkins	19.08.98	53.24	Caroline O'Shea	17.06.78
800m	2.00.69	Sonia O'Sullivan	28.07.94	2.05.72	Sonia O'Sullivan	18.07.87
1,000m	2.34.66	Sonia O'Sullivan	03.07.93			
1,500m	3.58.85	Sonia O'Sullivan	25.07.95	4.17.84	Natalie Davey	07.06.91
Mile	4.17.26	Sonia O'Sullivan	23.07.94			
2,000m	5.25.36	Sonia O'Sullivan	08.07.94			
3,000m	8.21.65	Sonia O'Sullivan	15.07.94	9.01.52	Sonia O'Sullivan	07.07.87
5,000m	14.41.40	Sonia O'Sullivan	01.09.95			
10,000m	31.08.41	Catherina McKiernan	17.06.95	33.45.79	Aisling Ryan	05.06.88
100m Hurdles	13.12	Susan Smith	09.08.98	13.90	Olive Burke	03.07.84
400m Hurdles	54.31	Susan Smith	12.08.98	59.45	Fiona Norwood	18.05.97
4x100m	45.60	National Team	11.06.94	47.6	BLOE Team	06.08.78
4x100m	= 47.8	Nenagh Olympic	01.05.80	48.92	Nenagh Olympic	23.08.81
	= 47.8	Crusaders	01.07.84			
4x400m	3.32.56	National Team	05.09.87	3.47.38	National Team	12.08.89
4x400m	3.44.73	Puma T.C.	05.06.88	3.57.30	Raheny Shamrocks	20.07.91
Marathon	2.23.44	Catherina McKiernan	28.09.97			
3km Walk	13.06.15	Lisa Sheridan	22.08.93	13.54.93	Gillian O'Sullivan	15.07.95
5km Walk	21.35.62	Deirdre Gallagher	23.06.96	23.29.73	Rosaleigh Comerford	24.08.96
10km Walk	47.09.1	Gillian O'Sullivan	03.05.97			
10km Walk Road	45.12	Deirdre Gallagher	24.02.96			
High Jump	1.89m	Laura Sharpe	03.07.94	1.84m	Brigid Corrigan	26.05.80
Long Jump	6.48m	Terri Horgan	14.06.92	5.97m	Claire Ingerton	19.07.91
Triple Jump	12.21m	Siobhan Hoey	18.07.94			
Shot	16.99m	Marita Walton	02.04.84	14.70m	Marita Walton	20.08.78
Discus	57.60m	Patricia Walsh	07.07.84	48.26m	Patricia Walsh	22.07.79
Javelin	50.42m	Mary T. Real	20.06.92	47.52m	Brenda Walsh	12.06.82
Hammer	56.22m	Olivia Kelleher	30.07.97	48.82m	Clare Thompson	13.07.97
Heptathlon	5394 pts	Sharon Foley	23/24.08.97	4962 pts	Brid Hallissey	5/6.07.86

Indoor Records

Event	Men's Record	Holder	Date	Women's Record	Holder	Date
60m	6.88	Gary Ryan	11.01.98	7.38	Michelle Carroll	27.02.93
200m	21.13	Gary Ryan	07.03.97	24.2	Michelle Carroll	16.02.80
400m	47.0	Fanahan McSweeney	15.03.70	53.45	Karen Shinkins	28.03.98
800m	1.47.6	Noel Carroll	09.03.69	2.02.87	Aisling Molloy	17.02.90
1,000m	2.20.2	Marcus O'Sullivan	25.01.85	-	-	-
1,500m	3.35.4	Marcus O'Sullivan	13.02.88	4.14.2	Mary Purcell	02.03.80
1 Mile	3.49.78	Eamonn Coghlan	27.02.83	4.32.4	Sinead Delahunty	22.02.97
2,000m	4.54.07	Eamonn Coghlan	20.02.87	5.56.32	Monica Joyce	18.01.85
3,000m	7.41.14	Frank O'Mara	10.03.91	8.46.19	Sonia O'Sullivan	08.03.97
5,000m	13.34.96	John Treacy	12.02.82	15.17.28	Sonia O'Sullivan	26.01.91
60m Hurdles	7.69	T.J. Kearns	09.03.91	8.44	Susan Smith	25.02.96
5,000m Walk	19.24.91	Jimmy McDonald	10.03.91	-	-	-
High Jump	2.26m	Mark Mandy	02.02.97	1.86m	Sharon Foley	03.03.96
Pole Vault	5.02m	John Hallissey	19.01.97	-	-	-
Long Jump	7.59m	Ciaran McDonagh	08.03.96	6.09m	Terri Horgan	03.02.90
Triple Jump	16.27m	Colm Cronin	10.03.78	12.38m	Siobhan Hoey	23.02.97
Shot	18.07m	Paul Quirke	01.02.91	17.06m	Marita Walton	26.02.82
Heptathlon	5492pts	Barry Walsh	13/14.03.93	-	-	-
Pentathlon	-	-	-	3909pts	Brid Hallissey	16.02.92

CHAMPIONSHIP MEDALLISTS

Indoor

Year	Championships	Event	Medal	Winner
1967	European Indoor Games	800m	Gold	Noel Carroll
1968	European Indoor Games	800m	Gold	Noel Carroll
1969	European Indoor Games	800m	Bronze	Noel Carroll
1970	European Indoor Championships	1,500m	Silver	Frank Murphy
1979	European Indoor Championships	1,500m	Gold	Eamonn Coghlan
1980	European Indoor Championships	1,500m	Silver	Ray Flynn
1980	European Indoor Championships	1500m	Bronze	Mary Purcell
1985	European Indoor Championships	1,500m	Silver	Marcus O'Sullivan
1987	World Indoor Championships	1,500m	Gold	Marcus O'Sullivan
1987	World Indoor Championships	3,000m	Gold	Frank O'Mara
1987	World Indoor Championships	3,000m	Silver	Paul Donovan
1989	World Indoor Championships	1,500m	Gold	Marcus O'Sullivan
1991	World Indoor Championships	3,000m	Gold	Frank O'Mara
1993	World Indoor Championships	1,500m	Gold	Marcus O'Sullivan
1997	World Indoor Championships	3,000m	Silver	Sonia O'Sullivan

Outdoor

Year	Championships	Event	Medal	Winner
	Senior			
1969	European Championships	1,500m	Silver	Frank Murphy
1978	European Championships	1,500m	Silver	Eamonn Coghlan
1981	World Cup	5,000m	Gold	Eamonn Coghlan
1983	World Championships	5,000m	Gold	Eamonn Coghlan
1984	Olympic Games	Marathon	Silver	John Treacy
1991	World Cup	5,000m	Silver	John Doherty
1993	World Championships	1,500m	Silver	Sonia O'Sullivan
1994	European Championships	3,000m	Gold	Sonia O'Sullivan
1995	World Championships	5,000m	Gold	Sonia O'Sullivan
1998	European Championships	5,000m	Gold	Sonia O'Sullivan
1998	European Championships	10,000m	Gold	Sonia O'Sullivan
1998	European Championships	5,000m	Bronze	Mark Carroll
1998	World Cup	5,000m	Gold	Sonia O'Sullivan
	Junior			
1975	European Junior Championships	5,000m	Silver	John Treacy
1985	European Junior Championships	3,000m	Gold	Nick O'Brien

Continued from previous page

Year	Championships	Event	Medal	Winner
1987	European Junior Championships	Decathlon	Bronze	Barry Walsh
1991	European Junior Championships	5,000m	Gold	Mark Carroll
1993	European Junior Championships	800m	Bronze	David Matthews
1994	World Junior Championships	High Jump	Silver	Antoine Burke
1997	European Junior Championships	1,500m	Bronze	Gareth Turnbull
	Youth			
1991	European Youth Olympics	Long Jump	Silver	Arlene Smith
1991	European Youth Olympics	800m	Silver	Claire Ingerton
1993	European Youth Olympics	800m	Silver	James Nolan
1995	European Youth Olympics	1,500m	Silver	Gareth Turnbull
1995	European Youth Olympics	1,500m	Silver	Maria Lynch
1995	European Youth Olympics	100m Hurdles	Bronze	Grainne Redmond
1997	European Youth Olympics	200m	Gold	Ciara Sheehy
1997	European Youth Olympics	1,500m	gold	Colm McLean
1998	World Youth Olympics	100m	Gold	Emily Maher
1998	World Youth Olympics	200m	Gold	Emily Maher
	Student			
1991	World Student Games	1,500m	Gold	Sonia O'Sullivan
1991	World Student Games	3,000m	Silver	Sonia O'Sullivan
1991	World Student Games	1,500m	Gold	Niall Bruton
1993	World Student Games	Discus	Bronze	Nick Sweeney

Cross Country

Year	Championships	Medal	Winner
	Senior Individual		
1978	World Championships	Gold	John Treacy
1979	World Championships	Gold	John Treacy
1992	World Championships	Silver	Catherina McKiernan
1993	World Championships	Silver	Catherina McKiernan
1994	World Championships	Silver	Catherina McKiernan
1994	European Championships	Gold	Catherina McKiernan
1995	World Championships	Silver	Catherina McKiernan
1998	World Championships (8km)	Gold	Sonia O'Sullivan
1998	World Championships (4,000m)	Gold	Sonia O'Sullivan
	Senior Team		
1971	Women's International Championships	Bronze	A O'Brien, P. Mullen, D. Foreman, J. McNicholl
1979	World Championships	Silver	J. Treacy, D. McDaid, G. Deegan, M. O'Shea, D. Walsh, T. Brien
1997	World Championships	Bronze	C. McKiernan, S. O'Sullivan, V. Vaughan, U. English
	Junior Individual		
1971	Junior International	Gold	John Hartnett
1974	World Junior Championships	Bronze	John Treacy
1975	World Junior Championships	Bronze	John Treacy
	Junior Team		
1969	Junior International	Silver	J. Hartnett, E. Leddy, P. Gilsenan, D. Murphy
1975	Junior Championships	Silver	J. Treacy, L. Kenny, G. Finnegan, G. Redmond

PAST NATIONAL CHAMPIONS

Men

	100m			200m		
Year	Winner	Club	Perf	Winner	Club	Perf
1997	Neil Ryan	Nenagh Olympic	10.53	Gary Ryan	Nenagh Olympic	21.02
1996	Neil Ryan	Nenagh Olympic	10.74	Gary Ryan	Nenagh Olympic	21.10
1995	Ian Cralg	Annadale Striders	10.67	Mark Allen	Annadale Striders	21.35
1994	Jeff Pamplin	DCH	10.94	Tom McGuirk	DCH	21.58
1993	Kieran Finn	Limerick	10.48	Kieran Finn	Limerick	21.42
1992	Neil Ryan	Nenagh Olympic	10.67	Mark Allen	Annadale Striders	21.78
1991	Carlton Haddock	Togher	10.91	Barry Martin	Redeemer	21.69
1990	Barry Martin	Redeemer	10.84	Barry Martin	Redeemer	21.41

Continued from previous page

Year	100m Winner	Club	Perf	200m Winner	Club	Perf
1989	Darren Haddock	Togher	11.14	Gerry Delaney	DCH	22.37
1988	Philip Snoddy	Annadale Striders	10.55	Philip Snoddy	Annadale Striders	20.50

Year	400m Winner	Club	Perf	800m Winner	Club	Perf
1997	Brian Forbes	Mid Ulster	47.06	David Matthews	UCD	1.50.53
1996	Eugene Farrell	DCH	47.56	David Matthews	UCD	1.48.10
1995	Stephen Newman	DCH	47.93	David Matthews	UCD	1.47.87
1994	Sean McAteer	Harolds Cross	47.17	David Matthews	UCD	1.49.81
1993	Sean McAteer	Harolds Cross	48.07	PJ O'Rourke	Nenagh Olympic	1 45.81
1992	Stephen Newman	DCH	48.04	Marcus O'Sullivan	Leevale	1.49.90
1991	Peter Sinclair	Banbridge	47.34	David Wilson	Annadale Striders	1.48.37
1990	Brendan Murphy	Cashel	47 63	PJ O'Rourke	Nenagh Olympic	1.51.39
1989	Brendan Murphy	Cashel	46.88	Marcus O'Sullivan	Leevale	1.50.33
1988	Gerry Delaney	DCH	46.85	Mark Kirk	Ballymena/Antrim	1.50.82

Year	1,500m Winner	Club	Perf	5,000m Winner	Club	Perf
1997	Niall Bruton	Clonliffe Harriers	3.42.67	Seamus Power	Kilmurray	14.07.00
1996	Niall Bruton	Clonliffe Harriers	3.41.68	John Daly	Nenagh Olympic	14.34.82
1995	Mark Carroll	Leevale	3.39.67	Frank O'Mara	Limerick	13.45.79
1994	Niall Bruton	Clonliffe Harriers	3.42.27	Corm Finnerty	Mullingar Harriers	13.50.66
1993	Niall Bruton	Clonliffe Harriers	3.50.93	Paul Donovan	GCH	14.36.95
1992	Garreth Barry	North Cork	3.47.30	Noel Richardson	Limerick	14.08.14
1991	Frank O'Mara	Limerick	3.41.21	Seamus Power	Treaty TC	14.02.94
1990	Anthony Spelman	GCH	3.46.89	Paul Donovan	GCH	14.00.62
1989	Gerry O'Reilly	Metro	3.43.02	Seamus Hynes	Limerick	14.19.14
1988	Frank O'Mara	Limerick	3.47.27	John Doherty	Leeds, England	13.43.29

Year	10,000m Winner	Club	Perf	100m Hurdles Winner	Club	Perf
1997	Noel Berkley	DSD	29.57.44	TJ Kearns	DCH	14.20
1996	Sean Dollman	Kentucky, USA	29.17.49	Peter Coghlan	Crusaders	14.08
1995	Noel Berkeley	DSD	29.55.57	Sean Cahill	Cushinstown	14.40
1994	Noel Berkeley	DSD	29.22.52	TJ Kearns	DCH	13.92
1993	Noel Berkeley	DSD	29.23.20	TJ Kearns	DCH	13.62
1992	Gerry McGrath	DSD	30.21.70	TJ Kearns	DCH	13.98
1991	Noel Richardson	Limerick	29.29.12	TJ Kearns	DCH	13.81
1990	Richard Mulligan	Clonliffe Harriers	30.06.52	TJ Kearns	DCH	14.02
1989	Richard Mulligan	Clonliffe Harriers	30.14.09	TJ Kearns	DCH	14.62
1988	Gerry Curtis	Donore	28.49.26	TJ Kearns	DCH	14.41

Year	400m Hurdles Winner	Club	Perf	3,000m Steeplechase Winner	Club	Perf
1997	Tom McGuirk	DCH	51.00	Patrick Davoren	Brighton, England	9.00.54
1996	Tom McGuirk	DCH	50.61	John Murray	DCH	8.39.24
1995	Tom McGuirk	DCH	50.97	John Murray	DCH	9.03.34
1994	Tom McGuirk	DCH	51.40	Liam O'Brien	East Cork	8.56.43
1993	Nigel Keogh	Blackheath, England	53.94	Enda Ftzpatrick	DCH	8.57.30
1992	Ciaran McDunphy	London Irish	53.41	Liam O'Brien	East Cork	9.00.40
1991	Ciaran McDunphy	Raheny Shamrocks	51.83	Liam O'Brien	East Cork	8.41.55
1990	Nigel Keogh	Blackheath, England	53.04	Kieran Stack	North Cork	8.40.94
1989	TJ Kearns	DCH	52.84	Kieran Stack	North Cork	8.50.37
1988	JJ Barry	DCH	52.82	Brendan Quinn	Waterford	8.42.83

Year	10k Walk Winner	Club	Perf	20k Walk Winner	Club	Perf
1997	Michael Casey	Sligo	44.03.62	Michael Casey	Sligo	1.27.56
1996	Jimmy McDonald	DCH	41.02.52	Jimmy McDonald	DCH	1.25.51
1995	Michael Casey	Sligo	41.30.73	Michael Casey	Sligo	1.29.20
1994	Michael Casey	Sligo	44.09.82	Pat Murphy	Castleisland	1.26.28
1993	Pat Murphy	Castleisland	44.21.56	Pat Murphy	Castleisland	1.33.32
1992	Michael Lane	Mullingar Harriers	46.57.99	Michael Lane	Mullingar Harriers	1.37.42

Continued from previous page

Year	10k Walk Winner	Club	Perf	20k Walk Winner	Club	Perf
1991	Jimmy McDonald	DCH	41.28.70	Bobby O Leary	Clonliffe Harriers	1.23.51
1990	Jimmy McDonald	DCH	41.55.05	Michael Lane	Mullingar Harriersl	1.31.51
1989	Jimmy McDonald	DCH	41.25.41	Michael Lane	Mullingar Harriers	1.27.05
1988	Jimmy McDonald	Slaneyside	42.07.37	Jimmy McDonald	Slaneyside	1.27.29

Year	Marathon Winner	Club	Perf	Long Jump Winner	Club	Perf
1997	Seamas O'Donnell	GCH	2.29.08	Garret Devlin	Ballymena	6.87
1996	Seamas O'Donnell	GCH	2.25.41	Ciaran McDonagh	Fr Murphy	7.74m
1995	Richard Mulligan	Clonliffe Harriers	2.27.11	Jonathon Kron	DCH	7.73m
1994	Eamon Tierney	Clonliffe Harriers	2.23.38	Jonathon Kron	DCH	7.12m
1993	Seamas O'Donnell	GCH	2.23.38	Jonathon Kron	DCH	7.40m
1992	Jerry Kiernan	Clonliffe Harriers	2.17.19	Jonathon Kron	DCH	7.26m
1991	Tom Hughes	Duncairn	2.14.46	Jonathon Kron	DCH	6.98m
1990	Roy Dooney	DCH	2.16.07	Jonathon Kron	DCH	7 54m
1989	John Griffn	St Johns	2.18.49	Billy Oakes	Leevale	6.71m
1988	John Woods	Liverpool, England	2.11.30	Billy Oakes	KCH	6.91m

Year	High Jump Winner	Club	Perf	Pole Vault Winner	Club	Perf
1997	Mark Mandy	Birchfield	2.20m	Dylan McDermott	Borrisokane	4.60m
1996	Mark Mandy	Cannock, England	2.23m	Dylan McDermott	Borrisokane	4.50m
1995	Mark Mandy	Cannock, England	2.13m	Neil Young	Lisburn	4.80m
1994	Kevin Keane	DCH	2.11m	Neil Young	Lisburn	4.60m
1993	Mark Mandy	Cannock, England	2.10m	Neil Young	Lisburn	4.40m
1992	Antoine Burke	Limerick	2.12m	Richard Ramsey	Annadale Striders	4.60m
1991	Brendan Reilly	Corby, England	2.17m	Mike Bull	North Down	4.30m
1990	Peter Minogue	Harolds Cross	2.00m	John Hallisey	Ferrybank	4.20m
1989	Simon Boyle	Annadale Striders	2.07m	Alan Burke	Hounslow	4.71m
1988	Peter Minogue	Harolds Cross	2.07m	Alan Burke	Hounslow	4.50m

Year	Shot Putt Winner	Club	Perf	Discus Winner	Club	Perf
1997	Nicky Sweeney	DSD	17.02m	Nick Sweeney	DSD	57.90m
1996	John Farrelly	DSD	15.12m	Nick Sweeney	DSD	60.66m
1995	Paul Quirke	Crusaders	17.04m	Nick Sweeney	DSD	57.42m
1994	Nicky Sweeney	DSD	17.37m	Nick Sweeney	DSD	60.36m
1993	Paul Quirke	Crusaders	17.54m	Nick Sweeney	DSD	57.30m
1992	Paul Quirke	Crusaders	17.08m	Nick Sweeney	DSD	58.14m
1991	Victor Costello	DSD	16.51m	Nick Sweeney	DSD	58.46m
1990	Victor Costello	DSD	16.85m	Paul Quirke	Crusaders	49 40m
1989	Victor Costello	DSD	16.05m	Frank O'Brien	Dungarvan	45.50m
1988	Victor Costello	Team Puma	16.49m	John Farrelly	Team Puma	46.96m

Year	Javelin Winner	Club	Perf	Hammer Winner	Club	Perf
1997	Terry McHugh	DCH	70.80m	Roman Linscheid	Donore Harriers	71.54m
1996	Terry McHugh	DCH	73.92m	Roman Linscheid	Donore Harriers	72.88m
1995	Terry McHugh	DCH	71.76m	Roman Linscheid	Donore Harriers	69.00m
1994	Terry McHugh	DCH	72.32m	Ronald Quinlan	Walkinstown	57.10m
1993	Terry McHugh	DCH	72.28m	Patrick McGrath	Raheny Shamrocks	65.46m
1992	Terry McHugh	DCH	75.40m	Patrick McGrath	Raheny Shamrocks	62.22m
1991	Terry McHugh	DCH	75.52m	Conor McCullough	Crusaders	64.88m
1990	Terry McHugh	DCH	75.90m	Conor McCullough	Crusaders	67.62m
1989	Terry McHugh	DCH	74.42m	Gary Halpin	KCH	63.72m
1988	Terry McHugh	DCH	69.20m	Conor McCullough	Crusaders	74.16m

Year	56lbs for Distance Winner	Club	Perf	56lbs for height Winner	Club	Perf
1997	John Menton	Donore Harriers	8.95m	Nick Sweeny	DSD	4.40m
1996	John Menton	Donore Harriers	8.73m	Seamus Fitzpatrick	North Laois	4.70m
1995	John Menton	Donore Harriers	8.33m	Pat Maher	Brow Rangers	4.55m
1994	Nick Sweeney §	DSD	9.23m	Pat Maher	Brow Rangers	4.61m

Continued from previous page

Year	56lbs for Distance Winner	Club	Perf	56lbs for height Winner	Club	Perf
1993	John Menton	Donore Harriers	8.61m	Paul Quirke	Crusaders	4.40m
1992	Sean Egan	Donore Harriers	7.04m	Pat Maher	Brow Rangers	4 35m
1991	John Menton	Donore Harriers	8 19m	Pat Maher	Brow Rangers	4.50m
1990	Pat Maher	Brow Rangers	8 14m	Pat Maher	Brow Rangers	4.20m
1989	John Dunlee	Unattached	8.22m	Pat Maher	KCH	4.57m
1988	John Dunlee	Kilorglin	8.61m	Pat Maher	Brow Rangers	4.62m

§ Light weight

Year	Triple Jump Winner	Club	Perf
1997	Patrick Shannon	Ballybrk	13.69m
1996	Michael McDonald	Border Harriers	15.04m
1995	Michael McDonald	Border Harriers	14.22m
1994	Michael McDonald	Ballymena/Antrim	15 45m
1993	Michael McDonald	Queens University	15.26m
1992	Jim Hayes	Waterford	14 59m
1991	Michael McDonald	Queens University	15.09m
1990	Michael McDonald	Ballymena/Antrim	14.82m
1989	Billy Oakes	Leevale	13.97m
1988	Michael McDonald	Ballymena/Antrim	15.45m

Women

Year	100m Winner	Club	Perf	200m Winner	Club	Perf
1997	Aoife Hearn	Waterford	11.88	Ciara Sheehy	West Dublin	24.31
1996	Lena Barry	Limerick Emerald	12.35	Jackqui Stokes	Ferrybank	24.46
1995	Michele Carroll	Crusaders	11.83	Michele Carroll	Crusaders	24.46
1994	Terri Horgan	DCH	12.18	Marissa Smith	Clonliffe Harriers	24.36
1993	Michele Carroll	Crusaders	11.74	Michele Carroll	Crusaders	24.25
1992	Michele Carroll	Crusaders	11.54	Michele Carroll	Crusaders	23.89
1991	Michele Carroll	Crusaders	11.79	Michele Carroll	Crusaders	24.18
1990	Marissa Smyth	Boyne	12.11	Marissa Smith	Boyne	24.29
1989	Michele Carroll	Crusaders	12.24	Michele Carroll	Crusaders	24.88
1988	Michele Carroll	Crusaders	11.86	Patricia Amond	DCH	23.47

Year	400m Winner	Club	Perf	800m Winner	Club	Perf
1997	Karen Shinkins	DCH	56.20	Amanda Crowe	Lisburn	2.07.46
1996	Emma Nicholson	DCH	54.79	Freda Davoren	UCC	2.05.65
1995	Michelle Carroll	Crusaders	54.18	Aisling Molloy	DSD	2.03.51
1994	Stephanie McCann	Lisburn	54.81	Aisling Molloy	DSD	2.04.90
1993	Stephanie McCann	Lisburn	55.68	Geraldine Nolan	KCH	2.08.12
1992	Michelle Carroll	Crusaders	54.51	Sonia O'Sullivan	Ballymore/Cobh	2.05.63
1991	Emma Nicholson	DCH	54.93	Aisling Molloy	DSD	2.02.08
1990	Bernadette Kavanagh	Lucan Harriers	55.16	Bernadette Kavanagh	Lucan	2.07.59
1989	Michelle Carroll	Crusaders	54.39	Urusla McKee	Lisburn	2.09.02
1988	Patricia Walsh	Team Puma	54.39	Aisling Molloy	Team Puma	2.05.48

Year	1,500m Winner	Club	Perf	3,000m/5,000m Winner	Club	Perf
1997	Valerie Vaughan	Blarne	4.23.50	Valerie Vaughan	Blarney	15.44.72
1996	Sonia O'Sullivan	Ballymore/Cobh	4.15.24	Catherina McKiernan	Cornafean	15.27.10
1995	Sonia O'Sullivan	Ballymore/Cobh	4.07.09	Teresa Duffy	Beechmount Harriers	16.15.94
1994	Sinead Delahunty	KCH	4.14.63	Geraldine Hendricken	St L. O'Toole	9.35 62
1993	Anita Philpott	North Cork	4.24.36	Catherina McKiernan	Cornafean	9.13.40
1992	Valerie Vaughan	Blarney Iniscarra	4.28.71	Catherina McKiernan	Cornafean	9.04.08
1991	Una English	DCH	4.22.69	Catherina McKiernan	Cornafean	9.10.93
1990	Sonia O'Sullivan	Ballymore/Cobh	4.00.44	Catherina McKiernan	Cornafean	9.16.60
1989	Valerie O'Mahoney	Togher	4.24 56	Roisin Smyth	DCH	9.27.39
1988	Monica Joyce	Westport	4.20.43	Rosie Lambe	Knockbridge	9.22.77

Marathon

Year	Winner	Club	Perf
1997	Donna McNulty	Foyle Valley	3.21.05
1996	Brid Murphy	Leevale	2.52.52
1995	Mary Jennings	Waterford	3.00.45
1994	Eleanor Hill	Bray	2.57.42
1993	Brid Murphy	Leevale	2.52.33
1992	Brid Murphy	Leevale	2.43.00
1991	Christine Kennedy	GCH	2.35.56
1990	Christine Kennedy	GCH	2.38.05
1989	Mary Ryan	Waterford	2.53.47
1988	Marie R. Murphy	Unatthed	2.40.48

100m Hurdles

Winner	Club	Perf
Gráinne Redmond	Cushinstown	14.29
Patricia Naughton	Nenagh Olympic	14.44
Susan Smith	Waterford	13.99
Patricia Naughton	Nenagh Olympic	14.47
Patricia Naughton	Nenagh Olympic	14.31
Susan Smith	Waterford	13.88
Susan Smlth	Waterford	14.00
Susan Smith	Waterford	14.41
Susan Smith	Waterford	14.04
Olive Burke	Limerick	14.00

400m hurdles

Year	Winner	Club	Perf
1997	Susan Smith	Waterford	56.55
1996	Susan Smith	Waterford	56.01
1995	Mandy Bloomer	Mountmellick	60.50
1994	Mandy Bloomer	Mountmellick	60.77
1993	Stephanie McCann	Lisburn	60.21
1992	Susan Smith	Waterford	60.31
1991	Lisa Nicholson	DCH	60.75
1990	Lisa Nicholson	DCH	59.46
1989	Barbara johnson	North Cork	59.97
1988	Barbara Johnson	North Cork	57.93

Triple Jump

Winner	Club	Perf
Siobhan Hoey	DCH	11.36m
Siobhan Hoey	DCH	11.95m
Siobhan Hoey	UCD	11.35m
Siobhan Hoey	UCD	12.10m
Siobhan Hoey	UCD	12.02m
Jocelyn Hanarahan	UCD	11.06m
Michelle Rea	Lisburn	11.70m
-	-	-
-	-	-
-	-	-

3000/5000m walk

Year	Winner	Club	Perf
1997	Perri Williams	St Senans	24.50.08
1996	Deirdre Gallagher	U.C.D	22.00.05
1995	Deirdre Gallagher	U.C.D	23.14.24
1994	Deirdre Gallagher	U.C.D	23.34.00
1993	Lisa Sheridan	DCH	23.05.10
1992	Perri Williams	St Senans	23.37.60
1991	Marie Walsh	Shelbourne	24.23.58
1990	Marie Walsh	Shelbourne	24.45.25
1989	Marie Walsh	Shelbourne	14.27.90
1988	Perri Williams	St Senans	14.21.72

10k walk

Winner	Club	Perf
Gillian O Sullivan	U.C.C	48.59
Gillian O'Sullivan	U.C.C	50.19
Deirdre Gallagher	U C D	49.08
Deirdre Gallagher	U.C.D.	49.08
Perri Williams	St Senans	51.43
Perri Williams	St Senans	49.33
Perri Williams	St Senans	50.43
Marie Walsh	Shelbourne	51.14
Marie Walsh	Shelbourne	49.46
Perri Williams	St. Senans	51.52

Long Jump

Year	Winner	Club	Perf
1997	Jacqui Stokes	Ferrybank	5.77m
1996	Jacqui Stokes	Ferrybank	5.97m
1995	Jacqui Stokes	Ferrybank	6.17m
1994	Jacqui Stokes	Ferrybank	6.00m
1993	Terri Horgan	DCH	6.29m
1992	Terri Horgan	DCH	6.05m
1991	Terri Horgan	DCH	6.19m
1990	Terri Horgan	DCH	6.31m
1989	Terri Horgan	Mallow	5.95m
1988	Terri Horgan	Mallow	6.27m

High Jump

Winner	Club	Perf
Sharon Foley	Lifford	1.75m
Breda Tierney-Browne	Nenagh	1.73m
Sharon Foley	Lifford	1.78m
Laura Sharpe	Navan	1.85m
Sharon Foley	Lifford	1.75m
Laura Sharpe	Navan	1.75m
Laura Sharpe	Navan	1.78m
Sharon Foley	Lifford	1.76m
Sharon Foley	Lifford	1.74m
Elizabeth Comerford	West Dublin	1.74m

Shot Putt

Year	Winner	Club	Perf
1997	Emma Gavin	Limerick	12.85m
1996	Emma Gavin	Limerick	12.45m
1995	Emma Gavin	Limerick	12.65m
1994	Kelly Kane	Sheffield, England	13.68m
1993	Kelly Kane	Blackpool, England	13.01m
1992	Mary Mahon	West Dublin	12.85m
1991	Marita Walton	KCH	14.02m
1990	Mary Mahon	West Dublin	12.13m
1989	Marita Walton	KCH	14.42m

Discus

Winner	Club	Perf
Ailish O'Brien	West Waterford	45.02m
Ailish O'Brien	West Waterford	41.06m
Ailish O'Brien	West Waterford	42.10m
Ailish O'Brien	West Waterford	42.46m
Mary Mahon	West Waterford	42.60m
Lorraine Shaw	DCH	46.32m
Lorraine Shaw	Gloucester	49.98m
Lorraine Shaw	Gloucester	45.24m
Ailish O'Brien	Dungarvan	41.78m

Year	Winner	Club	Perf	Winner	Club	Perf
1988	Marita Walton	KCH	14.89m	Marita Walton	KCH	47.64m

Year	Javelin Winner	Club	Perf	Hammer Winner	Club	Perf
1997	Alison Moffit	North Down	45.48m	Clara Thompson	Slaney Olympic	48.82m
1996	Alison Moffitt	North Down	49.10m	Julie Kirkpatrick	Lisburn	48.90m
1995	Dara Shakespeare	DSD	46.26m	Brenda Thompson	Slaney Olympic	44.28m
1994	Dara Shakespeare	DSD	50.26m	Brenda Thompson	Slaney Olympic	39.98m
1993	Mary-T Real	Limerick	47.48m	Brenda Thompson	Slaney Olympic	35.20m
1992	Mary-T Real	Limerick	47.74m	Lorraine Shaw	DCH	44.90m
1991	Mary-T Real	Limerick	47.38m	Elaine Hayes	North Laois	43.32m
1990	Mary-T Real	Limerick	45.74m	Elaine Hayes	North Laois	42.40m
1989	Dara Shakespeare	DSD	43.98m	Noreen Linehan	Eagle	36.84m
1988	Dara Shakespeare	Team Puma	43.76m	Breda Wall	Ferrybank	39.78m

Texaco Award Winners, Athletics

Year	Winner	Year	Winner
1958	Bertie Messitt	**1975**	Eamon Coughlan
1959	Ronnie Delaney	**1976**	Eamon Coughlan
1960	Sean Lawlor	**1977**	Eamon Coughlan
1961	Noel Carroll	**1978**	John Treacy
1962	S. O' Sullivan	**1979**	John Treacy
1963	Tom O' Riordan	**1980**	Eamon Coughlan
1964	Basil Clifford	**1981**	Eamon Coughlan
1965	Derek Graham	**1983**	Eamon Coughlan
1966	Mike Bull	**1984**	John Treacy
1967	Noel Carroll	**1987**	Frank O' Mara
1968	Frank Murphy	**1989**	Marcus O' Sullivan
1969	Frank Murphy	**1992**	Sonia O'Sullivan
1970	Mary Peters	**1993**	Sonia O'Sullivan
1971	Claire Walsh	**1994**	Sonia O'Sullivan
1972	Mary Peters	**1995**	Sonia O'Sullivan
1973	M. Tracey	**1997**	Catherina McKiernan
1974	Neil Cusack		

BADMINTON

Badminton Union of Ireland

Baldoyle Badminton Centre, Baldoyle Industrial Estate, Grange Road, Baldoyle, Dublin 13.
Tel./ Fax. (01) 8393028

Founded 1899
President .... Audrey E. Kinkead
General Secretary .... John Feeney
No. of Clubs 600
No. of Branches .... 4 (Connacht, Leinster, Munster & Ulster)
Number of Teams 500
Number of Members .... Men (20,500), Women (21,000)
Main Badminton Venues .... Baldoyle Badminton Centre, Dublin; Lisburn Racquets Club, Antrim;
.... Whitehall Road (Terenure), Dublin.
Connacht Branch:
President .... Aidan J. Cashin
Secretary .... Tony Kennedy
Leinster Branch:
President .... Mary Dinan
Chairman .... Norman Borton
General Secretary .... Dick O'Rafferty
Munster Branch:
President .... Martin Morrissey
Honorary Secretary .... John Griffin
Ulster Branch:
President .... D. Mullan
Chairman .... D. Gourlay
General Secretary .... A. E. Kinkead
International Statistics:
Senior Coach .... Ray Stevens
Best Result (team) .... European Seniors (excludes top 6 Counties) - Mixed Helvetia Cup Winners 1981
Best Result (team-women) .... World Ladies Team Championships (15th overall) - Uber Cup 1998
International Ranking (men) 29
International Ranking (women) 18
All Time Record Attendance (in Ireland) .... Ireland v Russia, Neptune Stadium (10th March 1990) 1,500

DOMESTIC RESULTS

Irish National Championships

LISBURN (JANUARY 31ST - FEBRUARY 1ST, 1998)

Result	Winner(s)	Runner-Up
Senior: Ladies Singles	Sonya McGinn (Kadca)	Keelin Fox (Mt. Pleasant)
Senior: Men's Singles	Michael Watt (Alpha)	Bruce Topping (Alpha)
Senior: Ladies Doubles	Claire Henderson (Alpha) &	Angela Carr (Mt. Pleasant) &
	Jayne Plunkett (Alpha)	Annette Taylor (Ailesbury)
Senior: Men's Doubles	Bruce Topping (Alpha) &	Mark Peard (Ailesbury) &
	Michael O'Meara (Mt. Pleasant)	Donie O'Halloran (Ailesbury)
Senior: Mixed Doubles	Bruce Topping (Alpha) &	Mark Peard (Ailesbury) &
	Michael O'Meara (Mt. Pleasant)	Elaine Kiely (UCD)

WHITEHALL ROAD - TERENURE, (JANUARY 10TH-11TH, 1998)

Result	Winner	Runner-Up
Junior: Ladies Singles	Sandra Lynch (UCD)	Caitriona O'Kelly (A/bury)
Junior: Men's Singles	Nigel Boyne (Kadca)	Brian Moore (Alpha)
Junior: Ladies Doubles	Pam Peard (Crawfordsburn) &	Ann Marie Reid (A/bury) &
	Vera Marron (Ailesbury)	Caitriona O'Kelly (A/bury)
Junior: Men's Doubles	Mark Dempsey (Mt. Pleasant) &	Nigel Boyne (Kadca) &
	Mark Gogarty (Mt. Pleasant)	Eamon Porter (Mt. Pleasant)
Junior: Mixed Doubles	Mark Dempsey (Mt. Pleasant) &	Joe Ledwidge (Terenure) &
	Sandra Lynch (UCD)	Sharon Smith (Terenure)

BALDOYLE BADMINTON CENTRE (JANUARY 17TH - 18TH, 1998)		
Result	**Winner**	**Runner-Up**
Under 19: Girls Singles	Keelin Fox (Mt. Pleasant)	Lyndsey Seaton (Alpha)
Under 19: Boys Singles	Thomas Ward (Stewarts)	Ciaran Darcy (Mt. Pleasant)
Under 19: Girls Doubles	Sarah Ross (Navan) & Keelin Fox (Mt. Pleasant)	Lyndsey Seaton (Alpha) & Ann Marie Reid (A/bury)
Under 19: Boys Doubles	Ciaran Darcy (Mt. Pleasant) & Neil Lynch (Naas)	Colm O'Brien & Sean Og Devanney (Stewarts)
Under 19: Mixed Doubles	Sean Og Devanney (Stewarts) & Keelin Fox (Mt. Pleasant)	Neil Tolerton (Alpha) & Lyndsey Seaton (Alpha)

LISBURN (NOVEMBER 29TH - 30TH, 1997)		
Result	**Winner**	**Runner-Up**
Under 17: Girls SIngles	Pamela Kinghorn (Alpha)	Ruth Fitzsimons (Terenure)
Under 17: Boys Singles	Ciaran Darcy (Mt. Pleasant)	Gareth Hickey (Carrigaline)
Under 17: Girls Doubles	Fiona Glennon (Kadca) & Teresa Donohue (Naas)	Lisa Lynas (Alpha) & Ruth Fitzsimons (Terenure)
Under 17: Boys Doubles	Ciaran Darcy (Mt. Pleasant) & Neil Lynch (Naas)	Thomas Ward (Stewarts) & Gareth Hickey (Carrigaline)
Under 17: Mixed Doubles	John Forde (Claregalway) & Aoife Aherne (Stewarts)	Ciaran Darcy (Mt. Pleasant) & Fiona Glennon (Kadca)

WATERFORD (JANUARY 27TH - 18TH FEBRUARY, 1998)		
Result	**Winner**	**Runner-Up**
Under 15: Girls Singles	Eimear Harte (Kinsale)	Caitriona Farrell (Kadca)
Under 15: Boys Singles	Darryl Eade (Ennis)	Amir Intisar (Ennis)
Under 15: Girls Doubles	Eimear Harte (Kinsale) & Kim Reville (Kadca)	Caitriona Farrell (Kadca) & Avril Buckley (Carrigtwohill)
Under 15: Boys Doubles	Darryl Eade (Ennis) & Amir Intisar (Ennis)	Aidan Robinson (Kadca) & Aaron Hogue (Kadca)
Under 15: Mixed Doubles	Darryl Eade (Ennis) & Eimear Harte (Kinsale)	Amir Intisar (Ennis) & Ruth Kilkenny (Killaloe)

GALWAY LTC (FEBRUARY 28TH - MARCH 1ST 1998)		
Result	**Winner**	**Runner-Up**
Under 13: Girls Singles	Ruth Connolly (Ramparts)	Jennifer Dunne (Stamullen)
Under 13: Boys Singles	Ciaran McDonnell (Edenderry)	Evan McMillan (Stewarts)
Under 13: Girls Doubles	Donna Scott (Alpha) & Jenny Ryan (Alpha)	Pamela Lynch (Hillview) & Ruth Connolly (Ramparts)
Under 13: Boys Doubles	Brian Kearney (Edenderry) & Ciaran McDonnell (Edenderry)	Philip Collins (Kinsale) & Ronan Mitchell (Kinsale)
Under 13: Mixed Doubles	Philip Collins (Kinsale) & Caroline Hayes (Carrigaline)	Ciaran McDonnell (Edenderry) & Ruth Connolly (Ramparts)

DOMESTIC RESULTS

IRISH CUPS

Venue (Date)	Category	Winners
Lisburn (March 29th, 1998)	Senior	Alpha
Sligo LTC (February 20th-22nd, 1998)	Junior	Mount Pleasant
Baldoyle (March 14th, 1998)	Intermediate	Kadca
Baldoyle (November 23rd, 1997)	Under 19	Alpha

BADMINTON UNION OF IRELAND INTER LEAGUE FINALS

Division	Winners	Results
Division 1	Carlow LTC	Round 1: (Galway LTC 5, Killenaule 2)
		Round 2: (Carlow LTC 6, Killenaule 1)
		Round 3: (Galway LTC 3, Carlow LTC 4)
Division 2	Roundwood	Round 1: (Loughrey 3, Killaloe 4)
		Round 2: (Roundwood 7, Loughreyy 0)
		Round 3: (Roundwood 4, Killaloe 0)
Division 3	Tullahought	Round 1: (Maugherow 6, Galbally 1)
		Round 2: (Tullahought 7, Galbally 0)
		Round 3: (Maugherow 2, Tullahought 4)
Division 4	Cortoon	Round 1: (Cortoon 5, Ballycommon 2)
		Round 2: (Dromconrath 5, Ballycommon 2)

Continued from previous page

Division	Winners	Results
		Round 3: (Cortoon 4, Drumconrath 1)
Division 5	Killoughy	Round 1: (Ballinrobe 4, Balckrock 3)
		Round 2: (Killoughy 4, Blackrock 3)
		Round 3: (Ballinrobe 0, Killoughy 4)
Division 6	Ballina Stephites	Round 1: (Ballina 4, Blackrock 3)
		Round 2: (Bagnelstown 5, Blackrock 2)
		Round 3: (Ballina 4, Bagnelstown 1)

INTERNATIONAL RESULTS

SENIOR RESULTS

Triangular - Ballymena (Dec. 18th, 1997)

Ireland 4 .... Wales 1
Ireland 4 .... Scotland 1

Thomas Cup - Norway (Feb. 14-16th, 1998)

Ireland 5 .... Estonia 0
Ireland 5 .... Brazil 0
Ireland 0 .... Norway 5

Uber Cup - Norway (Feb. 14th-19th, 1998)

Ireland 5 .... Azerbajian 0
Ireland 5 .... Spain 0
Ireland 5 .... Portugal 0
Ireland 0 .... Sweden 5
Ireland 0 .... Germany 5
Ireland 3 .... USA 2

European Seniors - Bulgaria (April 19th-21st, 1998)

Ireland 1 .... Switzerland 4
Ireland 1 .... Finland 4
Ireland 2 .... Poland 3
Ireland 2 .... Portugal 3

UNDER 19 RESULTS

Team Challenge - Leeds (APRIL 4th-5th, 1998)

Ireland 7 .... Scottish Midland 2
Ireland 7 .... Durham 2
Ireland 7 .... Lincolnshire 2
Ireland 1 .... Nottinghamshire 8
Ireland 2 .... Lothian 7
Ireland 5 .... Derbyshire 4

UNDER 17 RESULTS

Quadrangular - Irvine (Jan. 9th - 11th, 1998)

Ireland 3 .... England 6
Ireland 8 .... Wales 1
Ireland 2 .... Scotland 7

UNDER 15 RESULTS

Quadrangular - Cardiff (May 1st - 3rd, 1998)

Ireland 7 .... Scotland 3
Ireland 2 .... England 8
Ireland 4 .... Wales 6

BASKETBALL

Irish Basketball Association

National Basketball Arena, Tymon Park, Dublin 24. Tel. (01) 4590211 www.indigo.ie.iba

Founded	1945
Number of Clubs Affiliated to IBA	300
Number of Local Area Boards	15
Number of Clubs Affiliated to Local Boards	1,200
Number of Registered Players (Men)	5,341
Number of Registered Players (Women)	5,896
Number of Registered Players (Schools)	80,000
President	Finn Ahern
Chief Executive Officer	Scott McCarthy
General Secretary	Sheila Gilligan
Number of Coaches	1,100
Principal Venue	National Basketball Arena (capacity 2,500)
Men's Superleague Champions	Star of Sea - Belfast
Men's Cup Champions	Denny Notre Dame
Women's Superleague Champions	Snowcream Wildcats - Waterford
Women's Cup Champions	Snowcream Wildcats - Waterford
Men's National Team Coach	Enda Byrt
Women's National Team Coach	Gerry Fitzpatrick
Most Capped International (Men)	Mark Keenan (69 caps)
Most Capped International (Women)	Caroline Forde

1997/98 Irish Basketball Association Awards

Senior Player of the Year (Men)	Gareth Maguire, Star of the Sea
Senior Player of the Year (Women)	Jillian Hayes, Snowcream Wildcats - Waterford
Junior Player of the Year (Men)	Gary Dredge, Killester
Junior Player of the Year (Women)	Susan Moran, Tullamore
Coach of the Year (Men's team)	Danny Fulton, Star of the Sea
Coach of the Year (Women's team)	Gerry Fitzpatrick, Snowcream Wildcats
International Player of the Year (Women)	Susan Moran (Junior)
Superleague Club of the Year (Women)	Snowcream Wildcats
Division One Club of the Year 1997/98 (Men)	Sligo Dairies
Non National League Club of the Year	Blue Demons
International Player of the Year (Men)	Michael Bree (Junior)
Junior Official of the Year	Irene Mahony, Tralee
President's Award	Rowena Fahey, Midland Area
Tom Sullivan Award (for services to Schools Basketball)	John O'Mahony, Skibereen
Junior Schoolgirl of the Year	April Cahalane, Skibereen
Junior Schoolboy of the Year	Barry Glover, Marian
Senior Schoolgirl of the Year	Susan Moran, Tullamore
Senior Schoolboy of the Year	Johnathon Darcy, Ard Scoil Ris, Limerick
School of the Year (Girls)	Colaiste Iosagain, Dublin
School of the Year (Boys)	St. Mary's Moyderwell, Tralee

INTERNATIONAL RESULTS

European Men's Basketball Championship Preliminary Round, Helsinki

18.05.98	**Ireland 88**	**Switzerland 80**
	Callahan 23, Phelan 20, Powell 15, Maguire 12	
19.05.98	**Ireland 56**	**Cyprus 57**
	Powell 17, Callahan 12, Richardson 8, O'Connell 8	
21.05.98	**Ireland 66**	**Norway 69**
	Richardson 23, Phelan 11, Callahan 11	
22.05.98	**Ireland 73**	**Luxembourg 59**
	Phelan 19, Richardson 15, Powell 9	
23.05.98	**Ireland 74**	**Austria 89**
	Callahan 15, Maguire 12, Powell 12, Burke 9, O'Connell 9	
24.05.98	**Ireland 79**	**Finland 89**
	Callahan 21, Burke 15, O'Connell 14	

Women's Four Countries International Tournament, Tallaght

10.04.98 .... **Ireland 72** .... **Wales 37**
R. Kelly 12, E. Brophy 10, M. Maguire 9

11.04.98 .... **Ireland 76** .... **England 57**
S. Maguire 10, E. O'Gorman 18, J. Hayes 10, A. McNally 10

12.04.98 .... **Ireland 69** .... **Scotland 38**
S. Maguire 18, J. Hayes 12

Result. 1. Ireland **2.** England **3.** Scotland **4.** Wales
Most Valuable Player: Edel O'Gorman (Ireland)

Junior Women's Four Countries International Tournament, Cardiff

17.04.98 .... **Ireland 76** .... **Scotland 67**
18.04.98 .... **Ireland 84** .... **England 51**
19.04.98 .... **Ireland 92** .... **Wales 44**

Result. 1. Ireland **2.** England **3.** Scotland **4.** Wales

Schoolgirls Four Countries International Tournament, Cardiff

March 1998 .... **Ireland 80** .... **England 72**
March 1998 .... **Ireland 94** .... **Scotland 46**
March 1998 .... **Ireland 94** .... **Wales 36**

Result. 1. Ireland **2.** England **3.** Scotland **4.** Wales

Junior Men's Four Countries International Tournament, Aberdeen

17.04.98 .... **Ireland 97** .... **Scotland 47**
18.04.98 .... **Ireland 97** .... **Wales 33**
19.04.98 .... **Ireland 72** .... **England 81**

Result: 1. England **2.** Ireland **3.** Scotland **4.** Wales

Schoolboy's Four Countries International Tournament, Scotland

March 1998 .... **Ireland 118** .... **Wales 43**
March 1998 .... **Ireland 104** .... **Scotland 62**
March 1998 .... **Ireland 56** .... **England 63**

Result: 1. England **2.** Ireland **3.** Scotland **4.** Wales

DOMESTIC RESULTS

Budweiser Men's Superleague results 1997/98 Season

Home	Ballina	D'gannon	Killarney	Killester	Marian	Neptune	N. Dame	Vincent's	Star	Tralee
Ballina	•	114-89	81-77	85-102	81-77	99-89	78-92	85-87	74-90	130-97
Dungannon	85-77	•		83-78	86-85	76-67	81-93	74-85	77-87	101-83
Killarney	85-92	74-75	•	76-109	82-81	89-83	67-98	89-82	82-106	86-80
Killester	98-82	86-72	96-89	•	83-73	108-94	108-94	72-68	84-98	119-83
Marian	94-95	93-94	95-81	90-82	•	86-80	82-99	73-86	81-90	99-91
Neptune	103-86	81-84	96-90	104-81	74-75	•	95-112	84-87	91-107	95-88
Notre Dame	115-84	108-78	83-85	78-85	80-60	86-82	•	99-85	93-84	109-83
St Vincent's	96-115	90-81	109-95	91-82	91-93	78-88	100-69	•	62-90	97-87
Star of the Sea	108-94	110-90	96-50	113-80	124-88	97-77	100-83	91-76	•	92-89
Tralee	91-81	70-72	86-72	90-70	62-80	86-83	117-100	74-78	68-81	•

ESB Women's Superleague results 1997/98 Season

	Blarney	C'island	Killester	Limerick	Meteors	N. Mhuire	T. Rovers	Tralee	Wildcats
Blarney	•	97-50	57-71	94-52	54-56	53-98	68-57	59-44	60-105
Castleisland	67-91	•	42-70	49-90	51-81	61-119	72-94	63-67	67-146
Killester	58-56	61-39	•	77-63	52-72	47-74	58-77	94-56	53-90
Limerick	69-74	90-64	49-46	•	67-84	47-68	62-64	83-50	53-102
Meteors	66-46	97-57	73-38	76-40	•	56-62	55-81	80-41	46-52
Naomh Mhuire	63-53	79-62	66-36	91-59	62-52	•	57-59	104-58	56-67
Tolka Rovers	83-46	107-53	86-60	86-58	70-69	70-73	•	99-46	72-78
Tralee	51-64	53-58	58-79	50-57	39-72	52-76	56-89	•	40-84
Wildcats	81-62	123-23	75-51	107-34	83-61	72-64	83-58	106-42	•

Budweiser Men's Division One Home and Away Results 1997/98 Season

	C'island	Limerick	MSB	Sligo	St Gall's	T. Rovers	Tridents	Waterford
Castleisland	•	75-81	77-83	89-101	129-81	97-93	98-84	122-113
Limerick	81-72	•	94-82	81-98	102-75	73-76	65-72	74-82
MSB	93-79	67-81	•	106-87	121-82	88-92	82-67	91-70
Sligo	103-69	74-90	88-84	•	122-74	85-81	83-88	74-72
St Gall's	66-86	71-98	81-102	71-83	•	71-117	85-107	62-127
Tolka Rovers	104-97	85-103	83-84	85-102	101-88	•	87-73	109-78
Tridents	64-100	99-110	91-78	89-97	103-60	76-79	•	86-107
Waterford	67-61	95-87	88-75	91-85	95-75	112-107	106-87	•

Talka Rovers 118 **St Gall's** 59; **St Gall's** 60 **C'island** 71; **Waterford** 66 **Limerick** 71; **Talka Rovers** 96 **Sligo** 111; **MSB** 72 **Waterford** 75; **MSB** 102 **Tridents** 87; **Waterford** 104 **MSB** 86; **Tridents** 61 **MSB** 81; **Limerick** 112 **C'island** 89; **C'island** 112 **St Gall's** 71; **Sligo** 111 **Tridents** 85; **C'island** 80 **Limerick** 89.

1997/98 Final League Tables

MEN'S SUPERLEAGUE

	P	W	L	Pts
Star of the Sea	18	17	1	52
Notre Dame	18	13	5	44
St Vincent's	18	10	8	38
Killester	18	10	8	38
Dungannon	18	9	9	36
Ballina	18	8	10	34
Marian	18	7	11	32
Killarney	18	6	12	30
Neptune	18	5	13	28
Tralee	18	5	13	28

MEN'S DIVISION ONE

	P	W	L	Pts
Sligo	18	14	4	46
Waterford	18	13	5	44
Limerick	18	12	6	42
Tolka Rovers	18	10	8	38
MSB	18	10	8	38
Castleisland	18	8	10	34
Tridents	18	5	13	28
St Gall's	18	0	18	18

WOMEN'S SUPERLEAGUE

	P	W	L	Pts
Wildcats	16	16	0	48
Naomh Mhuire	16	13	3	42
Tolka Rovers	16	12	4	40
Meteors	16	10	6	36
Blarney	16	10	6	36
Killester	16	7	9	30
Limerick	16	5	11	26
Castleisland	16	1	15	18
Tralee	16	1	15	18

2 points are awarded for a win, one point is awarded for each fixture.

Sprite Cup Results, Senior Women

1st Round: Naomh Mhuire 109, Sporting Belfast 41; Tralee 57, Sligo 46; Wildcats bt Limerick; Tolka Rovers bt Castleisland.

Quarter Finals: Naomh Mhuire 58, Killester 56; New Ross 31, Tolka Rovers 80; Wildcats 80, Blarney 73; Tralee 45, Meteors 62.

Semi Finals: Wildcats 71, Meteors 60; Naomh Mhuire 64, Tolka Rovers 62.

Final: Naomh Mhuire 58, Wildcats 72.

Sprite Cup Results, Senior Men

1st Round: Castleisland 90, St. Vincent's 91; Notre Dame 97, Killarney 73; Killester 82, Tralee 90; UCD Marian 83, Star of the Sea 87; Waterford 88, Ballina 90; Blue Demons bt St. Gall's; Tolka Rovers bt Dungannon.

Quarter Finals: Notre Dame 90, Blue Demons 64; Tralee 76, Star of the Sea 97; Neptune 86, Ballina 74; Tolka Rovers 96, St. Vincent's 92.

Semi Finals: Star of the Sea 74, Notre Dame 77; Neptune 85, Tolka Rovers 78.

Final: Neptune 73, Notre Dame 79.

Sprite Cup Results, Junior Women

Semi-Finals: Blarney 48, Castlebar 68; Naomh Mhuire 72, Tullamore 78.

Final: Castlebar 64, Tullamore 82.

Sprite Cup Results, Junior Men

Semi-Finals: Blue Demons 89, Sligo 64; Killester 77, Limerick 56.

Final: Blue Demons 52, Killester 67.

PAST WINNERS

National Cup

Season	Men	Women
1983/84	St Vincent's	Naomh Mhuire
1984/85	Neptune	Meteors
1985/86	Blue Demons	Lee Strand Tralee
1986/87	Killester	Blarney
1987/88	Neptune	Castledermot
1988/89	Corinthians	Naomh Mhuire
1989/90	Neptune	Lee Strand Tralee
1990/91	Ballina	Blarney
1991/92	Neptune	Meteors
1992/93	St Vincent's	Lee Strand Tralee
1993/94	St Vincent's	Naomh Mhuire
1994/95	North Mon	Naomh Mhuire
1995/96	Ballina	Meteors
1996/97	Denny Notre Dame	Naomh Mhuire
1997/98	Denny Notre Dame	Wildcats

Superleague

Season	Men	Women
1982/83	Neptune	Meteors
1983/84	Blue Demons	Meteors
1984/85	Neptune	Meteors
1985/86	Neptune	Meteors
1986/87	Neptune	Lee Strand Tralee
1987/88	Neptune	Lee Strand Tralee
1988/89	Blue Demons	Blarney
1989/90	Neptune	Blarney
1990/91	Neptune	Blarney
1991/92	Ballina	Naomh Mhuire
1992/93	North Mon	Meteors
1993/94	St Vincent's	Lee Strand Tralee
1994/95	Neptune	Snowcream Wildcats
1995/96	Garveys Tralee	Snowcream Wildcats
1996/97	Neptune	Snowcream Wildcats
1997/98	Star of the Sea	Snowcream Wildcats

IBA PAST PRESIDENTS

Years	President
1945-52	Col. Joe Byrne
1952-55	George McLoughlin
1955-57	P.J. Nultley
1957-62	Murray L. Gordan
1962-65	M. Heffernan
1965-68	Harry Boland
1968-70	L. George Glaydon
1970-72	Dennis Foley
1972-73	Fr. Michael Casey
1973-75	Alf O'Riordan
1975-77	Tom Burke
1977-79	Frank Geelan
1979-80	Jim Lawlor
1980-82	Noel Keating
1982-88	Liam McGinn
1988-89	Mary Beehan
1989-93	Tony Keane
1993-96	Paul Meaney
1996-	Finn Ahern

BOWLING

Bowling League of Ireland

c/o 7 Glendoher Close, Dublin 16

Founded 1912
President .... R. J. O'Leary
PRO .... J. B. Duff
Number of Clubs .... 21 (19 in Dublin and 2 in Cork)
Number of Members 1,200
Number of Coaches 20
International Statistics:
Most Capped Male (international appearances) .... P. Smyth
Best International Result .... Winners of the Home Countries Championships (1981)
International Ranking .... Top 6

DOMESTIC RESULTS

Bowling League of Ireland Championships: Fáilte Park, Bray (27th July - 1st August 1998)

Result	Winner and Runner-Up	Score
Marper Cup: Senior Singles	B. Somers (Bray) beat P. Moorehead (Leinster)	21/13
Boyd Cup: Senior Pairs	D. Lloyd, G. Darcy (CYM) beat T. Donnelly, H. Barry (CYM)	32/12
Baird Cup: Senior Triples	B. Tormey, J. Kavanagh, T. Fitzpatrick (Leinster) beat C. Murphy, J. O'Sullivan, M. Keegan	25/5
Nassau Cup: Junior Singles	J. Hayden (Greystones) beat B. Larrigan (CYM)	21/18
Tyler Cup: Junior Pairs	C. Cushen, P. O'Looney (Westmanstown) beat B. Downey, K. McDunphy (Aer Lingus)	17/16

Ladies' Bowling League of Ireland

c/o 17 Kimmage Road West, Dublin 12. Tel. (01) 4555302

President .... Betty Kerrigan
Honorary Secretary .... June Fincher
Number of Clubs 18
Number of Senior Coaches 6
Number of Club Coaches 10
International Statistics:
Most Capped Competitor (international appearances) .... Phillis Nolan (Blackrock)
Best International Result .... Phillis Nolan (Gold) World Bowls Pairs 1988, 1992 and 1996 unbeaten (played with Margaret Johnston (Ballymoney)
International Ranking (over 5 years) .... 1st Phillis Nolan; 2nd Marie Barber; 3rd Christine O'Gorman; 4th Pat Murphy
Biggest International Victory .... World Bowls Pairs Winner unbeaten (1988, 1992 and 1996)
Biggest International Defeat .... Wales 1998 (Ireland had no winners in the British Isles Championships.

DOMESTIC RESULTS

Ladies' Bowling League of Ireland National Championships - CYM, Terenure (10th-14th August, 1998)

Result	Senior Winners	Runners-Up	Score
Senior Pairs:	M. Barber & P. Nolan (Blackrock)	M. Chappie & A. Newall (Dun Laoghaire)	20/16
Senior Triples:	M. Murphy, P. Murphy & J. Nolan (Blackrock)	B. Keogh, P. O'Toole & C. Sheppard (Bray)	21/16
Junior Pairs:	J. O'Looney & P. Ellis (Westmanstown)	J. Kane & M. O'Farrell (IGB)	20/18
Junior Triples:	N. French, J. Kane & M. O'Farrell (IGB)	E. Drohan, I. White & N. O'Reilly (Blackrock)	20/9
Junior Fours:	K. Maume, J. Manning, J. Moore & A. Brophy (B of I)	S. Horan, M. Wall, C. Carrigan & N. O'Reilly (Blackrock)	19/16

INTERNATIONAL RESULTS

British Isles Championship - Ayr, Scotland

Triple Winners .... E. Hingston, P. Dawson & C. O'Gorman (Blackrock Bowling Club)

NATIONAL SQUAD FACT FILE (as of 18th July, 1998)

Name	Club	Nationality	No. of Appearances
Phillis Nolan	Blackrock	Irish	18
Marie Barber	Blackrock	Irish	17
Christine O'Gorman	Blackrock	Irish	16
Pat Murphy	Blackrock	Irish	3
Marie Schofield	Blackrock	Irish	1
Margaret Murphy	Blackrock	Irish	1
Phyllis Brett	Bray	Irish	5
Pauline Day	Leinster	Irish	2
Muriel McCrudden	Crumlin	Irish	1
Pat McDonagh	Leinster	English	3

PAST PRESIDENTS

Year	Name	Club
1962	W. Allen	Leinster
1963	D. Maddocks	Kenilworth
1964	E. Hayes	Herbert Park
1965	A. Marsland	Crumlin
1966	R. Kennedy	Blackrock
1967	C. Robinson	Leinster
1968	D. Maddocks	Kenilworth
1969	N. Burnett	Herbert Park
1970	M. Cummins	Crumlin
1971	M. Masson	Blackrock
1972	A. Moran	Dunlaoghaire
1973	C. Robinson	Leinster
1974	H. Watts	Kenilworth
1975	B. McKeon	Herbert Park
1976	V. Hurley	Crumlin
1977	J. Drysdale	Blackrock
1978	G. Franck	Dunlaoghaire
1979	E. Greer	Leinster
1980	J. Fincher	Kenilworth
1981	N. Burnett	Herbert Park
1982	V. Hurley	Crumlin
1983	P. Marchant	Blackrock
1984	M. Stevens	Dunlaoghaire
1985	K. Donnelly	Bray
1986	M. Byrne	Leinster
1987	G. Blakeman	Kenilworth
1988	B. McKeon	Herbert Park
1989	C. Kane	Crumlin
1990	A. Prodohl	Blackrock
1991	M. Donaghy	Dunlaoghaire
1992	T. Devlin	Railway Union
1993	C. Redmond	St. James's Gate
1994	S. Heade	Leinster
1995	K. Savage	Kenilworth
1996	L. Allen	Herbert Park
1997	J. Doyle	Crumlin
1998	B. Kerrigan	CYM

RECORDS

Name	Club	Event	Year
Phillis Nolan	Blackrock	Winner - British Isles Singles	1992-93
Phillis Nolan, Marie Schofield, Pat Murphy, Margaret Murphy	Blackrock	Winners - British Isles Fours	1995-96
Phillis Nolan	Blackrock	Winner - Gold Pairs (Atlantic Rim, Florida)	1993
Phillis Nolan	Blackrock	Bronze - Singles & Pairs (Atlantic Rim, Durban)	1995

Irish Indoor Bowling Association

c/o 204 Kings Road, Knock, Belfast BT5 7HX.

Founded 1962
President .... R. McDermott
Secretary .... D. Hunter
Number of Clubs 1,084
Number of Members .... 30,000+
International Statistics:
Most Capped Competitor .... Dessie Hamilton & Tommy Johnston (1 series each)
International Ranking 1

PAST PRESIDENTS

Years	Name
1962-64	P. T. Watson
1964-66	R. E. Thompson
1966-81	J. A. Boomer
1981-97	S. Nash
1997-present	R. McDermott

irish amateur boxing: a sport in need of a radical overhaul

by **mick dowling**

FORMER IRISH INTERNATIONAL BOXER

THE noble art of self-defence has seen many changes over the past number of years, some of which are to be welcomed while others did not quite deliver in the way in which it was hoped.

In professional boxing, the shortening of championship fights from 15 to 12 rounds was a good move because it was generally in the later rounds, when boxers became tired, that serious damage occurred. One must question the fairly recent trend of fighters prolonging their careers into their late forties and in other cases, making comebacks, having been out of the sport for long periods.

Those of us who have been around the fight game for a long time are very aware of the dangers within the sport, and I can only try to imagine the damage it must be doing to those fighters. I feel the various bodies who control professional boxing - and God knows there are enough of them - have a moral duty to protect these fighters from themselves. Professional boxing has become a huge business with vast amounts of money coming from television rights etc, but while some fighters do well financially, many, many more end up penniless. As one former World Champion said: "The managers are the shrewd ones, they take the money, we take the risks."

Amateur Boxing is currently going through a difficult period. In the space of five years, the world-governing body, the Amateur International Boxing Association (AIBA), introduced two changes both of which had a dramatic effect on the sport. The first was the mandatory wearing of headguards at the Los Angeles Olympic Games in 1984, which was designed to make the sport safer. The second and more controversial change was the introduction, after the 1988 Seoul Olympics, of the computerised scoring system. This was designed to eliminate bad decisions; however, there is a growing band of opinion that these two changes have contributed in no small way to the problems which amateur boxing faces today.

While professional boxing is thriving with lots of television exposure and the showbiz style of presentation, amateur boxing lacks the glitz and glamour. It is my opinion that amateur boxing in this country needs a complete overhaul from top to bottom, and this is a view shared by many in the sport.

The Irish Amateur Boxing Association (IABA) have a stadium in a prime location with a value in excess of £7 million which lies empty 75% of the time. If it were a business, it would have gone bust years ago. A few miles down the road, Shelbourne Park is a classic example of what can be achieved if the right people are in place to plan and make decisions for the future, and, if that were not proof enough you could go a few miles in a different direction and you would find the impressive new National Basketball Arena which is always a hive of activity. If amateur boxing in Ireland is to regain its popularity and become the force it once was at international level, there are a number of issues which need to be tackled:

1. A revamped stadium is required urgently, this would act as a money earner for the association.

2. We need to stage four top class international competitions per year.

3. A proper PR system must be put in place to sell and promote these matches, and the National Championships.

I feel that with the arrival of a new professional gym in Dublin city centre, the time is now right for incentives in the form of Payment for Performance for our amateurs in the Championships and at International level. While the elite grants are to be welcomed, Payment for Performance might be a fairer way to distribute the much sought after Sports Council grants.

I would be of the opinion that if the IABA adopted the Payment for Performance system not only would it be seen as a more just way of distributing Sports Council Elite Athlete Grants but it would also lift our Championships and International matches to a much higher plane. If drastic changes are not made quickly, I think the IABA will find it even more difficult to stem the flow to the professional ranks.

As a small nation with a very small pool of top class boxers, the Association cannot afford to lose its star boxers at the rate at which it has been losing them. Therein lies just a few of the problems which need to be urgently addressed by the IABA.

Irish Amateur Boxing Association

National Boxing Stadium, South Circular Road, Dublin 8. Tel. (01) 4533371

Founded 1911
President .... Breandán Ó Conaire
Honorary Secretary .... Seán Crowley
Number of Provincial Councils .... 4 (Connacht, Leinster, Munster and Ulster)
Number of County Boards 26
Number of Clubs 330
Principal Venue .... The National Boxing Stadium (capacity 2,000)

NATIONAL CHAMPIONSHIP RESULTS

Irish Amateur Boxing Senior Final Results 1997/98

Venue: National Boxing Stadium, January 23, 1998. (stpd= stopped; retd= retired; c/back= count back)

Weight	Winner	Club	Runner Up	Club	Result
Light Flyweight, 48kg	J Rooney	Star (Belfast)			w/o
Flyweight, 51kg	M. Murphy	St Paul's (Waterford)	L. Cunningham	Saints (Belfast)	stpd r2
Bantamweight, 54kg	B. Dunne	CIE (Dublin)	M. Burke	Gorey (Wexford)	stpd r2
Featherweight, 57kg	P. O'Donnell	Dockers (Belfast)	T. Carlyle	Sacred Heart (Dublin)	5-4
Lightweight, 60kg	E. McEnaney	Dundalk (Louth)	A. Carlyle	Sacred Heart (Dublin)	13-12
Light Welterweight, 63.5kg	M. Wickham	Enniscorty (Wexford)	P. McCloskey	Derry	8-7
Welterweight, 67kg	N. Gough	St Paul's (Waterford)	F. Barret	Olympic (Galway)	25-8
Light Middleweight, 71kg	M. Roche	Sunnyside (Cork)	T. Fitzgerald	Ballyvolane (Cork)	24-1
Middleweight, 75kg	B. Magee	Holy Trinity (Belfast)	K. Walsh	St Colman's (Cork)	25-2
Light Heavyweight, 81kg	A. Sheerin	Swinford (Mayo)	A. Kelly	Offaly	15-11
Heavyweight, 91kg	J. Kiely	Corpus Christi (Limerick)	B. McGarrigle	Omagh (Tyrone)	21-9
Super Heavyweight, 91+kg	S. Reynolds	St Joseph's (Sligo)	J. Kinsella	Crumiln (Dublin)	23-14

Irish Amateur Boxing Intermediate Final Results 1997/98

Venue: National Boxing Stadium, 5th December, 1998. (stpd= stopped; retd= retired; c/back= count back)

Weight	Winner	Club	Runner Up	Club	Result
Light Flyweight, 48kg	J. Moore	St Francis (Limerick)			w/o
Flyweight, 51kg	D. Campbell	Glin	J. O'Donoghue	St Colamn's	20-8
Bantamweight, 54kg	B. Dunne	C.I.E.	W. White	Holy Family	18-8
Featherweight, 57kg	A. O'Donovan	Fr Horgan's	M. Burke	Gorey	12-11
Lightweight, 60kg	I. Hackett	Holy Family (Drogheda)	O. Kelly	Loughlynn	18-13
Light Welterweight, 63.5kg	P. Jennings	C.I.E.	J. McDonagh	Galway	9-5
Welterweight, 67kg	J. Moore	Arklow	C. Carmichael	Holy Trinity	10-9
Light Middleweight, 71kg	T. McDermott	Bishop Kelly	K. Whelan	Saviours Crystal	11-5
Middleweight, 75kg	J. McKay	H.M.L.	M. McAllister	Dockers	14-5
Light Heavyweight, 81kg	S. O'Grady	St Saviours	A. Reynolds	St Joseph's (Sligo)	stpd r2
Heavyweight, 91kg	E. Falvey	St Colmans	J. McDonagh	St Anne's (Westport)	stpd r2
Super Heavyweight, 91+kg	J. White	St Patrick's (Newry)	M. O'Gara	Claremorris	20-5

Irish Amateur Boxing Junior Final Results 1997/98

Venue: National Boxing Stadium, October 2, 1998. (stpd= stopped; retd= retired; c/back= count back)

Weight	Winner	Club	Runner Up	Club	Result
Light Flyweight, 48kg	H. Cunningham	Saints	J. Moore	St Francis	52-6
Flyweight, 51kg	D. Campbell	Glin	C. Price	Quarryvale	stpd r4
Bantamweight, 54kg	G. Brown	Crumlin	F. Maughan	C.I.E.	c/back
Featherweight, 57kg	D. Hamill	All Saints	G. Morrison	All Saints	stpd r4
Lightweight, 60kg	T. Hamill	All Saints	P. McCann	St Lukes	26-17
Light Welterweight, 63.5kg	C. Smithers	Bunclody	S. McKeown	Newry	31-21
Welterweight, 67kg	P. Quinn	Ardnaree	K. Lawless	Portlaoise	15-12
Light Middleweight, 71kg	M. Lee	Oughterard	H. Keogh	Ballymore	stpd r1
Middleweight, 75kg	L. Senior	Crumlin	P. McDermott	Holy Trinity	25-17
Light Heavyweight, 81kg	M. Mellon	Newry	M. Regan	Kiltogher	retd r2
Heavyweight, 91kg	S. O'Hagan	Bishop Kelly			w/o
Super Heavyweight, 91+kg	D. Nevin	Dunboyne	S. McDonagh	Westport	retd r4

National Boys Champions, 1997/98

Weight	Boys 1 Champion	Boys 2 Champion	Boys 3 Champion	Boys 4 Champion
27kgs	**Francis Campbell**	-	-	-
Club	South Meath	-	-	-
29kgs	**David Joyce**	**Dean Murphy**	-	-
Club	Brosna	St Saviours	-	-
31kgs	**Ian Gallagher**	**Pierce Murphy**	**Paul Hyland**	-
Club	Claremorris	St Agnes	Golden Cobra	-
33kgs	**Robert Ward**	**John Joe McDonagh**	**Conor Ahern**	**Patrick McDonagh**
Club	St Ronan's	Brosna	Baldoyle	Kilcullen
36kgs	**David Nevin**	**Shane Hickey**	**Thomas Whelan**	**Joseph Wiggins**
Club	Brosna	Brian Dillons	St Ibar's	Saints
39kgs	**Anthony Elliott**	**Darren Blade**	**Anthony Connolly**	**Thomas Lee**
Club	Muine Bheag	Minivea	St Ronan's	Oughterard
42kgs	**Edward Ward**	**Eric Donovan**	**John Kenneally**	**Franics McClurkin**
Club	Galway	St Michael's, Athy	Fr Horgan's	St Agnes'
45kgs	**James Sweeney**	**Thomas Nevin**	**John McDonagh**	**Kenneth O'Leary**
Club	Phoenix	South Meath	Roscommon	Bishopstown
48kgs	**Gerard McGilloway**	**Stephen O'Brien**	**Roy Sheahan**	**James Linden**
Club	Oak Leaf	Mullinahone	St Michael's Athy	Pegasus
51kgs	-	**Darren O'Neill**	**James Stephens**	**Austin O'Malley**
Club	-	Paulstown	Crumlin	St Anne's, Westport
54 kgs	**Simon Reilly**	-	**Andrew McLaughlin**	**Paul Ford**
Club	St Ronan's	-	Buncrana	Monivea
57kgs	-	**William Crampton**	**Brian Mulholland**	**Daniel Quinn**
Club	-	St Broghan's	Rosses	Glasnevin
60kgs	-	**Paul Conlon**	**Dermot Barrett**	**Alan Foley**
Club	-	Elphin	Olympic	St Michael's, Athy
63.5kgs	-	-	**Jamie Balfe**	**Gerard Gallagher**
Club	-	-	Ballymore	Dunfanaghy
67kgs	-	-	-	**Barry Reynolds**
Club	-	-	-	Dunkineely
71kgs	-	-	-	**Thomas Noone**
Club	-	-	-	Galway

National Youths Champions, 1997/98

Weight	Youths 1 Champion	Club	Youths 2 Champion	Club
39kgs	Mark Casey	H.M.L.	-	-
42kgs	Michael McCombe	St Agnes'	-	-
45kgs	Jamie Dowling	Paulstown	David Dunne	St Anne's Mountrath
48kgs	Martin Lindsay	Immaculata	Hugh Joyce	St Michael's Athy
51kgs	Dermot Lawlor	Muine Bheag	Gavin Brown	Crumlin
54kgs	Darren Nolan	St Ibar's/St Joseph's	Francis Maughan	C.I.E.
57kgs	Patrick Taylor	St Agnes'	Stephen Twohig	Sunnyside
60kgs	Cormac Ó Conaire	Bay City	Brian Corcoran	Quarryvale
63.5kgs	Thomas Blaney	Golden Cobra	Ciaran Smithers	Bunclody
67kgs	Ger McAuley	Star	Emmet Colgan	Avona
71kgs	Kenneth Egan	Neilstown	Paul McDermott	Holy Trinity
75kgs	Shane Farrell	Galway	Martin McDonagh	Kiltogher
81kgs	Brian Ferry	Dunfanaghy	Paul Hickey	Paulstown

INTERNATIONAL RESULTS

World Championships

Venue: Budapest, Hungary. 17-27 October, 1997.

Weight	Irish Competitor		Opponent	Score
54kgs	Damien McKenna	lost to	Shankuli Meretniynzov (Tkm)	5-9
67kgs	Neil Gough	beat	Vadim Mrzga (Bul)	6-4
	Neil Gough	beat	Leonard Bundu (Ita)	8-6
	Neil Gough	beat	A. Noorian (Iri)	10-9
	Neil Gough	lost to	Oleg Saitov (Rus)	2-6
75kgs	Brian Magee	lost to	Sergei Savitski (Bul)	5-6
81kgs	Stephen Kirk	beat	Sergei Mihaylov (Uzb)	stpd r4

Continued from previous page

Weight	Irish Competitor		Opponent	Score
	Stephen Kirk	beat	Z. Dimitrijevic (Aut)	6-2
	Stephen Kirk	beat	Tamer Erolov (Bul)	10-9
	Stephen Kirk	lost to	Alexander Lebziak (Rus)	stpd r2

Kirk won Bronze medal

European Senior Championships

Belarus. 17-24 May, 1998.				
Weight	**Irish Competitor**		**Opponent**	**Score**
54kgs	Bernard Dunne	lost to	Reidar Walstad (Norway)	2-9
60kgs	Eugene McEneaney	beat	Robert Maczik (Hungary)	9-8
	Eugene McEneaney	lost to	Artur Guevorkian (Armenia)	3-6
75kgs	Brian Magee	beat	Robert Gertis (Netherlands)	6-0
	Brian Magee	beat	Harold Gaisler (Germany)	6-4
	Brian Magee	beat	Dimitri Strelchinin (Russia)	6-1
	Brian Magee	lost to	Zoltan Erdie (Hungary)	2-10

Magee won Silver medal

Ireland v Wales

Venue: Swansea, Wales. 11 November, 1997				
Weight	**Irish Competitor**		**Opponent**	**Score**
54kgs	Martin Murphy	lost	D. Hayde	c/back
60kgs	Aodh Carlyle	beat	J. Hull	10-5
60kgs	Michael Hobbs	lost	A. Evans	6-14
63.5kgs	Mark Wickham	lost	V. Powell	stpd r5
67kgs	Francis Barrett	beat	C. Maddox	16-6
71kgs	Tom Fitzgerald	lost	A. Smith	13-16
75kgs	Tommy Donnelly	beat	S. Pepperall	10-4
75kgs	Ciprian Petrea	beat	D. Haines	3-0
81kgs	Adrian Sheerin	lost	S. Donaldson	9-10

Ireland 4 Wales 5

Ireland v France

Venue: Thourotte, France. 29 November, 1997.				
Weight	**Irish Competitor**		**Opponent**	**Score**
48kgs	James Rooney	lost	T. Gerome	2-1
51kgs	Liam Cunningham	lost	G. Franck	3-0
57kgs	Damien McKenna	lost	H. Mourad	3-0
60kgs	Eugene McEneaney	lost	Blain Willy	3-0
67kgs	Seán Barrett	lost	C. Christophe	2-1
67kgs	Francis Barrett	lost	B. Hussein	stpd r2
81kgs	Adrian Sheerin	beat	T. Henere	2-1
	Junior			
60kgs	Aodh Carlyle	beat	A. Mehdi	2-1
71kgs	Marvin Lee	beat	Z. Mohamed	3-0
75kgs	Tommy Sheahan	beat	B. Karim	2-1

France 6 Ireland 4

Ireland v Scotland

Venue: National Stadium, Dublin. 6 February, 1998				
Weight	**Irish Competitor**		**Opponent**	**Score**
57kgs	Terry Carlyle	beat	C. Docherty	15-11
63.5kgs	Mark Wickham	lost	L. Sharpe	5-9
63.5kgs	Paul McCloskey	beat	K. Green	stpd r4
67kgs	Francis Barrett	beat	A. Wolecki	retd r2
67kgs	Robert Murray	lost	L. Smith	9-14
75kgs	Brian Magee	beat	D. Feeney	stpd r2
81kgs	Seán O'Grady	beat	L. Ramsay	KO r5
91+kgs	Stephen Reynolds	beat	D.McKenna	stpd r3
91+kgs	John Kinsella	beat	K. Gault	stpd r1
	Juniors			
60kgs	Oisín Kelly	beat	B. Morrison	12-2
60kgs	Ronan Maher	beat	B. Hawthorne	8-3

Ireland 9 Scotland 2

Ireland v England

Venue: National Stadium, Dublin. 27 March, 1998				
Weight	**Irish Competitor**		**Opponent**	**Score**
54kgs	Bernard Dunne	beat	L. Pattison	stpd r3
57kgs	Michael Hobbs	lost	S. Bell	c/back
60kgs	Eugene McEneaney	lost	A. McLean	c/back
60kgs	Aodh Carlyle	beat	S. Lawton	14-7
63.5kgs	Mark Wickham	lost	N. Wright	8-15
63.5kgs	Michael Kelly	lost	K. Bennet	2-11
71kgs	Frank O'Brien	lost	M. Barker	6-11
75kgs	Brian Magee	beat	J. Twite	KO r1
81kgs	Seán Collier	beat	V. Jones	11-2
91kgs	John Kiely	lost	F. Okesola	KO r4

Ireland 4 England 6

Ireland v USA

Venue: San Jose, California. 12 March, 1998			
Weight	**Irish Competitor**		**Opponent**
54kgs	Bernard Dunne	beat	Saul Perez
57kgs	Michael Hobbs	lost	Terence Shepherd
63.5kgs	Paul McCloskey	lost	Keith Kemp
67kgs	Francis Barrett	lost	Sechen Powell
67kgs	Seán Barrett	lost	Reggie Davis
67kgs	Robert Murray	beat	Daniel Hernandez
71kgs	Frank O'Brien	beat	Tommie Stepp
75kgs	Kevin Walsh	lost	Quinton Smith
81kgs	Seán Collier	lost	Olanda Anderson
91+kgs	Tom Clare	lost	Dominick Guinn

Ireland 3 USA 7

Venue: Spokane, Washington. 13 March, 1998			
Weight	**Irish Competitor**		**Opponent**
54kgs	Bernard Dunne	lost	Cornelius Lock
57kgs	Michael Hobbs	lost	Jason Ingwaldson
63.5kgs	Paul McCloskey	lost	Larry Mosley
67kgs	Francis Barrett	lost	L.C. Shepherd
67kgs	Seán Barrett	lost	Sechen Powell
67kgs	Robert Murray	lost	Reggie Davis
71kgs	Frank O'Brien	beat	Darnell Wilson
75kgs	Kevin Walsh	lost	Randy Griffin

Ireland 1 USA 7

Ireland v New Zealand

Venue: Auckland, New Zealand. 12 March, 1998			
Weight	**Irish Competitor**		**Opponent**
57kgs	Terry Carlyle	beat	J.J. Tipare
60kgs	Declan Barrett	lost	R. Abubot
91kgs	Ben McGarrigle	lost	A. Stepford
91+kgs	John Kinsella	lost	F. Falomoe

Venue: Christchurch, New Zealand. 20 March, 1998			
Weight	**Irish Competitor**		**Opponent**
57kgs	Terry Carlyle	beat	N. Lopez
60kgs	Declan Barrett	lost	K. Fiawi
91kgs	Ben McGarrigle	lost	G. de Silva

IRISH SENIOR CHAMPIONS, 1987-97

Weight	1987	1988	1989	1990	1991
48kg	**PJ O'Halloran**	**W. McCullough**	**PJ O'Halloran**	**G. Waite**	**P. Cosgrove**
	St Munchin's	Albert Foundry	St Munchin's	Cairn Lodge	Cavan
51kg	**P. Buttimer**	**J. Lawlor**	**J. Lawlor**	**W. McCullough**	**P. Buttimer**
	Sunnyside	Darndale	Darndale	Albert Foundry	Sunnyside
54kg	**R. Nash**	**J. Lowey**	**R. Nash**	**J. Todd**	**J. Lawlor**
	Ring, Derry	Ledley Hall	Ring, Derry	Holy Family, Belfast	Darndale
57kg	**P. Fitzgerald**	**P. Fitzgerald**	**E. Bolger**	**R. Nash**	**P. Griffin**
	Arklow	Arklow	Wexford CBS	Ring, Derry	Drimnagh
60kg	**M. Carruth**	**M. Carruth**	**J. Erskine**	**J. Erskine**	**P. Ireland**
	Drimnagh	Drimnagh	Holy Family, Belfast	Holy Family, Belfast	St George's
63.5kg	**G. Joyce**	**G. Joyce**	**E. Fisher**	**M. Carruth**	**N. Gough**
	Sunnyside	Sunnyside	Holy Trinity, Belfast	Drimnagh	St Paul's Waterford
67kg	**B. Walsh**	**B. Walsh**	**J. Lowe**	**E. Fisher**	**B. Walsh**
	St Joseph's Wexford	St Joseph's Wexford	Holy Trinity, Belfast	Holy Trinity, Belfast	St Ibar's Wexford
71kg	**K. Joyce**	**K. Joyce**	**B. Walsh**	**B. Walsh**	**J. Lowe**
	Sunnyside	Sunnyside	St Joseph's Wexford	St Ibar's Wexford	Holy Trinity, Belfast
75kg	**R. Close**	**R. Close**	**D. Galvin**	**D. Galvin**	**D. Galvin**
	Ledley Hall	Ledley Hall	Moate	Moate	Moate
81kg	**J. O'Sullivan**	**J. O'Sullivan**	**J. O'Sullivan**	**P. McKay**	**M. Delaney**
	St Pat's Enniscorthy	St Pat's Enniscorthy	St Pat's Enniscorthy	Rathfriland	Ledley Hall
91kg	**J. Egan**	**J. Egan**	**J. Egan**	**J. O'Sullivan**	**R. Kane**
	Donore	Donore	Donore	St Pat's Enniscorthy	Avona
91+kg	**W. Clyde**	**S. McLaughlin**	**P. Douglas**	**P. Douglas**	**G. Douglas**
	Ballyclare	Errigal	Holy Family, Belfast	Holy Family, Belfast	St Pats, South Meath

Weight	1992	1993	1994	1995	1996
48kg	**M. McQuillan**	**M. McQuillan**	**M. McQuillan**	**J. Prior**	**J. Prior**
	Holy Family Drogheda	Holy Family Drogheda	Holy Family Drogheda	Darndale	Darndale
51kg	**P. Buttimer**	**D. Kelly**	**D. Kelly**	**D. Kelly**	**D. Kelly**
	Sunnyside	Holy Trinity, Belfast	Holy Trinity, Belfast	Holy Trinity, Belfast	Holy Trinity, Belfast
54kg	**W. McCullough**	**P. Buttimer**	**G. Waite**	**W. Valentine**	**D. McKenna**
	Albert Foundry	Sunnyside	Cairn Lodge	St Saviours, Dubln	Holy Family Drogheda
57kg	**P. Griffin**	**P. Griffin**	**P. Griffin**	**A. Patterson**	**A. Patterson**
	Drimnagh	Drimnagh	Mount Talins	St Pats Newry	St Pats Newry

Continued from previous page

Weight	1992	1993	1994	1995	1996
60kg	**M. Winters**	**M. Winters**	**G. Stevens**	**G. Stevens**	**M. Reneghan**
	Antrim	Antrim	Crumlin	Crumlin	Keady
63.5kg	**E. Magee**	**E. Magee**	**B. Walsh**	**G. McClarnon**	**F. Barrett**
	Sacred Heart Belfast	Sacred Heart Belfast	St Colman's	Clann Eireann Lurgan	Olympic
67kg	**M. Carruth**	**N. Gough**	**N. Gough**	**N. Sinclair**	**N. Gough**
	Drimnagh	St Paul's Waterford	St Paul's Waterford	Holy Family, Belfast	St Paul's Waterford
71kg	**J. Lowe**	**J. Webb**	**J. Webb**	**D. Higgins**	**D. Higgins**
	Holy Trinity, Belfast	Holy Trinity, Belfast	Holy Trinity, Belfast	Fermoy	Fermoy
75kg	**D. Galvin**	**D. Ryan**	**D. Galvin**	**B. Magee**	**B. Magee**
	Moate	Raphoe	Moate	Holy Trinity, Belfast	Holy Trinity, Belfast
81kg	**M. Delaney**	**M. Sutton**	**G. Joyce**	**S. Kirk**	**S. Kirk**
	Holy Trinity, Belfast	St Saviours	Sunnyside	Cairn Lodge	Cairn Lodge
91kg	**T. Curley**	**P. Douglas**	**P. Douglas**	**J. Clancy**	**C. O'Grady**
	St Agnes', Belfast	Holy Family Belfast	Holy Family Belfast	Kilfenora	St Saviours
91+kg	**K. McBride**	**D. Corbett**	**G. Douglas**	**P. Douglas**	**S. Murphy**
	Smithboro	Holy Family	St Pats, South Meath	Holy Family Belfast	St Michaels New Ross

1997 CHAMPIONS

Weight	Champion	Club
48kg	**J. Rooney**	Star
51kg	**L. Cunningham**	Saints
54kg	**D. Kelly**	Holy Trinity
57kg	**P. O'Donnell**	Dockers
60kg	**E. McEneaney**	Dealgan
63.5kg	**G. McClarnon**	Holy Family/Golden Gloves
67kg	**N. Gough**	St Paul's Waterford
71kg	**M. Roche**	Sunnyside
75kg	**B. Magee**	Holy Trinity, Belfast
81kg	**S. Kirk**	Cairn Lodge
91kg	**J. Kiely**	Corpus Christi, Limerick
91+kg	**S. Reynolds**	St Joseph's Sligo

TEXACO AWARD WINNERS, BOXING

Year	Winner
1958	Freddie Gilroy
1959	Freddie Gilroy
1960	Johnny Caldwell
1961	Johnny Caldwell
1962	Freddie Gilroy
1963	Mick Leahy
1964	*Jim McCourt
1965	*Gus Farrell
1966	*Jim McCourt
1967	John McCormick
1968	*Mick Dowling
1969	*Mick Dowling

Year	Winner
1970	*Mick Dowling
1971	Danny McAlinden
1972	Danny McAlinden
1975	Paddy Maguire
1977	*Phil Suttcliffe
1978	*Barry Mc Guigan
1979	*Terry Christle
1980	*Hugh Russell
1982	Barry McGuigan
1983	Barry McGuigan
1984	Barry McGuigan
1985	Barry McGuigan

Year	Winner
1986	Dave McAuley
1989	Dave McAuley
1990	Dave McAuley
1991	Dave McAuley
1992	*Michael Carruth
1993	Eamon Loughran
1994	Steve Collins
1995	Wayne McCullough
1996	Steve Collins

*Denotes amateur or was an amateur when the award was made.

IRISH MEDALLISTS AT OLYMPIC GAMES AND EUROPEAN CHAMPIONSHIPS

Name	Olympic Games	Venue	Medal	Weight
Michael Carruth	1992	Barcelona	Gold	67kg
Wayne McCullough	1992	Barcelona	Silver	54kg
Fred Tiedt	1956	Melbourne	Silver	67kg
John McNally	1952	Helsinki	Silver	54kg
Hugh Russell	1980	Moscow	Bronze	51kg
Jim McCourt	1964	Tokyo	Bronze	60kg
Fred Gilroy	1956	Melbourne	Bronze	54kg
Tony Byrne	1956	Melbourne	Bronze	60kg
John Caldwell	1956	Melbourne	Bronze	51kg

Continued from previous page

Name	European C'ships	Venue	Medal	Weight
Paul Griffin	1991	Sweden	Gold	57kg
Maxie McCullough	1949	Norway	Gold	60kg
Gerry O' Colmain	1947	Ireland	Gold	91kg
Jim Ingle	1939	Ireland	Gold	51kg
Paddy Dowdal	1939	Ireland	Gold	60kg
Terry Milligan	1953		Silver	63.5kg
John Kelly	1951		Silver	54kg
Peter Maguire	1947	Ireland	Silver	57kg
Damean Kelly	1995	Denmark	Bronze	51kg
Sean Casey	1985		Bronze	51kg
Kieran Joyce	1983		Bronze	71kg
Gerry Hawkins	1981		Bronze	48kg
Phil Sutcliffe	1977-79		Bronze	48 + 51kg
Niall McLoughlin	1971		Bronze	51kg
Mick Dowling	1965-71		Bronze	54kg
Jim McCourt	1965		Bronze	60kg
Harry Perry	1959	Lucerne	Bronze	67kg
Colm McCoy	1959	Lucerne	Bronze	75kg
Fred Tiedt	1957	Prague	Bronze	67kg
Terry Milligan	1951		Bronze	63.5kg
David Connell	1949-51		Bronze	60kg

CANOEING

Irish Canoe Union

House of Sport, Long Mile Road, Walkinstown, Dublin 12. Tel. (01) 4509838 Fax: (01)4601064 e-mail: icu@iol.ie

President....................John Carolan
Chairman....................Brendan O'Connell
Secretary....................John Keogh
Development Officer....................Stephen Hannon
Number of Associate Members....................4,000
Number of Instructors....................350
Number of Coaches for Competitive Canoeing....................23

MAIN CANOEING VENUES

● **LEIXLIP LAKE** Co. Kildare ● **RIVER LIFFEY** Co. Dublin ● **RIVER LEE** Co. Cork ● **RIVER AVONMORE** Co. Wicklow ● **RIVER BOYNE** Co. Meath ● **RIVER INNY** Co. Longford ● **BARROW RIVER** Cos. Carlow/Kildare ● **RIVER SUIR** Waterford ● **RIVER NORE** Co. Kilkenny ● **LAHINCH BEACH** Co. Clare ● **BUNDORAN BEACH** Co. Donegal

1997-98 INTERNATIONAL RESULTS

● **National Coach Co-ordinator:** Stephen Hannon ● **Marathon Race Coach:** Deaglan O'Driscoll ● **Polo Coach:** Maire Diggin, Carmel Vickens ● **Sprint Coach:** Kevin Murphy ● **Recreational Training:** Tom Ronayne

Date	Event	Venue	Result (Winner/Irish Placing)
07.06.98	World Cup Class A international race	Italy	Ian Wiley (1st)

1997-98 DOMESTIC RESULTS

Date	Event	Venue	Result (Winner/Irish Placing)
10.05.98	Irish Open	Liffey	Ian Wiley K1 class
10.05.98	Irish Open	Liffey	Tadhg McIntyre C1 class
05.09.98	39th annual Liffey Descent	Liffey	Malcolm Banks K1 class
05.09.98	39th annual Liffey Descent	Liffey	Alan and Ian Tordoff K2 class
05.09.98	39th annual Liffey Descent	Liffey	Michelle Barry women's K1 class

CRICKET

Irish Cricket Union

c/o John Wright, The Diamond, Malahide, Co. Dublin. Tel. (01) 8450710

Founded	1923
President	Enda McDermott
Chairman	Gavin Craig
Honorary Secretary	John Wright
Public Relations Officer	R. Walsh
Number of Clubs Affiliated to I.C.U.	170
Number of Teams	400
Number of Registered Players	9,000
Number of Coaches	70
Largest Attendance	4,000 (July 1993, Ireland v. Australia in Dublin)
Highest Score Recorded	198 (Ivan J. Anderson v. Canada XI, 1973)
Number of Provincial Unions	4 (Munster, Leinster, North-West and North)
National Coach	Mike Hendrick
Most Capped Player	D.A. Lewis (121 caps between 1984 and 1997)
Most Runs	4,275 (S.J.S. Warke, 1981-96)
Most Centuries	7 (I.J. Anderson, 1966-85)
Most Wickets	326 (J.D. Monteith, 1965-84)
Best Bowling Analyses	9-26 (F. Fee v. Scotland 1957)
Most Catches	57 (A.J. O'Riordan)
Quickest Century	51 minutes, 51 balls (J.A. Prior v. Warwickshire 1982)
Number International Matches played since 1855	502

1998 Champions

Competition	Winners	Runners Up
Royal Liver Irish Senior Cup	Strabane	Ballymena
Northern Cricket Union League	Ballymena	North of Ireland
Northern Cricket Union Senior Cup	Woodvale	Instonians
North-West Cricket Union League	Limavady	Strabane
North West Cricket Union Senior Cup	Brigade	Ardmore
Munster Cricket Union League	Cork County	
Munster Cricket Union Senior Cup	Cork County	Cork Church of Ireland
Leinster Conqueror Cup	Leinster	Malahide
Leinster Lewis Traub League	Malahide	Merrion
Leinster Whitney Moore & Keller League	Leinster	Carlisle
Interprovincial Champions 1998	North	South
World Ranking of the Irish Team		13th
Principal Grounds	Malahide, Leinster, Clontarf, Downpatrick, Eglinton and North of Ireland Cricket Clubs	

Provincial Officers	Chairman	Secretary	Treasurer
Leinster Union	D. Williams	Mr. J. Dawson	B. Murray
Munster Union	F. Lynch	P. Nicholson	P. Sommerville
Northern Union	H. McGrory	W. McCarroll	B. Milford
North West Union	B. Faulkner	J. Lindsay	J. Lindsay

1998 ROYAL LIVER IRISH SENIOR CUP RESULTS

Round 1

Y.M.C.A.	beat	Bready
Strabane	beat	Malahide
Woodvale	beat	Ardmore

Round 2

Limavady	beat	C.Y.M.
Lurgan	beat	Railway Union
Ballymena	beat	Leinster
Instonians	beat	North County
Phoenix	beat	Lisburn
Muckamore	beat	Old Belvedere
Y.M.C.A.	beat	The Hills
Glendermott	beat	Carlisle
N.I.C.C.	beat	Woodvale
Merrion	beat	Cliftonville
Downpatrick	beat	Coleraine
Brigade	beat	Cork County
Donemana	beat	Rush
Pembroke	beat	Eglinton
Clontarf	beat	Sion Mills
Strabane	beat	Waringstown

Round 3

Limavady	beat	Lurgan
Clontarf	beat	Merrion

Donemana	beat	N.I.C.C.
Ballymena	beat	Pembroke
Phoenix	beat	Downpatrick
Strabane	beat	Glendermott
Brigade	beat	Instonians
Y.M.C.A.	beat	Muckamore

Quarter Finals

Clontarf	beat	Limavady
Y.M.C.A.	beat	Phoenix
Strabane	beat	Brigade
Ballymena	beat	Donemana

Semi Finals

Strabane	beat	Y.M.C.A.
Ballymena	beat	Clontarf.

Final (see below)

1998 Royal Liver Irish Senior Cup Final

Strabane

Batsman			Runs
J. Gillespie	c Williams	b Kennedy D	37
C. McCrum	Retired Hurt		17
P. Gillespie	c Fullerton	b Kennedy D	34
Mark Gillespie	Not Out		47
K. Finlay	c Finlay	b Kennedy D	0
Michael Gillespie	Run Out		35
G. Porter	Not Out		2
T. Patton Jnr			
S. McCay			
P. McNamee			
T. Patton Snr			
Extras			17
Total	(50 Overs) for 4 wickets		189

Bowler	**O**	**M**	**R**	**W**
Adair	9	2	47	0
Glass	10	1	38	0
Finlay	6	0	18	0
Neill	10	5	10	0
McKee	5	1	28	0
Kennedy D.	10	2	46	3

Ballymena

Batsman			Runs
J. Ireland	c PattonT.Jnr	b Porter	16
S. Carruthers	LBW	b Patton T.Snr	5
R. Kennedy	st McNamee	b Patton T.Snr	37
D. Kennedy	LBW.	b Gillespie P.	28
C. Williams	c Sub.	b Gillespie Mk	6
M. Glass		b Gillespie Mk	6
M. Adair	c McDonnell	b Gillespie Mk	17
N. Fullerton		b Gillespie P	9
A. McKee	LBW	b Gillespie Mk	17
D. Finlay	Not Out		3
N. Neill	c......and	b Gillespie Mk	0
Extras			21
Total	(48.4 Overs)		165

Bowler	**O**	**M**	**R**	**W**
Patton T. Snr	10	2	36	2
Porter	10	1	31	1
Gillespie P	9	0	30	2
Gillespie Mark	9.4	2	33	5
McCay	10	1	29	0

Strabane won by 24 Runs. Man of the Match Mark Gillespie.

INTERNATIONAL RESULTS, 1998

Benson & Hedges Cup

01.05.98
Glamorgan 230-9 (R.D.B. Croft 67, P.A. Coltey 54)
Ireland 115.
Lost to Glamorgan by 115 Runs at Castle Avenue.

04.05.98
Essex 359-7 (D.D.J. Robinson 114; N. Hussain 71; R.C. Irani 69.
Ireland 188-7 (N.C. Johnson 53)
Lost to Essex by 171 Runs at Chelmsford.

06.05.98
Ireland 196-7 (A.R. Dunlop 59*)
Middlesex 199-4 (M.R. Ramprakash 55*)
Lost to Middlesex by 6 Wickets at Lords.

04/05.06.98
Ireland 267-6 dec. (S.G.Smyth 102; D.Heasley 71) and **176 - 6 dec.** (P.G. Gillespie 57).
M.C.C. 199-5 declared (R.J. Boon 81) and **187-8** (G.D. Hodgson 58; N.J.N. Trestrail 75; W.K.Mc Callan 4-33).
Drew with M.C.C at Lurgan.

24/25.06.98
Warwickshire 302-5 (N.V. Knight 143; N.M.K. Smith 52)
Ireland 261 (E.C. Joyce 73; A.F. Giles 4-29).
Lost to Warwickshire at Edgbaston by 41 Runs.

Triple Crown

30.06.98
Scotland 160-9 (B.M.W. Patterson 79)
Ireland 151. (P.G. Gillespie 55)
Lost to Scotland at Greenock by 9 runs

01.07.98
Ireland 171-9 (C. Dagnall 4-25).
ECB XI 167-9
Beat ECB XI at Linlithgow by 4 Runs

02.07.98
Ireland 224-6 (W.K. McCallan 100)
Wales 207 (W.K. McCallan 4-53)
Beat Wales at Paisley by 17 Runs

European Championships
The Hague, Holland

18.07.98
Ireland 203-5 (S.G. Smyth 52)
ECB XI 201-9 (S.J. Foster 84; M.J. Roberts 57)
Ireland beat ECB XI by 2 runs

19.07.98
Ireland 134
Holland 137-5
Ireland lost to Holland by 5 Wickets

21.07.98
Ireland 196-6
Denmark 197-7
Ireland lost to Denmark by 3 wickets

23.07.98
Scotland 211 (I.M. Stanger 57)
Ireland 191-7
Ireland lost to Scotland by 20 Runs

24.07.98
Ireland 242-4 (S.G. Smyth 93; J.A.M. Molins 70*)
Scotland 245-6 (G. Salmond 57;)
Ireland lost to Scotland by 4 Wickets

Tour by Australia A.

20-22.08.98
Australia A 309-6 declared (M.E. Hussey 125*; M.L. Hayden 68; R.J. Campbell 53; M.D. Dwyer 4-57) and **169 - 5 declared** (B.P. Julian 60*).
Ireland 132 (A. Dale 6-43) and 196.
Australia A beat Ireland by 150 Runs

23.08.98
Ireland 168-7 (25 Overs) (S.R.Waugh 67).
Match Abandoned.
Ireland v Australia A at Castle Avenue.

27.08.98
Ireland 192-7 (35 Overs)(W.K. McCallan 51; S.R. Waugh 50)
Australia A 195-7 (32.2 Overs) (D.R. Martyn 59*)
Australia A beat Ireland at Waringstown by 3 wickets

28.09.98
Ireland 138 (46.5 Overs) (A.R. Dunlop 57; C.R. Miller 4-28)
Australia A 140-2 (30.3 Overs) (M.E. Hussey 78*)
Australia A beat Ireland at Waringstown by 8 Wickets.

29.08.98
Australia A 268-8 (50 Overs) (D.R. Martyn 98, M.J. DiVenuto 52)
Ireland 98 (29.2 Overs)(S.G. Smyth 59; A. Symonds 4-13).
Australia A beat Ireland at Downpatrick by 170 Runs.

30.08.98
Ireland 128-8 (50 Overs) (B.E. Young 4-25)
Australia A 131-6 (31.1 Overs) (B.P. Julian 53*; M.D. Dwyer 3-19)
Australia A beat Ireland at Derry by 4 Wickets

Other Matches

06.06.98
Bangladesh 229 (W.K. McCallan 4-35);
Ireland 231-6 (P.G. Gillespie 92 N.D. Carson 52)
Beat Bangladesh by 4 wickets at Waringstown.

10.07.98
South Africa 333-9 (S.M. Pollock 116*; M.V. Boucher 79; G. Cooke 4-60)
Ireland 72-2 (Rain stopped play after 16.3 Overs)
Match abandoned v South Africa at Downpatrick.

12.07.98
South Africa 289-5 (D.C. Cullinan 117*; W.J. Cronje 74).
Ireland 226-9 (A.R. Dunlop 101*)
Lost to South Africa at Castle Avenue by 63 Runs

1998 INTERPROVINCIAL SERIES, FINAL TABLE

Team	Played	Won	Lost	Aband.	Pts
North	2	1	0	1	15
South	2	1	1	0	10
Development XI	2	0	1	1	5

SENIOR CRICKET CLUBS & SECRETARIES

Club	Match/Club Secretary	Union
Ardmore	R. Brolly	North West
Ballymena	J.C. McCullough	North
Bready	S. McConnell	North West
Brigade	D. Huey	North West
Carlisle	R. Davies	Leinster
Cliftonville	J. Heaney	North
Clontarf	Stella Downes	Leinster
Coleraine	Martin Clarke	North West
Cork County	D. Griffin	Munster
CYM	Michael Dalton	Leinster
Donemana	G. Walker	North West
Downpatrick	B. Hodges	North
Eglinton	J. Pierce	North West
Glendermott	G. Montgomery	North West
Instonians	J. Irvine	North
Leinster	H.A. Buttimer	Leinster
Limavady	Andrew Christie	North West
Lisburn	R. Simpson	North
Lurgan	W. Boyd	North
Malahide	Evelyn Harmon	Leinster
Merrion	Grenna Clarke	Leinster
Muckamore	J. Mulholland	North
North County	P. Murphy	Leinster
North of Ireland	A. Babbington	North
Old Belvedere	Anthony Brady	Leinster
Pembroke	Aidan Dempsey	Leinster
Phoenix	G.H. Black	Leinster
Railway Union	F.X. Carty	Leinster
Rush	Marese Armstrong	Leinster
Sion Mills	Bobby Rao	North West
Strabane	Terence Patton Jr.	North West
The Hills	Joe Clinton	Leinster
Waringstown	Joy Muir	North
Woodvale	I. Gourley	North
Y.M.C.A.	Richard Beamish	Leinster

IRISH CRICKET UNION, PAST PRESIDENTS

Year	President	Union
1924	R.M. Erskine	NCU
1925	Hon Judge Pigot	LCU
1926	R.M. Erskine	NCU
1927	Sir G. Colthurst	Cork
1928	Hon Judge Pigot	LCU
1929	Lord Justice Andrews	NCU
1930	Sir G. Colthurst	Cork
1931	R.H. Lambert	LCU
1932	R.H. Lambert	LCU
1933	Lord Justice Best	NCU
1934	Sir L. Goulding	LCU
1935	D.C. Lindsay	NCU
1945		
1946	S.H. Jackson	NCU
1947	R.H. Lambert	LCU
1948	W. Andrews	NCU
1949	J.G. Oulton	LCU
1950	J.C. Picken	NCU
1951	J.G Oulton	LCU
1952	W. Andrews	NCU
1953	L. Amoroso	LCU
1954	J. MacDonald	NCU
1955	W.P. Hone	LCU
1956	W. Pollock	NCU
1957	T.G. McVeagh	LCU
1958	T.G. McVeagh	LCU
1959	C. Nicholson	NWCU
1960	C. Nicholson	NWCU
1961	J.R. Gill	LCU
1962	Sir R. Kinahan	NCU
1963	C.C.G. O'Donnell	MCU
1964	T.W. Grainger	NCU
1965	J.B. Ganly	LCU
1966	E.D.R. Shearer	NCU
1967	K.P. Tanham	LCU
1968	A.H. Montgomery	NWCU
1969	T.A. Doyle	LCU
1970	D. Moreland	NCU
1971	A.P. Harris	MCU
1972	W. Ritchie	NCU
1973	A.B. Robertson	LCU
1974	J. Hunter	NWCU
1975	B.E. Kernan	LCU
1976	C. Cave	NCU
1977	T.A. Dunlop	LCU
1978	M. Nicholson	NWCU
1979	N.C. Mahony	MCU
1980	J.S. Pollock	NCU
1981	H.D. Cashell	LCU
1982	D.W. Todd	NWCU
1983	J.D. Caprani	LCU
1984	A.D. Rose	NCU
1985	F.A. Malin	LCU
1986	M. Bannigan	NWCU
1987	P.J. Dineen	MCU
1988	C. Walker	NCU
1989	W.I. Lewis	LCU
1990	G. Craig	NWCU
1991	K.F. O'Riordan	LCU
1992	H.C. McCall	NCU
1993	A. Linehan	NCU
1994	E. de'H Dexter	LCU
1995	A.J. O'Riordan	LCU
1996	M. Rea	NCU
1997	J.P. Wright	LCU
1998	E.A. McDermott	LCU

LCU = Leinster Cricket Union
MCU = Munster Cricket Union
NCU = Northern Cricket Union
NWCU = North West Cricket Union

IRISH CRICKET UNION, HONORARY SECRETARIES

Year	Honorary Secretary
1924-31	G.J. Bonass
1932-47	A.E. Bex
1948-53	H.D. Huet
1954-73	J.C. Boucher
1974-96	D. Scott
1997-	J. Wright

IRISH WOMEN'S CRICKET UNION

"Woodcroft", 50 St.Alban's Park, Sandymount, Dublin 4.

Founded 1982
President .... Hilary O'Reilly (South Leinster)
President Elect .... Mary Pat Moore (North Leinster)
Honorary Secretary .... Ursula Lewis (South Leinster)
Honorary Treasurer .... Elaine Coburn (South Leinster)
Number of Provincial Unions .... 3 (South Leinster, North Leinster and Ulster)
Number of Clubs 17
Number of Registered Players 1,500
Number of Teams:
- **League** 39
- **Interprovincial** 13
- **Schools** 57

Number of Coaches 1
Most Capped Player .... Mary Pat Moore (46)
Most Runs .... 956 (Mary Pat Moore)
Most Centuries .... 1 (Mary Pat Moore)
Most Wickets .... 40 (Susan Bray)
Best Bowling Analyses .... 5-27 (Susan Bray)
Biggest Attendance .... 300 (July 1995, European Cup final)

1998 Champions	Winners	Runners Up
Leinster Senior Cup	Clontarf	YMCA
Leinster Senior League	Malahide	Clontarf
Leinster U19 League	Merrion	
Leinster U15 League	Merrion	
Leinster U13 League	Clontarf/Merrion	

COMMUNITY GAMES

National Community Games

5 Lower Abbey Street, Dublin 1. Tel: (01) 8788095 Fax: (01) 8365205

Founded: .... 1967 (by Joseph Connolly in Dublin)
President: .... George O'Toole
Vice-President: .... Carmel Grealy
Chairman: .... Michael O'Grady
Vice-Chairman: .... Brian MacManus
General Administrator: .... Richard Farrell
General Treasurer: .... Margaret McDermott
Company Secretary: .... Maureen Quinlan
Asst. Gen. Secretary: .... Rose Mary O'Reilly
Games Director: .... Conal Duffy
PRO: .... Martina Mulhall
Marketing/Development Officer: .... Aoife Mac Eoin
Youth Officer: .... Yvonne Carroll
Number of Regions: .... 4 (Connacht, Leinster, Munster, Ulster)
Number of Community Games Areas: .... 800 areas in the 32 counties

● **Number of Children participating:** approximately 500,000 (aged 7 - 17 years) nationwide and approximately 6,000 at the national finals ● **Typical Year activities:** Area games (November-May) which take place within localities with a population of 6,000 or under, County Games (January-July) which take place at county level for individual and team competitions, Provincial Games (July) in which teams compete for a place in the national finals, National Games (last weekend in August, first weekend in September). ● **International Affiliations:** International Sport and Cultural Association.

NATIONAL FINAL RESULTS - TEAM EVENTS 1998

BADMINTON

U15 Mixed .... Meath *Julianstown*
2nd .... Galway *Claregalway-Lackagh*
3rd .... Tipperary *Powerstown / Lisronagh*
4th .... Monaghan *Clones*

BASKETBALL

U16 Boys .... Longford *North*
2nd .... Mayo *Ballina*
3rd .... Kerry *Castleisland*
4th .... Monaghan *Castleblayney*
U16 Girls .... Kerry *Castleisleand*
2nd .... Carlow *St. Mary's*
3rd .... Galway *Moycullen*
4th .... Monaghan *Castleblayney*
U13 Boys .... Kerry *Castleisland*
2nd .... Monaghan *Castleblayney*
3rd .... Dublin *St. Jude's*
4th .... Mayo *Castlebar*
U13 Girls .... Kerry *Castleisland*
2nd .... Louth *Kilsaran / Strabannon*
3rd .... Monaghan *Castleblayney*
4th .... Sligo *Calry*

CAMOGIE

U14 Girls .... Clare *Shannon*
2nd .... Kilkenny *Urlingford / Johnstown*
3rd .... Galway *Woodford*
4th .... Derry *Carntogher*

GAELIC FOOTBALL

U10 (Mixed) .... Tipperary *Carrick-on-Suir*
2nd .... Donegal *Ballyshannon*
3rd .... Laois *Stradbally*
4th .... Galway *Renmore*
U12 (Girls) .... Kerry *Ballyduff*
2nd .... Carlow *Bagenalstown*
3rd .... Mayo *Carra*
4th .... Monaghan *Tydavnet*

HANDBALL

U13 Boys .... Kerry *Ballymacelligot*
2nd .... Kilkenny *Clogh / Moneenroe*
3rd .... Tyrone *Carrickmore / Loughmacrory*
4th .... Roscommon *Ballaghadereen*
U13 Girls .... Kerry *Ballymacelligott*
2nd .... Carlow *Myshall*
3rd .... Roscommon *Roscommon Parish*
4th .... Donegal *Cloughaneely*
U15 Boys .... Roscommon *Ballaghadereen*
2nd .... Kilkenny *Clogh / Moneenroe*
3rd .... Kerry *Ballymacelligott*
4th .... Cavan *Kingscourt*
U15 Girls .... Roscommon *Roscommon Parish*
2nd .... Carlow *Myshall*
3rd .... Tipperary *Ballina*
4th .... Donegal *Cloughaneely*

HOCKEY

U16 Girls .... Dublin *Castleknock*
2nd .... Cork *Ballinlough*
3rd .... Galway *Renmore*
4th .... Derry *Steelstown*

HURLING

U14 Boys .... Galway *Clontuskert*
2nd .... Kilkenny *Castlewarren*
3rd .... Tipperary *Thurles*
4th .... Monaghan *Aughnamullen West*

PITCH & PUTT

U16 Boys .... Cork *Ballinacollig East*
2nd .... Sligo *Strandhill*

3rd ....Galway *Portumna*
4th ....Westmeath *Rochesfortbridge*
Best Individual ....Stephen Kavanagh *Cork*
U16 Girls ....Cork *Fermoy*
2nd..Offaly *Ferbane*
3rd ....Kerry *Ardfert / Kilmoley*
4th..Kildare *Maynooth*
Best Individual ....Hazel Hanrahan*Cork*

RUGBY

U11 Boys..Dublin *Clontarf*
2nd..Limerick *Kilmallock*
3rd ....Galway *Abbey-Knockmoy Monivea*

SOCCER

U15 Girls..............................Clare *Ennis St. John's*
2nd..............................Louth *Lorship / Cooley*
3rd ....Mayo *Foxford*
4th..............................Monaghan *Donaghmoyne*
U12 Girls ....Kildare *Confey*
2nd ....Galway *Mullagh*
3rd ....Cork *Watergrasshill*
4th..............................Monaghan *Donaghmoyne*
U12 Boys..............................Tipperary *Carrick-on-Suir*
2nd..Dublin *St. Jude's*
3rd ....Mayo *Castlebar*
4th..Antrim *Lower Falls*

TABLE TENNIS

U16 Boys......................Wexford *Rowe St. / Bride St.*
2nd..Cork *Blarney*
3rd..Donegal *Cavan*

4th..Sligo *Drumcliffe*
U16 Girls..Cork *Glanmire*
2nd..Cavan *St. Patrick's*
3rd..Sligo *Drumcliffe*
4th..Wexford *Ferns*

TENNIS (HARDCOURT)

U16 (panel of girls/boys)..........Wexford *Enniscorthy*
2nd..Sligo *Rosses Point*
3rd..Cavan *St. Patrick's*
4th ....Cork *Ballinlough*
U13 (panel of girls/boys)..............Kildare *Naas East*
2nd..............................Tipperary *Tipperary Town*
3rd..Sligo *Calry*
4th..Cavan *St. Patrick's*

VOLLEYBALL

U15 Boys ....Donegal *Milford*
2nd..............Clare *Lisdoonvarna / Doolin Kilshanny*
3rd..Leitrim *Drumshambo*
4th..Wexford *Taghmon*
U16 Girls..Kildare *Naas East*
2nd..Waterford *Lismore*
3rd..Leitrim *Drumshambo*
4th..Donegal *Milford*

❑

NATIONAL FINALS - INDIVIDUAL EVENTS, 1998

CYCLING

U16 Grand Prix Girls ....Margaret Coffey *Kerry*
2nd ....Marie Keenahan *Roscommon*
3rd..Ailsa Friel *Donegal*
4th..Rachel Hickey *Limerick*
U16 Grand Prix Boys ....Conor Murphy Monaghan
2nd..Paul Duffy Louth
3rd..Joseph Boyce Donegal
4th..Padraig Dennehy Kerry
U16 Grass 2km Boys ....Keith Jennings Sligo
2nd..Shaun Stewart Donegal
3rd ....Michael Nash Kerry
4th..Philip Byrne Tipperary
U16 Grass 2km Girls ....Etaoin Friel *Donegl*
2nd ....Edel Kelly *Sligo*
3rd ....Lisa Keavney *Roscommon*
4th ....Katie Moriarty *Kerry*

GYMNASTICS

U16 Girls ....Patricia Fogarty *Laois*
2nd..Emma Leahy *Wexford*
3rd..Michelle Kinch *Wicklow*
4th ....Stacey McCarthy *Cork*
U16 Boys..............................Dermot Boyle *Monaghan*
2nd ....Thomas David Kennedy *Limerick*
3rd ....Padraig Kavanagh *Wexford*
4th ....Eamonn Kearns *Wicklow*
U14 Girls ....Margaret O'Brien *Laois*
2nd..Teresa Murphy *Mayo*
3rd ....Catríona Barrett *Carlow*
4th ....Aoife Lavelle *Cavan*
U14 Boys..Philip Rooney *Galway*
2nd..Conor Moran *Carlow*
3rd..John O'Mahony *Cork*

4th..Gary Melly *Sligo*
U12 Girls ....Michelle Carey *Roscommon*
2nd ....Kelly Duggan *Waterford*
3rd..............................Lauren Mononey *Wexford*
4th..Maria Stacey *Dublin*
U12 Boys..Ian Whelan *Laois*
2nd..Dermott Bradley *Derry*
3rd..David Sheehan *Cork*
4th ....Paul Byrne *Carlow*
U10 Girls..Mary Barrett *Carlow*
2nd..Emma McGinley *Derry*
3rd ....Sheila Nolan *Wicklow*
4th ....Jade McNamara *Limerick*
U10 Boys..............................Liam McNamara *Tipperary*
2nd ....Thomas Kelly *Sligo*
3rd ....Aidan Killeen *Laois*
4th..Michael Linenau *Kerry*
U8 Girls..Tara Gilgan *Westmeath*
2nd..Amy Hennessy *Carlow*
3rd ....Eva Crowley *Cork*
4th..............................Rebecca O'Rourke *Kerry*
U8 Boys ....Ruairí Boyle *Derry*
2nd ....Adam Lindenau *Kerry*
3rd..Keith Moroney *Dublin*
4th..Kevin Mooney *Kildare*
Team Event..................Limerick *Askeaton / Ballysteen*
2nd..Sligo *KCA*
3rd ....Kerry *Killarney South*
4th..Monaghan *Killeevan*

JUDO

U16 Boys 25kg ....Conor Bradley *Derry*
2nd ....Andrew Jacob *Galway*
3rd ....Peter Moran *Dublin*

U16 Boys 30kg ....Jamie Whelan *Clare*
2nd ....Colm Gallagher *Derry*
3rd ....Max McKenna *Dublin*
U16 Girls 30kg ....Eimear O'Mahony *Kerry*
2nd...Amy Moran *Dublin*
3rd ....Laura Campion *Galway*
U16 Boys 35kg ....Daniel Barry *Dublin*
2nd ....Richard Gorry *Tipperary*
3rd ....Ryan McGarvey *Derry*
U16 Girls 35kg........................Laura O'Mahony *Kerry*
U16 Boys 40kg ....Adam McGrealy *Dublin*
2nd..Colm O'Mahony *Kerry*
3rd ....John Sheridan *Cavan*
U16 Girls 40kg ....Aislin Casey *Kerry*
2nd......................................Bronagh Gillespie *Derry*
3rd..Linda Hynes *Dublin*
U16 Boys 45kg ....Darren Flynn *Tipperary*
2nd ....Paul Donohoe *Dublin*
3rd.....................................Shane O'Flaherty *Galway*
U16 Girls 45kg ....Eilish McNulty *Galway*
2nd...Ciara Foley *Dublin*
3rd ....Lauren Hyland *Cavan*
4th ....Sophie Conway *Kerry*
U16 Boys 50kg..........................Roy Gorey *Tipperary*
2nd..Padraig Cahill *Cavan*
3rd ....Carl Boylon *Dublin*
U16 Girls 50kg.............................Mary Harte Galway
2nd ....Bernadette Coyle *Derry*
3rd ....Joanne Dillon *Kerry*
4th ....Sophie Conway *Kerry*
U16 Boys 55kg................................John O'Brien *Cork*
2nd...Tony Walsh *Dublin*
3rd..Terry Murphy *Derry*
U16 Girls 55kg...............................Nicola Lally Galway
2nd ....Aoife O'Connor *Dublin*
3rd..Valerie Brady *Derry*
4th ....Elaine Morrison *Derry*
U16 Boys Open ....Brian Ryan *Dublin*
2nd ....Brian Walsh *Cork*
U16 Girls Open ....

SWIMMING

U16 Freestyle Boys ....Peter Touhy *Mayo*
2nd ....Ken Grant *Waterford*
3rd ....Shaun Maguire *Donegal*
U16 Freestyle Girls...................Caitríona Kelly *Galway*
2nd ....Jennifer McLoughlin *Mayo*
3rd ....Eleanor Hogan *Meath*
U16 Backstroke Boys ....Colin Hedderman *Cork*
2nd....................................Stephen Murphy *Louth*
3rd ....Rory Ryan *Clare*
U16 Backstroke Girls.........Siobhán McNally *Longford*
2nd...............................Deirdre Hughes *Westmeath*
3rd ....Jenny Colville *Fermanagh*
U16 Butterfly Boys....Dara McGrenaghan *Fermanagh*
2nd ....Florry O'Connell *Kerry*
3rd..David O'Dowling *Cork*
U16 Butterfly Girls......................Suzanne Ryan *Meath*
2nd ....Sarah Ryan *Wexford*
3rd ....Helena Walsh *Mayo*
U14 Freestyle Boys.........Patrick McKenna *Monaghan*
2nd ....Barry Murphy *Dublin*
3rd ....Joseph Moran *Mayo*
U14 Freestyle Girls..............Louise McLoughlin *Mayo*
2nd ....Caoimhe McGrenaghan *Fermanagh*
3rd ....Ciara Kealy *Dublin*
U14 Backstroke Boys..........Ryan Whitley *Fermanagh*
2nd ....Michael O'Sullivan *Dublin*
3rd...Cian Holland *Mayo*
U14 Backstroke Girls ....Edel Langan *Dublin*
2nd ....Sinead Redmond *Kildare*
3rd ....Claire Delaney *Meath*
U14 Breaststroke Boys............Ciaran McArdle *Louth*
2nd ....James Corry *Donegal*
3rd ....Alan Feely *Mayo*
U14 Breaststroke Girls ....Orlaith Ryan *Laois*
2nd...Rebecca Jarvis *Cork*
3rd...Naomi Martin *Mayo*
U13 Squad (4x25) Boys ....Louth
2nd...Donegal
3rd..Fermanagh
U13 Squad (4x25) Girls ....Cork
2nd...Donegal
3rd...Dublin
U12 Freestyle Boys...................Darren McHugh *Mayo*
2nd ....Richard Dowling *Cork*
3rd ....Cian Scanlon *Dublin*
U12 Freestyle Girls ....Michelle Dunne *Dublin*
2nd ....Ruth Hegarty *Cork*
3rd..Kate Varley *Galway*
U12 Breaststroke Boys ....Ben Morris *Dublin*
2nd ....Colin Rea *Carlow*
3rd......................................David Edwards *Wexford*
U12 Breaststroke Girls ....Maeve Coughlan *Cork*
2nd...................Clíodhna Nic Chonmharia *Westmeath*
3rd ....Ailbhe Gannon *Mayo*

ATHLETICS (Track)

U17 Relay (4x100m) Boys ....Limerick
2nd...Cork
3rd..Carlow
4th..Laois
U17 Relay (4x100m) Girls...................................Carlow
2nd ....Tipperary
3rd ....Wexford
4th ....Galway
U17 Marathon (10,000m) Boys...William Harty *Water.*
2nd ....John Dooley *Tipperary*
3rd....................................Martin Fagin *Westmeath*
4th...Karol Duggan *Donegal*
U17 Marathon (6,000m) Girls..Madeline Dorney *Tipp.*
2nd..............................Sandra Rafferty *Westmeath*
3rd ....Fiona Kehoe *Wexford*
4th..Kate O'Neill *Dublin*
U17 Marathon Team Boys ....Waterford
2nd ....Tipperary
3rd ....Galway
4th...Cork
U17 Marathon Team Girls................................Limerick
2nd...Tipperary
3rd...Carlow
4th..Cork
U17 100m Boys ....Jer O'Donoghue *Kerry*
2nd.......................................David McWalter *Wicklow*
3rd......................................Richard Reville *Wexford*
4th......................................Joe McDonnell Waterford
U17 100m Girls...........................Sinead Swan *Wexford*
2nd ....Sarah O'Brien *Clare*
3rd ....Mary McLoone *Donegal*
4th ....Niamh Cummins *Waterford*

U16 1,500m Boys.........................Liam Reale *Limerick*
2nd ....Sean Connolly *Dublin*
3rd...Brian Lenihan *Kerry*
4th...Gerry O'Flaherty *Clare*
U16 1,500m Girls ....Deirdre Byrne *Wicklow*
2nd...Mary Cullen *Sligo*
3rd ....Jean Anne Healy *Kildare*
4th...Sheila Coyle *Louth*
U16 100m Boys ....Daragh Graham *Wicklow*
2nd...Mark Canning *Cork*
3rd...Stephen Foy *Westmeath*
4th ....Paul Hession *Galway*
U16 100m Girls ....Ann Maire Lynch *Kilkenny*
2nd...Grace Hennessy *Offaly*
3rd...Eibhlis Ahearne *Waterford*
4th ....Siobhan Martin *Tipperary*
U15 Relay (4x100m) Mixed ....Cork
2nd ....Dublin
3rd...Wicklow
4th...Tipperary
U14 Relay (4x100m) Boys ....Carlow
2nd...Kilkenny
3rd...Monaghan
4th...Wexford
U14 Relay (4x100m) Girls ....Wicklow
2nd ....Wexford
3rd...Limerick
4th...Clare
U14 Hurdles (80m) Boys ....Damien Munelly *Mayo*
2nd ....James McCarthy *Cork*
3rd...Maurice Donnohue *Kilkenny*
4th ....Noel Morrisey *Limerick*
U14 Hurdles (80m) Girls......Caoimhe McCarthy *Kerry*
2nd...Orla Doyle *Kilkenny*
3rd ....Jessica Zebo *Cork*
4th...Emer Ruane *Sligo*
U14 800m Boys.........................Baragh Greene *Louth*
2nd ....James Ledingham *Waterford*
3rd ....Christopher Sloan *Clare*
4th ....Paul Hickey *Westmeath*
U14 800m Girls ....Ciara McDermott *Mayo*
2nd ....Colette Corry *Clare*
....Lorraine Treacy *Galway*
....Sharon Monaghan *Meath*
U14 100m Boys.........................Philip Keane *Laois*
2nd ....Gearoid Burke *Galway*
3rd ....James Lambe *Monaghan*
4th...Conor McGuinness *Dublin*
U14 100m Girls ....Mandy Crowe *Tipperary*
2nd...Claire Murphy *Wicklow*
3rd...Sinead Mackey *Cork*
4th ....Mairead McNally *Monaghan*
U13 Walking (900m) Boys.................Ed Healy Dublin
2nd ....Owen Murphy Waterford
3rd...Kevin McMahon Limerick
4th...David Martyn Sligo
U13 Walking (900m) Girls...Sharon Lawless *Waterford*
2nd ....Carol Burtenshaw *Kildare*
3rd...Elaine Fitzpatrick *Clare*
4th...Clare Byrne *Carlow*
U12 Relay (4x100m) Boys.............................Cork
2nd ....Meath
3rd ....Monaghan
4th...Kerry

U12 Relay (4x100m) Girls.....................Roscommon
2nd...Clare
3rd...Donegal
4th ....Carlow
U12 600m Boys ....
U12 600m Girls ....Grace Eade *Clare*
2nd...Zoë Speare *Donegal*
3rd...Laura Crowe *Kerry*
4th...Nicloa O'Malley *Kildare*
U12 100m Boys ....Cedrick Kilbahu *Clare*
2nd...Donal Murphy *Louth*
3rd...Simon Gaynor *Tipperary*
4th...Greg O'Leary *Cork*
U12 100m Girls.........................Karen Considine *Cork*
2nd ....Caroline Kelly *Kerry*
3rd ....Ashling Doran *Roscommon*
4th...Ciara Simcock *Limerick*

ATHLETICS (Field)

U17 Javelin Girls ....Noreen Dwyer *Kerry*
2nd ....Michelle O'Donnell *Derry*
3rd...Karen Dunne *Tipperary*
4th ....Noeleen Nolan *Carlow*
U16 Discus (1 kg) Boys ....Robert Butler *Tipperary*
2nd...Geoffrey Mullins *Limerick*
3rd ....Keith Gilligan *Laois*
4th ....Cormac Gardiner *Meath*
U16 High Jump Boys.................Peter Condron *Laois*
2nd...Karl Casey *Galway*
3rd ....Graham Woodcock *Dublin*
4th ....Thomas Burke *Limerick*
U16 High Jump Girls...............Carol Loscher *Wicklow*
2nd...Maria O'Rourke *Carlow*
3rd ....Majella Kenny *Kildare*
4th...Deirdre Treacy *Tipperary*
U14 Long Jump Boys................Paul Murphy *Wexford*
2nd ....Patrick Corrigan *Cavan*
3rd ....Tom Shanahan *Limerick*
4th ....Owen O'Connell *Kerry*
U14 Long Jump Girls.....................Alison Miller *Laois*
2nd...Niamh *Condron*
3rd ....Sharon Heveran *Mayo*
4th ....Fiona McNally *Monaghan*
U14 Shot Putt (3.25kg) Boys ....Eoin Leen *Kerry*
2nd ....Jim Healy *Tipperary*
3rd ....John Dilworth *Cork*
4th...Rory Nolan *Wicklow*
U14 Shot Putt (3.25kg) Girls ......Sinead Murphy *Tipp.*
2nd...Laura McCarthy *Cork*
3rd ....Leanne Hayes *Laois*
4th ....Dawn Molloy *Wicklow*
U14 Long Puck Boys........Richard McGrath *Tipperary*
2nd...Sean Hurley *Cork*
3rd ....Eoin Somers *Carlow*
4th ....Enda Kavanagh *Wicklow*
U14 Long Puck Girls ....Sharon Kavanagh *Galway*
2nd ....Ann Marie Flattery *Longford*
3rd ....Emer McFadden *Dublin*
4th...Deirdre Ryan *Offaly*

❑

FAMOUS PEOPLE WHO HAVE COMPETED IN COMMUNITY GAMES

Patricia Breen .... World Draughts Champion
Michael Carruth .... Boxer, Olympic Gold medalist and World Champion
Eamon Coughlan .... World Champion athlete
Roísín Faulkner .... Current Ladies B junior handball world champion
John Donnelly .... Drummer, The Saw Doctors
Denis Irwin .... Manchester United and Republic of Ireland footballer
Roy Keane .... Manchester United and Republic of Ireland footballer
Sarah Kelleher .... International hockey player
Maeve McGrath .... Actress *Fair City*
Catherina McKiernan .... 1998 London Marathon winner
Emily Maher .... Olympic Youth gold medalist, sprinter
Adrian O'Connor .... Irish international swimmer
Sonia O'Sullivan .... World and European Champion athlete
Gary O'Toole .... International swimmer
Niall Quinn .... Sunderland and Republic of Ireland footballer
Stephen Roche .... Tour de France winning cyclist
Michelle Smith .... Triple Olympic Gold medalist, swimmer
Susan Smith .... Irish international athlete
Stephen Staunton .... Liverpool and Republic of Ireland footballer
John Treacy .... Olympic silver medalist, athlete

CROQUET

Croquet Association of Ireland (CAI)

c/o Carrickmines Croquet & Lawn Tennis Club, Glenamuck Road, Carrickmines, Co. Dublin.

Founded 1900
President .... Niall McInerney
Chairman .... Robert Barklie
Secretary .... Jane Shorten
Treasurer .... Gerry Reynolds
Selectors .... Ronan McInerney & Jane Shorten
Handicapper .... Ronan McInerney
Number of Associate Members .... 144.

CAI Affiliated Clubs

- **CARRICKMINES** .... c/o Alan McInerney, Carrickmines Croquet & Lawn Tennis Club.
- **HERBERT PARK** .... c/o Angela Crean, 212 Waterloo Road, Dublin 4.
- **KELLS** .... c/o Stephen Strong, Ballynamona House, Kells, Co. Meath.
- **NEWCASTLE** .... c/o Nathaniel Healy, Newcastle House, Newcastle, Co. Wicklow.
- **SHANKILL** .... c/o Simon Williams, 20 Aubrey Grove, Shankill, Co. Dublin.
- **TRINITY** .... c/o PO Box 63, Regent Hse, Trinity College Dublin.

Non-Affiliated Clubs

- **BALLYLISK** .... Ballylisk House, Portadown, Co. Armagh, Northern Ireland.
- **ARDIGEEN VALE** .... Ardigeen Croquet & Lawn Tennis Club, Timoleauge, Co. Cork.
- **RUSHBROOKE** .... Rushbrooke Croquet and Lawn Tennis Club, Cobh, Co. Cork.

1997-98 INTERNATIONAL RESULTS

Date	Event (Trophy)	Venue	Result
1997	Ireland v. USA (Carter Challenge)	-	Ireland 15: USA 12
1997	England v. Ireland (Vera Mcweeney)	Southport, England	Ireland won
1997	Ireland v. Scotland (Appleton)	Carrickmines, Dublin	Ireland won
1997	Home Internationals	-	Ireland 3rd (Eng 1st)
1997	Ireland v. Jersey	-	Ireland 11: Jersey 19
1997	B Internationals	-	Ireland 14: Scotland 5
Mar. 98	South Africa vs. Ireland	Cape Town, S. Africa (A)	South Africa 15: Ireland 7
May 98	Ireland v. Jersey	Carrickmines, Dublin (A/B)	Ireland won
Jun. 98	Home Internationals	Southport, England (A)	England - 1st, Ireland - 2nd
Jun. 98	Begium v. Ireland	Brussels, Belgium (B/C)	Ireland
Jul. 98	Scotland v. Ireland	Glasgow, Scotland (A/B)	Ireland
Aug. 98	Ireland v. England	Carrickmines, Dublin (A/B)	Ireland
Nov. 98	European Championships	Palermo	-

1997-98 DOMESTIC RESULTS - SINGLES WINNERS

Event	Winner
Championships of Ireland (1997) Singles	R. McInerney
Championships of Ireland (1997) Doubles	R. McInerney & M.E. O'Shaughnessy
Championships of Ireland (1997) CAI Silver Medal	S. Williams

Event	Winner
Championships of Ireland (August 1998) Singles	Simon Williams
Championships of Ireland (August 1998) Doubles	Simon Williams & Malcolm O'Connell
Championships of Ireland (August 1998) CAI Silver Medal	Jane Shorten

PAST SINGLES WINNERS, 1900-96

Year	Winner
1900	R.N. Roper
1901	C. Corbally
1902	R.N. Roper
1903	C. Corbally
1904	R.C.J. Beaton

Year	Winner
1905	H. Corbally
1906	C. Corbally
1907	T.J. Considine
1908	R.C.J. Beaton
1909	R.C.J. Beaton

Year	Winner
1910	R.C.J. Beaton
1911	C. Corbally
1910	R.C.J. Beaton
1913	H. Corbally
1914	W.F. Pim

Year	Winner
1919	J.A. McMordie
1920	J.A. McMordie
1921	R. Willington
1922	W.F. Pim
1923	H. Corbally
1924	H. Corbally
1925	H. Corbally
1926	H. Corbally
(won the trophy outright)	
1937	J.C. Windsor (Aus)
1938	D. Hopkins
1939	P. Duff Matthews
1940	Mrs W Fitzgerald
1941	B.T. O'Reilly
1942	Mrs W Fitzgerald
1943	P. Duff Mathews
1944	P. Duff Mathews
1945	P. Duff Mathews
1946	G.M. Fitpatrick
1947	P. Duff Mathews
1948	P. Duff Mathews
(won the trophy outright - re-presented as the Duff Mathews Perpetual Trophy)	
1949	P. Duff Mathews
1950	G.M. Fitpatrick
1951	G.M. Fitpatrick
1952	P. Duff Mathews
1953	P. Duff Mathews
1954	P. Duff Mathews
1955	Col. W. Beamish
1956	P. Duff Mathews
& W Kirk (NZ) *(divided)*	
1957	Cmdr. W. Beamish
1958	Mrs. KE Longman
1959	Mrs. E. Leonard
1960	Lady Fitzgerald
1961	R.J. Leonard
1962	Capt. H. Stoker
1963	D.F. Strachen
1964	D.F. Strachen
1965	D.F. Strachen
1966	D.F. Strachen
1967	D.F. Strachen
1968	D.B. O'Connor
1969	D.B. O'Connor
1970	Mrs. J. Jarden (NZ)
1971	D.B. O'Connor
1972	T.O. Read
1973	T.O. Read
1974	T.O. Read
1975	T.O. Read
1976	T.O. Read
1977	T.O. Read
1978	T.O. Read
1979	T.O. Read
1980	T.O. Read
1981	R.J. Murfitt (NZ)
1982	T.O. Read
1983	CM. von Schmieder
1984	G.P.N. Healy
1985	T.O. Read
1986	G.P.N. Healy
1987	F.J. Rogerson
1988	S. Williams
1989	CM. von Schmieder
1990	J.E. Guest (Eng)
1991	Lewis Palmer (Wales)
1992	F.J. Rogerson
1993	A Westerby (NZ)
1994	G. Noble (Eng)
1995	A.E. Cunningham
1996	R. McInerney

CYCLING

Federation of Irish Cyclists

Kelly Roche House, 619 North Circular Road, Dublin 1. Tel. (01) 8551522 Fax: (01) 8551771

Founded 1987
President .... Pat McQuaid
Honorary Secretary .... Jack Watson
PRO .... Tommy Campbell
Number of Clubs 125
Number of Regions .... 4 (Ulster, Leinster, Munster and Connaught)
Number of Members (per region) .... 750 (approx.)
All Time Record Attendance at Cycling .... Nissan '87 Final Stage (Kilkenny-Dublin)

Regional Statistics:

Ulster Cycling Federation:
Chairperson .... Tom Mateer
Secretary .... Julie Stevenson
Treasurer .... Oliver Hunter
PRO .... Patrick Clarke
Number of Clubs 28

Leinster Cycling Federation:
President .... Richard Beatty
Secretary .... Tommy Campbell
Treasurer .... Pat O'Callaghan
Number of Clubs 45

Munster Cycling Federation:
President/Chairman .... Jim Wilson
Honorary Secretary .... Jim March
Honorary Treasurer .... Peter Thornton
PRO .... John O'Mahony
Number of Clubs 38

Connaught Cycling Federation:
Chairman .... Seamus Quinn
Secretary .... Michael O'Sullivan
Treasurer .... Martin Connery
PRO .... Mary Scanlon
Number of Clubs 14

1998 Champions:
Call Card Classic League (Seniors) .... Brian Kenneally (Carrick Cidona)
Call Card Classic League (Juniors) .... Mark Scanlon (Sligo)

MAIN SENIOR ROAD RACING RESULTS 1998 (MEN)

Date	Event	Venue	Distance	Name (Club Name) Time
05 April	Des Hanlon Memorial	Carlow	87miles	T. Evans (Banbridge) 3:24:17
26 April	Noel Hammond Memorial	Ballyboughal	72miles	K. MacMahon (O'Mara's) 2:49:39
10 May	Shay Elliott Memorial	Bray	120kms	M. O'Donnell (Coors/Bray Wheelers) 2:17:38
16 - 24 May	FBD Milk Rás*	-	1,258kms	C. Power (Ireland) 29:44:49
07 June	Mayo Grand Prix	Castlebar	84 miles	T. Evans (Banbridge) 3:45:21
14 June	Noel Taggart Memorial	Banbridge	87 miles	T. Evans (Banbridge) 3:29:31
28 June	Irish Road Race C'ship	Collon	110 miles	R. Clarke (Premier) 4:19:34
04 July	Tour of the Mournes	Newry	75 miles	A. Duff (Bray) 3:06:02
19 July	Matt Corcoran	Naas	165kms	B. Kenneally (Carrick Cidona)
26 July	Harding G.P. Classic	Cork	160kms	B. Kenneally (Carrick Cidona)
02 August	Gene Moriarity Memorial	Killorglin	140kms	B. Kenneally (Carrick Cidona)
29 August	T. Given Memorial	Hillsborough	150kms	D. McVeigh (Dan Morrissey) 3:19:27
	West Down GP	Banbridge		N. Taggart (Banbridge)
	Tour of Midleton	Carrick-on-Suir		B. Kenneally (Carrick Cidona)
	Tour of Armagh	Carlow		D. McVeigh (Dan Morrissey)

**See full stage results of FBD Milk Rás below.*

FBD MILK RÁS DAY-BY-DAY RESULTS

Stage	1st	2nd	3rd	Overall Lead	Team
(1) Dublin-Navan-Dublin **Sat. 16 May** (112kms)	S. Kukk 2:17:38 (Estonia)	D. O'Loughlin (s/t) (Mayo)	K. Loubser (s/t) (South Africa)	S. Kukk Estonia	S. Africa
(2) Mullingar-Tubbercurry **Sun 17 May** (146kms)	J. Wright 3:12:54 UK Bentec	K. Loubser (s/t) South Africa	U. Hardier (+ 2sec) Germany	K. Loubser South Africa	S. Africa
(3) Tubbercurry-Westport **Mon 18 May** (170kms)	D. Williams 4:01:02 UK Bentec	J. Slagter (+2sec) Netherlands	C. Roshier (s/t) Surrey	K. Loubser South Africa	S. Africa
(4) Westport-Kilrush **Tue 19 May** (186kms)	P. Lernout 4:19:14 Belgium	S. Rifflet (s/t) France	C. Roshier (+ 2sec) Surrey	K. Loubser South Africa	S. Africa
(5) Listowel-C'townbere **Wed 20 May** (146kms)	T. Evans 3:31:57 Ireland	S. Kukk (s/t) Estonia	W. Randle (s/t) Manchester	S. Kukk Estonia	-
(6) Castletownbere-Mallow **Thur 21 May** (150kms)	P. Griffin 3:40:34 Carlow	J Wright (s/t) UK Bentec	D Williams (s/t) UK Bentec	S. Kukk Estonia	UK Bentec
(7) Mallow-New Ross **Fri 22 May** (154kms)	M. Fitzgerald 3:49:12 Dublin Usher	D. Hourigan (+6sec) Limerick	J. Slagter (s/t) Netherlands	S. Kukk Estonia	UK Bentec
(8) New Ross-Ballymore **Sat 23 May** (154kms)	J Wright 3:47:54 UK Bentec	M. Smith (+ 6sec) Mayo	J. Desjardines (s/t) France		
(9) Dublin City Centre **Sun 24 May** (40kms)	M. Fitzgerald 58:10 Dublin Usher	H Fledderus (s/t) Netherlands	H. Veenstra (s/t) Netherlands	C. Power Ireland	Ireland
OVERALL	**C. Power** 29:44:49 **Ireland**	**T. Evans** (+ 45sec) **Ireland**	S Rifflet (+ 60sec) France	-	**Ireland**

IRISH CYCLING RECORDS *(as at 1st December, 1996)*

Time Trials

Distance	Time	Date	Holder
10ml Senior	19.59	08.08.93	**Tommy Evans** - Banbridge CC
25ml Senior	51.24	27.06.95	**Philip Collins** - Amev IRC
50ml Senior	1.47.37		**Philip Collins** - Amev IRC
50 ml Ladies	2.09.59	21.08.94	**Claire Moore** - Dungannon Whs
100ml TT	4.07.58	06.08.89	**Joe Barr** - Top Team Cyprus
12 Hours Senior	250.95ml	18.08.57	**Maurice Donaldson** - Maryland Whs

Track Records

Distance	Time	Date	Holder
Flying Start	29.746 sec	500 metres	**Declan Lonergan**
Flying Start	1 min.08.801 sec	1,000 metres	**Liam Collins**
Standing Start	1 min.06.00 sec	1km	**Declan Lonergan**
Standing Start	4 min.35.54 sec	4km	**Philip Collins**
Standing Start	6min.31.22 sec	5km	**Simon Coughlan**
Standing Start	13 min.08.90 sec	10km	**Simon Coughlan**
Standing Start	26 min.31.71 sec	20km	**Simon Coughlan**
Standing Start	2hr.55 min.22.9sec	100km	**Laurence Roche**
Standing Start	1hr	43.527 kms	**Simon Coughlan**

Note: 500m Standing Start, minimum standard 35 sec

Place to Place records

Distance	Time	Date	Holder
Mizen Head/Fair Head	19.03.16	08.08.93	**Joe Barr/Clarke Bros**
Belfast/Dublin	4.00.28	05.11.95	**Tommy Evans/Banbridge CC**
Derry/Dublin	6.26.00	20.09.64	**Morris Foster/Cyprus**
Dublin/Waterford	3.55.17	20.09.92	**David Peelo/Sorrento**
Dublin/Cork	6.16.21	30.10.94	**Brian Lenehan/Cork CC**
Ladies	7.45.10	1953	**Eileen Sheridan/Hercules Cycles**
Dublin/Wexford	3.21.12	04.06.94	**David Peelo/Sorrento**
Dublin/Limerick	4.42.44	23.10.94	**David Peelo/Sorrento**
Dublin/Galway	5.30.27	25.09.94	**Mel Sutcliffe/Amev IRC**
Ladies	5.50.10	1952	**Eileen Sheridan/Hercules Cycles**
Galway/Limerick	2.39.22	06.09.93	**Maurice O'Keeffe/Lee Strand**

Record Standards *(as at 1st January, 1998)*

T.T.'s Distance	Individual	Team
10ml. Junior	22.00	1.07.30
10ml. Ladies	24.30	1.15.00
10ml. Veteran	21.15	1.06.16
25ml. Junior	56.00	2.49.30
25ml. Ladies	1.02.00	3.07.30
25ml. Veteran	54.45	2.45.45
50ml. Veteran	1.57.30	5.54.00

PAST PRESIDENTS: FEDERATION OF IRISH CYCLISTS

Year	President
1987-90	Liam King
1990-94	Jack Watson
1994-95	Billy Kennedy
1995-present	Pat McQuaid

DARTS

Irish National Darts Organisation

Raheen, Ballyneety, Co. Limerick, Republic of Ireland. Tel.: (061) 351018

Founded: 1979
President: .... Charlie Waters
Chairman: .... Liam Kerins
Secretary / PRO: .... John Keane
Number of Clubs: 1500
Number of teams: 2120
Number of provincial unions / regions: 4
Number of members (per region): .... Between 3000 and 6000
Main Venue: .... Limerick Inn Hotel, Limerick (700)
All time record attendance at Irish darts event: .... 900 in 1989 (Spa Hotel, Dublin).

INTERNATIONAL STATISTICS

National senior coach: .... John Joe O'Shea
Team manager: .... John Keane
Most capped competitors: .... John Joe O'Shea and Jack McKenna
Best international result (team): .... 1989 Bronze
Best international result (individual): .... 1989 Silver (Jack McKenna)
Best ever nternational ranking: 7th

1998 RESULTS - DOMESTIC

Ladies Intercounty Team Championship (winners) .... Kildare
Ladies Intercounty Team Championship (runners-up) .... Dublin
Mens Intercounty Team Championship (winners) .... Donegal
Mens Intercounty Team Championship (runners-up) .... Cork
Intercounty Youth Championship (winner) .... Keith Rooney
Ladies National Singles Championship .... Susan McKenna (Kildare)
Mens National Singles Championship .... Joe Beirn (Sligo)

1998 RESULTS - INTERNATIONAL

OSLO, NORWAY - EUROPEAN CUP

(Men) .... Team Event - 5th place .... **Overall Placing:** 10th
(Ladies) .... Team Event - 5th place .... **Overall Placing:** 11th

NATIONAL SQUAD FACT FILE (MEN)

Player	Team	D.O.B.	International. App.
Seamus Gormley	Connolly's, Cootehill, Co. Cavan	17/4/66.	8
Brendan Grace	Showboat, Waterford	5/12/65	3
John Burke	Lucan County Bar, Dublin	21/6/60	4
Jack McKenna	Arch Bar, Newbridge, Co. Kildare	10/3/42	Numerous

NATIONAL SQUAD FACT FILE (WOMEN)

Player	Team	D.O.B.	International App.
Maureen Kelly	Railway House, Bagenalstown, Co. Carlow	19/11/59	2
Marion McDermot		7/4/61	5

BEST INDIVIDUAL RESULT AT THE EUROPE CUP

Men: Jack McKenna. **Women:** Maureen Kelly.

PAST PRESIDENTS

Michael O'Sullivan (Cork); Jim Dowling (Cork); Paddy McGlynn (Dublin); Frank McGuire (Carlow).

THE YEAR IN PICTURES

TOUR DE FRANCE BEGINS IN IRELAND: The Tour de France began in Ireland in July, generating massive spectator interest. Pictured above is the peloton making their way over Wicklow Gap. On leaving Ireland after three days of racing, *Le Tour* descended into farce amid allegations of drug taking.

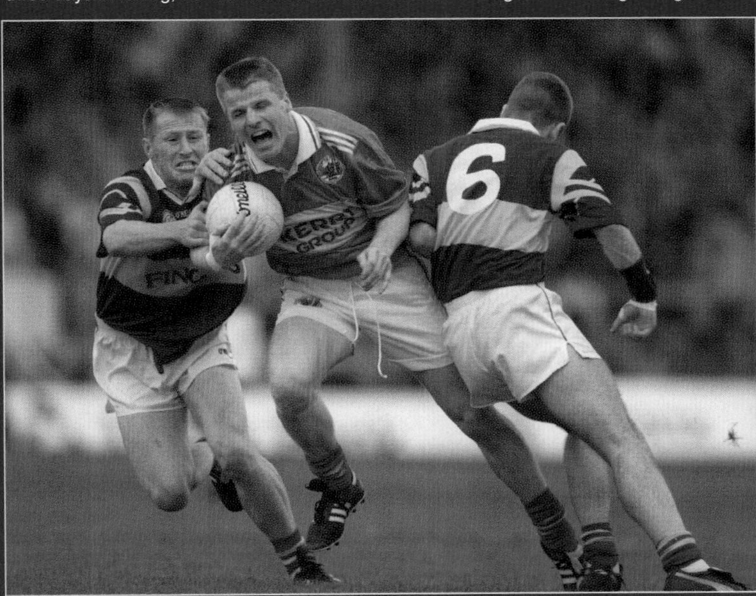

ALL IRELAND CHAMPIONS DETHRONED: Despite defeating Tipperary in the Munster Final, Kerry senior footballers crashed out in the All-Ireland semi-final, while Kildare marched onwards to their first All-Ireland final appearance since 1935. Pictured left, Eamonn Breen feels the brunt of a Tipperary challenge in the Munster Final.

THE WEST'S AWAKE!: Despite entering the All-Ireland Senior Football Final as underdogs Galway proved too good for the favourites, Kildare, and won by four points. Here, Kildare's Dermot Earley (L) and Galway's Jarlath Fallon duel for a high ball at midfield.

DE BRUIN BANNED: Triple-Olympic champion Michelle De Bruin was banned from competition for four years by FINA (the international governing body for swimming). De Bruin held a press conference in Dublin where she denied allegations of tampering with a urine sample and vowed to clear her name.

KILKENNY GIRL OLYMPIC YOUTH CHAMPION: Kilkenny's Emily Maher is greeted by family and friends on her return from the Youth Olympics in Moscow. Maher struck gold in both the 100m and 200m sprints.

OFFALY WIN NATIONAL FOOTBALL LEAGUE TITLE: Despite the best efforts of Derry midfielder Anthony Tohill, Offaly proved too much for league specialists Derry in the National League final. The game was played in torrential rain.

SHANNON CLAIM ALL-IRELAND LEAGUE TITLE: Frank McNamara gets the ball away as his side, Shannon, go on to claim rugby's All Ireland League title for the fourth year in a row.

GLORY DAYS BACK FOR SONIA: Sonia O'Sullivan breaks the tape at Marrakesh, Morocco, to win gold in the Women's 4km race at the IAAF World Cross Country Championships. O'Sullivan went on to collect a second gold in the 8km race and completed her season spectacularly in August by winning double gold in the European Championships.

OFFALY TAKE KILKENNY APART: Offaly hurlers became the first side to successfully avail of the 'back-door' ruling. Rejoining the All-Ireland series (and after an epic three match semi-final saga with Clare), they proceeded to the All-Ireland final and defeated Leinster champions Kilkenny on the scoreline of 2-16 to 1-13. Here Offaly forward Joe Errity brushes past Kilkenny's Canice Brennan and Willie O'Connor.

JORDAN TEAM GET IT RIGHT: Jordan driver Damon Hill leads his team-mate Ralf Schumacher to a historic one-two victory for Eddie Jordan's Formula One team at the Belgian Grand Prix at Spa Francorchamps.

IRELAND HOSTS TOUR DE FRANCE: Italian Marco Pantani pictured during the time trial held in Dublin city. Pantani, cycling for the Mercatay Uno-Bianchi team, was the eventual winner of the Tour.

BELFAST HOSTS NATIONAL SWIMMING CHAMPIONSHIPS: Swimming was the winner, after a year of ongoing controversies, when the National Championships in Belfast produced several national records - a fine display from Ireland's premier swimmers.

ANOTHER GREAT YEAR FOR HURLING: The standard of hurling was amazingly high yet again. One of the highlights of an epic year was the emergence of Waterford as the new pretenders. Pictured above, Gaway and Waterford players in a midfield tussle under the dropping ball.

TEARS IN BRUSSELS: Irish goalkeeper Shay Given is comforted by colleague Andy Townsend and physio Mick Byrne, following Ireland's exit from the World Cup qualifiers at the hands of Belgium.

SWAN JOY AT CHELTENHAM: Jockey Charlie Swan celebrates winning the Smurfit Champion Hurdle on Istabraq.

CORK WIN ALL-IRELAND: Cork were crowned 1998 All-Ireland Senior Camogie Champions following their win over Galway at Croke Park.

CHELTENHAM ACTION: The Queen Mother Chase proved to be a thrilling affair at Cheltenham. Here, Brian Harding leads the field on One Man - a lead they were to lose.

EURO TITLE FOR IRISH: Brian Kerr's Republic of Ireland U-16s were crowned soccer's European champions in Scotland when they defeated Italy in the final.

NATIONAL LEAGUE ACTION: Shamrock Rovers v St. Patrick's Athletic - Richard Purdy of Shamrock Rovers goes over the top for a spectacular header at the expense of St. Pat's Leon Braithwaite.

WORLD TITLE FOR IRISH RUGBY: The Irish U-19 rugby team celebrating at Dublin Airport, following their return from France where they won the IRB/FIRA World Junior Championships.

IRVINE'S FABULOUS YEAR: Dublin-based Eddie Irvine enjoyed his most successful year to date amassing seven podium finishes, including two second places, for Ferrari.

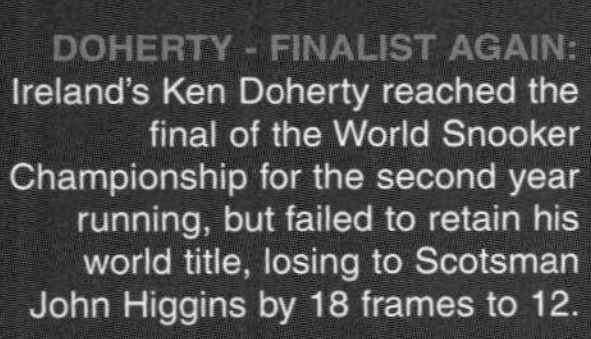

DOHERTY - FINALIST AGAIN: Ireland's Ken Doherty reached the final of the World Snooker Championship for the second year running, but failed to retain his world title, losing to Scotsman John Higgins by 18 frames to 12.

FIVE NATIONS ACTION: Victor Costello charges through the French at the Stad de France - a game Ireland were desperately unlucky to lose on the scoreline of 16 points to 18. Despite this and other spirited performances in the Five Nations series, the Irish rugby team finished with the Wooden Spoon.

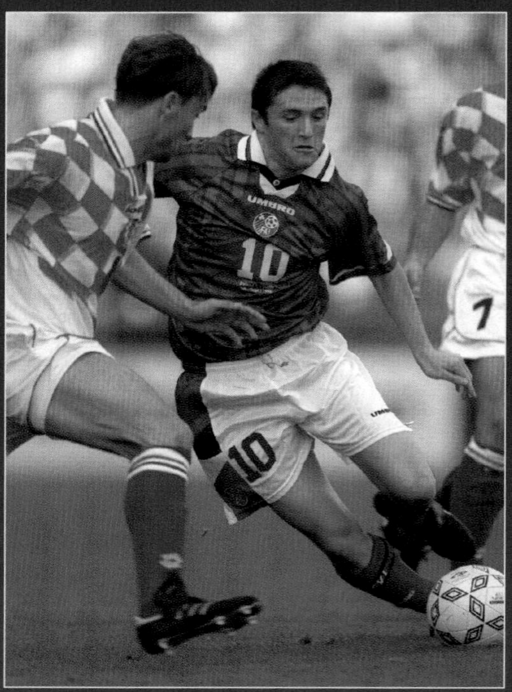

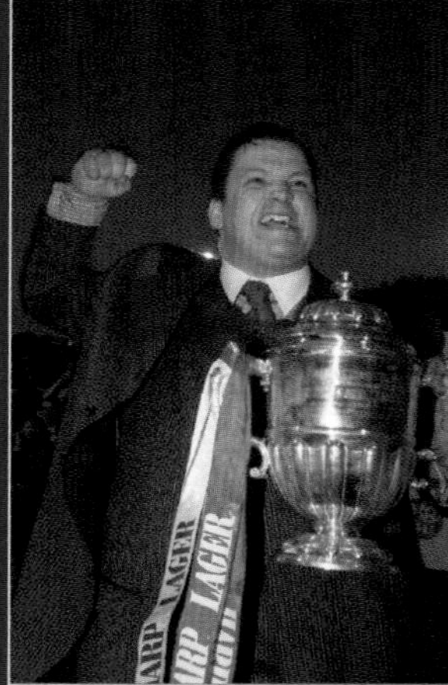

DOLAN CELEBRATES IN STYLE: St. Patrick's Athletic's flamboyant manager Pat Dolan celebrates winning the National League Premier Division title.

KEANE MAKES A NAME FOR HIMSELF: The Wolves' striker, Robbie Keane, emerged as a major figure on the Irish soccer scene, both at under-age and senior level. Here, he takes on Dario Simic of Croatia at Lansdowne Road in the Republic's winning opening game over Croatia for the European 2000 qualifying campaign.

WALLACE BROTHERS PSYCHE UP: Paul and Richard Wallace prepare for battle with the French at the Stad de France prior to their Five Nations game.

CORK CITY WIN CUP: The Cork City side who won the FAI Cup after a replay with Shelbourne FC.

PREMIER DIVISION ACTION: Jason Sherlock of UCD in action against Colin Hawkins of St. Patrick's Athletic.

HURLING PASSION: Committed action from the first Offaly / Clare All-Ireland hurling semi-final. Here, Brian Quinn and Sean McMahon of Clare tussle with Johnny Dooley of Offaly. The game ended in a draw.

KEANE DELIGHT: Robbie Keane celebrates in some style after scoring against Croatia at the European Championships in Cyprus. The Ireland U-18s went on to win the European Cup when they defeated Germany on penalties in the final.

McKIERNAN'S LONDON SUCCESS: Catherina McKiernan recorded a great victory at the London Marathon in April. The London race was only the second marathon raced by the Cavan athlete - she also won her debut marathon in Berlin in 1997.

SURFING UP A STORM: David O'Donnell, a member of the Guinness Irish surf team, puts in a practice run at Strandhill. He later competed with the team at the 1998 World Surfing Games in Portugal.

CLIFTONVILLE DELIGHT: Cliftonville FC bridged a 78-year gap by winning the Irish League. The North Belfast side, captained by Mickey Donnelly (R) secured a 1-1 draw with Glenavon and the defeat of arch rivals Linfield, on the same day, to bring the Gibson Cup to North Belfast for the first time since the 1909/10 season.

HORSESHOW SPECTACULAR: Robert Smith on Senator Mighty Blue, pictured in action at the Dublin Horseshow during The Kerrygold Challenge.

THE MAN IN THE MIDDLE: Action from the Ulster Senior Football final at Clones - Donegal v Derry. Here, referee Jim Curran gets into a tangle with Eamon Burns of Derry and Noel Hegarty and Jim McGuinness of Donegal. Derry went on to win the Ulster Final with a last minute goal from Joe Brolly.

EQUESTRIAN SPORT

Equestrian Federation of Ireland

Ashton House, Castleknock, Dublin 15. Tel. (01) 8387611 Fax. (01) 8382051

Founded 1931
President .... Lewis Lowry
Secretary .... Col. E. V. Campion
Number of Affiliated Associations 14
Main Venues .... Dublin, Millstreet, Cavan and Punchestown.
Past Presidents .... Conor Crowley, Bill Buller and Lewis Lowry (*present president*)

1998 FORMULA 1 WORLD CHAMPIONSHIP RESULTS

The 1998 Formula One Grand Prix circuit began in Melbourne, Australia on 8 March 1998, and the 16 race programme finished on 1 November 1998 in Japan.

- **AUSTRALIAN GRAND PRIX** (at Melbourne) 1st round - 8 March 1998: **Podium finish: 1** M Hakkinen (Fin) McLaren-Mercedes 1hr 31min 45.996s, **2** D Coulthard (Brit) McLaren-Mercedes 1hr 31min @ 0.700s, **3** H-H Frentzen (Ger) Williams-Mecachrome @8.668s, **4** E Irvine (Ire) Ferrari @9.747s, **8** D Hill (Brit) Jordan @ 48.898s, R. Schumacher (Ger) Jordan Not Classified.

- **BRAZILIAN GRAND PRIX** (at Interlagos) 2nd round - 29 March 1998: **Podium finish: 1** M Hakkinen (Fin) McLaren-Mercedes 1hr 37min 11.747s, **2** D Coulthard (Brit) McLaren-Mercedes @1.102s, **3** M Schumacher (Ger) Ferrari @ 1min 0.55s. **8** E Irvine (Ire) Ferrari @ 1 lap. D Hill (Brit) Jordan disqualified, R. Schumacher (Ger) Jordan not classified.

- **ARGENTINAN GRAND PRIX** (at Buenos Aires) 3rd round - 12 April 1998: **Podium finish: 1** M Schumacher (Ger) Ferrari 1hr 48min 36.175s, **2** M Hakkinen (Fin) McLaren-Mercedes @ 22.899s, **3** E Irvine (Ire) Ferrari @ 57.745s. **8** D Hill (Brit) Jordan @ 1 lap, R. Schumacher (Ger) Jordan Not Classified.

- **SAN MARINO GRAND PRIX** (at Imola) 4th round - 26 April 1998: **Podium finish: 1** D Coulthard (Brit) McLaren-Mercedes 1hr 34min 24.593s, **2** M Schumacher (Ger) Ferrari @ 4.554s, **3** E Irvine (Ire) Ferrari @ 51.776s, **7** R. Schumacher (Ger) Jordan @ 2 laps, **10** D Hill (Brit) Jordan @ 5 laps.

- **SPANISH GRAND PRIX** (at Barcelona) 5th round - 10 May 1998: **Podium finish: 1** M Hakkinen (Fin) McLaren-Mercedes 1hr 33min 37.621s, **2** D Coulthard (Brit) McLaren-Mercedes @ 9.439s, **3** M Schumacher (Ger) Ferrari @ 47.094s. **11** R. Schumacher (Ger) Jordan @ 2 laps, D Hill (Brit) Jordan Not Classified. E Irvine (Ire) Ferrari Not Classified.

- **MONACO GRAND PRIX** (at Monte Carlo) 6th round - 24 May 1998: **Podium finish: 1** M Hakkinen (Fin) McLaren-Mercedes 1hr 51min 23.595s, **2** G Fisichella (Ita) Benetton-Mecachrome @ 11.475s, **3** E Irvine (Ire) Ferrari @ 41.378s. 8 D Hill (Brit) Jordan @ 2 laps, R. Schumacher (Ger) Jordan Not Classified.

- **CANADIAN GRAND PRIX** (at Montreal) 7th round - 7 June 1998: **Podium finish: 1** M Schumacher (Ger) Ferrari 1hr 40min 57.355s, **2** G Fisichella (Ita) Benetton-Mecachrome @ 16.662s, **3** E Irvine (Ire) Ferrari @ 1min 0.058s, D Hill (Brit) Jordan Not Classified. R. Schumacher (Ger) Jordan Not Classified.

- **FRENCH GRAND PRIX** (at Magny Cours) - 8th round - 28 June 1998. **Podium finish: 1** M Schumacher (Ger) Ferrari 1hr 34min 45.026s, **2** E Irvine (Ire) Ferrari @ 19.575 s, **3** M Hakkinen (Fin) McLaren-Mercedes @ 19.747s 16 R. Schumacher (Ger) Jordan @ 3 laps, D Hill (Brit) Jordan Not Classified.

- **BRITISH GRAND PRIX** (at Silverstone) 9th round - 12 July 1998: **Podium finish: 1** M Schumacher (Ger) Ferrari 1hr 46min 52.450sec, **2** M Hakkinen (Fin) McLaren-Mercedes @ 22.465, **3** E Irvine (Ire) Ferrari @ 29.199s **6** R. Schumacher (Ger) Jordan @ 1 lap, D Hill (Brit) Jordan Not Classified.

- **AUSTRIAN GRAND PRIX** (at Zeltweg) 10th round - 26 July 1998: **Podium finish: 1** M. Hakkinen (Fin) McLaren-Mercedes 1hr 30min 44.086 s, **2** D. Coulthard (Brit) @ 5.289s, **3** M. Schumacher (Ger) Ferrari @ 39.093s, **4** E. Irvine (Ire) Ferrari at 43.977s, **5** R. Schumacher (Ger) Jordan @ 50.655s, **7** D. Hill (Brit) Jordan @ 1min 13.624s.

- **GERMAN GRAND PRIX** (at Hockenheim) 11th round - 2 August 1998: **Podium finish: 1** M. Hakkinen (Fin) McLaren-Mercedes 1hr 20min 47.984s, **2** D. Coulthard (Brit) McLaren-Mercedes @ 0.427s, **3** J. Villeneuve (Can) Williams-Mecachrome @ 2.578s, **4** D. Hill (Brit) Jordan @ 7.185s, **6** R. Schumacher (Ger) Jordan @ 29.739s, **8** E. Irvine (Ire) Ferrari @ 31.650s.

- **HUNGARIAN GRAND PRIX** (at Budapest) 12th round - 16 August 1998: **Podium finish: 1** M. Schumacher (Ger) Ferrari 1hr 45min 25.55s, **2** D. Coulthard (Brit) McLaren-Mercedes @ 9.433 s, **3** J. Villeneuve (Can) Williams-Mecachrome @ 44.444s, **4** D. Hill (Brit) Jordan @ 55.075s **9** R. Schumacher (Ger) Jordan @ 1 lap. E. Irvine (Ire) Ferrari, Not Classified.

- **BELGIAN GRAND PRIX** (at Spa-Francorchamps) 13th round - 30 August 1998: **Podium finish: 1** D. Hill (Brit)

Jordan 1hr 43mins 47.407s, **2** R. Schumacher (Ger) Jordan @ 0.932 s **3** J. Alesi (Fra) @ 7.240 s. E. Irvine (Ire) Ferrari, Not Classified.

■ **ITALIAN GRAND PRIX** (at Monza) 14th round - 13 September 1998: **Podium finish: 1** M. Schumacher (Ger) Ferrari 1hr 17mins 09.672s, **2** E. Irvine (Ire) Ferrari @ 37.977s, **3** R. Schumacher (Ger) Jordan @ 41.152 s, **6** D. Hill (Brit) Jordan @ 1min 06.688 secs.

■ **LUXEMBOURG GRAND PRIX** (at Nurburgring) 15th round - 27 September 1998: **Podium finish: 1** M. Hakkinen (Fin) McLaren 1hr 32mins 14.789s, **2** M. Schumacher (Ger) Ferrari @ 2.212s **3** D. Coulthard (Brit) McLaren @ 34.164s, **4** E. Irvine (Ire) Ferrari @ 58.183s, **9** D. Hill (Brit) Jordan @ 1 lap. R. Schumacher (Ger) Jordan, Not Classified.

■ **JAPANESE GRAND PRIX** (at Suzuka) 16th round - 1 November 1998: *(Result not available at time of going to press).*

1998 WORLD CHAMPIONSHIP, STANDINGS

DRIVERS' CHAMPIONSHIP*

Name	Aus	Bra	Arg	San	Esp	Mon	Can	Fra	Bri	Aus	Ger	Hun	Bel	Ita	Lux	Jap	Total
HAKKINEN, M.	10	10	6		10	10		4	6	10	10	1		3	10		90
SCHUMACHER, M.		4	10	6	4		10	10	10	4	2	10		10	6		86
COULTHARD, D.	6	6	1	10	6			1		6	6	6			4		52
IRVINE, E.	3		4	4		4	4	6	4	3				6	3		41
VILLENEUVE, J.	2			3	1	2		3		1	4	4					20
WURZ, A.		3	3		3		3	2	3								17
HILL, D.											3	3	10	1			17
FISICHELLA, G.		1				6	6		2						1		16
SCHUMACHER, R.									1	2	1		6	4			14
FRENTZEN, H-H	4	2		2								2	3		2		15
ALESI, J.			2	1									4	2			9
BARRICHELLO, R.					2		2										4
SALO, M.						3											3
DINIZ, P.						1							2				3
HERBERT, J.	1																1
MAGNUSSEN, J.							1										1
TRULLI, J.													1				1
NAKANO, S.																	0
PANIS, O.																	0
ROSSET, R.																	0
TAKAGI, T.																	0
TUERO, E.																	0
VERSTAPPEN, J.																	0

** Table above takes into account 15 out of 16 rounds. The result of the 16th round, the Japanese Grand Prix, (1 November 1998) not available at time of going to press.*

CONSTRUCTORS' CHAMPIONSHIP

Name	Aus	Bra	Arg	San	Esp	Mon	Can	Fra	Bri	Aus	Ger	Hun	Bel	Ita	Lux	Jap	Total
McLaren	16	16	7	10	16	10		5	6	16	16	7		3	14		142
Ferrari	3	4	14	10	4	4	14	16	14	7	2	10		16	9		127
Williams	6	2		5	1	2		3		1	4	6	3		2		35
Bennetton		4	3		3	6	9	2	5						1		33
Jordan									1	2	4	3	16	5			31
Sauber	1		2	1									4	2			10
Arrows						4							2				6
Stewart					2		3										5
Prost													1				1
Minardi																	0
Tyrrell																	0

JORDAN CONSTRUCTORS' WORLD C'SHIP RECORD

Year	Starts	Points	Poles	Wins	Constructors C'ship	Drivers	Engine
1991	31	13	0	0	5th	A. de Cesaris, B. Gachot	Ford

Continued from previous page

Year	Starts	Points	Poles	Wins	Constructors C'ship	Drivers	Engine
1992	28	1	0	0	13th	S. Modena, M. Gugelmin	Yamaha
1993	31	3	0	0	11th	R. Barrichello, T. Boutsen	Hart
1994	31	28	1	0	5th	R. Barrichello, E. Irvine	Peugeot
1995	34	21	0	0	6th	R. Barrichello, E. Irvine	Peugeot
1996	32	22	0	0	5th	R. Barrichello, M. Brundle	Peugeot
1997	34	33	0	0	5th	R. Schumacher, G. Fisichella	Peugeot
Total	**221**	**121**	**1**	**0**			

DRIVER CAREER STATISTICS to end of 1997 season

Driver	Races	C'ships	Wins	2nd	3rd	Poles	Points
Eddie Irvine (Ferrari)	65	0	0	1	10	0	52
Damon Hill (Jordan)	84	1	21	15	5	20	333
Ralph Schumacher (Jordan)	17	0	0	0	1	0	13

1997 WORLD CHAMPIONSHIP FINAL STANDINGS

Drivers' Championship

Position	Team	Points
1. J. Villeneuve (Can)	Williams Renault	81
2. H.H. Frentzen (Ger)	Williams Renault	42
3. D. Coulthard (Brit)	McLaren Mercedes	36
4. J. Alesi (Fra)	Benetton Renault	36
5. G. Berger (Aus)	Benetton Renault	27
6. M. Hakkinen (Fin)	McLaren Mercedes	27
7. E. Irvine (Irl)	Ferrari	24
8. G. Fisichella (Ita)	Jordan Peugeot	20
9. O. Panis (Fra)	Prost Mugen Honda	16
10. J. Herbert (Brit)	Sauber Petronas	15
11. R. Schumacher (Ger)	Jordan Peugeot	13
12. D. Hill (Brit)	Arrows Yamaha	7
13. R. Barrichello (Bra)	Stewart Ford	6
14. A. Wurz (Aus)	Benetton Renault	4
15. J. Trulli (Ita)	Prost Mugen Honda	3
16. M. Salo (Fin)	Tyrrell Ford	2
17. P. Diniz (Bra)	Arrows Yamaha	2
18. S. Nakano (Jap)	Prost Mugen Honda	2
19. N. Larini (Ita)	Sauber Petronas	1
Disqualified		
M. Schmacher (Ger)	Ferrari	78

Constructors' Championship

Position	Points
1. Williams-Renault	123
2. Ferrari	102
3. Benetton Renault	67
4. McLaren Mercedes	63
5. Jordan Peugeot	33
6. Prost Mugen Honda	21
7. Sauber Petronas	16
8. Arrows Yamaha	9
9. Stewart Ford	6
10. Tyrrell Ford	2

the challenges facing the gaa

by ***liam horan***

sports writer **IRISH INDEPENDENT**

THE GAA's uncertain relationship with modern technology came to light once again during 1998. Even though the debate about the use of video evidence in the GAA was settled almost two decades ago, there were still numerous dissenting voices when it was availed of to help with the investigation into the four minutes of wild swinging at the start of the Munster Hurling Final replay between Waterford and Clare. It was as if this was the very first time a GAA ruling body had bought a video and a remote control into a meeting-room to get to the heart of what happened in a violent incident. Video evidence has been used every single year, in numerous meeting-rooms up and down the country, since the early to mid-1980s. And the Munster Council had gone down the exact same road in 1995 when dealing with incidents in the senior hurling championship game between Waterford and Tipperary.

Shay Walsh, who this year won an All-Ireland senior football medal with Galway, enjoyed some mercy from the cameras in 1994. Sent off in the All-Ireland minor semi-final, the pictures showed clearly that he was attempting to play the ball and made no contact whatsoever with his opposite number. The mandatory two-week suspension was lifted, which was of little consolation to Shay and his defeated colleagues at the time, but it was one more case of a video being used in the boardroom.

In 1995, a procedural facility was found to allow a Leinster senior-football championship match, between Carlow and Laois, be replayed after the cameras clearly showed that Mick Turley's match-winning point for Laois was actually wide of the post.

Ergo, much of the hand-wringing and tch-tching which accompanied the Munster Council's decision to study video evidence this year was at best misplaced, and perhaps even orchestrated to deflect attention from the incidents on hand.

One simple precept governs this entire area and it is this: only those who are guilty, who aim a kick or swing the hurley, have something to fear from video evidence being used in their cases.

There are wider issues that the GAA must tackle, of course. The present system of administering justice is outmoded and unwieldy. The speed with which it moves - i.e. slow to very slow - serves only to prolong major controversies in the media. In this age of e-mails and fax machines, the process takes far too long and, apart from generating huge news interest, allows for all sorts of canvassing and revisionism to set in.

The delays have another bizarre effect. When the time comes for the matter to be dealt with, sometimes up to three weeks after the event, a groundswell of opinion has developed that the player, though clearly guilty, has 'suffered enough in the media' - and, thus, should be let off without a suspension at all!

It is clear the GAA must take a jackhammer to many of its present regulations governing discipline. There is no reason why a small group of people cannot sit in judgement of incidents within 24 hours of major inter-county matches. They should have the entire match available to them on video. They should have the referee's report (another area where the carrier pigeon seems to be the chosen speed). They should be able to call in players even shortly after the game to shed further light on incidents and, most importantly of all, they should have the power - and the obligation - to cite players whose misdemeanours come up on video.

The present system is haphazard. If a county does not kick up a storm about incidents, they pass off. If they do, the pressure comes on the ruling body to investigate. It's the 'make it up as you go along' system of dispensing justice. The GAA must be more rigorous in how it approaches all matches. Rules, regulations and procedures that worked fine 20 years ago have now been rendered outdated by a society awash with ever-improving technology, massive public and media interest in the games and the individual's greater understanding of his or her entitlement to fair play.

The year just over also yielded another huge controversy involving modern technology - that of the put-upon referee, up to his ears in bookings and scorekeeping, also having to take charge of timekeeping. The replay of the Clare-Offaly All Ireland hurling semi-final was declared void when the Galway referee, Jimmy Cooney, blew the final whistle two minutes short of full-time, not to mention a possible two more minutes of injury-time.

The error - as much that of the system, as Jimmy Cooney himself - may have cost Clare an All-ireland title. They were certainly on their way to the final at the time. The three games between Offaly and Clare pointed up most of the problems accruing from the archaic practice of the referee being the ultimate - and only - judge of time.

In the first match, Cooney blew up just a few seconds into injury-time, even though there were almost two minutes more of injury-time to be played. This was passed off at the time on the basis that injury-time is at the referee's own discretion - which it is not. So, over two days, the referee blew up early twice, the second a simple human error, the first never properly explained.

The phenomenon of a referee 'playing for a draw' is recognised in folkloric terms in the GAA, and I am not suggesting that Cooney did that the first day. But as long as the referee has the timekeeping under his control, some will be tempted to cut short when the teams are level - a draw has a sobering effect on everyone, even those who may have felt wronged by some of the referee's decisions during a game.

The Ladies Football Association got in ahead of the GAA by introducing a special timekeeper clock for all to see for their finals at the start of October. it is the way to go - there should never be disputes about timing. The speed of Gaelic football and hurling make every minute invaluable. The unexplained loss of two minutes of injury-time is simply not good enough.

There is no reason to be unduly optimistic that the GAA will embrace modern technology any more than it has. It is still struggling to convince senior officials that video evidence is an imperative. No clear initiative has emerged for the timekeeping to be taken out of the hands of the referee.

There is a deeper malaise underpinning all of this. The GAA is not concerned enough about its own discipline. If it were, it would have more regard for its system of deterrents. Deterrents come in the form of suspensions. At the moment, it is a thing of chance; a full swing of the hurley can cause a player to miss three months and no match, a relatively harmless second booking can result in a player missing a provincial final. The system of time-bans has been discredited in recent years to a laughable extent. And, yet, we await a move for a switch to match-bans. Until this simple step is taken, let alone the bigger picture involving modern technology, there will be glaring anomalies in the punishments handed out for similar offences.

I have been making this point for quite some time, and at the turn of the year it might be a good time to reiterate it: the biggest challenge facing the GAA at the minute is to get its system of discipline in order.

❑

Cumann Lúthchleas Gael

Páirc an Chrócaigh, Baile Átha Cliath 3. Tel. (01) 8363222

Founded	1884
President	Joe McDonagh
Director General	Liam Mulvihill
Public Relations Officer	Danny Lynch
Number of Provincial Councils	4
Number of Clubs	2,664
Number of Members	750,000
Number of Teams	20,000
Number of Coaches	2,000
Biggest Recorded Attendance	90,556 (Croke Park September 1961, Down v.Offaly)
Main Stadia	Croke Park (66,000), Semple Stadium Thurles (50,000)

1998 FINALISTS	**HURLING**		**FOOTBALL**	
	Winners	**Runners Up**	**Winners**	**Runners Up**
All-Ireland	Offaly	Kilkenny	Galway	Kildare
Connacht	Galway	Roscommon	Galway	Roscommon
Leinster	Kilkenny	Offaly	Kildare	Meath
Munster	Clare	Waterford	Kerry	Tipperary
Ulster	Antrim	Down	Derry	Donegal
National League	Cork	Waterford	Offaly	Derry
Railway Cup*	Munster	Leinster	Ulster	Leinster
All-Ireland Club	Birr (Offaly)	Sarsfields (Galway)	Corofin (Galway)	Erin's Isle (Dublin)

Top Scorer in 1998 Hurling Championship	John Troy (Offaly) 2-31
Top Scorers in 1998 Football Championship	Declan Browne (Tipperary) 2-29
1997 Player of the Year, Hurling	James O'Connor (Clare)
1997 Player of the Year, Football	Maurice Fitzgerald (Kerry)

*The Railway Cup Hurling result is from the 1997 season.

Attendances at GAA Championships 1996-98

1998 Total Championship Attendance	1,429,386
1997 Total Championship Attendance	1,337,345
1996 Total Championship Attendance	1,056,236

Provincial breakdown Figures in *italics* indicate number of fixtures played in each provincial championship

	1997				1998			
PROVINCE	**FOOTBALL**		**HURLING**		**FOOTBALL**		**HURLING**	
Connacht	71,000	*5*	2,500	*1*	119,000	*7*	2,000	*1*
Leinster	338,454	*14*	124,677	*7*	330,238	*12*	88,568	*5*
Munster	62,651	*6*	146,435	*5*	84, 725	*5*	221,689	*6*
Ulster	202,682	*11*	2,700	*2*	144,829	*8*	9,250	*4*
All-Ireland Series	182,042	*3*	204,204	*5*	169,457	*3*	259,630	*7*
Total	856,829	*39*	480,516	*20*	848,249	*35*	581,137	*23*

RESULTS

1998 Guinness Hurling Championship

Date	Round	Venue	Attend	Result			
Connacht							
11.07.98	Final	Dr Hyde Park, Roscommon	2,000	Roscommon	3-13	Galway	2-27
Leinster							
24.05.98	1st Round	Croke Park, Dublin	48,856§	Meath	0-8	Offaly	4-28
31.05.98	1st Round	Parnell Park, Dublin	10,000	Dublin	0-14	Kilkenny	4-23
14.06.98	Semi-final	Croke Park, Dublin	*46,078	Kilkenny	3-11	Laois	1-14
14.06.98	Semi-final	Croke Park, Dublin	*	Offaly	1-15	Wexford	0-17
05.07.98	Final	Croke Park, Dublin	32,490	Kilkenny	3-10	Offaly	1-11
Munster							
24.05.98	1st Round	Austin Stack Park, Tralee	4,106	Kerry	1-9	Waterford	0-20
31.05.98	1st Round	Gaelic Grounds, Limerick	34,480	Limerick	3-11	Cork	1-20
07.06.98	Semi-final	Páirc Uí Chaoimh, Cork	30,822	Waterford	0-21	Tipperary	2-12
21.06.98	Semi-final	Semple Stadium, Thurles	49,133	Clare	0-21	Cork	0-13
12.07.98	Final	Semple Stadium, Thurles	51,417	Clare	1-16	Waterford	3-10
19.07.98	Final (R)	Semple Stadium, Thurles	51,731	Clare	2-16	Waterford	0-10

Ulster

Date	Round	Venue	Attendance	Team	Score	Opponent	Score
14.06.98	Semi-final	Casement Park, Belfast	**250**	Antrim	0-19	London	0-19
21.06.98	Semi-final	Casement Park, Belfast	3,000	Derry	2-17	Down	0-18
21.06.98	Semi-final (R)	Casement Park, Belfast	*	Antrim	6-27	London	1-7
05.07.98	Final	Casement Park, Belfast	6,000	Antrim	1-19	Derry	2-13
All-Ireland Series							
26.07.98	Quarter-final	Croke Park, Dublin	26,052	Waterford	1-20	Galway	1-10
26.07.98	Quarter-final	Croke Park, Dublin	*	Offaly	2-18	Antrim	2-9
09.08.98	Semi-final	Croke Park, Dublin	37,124	Clare	1-13	Offaly	1-13
16.08.98	Semi-final	Croke Park, Dublin	50,856	Kilkenny	1-11	Waterford	1-10
22.08.98	Semi-final (R)	Croke Park, Dublin	38,015	Clare	1-16	Offaly	2-10†
29.08.98	Semi-final (R)	Semple Stadium, Thurles	42,092	Offaly	0-16	Clare	0-13
All-Ireland Final							
13.09.98		Croke Park, Dublin	65,491	Offaly	2-16	Kilkenny	1-13

(R)=Replay. † Match unfinished, replayed one week later. § Double header with Meath v Offaly Leinster SFC tie.

All-Ireland Hurling Final

CROKE PARK, 13 SEPTEMBER 1998. Attendance: 65,491. **Half time score:** Offaly 0-8, Kilkenny 1-7. **Full-time score:** Offaly 2-16, Kilkenny 1-13. **Booked:** Martin Hanamy (Offaly, 57 mins). **Sent off:** None. **Top Scorer:** Brian Whelehan (1-6, 3 frees). **Man-of-the-Match:** Brian Whelehan (Offaly). **Referee:** Dickie Murphy (Wexford). **Linesmen:** P. O'Connor (Limerick), S. McMahon (Clare).

The Teams

OFFALY

Stephen Byrne

Simon Whelahan **Kevin Kinahan** **Martin Hanamy**

Brian Whelehan (1-6) **Hubert Rigney (C)** **Kevin Martin**

Johnny Pilkington (0-1) **Michael Duignan** (0-2)

Johnny Dooley **Joe Errity** (1-2) **Gary Hanniffy**

John Troy (0-3) **Joe Dooley** (0-2) **Billy Dooley**

Subs: Paudie Mulhare for G. Hannify (30 mins); Darren Hannify for B. Dooley (61 mins); John Ryan for J. Dooley (67 mins). Subs not used: Eoin Kennedy, Barry Whelahan, Niall Claffey, Colm Cassidy, Killian Farrell, Noel Murphy, Cathal Murray, Eunan Martin, Ger Oakley.

Manager: Michael Bond.
Selectors: Pat McLoughney, Paudge Mulhare.

KILKENNY

Joe Dermody

Tom Hickey (C) **Pat O'Neill** **Willie O'Connor**

Michael Kavanagh **Canice Brennan** **Liam Keoghan**

Philip Larkin (0-1) **Peter Barry**

Brian McEvoy (0-3) **Andy Comerford** (0-1) **DJ Carey** (0-5)

Ken O'Shea (0-2) **PJ Delaney** **Charlie Carter** (1-1)

Subs: Niall Moloney for K. O'Shea (61 mins); John Costelloe for M. Kavanagh (67 mins). Subs not used: James McGarry, John Hoyne, Sean Ryan, Denis Byrne, Patsy Brophy, Liam Simpson, Dan O'Neill.

Manager: Kevin Fennelly.
Selectors: Mick McCarthy, Dick O'Neill.

Top Scorers 1998 Senior Hurling Championship

OVERALL

Rank & Name	County	Score	Total Pts
1 John Troy	Offaly	2-31	37
2 Paul Flynn	Waterford	1-30	33
3 James O'Connor	Clare	0-32	32
4 Gregory O'Kane	Antrim	1-29	32
5 DJ Carey	Kilkenny	3-22	31
6 Brian Whelehan	Offaly	2-21	27
7 Joe Dooley	Offaly	1-20	23
8 Oliver Collins	Derry	0-22	22
9 Tony Browne	Waterford	1-17	20
10 Charlie Carter	Kilkenny	2-14	20

INDIVIDUAL

Rank and Name	County	Score	Opposition
1 Daragh Coen	Galway	1-13	v Roscommon
2 Oliver Collins	Derry	0-12	v Down
3 John Troy	Offaly	1-9	v Meath
4 DJ Carey	Kilkenny	1-8	v Dublin
5 Paul Flynn	Waterford	0-10	v Tipp
6 Gregory O'Kane	Antrim	0-10	v Derry
7 Oliver Collins	Derry	0-10	v Antrim
8 Timmy Moloney	London	0-10	v Antrim
9 Gregory O'Kane	Antrim	1-7	v London
10 Paul Codd	Wexford	0-9	v Offaly

1998 Bank of Ireland Football Championship

Connacht

Date	Round	Venue	Attend	Result			
24.05.98	1st Round	McHale Park, Castlebar	30,000	Mayo	2-6	Galway	1-13
31.05.98	1st Round	Ruislip, London	2,000	London	1-7	Sligo	0-14
14.06.98	Semi-final	Seán McDermott Park, Carrick	12,000	Leitrim	0-5	Galway	1-16
28.06.98	Semi-final	Hyde Park, Roscommon	15,000	Roscommon	2-12	Sligo	1-15
05.07.98	Semi-final (R)	Markievicz Park, Sligo	12,000	Sligo	0-15	Roscommon	1-13
19.07.98	Final	Tuam Stadium	25,000	Galway	0-11	Roscommon	0-11
01.08.98	Final (R)	Hyde Park, Roscommon	23,000	Galway	1-17	Roscommon	0-17

Leinster

Date	Round	Venue	Attend	Result			
03.05.98	Preliminary	Cusack Park, Mullingar	5,677	Westmeath	1-18	Carlow	2-5
03.05.98	Preliminary	Kennedy Park, New Ross	5,000	Wexford	2-13	Longford	1-16
10.05.98	Preliminary (R)	Pearse Park, Longford	7,500	Longford	0-16	Wexford	2-7
17.05.98	Preliminary	Pearse Park, Longford	10,012	Westmeath	3-14	Longford	1-13
24.05.98	1st Round	Croke Park	§48,856	Meath	3-10	Offaly	0-7
31.05.98	1st Round	O'Rahilly Park, Drogheda	6,000	Louth	3-14	Wicklow	1-11
07.06.98	1st Round	Croke Park	*60,058	Laois	1-15	Westmeath	0-15
07.06.98	1st Round	Croke Park	*	Dublin	0-10	Kildare	0-10
21.06.98	1st Round (R)	Croke Park	58,247	Dublin	1-8	Kildare	0-12
28.06.98	Semi-final	Croke Park	41,384	Meath	0-15	Louth	1-11
19.07.98	Semi-final	Croke Park	25,000	Kildare	2-13	Laois	0-8
02.08.98	Final	Croke Park	62,504	Kildare	1-12	Meath	0-10

Munster

Date	Round	Venue	Attend	Result			
10.05.98	Preliminary	Gaelic Grounds, Limerick	2,730	Limerick	1-12	Tipperary	1-13
30.05.98	1st Round	Clonmel	2,000	Tipperary	1-16	Waterford	0-7
28.06.98	Semi-final	Gaelic Grounds, Limerick	8,738	Tipperary	1-16	Clare	0-12
05.07.98	Semi-final	Fitzgerald Stadium, Killarney	43,994	Kerry	1-14	Cork	1-11
02.08.98	Final	Semple Stadium, Thurles	27,263	Kerry	0-17	Tipperary	1-10

Ulster

Date	Round	Venue	Attend	Result			
17.05.98	Preliminary	Healy Park, Omagh	13,500	Tyrone	2-7	Down	0-15
24.05.98	1st Round	Casement Park, Belfast	6,000	Antrim	0-11	Donegal	1-11
31.05.98	1st Round	Celtic Park, Derry	12,000	Derry	3-13	Monaghan	0-11
07.06.98	1st Round	Breffni Park	12,000	Cavan	0-13	Fermanagh	0-11
14.06.98	1st Round	St Tighearnach's Park, Clones	24,303	Armagh	0-16	Down	0-11
21.06.98	Semi-final	St Tighearnach's Park, Clones	26,811	Donegal	0-15	Cavan	0-13
28.07.98	Semi-final	St Tighearnach's Park, Clones	21,846	Derry	2-13	Armagh	0-12
19.07.98	Final	St Tighearnach's Park, Clones	28,369	Derry	1-7	Donegal	0-8

All Ireland Series

Date	Round	Venue	Attend	Result			
23.08.98	Semi-final	Croke Park	38,569	Galway	0-16	Derry	1-8
30.08.98	Semi-final	Croke Park	65,002	Kildare	0-13	Kerry	1-9
27.09.98	Final	Croke Park	65,886	Galway	1-14	Kildare	1-10

(R)=Replay. §Double header with Offaly v Meath Leinster SHC.

All-Ireland Football Final

CROKE PARK, 27 SEPTEMBER 1998. Attendance: 65,886. **Half time score:** Galway 0-5, Kildare 1-5. **Full-time score:** Galway 1-14, Kildare 1-10. **Booked:** Ken Doyle (Kildare, 48 mins), Glen Ryan (Kildare, 57 mins) and Brian Lacey (KIldare, 59 mins). **Sent off:** None. **Top Scorer:** Padraic Joyce (Galway 1-2, 1 free). **Man-of-the-Match:** Michael Donnellan (Galway). **Referee:** John Bannon (Longford). **Linesmen:** N. Barrett (Cork), B. White (Wexford).

The Teams

GALWAY

Martin McNamara

Tomás Meehan | Gary Fahy | Tomás Mannion

Ray Silke (C) | John Divilly | Seán Óg de Paor 0-2

Kevin Walsh | Seán Ó Domhnaill 0-1

Michael Donnellan 0-2 | Jarlath Fallon 0-3 | Shay Walsh

Derek Savage | Padraic Joyce 1-2 | Niall Finnegan 0-4

Subs: Paul Clancy for S. Walsh (65 mins). Subs not used: Pat Comer, Brian Silke, Richie Fahy, Kevin Fallon, Damien Mitchell, Declan Meehan, Tommy Joyce, Fergal Gavin, Tommy Wilson, Pauric Boyce, Kevin T. MacDonnacha, Michael Geoghegan, Michael Cloherty, Robin Doyle.

Manager: John O'Mahony
Selectors: Stephen Joyce, Peter Warren.

KILDARE

Christy Byrne

Brian Lacey | Seamus Dowling | Ken Doyle

Anthony Rainbow | Glen Ryan (C) | John Finn

Niall Buckley 0-1 | Willie McCreery

Eddie McCormack 0-2 | Declan Kerrigan 0-1 | Dermot Earley 1-1

Martin Lynch | Karl O'Dwyer 0-2 | Padraig Graven

Subs: Pauric Brennan (0-3) for P. Graven (46 mins); Brian Murphy for M. Lynch (58 mins). Subs not used: Paul Flood, Davy Dalton, Martin Ryan, Paul McCormack, Derek Maher, Noel Donlon.

Manager: Mick O'Dwyer
Selectors: Pat Dunny, John Crofton, Pat McCarthy.

Top Scorers 1998 Football Championship

OVERALL

Rank & Name	County	Score	Total Pts
1 Declan Brown	Tipperary	2-29	35
2 Eddie Lohan	Roscommon	1-27	30
3 Padraic Joyce	Galway	1-23	26
4 Padraig Graven	Kildare	1-20	23
5 Niall Finnegan	Galway	1-19	22
6 Maurice Fitzgerald	Kerry	1-18	21
7 Ger Heavin	Westmeath	2-14	20
8 Dessie Barry	Longford	1-16	19
9 Padraig Davies	Longford	0-17	17
10 Paul Taylor	Sligo	0-17	17

INDIVIDUAL

Rank & Name	County	Score	Total Pts
1 Maurice Fitzgerald	Kerry	0-10	v Tipperary
2 Declan Brown	Tipperary	1-7	v Clare
3 Declan Brown	Tipperary	0-9	v Waterford
4 Dessie Barry	Longford	0-9	v Longford
5 Declan Brown	Tipperary	1-6	v Limerick
6 Eddie Lohan	Roscommon	1-6	v Sligo
7 Padraic Joyce	Galway	0-8	v Derry
8 Eddie Lohan	Roscommon	0-8	v Galway
9 Eddie Lohan	Roscommon	0-8	v Galway R
10 Paul Taylor	Sligo	0-8	v Roscommon R
11 Padraig Davis	Longford	0-8	v Wexford

A number of players also scored 1-5 which is equal to eight points.

U21 Results, 1998

FOOTBALL

Connacht Final

18.04.98 .... Galway 0-13 ...... Leitrim 1-7 .... Carrick

Leinster Final

12.04.98 .... Laois 1-13 .... Dublin 1-7 ...... Tullamore

Munster Final

11.04.98 .... Kerry 3-10 ... Tipperary 1-11 .... Tralee

Ulster Final

19.04.98 .... Armagh 1-8 .... Derry 0-10 .... Clones

All Ireland Semi-Final

25.04.98 .... Laois 0-13 .... Galway 1-9 .... Longford
02.05.98 .... Kerry 1-14 .... Armagh 0-9 .. Parnell Park

All-Ireland Final

09.05.98 .... Kerry 2-8 .... Laois 0-11 .... Limerick

HURLING

Munster Final

23.08.98 .... Cork 3-18 .... Tipperary 1-10 .... Cork

Leinster Final

19.07.98 .... Kilkenny 2-10 ... Dublin 0-12 .... Carlow

Ulster Final

18.07.98 .... Antrim 3-20 .... Down 4-8 .... Belfast

All Ireland Semi-Final

29.08.98 .... Galway 4-18 ... Kilkenny 3-7 .... Thurles
05.09.98 .... Cork 3-15 .... Antrim 0-11 .. Parnell Park

All-Ireland Final

20.09.98 .... Cork 2-15 .... Galway 2-10 .... Thurles

U18 Results, 1998

FOOTBALL

Connacht Final

19.07.98..Leitrim 0-8 ....Galway 0-7................Tuam

Leinster Final

02.08.98..Laois 2-9 ....Dublin 0-12........Croke Park

Munster Final

02.08.98..Kerry 2-11 ....Limerick 0-8.............Thurles

Ulster Final

19.07.98..Tyrone 4-9...........Antrim 2-2..............Clones

All Ireland Semi-Finals

23.08.98..Tyrone 1-14 ....Leitrim 1-3........Croke Park
30.08.98..Laois 1-10.............Kerry 2-5........Croke Park

All-Ireland Final

27.09.98 Tyrone 2-11.........Laois 0-11........Croke Park

HURLING

Leinster Final

05.07.98..Kilkenny 1-11..Wexford 1-11........Croke Park
18.07.98..Kilkenny 2-15....Wexford 0-6.............Carlow

Munster Final

12.07.98..Cork 3-13.............Clare 0-8.............Thurles

Ulster Final

05.07.98..Antrim 3-9............Derry 0-8 ....Casement Pk

All-Ireland Quarter Final

26.07.98..Galway 1-12...........Clare 2-8........Croke Park
25.07.98..Wexford 2-14.......Antrim 1-9..........Drogheda

All Ireland Semi-Finals

09.08.98..Cork 0-12 ....Wexford 0-10........Croke Park
16.08.98..Kilkenny 2-10...Galway 1-12........Croke Park

All-Ireland Final

13.09.98..Cork 2-15 ....Kilkenny 1-9.......Croke Park

National Hurling League Results

08.03.98: 1A: Clare 3-21, Antrim 2-7; Dublin 1-13, Galway 1-9; Offaly 0-13, Limerick 2-11. **1B:** Cork 0-16, Kilkenny 1-8; Tipperary 1-14, Waterford 1-17; Wexford 1-14, Laois 1-11. **2A:** Armagh 1-5, Derry 3-12; Carlow 2-13, Kerry 3-8; Monaghan 1-8, Wicklow 0-16. **2B:** Louth 0-10, Kildare 4-17; Tyrone 1-8, Meath 3-12; Westmeath 1-7, Down 1-9. **3:** Cavan 1-9, Donegal 0-8; Fermanagh 0-8, Leitrim 0-9; Longford 3-6, Mayo 2-11.

22.03.98: 1A: Antrim 2-11, Dublin 1-8; Galway 3-15, Offaly 1-12; Limerick 2-11, Clare 0-12. **1B:** Kilkenny 0-15, Wexford 0-9; Laois 1-13, Tipperary 1-13; Waterford 1-5, Cork 1-12. **2A:** Derry 2-12, Roscommon 1-12; Kerry 5-21, Armagh 0-11; Wicklow 1-14, Carlow 2-9. **2B:** Down 8-27, Louth 2-1; Kildare 0-15, London 2-10; Meath 2-6, Westmeath 1-10. **3:** Donegal 0-11, Sligo 3-5; Leitrim 0-7, Cavan 1-4; Mayo 0-14, Fermanagh 1-8.

29.03.98: 1A: Dublin 2-8, Clare 1-18; Galway 1-9, Limerick 1-10; Offaly 3-13, Antrim 0-9. **1B:** Laois 1-9, Waterford 4-11; Tipperary 3-13, Kilkenny 1-13; Wexford 1-11, Cork 1-11. **2A:** Armagh 0-2, Wicklow 3-13; Monaghan 0-3, Derry 5-16; Roscommon 2-12, Kerry 1-17. **2B:** London 0-8, Down 2-14; Louth 2-6, Meath 2-21; Tyrone 2-8, Kildare 0-10. **3:** Cavan 2-5, Mayo 1-7; Longford 0-13, Donegal 1-6; Sligo 1-5, Leitrim 2-5.

05.04.98: 2A: Derry 0-12, Carlow 1-15; Kerry 4-20, Monaghan 0-7; Wicklow 0-13, Roscommon 1-7. **2B:** Down 2-20, Tyrone 1-7; Kildare p-p Westmeath; Meath 2-12, London 2-14. **3:** Donegal 1-6, Fermanagh 2-9; Mayo 2-11, Sligo 1-2.

12.04.98: 1A: Antrim 1-12, Galway 2-19; Clare 1-13, Offaly 1-11; Limerick 0-11, Dublin 1-6. **1B:** Cork 2-11, Tipperary 2-10; Kilkenny 1-5, Laois 0-13; Waterford 0-13, Wexford 0-13.

16.04.98: 2B: Kildare 0-8, Westmeath 5-13.

19.04.98: 1A: Clare 0-19, Galway 2-15; Dublin 4-10, Offaly 1-13; Limerick 2-14, Antrim 2-8. **1B:** Cork 1-13, Laois 1-8; Waterford 2-18, Kilkenny 2-13; Wexford 2-13, Tipperary 0-10. **2A:** Derry 2-8, Wicklow 0-13; Monaghan 2-7, Armagh 1-8; Roscommon 1-4, Carlow 2-10. **2B:** Kildare 1-9, Meath 1-7; London 1-8, Westmeath 4-5; Tyrone 1-11, Louth 2-6. **3:** Donegal 1-2, Mayo 6-18; Longford 2-6, Cavan 2-11; Sligo 0-6, Fermanagh 1-13.

26.04.98: 2A: Armagh 0-7, Roscommon 4-12.

03-04.05.98: 2A: Carlow 5-16, Monaghan 0-6; Wicklow 0-15, Kerry 2-17. **2B:** Meath 2-11, Down 3-13; Westmeath 9-25, Tyrone 0-2; London bt Louth. **3:** Cavan 5-16, Sligo 0-5; Fermanagh 1-11, Longford 0-8; Mayo 2-18, Leitrim 1-3.

09-10.5.98: 2A: Carlow 5-25, Armagh 0-8; Kerry 2-16, Derry 1-13; Roscommon 3-6, Monaghan 3-9. **2B:** Down 4-17, Kildare 0-5; London 2-16, Tyrone 1-4; Westmeath 1-20, Louth 3-5. **3:** Fermanagh 1-3, Cavan 1-15; Leitrim 1-12, Donegal 2-5; Sligo 1-7, Longford 3-13.

17.5.98: 3 Longford 2-11, Leitrim 0-5.

KNOCKOUT STAGES

03.05.98: Semi-finals: Clare 0-10, Cork 2-15; Limerick 2-11, Tipperary 2-17.

17.05.98: Final: Cork 2-14, Waterford 0-13.

National Football League Results

19.10.97: Section A: Laois 2-11, Carlow 0-15; Mayo 1-10, Fermanagh 0-10; Galway 1-14, Leitrim 0-8; Kilkenny 2-3, Louth 3-17. **Section B:** Armagh 5-18, Antrim 2-7; Derry 0-10, Westmeath 0-10; Donegal 1-12, Longford 2-7; Meath 4-17, London 0-7. **Section C:** Kerry 1-12, Cavan 0-8; Offaly 1-12, Monaghan 1-8; Sligo 2-7, Dublin 0-12; Tyrone 2-16, Wexford 2-3. **Section D:** Clare 1-11, Roscommon 1-11; Cork 4-17, Tipperary 3-5; Waterford 2-5, Kildare 0-16; Wicklow 1-10, Down 0-10.

02.11.97: Section A: Laois 2-15, Kilkenny 0-6; Leitrim 2-9, Carlow 0-7; Louth 2-12, Fermanagh 3-8; Mayo 1-9, Galway 0-12. **Section B:** Armagh 4-17, London 0-3; Donegal 2-14, Derry 1-9; Longford 1-14, Antrim 3-5; Meath 2-16, Westmeath 0-12. **Section C:** Kerry 1-7, Wexford 0-5; Monaghan 2-8, Cavan 1-8; Offaly 1-11, Dublin 1-8; Tyrone 0-16, Sligo 0-12. **Section D:** Cork 0-14, Waterford 1-7; Down 2-10, Tipperary 1-7; Kildare 2-15, Limerick 1-6; Roscommon 1-7, Wicklow 0-10.

16.11.97: Section A: Galway 0-10, Laois 1-7; Leitrim 2-12, Fermanagh 2-7; Louth 1-15, Carlow 2-9; Mayo 2-17, Kilkenny 1-5. **Section B:** Armagh 3-1, Donegal 0-12; Derry 2-15, London 1-5; Longford 2-8, Westmeath 1-10; Meath 2-18, Antrim 1-8. **Section C:** Dublin 1-9, Wexford 0-4; Offaly 0-9, Kerry 1-4; Sligo 1-11, Monaghan 1-11; Tyrone 0-15, Cavan 0-9. **Section D:** Cork 0-13, Clare 0-8; Down 0-12, Waterford 0-5; Kildare 2-9, Tipperary 1-11; Roscommon 2-15, Limerick 0-7.

30.11.97: Section A: Laois 0-9, Fermanagh 0-8; Leitrim 3-20, Kilkenny 0-4; Louth 1-9, Galway 1-12. **Section B:** Antrim 1-8, Derry 0-14; Donegal 1-8, Meath 1-8; London 2-7, Longford 3-12; Westmeath 2-6, Armagh 1-11. **Section C:** Dublin 2-14, Cavan 0-8; Kerry 1-7, Sligo 0-11; Monaghan 2-13, Wexford 1-8; Tyrone 1-8, Offaly 1-10. **Section D:** Down 1-13, Cork 1-2; Kildare 0-13, Wicklow 0-10; Limerick 0-6, Clare 0-21; Roscommon 2-14, Waterford 0-6.

07.12.97: Section D: Cork 1-12, Limerick 0-7; Tipperary 1-7, Roscommon 0-7; Wicklow 2-4, Clare 1-10.

14.12.97: Section D: Down 0-12, Kildare 1-8.

01.02.98: Section D: Clare 1-8, Down 0-10; Kildare 0-8, Cork 0-9; Limerick 1-8, Wicklow 0-8; Waterford 0-7, Tipperary 2-12.

08.02.98: Section A: Mayo 0-14, Carlow 0-4.

15.02.98: Section A: Carlow 3-6, Kilkenny 1-9; Fermanagh 1-8, Galway 1-19; Laois 1-11, Louth 1-10; Mayo 1-9, Leitrim 0-9. **Section B:** Donegal 2-11, Westmeath 2-8; London 0-11, Antrim 3-9; Longford 0-10, Derry 0-13; Meath 1-7, Armagh 1-8. **Section C:** Cavan 4-11, Wexford 1-11; Dublin 0-12, Monaghan 2-12; Kerry 1-6, Tyrone 1-9; Sligo 0-12, Offaly 1-9. **Section D:** Cork 0-13, Roscommon 1-6; Kildare 1-15, Clare 0-13; Limerick 0-7, Tipperary 1-11; Wicklow 2-16, Waterford 2-6.

01.03.98: Section A: Galway 3-17, Carlow 0-4; Kilkenny 2-5, Fermanagh 3-14; Leitrim 2-7, Laois 2-7; Mayo 1-8, Louth 1-6. **Section B:** Antrim 0-7, Donegal 1-15; Armagh 2-15, Longford 0-12; Derry 1-7, Meath 0-7; Westmeath 3-19, London 1-6. **Section C:** Monaghan 0-10, Kerry 2-9; Offaly 1-11, Cavan 0-11; Tyrone 1-13, Dublin 1-7; Wexford 1-10, Sligo 0-15. **Section D:** Clare 1-20, Waterford 1-4; Down 0-19, Limerick 1-6; Roscommon 0-11, Kildare 1-10; Tipperary 0-11, Wicklow 3-7.

15.03.98: Section A: Carlow 2-7, Fermanagh 1-10; Kilkenny 0-6, Galway 1-18; Louth 1-7, Leitrim 2-6; Mayo 1-14, Laois 2-10. **Section B:** Derry 1-15, Armagh 2-10; London 1-6, Donegal 2-15; Longford 1-9, Meath 1-18; Westmeath 1-12, Antrim 0-9. **Section C:** Cavan 2-9, Sligo 0-9; Dublin 0-18, Kerry 1-3; Tyrone 0-11, Monaghan 2-6; Wexford 0-11, Offaly 1-16; **Section D:** Roscommon 1-7, Down 1-12; Waterford 3-9, Limerick 2-12; Wicklow 1-12, Cork 1-11.

05.04.98: Section D: Clare 0-7, Tipperary 1-7.

Quarter-finals: 05.04.98: Donegal 2-14, Cork 1-9; Down 1-8, Monaghan 2-6; Mayo 0-10, Derry 1-9; Offaly 1-11, Galway 0-10.

Semi-finals: 12.04.98: Derry 1-12, Monaghan 0-8; Donegal 1-14, Offaly 3-10.

Final: 26.04.98: Offaly 0-9, Derry 0-7.

National Hurling League final tables 1997/98

DIVISION 1A	P	W	D	L	Pts
Limerick	5	5	0	0	10
Clare	5	3	0	2	6
Galway	5	3	0	2	6
Dublin	5	2	0	3	4
Offaly	5	1	0	4	2
Antrim	5	1	0	4	2

DIVISION 1B	P	W	D	L	Pts
Cork	5	4	1	0	9
Waterford	5	3	1	1	7
Wexford	5	2	2	1	6
Tipperary	5	1	1	3	3
Laois	5	1	1	3	3
Kilkenny	5	1	0	4	2

DIVISION 2A	P	W	D	L	Pts
Kerry	6	5	0	1	10
Carlow	6	5	0	1	10
Wicklow	6	4	0	2	8
Derry	6	4	0	2	8
Monaghan	6	2	0	4	4
Roscommon	6	1	0	5	2
Armagh	6	0	0	6	0

DIVISION 2B	P	W	D	L	Pts
Down	6	6	0	0	12
Westmeath	6	5	0	1	10
London	6	4	0	2	8
Tyrone	6	2	0	4	4
Meath	6	2	0	4	4
Kildare	6	2	0	4	4
Louth	6	0	0	6	0

DIVISION 3	P	W	D	L	Pts
Cavan	6	5	1	0	11
Mayo	6	5	0	1	10
Leitrim	6	3	1	2	7
Fermanagh	6	3	0	3	6
Longford	6	3	0	3	6
Sligo	6	1	0	5	2
Donegal	6	0	0	6	0

National Football League final tables 1997/98

SECTION A

	P	W	D	L	Scr	Con	Ave	Pts
Mayo	7	6	1	0	7-81	4-56	1.5	13
Galway	7	5	2	0	7-102	4-51	1.952	12
Laois	7	4	2	1	10-70	4-70	1.219	10
Leitrim	7	4	1	2	11-71	7-55	1.368	9
Louth	7	3	0	4	10-76	12-57	1.139	6
Fermanagh	7	1	1	5	10-65	10-74	1.01	3
Carlow	7	1	1	5	7-52	11-82	0.634	3
Kilkenny	7	0	0	7	6-38	17-107	0.354	0

SECTION B

	P	W	D	L	Scr	Con	Ave	Pts
Donegal	7	6	1	0	9-87	10-46	1.5	13
Derry	7	5	1	1	5-83	6-64	1.195	11
Armagh	7	5	0	2	18-80	6-62	1.717	10
Meath	7	4	1	2	11-91	5-59	1.675	9
Longford	7	3	0	4	9-72	10-80	0.918	6
Westmeath	7	2	1	4	9-77	8-71	1.094	5
Antrim	7	1	0	6	10-53	10-102	0.628	2
London	7	0	0	7	5-45	21-104	0.359	0

SECTION C

	P	W	D	L	Scr	Con	Ave	Pts
Offaly	7	6	1	0	6-78	4-62	1.297	13
Monaghan	7	4	1	2	10-68	6-71	1.101	9
Dublin	7	4	0	3	5-80	7-48	1.376	8
Tyrone	7	4	0	3	5-78	7-53	1.256	8
Sligo	7	3	2	2	3-77	6-74	0.934	8
Kerry	7	3	0	4	8-48	1-70	0.986	6
Cavan	7	2	0	5	7-64	7-78	0.841	4
Wexford	7	0	0	7	5-52	11-87	0.558	0

SECTION D

	P	W	D	L	Scr	Con	Ave	Pts
Down	8	6	0	2	4-98	7-53	1.486	12
Cork	8	6	0	2	7-100	7-66	1.39	12
Kildare	8	6	0	2	7-94	4-77	1.292	12
Clare	8	4	1	3	4-98	6-70	1.25	9
Wicklow	8	4	1	3	9-77	6-76	1.106	9
Tipperary	8	4	0	4	10-71	11-71	0.971	8
Roscommon	8	2	2	4	8-78	4-76	1.159	6
Limerick	8	1	1	6	5-59	9-119	0.506	3
Waterford	8	0	1	7	9-49	9-116	0.531	1

All-Ireland Club Championships

FOOTBALL

Connacht Final

Corofin, Galway ...2-10 Allen Gaels, Leitrim............0-11

Leinster Final

Erin's Isle, Dublin .0-11 Strabannon Parnell's, Louth .0-8

Munster Final

Castlehaven, Cork1-14 Fethard, Tipperary 1-8

Ulster Final

Dungiven, Derry...0-14 Errigal Ciaran, Tyrone 1-8

All Ireland Quarter-Final

Castlehaven.......0-15 Tir Chonaill Gaels, London ..0-8

All Ireland Semi-Final

Erin's Isle ....2-12 Castlehaven 0-17

Corofin .... 0-11 Dungiven 0-9

All-Ireland Final

Corofin ....0-15 Erin's Isle 0-10

HURLING

Connacht Final

Sarsfields, Galway ...5-15 Tooreen, Mayo 1-5

Leinster Final

Birr, Offaly ....0-11 Castletown, Laois...........0-5

Munster Final

Clarecastle, Clare ....2-11 Patrickswell, Limerick ...0-15

Ulster Final

Dunloy, Antrim..........3-16 Lavey, Derry 4-10

All Ireland Quarter-Final

Clarecastle ....2-24 St Gabriel's, London.......1-7

All Ireland Semi-Finals

Birr...........................1-15 Clarecastle ....3-9 (Draw)

Sarsfields ....3-14 Dunloy ....4-11 (Draw)

Birr...........................0-12 Clarecastle ....0-11 aet

Sarsfields ....1-15 Dunloy 1-11

All-Ireland Final

Birr...........................1-13 Sarsfields 0-9

Third Level Results, 1998

HURLING

Fitzgibbon Cup

Semi-Finals: UCC ....3-14 UCD 1-6

Waterford IT 1-11 Garda College 1-9

Final: ....UCC ....2-17 Waterford IT 0-13

Ryan Cup

Final: ....DCU ....3-8 Limerick IT.................2-8

FOOTBALL

Sigerson Cup

Semi-Finals: UUJ ....1-8 Queen's 2-3

IT Tralee ....2-12 Athlone IT.......................0-6

Final: ....IT Tralee ......0-10 UUJ 0-8

Trench Cup

Final: ....UCC ....4-4 Cork IT 2-7

Railway Cup 1998, Football

25.01.98 SEMI-FINAL: Fitzgerald Stadium, Killarney. Leinster 2-8, Munster 0-12.

Leinster: C. Byrne (Kildare), C. Daly (Offaly), D. Fay (Meath), M. O'Reilly (Meath), D. Lalor (Laois), G. O'Neill (Louth), F. Cullen (Offaly 0-1), J. McDermott (Meath 0-1), N. Buckley (Kildare 0-1), C. Whelan (Dublin 1- 0), B. Stynes (Dublin), D. Darcy (Dublin 0-2, both frees), V. Claffey (Offaly), T. Dowd (Meath 1-1), K. O'Brien (Wicklow 0-2). **Subs:** G. Ryan (Kildare) for O'Reilly (half-time), P. Brady (Offaly) for Claffey (39 mins), S. Grennan (Offaly) for Darcy (56 mins).

Munster: D. O'Keeffe (Kerry), B. Keating (Clare), B. O'Shea (Kerry), S. Stack (Kerry), S. Moynihan (Kerry 0-1), L. Flaherty (Kerry), E. Breen (Kerry), D. Ó Sé (Kerry 0-1), F. Collins (Cork), J. Kavanagh (Cork 0-6, four frees), F. McInerney (Clare), D. Foley (Tipperary), M.F. Russell (Kerry), P. Hegarty (Cork), M. Daly (Clare 0-2 both frees).

Subs: J. Crowley (Kerry) for Hegarty (21 mins), W. Kirby (Kerry) for Collins (half-time), D. Ó Cinnéide (Kerry) for Foley (41 mins).

25.01.98 SEMI-FINAL: Dr Hyde Park Roscommon. Connacht 0-15, Ulster 0-15 (aet)
Connacht: P. Burke (Mayo), K. Mortimer (Mayo), G. Fahy (Galway), F. Costello (Mayo), D. Heaney (Mayo), J. Nallen (Mayo), S. de Paor (Galway 0-2), P. Fallon (Mayo), D. Brady (Mayo), L. Dowd (Roscommon 0-1), E. O'Hara (Sligo 0-1), C. McManaman (Mayo 0-1), C. McDonald (Mayo), A. Cullen (Leitrim 0-3), P. Taylor (Sligo 0-5, all frees). **Subs:** J. Horan (Mayo 0-2) for McDonald (38 mins), B. Walshe (Sligo) for Dowd (53 mins), D. Donlon (Roscommon) for Horan (71 mins), D. Mitchell (Galway) for Brady (87 mins).
Ulster: F. McConnell (Tyrone), P. Devlin (Tyrone), J.J. Doherty (Donegal), G. Coleman (Derry), N. Hegarty (Donegal), H. Downey (Derry), K. McGeeney (Armagh), J. Burns (Armagh), D. McCabe (Cavan 0-3, two frees), P. Reilly (Cavan), P. Canavan (Tyrone), P. McGrane (Armagh 0-1), R. Gallagher (Fermanagh 0-3, two frees), T. Boyle (Donegal 0-6, five frees), M. Linden (Down). **Subs:** A. Tohill (Derry) for Linden (37 mins), J. McGuinness (Donegal) for Reilly (56 mins), G. Cavlan (Tyrone 0-2) for Gallagher (59 mins), C. Lawn (Tyrone) for Doherty (76 mins), P. Brewster (Fermanagh) for Hegarty (76 mins).

01.02.98 SEMI-FINAL REPLAY: St. Tiergnach's Park, Clones. Ulster 0-20, Connacht 1-14 (aet)
Ulster: F. McConnell (Tyrone), P. Devlin (Tyrone), C. Lawn (Tyrone), J.J. Doherty (Donegal), N. Hegarty (Donegal 0-1), H. Downey (Derry), K. McGeeney (Armagh), J. Burns (Armagh), A. Tohill (Derry), D. McCabe (Cavan 0-1, free), G. Cavlan (Tyrone 0-3, one free), P. McGrane (Armagh), P. Reilly (Cavan), T. Boyle (Donegal 0-12, 10 frees), P. Canavan (Tyrone). **Subs:** D. Marsden (Armagh 0-1) for Reilly (37 mins), P. Brewster (Fermanagh) for Burns (50 mins), J. McGuinness (Donegal 0-2) for McCabe (48 mins), Reilly for McGrane (84 mins).
Connacht: P. Burke (Mayo), K. Mortimer (Mayo), G. Fahy (Galway), F. Costello (Mayo), D. Donlon (Roscommon), D. Mitchell (Galway), S. de Paor (Galway), P. Fallon (Mayo 0-1), J. Nallen (Mayo), A. Rooney (Leitrim 0-1), E. O'Hara (Sligo 0-2), C. McManaman (Mayo 0-2), M. Sheridan (Mayo 0-5, four frees), A. Cullen (Leitrim 0-2), L. Dowd (Roscommon 1-0). **Subs:** B. Walsh (Sligo 0-1) for Rooney (45 mins), K. Murray (Leitrim) for Donlon (76 mins), B. Kilcoyne (Sligo) for Walsh (87 mins).

08.02.98 FINAL: St Tiergnach's Park, Clones. Ulster 0-20, Leinster 0-17 (aet)
Ulster: F. McConnell (Tyrone), J.J. Doherty (Donegal), C. Lawn (Tyrone), P. Devlin (Tyrone), K. McGeeney (Armagh), H. Downey (Derry), N. Hegarty (Donegal), J. Burns (Armagh), A. Tohill (Derry), J. McGuinness (Donegal), G. Cavlan (Tyrone 0-4, one free, one 45), P. McGrane (Armagh 0-2), D. McCabe (Cavan 0-4, three frees, one sideline), T. Boyle (Donegal 0-6, all frees), P. Canavan (Tyrone 0-3, one penalty). **Subs:** G. Coleman (Derry 0-1) for Lawn (10 mins), P. Brewster (Fermanagh) for Burns (42 mins), M. Linden (Down) for McGuinness (52 mins), J. McGuinness (Donegal) for McGrane (81 mins), D. Marsden (Armagh) for Boyle (84 mins), B Morris (Cavan) (91 mins).
Leinster: C. Byrne (Kildare), C. Daly (Offaly), D. Fay (Meath), M. O'Reilly (Meath), D. Lalor (Laois 0-2), G. O'Neill (Louth), F. Cullen (Offaly), J. McDermott (Meath), N. Buckley (Kildare), C. Whelan (Dublin 0-2), B. Stynes (Dublin), T. Giles (Meath 0-4, three frees), T. Dowd (Meath 0-2), D. Darcy (Dublin 0-4), K. O'Brien (Wicklow 0-3). **Subs:** S. Grennan (Offaly) for Stynes (47 mins), G. Geraghty (Meath) for Whelan (53 mins), P. Brady (Offaly) for Darcy (60 mins), K. Reilly (Louth) for Buckley (69 mins), V. Claffey (Offaly) for Grennan (75 mins), J. Kenny (Offaly) for O'Reilly (75 mins).

Railway Cup 1997, Hurling Final

09.11.97 FINAL: Ballinasloe, Co. Galway. Munster 0-14, Leinster 0-10
Munster: D. Fitzgerald (Clare), S. McDonagh (Limerick), B. Lohan (Clare), M. Ryan (Tipperary), D. Clarke (Limerick), L. Doyle (Clare), T. Brown (Waterford), O. Moran (Limerick), C. Lynch (Clare, 0-1), T. Dunne (Tipperary, 0-1), K. McGrath (Waterford, 0-2), M. Galligan (Limerick, 0-7 6 frees), M. Cleary (Tipperary), N. Gilligan (Clare, 0-2), S. McGrath (Cork, 0-1). **Subs:** C. Bonnar (Tipperary), for O. Moran; D. Forde (Clare) for M. Cleary.
Leinster: R. Cashin (Laois), B. Maher (Laois), S. Power (Dublin), L. Simpson (Kilkenny), N. Rigney (Offaly), C. Byrne (Kildare), R. Boland (Dublin), A. Comerford (Kilkenny), O. Dowling (Laois), Johnny Dooley (Offaly, 0-10, 9 frees), D. Rooney (Laois), C. McCann (Dublin), R. McCarthy (Wexford), C. Brennan (Kilkenny), C. Carter (Kilkenny). **Subs:** G. Ennis (Dublin), for McCann; C. Cassidy (Offaly) for Byrne; J. Troy (Offaly) for Rooney.
Referee: Jimmy Cooney (Galway).

ALL-IRELAND FINAL RESULTS SINCE 1887

	HURLING					FOOTBALL				
Year	**Winners**			**Runners Up**	**Attend.**	**Winners**			**Runners Up**	**Attend.**
1887	Tipperary	1-1	0-0	Galway	-	Limerick	1-4	0-3	Louth	-
1888	C'ship unfinished					C'ship unfinished				
1889	Dublin	5-1	1-6	Clare	-	Tipperary	3-6	0-0	Laois	-
1890	Cork	1-6	2-2	Wexford	-	Cork	2-4	0-1	Wexford	-
1891	Kerry	2-3	1-5	Wexford	-	Dublin	2-1	1-9*	Cork	-
1892	Cork	2-4	1-1†	Dublin	-	Dublin	1-4	0-3	Kerry	-
1893	Cork	6-8	0-2	Kilkenny	-	Wexford	1-1	0-2	Cork	-
1894	Cork	5-20	2-0	Dublin	-	Dublin	0-5	1-2†	Cork	-
1895	Tipperary	6-8	1-10	Kilkenny	-	Tipperary	0-4	0-3	Meath	-
1896	Tipperary	8-14	0-4	Dublin	-	Limerick	1-5	0-7	Dublin	-
1897	Limerick	3-4	2-4	Kilkenny	-	Dublin	2-6	0-2	Cork	-
1898	Tipperary	7-13	3-10	Kilkenny	-	Dublin	2-8	0-4	Waterford	-
1899	Tipperary	3-12	1-4	Wexford	-	Dublin	1-10	0-6	Cork	-
1900	*Tipperary*	*6-13*	*1-5*	*Galway*	-	*Tipperary*	*2-20*	*0-1*	*Galway*	-
1900	Tipperary	2-5	0-6	London	-	Tipperary	3-7	0-2	London	-
1901	*Cork*	*2-8*	*0-6*	*Wexford*	-	*Dublin*	*1-2*	*0-4*	*Cork*	-
1901	London	1-5	0-4	Cork	-	Dublin	0-14	0-2	London	-
1902	*Cork*	*2-6*	*0-1*	*Dublin*	-	*Dublin*	*0-6*	*0-5*	*Tipperary*	-
1902	Cork	2-13	0-0	London	-	Dublin	2-8	0-4	London	-
1903	*Cork*	*8-9*	*0-8*	*Kilkenny*	-	*Kerry*	*0-8*	*0-2*	*Kildare*	-
1903	Cork	3-16	1-1	London	-	Kerry	**0-8**	**0-2§**	Kildare	-
1904	Kilkenny	1-9	1-8	Cork	-	Kerry	0-5	0-2	Dublin	-
1905	Kilkenny	**7-7**	**2-9**	Cork	-	Kildare	1-7	0-5	Kerry	-
1906	Tipperary	3-16	3-8	Dublin	-	Dublin	0-5	0-4	Cork	-
1907	Kilkenny	3-12	4-8	Cork	-	Dublin	0-5	0-4	Cork	-
1908	Tipperary	**3-15**	**1-5**	Dublin	-	Dublin	1-10	0-4	London	-
1909	Kilkenny	4-6	0-12	Tipperary	-	Kerry	1-9	0-6	Louth	-
1910	Wexford	7-0	6-2	Limerick	-	Louth	w.o		Kerry	-
1911	Kilkenny	3-3	2-1	Tipperary	-	Cork	6-6	1-2	Antrim	-
1912	Kilkenny	2-1	1-3	Cork	18,000	Louth	1-7	1-2	Antrim	13,000
1913	Kilkenny	2-4	1-2	Tipperary	15,000	Kerry	2-2	0-3	Wexford	17,000
1914	Clare	5-1	1-0	Laois	12,000	Kerry	**2-3**	**0-6**	Wexford	20,000
1915	Laois	6-2	4-1	Cork	15,000	Wexford	2-4	2-1	Kerry	27,000
1916	Tipperary	5-4	3-2	Kilkenny	5,000	Wexford	2-4	1-2	Mayo	3,000
1917	Dublin	5-4	4-2	Tipperary	11,000	Wexford	0-9	0-5	Clare	6,500
1918	Limerick	9-5	1-3	Wexford	12,000	Wexford	0-5	0-4	Tipperary	12,000
1919	Cork	6-4	2-4	Dublin	32,000	Kildare	2-5	0-1	Galway	32,000
1920	Dublin	4-9	4-3	Cork	22,000	Tipperary	1-6	1-2	Dublin	17,000
1921	Limerick	8-5	3-2	Dublin	18,000	Dublin	0-6	0-4	Galway	11,792
1922	Kilkenny	4-2	2-6	Tipperary	26,119	Dublin	0-6	0-4	Galway	11,792
1923	Galway	7-3	4-5	Limerick	21,000	Dublin	1-5	1-3	Kerry	20,000
1924	Dublin	5-3	2-6	Galway	9,000	Kerry	0-4	0-3	Dublin	28,844
1925	Tipperary	5-6	1-5	Galway	23,000	Galway	3-2	1-2	Cavan	17,800
1926	Cork	4-6	2-0	Kilkenny	25,000	Kerry	1-4	0-4	Kildare	35,500
1927	Dublin	4-8	1-3	Cork	23,824	Kildare	0-5	0-3	Kerry	36,529
1928	Cork	6-12	1-0	Galway	15,259	Kildare	2-6	2-5	Cavan	24,700
1929	Cork	4-9	1-3	Galway	14,000	Kerry	1-8	1-5	Kildare	43,839
1930	Tipperary	2-7	1-3	Dublin	21,730	Kerry	3-11	0-2	Monaghan	33,280
1931	Cork	**5-8**	**3-4§**	Kilkenny	31,935	Kerry	1-11	0-8	Kildare	42,350
1932	Kilkenny	3-3	2-3	Clare	34,392	Kerry	2-7	2-4	Mayo	25,816
1933	Kilkenny	1-7	0-6	Limerick	45,176	Cavan	2-5	1-4	Galway	45,188
1934	Limerick	5-2	2-6	Dublin	30,250	Galway	3-5	1-9	Dublin	36,143
1935	Kilkenny	2-5	2-4	Limerick	46,591	Cavan	3-6	2-5	Kildare	50,380
1936	Limerick	5-6	1-5	Kilkenny	51,235	Mayo	4-11	0-5	Laois	50,168
1937	Tipperary	3-11	0-3	Kilkenny	43,638	Kerry	**4-4**	**1-7**	Cavan	51,234
1938	Dublin	2-5	1-6	Waterford	37,129	Galway	**2-4**	**0-7**	Kerry	47,581
1939	Kilkenny	2-7	3-3	Cork	39,302	Kerry	2-5	2-3	Meath	46,828
1940	Limerick	3-7	1-7	Kilkenny	49,260	Kerry	0-7	1-3	Galway	60,821
1941	Cork	5-11	0-6	Dublin	26,150	Kerry	1-8	0-7	Galway	45,512
1942	Cork	2-14	3-4	Dublin	27,313	Dublin	1-10	1-8	Galway	37,105

Continued from previous page

Year	HURLING Winners			Runners Up	Attend.	FOOTBALL Winners			Runners Up	Attend.
1943	Cork	5-16	0-4	Antrim	48,843	Roscommon	**2-7**	**2-2**	Cavan	47,193
1944	Cork	2-13	1-2	Dublin	26,896	Roscommon	1-9	2-4	Kerry	79,245
1945	Tipperary	5-6	3-6	Kilkenny	69,459	Cork	2-5	0-7	Cavan	67,329
1946	Cork	7-5	3-8	Kilkenny	64,415	Kerry	**2-8**	**0-10**	Roscommon	65,661
1947	Kilkenny	0-14	2-7	Cork	61,510	Cavan	2-11	2-7	Kerry	34,941
1948	Waterford	6-7	4-2	Dublin	61,742	Cavan	4-5	4-4	Mayo	74,645
1949	Tipperary	3-11	0-3	Laois	67,168	Meath	1-10	1-6	Cavan	79,460
1950	Tipperary	1-9	1-8	Kilkenny	67,629	Mayo	2-5	1-6	Louth	76,174
1951	Tipperary	7-7	3-9	Wexford	68,515	Mayo	2-8	0-9	Meath	78,201
1952	Cork	2-14	0-7	Dublin	64,332	Cavan	**0-9**	**0-5**	Meath	62,515
1953	Cork	3-3	0-8	Galway	71,195	Kerry	0-13	1-6	Armagh	86,155
1954	Cork	1-9	1-6	Wexford	84,856	Meath	1-13	1-7	Kerry	75,276
1955	Wexford	3-13	2-8	Galway	72,854	Kerry	0-12	1-6	Dublin	87,102
1956	Wexford	2-14	2-8	Cork	83,096	Galway	2-13	3-7	Cork	70772
1957	Kilkenny	4-10	3-12	Waterford	70,594	Louth	1-9	1-7	Cork	72,732
1958	Tipperary	4-9	2-5	Galway	47,276	Dublin	2-12	1-9	Derry	73,371
1959	Waterford	3-12	1-10	Kilkenny	77,285	Kerry	3-7	1-4	Galway	85,897
1960	Wexford	2-15	0-11	Tipperary	77,154	Down	2-10	0-8	Kerry	87,768
1961	Tipperary	0-16	1-12	Dublin	67,866	Down	3-6	2-8	Offaly	90,556
1962	Tipperary	3-10	2-11	Wexford	75,039	Kerry	1,12	1-4	Roscommon	75,771
1963	Kilkenny	4-17	6-8	Waterford	73,123	Dublin	1-9	0-10	Galway	87,106
1964	Tipperary	5-13	2-8	Kilkenny	71,282	Galway	0-15	0-10	Kerry	76,498
1965	Tipperary	2-16	0-10	Wexford	67,498	Galway	0-12	0-9	Kerry	77,735
1966	Cork	3-9	1-10	Kilkenny	68,249	Galway	1-10	0-7	Meath	71,569
1967	Kilkenny	3-8	2-7	Tipperary	64,241	Meath	1-9	0-9	Cork	70,343
1968	Wexford	5-8	3-12	Tipperary	63,461	Down	2-12	1-13	Kerry	71,294
1969	Kilkenny	2-15	2-9	Cork	66,844	Kerry	0-10	0-7	Offaly	67,828
1970	Cork	6-21	5-10	Wexford	65,062	Kerry	2-19	0-18	Meath	71,775
1971	Tipperary	5-17	5-14	Kilkenny	61,393	Offaly	1-14	2-8	Galway	70,789
1972	Kilkenny	3-24	5-11	Cork	66,137	Offaly	**1-19**	**0-13**	Kerry	66,136
1973	Limerick	1-21	1-14	Kilkenny	58,009	Cork	3-17	2-13	Galway	73,308
1974	Kilkenny	3-19	1-13	Limerick	62,071	Dublin	0-14	0-6	Galway	71,898
1975	Kilkenny	2-22	2-10	Galway	63,711	Kerry	2-12	0-11	Dublin	66,346
1976	Cork	2-21	4-11	Wexford	62,684	Dublin	3-8	0-10	Kerry	73,588
1977	Cork	1-17	3-8	Wexford	63,168	Dublin	5-12	3-6	Armagh	66,542
1978	Cork	1-15	2-8	Kilkenny	64,155	Kerry	5-11	0-9	Dublin	71,503
1979	Kilkenny	2-12	1-8	Galway	53,535	Kerry	3-13	1-8	Dublin	72,185
1980	Galway	2-15	3-9	Limerick	64,895	Kerry	1-9	1-6	Roscommon	63,854
1981	Offaly	2-12	0-15	Galway	71,384	Kerry	1-12	0-8	Offaly	61,489
1982	Kilkenny	3-18	1-13	Cork	59,550	Offaly	1-15	0-17	Kerry	62,309
1983	Kilkenny	2-14	2-12	Cork	58,381	Dublin	1-10	1-8	Galway	71,988
1984	Cork	3-16	1-12	Offaly	59,814	Kerry	0-14	1-6	Dublin	68,365
1985	Offaly	2-11	1-12	Galway	61,451	Kerry	2-12	2-8	Dublin	69,389
1986	Cork	4-13	2-15	Galway	63,451	Kerry	2-15	1-10	Tyrone	68,628
1987	Galway	1-12	0-9	Kilkenny	65,586	Meath	1-14	0-11	Cork	68,431
1988	Galway	1-15	0-14	Tipperary	63,545	Meath	**0-13**	**0-12**	Cork	64,069
1989	Tipperary	4-24	3-9	Antrim	65,496	Cork	0-17	1-11	Mayo	65,519
1990	Cork	5-15	2-21	Galway	63,954	Cork	0-11	0-9	Meath	65,723
1991	Tipperary	1-16	0-15	Kilkenny	64,500	Down	1-16	1-14	Meath	64,512
1992	Kilkenny	3-10	1-12	Cork	64,354	Donegal	0-18	0-14	Dublin	64,547
1993	Kilkenny	2-17	1-15	Galway	63,460	Derry	1-14	2-8	Cork	64,500
1994	Offaly	3-16	2-13	Limerick	56,458	Down	1-12	0-13	Dublin	58,684
1995	Clare	1-13	2-8	Offaly	65,092	Dublin	1-10	0-12	Tyrone	65,983
1996	Wexford	1-13	0-14	Limerick	65,847	Meath	**2-9**	**1-11**	Mayo	65,802
1997	Clare	0-20	2-13	Tipperary	65,575	Kerry	0-13	1-7	Mayo	65,601
1998	Offaly	2-16	1-13	Kilkenny	65,491	Galway	1-14	1-10	Kildare	65,886

Scores in **bold** are replays (see results below).
§ denotes result of second replay (see results below).
* Until 1892 a goal outweighed any number of points, therefore in 1891 Dublin's 2-1 beat Cork's 1-9. From 1892 until 1896 a goal was worth five points, since 1896 a goal has been worth three points.

† Denotes unfinished game, title awarded

•In 1888 the GAA embarked on a tour of the United States and both the hurling and football championships remained unfinished.

•From 1900 to 1903 the All-Ireland title was played for by the champions of Ireland and London, the results of the three so-called 'Home Finals' in both hurling and football are in italics in the table above.

HURLING REPLAYS: 1902 Cork 1-7, Dublin 1-7; **1905** Kilkenny 3-13, Cork 5-10 (disputed match); **1908** Tipperary 2-5, Dublin 1-8; **1931** Cork 1-6, Kilkenny 1-6, 1st replay Cork 2-5, Kilkenny 2-5.

FOOTBALL REPLAYS: 1903 Kerry 1-4, Kildare 1-3 (disputed goal), 1st replay Kerry 0-7, Kildare 1-4; **1914** Kerry 1-3, Wexford 0-6; **1937** Kerry 2-5, Cavan 1-8; **1938** Galway 3-3, Kerry 2-6; **1943** Roscommon 1-6, Cavan 1-6; **1946** Kerry 2-4, Roscommon 1-7; **1952** Cavan 2-4, Meath 1-7; **1972** Offaly 1-13, Kerry 1-13; **1988** Meath 0-12, Cork 1-9; **1996** Meath 1-9, Mayo 0-12.

Finals held at venues other than Croke Park* (*Excludes 'Home Finals')

Venue	Hurling	Football
Athy	1908	1906, 1907
Birr	1887	-
Carrick-on-Suir	1904	-
Clonskeagh	-	1897
Clonturk Park	1890-92, 1894	1890
Cork	1909	1904
Dungarvan	1907, 1911	-
Inchicore	1889	1889
Jones's Road	1895, 1896, 1898-1903, 1910	1895-1901, 1908
Killarney	1937	-
Kilkenny	1906	-
Phoenix Park	1893	1893
Polo Grounds, New York	-	1947
Thurles	1984	1894,1905
Tipperary	1897	

National Hurling League Winners

Year	Winners
1926	Cork
1928	Tipperary
1929	Dublin
1930	Cork
1932	Galway
1933	Kilkenny
1934	Limerick
1935	Limerick
1936	Limerick
1937	Limerick
1938	Limerick
1939	Dublin
1940	Cork
1941	Cork
1946	Clare
1947	Limerick
1948	Cork
1949	Tipperary
1950	Tipperary
1951	Galway
1952	Tipperary
1953	Cork
1954	Tipperary
1955	Tipperary
1956	Wexford
1957	Tipperary
1958	Wexford
1959	Tipperary
1960	Tipperary
1961	Tipperary
1962	Kilkenny
1963	Waterford
1964	Tipperary
1965	Tipperary
1966	Kilkenny
1967	Wexford
1968	Tipperary
1969	Cork
1970	Cork
1971	Limerick
1972	Cork
1973	Wexford
1974	Cork
1975	Galway
1976	Kilkenny
1977	Clare
1978	Clare
1979	Tipperary
1980	Cork
1981	Cork
1982	Kilkenny
1983	Kilkenny
1984	Limerick
1985	Limerick
1986	Kilkenny
1987	Galway
1988	Tipperary
1989	Galway
1990	Kilkenny
1991	Offaly
1992	Limerick
1993	Cork
1994	Tipperary
1995	Kilkenny
1996	Galway
1997	Limerick
1998	Cork

National Football League Winners

Year	Winners
1927	Laois
1928	Kerry
1929	Kerry
1931	Kerry
1932	Kerry
1933	Meath
1934	Mayo
1935	Mayo
1936	Mayo
1937	Mayo
1938	Mayo
1939	Mayo
1940	Galway
1941	Mayo
1946	Meath
1947	Derry
1948	Cavan
1949	Mayo
1950	New York
1951	Meath
1952	Cork
1953	Dublin
1954	Mayo
1955	Dublin
1956	Cork
1957	Galway
1958	Dublin
1959	Kerry
1960	Down
1961	Kerry
1962	Down
1963	Kerry
1964	New York
1965	Galway
1966	Longford
1967	New York
1968	Down
1969	Kerry
1970	Mayo
1971	Kerry
1972	Kerry
1973	Kerry
1974	Kerry
1975	Meath
1976	Dublin
1977	Kerry
1978	Dublin
1979	Roscommon
1980	Cork
1981	Galway
1982	Kerry
1983	Down
1984	Kerry
1985	Monaghan
1986	Laois
1987	Dublin
1988	Meath
1989	Cork
1990	Meath
1991	Dublin
1992	Derry
1993	Dublin
1994	Meath
1995	Derry
1996	Derry
1997	Kerry
1998	Offaly

All Ireland Minor Hurling Champions since 1928

Year	Winners
1928	Cork
1929	Waterford
1930	Tipperary
1931	Kilkenny
1932	Tipperary
1933	Tipperary
1934	Tipperary
1935	Kilkenny
1936	Kilkenny
1937	Cork
1938	Cork
1939	Cork
1940	Limerick
1941	Cork
1945	Dublin
1946	Dublin
1947	Tipperary
1948	Waterford
1949	Tipperary
1950	Kilkenny
1951	Cork
1952	Tipperary
1953	Tipperary
1954	Dublin
1955	Tipperary
1956	Tipperary
1957	Tipperary
1958	Limerick
1959	Tipperary
1960	Kilkenny
1961	Kilkenny
1962	Kilkenny
1963	Wexford
1964	Cork
1965	Dublin
1966	Wexford
1967	Cork
1968	Wexford
1969	Cork
1970	Cork
1971	Cork
1972	Kilkenny
1973	Kilkenny
1974	Cork
1975	Kilkenny
1976	Tipperary
1977	Kilkenny
1978	Cork
1979	Cork
1980	Tipperary
1981	Kilkenny
1982	Tipperary
1983	Galway
1984	Limerick
1985	Cork
1986	Offaly
1987	Offaly
1988	Kilkenny
1989	Offaly
1990	Kilkenny
1991	Kilkenny
1992	Galway
1993	Kilkenny
1994	Galway
1995	Cork
1996	Tipperary
1997	Clare
1998	Cork

All Ireland Minor Football Champions since 1929

Year	Winners	Year	Winners	Year	Winners
1929	Clare	1955	Dublin	1978	Mayo
1930	Dublin	1956	Dublin	1979	Dublin
1931	Kerry	1957	Meath	1980	Kerry
1932	Kerry	1958	Dublin	1981	Cork
1933	Kerry	1959	Dublin	1982	Dublin
1934	Tipperary	1960	Galway	1983	Derry
1935	Mayo	1961	Cork	1984	Dublin
1936	Louth	1962	Kerry	1985	Mayo
1937	Cavan	1963	Kerry	1986	Galway
1938	Cavan	1964	Offaly	1987	Down
1939	Roscommon	1965	Derry	1988	Kerry
1940	Louth	1966	Mayo	1989	Derry
1941	Roscommon	1967	Cork	1990	Meath
1945	Dublin	1968	Cork	1991	Cork
1946	Kerry	1969	Cork	1992	Meath
1947	Tyrone	1970	Galway	1993	Cork
1948	Tyrone	1971	Mayo	1994	Kerry
1949	Armagh	1972	Cork	1995	Westmeath
1950	Kerry	1973	Tyrone	1996	Laois
1951	Roscommon	1974	Cork	1997	Laois
1952	Galway	1975	Kerry	1998	Tyrone
1953	Mayo	1976	Galway		
1954	Dublin	1977	Down		

All-Ireland Hurling Club Championship Final Results since 1971

Year	Winners	County		Runners Up	County	
1971	Roscrea	Tipperary	4-5	St Rynagh's	Offaly	2-5
1972	Blackrock	Cork	5-13	Rathnure	Wexford	6-9
1973	Glen Rovers	Cork	2-18	St Rynagh's	Offaly	2-8
1974	Blackrock	Cork	3-8*	Rathnure	Wexford	1-9
1975	St Finbarrs	Cork	3-8	The Fenians	Kilkenny	1-6
1976	James Stephens	Kilkenny	2-10	Blackrock	Cork	2-4
1977	Glen Rovers	Cork	2-12	Camross	Laois	0-8
1978	St Finbarrs	Cork	2-7	Rathnure	Wexford	0-9
1979	Blackrock	Cork	5-7	Shamrocks	Kilkenny	5-5
1980	Castlegar	Galway	1-11	Ballycastle	Antrim	1-8
1981	Ballyhale Shamrocks	Kilkenny	1-15	St Finbarr's	Cork	1-11
1982	James Stephens	Kilkenny	3-13	Mount Sion	Waterford	3-8
1983	Loughgiel Shamrocks	Antrim	2-12*	St Rynagh's	Offaly	1-12
1984	Ballyhale Shamrocks	Kilkenny	1-10*	Gort	Galway	0-7
1985	St Martin's	Kilkenny	1-13*	Castlegar	Galway	1-10
1986	Kilruane McDonagh's	Tipperary	1-15	Buffers Alley	Wexford	2-10
1987	Borrisoleigh	Tipperary	2-9	Rathnure	Wexford	0-9
1988	Midleton	Cork	3-8	Athenry	Galway	0-9
1989	Buffers Alley	Wexford	2-12	O'Donovan Rossa	Antrim	0-12
1990	Ballyhale Shamrocks	Kilkenny	1-16	Ballybrown	Limerick	0-16
1991	Glenmore	Kilkenny	1-13	Patrickswell	Limerick	0-12
1992	Kiltormer	Galway	0-15	Birr	Offaly	1-8
1993	Sarsfields	Galway	1-17	Kilmallock	Limerick	2-7
1994	Sarsfields	Galway	1-14	Toomevara	Tipperary	3-6
1995	Birr	Offaly	3-13*	Dunloy	Antrim	2-3
1996	Sixmilebridge	Clare	5-10	Dunloy	Antrim	2-6
1997	Athenry	Galway	0-14	Wolfe Tone's	Clare	1-8
1998	Birr	Offaly	1-13	Sarsfields	Galway	0-9

*Denotes result of replayed final.

All-Ireland Football Club Championship Final Results since 1971

Year	Winners	County		Runners Up	County	
1971	East Kerry	Kerry	5-9	Bryansford	Down	2-7
1972	Bellaghy	Derry	0-15	UCC	Cork	1-11
1973	Nemo Rangers	Cork	4-6*	St Vincent's	Dublin	0-10

Year	Winners	County		Runners Up	County	
1974	UCD	Dublin	0-14*	Clan na Gael	Armagh	1-4
1975	UCD	Dublin	1-11	Nemo Rangers	Cork	0-12
1976	St Vincent's	Dublin	4-10	Roscommon Gaels	Roscommon	0-5
1977	Austin Stack's	Kerry	1-13	Ballerin	Derry	2-7
1978	Thomond College	Limerick	2-14	St John's	Antrim	1-3
1979	Nemo Rangers	Cork	2-9	Scotstown	Monaghan	1-3
1980	St Finbarr's	Cork	3-9	St Grellans	Galway	0-8
1981	St Finbarr's	Cork	1-9	Walterstown	Meath	0-6
1982	Nemo Rangers	Cork	6-11	Garymore	Mayo	1-8
1983	Portlaoise	Laois	0-12	Clann na Gael	Roscommon	2-0
1984	Nemo Rangers	Cork	2-10	Walterstown	Meath	0-5
1985	Castleisland Desmonds	Kerry	2-2	St Vincent's	Dublin	0-7
1986	Burren	Down	1-10	Castleisland Desmonds	Kerry	1-6
1987	St Finbarr's	Cork	0-10	Clann na Gael	Roscommon	0-7
1988	Burren	Down	1-9	Clann na Gael	Roscommon	0-8
1989	Nemo Rangers	Cork	1-13	Clann na Gael	Roscommon	1-3
1990	Baltinglass	Wicklow	2-7	Clann na Gael	Roscommon	0-7
1991	Lavey	Derry	2-9	Salthill	Galway	0-10
1992	Dr Crokes Killarney	Kerry	1-11	Thomas Davis	Dublin	0-13
1993	O'Donovan Rossa	Cork	1-7*	Éire Óg	Carlow	0-8*
1994	Nemo Rangers	Cork	3-11	Castlebar Mitchels	Mayo	0-8
1995	Kilmacud Crokes	Dublin	0-8	Bellaghy	Derry	0-5
1996	Laune Rangers	Kerry	4-5	Éire Óg	Carlow	0-11
1997	Crossmaglen Rangers	Armagh	2-13	Knockmore	Mayo	0-11
1998	Corofin	Galway	0-15	Erin's Isle	Dublin	0-10

*Denotes result of replayed final.

Railway Cup Winners, Hurling

Year	Winners	Year	Winners	Year	Winners
1927	Leinster	1952	Munster	1977	Leinster
1928	Munster	1953	Munster	1978	Munster
1929	Munster	1954	Leinster	1979	Leinster
1930	Munster	1955	Munster	1980	Connacht
1931	Munster	1956	Leinster	1981	Munster
1932	Leinster	1957	Munster	1982	Connacht
1933	Leinster	1958	Munster	1983	Connacht
1934	Munster	1959	Munster	1984	Munster
1935	Munster	1960	Munster	1985	Munster
1936	Leinster	1961	Munster	1986	Connacht
1937	Munster	1962	Leinster	1987	Connacht
1938	Munster	1963	Munster	1988	Leinster
1939	Munster	1964	Leinster	1989	Connacht
1940	Munster	1965	Leinster	1990	No Competition
1941	Leinster	1966	Munster	1991	Connacht
1942	Munster	1967	Leinster	1992	Munster
1943	Munster	1968	Munster	1993	Leinster
1944	Munster	1969	Munster	1994	Connacht
1945	Munster	1970	Munster	1995	Munster
1946	Munster	1971	Leinster	1996	Munster
1947	Connacht	1972	Leinster	1997	Munster
1948	Munster	1973	Leinster		
1949	Munster	1974	Leinster		
1950	Munster	1975	Leinster		
1951	Munster	1976	Munster		

Overall:

Connacht 9 Leinster 20
Munster 41 Ulster 0

Railway Cup Winners, Football

Year	Winners	Year	Winners	Year	Winners
1927	Munster	1933	Leinster	1939	Leinster
1928	Leinster	1934	Connacht	1940	Leinster
1929	Leinster	1935	Leinster	1941	Munster
1930	Leinster	1936	Connacht	1942	Ulster
1931	Munster	1937	Connacht	1943	Ulster
1932	Leinster	1938	Connacht	1944	Leinster

Continued from previous page

Year	Winners
1945	Leinster
1946	Munster
1947	Ulster
1948	Munster
1949	Munster
1950	Ulster
1951	Connacht
1952	Leinster
1953	Leinster
1954	Leinster
1955	Leinster
1956	Ulster
1957	Connacht
1958	Connacht
1959	Leinster
1960	Ulster
1961	Leinster
1962	Leinster
1963	Ulster
1964	Ulster
1965	Ulster
1966	Ulster
1967	Connacht
1968	Ulster
1969	Connacht
1970	Ulster
1971	Ulster
1972	Munster
1973	Combined Universities
1974	Leinster
1975	Munster
1976	Munster
1977	Munster
1978	Munster
1979	Ulster
1980	Ulster
1981	Munster
1982	Munster
1983	Ulster
1984	Ulster
1985	Leinster
1986	Leinster
1987	Leinster
1988	Leinster
1989	Ulster
1990	No Competition
1991	Ulster
1992	Ulster
1993	Ulster
1994	Ulster
1995	Ulster
1996	Leinster
1997	Leinster
1998	Ulster

Overall:

Connacht	9	Universities	1
Munster	13	Leinster	24
		Ulster	24

AWARDS

The Eircell All-Star Awards, 1997

FOOTBALL AWARDS

Declan O'Keefe (Kerry)

Kenneth Mortimer (Mayo) · **Davy Dalton** (Kildare) · **Cathal Daly** (Offaly)

Seamus Moynihan (Kerry) · **Glen Ryan** (Kildare) · **Eamonn Breen** (Kerry)

Pat Fallon (Mayo) · **Niall Buckley** (Kildare)

Pa Laide (Kerry) · **Trevor Giles** (Meath) · **Dermot McCabe** (Cavan)

Joe Brolly (Derry) · **Brendan Reilly** (Meath) · **Maurice Fitzgerald** (Kerry)

Footballer of the Year: Maurice Fitzgerald (Kerry)

HURLING AWARDS

Damien Fitzhenry (Wexford)

Paul Shelley (Tipperary) · **Brian Lohan** (Clare) · **Willie O'Connor** (Kilkenny)

Liam Doyle (Clare) · **Sean McMahon** (Clare) · **Liam Keoghan** (Kilkenny)

Colin Lynch (Clare) · **Tommy Dunne** (Tipperary)

James O'Connor (Clare) · **Declan Ryan** (Tipperary) · **John Leahy** (Tipperary)

Kevin Broderick (Galway) · **Ger O'Loughlin** (Clare) · **DJ Carey** (Kilkenny)

Hurler of the Year: James O'Connor (Clare)

Number of All-Star Winners by County

FOOTBALL

County	No.
Kerry	80
Dublin	67
Cork	45
Meath	36
Offaly	30
Derry	21
Mayo	20
Down	19
Galway	19
Roscommon	14
Donegal	12
Tyrone	12
Armagh	7
Monaghan	6
Kildare	5
Cavan	2
Laois	2
Leitrim	2
Sligo	2
Antrim	1
Clare	1
Fermanagh	1
Wicklow	1

HURLING

County	No.
Kilkenny	85
Cork	72
Galway	59
Tipperary	46

Continued from previous page

HURLING County	No.
Limerick	40
Offaly	32
Clare	29
Wexford	28

HURLING County	No.
Antrim	5
Waterford	4
Dublin	2
Down	1

HURLING County	No.
Laois	1
Westmeath	1

Texaco Award Winners, Gaelic Football

Year	Winner	County
1958	Jim McKeever	Derry
1959	Sean Murphy	Kerry
1960	Jim McCartan	Down
1961	Jim McCartan	Down
1962	Mick O' Connell	Kerry
1963	Lar Foley	Dublin
1964	Noel Tierney	Galway
1965	Martin Newell	Galway
1966	Mattie McDonagh	Galway
1967	Bertie Cunningham	Meath
1968	Sean O' Neill	Down
1969	Mick O'Dwyer	Kerry
1970	Tom Prendergast	Kerry
1971	Eugene Mulligan	Offaly
1972	Willie Bryan	Offaly
1973	Billy Morgan	Cork
1974	Kevin Heffernan	Dublin
1975	John O' Keeffe	Kerry
1976	Jimmy Keaveney	Dublin
1977	Jimmy Keaveney	Dublin

Year	Winner	County
1978	Pat Spillane	Kerry
1979	Mikey Sheehy	Kerry
1980	Jack O' Shea	Kerry
1981	Jack O' Shea	Kerry
1982	Martin Furlong	Offaly
1983	Tommy Drumm	Dublin
1984	Jack O' Shea	Kerry
1985	Jack O' Shea	Kerry
1986	Pat Spillane	Kerry
1987	Brian Stafford	Meath
1988	Robbie O' Malley	Meath
1989	Teddy McCarthy	Cork
1990	Shay Fahy	Cork
1991	Colm O' Rourke	Meath
1992	Martin Mc Hugh	Donegal
1993	Henry Downey	Derry
1994	Mickey Linden	Down
1995	Paul Curran	Dublin
1996	Martin O'Connell	Meath
1997	Maurice Fitzgerald	Kerry

Texaco Award Winners, Hurling

Year	Winner	County
1958	Tony Wall	Tipperary
1959	Christy Ring	Cork
1960	Nick O' Donnell	Wexford
1961	Liam Devaney	Tipperary
1962	Donie Nealon	Tipperary
1963	Seamus Cleere	Kilkenny
1964	John Doyle	Tipperary
1965	Jimmy Doyle	Tipperary
1966	Justin Mc Carthy	Cork
1967	Ollie Walsh	Kilkenny
1968	Dan Quigley	Wexford
1969	Ted Carroll	Kilkenny
1970	Pat Mc Donnell	Cork
1971	Michael 'Babs' Keating	Tipperary
1972	Eddie Keher	Kilkenny
1973	Eamonn Grimes	Limerick
1974	Pat Henderson	Kilkenny
1975	Liam O' Brien	Kilkenny
1976	Tony Doran	Wexford
1977	Denis Coughlan	Cork

Year	Winner	County
1978	John Horgan	Cork
1979	Ger Henderson	Kilkenny
1980	John Connolly	Galway
1981	Pat Delaney	Offaly
1982	Noel Skehan	Kilkenny
1983	Frank Cummins	Kilkenny
1984	John Fenton	Cork
1985	Eugene Coughlan	Offaly
1986	Ger Cunningham	Cork
1987	Joe Cooney	Galway
1988	Tony Keady	Galway
1989	Nicky English	Tipperary
1990	Tony O' Sullivan	Cork
1991	Pat Fox	Tipperary
1992	Brian Corcoran	Cork
1993	D.J. Carey	Kilkenny
1994	Brian Whelehan	Offaly
1995	Seanie McMahon	Clare
1996	Larry O'Gorman	Wexford
1997	Jamesie O'Connor	Clare

Past Presidents of the GAA

Year	President	County
1884	Maurice Davin	Tipperary
1887	Eamonn Bennet	Clare
1888	Maurice Davin	Tipperary
1889	Peter Kelly	Galway
1895	Frank Dineen	Limerick
1898	Michael Deering	Cork
1901	James Nowlan	Kilkenny

Year	President	County
1921	Daniel McCarthy	Dublin
1924	Patrick Breen	Wexford
1926	William Clifford	Limerick
1928	Seán Ryan	Dublin
1932	Seán McCarthy	Cork
1935	Bob O'Keefe	Laois
1938	Pádraig McNamee	Antrim

Continued from previous page

Year	President	County
1943	Seamus Gardiner	Tipperary
1946	Dan O'Rourke	Roscommon
1949	Michael Kehoe	Wexford
1952	Michael O'Donoghue	Waterford
1955	Seamus McFerran	Antrim
1958	Dr. J.J. Stuart	Dublin
1961	Hugh Byrne	Wicklow
1964	Alf Murray	Armagh
1967	Seamus Ó Riain	Tipperary
1970	Pat Fanning	Waterford
1973	Dr. Donal Keenan	Roscommon
1976	Con Murphy	Cork
1979	Paddy McFlynn	Down
1982	Paddy Buggy	Kilkenny
1985	Dr. Mick Loftus	Mayo
1988	John Dowling	Offaly
1991	Peter Quinn	Fermanagh
1994	Jack Boothman	Wicklow
1997-	Joe McDonagh	Galway

Past Directors General

Year	Director General	County
1884	Maurice Davin	Tipperary
1884-85	Michael Cusack	Clare
1884-85	John McKay	Cork
1884-87	John W. Power	Kildare
1885-87	J.B. O'Reilly	Dublin
1885-89	Timothy O'Riordan	Cork
1887-88	James Moore	Louth
1888-89	William Prendergast	Tipperary
1889-90	P.R. Cleary	Limerick
1890-92	Maurice Moynihan	Kerry
1891-94	Patrick Tobin	Dublin
1894-95	David Walsh	Cork
1895-98	Richard Blake	Meath
1898-1901	Frank Dineen	Limerick
1901-29	Luke O'Toole	Dublin
1929-64	Pádraic Ó Caoimh	Cork
1964-79	Seán Ó Síocháin	Cork
1979-	Liam Mulvihill	Longford

COUNTY BY COUNTY STATISTICS

ANTRIM Colours: Saffron & White. **Ground:** Casement Park, Belfast. **Capacity:** 21,000; **Number of Clubs:** 108; **1997 County SFC Champions:** St Paul's; **1997 County SHC Champions:** Dunloy. **All-Ireland SFC Titles:** 0; **All-Ireland SHC Titles:** 0. **Performance 1998 SFC:** Eliminated 1st round Ulster Championship. **Performance 1998 All-Ireland SHC:** Ulster Champions, Eliminated All-Ireland Quarter Final. **NFL Titles:** 0; **NHL Titles:** 0. **Performance 1997/98 NFL:** 7th Section B. **Performance 1997/98 NHL:** 6th Division 1A.

ARMAGH Colours: Orange & White. **Ground:** Athletic Grounds, Armagh. **Capacity:** 18,000; **Number of Clubs:** 55; **1997 County SFC Champions:** Crossmaglen Rangers; **1997 County SHC Champions:** Keady. **All-Ireland SFC Titles:** 0; **All-Ireland SHC Titles:** 0. **Performance 1998 SFC:** Eliminated semi-final Ulster Championship. **Performance 1998 All-Ireland SHC:** N/a **NFL Titles:** 0; **NHL Titles:** 0. **Performance 1997/98 NFL:** 3rd Section B. **Performance 1997/98 NHL:** 7th Division 2A.

CARLOW Colours: Red, Green & Yellow. **Ground:** Dr Cullen Park, Carlow. **Capacity:** 10,000; **Number of Clubs:** 35; **1997 County SFC Champions:** Old Leighlin; **1997 County SHC Champions:** St Mullins. **All-Ireland SFC Titles:** 0; **All-Ireland SHC Titles:** 0. **Performance 1998 SFC:** Eliminated Preliminary Round Leinster Championship. **Performance 1998 All-Ireland SHC:** N/a. **NFL Titles:** 0; **NHL Titles:** 0. **Performance 1997/98 NFL:** 7th Section A. **Performance 1997/98 NHL:** 2nd Division 2A.

CAVAN Colours: Blue & White. **Ground:** Breffni Park, Cavan. **Number of Clubs:** 59; **1997 County SFC Champions:** Gowna; **1997 County SHC Champions:** Mullahoran. **All-Ireland SFC Titles:** 5, 1933, 1935, 1947, 1948, 1952; **All-Ireland SHC Titles:** 0. **Performance 1998 SFC:** Eliminated Semi-final Ulster Championship. **Performance 1998 All-Ireland SHC:** N/a. **NFL Titles:** 1, 1948; **NHL Titles:** 0. **Performance 1997/98 NFL:** 7th Section C. **Performance 1997/98 NHL:** 1st Division 3.

CLARE Colours: Gold & Blue. **Ground:** Cusack Park, Ennis. **Number of Clubs:** 90; **1997 County SFC Champions:** Cooraclare; **1997 County SHC Champions:** Clarecastle. **All-Ireland SFC Titles:** 0; **All-Ireland SHC Titles:** 3, 1914, 1995, 1997; **Performance 1998 SFC:** Eliminated Munster Semi-final. **Performance 1998 All-Ireland SHC:** Munster champions, Eliminated All-Ireland semi-final. **NFL Titles:** 0; **NHL Titles:** 3. 1946, 1977, 1978. **Performance 1997/98 NFL:** 4th Section D. **Performance 1997/98 NHL:** Beaten semi-finalists.

CORK Colours: Red & White. **Ground:** Pairc Uí Chaoimh. **Capacity:** 43,500; **Number of Clubs:** 264; **1997 County SFC Champions:** Castlehaven; **1997 County SHC Champions:** Sarsfield. **All-Ireland SFC Titles:** 6, 1890, 1911, 1945, 1973, 1989, 1990; **All-Ireland SHC Titles:** 27, 1890, 1892, 1893, 1894, 1902, 1903, 1919, 1926,

1928, 1929, 1931, 1941, 1942, 1943, 1944, 1946, 1952, 1953, 1954, 1966, 1970, 1976, 1977, 1978, 1984, 1986, 1990. **Performance 1998 SFC:** Eliminated semi-final Munster Championship. **Performance 1998 All-Ireland SHC:** Eliminated Munster semi-final. **NFL Titles:** 4, 1952, 1956, 1980, 1989; **NHL Titles:** 14, 1926, 1930, 1940, 1941, 1948, 1953, 1969, 1970, 1972, 1974, 1980, 1981, 1993, 1998. **Performance 1997/98 NFL:** Beaten quarter-finalists. **Performance 1997/98 NHL:** NHL Champions.

DERRY Colours: White & Red. **Ground:** Celtic Park, Derry. **Capacity:** 15,000; **Number of Clubs:** 60; **1997 County SFC Champions:** Kevin Lynch's, Dungiven; **1997 County SHC Champions:** Lavey. **All-Ireland SFC Titles:** 1, 1993; **All-Ireland SHC Titles:** 0. **Performance 1998 SFC:** Ulster Champions, eliminated All-Ireland semi-final. **Performance 1998 All-Ireland SHC:** Beaten Ulster finalists. **NFL Titles:** 4, 1947, 1992, 1995, 1996; **NHL Titles:** 0. **Performance 1997/98 NFL:** Beaten finalists. **Performance 1997/98 NHL:** 4th Division 2A.

DONEGAL Colours: Green & Gold. **Ground:** McCumhaill Park, Ballybofey. **Capacity:** 15,000; **Number of Clubs:** 63; **1997 County SFC Champions:** Aodh Ruadh, Ballyshannon; **1997 County SHC Champions:** Burt. **All-Ireland SFC Titles:** 1, 1992; **All-Ireland SHC Titles:** 0. **Performance 1998 SFC:** Beaten Ulster finalists. **Performance 1998 All-Ireland SHC:** N/a. **NFL Titles:** 0; **NHL Titles:** 0. **Performance 1997/98 NFL:** Beaten semi-finalists. **Performance 1997/98 NHL:** 7th Division 3.

DOWN Colours: Red & Black. **Ground:** Pairc an Iúir. **Capacity:** 11,000; **Number of Clubs:** 70; **1997 County SFC Champions:** Burren; **1997 County SHC Champions:** Ballygalget. **All-Ireland SFC Titles:** 5, 1960, 1961, 1968, 1991, 1994; **All-Ireland SHC Titles:** 0. **Performance 1998 SFC:** Eliminated first round Ulster Championship. **Performance 1998 All-Ireland SHC:** Eliminated Ulster semi-final. **NFL Titles:** 4, 1960, 1962, 1968, 1983.; **NHL Titles:** 0. **Performance 1997/98 NFL:** Beaten quarter-finalists. **Performance 1997/98 NHL:** 1st Division 2B.

DUBLIN Colours: Sky Blue & Navy. **Ground:** Parnell Park. **Capacity:** 10,000; **Number of Clubs:** 270; **1997 County SFC Champions:** Erin's Isle; **1997 County SHC Champions:** O'Toole's. **All-Ireland SFC Titles:** 22, 1891, 1892, 1894, 1897, 1898, 1899, 1901, 1902, 1906, 1907, 1908, 1921, 1922, 1923, 1942, 1958, 1963, 1974, 1976, 1977, 1983, 1995; **All-Ireland SHC Titles:** 6, 1889, 1917, 1920, 1924, 1927, 1938. **Performance 1998 SFC:** Eliminated first round Leinster Championship. **Performance 1998 All-Ireland SHC:** Eliminated first round Leinster championship. **NFL Titles:** 8, 1953, 1955, 1958, 1976, 1978, 1987, 1991, 1993; **NHL Titles:** 2. 1929, 1939. **Performance 1997/98 NFL:** 3rd Section C. **Performance 1997/98 NHL:** 4th Division 1A.

FERMANAGH Colours: Green & White. **Ground:** Brewster Park, Enniskillen. **Number of Clubs:** 50; **1997 County SFC Champions:** Newtownbutler; **1997 County SHC Champions:** Lisbellaw. **All-Ireland SFC Titles:** 0; **All-Ireland SHC Titles:** 0. **Performance 1998 SFC:** Eliminated first round Ulster Championship. **Performance 1998 All-Ireland SHC:** N/a. **NFL Titles:** 0; **NHL Titles:** 0. **Performance 1997/98 NFL:** 6th Section A. **Performance 1997/98 NHL:** 4th Division 3.

GALWAY Colours: Maroon & White. **Ground:** St Jarlath's Stadium, Tuam. **Capacity:** 25,000; **Number of Clubs:** 88; **1997 County SFC Champions:** Corofin; **1997 County SHC Champions:** Sarsfields. **All-Ireland SFC Titles:** 8, 1925, 1934, 1938, 1956, 1964, 1965, 1966, 1998; **All-Ireland SHC Titles:** 4, 1923, 1980, 1987, 1988. **Performance 1998 SFC:** Connacht and All-Ireland Champions. **Performance 1998 All-Ireland SHC:** Eliminated All-Ireland quarter final. **NFL Titles:** 4, 1940, 1957, 1965, 1981; **NHL Titles:** 6. 1932, 1951, 1975, 1987, 1989, 1996. **Performance 1997/98 NFL:** Beaten quarter-finalists. **Performance 1997/98 NHL:** 3rd Division 1A.

KERRY Colours: Green & Gold. **Ground:** Fitzgerald Stadium, Killarney. **Number of Clubs:** 89; **1997 County SFC Champions:** Laune Rangers; **1997 County SHC Champions:** Ballyheigue. **All-Ireland SFC Titles:** 31,1903, 1904, 1909, 1913, 1914, 1924, 1926, 1929, 1930, 1931, 1932, 1937, 1939, 1940, 1941, 1946, 1953, 1955, 1959, 1962, 1969, 1970, 1975, 1978, 1979, 1980, 1981, 1984, 1985, 1986, 1997; **All-Ireland SHC Titles:** 1, 1891. **Performance 1998 SFC:** Munster Champions, Eliminated All-Ireland semi-final. **Performance 1998 All-Ireland SHC:** Eliminated first round Munster Championship. **NFL Titles:** 16, 1928, 1929, 1931, 1932, 1959, 1961, 1963, 1969, 1971, 1972, 1973, 1974, 1977, 1982, 1984, 1997; **NHL Titles:** 0. **Performance 1997/98 NFL:** 6th Section C. **Performance 1997/98 NHL:** 1st Division 2A.

KILDARE Colours: White. **Ground:** Newbridge. **Capacity:** 15,000; **Number of Clubs:** 70; **1997 County SFC Champions:** Clane; **1997 County SHC Champions:** Naas. **All-Ireland SFC Titles:** 4, 1905, 1919, 1927, 1928; **All-Ireland SHC Titles:** 0. **Performance 1998 SFC:** Leinster Champions and beaten All-Ireland finalists. **Performance 1998 All-Ireland SHC:** N/a. **NFL Titles:** 0; **NHL Titles:** 0. **Performance 1997/98 NFL:**

Third Section D. **Performance 1997/98 NHL:** 6th Division 2B.

KILKENNY Colours: Black & Amber. **Ground:** Nowlan Park, Kilkenny. **Capacity:** 30,000; **Number of Clubs:** 27; **1997 County SFC Champions:** Dicksboro; **1997 County SHC Champions:** Dunnamaggin. **All-Ireland SFC Titles:** 0; **All-Ireland SHC Titles:** 25, 1904, 1905, 1907, 1909, 1911, 1912, 1913, 1922, 1932, 1933, 1935, 1939, 1947, 1957, 1963, 1967, 1969, 1972, 1974, 1975, 1979, 1982, 1983, 1992, 1993. **Performance 1998 SFC:** N/a. **Performance 1998 All-Ireland SHC:** N/a. **NFL Titles:** 0; **NHL Titles:** 9. 1933, 1962, 1966, 1976, 1982, 1983, 1986, 1990, 1995. **Performance 1997/98 NFL:** 8th Section A. **Performance 1997/98 NHL:** 6th Division 2A.

LAOIS Colours: Blue & White. **Ground:** O'Moore Park, Portlaoise. **Number of Clubs:** 88; **1997 County SFC Champions:** Stradbally; **1997 County SHC Champions:** Castletown. **All-Ireland SFC Titles:** 0; **All-Ireland SHC Titles:** 1, 1915. **Performance 1998 SFC:** Eliminated semi-final Leinster Championship. **Performance 1998 All-Ireland SHC:** Eliminated semi-final Leinster Championship. **NFL Titles:** 2, 1927, 1986; **NHL Titles:** 0. **Performance 1997/98 NFL:** 3rd Section A. **Performance 1997/98 NHL:** 5th Division 1B.

LEITRIM Colours: Green & Gold. **Ground:** Pairc MacDiarmada, Carrick-on-Shannon. **Capacity:** 12,000; **Number of Clubs:** 33; **1997 County SFC Champions:** Allen Gaels; **1997 County SHC Champions:** St Mary's. **All-Ireland SFC Titles:** 0; **All-Ireland SHC Titles:** 0. **Performance 1998 SFC:** Eliminated Connacht semi-final. **Performance 1998 All-Ireland SHC:** N/a. **NFL Titles:** 0; **NHL Titles:** 0. **Performance 1997/98 NFL:** 4th Section A. **Performance 1997/98 NHL:** 3rd Division 3.

LIMERICK Colours: Green & White. **Ground:** Gaelic Grounds, Limerick. **Capacity:** 36,000; **Number of Clubs:** 117; **1997 County SFC Champions:** Galbally; **1997 County SHC Champions:** Patrickswell. **All-Ireland SFC Titles:** 2, 1887, 1896; **All-Ireland SHC Titles:** 7, 1897, 1918, 1921, 1934, 1936, 1940, 1973. **Performance 1998 SFC:** Eliminated Preliminary round Munster Championship. **Performance 1998 All-Ireland SHC:** Eliminated 1st round Munster Championship. **NFL Titles:** 0; **NHL Titles:** 11. 1934, 1935, 1936, 1937, 1938, 1947, 1971, 1984, 1985, 1992, 1997. **Performance 1997/98 NFL:** 8th Section D. **Performance 1997/98 NHL:** Beaten semi-finalists.

LONGFORD Colours: Blue & Gold. **Ground:** Pearse PArk, Longford. **Capacity:** 8,000; **Number of Clubs:** 52; **1997 County SFC Champions:** Fr Manning Gaels; **1997 County SHC Champions:** Longford Slashers. **All-Ireland SFC Titles:** 0; **All-Ireland SHC Titles:** 0. **Performance 1998 SFC:** Eliminated Preliminary round Leinster Championship. **Performance 1998 All-Ireland SHC:** N/a. **NFL Titles:** 1, 1966; **NHL Titles:** 0. **Performance 1997/98 NFL:** 5th Section B. **Performance 1997/98 NHL:** 5th Division 3.

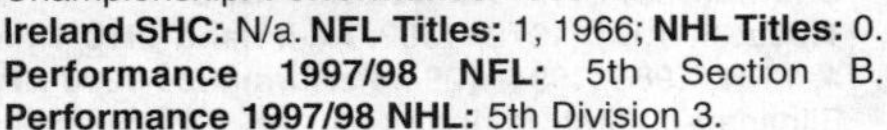

LOUTH Colours: White and Red. **Ground:** Drogheda. **Capacity:** 22,000; **Number of Clubs:** 51; **1997 County SFC Champions:** Stabannon Parnells; **1997 County SHC Champions:** Naomh Mhuire. **All-Ireland SFC Titles:** 3, 1910, 1912, 1957; **All-Ireland SHC Titles:** 0. **Performance 1998 SFC:** Eliminated Leinster semi-final. **Performance 1998 All-Ireland SHC:** N/a. **NFL Titles:** 0; **NHL Titles:** 0. **Performance 1997/98 NFL:** 5th Section A. **Performance 1997/98 NHL:** 7th Division 2B.

MAYO Colours: Green & Red. **Ground:** McHale Park, Castlebar. **Number of Clubs:** 52; **1997 County SFC Champions:** Knockmore; **1997 County SHC Champions:** Tooreen. **All-Ireland SFC Titles:** 3, 1936, 1950, 1951; **All-Ireland SHC Titles:** 0. **Performance 1998 SFC:** Eliminated first round Connacht Championship. **Performance 1998 All-Ireland SHC:** N/a. **NFL Titles:** 10, 1934, 1935, 1936, 1937, 1938, 1939, 1941, 1949, 1954, 1970; **NHL Titles:** 0. **Performance 1997/98 NFL:** Beaten quarter-finalists. **Performance 1997/98 NHL:** 2nd Division 3.

MEATH Colours: Green & Gold. **Ground:** Pairc Tailteann, Navan. **Number of Clubs:** 145; **1997 County SFC Champions:** Navan O'Mahony's; **1997 County SHC Champions:** Rathmolyon. **All-Ireland SFC Titles:** 6, 1949, 1954, 1967, 1987, 1988, 1996; **All-Ireland SHC Titles:** 0. **Performance 1998 SFC:** Beaten Leinster finalists. **Performance 1998 All-Ireland SHC:** Eliminated 1st Round Leinster Championship. **NFL Titles:** 7, 1933, 1946, 1951, 1975, 1988, 1990, 1994; **NHL Titles:** 0. **Performance 1997/98 NFL:** 4th Section B. **Performance 1997/98 NHL:** 5th Division 2B.

MONAGHAN Colours: White & Blue. **Ground:** Castleblaney. **Capacity:** 23,000. **Number of Clubs:** 50; **1997 County SFC Champions:** Clontibret; **1997 County SHC Champions:** Clontibret O'Neills. **All-Ireland SFC Titles:** 0; **All-Ireland SHC Titles:** 0. **Performance 1998 SFC:** Eliminated first round Ulster Championship. **Performance 1998 All-Ireland SHC:** N/a. **NFL Titles:** 1, 1985; **NHL Titles:** 0. **Performance 1997/98 NFL:** Beaten quarter-finalists. **Performance 1997/98 NHL:** 5th Division 2A.

OFFALY Colours: Green, White & Gold. **Ground:** Pairc Uí Conchuir, Tullamore. **Capacity:** 25,000. **Number of Clubs:** 65; **1997 County SFC Champions:** Edenderry; **1997 County SHC Champions:** Birr. **All-Ireland SFC Titles:** 3, 1971, 1972, 1982; **All-Ireland SHC Titles:** 4, 1981, 1985, 1994, 1998. **Performance 1998 SFC:** Eliminated first round Leinster Championship. **Performance 1998 All-Ireland SHC:** Beaten Leinster finalists and All-Ireland Champions. **NFL Titles:** 1, 1998; **NHL Titles:** 1, 1991. **Performance 1997/98 NFL:** Champions. **Performance 1997/98 NHL:** 5th Division 1A.

ROSCOMMON Colours: Gold & Blue. **Ground:** Dr Hyde Park, Roscommon. **Capacity:** 23,000. **Number of Clubs:** 56; **1997 County SFC Champions:** St Brigids; **1997 County SHC Champions:** Four Roads. **All-Ireland SFC Titles:** 2, 1943, 1944; **All-Ireland SHC Titles:** 0. **Performance 1998 SFC:** Beaten Connacht finalists. **Performance 1998 All-Ireland SHC:** Beaten Connacht finalists. **NFL Titles:** 1, 1979; **NHL Titles:** 0. **Performance 1997/98 NFL:** 7th Section D. **Performance 1997/98 NHL:** 6th Division 2A.

SLIGO Colours: White & Black. **Ground:** Markevicz Park, Sligo. **Capacity:** 13,000. **Number of Clubs:** 51; **1997 County SFC Champions:** Tourlestrane; **1997 County SHC Champions:** Tubbercurry. **All-Ireland SFC Titles:** 0; **All-Ireland SHC Titles:** 0. **Performance 1998 SFC:** Eliminated semi-final Connacht Championship. **Performance 1998 All-Ireland SHC:** N/a. **NFL Titles:** 0; **NHL Titles:** 0. **Performance 1997/98 NFL:** 5th Section C. **Performance 1997/98 NHL:** 6th Division 3.

TIPPERARY Colours: Blue & Gold. **Ground:** Semple Stadium, Thurles. **Capacity:** 50,000. **Number of Clubs:** 65; **1997 County SFC Champions:** Fethard; **1997 County SHC Champions:** Clonoulty Rossmore. **All-Ireland SFC Titles:** 4, 1889, 1895, 1900, 1920; **All-Ireland SHC Titles:** 24, 1887, 1895, 1896, 1898, 1899, 1900, 1906, 1908, 1916, 1925, 1930, 1937, 1945, 1949, 1950, 1951, 1958, 1961, 1962, 1964, 1965, 1971, 1989, 1991. **Performance 1998 SFC:** Beaten Munster finalists. **Performance 1998 All-Ireland SHC:** Eliminated Munster semi-final. **NFL Titles:** 0; **NHL Titles:** 16. 1928, 1949, 1950, 1952, 1954, 1955, 1957, 1959, 1960, 1961, 1964, 1965, 1968, 1979, 1988, 1994. **Performance 1997/98 NFL:** 6th Section D. **Performance 1997/98 NHL:** 4th Division 1B.

TYRONE Colours: White & Red. **Ground:** Healy Park, Omagh. **Capacity:** 20,000. **Number of Clubs:** 68; **1997 County SFC Champions:** Errigal Ciaran; **1997 County SHC Champions:** Dungannon. **All-Ireland SFC Titles:** 0; **All-Ireland SHC Titles:** 0. **Performance 1998 SFC:** Eliminated Preliminary round Ulster Championship. **Performance 1998 All-Ireland SHC:** N/a. **NFL Titles:** 0; **NHL Titles:** 0. **Performance 1997/98 NFL:** 4th Section C. **Performance 1997/98 NHL:** 4th Division 2B.

WATERFORD Colours: White & Blue. **Ground:** Walsh Park, Waterford. **Capacity:** 17,000. **Number of Clubs:** 57; **1997 County SFC Champions:** The Nire; **1997 County SHC Champions:** Ballygunner. **All-Ireland SFC Titles:** 0; **All-Ireland SHC Titles:** 2, 1948, 1959. **Performance 1998 SFC:** Eliminated first round Munster Championship. **Performance 1998 All-Ireland SHC:** Beaten Munster finalists and eliminated All-Ireland semi-final. **NFL Titles:** 0; **NHL Titles:** 1. 1963. **Performance 1997/98 NFL:** 9th Section D. **Performance 1997/98 NHL:** Beaten finalists.

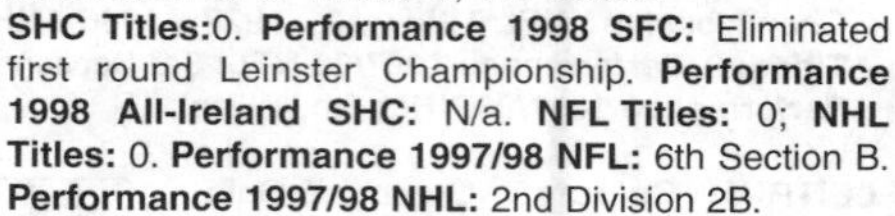

WESTMEATH Colours: Maroon & White. **Ground:** Mullingar. **Capacity:** 11,000. **Number of Clubs:** 44; **1997 County SFC Champions:** Moate; **1997 County SHC Champions:** Lough Lene Gaels. **All-Ireland SFC Titles:** 0; **All-Ireland SHC Titles:**0. **Performance 1998 SFC:** Eliminated first round Leinster Championship. **Performance 1998 All-Ireland SHC:** N/a. **NFL Titles:** 0; **NHL Titles:** 0. **Performance 1997/98 NFL:** 6th Section B. **Performance 1997/98 NHL:** 2nd Division 2B.

WEXFORD Colours: Purple & Gold. **Ground:** Wexford Park. **Number of Clubs:** 178; **1997 County SFC Champions:** Kilanerin; **1997 County SHC Champions:** Oulart-the-Ballagh. **All-Ireland SFC Titles:** 5, 1893, 1915, 1916, 1917, 1918; **All-Ireland SHC Titles:** 6, 1910, 1955, 1956, 1960, 1968, 1996. **Performance 1998 SFC:** Eliminated Preliminary Round Leinster Championship. **Performance 1998 All-Ireland SHC:** Eliminated Leinster semi-final. **NFL Titles:** 0; **NHL Titles:** 4. 1956, 1958, 1967, 1973. **Performance 1997/98 NFL:** 8th Section C. **Performance 1997/98 NHL:** 3rd Division 1B.

WICKLOW Colours: Blue & Gold. **Ground:** Aughrim. **Capacity:** 10,000. **Number of Clubs:** 66; **1997 County SFC Champions:** Rathnew; **1997 County SHC Champions:** Kiltegan. **All-Ireland SFC Titles:** 0; **All-Ireland SHC Titles:** 0. **Performance 1998 SFC:** Eliminated First Round Leinster Championship. **Performance 1998 All-Ireland SHC:** N/a. **NFL Titles:** 0; **NHL Titles:** 0. **Performance 1997/98 NFL:** 5th Section D. **Performance 1997/98 NHL:** 3rd Division 2A.

CAMOGIE

Cumann Camógaíochta na nGael,

Páirc an Chrócaigh, Áth Cliath 3. Tel. (01) 8554257

Founded	1904
President	Fileas Ní Bhreasláin
Secretary	Síle De Bhailís
Public Relations Officer	P.J. Fulham
Number of Affiliated Clubs	498 (including 28 abroad)
Number of Members	78,000

1998 CHAMPIONS	Winners	Runners Up
All-Ireland, Senior	Cork	Galway
All-Ireland, Intermediate	Down	Cork
All-Ireland, Junior	Galway	Tipperary
All-Ireland, Minor	Cork	Derry
Most Senior All-Ireland Titles		Dublin (26)
Most Junior All-Ireland Titles		Galway (6)
Most Minor All-Ireland Titles		Cork (9)
Attendance 1998 All-Ireland Finals		10,436

1998 RESULTS

Bord na Gaeilge All-Ireland Senior Camogie Championship

First Round					
04.07.98	Cork	3-18	Dublin	1-13	O'Toole Park, Dublin
04.07.98	Clare	1-13	Wexford	1-9	Sixmilebridge, Clare
04.07.98	Tipperary	3-11	Kilkenny	3-10	Semple Stadium, Thurles
05.07.98	Galway	1-15	Limerick	2-10	Mary Immaculate College, Limerick
Semi-Finals					
01.08.98	Galway	2-11	Tipperary	0-14	Nowlan Park, Kilkenny
01.08.98	Cork	2-13	Clare	1-9	Nowlan Park, Kilkenny

Bord na Gaeilge All-Ireland Senior Camogie Championship Final

CROKE PARK, 6 SEPTEMBER 1998. Attendance: 10,436. **Half time score:** Cork 2-7, Galway 0-9. **Full time score:** Cork 2-13, Galway 0-15. **Booked:** None. **Sent-off:** None. **Top Scorer:** Lynn Dunlea (Cork 0-9, 6 frees). **Referee:** John Morrissey (Tipperary). **Lineswomen:** Miriam O'Callaghan (Offaly); Marie O'Connell (Dublin).

CORK

Cora Keohane

Eithne Duggan (c)

Denise Cronin **Vivienna Harris** **Mags Finn**

Ursula Troy (0-1) **Mary O'Connor** (0-1) **Linda Mellerick** (0-1)

Sinead O'Callaghan **Fiona O'Driscoll** (0-1) **Irene O'Keefe** (2-0)

Lynn Dunlea (0-9)

Subs: Miriam Deasy for U. Troy (44mins); **Not used:** L. Nolan; P. O'Connor; C. Harrington; S. Dunlea; L. O'Sullivan; M. Burke; T. Doyle.

Manager: Tom Nott.

GALWAY

Louise Curry

Olivia Broderick (c)

Anne Broderick **Tracey Laheen** **Pamela Nevin**

Therese Maher (0-2) **Sharon Glynn** (0-1) **Áine Hillary** (0-1)

Colette Nevin (0-8) **Imelda Hobbins** (0-1) **Veronica Curtin** (0-1)

Ann Forde (0-1)

Subs: Denise Gilligan for T. Maher (47mins); **Not used:** O. Coen; Ann Hardiman; F. Ryan; M. Meehan; S. Ward; C. Hannon; H. Ryan.

Manager: Tony Ward.

All-Ireland Intermediate Camogie Championship

Date	Team	Score	Team	Score	Venue
First Round					
18.07.98	Limerick	1-16	Galway	0-15	Loughrea, Co. Galway
19.07.98	Cork	4-16	Armagh	0-6	Ballincollig, Co. Cork
19.07.98	Antrim	3-8	Dublin	2-9	
Semi-Finals					
30.08.98	Down	2-14	Antrim	3-10	Ballycastle, Co. Antrim
30.08.98	Cork	3-5	Limerick	1-10	Adare, Co. Limerick
Final					
20.08.98	Down	1-12	Cork	1-8	Páirc Uí Rinn, Cork

All-Ireland Junior Camogie Championship

Date	Team	Score	Team	Score	Venue
Semi-Finals					
16.08.98	Galway	3-10	Carlow	1-11	The Hurling Grounds, Co. Carlow
16.08.98	Tipperary	3-10	Derry	2-13 (Draw)	The Ragg, Thurles
30.08.98	Tipperary	2-9	Derry	0-11	Bellaghy, Co. Derry
Final					
06.09.98	Galway	3-11	Tipperary	2-10	Croke Park

All-Ireland Minor (U16) Camogie Championship

Date	Team	Score	Team	Score	Venue
Semi-Finals					
19.07.98	Derry	2-8	Kilkenny	1-7	Castledawson, Co. Derry
26.07.98	Cork	0-13	Galway	1-9	Loughrea, Co. Galway
Final					
22.08.98	Cork	3-18	Derry	1-5	Ballincollig, Co. Cork

Senior National League

Section A	Points
Galway	8
Antrim	5
Down	3
Dublin	2
Armagh	0

Section B	Points
Cork	8
Kilkenny	4
Tipperary	4
Clare	4
Wexford	0

Date	Team	Score	Team	Score
Semi-Finals				
10.05.98	Galway	3-11	Kilkenny	1-14
10.05.98	Cork	2-15	Antrim	2-12
Final				
29.05.98	Cork	1-16	Galway	2-9

Junior National League

Zone A	Points
Cork	8
Tipperary	6
Clare	2
Limerick	2
Kilkenny	0

Zone B	Points
Down	8
Derry	6
Antrim	4
Tyrone	2
Donegal	0

Zone C	Points
Wexford	6
Carlow	5
Armagh	4
Kildare	3
Dublin	2

Zone D	Points
Galway	8
Offaly	6
Cavan	4
Westmeath	2
Roscommon	0

Date	Team	Score	Team	Score
Quarter-Finals				
26.04.98	Cork	4-13	Carlow	3-3
26.04.98	Tipperary	2-15	Wexford	2-7
26.04.98	Down	5-12	Offaly	1-10
26.04.98	Galway	1-10	Derry	0-7
Semi-Finals				
17.05.98	Cork	3-10	Galway	1-9
17.05.98	Down	4-12	Tipperary	1-10
Final				
30.05.98	Down	0-20	Cork	0-12

PREVIOUS CHAMPIONSHIP WINNERS

Senior Championship

Year	Result			
1932	Dublin	3-2	Galway	0-2
1933	Dublin	9-2	Galway	4-0
1934	Cork	4-3	Louth	1-4
1935	Cork	3-4	Dublin	4-0
1936	Cork	6-4	Louth	3-3
1937	Dublin	9-4	Galway	1-0
1938	Dublin	5-0	Cork	2-3
1939	Cork	6-1	Galway	1-1
1940	Cork	4-1	Galway	2-2
1941	Cork	7-5	Dublin	1-2
1942	Dublin	4-1	Cork	2-2
1943	Dublin	8-0	Cork	1-1
1944	Dublin	5-4	Antrim	0-0
1945	Antrim	5-2	Waterford	3-2
1946	Antrim	4-1	Galway	2-3
1947	Antrim	2-4	Dublin	2-1
1948	Dublin	11-4	Down	4-2
1949	Dublin	8-6	Tipperary	4-1
1950	Dublin	6-5	Antrim	4-1
1951	Dublin	8-6	Antrim	4-1

Year	Result			
1952	Dublin	5-1	Antrim	4-2
1953	Dublin	8-4	Tipperary	1-3
1954	Dublin	10-4	Derry	4-2
1955	Dublin	9-2	Cork	5-6
1956	Antrim	5-3	Cork	4-2
1957	Dublin	3-3	Antrim	3-1
1958	Dublin	5-4	Tipperary	1-1
1959	Dublin	11-6	Mayo	1-3
1960	Dublin	6-2	Galway	2-0
1961	Dublin	7-2	Tipperary	4-1
1962	Dublin	5-5	Galway	2-0
1963	Dublin	7-3	Antrim	2-5
1964	Dublin	7-4	Antrim	3-1
1965	Dublin	10-1	Tipperary	5-3
1966	Dublin	2-2	Antrim	0-6
1967	Antrim	3-9	Dublin	4-2
1968	Wexford	4-2	Cork	2-5
1969	Wexford	4-4	Antrim	4-2
1970	Cork	5-7	Kilkenny	3-2
1971	Cork	4-6	Wexford	1-2
1972	Cork	2-5	Kilkenny	1-4
1973	Cork	2-5	Antrim	3-1
1974	Kilkenny	3-3	Cork	1-5
1975	Wexford	4-3	Cork	1-2
1976	Kilkenny	0-6	Dublin	1-2
1977	Kilkenny	3-4	Wexford	1-3
1978	Cork	6-4	Dublin	1-2
1979	Antrim	2-3	Tipperary	1-3
1980	Cork	1-8	Limerick	2-2
1981	Kilkenny	1-9	Cork	0-7
1982	Cork	2-7	Dublin	2-6
1983	Cork	2-5	Dublin	1-6
1984	Dublin	5-9	Tipperary	2-4
1985	Kilkenny	0-13	Dublin	1-5
1986	Kilkenny	2-12	Dublin	2-3
1987	Kilkenny	3-10	Cork	1-7
1988	Kilkenny	4-11	Cork	3-8
1989	Kilkenny	3-10	Cork	2-6
1990	Kilkenny	1-14	Wexford	0-7
1991	Kilkenny	3-8	Cork	0-10
1992	Cork	1-20	Wexford	2-6
1993	Cork	3-15	Galway	2-8
1994	Kilkenny	2-11	Wexford	0-8
1995	Cork	4-8	Kilkenny	2-10
1996	Galway	4-8	Cork	1-15
1997	Cork	0-15	Galway	2-5
1998	Cork	2-13	Galway	0-15

Intermediate Championship

Year	Result			
1992	Dublin	4-11	Down	4-4
1993	Clare	1-8	Dublin	1-5
1994	Armagh	7-11	Kildare	3-11
1995	Clare	1-10	Tipperary	1-9
1996	Limerick	2-10	Down	1-6
1997	Tipperary	2-19	Clare	2-12
1998	Down	1-12	Cork	1-8

Junior Championship

Year	Result			
1968	Down	2-3	Cork	1-1
1969	Derry	4-2	Cork	2-4
1970	Dublin	4-2	Armagh	3-3
1971	Dublin	2-2	Cork	1-2
1972	Galway	3-6	Wexford	2-1
1973	Cork	4-4	Galway	1-4
1974	Clare	3-2	Dublin	3-0
1975	Dublin	5-0	Down	0-3
1976	Down	3-4	Wexford	3-3
1977	Limerick	2-7	Wexford	3-1
1978	Derry	3-4	Cork	1-4
1979	Galway	4-3	Cork	3-2
1980	Cork	4-4	Tyrone	1-4
1981	Clare	3-2	Antrim	0-7
1982	Louth	1-7	Cork	1-6
1983	Cork	2-5	Dublin	2-3
1984	Cork	5-8	Cavan	2-2
1985	Galway	8-7	Armagh	3-7
1986	Clare	1-13	Kildare	3-4
1987	Kildare	2-10	Armagh	0-7
1988	Galway	3-4	Limerick	1-5
1989	Kildare	3-11	Galway	1-3
1990	Kildare	2-14	Tipperary	3-7
1991	Down	3-13	Tipperary	2-14
1992	Tipperary	6-13	Galway	2-7
1993	Armagh	2-10	Galway	0-6
1994	Galway	2-10	Limerick	1-11
1995	Limerick	3-7	Roscommon	4-3
1996	Cork	6-5	Roscommon	2-7
1997	Antrim	7-11	Cork	2-10
1998	Galway	3-11	Tipperary	2-10

Minor Championship

Year	Result			
1974	Down	3-0	Cork	0-1
1975	Cork	6-2	Galway	0-3
1976	Cork	4-6	Down	2-1
1977	Galway	5-4	Dublin	2-1
1978	Cork	5-1	Dublin	3-4
1979	Cork	5-3	Cavan	3-0
1980	Cork	5-5	Cavan	0-2
1981	Galway	3-4	Antrim	3-3
1982	Dublin	5-2	Galway	2-3
1983	Cork	3-3	Dublin	2-3
1984	Cork	2-12	Galway	5-0
1985	Cork	3-8	Galway	2-3
1986	Galway	2-8	Wexford	1-4
1987	Galway	1-11	Cork	3-3
1988	Kilkenny	5-6	Armagh	2-5
1989	Kilkenny	9-10	Tipperary	3-8
1990	Tipperary	2-11	Kilkenny	3-6
1991	Kilkenny	4-12	Galway	3-7

Continued from previous page

Year	Result			
1992	Tipperary	4-9	Kilkenny	1-3
1993	Tipperary	3-10	Galway	2-9
1994	Galway	7-13	Tipperary	3-9
1995	Wexford	2-9	Galway	1-7
1996	Galway	3-16	Tipperary	4-11
1997	Galway	2-14	Cork	1-6
1998	Cork	3-18	Derry	1-5

CUMANN PEÍL GAEL NA mBAN

(The Ladies Gaelic Football Association)

House of Sport, Long Mile Road, Dublin 12. Tel. (01) 4569113.

Founded	1974
President	Noel Murray
Secretary	Helen O'Rourke
Treasurers	Mick Fitzgerald and Peter Rice
Public Relations Officer	Finbarr O'Driscoll
Number of Affiliated Clubs	600
Number of Members	70,000

1998 ALL-IRELAND CHAMPIONS	Winners	Runners Up
Senior	Waterford	Monaghan
Intermediate	Cork	Laois
Junior	Louth	Roscommon
Minor (U18)	Monaghan	Mayo
Under 16	Waterford	Monaghan
Under 14	Waterford	Meath
Interprovincial Champions (Senior)	Leinster	Connacht

1998 RESULTS

All-Ireland Senior Championship

MUNSTER

Semi-Final	Waterford	3-18	Cork	1-0
Semi-Final	Clare	1-12	Kerry	0-9
Final	Waterford	4-11	Clare	3-7

LEINSTER

Quarter-Final	Dublin	4-8	Laois	0-6
Quarter-Final	Longford	5-14	Westmeath	4-8
Semi-Final	Dublin	3-11	Longford	0-6
Semi-Final	Meath	2-10	Wexford	2-6
Final	Meath	2-12	Dublin	3-6

ALL-IRELAND SERIES

Semi-Final	Waterford	1-15	Mayo	1-4
Semi-Final	Monaghan	0-13	Meath	1-8
Final	Waterford	1-16	Monaghan	4-7
Final (Replay)	Waterford	2-14	Monaghan	3-8

Other Results

ALL-IRELAND INTERMEDIATE FINAL

Cork ....4-14 .....Laois........3-7

ALL-IRELAND JUNIOR FINAL

Louth ....4-8 .....Roscommon........2-9

ALL-IRELAND UNDER 18 FINAL

Monaghan ....2-11 .....Mayo........3-4

ALL-IRELAND UNDER 16 FINAL

Waterford........6-8 .....Monaghan........3-6

ALL-IRELAND UNDER 14 FINAL

Waterford........3-8 .....Meath........3-7

INTERPROVINCIAL CHAMPIONSHIP FINAL

Leinster ....3-14 .....Connacht........0-12

RECORDS

All-Ireland Senior Championship

Year	Winners	Runners Up
1974	Tipperary	Offaly
1975	Tipperary	Galway
1976	Kerry	Offaly
1977	Cavan	Roscommon
1978	Roscommon	Tipperary
1979	Offaly	Tipperary
1980	Tipperary	Cavan
1981	Offaly	Cavan
1982	Kerry	Offaly
1983	Kerry	Wexford
1984	Kerry	Leitrim
1985	Kerry	Laois

Continued from previous page

Year	Winners	Runners Up
1986	Kerry	Wexford
1987	Kerry	Westmeath
1988	Kerry	Laois
1989	Kerry	Wexford
1990	Kerry	Laois
1991	Waterford	Laois
1992	Waterford	Laois
1993	Kerry	Laois
1994	Waterford	Monaghan
1995	Waterford	Monaghan
1996	Monaghan	Laois
1997	Monaghan	Waterford
1998	Waterford	Monaghan

National League

Year	Winners	Runners Up
1979	Tipperary	Galway
1980	Kerry	Offaly
1981	Kerry	Tipperary
1982	Kerry	Tipperary
1983	Kerry	Leitrim
1984	Kerry	Laois
1985	Kerry	Leitrim
1986	Wexford	Laois
1987	Kerry	Laois
1988	Kerry	Waterford
1989	Kerry	Waterford
1990	Kerry	Waterford
1991	Kerry	Waterford
1991	Kerry	Waterford
1992	Waterford	Laois
1993	Laois	Cork
1994	Monaghan	Mayo
1995	Waterford	Mayo
1996	Monaghan	Mayo
1997	Monaghan	Waterford
1998	Waterford	Clare

All-Ireland Junior Championship

Year	Winners	Runners Up
1986	Waterford	Wexford
1987	Mayo	Wexford
1988	Leitrim	London
1989	Dublin	Clare
1990	Wicklow	London
1991	Clare	London
1992	Monaghan	London
1993	London	Donegal
1994	Meath	Donegal
1995	Cork	Tyrone
1996	Clare	Longford
1997	Longford	Tyrone
1998	Louth	Roscommon

Interprovincial Senior Championship

Year	Winners	Runners Up
1976	Munster	Leinster
1977	Munster	Connacht
1978	Connacht	Leinster
1979	Connacht	Leinster
1980	Munster	Leinster
1981	Munster	Ulster
1982	Leinster	Munster
1983	Leinster	Munster
1984	Munster	Connacht
1985	Munster	Leinster
1986	Munster	Leinster
1987	Munster	Leinster
1988	Munster	Leinster
1989	Leinster	Connacht
1990	Leinster	Munster
1991	Munster	Leinster
1992	Leinster	Munster
1993	Munster	Leinster
1994	Leinster	Munster
1995	Munster	Leinster
1996	Munster	Combined Colleges
1997	Connacht	Combined Colleges
1998	Leinster	Connacht

Past Presidents

Year	President	County
1974	Jim Kennedy	Tipperary
1977	Jim Kenny	Offaly
1979	Tom Dowd	Cavan
1982	Mick Fitzgerald	Kerry
1985	Pat Quill	Wexford
1988	Mary Wheatley	Laois
1991	Peter Rice	Wexford
1994	Helen O'Rourke	Dublin
1997	Noel Murray	Waterford

Past Secretaries

Year	Secretary	County
1974	Margaret Colleran	Galway
1975	Mary Nevin	Offaly
1976	Marie Holland	Roscommon
1978	Veronica Sharkey	Cavan
1979	Agnes Gorman	Offaly
1985	Barbara Reaney	Galway
1985	Agnes Gorman	Offaly
1987	Christy Byrne	Westmeath
1997	Helen O'Rourke	Dublin

Golfing Union of Ireland

Glencar House, 81 Eglinton Road, Donnybrook, Dublin 4. Tel. (01) 2694111

Founded	1891
Number of Affiliated Clubs	367
President	Percy Shannon, Mallow
President Elect	Tom Grealy, Roscommon
Honorary Secretary	Gerard O'Brien, Clontarf
Honorary Treasurer	Rollo McClure, Malone
International Team Captain	M. Craddock, Malahide
Youths Team Captain	J.E. Brett, Douglas
Boys Captain	J. Greene, Grange
Number of Coaches	5
Number of Club Members	125,061
Oldest Club with a Continuous Existence	Royal Belfast (1881)

1998 CHAMPIONS	Winner	Runner Up
East of Ireland Amateur Open	Garth McGimpsey (Bangor)	E. McMenamin (Ballybofey)
North of Ireland Amateur Open	Paddy Gribben (Warrenpoint)	D. Gibson (Downpatrick)
West of Ireland Amateur Open	Noel Fox (Portmarnock)	Pat Lyons (Cork)
South of Ireland Amateur Open	Johnny Foster (Ballyclare)	Andrew McCormick (Scrabo)
Irish Amateur Open	Michael Hoey (Shandon Park)	G. Cullen (Beaverstown)
Irish Amateur Close	Eddie Power (Kilkenny)	Bryan Omelia (Newlands)
Senior Interprovincial	Leinster	Ulster

East of Ireland Championship (Baltray, Co. Louth. May 30-June 1 1998)

Player	Club	Scores
292 (level)		
G. McGimpsey	Bangor	72...75...73...72
296 (+4)		
E. McMenamin	Ballybofey	74...76...71...75
298 (+6)		
C. Mallon	North West	78...75...71...75
299 (+7)		
A. Morrow	Portmarnock	75...73...75...76
G. Cullen	Beaverstown	73...72...79...75
301 (+9)		
K. Bornemann	Douglas	74...77...76...74
302 (+10)		
P. Gribben	Warrenpoint	74...79...72...77
A. McCormick	Scrabo	75...75...76...76
303 (+11)		
M. Hoey	Shandon Park	75...79...75...74
B. Ronan	Co. Louth	74...79...78...72
304 (+12)		
E. O'Sullivan	The Island	78...75...76...75
305 (+13)		
D. Quillan	Elm Park	76...77...74...78
R. Leonard	Univ. of Ulster	77...76...76...76
P. Rodgers	Dundalk	77...76...79...73
J.P. Fitzgerald	Co. Louth	76...76...77...76
L. Brady	Royal Dublin	72...77...80...76
J. Gannon	Co. Louth	74...74...78...79
A. Morris	Belvoir Park	76...71...85...73

North of Ireland Championship (Royal Portrush, Co. Antrim. June 13-17)

Third Round					
D. Coyle	Dundalk	bt	E. Brady	Royal Dublin	2 and 1
L. Dalton	Waterford	bt	R. Flood	Stackstown	4 and 3
R. Elliott	Royal Portrush	bt	R. McDowell	Royal Belfast	2 holes
D. Gibson	Downpatrick	bt	G. McDowell	Rathmore	4 and 3
P. Gribben	Warrenpoint	bt	C. Moriarity	Clandeboye	2 holes
G. McGimpsey	Bangor	bt	D. Quilligan	Elm Park	9 and 7
A. Morris	Belvoir Park	bt	G. Reynolds	Rothesay	4 and 2
B. Omelia	Newlands	bt	C. Devlin	Ballymena	4 and 3
Quarter Finals					
R. Elliott	Royal Portrush	bt	B. Omelia	Newlands	6 and 5
D. Gibson	Downpatrick	bt	L. Dalton	Waterford	4 and 3
P. Gribben	Warrenpoint	bt	D. Coyle	Dundalk	1 hole
G. McGimpsey	Bangor	bt	A. Morris	Belvoir Park	6 and 4
Semi Finals					
P. Gribben	Warrenpoint	bt	G. McGimpsey	Bangor	5 and 4
D. Gibson	Downpatrick	bt	R. Elliott	Royal Portrush	2 and 1
Final					
P. Gribben	Warrenpoint	bt	D. Gibson	Downpatrick	5 and 4

South of Ireland Championship (Lahinch, Co. Clare. July 25-29, 1998)

Fifth Round

Justin Kehoe	Birr	beat	John Hutchinson	Royal Dublin	1 hole
Karl Bornemann	Douglas	beat	Dermot Snow	Portmarnock	at 20th
Bryan Ronan	Co. Louth	beat	C. Devlin	Ballymena	2 holes
Johnny Foster	Ballyclare	beat	Enda McMenamin	Ballybofey	3 and 2
Andrew McCormick	Scrabo	beat	Garret Mallon	North West	4 and 3
Jody Fanagan	Milltown	beat	Richard Elliott	Royal Portrush	7 and 6
Pat Killeen	Claremorris	beat	Timmy Rice	Limerick	2 and 1
Eamon Brady	Royal Dublin	beat	Fergal Deasy	Cork	2 and 1

Quarter Finals

Karl Bornemann	Douglas	beat	Justin Kehoe	Birr	3 and 2
Johnny Foster	Ballyclare	beat	Bryan Ronan	Co. Louth	1 hole
Andrew McCormick	Scrabo	beat	Jody Fanagan	Milltown	3 and 2
Eamon Brady	Royal Dublin	beat	Pat Killeen	Claremorris	2 and 1

Semi Finals

Johnny Foster	Ballyclare	beat	Karl Bornemann	Douglas	2 holes
Andrew McCormick	Scrabo	beat	Eamon Brady	Royal Dublin	3 and 2

Final

Johnny Foster	Ballyclare	beat	Andrew McCormick	Scrabo	2 holes

West of Ireland Championship (Enniscrone, Co. Sligo. April 10-14, 1998)

Third Round

Stephen Browne	Hermitage	beat	John Hutchinson	Royal Dublin	2 and 1
Colin Cunningham	Mullingar	beat	John Brady	Edenderry	at 20th
Jody Fanagan	Milltown	beat	Mark Campbell	Stackstown	2 and 1
Pat Lyons	Cork	beat	Graeme McDowell	Rathmore	4 and 2
Noel Fox	Portmarnock	beat	Pat Murray	Tipperary	1 hole
Eddie Power	Kilkenny	beat	Alan Thomas	Tramore	2 and 1
Henri Salonen	Finland	beat	Chris Brown	Royal Portrush	5 and 4
Michael Sinclair	Knock	beat	Pat Kileen	Claremorris	1 hole

Quarter Finals

Jody Fanagan	Milltown	beat	Michael Sinclair	Knock	1 hole
Noel Fox	Portmarnock	beat	Henri Salonen	Finland	1 hole
Pat Lyons	Cork	beat	Stephen Browne	Hermitage	3 and 2
Eddie Power	Kilkenny	beat	Colin Cunningham	Mullingar	4 and 3

Semi Finals

Noel Fox	Portmarnock	beat	Jody Fanagan	Milltown	at 19th
Pat Lyons	Cork	beat	Eddie Power	Kilkenny	4 and 2

Final

Noel Fox	Portmarnock	beat	Pat Lyons	Cork	2 and 1

Irish Amateur Open Championship (Royal Dublin. May 9-10, 1998)

286 (-2)					
M. Hoey	Shandon Park	72	69	74	71
288 (level)					
G. Cullen	Beaverstown	71	72	71	74
291 (+3)					
B. Omelia	Newlands	73	71	76	71
293 (+5)					
S. Paul	Tandragee	75	71	74	73
294 (+6)					
A. Morrow	Portmarnock	73	72	73	76
295 (+7)					
A. Thomas	Tramore	70	80	70	75
296 (+8)					
G. McGimpsey	Bangor	74	77	72	73
297 (+9)					
P. Lyons	Cork	75	73	72	77
G. McNeill	Waterford	70	76	77	74
298 (+10)					
G. Murphy	Monkstown	77	77	71	73
D. De Vooght	Belgium	76	72	74	76
299 (+11)					
E. Gibstein	U.S.A.	76	77	70	76
E. McMenamin	Ballybofey	76	74	73	76
300 (+12)					
D. Jones	City of Derry	73	75	74	78
P. Murray	Tipperary	75	75	77	73
E. Power	Kilkenny	77	76	74	73
C. Zaretti	Italy	77	77	71	75

Irish Amateur Close Championship (The Island, Dublin. July 13-17, 1998)

Third Round

E. Power	Kilkenny	beat	D. Sugrue	Killarney	2 holes
M. McGinley	Grange	beat	P. Murray	Tipperary	1 hole
G. Cullen	Beaverstown	beat	E. McMenamin	Ballybofey	at 21st
B. Ronan	Co. Louth	beat	M. Horan	Birr	5 and 4

M. Hoey	Shandon Park	beat	A. Lynch	University of Stirling	2 and 1
R. Symes	Shandon Park	beat	D. Dudley	Douglas	3 and 2
D. Coyle	Dundalk	beat	C. McElderry	Royal Portrush	2 and 1
B. Omelia	Newlands	beat	J. Mulready	Castle	4 and 2
Quarter Finals					
Eddie Power	Kilkenny	beat	M. McGinley	Grange	7 and 6
G. Cullen	Beaverstown	beat	Bryan Ronan	Co. Louth	at 20th
Michael Hoey	Shandon Park	beat	R. Symes	Shandon Park	1 hole
Bryan Omelia	Newlands	beat	D. Coyle	Dundalk	2 and 1
Semi Finals					
Eddie Power	Kilkenny	beat	G. Cullen	Beaverstown	2 holes
Bryan Omelia	Newlands	beat	Michael Hoey	Shandon Park	1 hole
Final					
Eddie Power	Kilkenny	beat	Bryan Omelia	Newlands	1 hole

1998 CUPS & SHIELDS

Athlone Golf Club 17-19 September

THE JIMMY BRUEN SHIELD

Semi-Finals

Portumna 3, Co. Cavan 2.

Moate 3, Muskerry 2.

Final

Moate 3½, Portumna 1½.

(Moate names first) P. Geraghty & M. Glennon bt J. Harte & N. Kilkenny 5/4; D. Fitzpatrick & T. Rosney bt F. McClearn & L. smith 3/2; A. Lynch & G. Digan lost to M. Carty & D. Burke 2 holes; K. Heavin & T. Higgins bt J. Slattery & F. Kilkenny 1 hole; L. Cunningham & T. Flattery halved with P. Quinlan & P. O'Rourke.

THE PIERCE PURCELL SHIELD

Semi-Finals

Woodbrook 3, Galway 2.

Nenagh 3, Nuremore 2.

Final

Nenagh 3½,Woodbrook 1½.

(Nenagh names first) T. Finan & S. O'Donoghue lost to T. Kelly & M. Mee 6/5; T. Grace & L. Hackett bt M. Hughes & P. Miley 3/2; P. Martin & T. Gaynor bt T. Pitt & C. Blair 4/3; P. Maloney & J. Hickey bt J. Murphy & D. Marsh 1 hole; D. Ryan & B. Galvin halved with E. Sweeney & N. Murphy.

THE SENIOR CUP

Semi-Finals

Cork 3½, Connemara 1½

Shandon Park 3, Portmarnock 2

Final

Cork 4, Shandon Park 1

(Cork names first) P. Dooley lost to N. Anderson 3/2; T. Cleary bt R. Symes 3/2; M. Owens bt P. Purdy 1 hole; G. O'Flaherty bt G. Lynas 2/1; P. Lyons bt B. Hobson 4/3.

THE JUNIOR CUP

Semi-Finals

Old Conna 3, Cork 2.

Tuam 3½, Strabane 1½.

Final

Old Conna 3, Tuam 2.

(Old Conna names first) G. O'Gorman bt O. McDonagh 1 hole; D. Mason lost to D. Coyne 6/4; M. Kynes lost to D. Scully 4/3; D. Leonard bt B. Cunniffe 1 hole; P. McDonald bt J.C. Davin 7/6.

THE BARTON SHIELD

Semi-Finals

Co. Sligo beat Grange 5 holes.

Warrenpoint beat Limerick at 19th hole.

Final

Warrenpoint beat Co. Sligo 1 hole.

(Warrenpoint names first) D. Dunne & T. Ford bt H. Armstrong & B. Orr 1 hole; K. Kearney & S. Heavey lost to P. Gribben & C. Campbell 2 holes.

INTERNATIONAL RESULTS, 1998

Home Internationals Royal Porthcawl, Wales. 9-11 September 1998.

Irish Team

Eamon Brady, Johnny Foster, Noel Fox, Paddy Gribben, David Jones, Ken Kearney, Andrew McCormick, Garth McGimpsey, John Morris, Eddie Power. Mick Craddock (c).

Ireland v Scotland. 09.09.98

Foursomes Result: Ireland 4, Scotland 1.
Singles Result: Ireland 7, Scotland 3.
Final Result: Ireland 11, Scotland 4.

Ireland v Wales. 10.09.98

Foursomes Result: Ireland 3, Wales 2.
Singles Result: Ireland 4½, Wales 5½.
Final Result: Ireland 7½, Wales 7½.

Ireland v England. 11.09.98

Foursomes Result: Ireland 3½, England 1½.
Singles Result: Ireland 3½, England 6½.
Final Result: Ireland 7, England 8.

FINAL STANDINGS

Position	Matches
1. England	3
2. Ireland	1½
3. Wales	1½
4. Scotland	0

IRISH CHAMPIONSHIP WINNERS

	Close Championship			Open Championship		
Year	Venue	Winner	Club	Venue	Winner	Club
1892	-	-	-	Portrush	A. Stuart	Hon. Co. Edinburgh
1893	Portrush	T. Dickson	Co Down	Newcastle	J. Ball Jr	Royal Liverpool
1894	Newcastle	R. Magill	Co Down	Dollymount	J. Ball Jr	Royal Liverpool
1895	Dollymount	W.H. Webb	Royal Portrush	Portrush	W.B. Taylor	Carlton
1896	Portrush	J.S. Moore	Dublin University	Newcastle	W.B. Taylor	Carlton
1897	Newcastle	H.E.Reade	Royal Belfast	Dollymount	H.H. Hilton	Royal Liverpool
1898	Dollymount	W.H. Webb	Royal Portrush	Portrush	W.B. Taylor	Carlton
1899	Portrush	H.E. Reade	Royal Belfast	Portmarnock	J. Ball Jr	Royal Liverpool
1900	Portmarnock	G.N. Henry	Portmarnock	Newcastle	H.H. Hilton	Royal Liverpool
1901	Newcastle	W.H. Boyd	Portmarnock	Dollymount	H.H. Hilton	Royal Liverpool
1902	Dollymount	F.B.Newett	Malone	Portrush	H.H. Hilton	Royal Liverpool
1903	Portrush	H.E.Reade	Royal Belfast	Portmarnock	Geo Wilkie	Leven Thistle
1904	Portmarnock	H.A. Boyd	Portmarnock	Newcastle	J.S. Worthington	Royal Mid-Surrey
1905	Newcastle	F.B. Newett	Malone	Dollymount	H.A. Boyd	Portmarnock
1906	Dollymount	H.A. Boyd	Portmarnock	Portrush	H.H. Barker	Huddersfield
1907	Portrush	H.M. Cairnes	Portmarnock	Portmarnock	J. Douglas Brown	Murrayfield
1908	Portmarnock	L.O. Munn	Dublin University	Newcastle	J.F. Mithchell	Royal Musselburgh
1909	Newcastle	J.F. Jameson	Malahide	Dollymount	L.O. Munn	North West
1910	Dollymount	J.F. Jameson	Malahide	Portrush	L.O. Munn	North West
1911	Portrush	L.O. Munn	North-West	Portmarnock	L.O. Munn	North West
1912	Castlerock	A.H. Craig	Fortwilliam	Newcastle	Gordon Lockhart	Prestwick St Nicholas
1913	Portmarnock	L.O. Munn	Royal Dublin	Dollymount	C.A. Palmer	Handsworth
1914	Hermitage	L.O. Munn	North-West			NO CHAMPIONSHIP
1915-18			NO C'SHIP			NO CHAMPIONSHIP
1919	Portmarnock	E.F. Carter	Royal Portrush	Portrush	C. Bretherton	Handsworth
1920	Castlerock	C.O. Hezlet	Royal Portrush	Portmarnock	G.N.C. Martin	Royal Portrush
1921	Portmarnock	E.F. Carter	Royal Dublin	Newcastle	D. Wilson Smyth	Royal Co. Down
1922	Portrush	E.M. Munn	North-West	Portrush	Alfred Lowe	Malone
1923	Milltown	J.D. MacCormack	Hermitage	Newcastle	G.N.C. Martin	Royal Portrush
1924	Newcastle	J.D. MacCormack	Hermitage	Dollymount	E.F. Spiller	North West
1925	Portmarnock	C.W. Robertson	Delgany	Portrush	T.A. Torrance	Sandy Lodge
1926	Portrush	A.C. Allison	Royal Portrush	Portmarnock	C.O. Hezlet	Royal Portrush
1927	Cork	J.D. MacCormack	Hermitage	Newcastle	R.M. McConnell	Royal Portrush
1928	Castlerock	E.B. Soulby	Fortwilliam	Dollymount	G.S. Noon	Edinburgh Burgess
1929	Dollymount	E.B. Soulby	Fortwilliam	Portrush	C.O. Hezlet	Royal Portrush
1930	Lahinch	J. Burke	Lahinch	Portmarnock	William Sutton	Timperley
1931	Rosses Point	J. Burke	Lahinch	Newcastle	E.A. McRuvie	Leven Thistle
1932	Portrush	J. Burke	Lahinch	Dollymount	J. McLean	Hayston
1933	Cork	J. Burke	Lahinch	Newcastle	J. McLean	Hayston
1934	Rosslare	J.C. Brown	Waterford	Portmarnock	H. Thomson	Williamwood
1935	Galway	R.M. McConnell	Royal Portrush	Portrush	H. Thomson	Williamwood
1936	Castlerock	J. Burke	Newlands	Portmarnock	J.C. Brown	Waterford
1937	Ballybunion	J. Bruen Jr	Muskerry	Dollymount	J. Fitzsimmons	Bushfoot
1938	Castle	J. Bruen Jr	Muskerry	Newcastle	J. Bruen Jr	Cork
1939	Rosses Point	G.H. Owens	Skerries	Portmarnock	C'ship cancelled	
1940	Dollymount	J. Burke	Castletroy			NO CHAMPIONSHIP
1941-45		NO CHAMPIONSHIP				NO CHAMPIONSHIP
1946	Dollymount	J. Burke	Castletroy	Portrush	J.B. Carr	Sutton
1947	Lahinch	J. Burke	Castletroy	Dollymount	J. Burke	Limerick
1948	Portrush	C. Ewing	Co. Sligo	Newcastle	Cecil Ewing	Co. Sligo
1949	Galway	J.P. Carroll	Sutton	Killarney	W.M. O'Sullivan	Killarney
1950	Baltray	B. Herlihy	Portmarnock	Rosses Point	J.B. Carr	Sutton
1951	Cork	M. Power	Muskerry	Portmarnock	Cecil Ewing	Co. Sligo
1952	Craigivad	T.W. Egan	Monkstown	Portrush	N.V. Drew	Bangor
1953	Rosses Point	J. Malone	Portmarnock	Killarney	N.V. Drew	Bangor
1954	Carlow	J.B. Carr	Sutton	Dollymount	J.B. Carr	Sutton
1955	Lahinch	R. Mahon	Portmarnock	Newcastle	J.F. Fitzgibbon	Cork
1956	Malone	A.G.H. Love	Knock	Portmarnock	J.B. Carr	Sutton
1957	Galway	J.B. Carr	Sutton	Portrush	J.L. Bamford	Royal Portrush
1958	Ballybunion	C. Ewing	Co Sligo	Dollymount	T. Craddock	Malahide

Continued from previous page

Year	Close Championship Venue	Winner	Club	Open Championship Venue	Winner	Club
1959	Portmarnock	T. Craddock	Malahide	Newcastle	J. Duncan	Shandon Park
1960	Portstewart	M. Edwards	Shandon Park			NO CHAMPIONSHIP
1961	Rosses Point	D. Sheahan	Grange & U.C.D.			NO CHAMPIONSHIP
1962	Baltray	M. Edwards	Shandon Park			NO CHAMPIONSHIP
1963	Killarney	J.B. Carr	Sutton			NO CHAMPIONSHIP
1964	Newcastle	J.B. Carr	Sutton			NO CHAMPIONSHIP
1965	Rosses Point	J.B. Carr	Sutton			NO CHAMPIONSHIP
1966	Dollymount	D. Sheahan	Grange			NO CHAMPIONSHIP
1967	Lahinch	J.B. Carr	Sutton			NO CHAMPIONSHIP
1968	Portrush	M.D. O'Brien	New Ross			NO CHAMPIONSHIP
1969	Rosses Point	V. Nevin	Limerick			NO CHAMPIONSHIP
1970	Grange	D. Sheahan	Grange			NO CHAMPIONSHIP
1971	Ballybunion	R.M. Kane	Malahide			NO CHAMPIONSHIP
1972	Newcastle	K. Stevenson	Banbridge			NO CHAMPIONSHIP
1973	Rosses Point	R.K.M. Pollin	Royal Belfast			NO CHAMPIONSHIP
1974	Portmarnock	R.M. Kane	Ealing			NO CHAMPIONSHIP
1975	Cork	M.D. O'Brien	New Ross			NO CHAMPIONSHIP
1976	Portrush	D. Brannigan	Bettystown & L'town			NO CHAMPIONSHIP
1977	Westport	M.A. Gannon	Co Louth			NO CHAMPIONSHIP
1978	Carlow	M.F. Morris	Portmarnock			NO CHAMPIONSHIP
1979	Ballybunion	J. Harrington	Adare Manor			NO CHAMPIONSHIP
1980	Newcastle	R. Rafferty	Warrenpoint			NO CHAMPIONSHIP
1981	Rosses Point	D. Brannigan	Bettystown & L'town			NO CHAMPIONSHIP
1982	Woodbrook	P. Walton	Malahide			NO CHAMPIONSHIP
1983	Killarney	T.Corridan	Castletroy			NO CHAMPIONSHIP
1984	Malone	T.B.C. Hoey	Shandon Park			NO CHAMPIONSHIP
1985	Westport	D.F. O'Sullivan	Cork			NO CHAMPIONSHIP
1986	Dollymount	J. McHenry	Douglas			NO CHAMPIONSHIP
1987	Tramore	E. Power	Tramore			NO CHAMPIONSHIP
1988	Portrush	G. McGimpsey	Bangor			NO CHAMPIONSHIP
1989	Rosses Point	P. McGinley	Grange			NO CHAMPIONSHIP
1990	Baltray	D. Clarke	Dungannon			NO CHAMPIONSHIP
1991	Ballybunion	G. McNeill	Warrenpoint			NO CHAMPIONSHIP
1992	Portstewart	G. Murphy	Kilkenny			NO CHAMPIONSHIP
1993	Enniscrone	E. Power	Tramore			NO CHAMPIONSHIP
1994	Portmarnock	D. Higgins	Waterville			NO CHAMPIONSHIP
1995	Lahinch	P. Harrington	Stackstown	Fota Island	P. Harrington	Stackstown
1996	Royal Co. Down	P. Lawrie	U.C.D.	Fota Island	K. Nolan	Bray
1997	Westport	K. Kearney	Co. Sligo	Fota Island	K. Nolan	Bray

PROVINCIAL CHAMPIONSHIP WINNERS SINCE 1948

Year	West of Ireland	East of Ireland	South of Ireland	North of Ireland
1948	J.B. Carr	J.B. Carr	J.B. Carr	J. Fitzsimmons
1949	C. Ewing	M.Ferguson	J.P. Carroll	F. Webster
1950	C. Ewing	J.P. Carroll	M. Power	N.V. Drew
1951	J.B. Carr	M.Power	G. Gilligan	W. Meharg
1952	J.C. Brown	N.V. Drew	M. Power	N. V. Drew
1953	J.B. Carr	J.P .Carroll	P.J. Leydon	C. Knox
1954	J.B. Carr	B.J. Scannell	P. Bulger	J.L. Bamford
1955	W.I. Forsythe	B.J. Scannell	P.J. Leydon	R McK Fleury
1956	J.B. Carr	J.B. Carr	P.J. Leydon	M. Edwards
1957	J.R. Mahon	J.B. Carr	P.J. Leydon	M. Edwards
1958	J.B. Carr	J.B. Carr	J.C. Brown	T.E. Dijon
1959	W.J.J. Ferguson	T. Craddock	G. Roberts	J. Duncan
1960	J.B. Carr	J.B. Carr	P. Sullivan	W.H.E. Rainey
1961	J.B. Carr	J.B. Carr	M. Guerin	J. Duncan

Continued from previous page

Year	West of Ireland	East of Ireland	South of Ireland	North of Ireland
1962	J.B. Carr	T.W. Egan	M. Guerin	J.F.D. Madeley
1963	R.M. Craigan	G.N. Fogarty	M. Guerin	J.F.D. Madeley
1964	B.P. Malone	J.B. Carr	W.A. Kelleher	F.A. McCorty
1965	R.M. Craigan	T. Craddock	R. de L Staunton	W.H.E. Rainey
1966	J.B. Carr	T. Craddock	J.B. Carr	B. Edwards
1967	R.K.M. Pollin	N. Fogarty	G.N. Fogarty	W.R.A. Tennant
1968	D.A. Nelson	P. Caul	J.D. Smyth	M.J.C. Hoey
1969	R.K.M. Pollin	J.B. Carr	J.B. Carr	M.J.C. Hoey
1970	J. McTear	R.J. Carr	J.E. O'Leary	J. Faith
1971	R.J. Carr	P. Mulcare	P. Mulcare	R.K.M. Pollin
1972	V. Nevin	P. Mulcare	R. deL Staunton	J.L. Bamford
1973	H.B. Smyth	P. Mulcare	M.A. Gannon	B. Edwards
1974	M.A. Gannon	H.B. Smyth	D.C. Long	B.J.S Kissock
1975	I.A. Elliott	A.J.C. Morrow	B.P. Malone	J. Heggarty
1976	D. Branigan	D. White	V. Nevin	B.J.S. Kissock
1977	T.B.C. Hoey	T. Cleary	L. MacNamara	D.J.F. Young
1978	B.V.M. Reddan	M.A. Gannon	V. Nevin	G. McGimpsey
1979	D.C. Long	A.D. Pierse	P. O'Rourke	T.B.C. Hoey
1980	A.D. Pierse	P. Caul	M. Burns	M. Malone
1981	D. Branigan	D. Brannigan	P. O'Rourke	D.C. Long
1982	A.D. Pierse	M.F. Sludds	M.F. Morris	D.C. Long
1983	C. Glasgow	A.J.C. Morrow	A.C.J. Morrow	T.B.C. Hoey
1984	G. McGimpsey	B.Reddan	N.H. Anderson	G. McGimpsey
1985	J. Feeney	F. Ronan	P. O'Rourke	I.A. Elliott
1986	P. Rayfus	P.F. Hogan	J. McHenry	D.W. Ballentine
1987	N. McGrane	P. Rayfus	B.V.M. Reddan	A.D. Pierse
1988	G. McGimpsey	G. McGimpsey	M.A. Gannon	N.H. Anderson
1989	P. McInerney	D. Clarke	S. Keenan	N.H. Anderson
1990	N. Goulding	D.F. O'Sullivan	D. Clarke	D. Clarke
1991	N. Goulding	P. Hogan	P. McGinley	G. McGimpsey
1992	K. Kearney	R. Burns	L. MacNamara	G. McGimpsey
1993	G. McGimpsey	R. Burns	P. Sheehan	G. McGimpsey
1994	P. Harrington	G. McGimpsey	D. Higgins	N. Ludwell
1995	E. Brady	D. Branigan	J. Fanagan	K. Nolan
1996	G. McGimpsey	N. Fox	A. Morrow	M. McGinley
1997	J. Fanagan	S. Quinlivan	P. Collier	M. Sinclair

Senior Interprovincial Championship Winners

Year	Winners
1939	Leinster
1940-55	No Championship
1956	Leinster/Munster/Ulster
1957	Munster/Ulster
1958	Ulster
1959	Ulster
1960	Leinster/Munster/Ulster
1961	Ulster
1962	Leinster
1963	Leinster
1964	Leinster
1965	Leinster
1966	Leinster/Munster
1967	Connacht
1968	Leinster
1969	Leinster
1970	Ulster

Year	Winners
1971	Leinster
1972	Leinster
1973	Munster
1974	Munster
1975	Ulster
1976	Leinster
1977	Ulster
1978	Leinster/Munster/Ulster
1979	Ulster
1980	Munster
1981	Leinster
1982	Ulster
1983	Connacht
1984	Munster
1985	Ulster
1986	Leinster
1987	Ulster

Year	Winners
1988	Ulster
1989	Leinster
1990	Ulster
1991	Ulster
1992	Munster
1993	Munster
1994	Ulster
1995	Munster
1996	Munster
1997	Munster

Province	Overall Outright	Tied
Connacht	2	-
Leinster	13	4
Munster	9	5
Ulster	14	4

WALKER CUP

Irish Players 1924-97

Years	Name	Matches	Won	Halved	Lost	Points
1924, '28, '28	Charles Hezlett	6	0	1	5	1
1928	Noel Martin	1	0	0	1	0
1932	John Burke	2	0	1	1	1
1936, '38, '47, '49, '51, '53, '55	Cecil Ewing	10	1	2	7	4
1938, '49, '51	Jimmy Bruen	5	0	1	4	1
1947, '49, '51, '53, '55, '57, '59, '61, '63, '67	Joe Carr*	20	5	1	14	11
1949, '51	Max McCready	3	0	0	3	0
1953	Norman Drew	1	0	0	1	0
1963	David Madeley	2	0	1	1	1
1963	David Sheahan	4	2	0	2	4
1967, '69	Tom Craddock	6	2	1	3	5
1971	Roddy Carr	4	3	1	0	7
1975	Pat Mulcare	3	2	0	1	4
1981	Ronan Rafferty	4	2	0	2	4
1981, '83	Philip Walton	8	6	0	2	12
1983	Arthur Pierse	3	0	1	2	1
1985, '89, '91	Garth McGimpsey	8	3	2	3	8
1987	John McHenry	4	2	0	2	4
1989	Eoghan O'Connell	4	3	1	0	7
1991, '93, '95	Padraig Harrington	9	3	1	5	7
1991	Paul McGinley	3	1	0	2	2
1993	Raymond Burns	2	1	0	1	2
1995	Jody Fanagan	3	3	0	0	6
1997	Richard Coughlan	4	0	1	3	1
1997	Keith Nolan	3	0	0	3	0

* Joe Carr was non-playing captain of the Walker Cup team in 1965

Results 1924-97

Year	Venue	GB & Ireland	USA
1922	Long Island, New York	4	8
1923	St. Andrews	5½	6½
1924	Garden City, New York	3	9
1926	St. Andrews	5½	6½
1928	Chicago	1	11
1930	Sandwich	2	10
1932	Brookline, Massachusetts	2½	9½
1934	St. Andrews	2½	9½
1936	Pine Valley, New Jersey	1½	10½
1938	St. Andrews	7½	4½
1947	St. Andrews	4	8
1949	Winged Foot, New York	2	10
1951	Royal Birkdale	4½	7½
1953	Kittansett, Massachusetts	3	9
1955	St. Andrews	2	10
1957	Minikhada	3½	8½
1959	Muirfield	3	9
1961	Seattle, Washington	1	11
1963	Turnberry	8	12
1965	Baltimore, Maryland	11	11
1967	Sandwich	7	13
1969	Milwaukee, Wisconsin	8	10
1971	St. Andrews	13	11
1973	Brookline, Massachusetts	10	14
1975	St. Andrews	8½	15½
1977	Shinnecock Hills, New York	8	16
1979	Muirfield	8½	15½
1981	Cypress Point	9	15
1983	Hoylake	10½	13½
1985	Pine Valley, New Jersey	11	13
1987	Sunningdale	7½	16½
1989	Peachtree, Georgia	12½	11½
1991	Portmarnock	10	14
1993	Interlachen, Minnesota	3½	6½
1995	Royal Portcawl	14	10
1997	Quaker Ridge, New York	6	18

TEXACO AWARD WINNERS, GOLF

Year	Winner
1958	Harry Bradshaw
1959	Christy O' Connor Snr
1960	*Joe Carr
1961	Christy O' Connor Snr
1962	*David Sheahan
1963	*Philomena Garvey
1964	Jimmy Martin
1965	*Tom Craddock
1966	Christy O' Connor Snr
1967	*Cecil Ewing
1968	Elaine Bradshaw
1969	*Vincent Nevin
1970	Christy O' Connor Snr
1971	Roddy Carr
1972	Jimmy Kinsella
1973	Maisie Mooney
1975	Christy O' Connor Jnr
1976	Eamon Darcy
1977	Christy O' Connor Jnr
1979	Des Smyth
1980	*Ronan Rafferty
1981	*Philip Walton
1983	Philip Walton
1986	*Claire Hourihan

Continued from previous page

Year	Winner
1987	Eamon Darcy
1988	Des Smyth
1989	Ronan Rafferty
1990	David Feherty
1991	David Feherty
1992	Christy O' Connor Jnr
1993	Darren Clarke
1995	Philip Walton
1996	Padraig Harrington

*Denotes amateur, or had amateur status when award was made.

GOLFING UNION OF IRELAND PROVINCIAL OFFICERS

	Chairman	Honorary Treasurer	Honorary Secretary
Connacht	Michael P. O'Donoghue	Frederick W. Perry	Frederick W. Perry
Leinster	Patrick L. Murphy	Darry Doyle	Albert Lee
Munster	John V. Lynch	Bernard P. Hynes	Sean McMahon
Ulster	William G. Black	Cecil Lindsay	Lindsay Shanks

PRESIDENTS OF THE GOLFING UNION OF IRELAND

Years	President
1891-1905	Lord Ranfurly
1906-25	Sir. D. Plunkett Barton
1926-28	Hugh C. Kelly
1929-31	Beamish A. Morrison
1932-35	D. Wilson Smyth
1936-37	William Fitzsimmons
1938-41	George Crosbie
1942-45	Thomas P. Toher
1946-47	James Henderson
1948-49	Pierce F. Purcell
1950-51	Redmond Simcox
1952-53	Sir William Neill
1954-55	Michael G. O'Malley
1956-57	Robert E. Davitt
1958-59	William O'Sullivan
1960-62	David L. Baine
1963-64	Michael J. Murphy
1965-66	Thomas P. Brindley
1967	Thomas E. O'Donnell
1968	H. Max Hadden
1969	William J. Gill
1970	Cecil Ewing
1971	Gerald H. Owens
1972	Thomas Montgomery
1973	Patrick J. McPolin
1974	Maurice DeLacy Staunton
1975	Peter V. Lyons
1976	John G. McEverl
1977	Patrick J. Foley
1978	Thomas J. Rogers
1979	Brendan J. Scannell
1980	Michael C. McAuley
1981	John P. McInerney
1982	Frederick W. Perry
1983	Michael P. Fitzpatrick
1984	William J.J. Ferguson
1985	Francis W. Bowen
1986	Michael J. Hennelly
1987	J. Gerard O'Brien
1988	Barry T. Crymble
1989	Joseph M. Quinlan
1990	Gerard D. Golden
1991	Desmond Rea O'Kelly
1992	Liam Reidy
1993	J.L. Ian Bamford
1994	John F. O'Reilly
1995	Declan J. Howley
1996	Eamonn Curran
1997	Peter O'Hara
1998	J. Percy Shannon

HONORARY TREASURERS OF THE GOLFING UNION OF IRELAND

Years	Treasurer
1891-1911	Hugh C. Kelly
1912-29	William B. Fennell
1930	Arthur H. Moody
1931-36	Charles S. Harden
1937-45	William F. Neill
1946-47	Frank J. Byrne
1948-52	Alfred S.G. Adams
1953-67	Hugh Stevenson
1968-73	Charles H. Adams
1974-92	David M. McAuley
1993-	Rollo McClure

HONORARY SECRETARIES

Years	Secretary
1891-98	George Comba
1899-1905	Hugh J. Daly
1906-20	Rev. John L. Morrow
1921-26	George Price
1927-47	Alan B. Kidd
1948	John Roy
1949-67	William J. Gill
1968-69	Thomas P. Brindley
1970-74	William J. Gill
1975	William J. Gill & Desmond Rea O'Kelly
1976-88	Desmond Rea O'Kelly
1989	Desmond Rea O'Kelly & J. Gerard O'Brien
1990-	J. Gerard O'Brien

Irish Ladies Golf Union

1 Clonskeagh Square, Clonskeagh Road, Dublin 14. Tel. (01) 2696244

Founded	1893
President	Juliett McHugh
Secretary	M.P. Turvey
Number of Affiliated Clubs	333
Number of Club Members	42,500

1998 CHAMPIONS	**Winner(s)**	**Runner(s) Up**
Irish Ladies Close Championship	Lillian Behan (The Curragh)	Oonagh Purfield (Co. Louth)
Irish Open Stroke Play Championship	S. Fanagan O'Brien (Milltown)	Lillian Behan (The Curragh)
Senior Cup Championship	Royal Co. Down	Co. Louth
Interprovincial Championship	Leinster	Ulster
Irish Girls Interprovincials	Leinster	Munster
Schools Championship	Laurel Hill College, Limerick	Santa Sabina, Sutton
Connacht Senior Championship	Deirdre Smith (Co. Louth)	Emma Dickson (Royal Co. Down)
Leinster Senior Championship	Alison Coffey (Warrenpoint)	Lillian Behan (The Curragh)
Midland Senior Championship	Hanoria Fogarty (Castlecomer)	Mary Norton (Kilkenny)
Munster Senior Championship	Barbara Hackett (Castletroy)	
Ulster Senior Championship	Alison Coffey (Warrenpoint)	Emma Dickson (Royal Co. Down)

ILGU District Statistics

Irish Ladies Golf Union, Midland District

c/o Honorary Secretary, Cloonagoose, Borris, Co. Carlow. Tel. (0503) 73577

Founded	1935
Honorary Secretary	Netta Colgan
Number of Clubs	52
Number of Interprovincial Victories	N/a

Irish Ladies Golf Union, Western District

c/o Honorary Secretary, Ellison Street, Castlebar, Co. Mayo. Tel. (094) 21410.

Founded	1927
Chairperson	Dr Helen Cleary
Honorary Secretary	Ms Margaret Tighe
Number of Clubs	48
Number of Members	5,000 (approx)
Number of Interprovincial Victories	0

Irish Ladies Golf Union, Southern District

c/o Mary Power, 36 Tracton Avenue, Montenotte, Cork. Tel. (021) 551977

Chairperson	Joan Bouchier-Hayes
Honorary Secretary	Mary Power
Number of Affiliated Clubs	71
Number of Interprovincial Victories	5

Irish Ladies Golf Union, Eastern District

c/o Liz Foley, 10 Vale View Avenue The Park, Cabintely, Dublin 18. Tel. (01) 2856853

Founded	mid 1930s
Chairperson	Margaret Keogh
Honorary Secretary	Liz Foley
Number of Affiliated Clubs	92
Number of Interprovincial Victories	24

Irish Ladies Golf Union, Northern District

Founded	1893
Chairperson	Mrs Dorothy Russell
Honorary Secretary	Brigid McCaw
Number of Interprovincial Victories	4

DOMESTIC RESULTS

Irish Ladies Senior Cup Dundalk Golf Club 27-28 June

Semi Finals

Co. Louth ....bt ..The Curragh..................4-1
Royal Co. Down...........bt ..Killarney..................3½-1½

Final

Royal Co. Down...........bt ..Co. Louth 3½-1½

Irish Ladies Close Championship Clandeboye Golf Club 19-23 May, 1998

Semi Finals

Oonagh Purfield..........................Co. Louth ....beat......Paula Gorman ....Elm Park........3 and 2
Lillian Behan ....The Curragh .....beat......M. McEvoy ....Bangor........3 and 2

Final

Lillian Behan ....The Curragh .....beat......Oonagh Purfield....................Co. Louth.........at 19th

Irish Ladies Open Championship Waterford Castle. 24-26 July, 1998

141

S. Fanagan O'Brien............Milltown..................74...67

147

L. Behan..........................The Curragh............72...75

148

E. Dowdall ....Wexford.................72...76

149

J. Smith ....Gullane...................76...73

150

S. Wood.............................Aberdeen ....76...74

151

D. Smith............................Co. Louth................75...76

152

M. McGreevy ....Rosmore ....76...77
A. Coffey...........................Warrenpoint ....78...74

153

Y. Cassidy..........................Dundalk..................77...76

154

S. Keane............................The Curragh............81...73
C. Hargan..........................Dundee ....78...76
J. O'Brien...........................Thurles....................80...74
G. Hegarty..........................Greencastle.............75...79

155

E. Murphy...........................Cork ....79...76
H. Kavanagh.......................Grange ....78...77
T. Mangan...........................Ennis......................80...75

Heavy rain forced the abandonment of the third and final round.

INTERNATIONAL RESULTS

Home Internationals Burnham and Barrow. 9-11 September 1998.

Irish Team

Lillian Behan, Elaine Dowdall, Hazel Kavanagh, Suzanne O'Brien, Oonagh Purfield, Alison Coofey, Michelle McGreevy.

Ireland v. England. 09.09.98

Foursomes Result: Ireland 1½, England 1½.
Singles Result: Ireland 2 ½, England 3½.
Final Result: Ireland 4, England 5.

Ireland v. Scotland. 10.09.98

Foursomes Result: Ireland 1½, Scotland 1½.
Singles Result: Ireland 3, Scotland 3.
Final Result: Ireland 4½, Scotland 4½.

Ireland v. Wales. 11.09.98

Foursomes Result: Ireland 3, Wales 0.
Singles Result: Ireland 3, Wales 3.
Final Result: Ireland 6, Wales 0.

FINAL STANDINGS

Position	Matches Won
1. England	3
2. Ireland	1½
3. Scotland	1
4. Wales	½

RECORDS

Irish Ladies Close Championship

Year	Winner
1894	Miss C. Mulligan
1895	Miss Cox
1896	Miss N. Graham
1897	Miss N. Graham
1898	Miss J. Magill
1899	Miss M. Hazlet
1900	Miss R. Adair
1901	Miss R. Adair
1902	Miss R. Adair
1903	Miss R. Adair
1904	Miss M. Hezlet
1905	Miss M. Hezlet
1906	Miss N. Hezlet
1907	Miss F. Walker-Leigh
1908	Miss M. Hezlet
1909	Miss A. Ormsby
1910	Miss M. Harrison
1911	Miss M. Harrison
1912	Miss M. Harrison
1913	Miss J. Jackson
1914	Miss J. Jackson
1915-18	No Championship
1919	Miss J. Jackson
1920	Miss J. Jackson
1921	Miss Stuart French
1922	Mrs Claude Gotto
1923	Miss J. Jackson
1924	Miss C.G. Thornton
1925	Miss J Jackson
1926	Miss P. Jameson
1927	Miss McLoughlin
1928	Mrs W. Dwyer
1929	Mrs M. A. Hall

Year	Winner
1930	Mrs J. B. Walker
1931	Miss E. C. Pentony
1932	Miss B. Latchford
1933	Miss E. C. Pentony
1934	Mrs P. Shelock Fletcher
1935	Miss D. Ferguson
1936	Miss C. Tiernan
1937	Mrs H. V. Glendinning
1938	Mrs. J. Black
1939	Miss C. MacGeagh
1940-45	No Championship
1946	Miss P. Garvey
1947	Miss P. Garvey
1949	Miss C Smye
1950	Miss P. Garvey
1951	Miss P. Garvey
1952	Miss. D. Foster
1953	Miss P. Garvey
1954	Miss P. Garvey
1955	Miss P. Garvey
1956	Miss P. O'Sullivan
1957	Miss P. Garvey
1958	Miss P. Garvey
1959	Miss P. Garvey
1960	Miss P. Garvey
1961	Mrs P.G. MacCann
1962	Miss P. Garvey
1963	Miss P. Garvey
1964	Mrs Z. Fallon
1965	Miss E. Purcell
1966	Miss E. Bradshaw
1967	Mrs G. Brandom
1968	Miss E. Bradshaw
1969	Miss M. McKenna
1970	Miss P. Garvey
1971	Miss E. Bradshaw
1972	Miss M. McKenna
1973	Miss M. Mooney
1974	Miss M. McKenna
1975	Miss M. Gorry
1976	Miss C. Nesbitt
1977	Miss M. McKenna
1978	Miss M. Gorry
1979	Miss M. McKenna
1980	Miss C. Nesbitt
1981	Miss M. McKenna
1982	Miss M. McKenna
1983	Miss C. Hourihane
1984	Miss C. Hourihane
1985	Miss C. Hourihane
1986	Mrs T. O'Reilly
1987	Miss C. Hourihane
1988	Miss L. Bolton
1989	Miss M. McKenna
1990	Miss E.R. McDaid
1991	Miss C. Hourihane
1992	Mrs E.R. Power
1993	Miss E. Higgins
1994	Mrs Laura Webb
1995	Mrs E.R. Power
1996	B. Hackett
1997	S. Fanagan

Irish Ladies Open Championship

Year	Winner
1993	Tracy Eakin
1994	Hazel Kavanagh
1995	Naoimh Quigg
1996	Eileen Rose Power
1997	Yvonne Cassidy

Provincial Championship Winners

Year	Ulster*	Midland	Munster	Leinster	Connacht
1939	T. Marks	E. O'Henry	-	-	-
1940	WWII	N. L. Todd	-	-	-
1941	WWII	B. Hynes	-	-	-
1942	WWII	-	-	-	-
1943	WWII	M. M. Murphy	-	-	-
1944	WWII	N. L. Todd	-	-	-
1945	WWII	N. L. Todd	-	-	-
1946	WWII	K. Keogh	-	-	-
1947	Z. Bolton	M. M. Earner	-	-	-
1948	Z. Bolton	M. Kiely	-	-	-
1949	Z. Bolton	K. Doyle/A. O'Donohoe	S. McCloughry	-	-
1950	Z. Bolton	A McCarthy	J. K. Brice	-	-
1951	M. G. Smyth	Phil Garvey	Philomena Garvey	-	-
1952	D. Foster	P. G. McCann	M. O'Riordan	-	-
1953	D. Foster	Pat O'Sullivan	Pat O'Sullivan	-	-
1954	T. Marks	Pat O'Sullivan	Pat O'Sullivan	-	-
1955	T. Marks	R. Bayly	Z. Fallon	-	-
1956	Z. Bolton	M. Earner	Z. Fallon	P. Fletcher	-
1957	A. R. Humphries	P. McCann	Z. Fallon	V. Reddan	-
1958	M. G. Smyth	P. McCann	P. G. McGann	P. G. MacCann	-
1959	M. G. Smyth	A. O'Brien	Z. Fallon	Miss Brooks	-
1960	Z. Bolton	P. G. McCann	Pat Quinlan	M. Earner	-
1961	Not Played	Pat O'Sullivan	Z. Fallon	M. Earner	-
1962	A. Sweeney	Oonagh Heskin	H. E. Colhon	I. Burke	-
1963	A. Sweeney	E. J. Fagan	A. O'Brien	I Burke	-
1964	H. Colhoun	Ita Burke	A. J. Elmes	I. Burke	-
1965	S. Owen	J. Lambert	Ita Burke	B. Hyland	-
1966	J. Beckett	P. Quinlan	Pat Quinlan	B. Hyland	-
1967	E. Barnett	P. Quinlan	A. O'Brien	I. Burke	-
1968	C. McAuley	D. V. Hickey	A. J. Elmes	E. Bradshaw	-
1969	D. Madeley	P. Flanagan	O. Heskin	E Bradshaw	-
1970	C. McAuley	E. J. Fagan	A. Heskin	V. Singleton	-
1971	M. McConnell	Carol Smyth	A. Heskin	J. Mark	-

Continued from previous page

Year	Ulster*	Midland	Munster	Leinster	Connacht
1972	S. Morton	V. Hassett	A. J. Elmes	M. Earner	-
1973	P. Rooney	Therese Moran	Valerie Hassett	M. Earner	Mrs Winslow
1974	A. McLean	Mary Gorry	A. Heskin	S. Gorman	M. O'Donnell
1975	L. Malone	Lilian Malone	A. Heskin	Dr G. Costello	I. Hadden
1976	C. Nesbitt	Ivy Hadden	R. Hegarty	S Gorman	M. O'Donnell
1977	S. Morton	Maisie Lambe	Valerie Hassett	M. Gorry	M. Keon
1978	C. Nesbitt	K. Reilly	A. Heskin	S. O'Brien-Kenney	J. McHugh
1979	M. Gorry	Mary Gorry	R. Hegarty	M. Gorry	M. Gorry
1980	M. Madill	J. Gillespie	B. Gleeson	C. Hourihane	B. Gearty
1981	L. Starrett	A. Reynolds	R. Brennan	M. McKenna	J. Gillespie
1982	C. Robinson	Charlotte Daly	E. Higgins	M. McKenna	P. Wickham
1983	M. Madill	Brigid Gleeson	B. Gleeson	P. Wickham	L. Sweeney
1984	L. Starrett	S. O'Brien-Kenney	A. O'Sullivan	L. Behan	L. Sweeney
1985	M. Gamer	Brigid Gleeson	Eileen Rose McDaid	C. Hourihane	P. Wickham
1986	J. Allen	S. O'Brien-Kenney	C. Keating	Y. McQuillan	Y. McQuillan
1987	Vari McGreevy	Rita Walsh	B. Gleeson Healy	S. Gorman	P. Wickham
1988	Debbie Hanna	Karen Maguire	E. Higgins	M. McKenna	D. McCarthy
1989	Laura Bolton	Irene Murphy	A. O'Sullivan	M. McKenna	D. Mahon
1990	Paula Gorman	Susanne Kenny	E. Higgins	M. McKenna	P. Wickham
1991	Laura Bolton	Lynn Sweeney	Tricia Mangan	D. McCarthy	R. MacGuigan
1992	Vari McGreevy	Lynn Sweeney	Tricia Mangan	T. Eakin	S. Kearney
1993	Paula Gorman	Louise Darcy	Eileen Rose Power	M. McKenna	Geraldine Doran
1994	Laura Webb	Brenda Burke		Yvonne Cassidy	Geraldine Doran
1995	Laura Webb	Elaine Dowdall	Ada O'Sullivan	Hazel Kavanagh	Ruth MacGuigan
1996	M. McGreevy	Lillian Behan	Eavan Higgins	Suzanne O'Brien	Sinead Keane
1997	Laura Webb	Orla Barry	Eileen Rose Power	Hazel Kavanagh	Lillian O'Brien
1998	Alison Coffey	Hanoria Fogarty	Barbara Hackett	Alison Coffey	D. Smith

*The following are Ulster Senior Championship Winners 1923-38

Year	Winner
1923	Mrs D.B. Corbett
1924	Miss J. Rice
1925	Miss J. Rice
1926	Not available
1927	Miss J. Rice
1928	Miss B. Gardiner
1929	Miss J. Rice
1930	Mrs T. Marks (nee Rice)
1931	Miss D. Ferguson
1932	Mrs T. Marks
1933	Miss D. Ferguson
1934	Miss J. Mitchell
1935	Mrs. L. Lee (nee Gardiner)
1936	Mrs T. Marks
1937	Miss E. Ellis
1938	Mrs T. Marks

Interprovincial Champions

Year	Winner
1964	Leinster
1965	Leinster
1966	Leinster
1967	Leinster
1968	Leinster
1969	No Match
1970	Leinster
1971	Ulster
1972	No Match
1973	Leinster
1974	Leinster
1975	Leinster
1976	Leinster
1977	Ulster
1978	Leinster
1979	Leinster
1980	Munster
1981	Ulster
1982	Leinster
1983	Leinster
1984	Leinster
1985	Munster
1986	Munster
1987	Leinster
1988	Leinster
1989	Ulster
1990	Leinster
1991	Munster
1992	Leinster
1993	Munster
1994	Leinster
1995	Leinster
1996	Leinster
1997	Leinster

Curtis Cup, Irish Players 1932-98

Years	Name	Matches	Won	Halved	Lost	Points
1934, '36, '38	J.B. Pat Walker	6	2	1	3	5
1938, '48	Clairre Tiernan	3	2	1	0	5
1948, '50, '52, '54, '56, '60	Philomena Garvey	11	2	1	8	5
1966	Ita Burke	3	2	0	1	4
1970, '71, '74, '76, '78, '80, '82, '84, '86	Mary McKenna	30	10	4	16	22
1980	Claire Nesbitt	3	0	2	1	2
1980	Maureen Madill	4	0	1	3	1

Continued from previous page

Years	Name	Matches	Won	Halved	Lost	Points
1984, '86, '88, '92	Claire Hourihane	8	3	2	3	8
1986	Lillian Behan	4	3	0	1	6
1994	Eileen Rose Power					

Ireland had no playing representatives on the 1996 or 1998 Curtis Cup however, Elm Park's Ita Butler was non-playing captain on both occasions.

PAST PRESIDENTS

Years	President
1893-1902	The Countess of Annesley
1903-19	Lady de Ros
1920-24	Miss Leah Garratt
1925-30	Miss Helen Cox
1931-33	Mrs Cuthell
1934-39	Miss Edith Gregg
1940-46	Miss Eleanor Tivy
1947-52	Mrs G.H.C. Townsend
1953-58	Miss Daisy Ferguson
1959-64	Mrs J. Conroy
1965-67	Miss Eileen Murphy
1968-70	Miss M.G. Smyth
1971-73	Mrs J. Connolly
1974-76	Mrs J. F. Hegarty
1977-78	Mrs E. Maher
1979-80	Dr S.E.K. Meharg
1981-82	Mrs I. Wallace
1983-84	Mrs P. Fletcher
1985-86	Mrs E.M. Bruen
1987-88	Mrs E. Connolly
1989-90	Mrs M. McLeod
1991-92	Mrs M. Prendiville
1993-94	Mrs A. Tunney
1995-96	Mrs C. Holmes
1997-98	Mrs J. McHugh

EUROPEAN TOUR EVENTS HELD IN IRELAND (PRO)

Murphy's Irish Open (Druids Glen) July 2-5 1998

Pos	Player	R1	R2	R3	R4
278					
1.	D. Carter	68	72	67	71
2.	C. Montgomerie	65	74	71	68
	(Carter won at first play-off hole)				
280					
=3.	**J. McHenry (Irl)**	70	68	70	72
=3.	P. Baker	69	75	66	70
281					
5.	C. Hainline (USA)	70	68	72	71
282					
=6.	J. Coceres (Arg)	75	67	70	70
=6.	G. Orr	70	69	72	71
283					
8.	P. Lonard (Aus)	69	74	70	70
284					
=9.	J.M. Olazabal (Esp)	73	72	71	68
=9.	R. Claydon	71	71	73	69
=9.	D. Cooper	73	70	72	69
=9.	I. Garbutt	73	69	71	71
=9.	I. Woosnam	73	74	65	72
=9.	S. Webster	71	70	70	73
285					
15.	L. Westwood	70	73	73	69
286					
=16.	K. Eriksson (Swe)	71	74	72	69
=16.	P. Quirici (Swi)	72	75	70	69
=16.	B. Davis	71	71	73	71
=16.	M. A. Jimenez (Esp)	71	71	72	72
=16.	S. Richardson	68	71	74	73
=16.	J. Payne	71	71	71	73
=16.	P. Broadhurst	70	71	72	73
=16.	P. O'Malley (Aus)	74	70	69	73
=16.	B. Lane	70	75	62	79
287					
=25.	M. Davis	68	75	72	72
=25.	**E. Darcy (Irl)**	74	72	69	72
288					
=27.	A. Kankkonen (Fin)	74	71	73	70
=27.	E. Romero (Arg)	74	71	71	72
=27.	N. Faldo	75	72	67	74
=27.	T. Johnstone (Zim)	71	67	71	73
=27.	D. Lynn	68	76	70	74
289					
32.	S. Allan (Aus)	69	71	78	71
290					
=33.	P. Senior (Aus)	75	71	73	71
=33.	E. Els (SA)	71	71	70	78
291					
=35.	D. Hospital (Esp)	74	72	74	71
=35.	J. Rivero (Esp)	69	75	74	73
=35.	G. Chalmers (Aus)	69	75	72	75
=35.	V. Phillips	71	72	71	77
292					
=39.	J. Sandelin (Swe)	69	75	76	72
=39.	J. Spence	72	74	74	72
=39.	M. McNulty (Zim)	71	74	74	73
=39.	M. Jonzon (Swe)	75	70	72	75
=39.	S. Tinning (Den)	75	71	71	75
=39.	D. Gilford	73	71	72	76
=39.	**K. Nolan (Irl)**	71	74	71	76
293					
=46.	I. Garrido (Esp)	74	69	78	72
=46.	S. Struver (Ger)	72	74	75	72
=46.	R. Green (Aus)	71	73	75	74
=46.	M. Roe	74	71	73	75
=46.	N. Fasth (Swe)	73	69	75	76
294					
=51	C. Suneson (Esp)	72	75	74	73
=51.	P. Affleck	70	77	72	75
295					
=53.	C. Watts	72	72	77	74
=53.	D. Robertson	74	72	74	75
=53.	R. Chapman	73	72	73	77
=53.	K. Tomori (Jpn)	70	73	72	80
=53.	**D. Higgins (Irl)**	75	69	72	79
296					
=58.	R. Allenby (Aus)	73	73	77	73
=58.	R. Burns (Ire)	74	71	73	78
297					
=60.	A. Cejka (Ger)	72	70	77	78
=60.	* S. Garcia (Esp)	68	73	75	81
=60.	F. Tarnaud (Fra)	69	74	72	82
298					
=62.	F. Jacobson (Swe)	73	70	81	74
=62.	O. Edmond (Fra)	71	71	79	77
299					
64.	S. Torrance	71	76	76	76
300					
=65.	S. Ames (Tri)	68	78	78	76
=65.	P. Price	70	72	81	77
301					
67.	N. Joakimides (Fra)	75	72	77	77
302					
68.	J. Lomas	75	72	74	81
303					
69.	A. Cabrera (Arg)	75	72	77	79
307					
70.	A. Oldcorn	74	72	80	81

* Denotes Amateur

All golfers are British unless stated

153 golfers entered the tournament.

Other Irish Finishers (cut was 147)

Pos	Player	R1	R2
=71.	Paul McGinley	73	75
=80.	Christy O'Connor Jnr	78	71
=80.	Darren Clarke	74	75
=80.	Leslie Walker	75	74
=80.	Francis Howley	74	75
=89.	Damian McGrane	74	76
=89.	Robert Giles	73	77
=99.	Des Smyth	78	73
=112.	Jimmy Heggarty	75	77
=112.	Padraig Harrington	81	71
=112.	Damian Mooney	75	77
=120.	Philip Walton	73	80
=120.	Stephen Hamill	79	74
=129.	Leslie Robinson	79	75

=137.	Gary Murphy	77...78
=137.	Graham Spring	77...78
=140.	* Noel Fox	78...79
146.	Peter Lawrie	82...80
=148.	Paul Russell	83...82
=148.	* Michael Hoey	87...80

Top 16 & Irish Money Winners from the Murphy's Irish Open

		£
1.	David Carter	159,991
2.	Colin Montgomerie	106,631
=3.	Peter Baker	53,996
=3.	John McHenry	53,996
5.	Craig Hainline	40,797
=6.	José Coceres	31,197
=6.	Gary Orr	31,197
8.	Peter Lonard	23,998
=9.	Derrick Cooper	17,490
=9.	Ian Woosnam	17,490
=9.	José Maria Olazabal	17,490
=9.	Steve Webster	17,490
=9.	Russell Claydon	17,490
=9.	Ian Garbutt	17,490
15.	Lee Westwood	14,085
=16.	Klaus Eriksson	11,716
=16.	Barry Lane	11,716
=16.	Brian Davis	11,716
=16.	Paul Broadhurst	11,716
=16.	Miguel Angel Jiménez	11,716
=16.	Paolo Quirici	11,716
=16.	Peter O'Malley	11,716
=16.	Steven Richardson	11,716
=16.	Jim Payne	11,716
	Other Irish Money Winners	
=25.	Eamon Darcy	9,935
=39.	Keith Nolan	6,143
=53.	David Higgins	3,647
=58.	Raymond Burns	3,023

SMURFIT EUROPEAN OPEN (K Club, Kildare) 20-23 August 1998

	275 (-13)	
1.	M. Gronberg (Swe)	68...71...67...69
	285 (-3)	
=2.	M.A. Jimenez (Esp)	73...72...71...69
=2.	P. Price	72...74...68...71
	286 (-2)	
4.	**Darren Clarke (Irl)**	69...74...70...73
	287 (-1)	
=5.	A. Cabrera (Arg)	72...73...75...67
=5.	C. Hainline (USA)	71...69...69...78
	288 (Level)	
=7.	J. Van de Velde (Fra)	78...69...69...72
=7.	P. Broadhurst	72...73...71...72
=7.	B. Langer (Ger)	73...65...75...75
	289 (+1)	
=10.	C. Rocca (Ita)	72...73...72...72
=10.	S. Torrance	71...76...70...72
=10.	D. Gilford	75...74...68...72
=10.	B. Lane	75...69...72...73
=10.	P. Lawrie	72...72...72...73
=10.	J. Rivero (Esp)	72...66...75...76
	290 (+2)	
=16.	E. Romero (Arg)	74...73...76...67
=16.	S. Luna (Esp)	72...73...76...69
=16.	P. Haugsrud (Nor)	72...73...73...72
=16.	P. Baker	72...76...70...72
	291 (+3)	
=20.	J. Corceres (Arg)	74...75...69...73
=20.	R. Wessels (RSA)	71...71...73...76
=20.	**Paul McGinley (Irl)**	72...72...71...76
	292 (+4)	
=23.	J. Sandelin (Swe)	72...77...73...70
=23.	J. Wade (Aus)	76...69...76...71
=23.	F. Tarnaud (Fra)	73...74...74...71
=23.	**Padraig Harrington (Irl)**	71...74...74...73
=23.	T. Bjorn (Den)	76...70...69...77
	293 (+5)	
=28.	G. Owen	72...75...73...73
=28.	P. Hedblom (Swe)	76...72...72...73
=28.	M. Tunnicliff	74...74...72...73
=28.	P. Fulke (Swe)	78...71...70...74
	294 (+6)	
=32.	S. Henderson	75...73...73...73
=32.	S. Tinning (Den)	73...75...73...73
=32.	M. James	75...71...73...75
=32.	S. Leaney (Aus)	77...70...72...75
=32.	F. Cea (Esp)	71...75...72...76
	295 (+7)	
=36.	S. Grappasonni (Ita)	74...75...74...72
=36.	J.M. Olazabal (Esp)	75...73...75...72
=36.	R. Boxall	77...72...73...73
=36.	I. Garbutt	74...75...73...73
=36.	I. Garrido (Esp)	77...71...72...75
=36.	G. Nicklaus (USA)	74...66...77...78
=36.	I. Woosman	73...70...72...80
	296 (+8)	
=42.	P. Affleck	77...72...74...73
=42.	W. Westner (RSA)	75...73...74...74
=42.	M. Davis	73...74...74...75
=42.	T. Levet (Fra)	73...76...72...75
=42.	J. Payne	73...75...75...76
	297 (+9)	
=47.	P. Eales	74...75...76...72
=47.	J. Spence	75...71...75...76
	298 (+10)	
=49.	S. Ames (Tri)	73...76...76...73
=49.	S. Struver (Ger)	77...71...75...75
	299 (+11)	
=51.	D. Edlund (Swe)	76...73...75...75
=51.	K. Brink (Swe)	75...74...75...75
=51.	A. Beal	78...70...75...76
=51.	M. Mackenzie	71...77...74...77
	300 (+12)	
=55.	D. Carter	74...75...77...74
=55.	R. Jacquelin	76...73...76...75
=55.	D. Grane	74...74...76...76
=55.	**Philip Walton (Irl)**	76...71...75...78
	302 (+14)	
=59.	**Des Smyth (Irl)**	73...75...79...75
=59.	D. Lynn	76...73...78...75

=59. ....R. Chapman ....75...71...77...79

306 (+18)

=62. ....D. Robertson..........................74...73...77...82
=62. ....P. Senior (Aus).......................76...73...75...82

307 (+19)

64. ....S. Kjeldsen (Den) ....75...74...75...83

Retired: L.Westwood
All golfers are British unless stated.
156 golfers were entered in the tournament.

Other Irish finishers (cut was149)

=91. ....Eamon Darcy ....73...79
=117. .....Christy O'Connor Jnr ....74...81
=130. .....John McHenry.....................................78...80
=142. .....Stephen Hamill.......................................82...78
145. ....Raymond Burns ....81...80

Top 16 & Irish Money Winners from the Smurfit European Open

£

1. ....Mathias Grönberg 208,300
=2. ....Miguel Angel Jiménez.......................108,562
=2. ....Philip Price 108,562
4. ....Darren Clarke...62,500
=5. ....Angel Cabrera 48,375
=5. ....Craig Hainline..48,375
=7. ....Jean van de Velde.................................32,216
=7. ....Paul Broadhurst.......................................32,216
=7. ....Bernhard Langer 32,216
=10. ....Paul Lawrie...21,187
=10. ....José Rivero 21,187
=10. ....David Gilford...21,187
=10. ....Barry Lane..21,187
=10. ....Constatino Rocca.....................................21,187
=10. ....Sam Torrance 21,187
=16. ....Peter Baker..16,512
=16. ....Eduardo Romero 16,512
=16. ....Per Haugsrud 16,512
=16. ....Santiago Luna 16,512

Other Irish Money Winners

=20. ....Paul McGinley 14,625
=23. ....Padraig Harrington 13,125
=57. ....Philip Walton...3,968
=61. ....Des Smyth...3,500

INTERNATIONAL TEAM EVENTS

Dunhill Cup (St Andrews, Scotland) October 16-18, 1997

16.10.97: South Africa 2, Ireland 1.

Paul McGinley lost to R. Goosen 71-70.
Padraig Harrington bt D. Frost 67-69.
Darren Clarke lost to E. Els 71-66.

17.10.97: Ireland 1, Scotland 2.

Paul McGinley bt R. Russell 69-74.
Darenn Clarke lost to G. Brand Jnr 77-73.
Padraig Harrington lost to C. Montgomerie 76-72.

18. Ireland 2, Germany 1.

Darren Clarke bt A. Gejka 68-74.
Padraig Harrington bt S. Struver 66-69.
Paul McGinley lost to T. Gogele 71-67

FINAL STANDINGS GROUP THREE

Position	Matches Won
1. South Africa	3
2. Scotland	2
3. Ireland	1
4. Germany	0

Final: South Africa bt Sweden 2-1.

The Golf World Cup (Kiawah Island, South Carolina) November 20-23, 1997

545 Ireland
P. Harrington (71 67 68 67), P. McGinley (66 70 68 68)

550 Scotland
C. Montgomerie (68 66 66 66), R. Russell (66 72 74 72)

551 United States
D. Love (65 69 74 65), J. Leonard (72 69 67 70)

554 Wales
P. Price (72 68 69 66), I. Woosnam (74 72 69 64)

Germany
A. Cejka (63 68 65 72), S. Struver (70 75 67 74)

555 Spain
I. Garrido (67 67 69 67), M.A. Martin (68 74 71 72)

559 England
M. James (68 73 70 66), P. Broadhurst (68 74 68 72)

561 Zimbabwe
T. Johnstone (73 67 72 68), M. McNulty (68 74 71 68)

562 New Zealand
G. Waite (70 70 69 67), M. Long (69 75 67 75)

South Africa
E. Els (73 68 69 69), W. Westner (68 71 72 72)

Top 10 Individuals

266 ....C. Montgomerie (Sco) ....68...66...66...66
268 ....A. Cejka (Ger)............................63...68...65...72
270 ....I. Garrido (Esp)..........................67...67...69...67
272 ....P. McGinley (Irl) ....66...70...68...68
273 ....P. Harrington (Irl) ....71...67...68...67

D. Love (USA)........................65...69...74...65
275 ....T. Bjorn (Den) ....69...72...67...67
P. Price (Wal) ....72...68...69...66
276 ....G. Waite (NZ)........................70...70...69...67
277 ....J. Corceres (Arg) ....72...69...69...67
M. James (Eng) ....68...73...70...66

OTHER RESULTS

IRISH SENIORS OPEN (Woodbrook Co. Dublin) May 15-17 1998

208 (-8)

1. J. McDermott ....Ireland ....70...72...66
=2. T. Gale ....Australia ....71...68...69
=2. N. Ratcliffe ....Australia ....68...69...71
(McDermott won at fifth play-off hole)

210 (-6)

4. B. Waites ....England ....68...70...72

211 (-5)

5. T. Horton....................England ....72...67...72

213 (-3)

6. M. Slater ....England ....72...74...67

214 (-2)

=7. B. Barnes..............Scotland ....74...71...69
=7. J.R. Delich ..............U.S.A. ....71...71...72
=7. I. Richardson ....England ....70...72...72
=7. R. Lendzion ..............U.S.A. ....69...70...75
=7. A. Garrido ....Spain ....72...66...76

Smurfit Irish PGA Championship (Fota Island) October 9-12, 1997

285

1. ....P. McGinley ....70...66...75...74

286

=2. ....D. Higgins ....72...70...75...69
=2. ....J. McHenry ....71...75...71...69
=2. ....S. Hamill ....71...68...73...74

287

5. ....D. Smyth ....71...69...77...70

288

=6. ....E. Darcy ....73...73...72...70
=6. ....P. Harrington ....72...76...69...71

290

8. ....W. O'Callaghan ....76...70...72...72

291

9. ....D. Jones ....75...78...66...72

292

=10. ....J. Kelly ....78...71...71...72
=10. ....P. Walton ....73...74...72...73

293

12. ....J. Heggarty ....76...75...71...71

294

=13. ....D. McFarlane ....73...76...72...73
=13. ....D. Mooney.....................................72...78...70...74

295

=15. ....J. Dignam......................................70...77...75...73
=15. ....M. Sludds......................................75...74...73...73

296

=17. ....P. Russell ....75...78...71...72
=17. ....G. Loughrey ....72...78...70...76

297

19. ....K. O'Donnell ....73...78...72...74

298

=20. ....K. Morris ....75...81...71...71
=20. ....P. Hanna ....78...78...69...73

300

=22. ....D. Walker ....78...77...74...71
=22. ....L. Walker ....76...76...75...73
=22. ....K. Dorrian ....76...72...77...75
=22. ....P. Leonard...78...76...71...75
=22. ....P. Townsend ....74...76...73...77

301

=27. ....G. McNeill ....74...77...78...72
=27. ....E. Doyle ....75...78...75...73
=27. ....L. McCool ....74...76...77...74

302

=30. ....M. Allan..76...78...76...72
=30. ....N. Manchip ....76...75...78...73
=30. ....G. Burke ....73...79...76...74

Level par = 288.

IRISH WOMEN'S OPEN (BALLYLIFFIN, CO. DONEGAL) SEPT 3-6, 1998.

214

1. ....S. Gustafson (Swe)...............................68...78...68
2. ....I. Tinning (Den) ....73...73...68
Gustafson won at first play off hole.

218

3. ....A. Gottmo (Swe) ....70...78...70

220

4. ....**Aideen Rogers (Irl)** ....73...76...71

221

5. ....J. Forbes (Scot) ....78...74...69

221

=6. ....L. Davies (Eng) ....77...75...70
=6. .........M.T. Pistolet-Boselli (Fra).............75...76...71
=6. ....R. Carriedo (Esp).............................71...76...75

223

9. ....M. Hageman (Neth) ....75...74...74

224

=10. ....L. Greve (Den) ....75...77...72
=10. ....J. Head (Eng)..72...79...73
=10. ....K. Larsson (Swe) ....76...74...74
=10. .......A.M. Knight (Aus)..73...76...75
=10. ....A. Larraneta (Esp) ....73...75...76

Top 10 and Irish Money Winners

		£
1.	S. Gustafson (Swe)	12,000
2.	I. Tinning (Den)	8,729
3.	A. Gottmo (Swe)	6,020
4.	**Aideen Rogers (Irl)**	4,664
5.	J. Forbes (Scot)	3,646

=6.	L. Davies (Eng)	2,580
=6.	M.T. Pistolet-Boselli (Fra)	2,580
=6.	R. Carrriedo (Esp)	2,580
9.	M. Hageman (Neth)	1,926
=10.	L. Greve (Den)	1,499
=10.	J. Head (Eng)	1,499
=10.	K. Larsson (Swe)	1,499
=10.	A.M. Knight (Aus)	1,499
=10.	A. Larraneta (Esp)	1,499

Other Irish Money Winners

=41.	Tracey Eakin (Irl)	543
=46.	L. McCool (Irl)	404
=53	Barbara Hackett (Irl)	344

EUROPEAN TOUR PERFORMANCES1998 (IRISH PLAYERS)

BURNS, RAYMOND Tournaments Entered: 27; **Cuts Made:** 8; **No. of Top Ten Finishes:** 0; **Best Finish:** 29th, Portuguese Open; **Next Five Best Finishes:** 35th Moroccan Open; 58th Murphy's Irish Open; 61st Volvo PGA Championship; 64th Dubai Desert Classic. **Total Prizemoney:** £16,564.

CLARK, CAMERON Tournaments Entered: 7; **Cuts Made:** 1; **No. of Top Ten Finishes:** 0; **Best Finish:** 40th, Portuguese Open; **Next Five Best Finishes:** 71st Maderia Island Open; 92nd Turespana Masters Open Baleares; 103rd Moroccan Open; 126th British Masters; 132nd Cannes Open. **Total Prizemoney:** £2,170.

CLARKE, DARREN Tournaments Entered: 17; **Cuts Made:** 16; **No. of Top Ten Finishes:** 8; **Best Finish:** 1st Benson & Hedges International; **Next Five Best Finishes:** 2nd Deutsche Bank Open; 2nd Dutch Open; 2nd Scandinavian Masters; 3rd European Masters; 4th Smurfit European Open. **Total Prizemoney:** £616,867.

DARCY, EAMONN Tournaments Entered: 19; **Cuts Made:** 12; **No. of Top Ten Finishes:** 0; **Best Finish:** 11th Spanish Open; **Next Five Best Finishes:** 16th Cannes Open; 20th German Open; 25th Murphy's Irish Open; 26th International Open; 36th English Open. **Total Prizemoney:** £62,572.

HARRINGTON, PADRAIG Tournaments Entered: 22; **Cuts Made:** 17; **No. of Top Ten Finishes:** 3; **Best Finish:** 2nd German Open; **Next Five Best Finishes:** 3rd Heineken Classic; 8th German Masters; 8th Johnnie Walker Classic; 11th Volvo PGA Championship; 17th Qatar Masters. **Total Prizemoney:** £189,792.

HIGGINS, DAVID Tournaments Entered: 10; **Cuts Made:** 4; **No. of Top Ten Finishes:** 0; **Best Finish:** 16th Cannes Open; **Next Five Best Finishes:** 51st Madeira Island Open; 53rd Murphy's Irish Open; 66th German Open; 70th French Open; 97th Portuguese Open. **Total Prizemoney:** £9,514.

HOWLEY, FRANCIS Tournaments Entered: 12; **Cuts Made:** 4; **No. of Top Ten Finishes:** 0; **Best Finish:** 42nd French Open; **Next Five Best Finishes:** 56th Moroccan Open; 70th Madeira Island Open; 78th Cannes Open; 80th Murphy's Irish Open; 101st Italian Open. **Total Prizemoney:** £5,306.

McGINLEY, PAUL Tournaments Entered: 23; **Cuts Made:** 18; **No. of Top Ten Finishes:** 3; **Best Finish:** 3rd Turespana Masters Open Baleares; **Next Five Best Finishes:** 6th German Masters; 10th Volvo PGA Championship; 13th Italian Open; 16th Scandinavian Masters; 20th Smurfit European Open. **Total Prizemoney:** £189,470.

O'CONNOR JNR, CHRISTY Tournaments Entered: 8; **Cuts Made:** 2; **No. of Top Ten Finishes:** 1; **Best Finish:** 10th English Open; **Next Five Best Finishes:** 27th Cannes Open; 76th Portuguese Open; 80th Murphy's Irish Open; 80th Benson & Hedges International Open; 84th Dubai Desert Classic. **Total Prizemoney:** £14,440.

RAFFERTY, RONAN Tournaments Entered: 6 **Cuts Made:** 2; **No. of Top Ten Finishes:** 0; **Best Finish:** 41st English Open; **Next Five Best Finishes:** 69th Italian Open; 99th Benson & Hedges International Open; 102nd Deutsche Bank Open; 106th Volvo PGA Championship; 137th Heineken Classic. **Total Prizemoney:** £4,564.

SMYTH, DES Tournaments Entered: 21; **Cuts Made:** 10; **No. of Top Ten Finishes:** 0; **Best Finish:** 14th British Open. **Next Five Best Finishes:** 14th Moroccan Open; 25th Scandinavian Masters; 3rd Dubai Desert Classic; 40th Portuguese Open; 52nd Benson & Hedges International. **Total Prizemoney:** £53,531.

WALTON, PHILIP Tournaments Entered: 22; **Cuts Made:** 10; **No. of Top Ten Finishes:** 1; **Best Finish:** 4th Deutsche Bank Open. **Next Five Best Finishes:** 11th Dutch Open; 11th French Open; 33rd Lancome Trophy; 36th British Open; 40th Qatar Masters. **Total Prizemoney:** £98,715.

All details correct as far as 1998 German Masters.

GREYHOUNDS

Bord na gCon (Irish Greyhound Board)

104 Henry Street, Limerick. Tel. (061) 316788

Founded 1958
Chairman .... Paschal Taggert
Chief Executive .... Michael J. Field
Number of Meetings (per annum) 1,800
Number of Races 16,300
Total Prizemoney £2.2m
Betting (Tote & Bookmaker) £29m
Main Tracks .... Shelbourne Park & Harolds Cross, Dublin; Cork; Limerick; Lifford; Dundalk; Tralee and Waterford
Irish Derby Winner .... Eyeman 30.09secs. (550 yds.)
Irish Laurels Winner .... Mr. Pickwick 29.29 secs. (525 yds.)

GYMNASTICS

Irish Amateur Gymnastics Association

c/o House of Sport, Long Mile Road, Dublin 12. Tel. (01) 4501805 Fax (01) 4502805

Founded 1964
President .... Pat O'Brien
Secretary (Finance) .... Charles Appenzeller
Administration .... Shay McDonald
Number of Clubs 50
Number of Regions .... 7 (Midlands, North Dublin, North East, North West, South Dublin, South East and Southern)
Main Stadium .... Basketball Arena, Tallaght

Midlands:
- **Representative** .... Tony Halpenny
- **Secretary** .... Caroline Killeen
- **Number of Clubs** 6

North Dublin:
- **Representative** .... Audrey Farrelly
- **Secretary** .... Ruth Brady
- **Number of Clubs** 8

North East:
- **Representative** .... Monica Boyle
- **Secretary** .... vacant
- **Number of Clubs** 6

North West:
- **Representative** .... Dickie Kennedy
- **Secretary** .... Eileen Murphy
- **Number of Clubs** 6

South Dublin:
- **Representative & Secretary** .... Joe Corbett
- **Number of Clubs** 15

South East:
- **Representative & Secretary** .... David Aulsberry
- **Number of Clubs** 6

Southern:
- **Representative** .... Mairead O'Callaghan
- **Secretary** .... Carolyn O'Brien
- **Number of Clubs** 11

IRISH TITLE HOLDERS: Ladies Artistic Gymnastics

National Apparatus Champion 1997

Level	Name	Club
Senior - Vault	Elaine Duggan	Douglas
Senior - A/Bars	Elaine Duggan	Douglas
Senior - Beam	Elaine Duggan	Douglas
Senior - Floor	Elaine Duggan	Douglas
Junior - Vault	Roisin Morris	Trojan
Junior - A/Bars	Denise O'Connor	Douglas
Junior - Beam	Denise O'Connor	Douglas
	Amanda Cummins	Grange
Junior - Floor	Roisin Morris	Trojan

National Individual Champion 1997 (senior)

Level	Name	Club
Elaine Duggan		Douglas

National Individual Champion 1997 (junior)

Level	Name	Club
Denise O'Connor		Douglas

Young Gymnast of the Year 1997

Level	Name	Club
Theresa Murphy		Nadia

Intermediate 1
Single Piece Apparatus Junior Code Champions '98

Level	Name	Region
Under 16 - Vault	Margaret O'Brien	Midlands
Under 16 - Bars	Sheila Quinlan	Southern
Under 16 - Beam	Yvonne Kiely	Southern
Over 16 - Vault	Caroline Hanley	South Dublin
Over 16 - Bars	Aoife Heaslip	South Dublin
Over 16 - Beam	Una Kennedy	North West
Over 16 - Floor	Aoife Heaslip	South Dublin

Intermediate 2
Junior Code Single Apparatus Champions 1997

Level	Name	Region
Under 12 - Vault	Chloe Hegarty	Southern

Continued from previous page

Intermediate 2 Junior Code Single Apparatus Champions 1997		
Level	**Name**	**Region**
Under 12 - Bars	Petra McLoughlin	North West
Under 12 - Beam	Ciara Morris	South Dublin
Under 12 - Floor	Petra McLoughlin	North West

Junior Code Team Championships and National Team Championships 1998		
Level (basic 1)	**Name**	**Region**
Novice B-under 8	Sarah Wedel	Southern
Novice B-under 10	Jennifer Johnston	South Dublin
Novice B-over 10	Aishling Moloney	Southern
Novice B-under 12	Christina O'Driscoll	Southern
Novice B-over 12	Triona McMenamin	North West

Junior Code Team Championships and National Team Championships 1998		
Level (basic 2)	**Name**	**Region**
Novice A-under 9	Sarah Monaghan	South Dublin
Novice A-under 12	Karen Garvey	Southern
Novice A-under 15	Amanda Browne	North West
Novice A-over 15	Pamela Farrell	Southern
Level (basic 3-three piece set)	**Name**	**Region**
Level 4	under 12	Southern
Level 4	over 12	North West
Level 5	under 12	Southern
Level 5	over 12	Southern
Level 6	under 10	Southern
Level 6	under 12	South Dublin

Mens Artistic Gymnastics

Young Gymnast of the Year 1997	
Ian Whelan	Portlaoise

All-Ireland Novice Champions		
Level	**Name**	**Club**
Under 8	Matthew Condell	Janz
Under 10	Tom Campbell	Carrigaline
Under 12	Niall McCooey	Killevan
Under 14	John Creehan	Coolmine
Under 16	Frank O'Leary	Bandon

National Individual Champions		
Level	**Name**	**Club**
Senior	Conal Kelly	Coolmine
Youth	Shane Butler	Coolmine
Intermediate	Fiachra Harnett	Coolmine
Primary	Ian Whelan	Portlaoise

National Four Piece Champions		
Level	**Name**	**Club**
Under 8	Owen Cody	Coolmine
Under 10	Ronan McGivern	Coolmine
Under 12	Jamie O'Toole	Carrigaline

Carrigaline Cup 'A Section' Champions		
Level	**Name**	**Club**
Primary 4	Aidan Killeen	Portlaoise
Primary 3	Stephan White	Carrigaline
Primary 2	Ian Whelan	Portlaoise
Primary 1	Conor Moran	Portlaoise
Intermediate	Olan Lotty	Douglas

Carrigaline Cup 'B Section' Champions		
Level	**Name**	**Club**
Under 8	Michael Lindenau	Kingdom
Under 10	Tom Campbell	Carrigaline
Under 12	Eoin McInerney	Carrigaline
Under 14	Glen Wall	Coolmine

HOCKEY

Irish Ladies Hockey Union

95 Sandymount Road, Dublin 4. Tel. (01) 6606780

Founded	1894
President	Grace Redmond
Honorary Secretary	Joan McCloy
Honorary Treasurer	Rita Parsons
Public Relations Officer	Irene Johnston
Number of Clubs	126
Number of Provincial Unions	5 (Ulster, Munster, Leinster, Connacht and South-East)
Number of Members	30,000 (of which 20,364 are registered as players)

1998 CHAMPIONS	Winners	Runners Up
Irish Senior Cup	Pegasus	Old Alexandra.
Irish Senior League	Pegasus	Hermes
Irish Junior Cup	Pembroke Wanderers II	Old Alexandra II
Irish Junior League	Pembroke Wanderers II	Pegasus II
Irish Schools Cup	Regent House	Mount Mercy
Senior Interprovincial	Leinster	Munster
Leinster Senior Cup	Muckross	Loreto
Ulster Senior Cup	Pegasus	Randalstown
Munster Senior Cup	Harlequins	University College Cork
Connacht Senior Cup	National University of Ireland, Galway	Yeats County
Inter varsity	Trinity College, Dublin	
Main Stadium	University College Dublin, Belfield. Capacity 1,500	

INTERNATIONAL	
Irish Senior Ladies Coach	Terry Gregg
Number of Coaches	10
Most Capped Player	Mary Logue (116)
Top Scorer	Sarah Kelleher
International Ranking	14th
Biggest Attendance	6,000 (August 1994, Women's Hockey World Cup final)
Biggest Recorded Victories	11-0 (v. Wales 28.02.1907 and v. Poland 18.04.1997)

Provincial Officers	President	Hon Secretary	Hon Treasurer
Connacht	Dr Rosamund Jennings	Mary Canavan	Bridie Burke
Leinster	Doreen Howe	Puth Potterton	Ann Jarvis
Munster	Maeve Hyland	Sally Kavanagh	Toni Canavan
South-East	Ethel Telford	Mary McCormack	Jo O'Sullivan
Ulster	Norma Gartside	Jennifer Patterson	Linda Johnston

IRISH SENIOR CUP RESULTS, 1998

First Round

Ards	3	Pembroke Wanderers	1
NUI Galway	0	Randalstown	8
Victorians	4	North Down	0
Old Alexandra	3	Cork Church of Ireland	0
Harlequins	0	Trinity	2
Greenfields	0	Glenanne	4
UCC	4	Railway Union	1
Catholic Institute	0	Pegasus	8

Second Round

Yeats County	2	Belvedere	3
Collegians	1	Muckross	0
Portadown	1	UCC	2
Hermes	1	Randalstown	2
Victorians	0	Glenanne	1
Trinity	1	Pegasus	5
Ards	1	Old Alexandra	1
Old Alexandra	2	Ards	1 (Replay)
Coleraine	1	Loreto	5

Quarter-Finals

Glenanne	0	Randalstown	3
Collegians	1	UCC	2
Loreto	0	Old Alexandra	1
Pegasus	7	Belvedere	0

Semi-Finals

UCC	0	Old Alexandra	1
Pegasus	3	Randalstown	1

Final

Pegasus	5	Old Alexandra	0

INTERNATIONAL RESULTS 1998, IRISH SENIOR TEAM

Date	Result				Venue
03.05.98	Ireland	1	Scotland	2	Dundee, Scotland
08.05.98	Ireland	5	Italy	1	UCD Belfield, Dublin

Continued from previous page

Date	Result				Venue
09.05.98	Ireland	5	France	0	UCD Belfield, Dublin
10.05.98	Ireland	5	Wales	1	UCD Belfield, Dublin
05.07.98	Ireland	1	Wales	0	European Qualifier, Helsinki
07.07.98	Ireland	1	Belarus	1	European Qualifier, Helsinki
09.07.98	Ireland	1	Czech Republic	2	European Qualifer, Helsinki
10.07.98	Ireland	6	Belarus	1	European Qualifer, Helsinki

Ireland came 3rd overall and qualified for the 1999 European Cup.

International Results 1998, Irish U21 Team

Date	Result				Venue
21.12.97	Ireland	0	Italy	0	Catania, Italy
22.12.97	Ireland	1	Italy	1	Catania, Italy
02.05.98	Ireland	0	Germany	2	Belfast
03.05.98	Ireland	1	Germany	0	Belfast
27.06.98	Ireland	1	Canada	0	Stirling, Scotland
28.06.98	Ireland	1	Wales	2	Stirling, Scotland
29.06.98	Ireland	1	Scotland	1	Stirling, Scotland
24.07.98	Ireland	2	Wales	2	Cardiff, Wales
25.07.98	Ireland	1	Spain	2	Cardiff, Wales
26.07.98	Ireland	5	Scotland	0	Cardiff, Wales
09.08.98	Ireland	1	Germany	3	European Junior Nations Cup, Belfast
10.08.98	Ireland	0	Spain	3	European Junior Nations Cup, Belfast
12.08.98	Ireland	3	England	3	European Junior Nations Cup, Belfast
14.08.98	Ireland	2	Czech Republic	2*	European Junior Nations Cup, Belfast
15.08.98	Ireland	2	Belarus	0	European Junior Nations Cup, Belfast

*Ireland lost on penalty strokes.

IRISH SENIOR CUP WINNERS

Year	Winners
1903	Merton
1904	Merton
1905	Killiney
1906	Alexandra College
1907	Alexandra College
1908	Excelsior
1909	Killiney
1910	Cork
1911	Cork
1912	Killiney
1913	Knock
1914	Killiney
1915-19	World War I
1920	Maids
1921	Knock
1922	Old College
1923	Maids
1924	Old College
1925	Knock
1926	Queens
1927	Queens
1928	Knock
1929	Queens
1930	Maids
1931	Pembroke Wanderers
1932	Ards
1933	Cork
1934	Cork
1935	Maids
1936	Muckross
1937	Pembroke Wanderers
1938	Muckross
1939	Muckross
1940	Loreto Past
1941-45	World War II
946	Loreto Past
1947	Pembroke Wanderers
1948	Pembroke Wanderers
1949	Pembroke Wanderers
1950	Pembroke Wanderers
1951	UCD
1952	Pembroke Wanderers
1953	Loreto Past
1954	Muckross
1955	Instonians
1956	Loreto Past
1957	St. Dominicks PP
1958	Loreto Past
1959	Muckross
1960	Loreto Past
1961	Muckross
1962	Victorians
1963	Muckross
1964	Ards
1965	Pembroke Wanderers
1966	Muckross
1967	Pembroke Wanderers
1968	Muckross
1969	Muckross
1970	Pembroke Wanderers
1971	Muckross
1972	Portadown
1973	Pembroke Wanderers
1974	Pegasus
1975	Pembroke Wanderers
1976	Muckross
1977	Portadown
1978	Pegasus
1979	Muckross
1980	Portadown
1981	Pegasus
1982	Muckross
1983	Portadown
1984	Pegasus
1985	Portadown
1986	Portadown
1987	Pegasus
1988	Old Alexandra
1989	Pegasus
1990	Portadown
1991	Old Alexandra
1992	Pegasus
1993	Portadown
1994	Muckross
1995	Pegasus
1996	Pegasus
1997	Hermes
1998	Pegasus

The winners of the Irish Senior Cup are presented with the Kate Russell Cup.

IRISH JUNIOR CUP WINNERS

Year	Winners
1909	Phoenix H.C.
1910	Warington
1911	Orwell
1912	Ballinasloe Asylum
1913	Not recorded
1914	Celbridge College School
1915	Alexandra College II
1916-19	World War I
1920	Alexandra College II
1921	Alexandra College II
1922	Royal College of Surgeons
1923	Maids II
1924	Monkstown II
1925	Glenola
1926	North West
1927	Not played
1928	Instonians
1929	Holywood
1930	Derry
1931	Old Ursulines/North West
1932	Optimists II
1933	Ursuline Convent, Cork
1934	North West
1935	South Antrim
1936	Ewarts "A"
1937	Muckross II
1938	Newcomes II
1939	Muckross III

Year	Winners
1940-45	World War II
1946	Loreto Past II
1947	Maids II
1948	Loreto Past II
1949	Pembroke Wanderers II
1950	Catholic Inst.
1951	Ormiston
1952	Waterford Ladies
1953	Waterford Ladies/Ormiston
1954	Waterford Ladies
1955	Loreto Past III
1956	Pembroke Wanderers III
1957	Muckross III
1958	Muckross III
1959	Pembroke Wanderers III
1960	Lurgan
1961	Pembroke Wanderers III
1962	Pembroke Wanderers III
1963	Maids II
1964	St. Raphaels P.E.C.
1965	St. Raphaels P.E.C.
1966	Portadown II
1967	Railway Union II
1968	Old Ursulines II
1969	Pegasus II
1970	Ling PTC II
1971	U.C.P.E.
1972	Belvedere

Year	Winners
1973	Pegasus II
1974	Pegasus II
1975	Maids
1976	Carrick
1977	Railway Union II
1978	Portadown II
1979	Hermes
1980	Old Ursulines
1981	Our Lady's
1982	Portadown II
1983	Londonderry
1984	Glenanne
1985	Old Ursulines
1986	Pembroke Wanderers II
1987	Pembroke Wanderers II
1988	Portadown II
1989	Portadown II
1990	Harlequins II
1991	Kilkenny
1992	Harlequins II
1993	Pegasus II
1994	Pembroke Wanderers II
1995	Pegasus II
1996	Pegasus II
1997	Pegasus II
1998	Pembroke Wanderers II

The winners of the Irish Junior Cup are presented with the White Cup.

IRISH SENIOR LEAGUE WINNERS

Year	Winners
1991	Pegasus
1992	Muckross
1993	Randalstown
1994	Randalstown

Year	Winners
1995	Muckross
1996	Muckross
1997	Muckross
1998	Pegasus

The winners of the Irish Senior League are presented with the Audrey Murphy Cup

IRISH JUNIOR LEAGUE WINNERS

Year	Winners
1987	Portadown
1988	Portadown
1989	Muckross
1990	Pegasus II
1991	Mid Antrim

Year	Winners
1992	Pegasus II
1993	Collegians II
1994	North Kildare
1995	Pegasus II
1996	Pegasus II

Year	Winners
1997	Pegasus II
1998	Pembroke Wanderers II

The winners of the Irish Junior League are presened with the May Costley Cup.

INTERPROVINCIAL WINNERS, SENIOR

Year	Winners
1920	Leinster
1921	Ulster
1922	Leinster
1923	Leinster/Ulster
1924	Ulster
1925	Ulster
1926	Leinster
1927	Munster
1928	Ulster
1929	Ulster
1930	Abandoned - bad weather
1931	Not recorded
1932	Leinster

Year	Winners
1933	Munster
1934	Leinster
1935	Leinster
1936	Leinster
1937	Leinster/Ulster
1938	Leinster
1939	Leinster
1940-41	No competition
1942	Leinster
1943	Leinster
1944	Leinster/Ulster
1945	Leinster
1946	Leinster

Year	Winners
1947	Leinster
1948	Leinster
1949	Leinster
1950	Leinster
1951	Leinster
1952	Leinster
1953	Ulster
1954	Ulster
1955	Ulster
1956	Leinster
1957	Ulster
1958	Ulster
1959	Ulster

Year	Winners
1960	Leinster
1961	Leinster
1962	Ulster
1964	Ulster
1965	Leinster
1966	Munster
1967	Leinster
1968	Ulster
1969	Ulster
1970	Ulster
1971	Ulster
1972	Ulster
1973	Ulster
1974	Leinster
1975	Munster
1976	Ulster
1977	Ulster
1978	Ulster
1979	Ulster
1980	Ulster
1981	Leinster
1982	Leinster
1983	Ulster
1984	Ulster
1985	Ulster
1986	Leinster
1987	Ulster
1988	Leinster
1989	Ulster
1990	Ulster
1991	Leinster
1992	Leinster
1993	Ulster
1994	Leinster
1995	Munster
1996	Ulster
1997	Leinster
1998	Leinster

Results from 1901 to 1919 are not recorded.

The Stephen Doyle Memorial Cup is prsented to the Senior Interprovincial Champions.

INTERPROVINCIAL WINNERS, JUNIOR

Year	Winners
1922	Leinster/Connacht
1923	Ulster
1924	Ulster/Leinster
1925	Leinster
1926	Ulster
1927	Ulster
1928	Unfinished
1929	Not recorded
1930	Ulster
1931	Ulster
1932	Leinster
1933	Leinster
1934	Ulster
1935	Leinster
1936	Leinster
1937	Ulster
1938	Ulster
1939	Leinster
1940	South East
1941	South East
1942	Leinster
1943	North West
1944	Leinster
1945	Leinster
1946	South East
1947	Abandoned - bad weather
1948	Leinster
1949	Ulster/Munster
1950	South East
1951	Ulster
1952	Leinster
1953	Leinster/Munster
1954	Leinster
1955	Ulster
1956	Ulster
1957	South East
1958	Ulster
1959	Leinster
1960	Not recorded
1961	Leinster/Ulster
1962	Ulster
1963	Ulster/Leinster
1964	Leinster
1965	Leinster
1966	Ulster
1967	Ulster
1968	Ulster/Leinster
1969	Ulster/Munster
1970	Leinster
1971	Ulster
1972	Connacht
1973	Connacht/Ulster
1974	Ulster/Leinster
1975	South East
1976	Ulster
1977	Ulster
1978	Ulster
1979	Ulster
1980	Ulster
1981	Leinster
1982	South-East
1983	Leinster
1984	Ulster
1985	Ulster
1986	Leinster
1987	Ulster
1988	Ulster
1989	Ulster
1990	Ulster
1991	Ulster
1992	Ulster
1993	Ulster
1994	South-East
1995	Ulster
1996	Ulster
1997	Ulster
1998	Leinster

Results from the early years of the Junior Interprovincial competition are not recorded.

The winners of the Junior Interprovincial Championship are presented with The Munster Cup.

PAST PRESIDENTS OF THE IRISH LADIES HOCKEY UNION

Term	President	Union
1894-1900	Mrs A.H. Strangeways	Leinster
1900-01	Miss F.M.Staunell	Leinster
1901-02	Miss M.L. Martin	Leinster
1902-03	Miss S.F. Robb	Ulster
1903-04	Mrs J. Cleeve	Munster
1904-05	Mrs G. Galhaith	Connacht
1905-14	Miss H.M. White	Leinster
1914-20	First World War	
1920-21	Mrs E. Charley	Ulster
1921-22	Mrs F. Evans	Leinster
1922-23	Mrs M.S. Gosset	Leinster
1923-25	Miss I.A. Cumnins	Munster
1925-26	Mrs E. Charters	Ulster
1926-27	Mrs A.I. Weir	Leinster
1927-28	Mrs E.M. Williams	Munster
1928-29	Mrs A.K. Cross	Connacht
1929-30	Mrs E. Charters	Ulster
1930-31	Mrs E.V. Hanna	Leinster
1931-32	Mrs E.M. Williams	Munster
1932-33	Miss M. Gaffikin	Ulster
1933-34	Miss M.S. Gosset	Leinster
1934-35	Mrs E.M. Williams	Munster

Term	President	Union
1935-36	Miss I. Brandon	Ulster
1936-37	Mrs C.H. Pilkington	Leinster
1937-38	Mrs M.S. Cummins	Munster
1938-39	Mrs P. Strahan	Ulster
1939-40	Mrs F. Carroll	Leinster
1940-41	Mrs E. Sullivan	Munster
1941-42	Miss I. Young	Ulster
1942-43	Mrs F. Carroll	Leinster
1943-44	Mrs E. Sullivan	Munster
1944-45	Mrs W. Templeton	Ulster
1945-46	Miss D. Ennis	Leinster
1946-47	Dr. A.H. Ledlie	Munster
1947-48	Miss M. White	Ulster
1948-49	Miss D. Ennis	Leinster
1949-50	Miss A. Moore	Munster
1950-51	Mrs C.N. Grant	Ulster
1951-52	Mrs A.P. McWeeney	Leinster
1952-53	Mrs N. Cummins	Munster
1953-54	Mrs C.W. Grant	Ulster
1954-55	Miss N. Kehoe	Leinster
1955-56	Mrs J. O'Sullivan	Munster
1956-57	Mrs M. Hopkins	Ulster
1957-58	Miss B. Magee	Leinster
1958-59	Miss S.A. Murphy	Munster
1959-60	Miss E. Miller	South East
1960-61	Miss J. Turner	Ulster
1961-62	Miss A. Burn	Leinster
1962-63	Miss L. Moran	Munster
1963-64	Mrs E. McNamara	Connacht

Term	President	Union
1964-65	Miss E. Miller	South East
1965-66	Mrs W. Templeton	Ulster
1966-67	Miss K. Russell	Leinster
1967-68	Mrs M. Power	Munster
1968-69	Mrs M. Duignan	Connacht
1969-70	Miss E. Miller	South East
1970-71	Prof. F. McKeown	Ulster
1971-73	Miss P. Bourke	Leinster
1973-74	Miss J. Dorgan	Munster
1974-75	Mrs E. McNamara	Connacht
1975-76	Mrs S. Torrie	South East
1976-77	Mrs W. Templeton	Ulster
1977	Miss C. McTavish	Ulster
1977-78	Miss J. O'Reilly	Leinster
1978-79	Mrs C. Reid	Munster
1979-80	Mrs A. Lupton	Connacht
1980-81	Mrs M. Hofmeester	Ulster
1981-82	Mrs E. Hudson	Leinster
1982-83	Mrs E. O'Flynn	Munster
1983-84	Mrs M. Costello	Connacht
1984-85	Mrs H. O'Neill	Ulster
1985-86	Miss G. Ruddock	Leinster
1986-87	Mrs A. Lane	Munster
1987-89	Mrs J. Smith	Connacht
1989-91	Mrs R. Brosnan	South East
1991-93	Mrs J. McCloy	Ulster
1993-95	Mrs I. Johnston	Leinster
1995-97	Mrs Anita Manning	Munster
1997-98	Mrs Grace Redmond	Leinster

Irish Hockey Union

6A Woodbine Park, Blackrock, Co. Dublin. Tel. (01) 2600028

Founded 1893
President .... John Dennis
Honorary Secretary .... J. Andrew Kershaw
Honorary Treasurer .... Frank Hollway
Public Relations Officer .... Dixon Rose
Number of Clubs 76
Number of Provincial Unions .... 3 (Ulster, Munster and Leinster)
Main Stadium .... University College Dublin, Belfield. Capacity 1,500

1998 WINNERS	Winners	Runners Up
Irish Senior Cup	Instonians	Three Rock Rovers
Irish League	Instonians	Cork Church of Ireland
Irish Junior Cup	Three Rock Rovers II	Annadale II
Irish Schools Cup	Bangor Grammar	St Andrew's College
Leinster Senior Cup	Pembroke Wanderers	Glenanne
Ulster Senior Cup (Kirk)	Lisnagarvey	Annadale
Ulster Senior Cup (Anderson)	Banbridge	Cliftonville
Munster Senior Cup	Cork Church of Ireland	Harlequins

INTERNATIONAL

Irish Senior Coach .... John Clarke
Number of Senior Coaches 19
Most Capped Player .... Marty Sloan (149 caps)
Top Scorer .... Jimmy Kirkwood
Biggest Attendance .... 5,000 (1995, European Nations Cup finals)

Provincial Officers	President	Honorary Secretary	Honorary Treasurer
Leinster	Stuart Margetson	Paul M. Foster	Michael O'Brien
Munster	Fred Treacy	Finbarr Kelleher	Stuart Egner
Ulster	Peter S. Wood	W.R. Carson Clarke	G.R. Colvin

INTERNATIONAL RESULTS

Senior Team

Senior

Ireland	1	Scotland	2
Ireland	1	Wales	1
Ireland	0	Belgium	1

Under 21

Ireland	3	France	6
Ireland	4	Wales	0
Ireland	0	Scotland	0
Ireland	4	Scotland	3
Ireland	5	Belgium	1
Ireland	7	Czech Republic	0
Ireland	3	Wales	4
Ireland	11	Denmark	1
Ireland	3	Italy	1
Ireland	4	France	0

Under 18

Ireland	4	Scotland	3
Ireland	3	England	5
Ireland	2	Wales	0

Under 16

Ireland	3	Scotland	0
Ireland	1	England	2
Ireland	1	Wales	1

DOMESTIC RESULTS

1998 Irish Senior Cup

First Round

Avoca	0	Cork C.o.I.	0 aet
Cork C.o.I.	3	Avoca	1 (R)
Carlow	3	Kilkenny	3 aet
Kilkenny	bt	Carlow	
Collegians	2	Civil Service	3
Eastern Health	0	Cliftonville	12
Holywood	0	Cookstown	4
Instonians	8	Clontarf	0
Lisnagarvey	4	St James' Gate	0
North Down	4	Portadown	2
Parkview	5	Ballynahinch	0
Pembroke Wanderers	6	Phoenix Park	0
Queen's University	1	Down	2
Railway Union	6	Kilkeel	2
Three Rock Rovers	5	YMCA	0
UCC	0	Raphoe	4

Second Round

Three Rock Rovers	4	NICS	3
Pembroke Wanderers	3	Mossley	1
Cliftonville	4	Antrim	2
Annadale	3	Newry	1
Corinthians	2	Lisnagarvey	1 aet
Raphoe	2	Glenanne	1 aet
RUC	4	Suttonians	2
Instonians	5	UCD	1
Monkstown	5	Down	0
Belvedere	2	Kilkenny	0
Cookstown	7	Aer Lingus	0
Parkview	4	Portrane	0
Railway Union	2	Bangor	2 aet
Bangor	4	Railway Union	4 (R)

Bangor won 5-4 on penalty strokes

Banbridge	0	Dublin University	1
Harlequins	3	Cork C.o.I.	1
North Down	7	Catholic Institute	0

Third Round

Three Rock Rovers	4	Bangor	1
Corinthians	2	Monkstown	1
Belvedere	2	Belvedere	3 aet
Annadale	4	Cliftonville	2
Dublin University	2	Parkview	2 aet
Parkview	4	Dublin University	0 (R)
Instonians	2	Cookstown	0
North Down	0	Pembroke Wanderers	6
Raphoe	4	RUC	0

Quarter Final

Annadale	6	Parkview	0
Instonians	1	Raphoe	0
Pembroke Wanderers	3	Corinthinans	1
Three Rock Rovers	3	Harlequins	2 aet

Semi Finals

Annadale	2	Three Rock Rovers	3
Instonians	3	Pembroke Wanderers	2 aet

Final

Instonians	3	Three Rock Rovers	2

IRISH SENIOR CUP WINNERS

Year	Winners
1894	Dundrum
1895	Dublin University
1896	Dundrum
1897	Dublin University
1898	Three Rock Rovers
1899	Dublin University
1900	Palmerston
1901	Dublin University
1902	Dublin University
1903	Palmerston
1904	Palmerston
1905	Palmerston
1906	Dublin University
1907	Banbridge
1908	Three Rock Rovers
1909	Dundrum
1910	Monkstown
1911	Royal Hibernians
1912	Queen's University, Belfast
1913	Royal Hibernians
1914	Monkstown
1915-19	WWI - No Competition
1920	Royal Hibernians
1921	Royal Hibernians
1922	Limerick PYMA
1923	Banbridge
1924	Banbridge
1925	Lisnagarvey
1926	Banbridge
1927	Lisnagarvey
1928	Limerick PYMA
1929	Railway Union
1930	Railway Union
1931	Railway Union
1932	Cliftonville
1933	Pembroke Wanderers
1934	Dublin University
1935	Dublin University
1936	Dublin University

Year	Winners
1937	Pembroke Wanderers
1938	Railway Union
1939	Three Rock Rovers
1940	Dublin YMCA
1941	Lisnagarvey & Limerick PYMA
1942	Dublin University
1943	Dublin University
1944	Dublin YMCA
1945	Lisnagarvey
1946	Lisnagarvey
1947	Dublin University
1948	Banbridge
1949	Dublin YMCA
1950	Dublin YMCA
1951	Lisnagarvey
1952	Lisnagarvey
1953	Three Rock Rovers
1954	Dublin YMCA
1955	Lansdowne
1956	Banbridge
1957	Dublin YMCA
1958	Lisnagarvey
1959	Three Rock Rovers
1960	Lisnagarvey
1961	Belfast YMCA
1962	Three Rock Rovers & Lisnagarvey
1963	Three Rock Rovers
1964	Three Rock Rovers
1965	Dublin YMCA
1966	Lisnagarvey
1967	Cork Church of Ireland
1968	Cork Church of Ireland
1969	Cork Church of Ireland
1970	Lisnagarvey
1971	Lisnagarvey
1972	Queen's University, Belfast
1973	Pembroke Wanderers
1974	Three Rock Rovers
1975	Cliftonville
1976	Cliftonville
1977	Belfast YMCA
1978	Dublin YMCA
1979	Dublin YMCA
1980	Belfast YMCA
1981	Queen's University, Belfast
1982	Banbridge
1983	Belfast YMCA
1984	Banbridge
1985	Belfast YMCA
1986	Banbridge
1987	Cookstown
1988	Lisnagarvey
1989	Lisnagarvey
1990	Lisnagarvey
1991	Lisnagarvey
1992	Lisnagarvey
1993	Lisnagarvey
1994	Lisnagarvey
1995	Instonians
1996	Avoca
1997	Lisnagarvey
1998	Instonians

IRISH JUNIOR CUP WINNERS

Year	Winners
1895	Beechfield
1896	Sandymount
1897	Avoca School
1898	Three Rock Rovers II
1899	Dublin University II
1900	Corinthians II
1901	Dublin University II
1902	Dublin University II
1903	Dublin University II
1904	Kingston Grammar School
1905	Naas
1906	Monkstown II
1907	Dublin University II
1908	Monkstown II
1909	Monkstown II
1910	Three Rock Rovers II
1911	Dublin University II
1912	Three Rock Rovers
1913	Dublin University II
1914	Ballinasloe Asylum
1915-19	WWI - No Competition
1920	Three Rock Rovers II
1921	Dublin University II
1922	Waterford
1923	College of Science
1924	Pembroke Wanderers II
1925	Railway Union II
1926	Pembroke Wanderers II
1927	Killyleagh
1928	Ards
1929	Banbridge II
1930	Naas
1931	Cork Old Grammarians II
1932	Portrush
1933	Portrane Asylum
1934	Portrane Asylum
1935	Newry Olympic
1936	Newry Olympic
1937	Parkview
1938	Pembroke Wanderers II
1939	Maryborough
1940	Maryborough
1941	Maryborough
1942	Pembroke Wanderers
1943	Portrush
1944	Mossley
1945	Down
1946	Portrush
1947	Antrim II
1948	Antrim II
1949	Banbridge II
1950	Glenanne
1951	Monkstown
1952	RUC
1953	Banbridge II
1954	Dublin YMCA II
1955	Lisnagarvey II
1956	Lisnagarvey II
1957	Railway Union II
1958	Lisnagarvey II
1959	Lisnagarvey II
1960	Lisnagarvey II
1961	Pembroke Wanderers II
1962	Lisnagarvey II
1963	Lisnagarvey II
1964	Cliftonville II
1965	Avoca II
1966	Mossley II
1967	Lisnagarvey II
1968	Cork Church of Ireland II
1969	Monkstown III
1970	Lisnagarvey II
1971	Lorraine
1972	Lisnagarvey II
1973	Lisnagarvey II
1974	Lisnagarvey II
1975	Railway Union II
1976	Antrim II
1977	Lisnagarvey II
1978	Instonians II
1979	Three Rock Rovers II
1980	Instonians II
1981	Belfast YMCA
1982	Newry Olympic
1983	Cookstown II
1984	Cork Chuch of Ireland
1985	Cookstown II
1986	Mossley II
1987	Lisnagarvey II
1988	Aer Lingus
1989	Banbridge II
1990	Lisnagarvey II
1991	Holywood 87 II
1992	Holywood 87 II
1993	Cork Church of Ireland II
1994	Banbridge II
1995	Glenanne II
1996	Pembroke Wanderers II
1997	Avoca II
1998	Three Rock Rovers II

PAST PRESIDENTS OF THE IRISH HOCKEY UNION

Term	President
1893-1905	Rev T.B. Gibson
1905-20	W.I. Graham
1920-24	T.S.C. Dagg
1924-25	R.A.Burke
1925-26	J.E. Milles
1926-27	E.L.Wickham
1927-28	A.G. Burney
1928-29	J.W. Crawford
1929-30	J.E. McCausland
1930-31	T.S.C. Dagg
1931-32	A. Rose
1932-33	T.J. Bennett
1933-34	W.E. Graham
1934-35	R.H. Coulter
1935-36	H. Turpin
1936-37	A.G. Fitt
1937-38	W.G. McDonnell
1938-39	C.S. Waugh
1939-47	A.C. Montgomery
1947-48	H. Turpin
1948-49	W.R. Millar
1949-50	G.D. Findlater
1950-51	R.K. Megran
1951-52	R.H.H. Russell
1952-53	R. Collins
1953-54	M.C. O'Donoghue
1954-55	W.A. Shooter
1955-56	E. Roughan Banim
1956-57	W.R. Millar
1957-58	G.D.M. Beard
1958-59	Dr J.C.S. Ritchie
1959-61	E. Roughan Banim
1961-63	L.S. Bowers
1963-65	W.A. Carpenter
1965-67	A.F. Hayes
1967-68	Dr B. Blake
1968-69	L.F. Orr
1969-70	R.L. Williams
1970-71	W.P. Jordan
1971-72	Dr B. Blake
1972-73	D.J. Keane
1973-74	W.A. Carpenter
1974-75	H.D. Simon
1975-76	P. Shiel
1976-77	W.R.T. Dowdall
1977-78	W.A. Kirk
1978-79	R.G. Blowers
1979-80	B.R. George
1980-81	F.A. Glasby
1981-83	G.J. Cooke
1983-85	T.A. Wynne
1985-87	A.D. Rose
1987-89	D.G. Price
1989-91	W.R. Howard
1991-93	C.H. Tipping
1993-95	B.P. Hanna
1995-97	M.A. Gallagher
1997-	J. Dennis

HORSE RACING

Irish Horseracing Authority

Leopardstown Racecourse, Foxrock, Dublin 18. Tel. (01) 2892888

Founded .... 1994 (replaced the Racing Authority)
Chairman .... Denis Brosnan
Chief Executive .... Noel Ryan
Secretary .... Paddy Walsh
Number of Meetings (1997) 256
Number of Races (1997) 1,794
Total betting (1997) £552,728,300
On-course .... £104,728 ,300
Off-course £448,000,000
Total Prizemoney £15,003,000
Total Attendances for 1997 1,164,724
Main tracks .... The Curragh, Leopardstown, Fairyhouse, Punchestown and Ballybrit

NATIONAL HUNT

Number of Races 1,102
Total Prizemoney £7,131,000
Champion National Hunt Jockey (1996/97) .... Charlie Swan (126 winners)
Champion National Hunt Trainer (1996/97) .... Aidan O'Brien (76 winners)

1998 Winners	Winner	Jockey	Trainer
Jameson Grand National	Bobbyjo	Paul Carberry	Tommy Carberry
Powers Gold Cup	Delphi Lodge	Tommy Treacy	Tom Taafe
Hennessy Gold Cup	Dorans Pride	Richard Dunwoody	Michael Hourigan
Ladbroke Champion Hurdle	Graphic Equaliser	Conor O'Dwyer	Arthur Moore
A.I.G. Champion Hurdle	Istabraq	Charlie Swan	Aidan O'Brien
Compaq Galway Plate	Amlah	Brendan Powell	Philip Hobbs

FLAT

Number of Races 692
Total Prizemoney £7,872,000
Champion Flat Jockey (1997) .... Christy Roche (93 winners)
Champion Flat Trainer (1997) .... Aidan O'Brien (70 winners)

1998 Winners	Winner	Jockey	Trainer
Budweiser Irish Derby	Dream Well	Cash Asmussen	Pascal Bary
Heinz 57 Phoenix Stakes	Lavery	Walter Swinburn	Aidan O'Brien
Irish Oaks	Winona	Johnny Murtagh	John Oxx
Irish 2,000 Guineas	Tarascon	Jamie Spencer	Tommy Stack
Irish 1,000 Guineas	Desert Prince	Olivier Peslier	David Loder
Irish St. Leger	Kayf Tara	John Reid	S. Bin Suroor
National Stakes	Mus-if	Mick Kinane	Dermot Weld

1998 Results

National Hunt

10.01.98 **Ladbroke Handicap Hurdle.** Leopardstown, 2m. Going: Heavy.

	S.P.	Jockey	Trainer
1. Graphic Equaliser (6, 10-0)	5/1 fav	Conor O'Dwyer	Athur Moore
2. Notcomplainingbut (7, 10-13)	14/1	Tommy Treacy	Paddy Mullins
3. Lady Daisy (9, 11-9)	25/1	Jason Titley	A. Mullins

20 Ran

13.01.98 **Jameson Irish Grand National.** Fairyhouse, 3m 5F. Going: Yielding.

	Jockey	Trainer
1. Bobbyjo (8, 11-3)	Paul Carberry	Tommy Carberry
2. Pappillon (7, 12-0)	Ruby Walsh	Ted Walsh
3. Call It A Day (8, 11-12)	Charlie Swan	David Nicholson

20 Ran

29.07.98 **Compaq Galway Plate Handicap Chase.** Galway, 2m 6F. Going: Good to yielding.

	S.P.	Jockey	Trainer
1. Amlah (6, 9-13)	16/1	Brendan Powell	Philip Hobbs
2. Lucky Town (7, 10-7)	9/2 fav	David Casey	Enda Bolger
3. Corket (8, 10-4)	8/1	Tony Dobbin	Frances Crowley

22 Ran

30.07.98 **Guinness Galway Handicap Hurdle.** Galway, 2m. Going: Good to yielding.

1. Black Queen (7, 10-2) ..... 10/1 ..... Shay Barry ..... John Kiely
2. Tidjani (6, 9-13) ..... 10/1 ..... F. Berry ..... Frank Berry
3. Shantarini (4 10-5) ..... 9/1 ..... K.P. Gaule ..... S. Donohoe

24 Ran

14.04.98 **Power Gold Cup.** Fairyhouse, 2m 4F. Going: Good to yielding.

1. Delphi Lodge (8, 11-7) ..... 9/1 ..... Tommy Treacy ..... Tom Taafe
2. Tempo (6, 11-7) ..... 10/1 ..... K.F. O'Brien ..... F. Sutherland
3. Fiddlers Tune (8, 11-7) ..... 8/1 ..... Richard Dunwoody ..... M. Cunningham

11 Ran

23.09.98 **Guinness Kerry National Handicap chase.** Listowel, 3m. Going: Good.

1. Treble Bob (Bl) (8, 9-7) ..... 8/1 ..... Shay Barry ..... Dermot Weld
2. Oakler (Bl) (8, 9-8) ..... 12/1 ..... Tommy Teracy ..... Frances Crowley
3. Lucky Town (Bl) (7, 10-8) ..... 6/1 ..... David Casey ..... Enda Bolger

18 Ran

Flat

23.05.98 **Hibernia Foods Irish 2,000 Guineas.** The Curragh, 1m. Going: Good to Firm.

1. Desert Prince (9-0) ..... 8/1 ..... Olivier Peslier ..... David Loder
2. Fa-Eq (9-0) ..... 7/2 ..... Frankie Dettori ..... Saeed bin Suroor
3. Second Empire (9-0) ..... 4/5 fav ..... Christy Roche ..... Aidan O'Brien

7. Ran

24.05.98 **Airlie Coolmore Irish 1,000 Guineas.** The Curragh, 1m. Going: Good to Firm.

1. Tarascon (9-0) ..... 12/1 ..... Jamie Spencer ..... Tommy Stack
2. Kitza (9-0) ..... 16/1 ..... J.A. Heffernan ..... Aidan O'Brien
3. La Nuit Rose ..... 9/4 fav ..... Frankie Dettori ..... Saeed bin Suroor

13 Ran

28.06.98 **Budweiser Irish Derby.** The Curragh, 1m 4f. Going: Soft to Heavy.

1. Dream Well (9-0) ..... 2/1 fav ..... Cash Asmussen ..... Pascal Bary
2. City Honurs (9-0) ..... 4/1 ..... Frankie Dettori ..... Saeed bin Suroor
3. Desert Fox (9-0) ..... 40/1 ..... Kevin Manning ..... Aidan O'Brien

10 Ran

12.07.98 **Kildangan Stud Irish Oaks.** The Curragh, 1m 4f. Going: Yielding.

1. Winona (9-0) ..... 12/1 ..... Johnny Murtagh ..... John Oxx
2. Kitza (9-0) ..... 10/1 ..... Mick Kinane ..... Aidan O'Brien
3. Bahr (9-0) ..... 4/5 fav ..... Frankie Dettori ..... Saeed bin Suroor

9 Ran

09.08.98 **Heinz 57 Phoenix Stakes.** Leopardstown, 6f. Going: Good to firm.

1. Lavery (9-0) ..... 14/1 ..... Walter Swinburn ..... Aidan O' Brien
2. Access All Areas (9-0) ..... 7/2 ..... Pat Eddery ..... John Mulhern
3. Polaire (8-11) ..... 20/1 ..... Stephen Craine ..... K. Prendergast

11 Ran

19.09.98 **Jefferson Smurfit Irish St Leger.** Curragh, 1m 6f. Going: Yielding to soft.

1. Kayf Tara (9-0) ..... 4/1 ..... John Reid ..... Saeed bin Suroor
2. Silver Patriarch (9-0) ..... 6/4 fav ..... Pat Eddery ..... John Dunlop
3. Delilah (9-0) ..... 4/1 ..... Tim Sprake ..... Sir M. Stoute

7 Ran

20.09.98 **Aga Khan Studs National Stakes.** Curragh, 1m. Going: Yielding.

1. Mus-If (9-0) ..... 8/1 ..... Mick Kinane ..... Dermot Weld
2. Coliseum (9-0) ..... 4/7 fav ..... Johnny Murtagh ..... Aidan O'Brien
3. Festival Hall (9-0) ..... 14/1 ..... Kieren Fallon ..... Aidan O'Brien

9 Ran

RECORDS

Irish National Hunt Winners

JAMESON IRISH GRAND NATIONAL 3 miles 5 furlongs at Fairyhouse

Year	Winner	Jockey	Trainer
1967	Vulpine	M. Curran	P. Mullins
1968	Herring Gull	J. Crowley	P. Mullins
1969	Sweet Dreams	R. Coonan	K. Bell
1970	Garoupe	C. Finnegan	F. Flood
1971	King's Sprite	A.L. Moore	G. Wells

Continued from previous page

JAMESON IRISH GRAND NATIONAL 3 miles 5 furlongs at Fairyhouse

Year	Winner	Jockey	Trainer
1972	Dim Wit	M. Curran	P. Mullins
1973	Tartan Ace	J. Cullen	T. Costello
1974	Colebridge	E. Wright	J. Dreaper
1975	Brown Lad	T. Carberry	J. Dreaper
1976	Brown Lad	T. Carberry	J. Dreaper
1977	Billycan	M. Morris	A. Maxwell
1978	Brown Lad	G. Dowd	J. Dreaper
1979	Tied Cottage	Owner	D.L. Moore
1980	Daletta	J.P. Harty	G.St.J. Williams
1981	Luska	T.V. Finn	P. Mullins
1982	King Spruce	G. Newman	M.J. O'Brien
1983	Bit of a Skite	T. J. Ryan	E.J. O'Grady
1984	Bentom Boy	Mrs A. Ferris	W.E. Rooney
1985	Rhyme 'N' Reason	G. Bradley	D. Murray-Smith
1986	Insure	M. Flynn	P. Hughes
1987	Brittany Boy	T.J. Taaffe	K. Hitchmough
1988	Perris Valley	B. Sheridan	D. K. Weld
1989	Maid of Money	A. Powell	J. Fowler
1990	Desert Orchid	R. Dunwoody	D.R. Elsworth
1991	Omerta	A. Maguire	M.C. Pipe
1992	Vanton	J.F. Titley	M.J. O'Brien
1993	Ebony Jane	C.F. Swan	F. Flood
1994	Son Of War	F. Woods	P. McCreery
1995	Flashing Steel	J. Osborne	J. Mulhern
1996	Feathered Gale	F. Woods	A.L. Moore
1997	Mudahim	J.F. Titley	Mrs J. Pitman

GUINNESS GALWAY HURDLE
2 miles at Galway

Year	Winner	Jockey	Trainer
1984	Tara Lee	J.P. Byrne	W. Durkan
1985	Strathline	T. Carmody	D. K. Weld
1986	Rushmoor	P. Scudamore	R. Peacock
1987	Belsir	P. Gill	R. Nevin
1988	Try A Brandy	H. Rogers	M. Dunne
1989	I'm Confident	F.J. Flood	M. McDonogh
1990	Athy Spirit	T.J. Taaffe	W. Fennin
1991	Sagaman	P. Fenton	L. J. Codd
1992	Natalies Fancy	J. Titley	P. G. Kelly
1993	Camden Buzz	C.F. Swan	P. Mullins
1994	Oh So Grumpy	M. Dwyer	J. Harrington (Mrs.)
1995	No Tag	J.F. Titley	P. G. Kelly
1996	Mystical City	D.J. Casey	W. P. Mullins
1997	Toast the Spreece	A.P. McCoy	A. P. O'Brien

DIGITAL GALWAY PLATE
2 miles five furlongs at Galway

Winner	Jockey	Trainer
Master Player	J.P. Byrne	T. Bergin
Chow Mein	T. Morgan	D.T. Hughes
Boro Quarter	P. Kavanagh	P. Mullins
Randoss	K. Morgan	A. Collen
Afford A King	P. Gill	A. Mullins
Bold Flyer	Miss S. Collen	J. Dreaper
Kiichi	B. Sheridan	D.K. Weld
Firion's Law	M. Flynn	V. Bowens
The Gooser	A. Maguire	P. Mullins
General Idea	A. Maguire	D.K. Weld
Feathered Gale	F. Woods	A.L. Moore
Life of A Lord	T. Horan	A.P. O'Brien
Life of A Lord	C.F. Swan	A.P. O'Brien
Stroll Home	P. Carberry	J.J. Mangan

LADBROKE HANDICAP HURDLE
2 miles at Leopardstown

Year	Winner	Jockey	Trainer
1983	Fredcoteri	T.J. Taaffe	A.L. Moore
1984	Fredcoteri	T.J. Taaffe	A.L. Moore
1985	Hansel Prince	A. Powell	A. Redmond
1986	Bonalma	T.J. Taaffe	A.L. Moore
1987	Barnbrook Again	C.E. Brown	D.R. Elsworth
1988	Roark	T.J. Taaffe	A.L. Moore
1989	Redundant Pal	P. Kavanagh	P. Mullins
1990	Redundant Pal	C. O'Dwyer	P. Mullins
1991	The Illiad	P. McWilliams	A. Geraghty
1992	How's The Boss	J.F. Titley	J. Brassil
1993	Glencloud	G.M. O'Neill	N. Meade
1994	Atone	K.F. O'Brien	J. R. Cox
1995	Anusha	J.P. Broderick	M. Hourigan

AIG CHAMPION HURDLE
2 miles at Leopardstown

Winner	Jockey	Trainer
Dawn Run	J.J. O'Neill	P. Mullins
Fredcoteri	T.J. Taaffe	A.L. Moore
Herbert United	H. Rogers	D. McDonogh
Deep Idol	B. Sheridan	P.D. Osborne
Classical Charm	K. Morgan	J.A. McConnell
Kingsmill	D. Murphy	T. Stack
Nomadic Way	B.G. Powell	B. Hills
Nordic Surprise	C.F. Swan	J. Bolger
Chirkpar	L.P. Cusack	J. Bolger
Royal Derbi	D. Murphy	N. Callaghan
Fortune and Fame	A. Maguire	D.K. Weld
Fortune and Fame	M. Dwyer	D.K. Weld

Continued from previous page

LADBROKE HANDICAP HURDLE
2 miles at Leopardstown

Year	Winner	Jockey	Trainer
1996	Dance Beat	A. Powell	Mrs J. Harrington
1997	Master Tribe	N. Williamson	Mrs J. Pitman

AIG CHAMPION HURDLE
2 miles at Leopardstown

Winner	Jockey	Trainer
Collier Bay	J. Osborne	J. Old
Cockney Lad	R. Hughes	N. Meade

HENNESSY GOLD CUP
3 miles at Leopardstown

Year	Winner	Jockey	Trainer
1987	Forgive 'N' Forget	M. Dwyer	J.G. FitzGerald
1988	Playsehool	P. Nicholls	D.H. Barons
1989	Carvill's Hill	K. Morgan	J. Dreaper
1990	Nick The Brief	M.M. Lynch	Owner
1991	Nick The Brief	R.J. Supple	Owner
1992	Carvill's Hill	P. Scudamore	M.C. Pipe
1993	Jodami	M. Dwyer	P. Beaumont
1994	Jodami	M. Dwyer	P. Beaumont
1995	Jodami	M. Dwyer	P. Beaumont
1996	Imperial Call	C. O'Dwyer	F. Sutherland
1997	Danoli	T.P. Treacy	T. Foley

Irish Flat Winners

IRISH DERBY 1 mile four furlongs at The Curragh.

Year	Winner	Jockey	Trainer
1957	Ballymoss	T.P. Burns	M.V. O'Brien
1958	Sindon	L. Ward	M. Dawson
1959	Fidalgo	J. Mercer	H. Wragg
1960	Chamour	G. Bougoure	A.S. O'Brien
1961	Your Highness	H. Holmes	H. Cottrill
1962	Tambourine II	R. Poincelet	E. Pollet
1963	Ragusa	G. Bougoure	P.J. Prendergast
1964	Santa Claus	W. Burke	J.M. Rogers
1965	Meadow Court	L. Piggott	P.J. Prendergast
1966	Sodium	F. Durr	G. Todd
1967	Ribocco	L. Piggott	R.J. Houghton
1968	Ribero	L. Piggott	R.J. Houghton
1969	Prince Regent	G. Lewis	E. Pollet
1970	Nijinsky	L. Ward	M.V. O'Brien
1971	Irish Ball	A. Gilbert	P. Lallei
1972	Steel Pulse	W. Williamson	A. Breasley
1973	Weaver's Hall	G. McGrath	S. McGrath
1974	English Prince	Y. St. Martin	P. Walwyn
1975	Grundy	P. Eddery	P. Walwyn
1976	Malacate	P. Paquet	F. Boutin
1977	The Minstrel	L. Piggott	M.V. O'Brien
1978	Shirley Heights	G. Starkey	J. Dunlop
1979	Troy	W. Carson	W. Hern
1980	Tyrnavos	A. Murray	B. Hobbs
1981	Shergar	L. Piggott	M. Stoute
1982	Assert	C. Roche	D. O'Brien
1983	Shareef Dancer	W.R. Swinburn	M. Stoute
1984	El Gran Senor	P. Eddery	M.V. O'Brien
1985	Law Society	P. Eddery	M.V. O'Brien
1986	Shahrastani	W.R. Swinburn	M. Stoute
1987	Sir Harry Lewis	J. Reid	B. Hills
1988	Kahyasi	R. Cochrane	L. Cumani
1989	Old Vic	S. Cauthen	H. Cecil
1990	Salsabil	W. Carson	J. Dunlop
1991	Generous	A. Munro	P. Cole
1992	St. Jovite	C. Roche	J. Bolger
1993	Commander in Chief	P. Eddery	H. Cecil
1994	Balanchine	L. Dettori	H. Ibrahim
1995	Winged Love	O. Peslier	A. Fabre
1996	Zagreb	P. Shanahan	D.K. Weld
1997	Desert King	C. Roche	A.P. O'Brien

2,000 GUINEAS 1 mile at the Curragh

Year	Winner	Jockey	Trainer
1957	Jack Ketch	C. Smirke	E. Quirke
1958	Hard Ridden	C. Smirke	J.M. Rogers
1959	El Toro	T.P. Burns	M.V. O'Brien
1960	Kythnos	R. Hutchinson	P.J. Prendergast
1961	Light Year	G. Bougoure	A.S. O'Brien
1962	Arctic Storm	W. Williamson	J. Oxx
1963	Linacre	P. Matthews	P.J. Prendergast
1964	Santa Claus	W. Burke	J.M. Rogers
1965	Green Banner	N. Brennan	K. Kerr
1966	Paveh	T.P. Burns	T.D. Ainsworth
1967	Athentone Wood	R.F. Parnell	S. Quirke
1968	Mistigo	R.F. Parnell	S. Quirke
1969	Right Tack	G. Lewis	J. Sutcliffe, Jnr
1970	Decies	L. Piggott	B. van Cutsem
1971	King's Company	F. Head	G.W. Robinson
1972	Ballymore	C. Roche	P.J. Prendergast
1973	Sharp Edge	J. Mercer	W. Hern
1974	Furry Glen	G. McGrath	S. McGrath
1975	Grundy	P. Eddery	P. Walwyn
1976	Northern Treasure	G. Curran	K. Prendergast
1977	Pampapaul	G. Dettori	S. Murless
1978	Jaazeiro	L. Piggot	M.V. O'Brien
1979	Dickens Hill	A. Murray	M. O'Toole
1980	Nikoli	C. Roche	P.J. Prendsergast
1981	King's Lake	P. Eddery	M.V. O'Brien
1982	Dara Monarch	M.J. Kinane	L. Browne
1983	Wassl	A. Murray	J. Dunlop
1984	Sadler's Wells	G. McGrath	M.V. O'Brien
1985	Triptych	C. Roche	D. O'Brien
1986	Flash of Steel	M.J. Kinane	D. Weld
1987	Don't Forget Me	W. Carson	R. Hannon
1988	Prince of Birds	D. Gillespie	M.V. O'Brien
1989	Shaadi	W.R. Swinburn	M. Stoute
1990	Tirol	P. Eddery	R. Hannon
1991	Fourstars Allstar	M. Smith	L. O'Brien
1992	Rodrigo De Triano	L. Piggott	P. Chapple-Hyam
1993	Barathea	M. Roberts	L. Cumani
1994	Turtle Island	J. Reid	P. Chapple-Hyam
1995	Spectrum	J. Reid	P. Chapple-Hyam
1996	Spinning World	C. Asmussen	J. Peas
1997	Desert King	C. Roche	A.P. O'Brien

1,000 GUINEAS 1 Mile at the Curragh

Winner	Jockey	Trainer
Even Star	F. Durr	R. Day
Butiba	J. Massard	A. Head
Fiorentina	G. Moore	A. Head
Zenobia	L. Ward	T. Shaw
Lady Senator	T. Gosling	P. Ashworth
Shandon Belle	T.P. Burns	R.Fetherstonhaugh
Gazpacho	F. Palmer	P.J. Prendergast
Royal Danseuse	J. Roe	S. McGrath
Ardent Dancer	W. Rickaby	T. Gosling
Valoris	J. Power	M.V. O'Brien
Lacquer	R. Hutchinson	H. Wragg
Front Row	E. Eldin	R. Jarvis
Wenduyne	W. Williamson	P.J. Prendergast
Black Satin	R. Hutchinson	J. Dunlop
Favoletta	L. Piggott	H. Wragg
Pidget	W. Swinburn	K. Prendergast
Cloonagh	G. Starkey	H. Cecil
Gaily	R. Hutchinson	W. Hern
Miralla	R. F. Parnell	H. Nugent
Sarah Siddons	C. Roche	P.J. Prendergast
Lady Capulet	T. Murphy	M.V. O'Brien
More So	C. Roche	P.J. Prendergast
Godetia	L. Piggott	M.V. O'Brien
Cairn Rouge	A. Murray	M. Cunningham
Arctique Royale	G. Curran	K. Prendergast
Princess Polly	W. Swinburn	D. Weld
L'Attrayante	A. Badel	O. Douieb
Katies	P. Robinson	M. Ryan
Al Bahathri	A. Murray	H.T. Jones
Sonic Lady	W.R. Swinburn	M. Stoute
Forest Flower	T. Ives	I. Balding
Trusted Partner	M.J. Kinane	D.K. Weld
Ensconse	R. Cochrane	L. Cumani
In The Groove	S. Cauthen	D. Elsworth
Kooyonga	W.J. O'Connor	M. Kauntze
Marling	W.R. Swinburn	G. Wragg
Nicer	M. Hills	B. Hills
Mehthaaf	W. Carson	J. Dunlop
Ridgewood Pearl	C. Roche	J.M. Oxx
Matiya	W. Carson	B. Hanbury
Classic Park	S. Craine	A.P. O'Brien

IRISH OAKS 1 mile 4 furlongs at the Curragh

Year	Winner	Jockey	Trainer
1957	Silken Glider	J. Eddery	S. McGrath
1958	Amante	L. Ward	A. Head
1959	Discorea	E. Mercer	H. Wragg
1960	Lynchris	W. Williamson	J. Oxx
1961	Ambergris	J. Lindley	H. Wragg
1962	French Cream	W. Rickaby	G. Brooke
1963	Hibernia III	W. Williamson	J. Oxx
1964	Ancasta	J. Purtell	M.V. O'Brien
1965	Aurabella	L. Ward	M.V. O'Brien
1966	Merry Mate	W. Williamson	J. Oxx
1967	Pampalina	J. Roe	J. Oxx
1968	Celina	A. Barclay	N. Murless
1969	Gaia	L. Ward	M.V. O'Brien
1970	Santa Tina	L. Piggott	C. Milbanks
1971	Altesse Royale	G. Lewis	N. Murless
1972	Regal Exception	M. Philipperon	J. Fellows
1973	Dahlia	W. Pyers	M. Zilber
1974	Dibidale	W. Carson	B. Hills

IRISH ST LEGER 1 mile 6 furlongs at the Curragh

Winner	Jockey	Trainer
Ommeyad	J. Massard	A. Head
Royal Highway	N. Brennan	S. Murless
Barclay	G. Bougoure	M.V. O'Brien
Lynchris	W. Williamson	J. Oxx
Vimadee	T.P. Burns	T. Burns
Arctic Vale	P. Matthews	P.J. Prendergast
Christmas Island	G. Bougoure	P.J. Prendergast
Biscayne	W. Williamson	J. Oxx
Craighouse	J. Mercer	W. Hern
White Gloves	L. Ward	M.V. O'Brien
Dan Kano	L. Piggott	J. Lenehan
Giolla Mear	F. Berry	M. Hurley
Reindeer	L. Ward	M.V. O'Brien
Allangrange	G. McGrath	S. McGrath
Parnell	A. Simpson	S. Quirke
Pidget	T.P. Burns	K. Prendergast
Conor Pass	P. Jarman	K. Prendergast
Mistigri	C. Roche	P.J. Prendergast

Continued from previous page

IRISH OAKS 1 mile 4 furlongs at the Curragh				IRISH ST LEGER 1 mile 6 furlongs at the Curragh		
Year	**Winner**	**Jockey**	**Trainer**	**Winner**	**Jockey**	**Trainer**
1975	Juliette Marny	L. Piggott	J. Tree	Caucasus	L. Piggott	M.V. O'Brien
1976	Lagunette	P. Paquet	F. Boutin	Meneval	L. Piggott	M.V. O'Brien
1977	Olwyn	J. Lynch	R. Boss	Transworld	T. Murphy	M.V. O'Brien
1978	Fair Salinia	G. Starkey	M. Stoute	M-Lolshan	B. Taylor	R. Price
1979	Godetia	L. Piggott	M. V. O'Brien	Niniski	W. Carson	W. Hern
1980	Shoot A Line	W. Carson	W. Hern	Gonzales	R. Carroll	M.V. O'Brien
1981	Blue Wind	W. Swinburn	D. K. Weld	Protection Racket	B. Taylor	J. Hindley
1982	Swiftfoot	W. Carson	W. Hern	Touching Wood	P. Cook	H.T. Jones
1983	Give Thanks	D. Gillespie	J. Bolger	Mountain Lodge	D. Gillespie	J. Dunlop
1984	Princess Pati	P. Shanahan	C. Collins	Opale	D. McHargue	A. Stewart
1985	Helen Street	W. Carson	W. Hern	Leading Counsel	P. Eddery	M.V. O'Brien
1986	Colorspin	P. Eddery	M. Stoute	Authaal	C. Roche	D. O'Brien
1987	Unite	W.R. Swinburn	M. Stoute	Eurobird	C. Asmussen	J. M. Oxx
1988	Dimineuendo*	S. Cauthen	H. Cecil	Dark Lomond	D. Gillespie	M.V. O'Brien
	Melodist*	W.R. Swinburn	M. Stoute			
1989	Alydaress	M.J. Kinane	H. Cecil	Petite Ile	R. Quinton	J. M. Oxx
1990	Knight's Baroness	T. Quinn	P. Cole	Ibn Bey	T. Quinn	P. Cole
1991	Possessive Dancer	S. Cauthen	A. A. Scott	Turgeon	A. Cruz	J.E. Pease
1992	User Friendly	G. Duffield	C. Brittain	Mashaallah	S. Cauthen	J. Gosden
1993	Wemyss Bight	P. Eddery	A. Fabre	Vintage Crop	M.J. Kinane	D.K. Weld
1994	Bolas	P. Eddery	B. Hills	Vintage Crop	M.J. Kinane	D.K. Weld
1995	Pure Grain	J. Reid	M. Stoute	Strategic Choice	T. Quinn	P. Cole
1996	Dance Design	M.J. Kinane	D. K. Weld	Oscar Schindler	S. Craine	K. Prendergast
1997	Ebayiyla	J.P. Murtagh	J. M. Oxx	Oscar Schindler	S. Craine	K. Prendergast

* Dead Heat

ICE HOCKEY

Northern Ireland Ice Hockey

c/o 88 Coronation Park, Dundonald, Belfast BT16 0HF. Tel. (01232) 483859

PRO & Coach..Jim Graves
Number and Names of Teams ....6 - Coleraine - (1 senior, Coleraine Jets & 2 junior);
....Dundonald - (3 junior, Kestrels, under 15; Hawks, under 17; Goldwings, under 21)
Capacity of Ice Hockey Venues ....Coleraine Jet Centre (300); Dundonald Ice Bowl (1,500)

MOTOR CYCLING

Motor Cycle Union of Ireland

35 Lambay Road, Glasnevin, Dublin 9. Tel. (01) 8378090
7 St. Bennet's Avenue, Donaghadee, Co. Down.Tel. (01247) 883477

Founded 1902
Number of Centres .... 2: Southern (i.e. Leinster, Connacht and Munster) and Ulster
Number of Clubs 66
Number of Members .... 1,700 (Competition Licence Holders)
President .... Sam McClelland
Secretary .... Andrew Campbell
Public Relations Officer .... Harry Havelin
Number of Coaches 2
Biggest Attendance .... 100,000 (at North-West 200 Road Races, Portrush Co. Antrim)
Main Venues (Short Circuit) .... Mondello Park, Naas; Nutts Corner, Co. Antrim; Bishopscourt, Downpatrick.
Main Venues (Road Racing) .... Cookstown, Tandragee, Portstewart, Skerries, Kells, Monaghan

IRISH CHAMPIONS 1998

1998 Irish Motor Cycle Road Racing Championships, Final Positions

Class	1st	Pts	2nd	Pts	3rd	Pts
125 c.c.	Owen McNally	236	Gary Dynes	181	Mark Curtin	136
200 c.c.	Ray Hanna	215	Barry Davidson	171	Gordon Taylor	145
250 c.c.	Gary Dynes	217	Owen McNally	177	Denis McCullough	142
Junior Class	R.J. Hazelton	220	Geoff McMullan	211	Trevor Ferguson	78
Supersport 600	Richard Britton	217½	Adrian Archibald	217	John Donnan	120½
Open	James Courtney	236	Richard Britton	162	Adrian Archibald	149
201-400 c.c. Support Class	Andrew McClean	250	David Guiney	149	Alex McVicker	71
401-750 c.c. Support Class	George Jeffers	194	Barry Maguire	164	Colin Rodgers	127

1998 Irish Motor Cycle Short Circuit Championships, Final Positions

Class	1st	Pts	2nd	Pts	3rd	Pts
125 c.c.	Paul Robinson		....		....	
250/350 c.c.	John Creith		....		....	
600c.c.	Kieran McCrory		....		....	
Senior	Michael Swann		....		....	
Sidecar	Charlie O'Neill/Peter O'Neill		....		....	
125 Superking	Owen McNally	343	Paul Robinson	253	Robert Dunlop	179
Regal 600	Richard Britton	294½	Adrian Archibald	276	James Courtney	256
Joe Lindsay Memorial Series	James Courtney	247	Rodney McCurdy	231	Richard Britton	216

INTERNATIONAL NORTH WEST 200 ROAD RACES

Portstewart-Coleraine-Portrush Circuit, Co. Derry. May 16, 1998.

Race	1st	Team	Ave mph	2nd	Team	Ave mph	3rd	Team	Ave mph
250 c.c.	W. Coulter	Honda	112.20	I. Lougher	Honda	112.18	R.Farquhar	Honda	111.91
Mobil 1 Superbike	I. Simpson	Honda	118.13	M. Rutter	Honda	116.20	B. Jackson	Kawas	116.18
Regal 600 Race	I. Simpson	Honda	113.54	S. Plater	Honda	113.53	M. Rutter	Honda	113.52
125 c.c.	Abandoned								
Production	M. Rutter	Honda	118.49	D. Jeffries	Yamaha	114.55	S. Plater	Honda	112.75
NW200 Superbike	M. Rutter	Honda	118.49	I. Simpson	Honda	118.47	I. Duffus	Honda	117.23

NATIONAL ROAD RACING CHAMPIONS SINCE 1991

	1991	1992	1993	1994	1995	1996	1997
Trials	M. Harris	I.Callaghan	I. Callaghan	M. Harris	P. McLoughlin	A. Perry	A. Perry
125 cc	J. Dunlop	D. McCullough	R. Dunlop	P. Owens	D. McCullough	D. McCullough	D. McCullough
200 cc	F. McConnell	T. Ritchie	T. Ritchie	T. Ritchie	B. Campbell	B. Campbell	G. Purdy
250 cc	P. McCallen	P. McCallen	J. Dunlop	J. Courtney	J. Courtney	G. Dynes	G. Dynes
350 cc	L. McMaster	D. McCullough	T. Keyes	-	-	-	-
600 cc	P. McCallen	D. Young	J. Dunlop	D. Young	D. Young	D. Young	A. Archibald
750 cc	P. McCallen	D. Young	-	D. Young	-	-	-

Continued on next page

	1991	1992	1993	1994	1995	1996	1997
Junior	-	-	-	T. Keyes	R.J. Hazelton	N. Watt	R.J. Hazelton
Senior	-	-	D. Young	-	J. Courtney	D. Young	J. Courtney

IRISH WINNERS AT ISLE OF MAN T.T. RACES

Year	Class	Winner	Team	Speed (m.p.h.)
1922	Senior	Alec Bennett	Sunbeam	58.31
1923	Junior	Stanley Woods	Cotton	55.74
1924	Senior	Alec Bennett	Norton	61.64
1926	Junior	Alec Bennett	Velocette	66.70
	Lightweight	Charlie Johnston	Cotton	60.24
	Senior	Stanley Woods	Norton	67.54
1927	Senior	Alec Bennett	Norton	68.41
1928	Junior	Alec Bennett	Velocette	68.65
1930	Junior	Henry G. Tyrell-Smith	Rudge	71.08
1932	Junior	Stanley Woods	Norton	77.16
	Senior	Stanley Woods	Norton	79.38
1933	Junior	Stanley Woods	Norton	78.08
	Senior	Stanley Woods	Norton	81.04
1935	Lightweight	Stanley Woods	Moto Guzzi	71.56
	Senior	Stanley Woods	Moto Guzzi	84.68
1938	Junior	Stanley Woods	Velocette	84.80
1939	Junior	Stanley Woods	Velocette	83.19
1947	Lightweight	Manliff Barrington	Moto Guzzi	73.22
1948	Senior	Artie Bell	Norton	84.97
1949	Lightweight	Manliff Barrington	Moto Guzzi	77.99
1950	Junior	Artie Bell	Norton	86.32
1951	Lightweight (125 c.c.)	Cromie McCandless	Mondial	74.85
1952	Senior	Reg Armstrong	Norton	92.97
1966	50 c.c.	Ralph Bryans	Honda	85.66
1973	125 c.c.	Tommy Robb	Yamaha	88.90
1976	Senior	Tom Herron	Yamaha	105.15
	250 c.c.	Tom Herron	Yamaha	103.55
1977	Jubilee	Joey Dunlop	Yamaha	108.86
1978	Senior	Tom Herron	Suzuki	111.74
1980	Classic	Joey Dunlop	Yamaha	112.72
1982	Senior	Norman Brown	Suzuki	110.98
	Junior	Con Law	Waddon	105.32
1983	Formula One	Joey Dunlop	Honda	114.03
	Junior	Con Law	EMC	108.09
1984	Formula One	Joey Dunlop	Honda	111.68
	Classic Race (350 c.c.)	Steve Cull	Aermacchi	94.26
1985	Formula One	Joey Dunlop	Honda	113.95
	Junior	Joey Dunlop	Honda	109.91
	Senior	Joey Dunlop	Honda	113.69
1986	Formula One	Joey Dunlop	Honda	112.96
	Sidecar Race "A"	Lowry Burton/Pat Cushnahan	Yamaha	104.53
	Formula Two	Brian Reid	Yamaha	109.72
	Junior	Steve Cull	Honda	109.62
1987	Formula One	Joey Dunlop	Honda	115.03
	Junior	Eddie Laycock	EMC	108.52
	Sidecar Race "B"	Lowry Burton/Pat Cushnahan	Yamaha	105.53
	Senior	Joey Dunlop	Honda	99.85
1988	Formula One	Joey Dunlop	Honda	116.25
	Junior	Joey Dunlop	Honda	111.87
	Senior	Joey Dunlop	Honda	117.38
1989	Supersport 400	Eddie Laycock	Suzuki	105.27
	125 c.c.	Robert Dunlop	Honda	102.58
	Junior	Johnny Rea	Yamaha	112.12
1990	125 c.c.	Robert Dunlop	Honda	103.41
	Supersporrt 600	Brian Reid	Yamaha	111.98

Continued on next page

Year	Class	Winner	Team	Speed (m.p.h.)
1991	125 c.c.	Robert Dunlop	Honda	103.68
	Junior	Robert Dunlop	Yamaha	114.89
1992	Formula One	Phillip McCallen	Honda	119.80
	Supersport 400	Brian Reid	Yamaha	110.50
	125 c.c.	Joey Dunlop	Honda	106.49
	Junior	Brian Reid	Yamaha	115.13
	Supersport 600	Phillip McCallen	Honda	115.04
1993	125 c.c.	Joey Dunlop	Honda	107.26
	Junior	Brian Reid	Yamaha	115.14
	Senior	Phillip McCallen	Honda	118.32
1994	125 c.c.	Joey Dunlop	Honda	105.74
	Junior	Joey Dunlop	Honda	114.67
1995	Formula One	Phillip McCallen	Honda	117.84
	Lightweight	Joey Dunlop	Honda	115.68
	Senior	Joey Dunlop	Honda	119.11
1996	125 c.c.	Joey Dunlop	Honda	
	250 c.c.	Joey Dunlop	Honda	
	600 c.c.	Phillip McCallen	Honda	
	Production Race	Phillip McCallen	Honda	
	Formula One	Phillip McCallen	Honda	
1997	250 c.c.	Joey Dunlop	Honda	
	Production Race	Phillip McCallen	Honda	
	Formula One	Phillip McCallen	Honda	
1998	250 c.c.	Joey Dunlop	Honda	
	125 c.c.	Robert Dunlop	Honda	

PAST PRESIDENTS

Year	President
1912	R.C. Lindsay
1913	J.G. Drury
1915	R.G. Lindsay
1922	R. McLardy
1923	T.W. Murphy
1924	D.A. Boyd
1925	E.F. Keating
1926	D.A. Boyd
1927	E.H. Hill
1928	R.H. Wright
1929	J.J. Beggan
1930	R.H. Wright
1931	S.S. Russell
1932	R.H. Wright
1933	J.J. Sheil
1934	R.H. Wright
1935	T.W. Murphy
1936	R.H. Wright
1937	J. Irvine
1938	R.H. Wright
1939	S.D. Campbell
1940	R.H. Wright
1941	A. Harrison
1942	T. Stewart
1943	T.W. Murphy
1944	R.H. Wright
1945	E.P. Hurst
1946	R.H. Wright
1947	A.H.L. Archer
1948	R.H. Wright
1949	V.F. Ross
1950	R.H. Wright
1951	W.V.L. Bowie
1952	R.H. Wright
1953	G.A. Mangan
1954	M. Wilson
1955	G.A. Mangan
1956	M. Wilson
1957	A.H.L. Archer
1958	W.A. McMaster
1959	E.P. Gill
1960	H.H. Palmer
1961	V.M.L. O'Reilly
1962	W.J. Hagen
1963	D.C. Ewen
1964	T.J.B. Stronge
1965	J.J. O'Neill
1966	W.R. Mann
1967	A. Jolly
1968	J. Hunter
1969	E.I. Gibson
1970	J.K. Martin
1971	M. Bryan
1972	D.D.H. Fleck
1973	H. Lambert
1974	R. Brown
1975	D. Long
1976	A.G. Fox
1977	R. Alton
1978	V.Neill
1979	G. Rogers
1980	D.H. Elliott
1981	D.R. Felton
1982	R.J. Hewitt
1983	E. Callaghan
1984	S. Steel
1985	G. Martin
1986	T. Steele
1987	S. O'Reilly
1988	J.K. Agnew
1989	S. Bissett
1990	W.J. Hutton
1991	S. Bisset
1992	A.J. Armstrong
1993	S. Bisset
1994	S.H. Healy
1995	S. Bisset
1996	F. Semple
1997	S. Bissett
1998	A.S. McClelland

Royal Irish Automobile Club

Motor Sport Department, 34 Dawson Street, Dublin 2. Tel. (01) 6775628

Founded...1901
Number of Clubs...35
Total Membership...2,800
Chairman Motor Sport Commission...Michael FitzSimons
Secretary...Alex Sinclair
Biggest Recorded Attendance...100,000 (Phoenix Park, 1929 Irish Grand Prix)
Main Venue...Mondello Park, Naas, Co. Kildare
Irish Land Speed Record, flying kilometre...179.31mph (20.08.94 Brendan O'Mahony in a Porsche 962)

R.I.A.C. NATIONAL CHAMPIONS

Event	1st	2nd	3rd
Motorsport Championship (Sexton Trophy)	Neil Shanahan	n/a	n/a
Hill Climb Championship (Keane Trophy)	Ronnie Maybin	Donal Griffin	Padraig Forde
Touring Cars Championship	Ed O'Connor	Michael Cullen	David Kerrigan
Hewison Championship	Peter Grimes	Eamonn Byrne	J.J. Farrell
Navigation Rally Championship	Damien Courtney/ Aiden Courtney	Bertie Wedlock/ Paul Hughes	Raymond O'Neill/ Harry Bleakley
Vard Rally Championship	John Gileece/ Michael Gibson	Michael Barrable/ Hugh McPhillips	Frank O'Mahony/ Hugh McVeigh
Forestry Championship	John McKeown/ Padraig Barry	Dermot Kelly/ Kevin Casey	Dominic McNeill/ Martin Carey
Rallycross	Dermot Carnegie	Laurence Gibson	David Francis

FORMER CHAIRMEN OF MOTOR SPORT COMMISSION

Edmund Gill; Reg Redmond; Dudley Reynolds; Peter Jenkins; Michael FitzSimons.

SELECTED RALLY RESULTS 1998

GALWAY INTERNATIONAL RALLY 20-22 February: **1.** A. McHale & B. Murphy (Toyota Celica GT4) 1hr 45mins 0secs; **2.** B. Fisher & R. Kennedy (Subaru Impreza) 1hr 46mins 05secs; **3.** A. Nesbitt & J. O'Brien (Toyota Celica GT4) 1hr 47mins 27secs.

CIRCUIT OF IRELAND 10-13 April: **1.** A. McHale & B. Murphy (Toyota Celica GT4) 3hrs 56mins 55secs*; **2.** B. Fisher & R. Kennedy (Subaru Impreza) 3hrs 56m 56secs; **3.** A. Nesbitt & J. O'Brien (Toyota Celica GT4) 4hrs 1min 58secs.

*McHale had a 20 second penalty lifted on appeal.

KILLARNEY INTERNATIONAL RALLY OF THE LAKES 2-3 May: **1.** J. Lecky & G. Millar (Subaru Impreza) 2hrs 33mins 36secs; **2.** A. McHale & B. Murphy (Toyota Celica GT4) 2hrs 35mins 28secs; **3.** A. Nesbitt & J. O'Brien (Toyota Celica GT4) 2hrs 36mins 17secs.

DONEGAL INTERNATIONAL RALLY 19-21 June: **1.** A. Nesbitt & J. O'Brien (Toyota Celica GT4) 2hrs 40mins 48 secs; **2.** A. McHale & B. Murphy (Toyota Celica GT4) 2hrs 41mins 55 secs; **3.** E. Boland & D. Morrissey (Ford Escort) 2hrs 44mins 18secs.

CORK 20 INTERNATIONAL RALLY 2-4 October: **1.** I. Greer & D. Beckett (Toyota Celica GT4) 2hrs 8mins 52secs; **2.** B. Fisher & R. Kennedy (Subaru Impreza) 2hrs 10mins 5 secs; **3.** L. O'Callaghan & H. McPhilips (Ford Escort Maxi) 2hrs 14mins 52secs.

1998 TOSHIBA TARMAC CHAMPIONS

Class	Winner
Overall	Austin McHale
Formula 2	Liam O'Callaghan
Group N	Derek mcGarrity
Class 2	Philip Wilson
Class 3	Gearoid Walsh
Class 5	Barry Gambel

Class	Winner
Class 6	Simon Welby
Class 9	Sammy Fisher
Class 10	Tommy McDonald
Class 12	Joe McGurk
Class 13	Fergal Allen
Modified	Uel Williamson
Historic	Dessie Nutt

NETBALL

Northern Ireland Netball Association

Netball Office, House of Sport, Upper Malone Road, Belfast BT9 5LA. Tel. (01232) 383806

Founded 1949
President .... Maureen Drennan
Secretary .... Claire Curran
PRO .... Rosemary McWhinney
Number of Clubs 35
Number of Teams 54
Number of Members 1,000
Number of Coaches 40
Number of Main Venues and Capacities .... 5 - Northern Ireland Badminton Centre, Lisburn (1,000); Maysfield Leisure Centre, Belfast (1,000); Omagh Leisure Centre (500); Templemore Leisure Centre, Derry (800); Methodist College, Belfast (400).

International Statistics:

National Senior Coach .... Marion Lofthouse
Most Capped Players (international appearances) .... Elizabeth Rodgers
Top International Scorer .... Helen McCambridge
Best International Result (team) .... Northern Ireland 44, England 54
International Ranking .... World (18); Europe (4)
All Time Record Attendance .... Northern Ireland v Jamaica, Maysfield (October 1996) 1,100

DOMESTIC RESULTS

Northern Ireland League Finals (Lisburn)

(Saturday 7th March 1998)

Results	Teams	Score
Minor Final	Lismore beat OLSPCK, Knock	19/18
Junior Final	St. Brigid's, Omagh beat OLSPCK, Knock	20/12
Intermediate Final	St. Brigid's, Omagh beat St. MacNissis	36/28
Senior Final	Lismore beat Loreto Grammar, Omagh	38/20

All-Ireland Finals (Dublin)

Results	Teams	Score
Minor Final	Lismore beat Mount Anville	18/13
Junior Final	St. Brigid's, Omagh beat Rathdown	25/14
Intermediate Final	St. Brigid's, Omagh beat Mount Anville	28/27
Senior Final	Lismore beat Mount Anville	37/34

Northern Ireland Cup (Lisburn Racquets Club)

Results	Teams	Score
Minor Section	Lismore beat OLSPCK	26/19
Junior Section	St. Brigid's, Omagh beat St. Mary's, Lurgan	19/17
Intermediate Section	St. Brigid's, Omagh beat Lismore	34/23
Senior Section	Lismore beat Sullivan	41/21

INTERNATIONAL RESULTS

Federation of European Championships 26th February 1998 (Gateshead)

Results	Teams	Score
Under 17	Northern Ireland beat Scotland	27/23
Under 17	Northern Ireland beat Malta	60/4
Under 17	Wales beat Northern Ireland	27/22
Under 17	England beat Northern Ireland	42/12

Federation of European Championships 17-19th April 1998 (Cardiff)

Results	Teams	Score
Open	Wales beat Northern Ireland	72/34
Open	England beat Northern Ireland	84/19
Open	Northern Ireland beat Malta	67/51

Continued from previous page

Results	Teams	Score
Open	Scotland beat Northern Ireland	51/46

Federation of European Championships 27-28th March 1998 (Edinburgh)

Results	Teams	Score
Under 19	Scotland beat Northern Ireland	38/29
Under 19	England beat Northern Ireland	63/17
Under 19	Wales beat Northern Ireland	47/28

ORIENTEERING

Irish Orienteering Association (IOA)

c/o AFAS, The House of Sport, Longmile Road, Walkinstown, Dublin 12. Tel: (01) 4509845 Fax: (01) 4502805. Orienteering Information (24 hr): (01) 4569099. e-mail: irishoa@tinet.ie

Founded 1970
Chairman .... Bernard Creedon
Honorary Secretary .... Ken Griffin
Public Relations Officer .... John McCullough
Number of Regions .... 3 + Northern Ireland (See Regional Associations)
Affiliations .... International Orienteering Federation (since 1975)
National Coaching Officer .... Frank Ryan
Most Capped Competitor .... Eileen Loughman (Curragh-Naas OC) represented Ireland at a world record total of 12 successive WOCs (1976-97)
Best International Result in 1998 .... Colm Rothery 22nd in the World Cup series (held in Ireland in May)

What is Orienteering: It's competitive navigation on foot, usually through forests and the countryside, using special Orienteering or 'O' maps, which are far more detailed than Ordnance Survey maps, featuring additional symbols and colours. Orienteering has many levels of participation from just an enjoyable visit to the forest to serious competition at local, regional, national and international competitions.

Regional Associations

CONNACHT ORIENTEERING ASSOCIATION *P. Higgins, 24 Alverno Ave, Athlone, Co. Westmeath* **Clubs:** (4) Forest Warriors OC, Galway RTC Orienteers, Sligo Orienteering Club, UCG Orienteers.

LEINSTER ORIENTEERING ASSOCIATION *V. Murtagh, 19 The Cloisters, Terenure, Dublin 6W Tel: (01) 4908237* **Clubs:** (11) Ajax Orienteers, Athlone RTC Orienteers, Curragh-Naas Orienteers, Defence Forces, Dublin University Orienteers, Fingal Orienteers, Great Eastern Navigators, Midland Navigators, Setanta Orienteers, Three Rock OC, UCD Orienteers.

MUNSTER ORIENTEERING ASSOCIATION *J. Muckian, 13 Elmvale Close, Wilton Cork. Tel: (021) 343384* **Clubs:** (10) Bishopstown OC, Blackwater Valley OC, Cork Orienteers, Former UCCO, Kerry Orienteers, Lee Orienteers, Southern Orienteers, Thomond Orienteers, UCC Orienteers, Waterford Orienteers.

NORTHERN IRELAND ORIENTEERING ASSOCIATION *V. Cordner, 19 Derrygavad Rd., Annaghmore, Co. Armagh BT62 1ND Tel: (01762) 328749* **Affiliated to:** British Orienteering Federation. **Clubs** (3) Fermanagh Orienteers, Lagan Valley Orienteers, North West OC.

1998 INTERNATIONAL RESULTS

Date	Competition	Course Length	Distance climbed	Best Irish Result
Orienteering World Cup Results, Killarney				
22-25 May	Men's Classic A Final	11.745km	515m	John Feehan (51st)
22-25 May	Women's Classic A Final	7.905km	303m	Una Creagh (44th)
22-25 May	Women's Classic A Final	7.905km	303m	Toni O'Donovan (59th)
Orienteering World Cup Results, Lake District, England				
28-30 May	Men's Classic A Final	13.00km	875m	John Feehan (54th)
28-30 May	Men's Classic A Final	13.00km	875m	Colm Rothery (62nd)
28-30 May	Men's Classic A Final	13.00km	875m	Bill Edwards (63rd)
28-30 May	Men's Classic A Final	13.00km	875m	James Logue (64th)
28-30 May	Women's Classic A Final	9.00km	590m	Una Creagh (68th)
28-30 May	Women's Classic A Final	9.00km	590m	Toni O' Donovan (70th)
28-30 May	Women's Classic A Final	9.00km	590m	Eadaoin Morrish (77th)
28-30 May	Women's Classic A Final	9.00km	590m	Julie Cleary (78th)
28-30 May	Women's Classic A Final	9.00km	590m	Nina Phillips (81st)
28-30 May	Men's Short Distance A Final	5.20km	225m	Colm Rothery (22nd)
28-30 May	Men's Short Distance A Final	5.20km	225m	Marcus Pinker (54th)
28-30 May	Women's Short Distance A Final	4.35km	180m	Una Creagh (55th)
World University Orienteering Championships, Trondheim, Norway				
10-15 Aug.	Men's Classic Distance	13.31km	465m	Marcus Pinker (33rd)
10-15 Aug.	Women's Classic Distance	-	-	Toni O'Donovan (60th)
10-15 Aug.	Women's Classic Distance	-	-	Ailbhe Creedon (77th)
10-15 Aug.	Men's Short Distance A Final	-	-	Marcus Pinker (32nd)

1998 IRISH CHAMPIONSHIP RESULTS

2nd May 1998, Slieve Gullion, Co. Armagh

MEN'S RESULTS:

Overall - 1st Bill Edwards (CORKO), 2nd John Feehan (AJAX), 3rd Colm Rothery (AJAX).

Event	Course length	Distance climbed	Winner	Club	Time
UNDERAGE					
M10A	1.6km	30m	Barry Healy	GEN	24:36
M12A	2.6km	70m	Padraig O'Brien	BOC	46:08
M14A	4.2km	155m	Niall Walsh	3ROC	45:01
M16A	5.3km	200m	Jonathan Lucey	BOC	48:00
M18A	7.4km	270m	Alan Barry	CORKO	66:40
COMPETITION					
M20L	9.0km	365m	Shane Lynch	DUO	85:38
M21E	11.5km	420m	Bill Edwards	CORKO	78:38
M21L	9.0km	365m	Hugh McLindon	3ROC	80:55
M21S	6.8km	230m	Geoff Somerville	LVO	58:10
VETERAN					
M35L	9.0km	365m	Dave Weston	SET	92:01
M35S	5.9km	220m	Ronan Cleary	3ROC	62:12
M40L	8.2km	320m	Liam O'Brian	CORKO	67:52
M45L	7.4km	270m	Denis Reidy	AJAX	61:54
M45S	4.2km	210m	Anthony McGonagle	NWOC	45:09
M50L	6.8km	230m	Wilbert Hollinger	LVO	68:16
M55L	6.4km	220m	Ted Feehan	BVOC	56:51
M60L	5.3km	200m	Maxwell Reed	FERMO	51:18
M65L	4.2km	210m	Fred Calnan	CORKO	68:30
M70L	4.2km	210m	Norman Ervine	LVO	60:53

WOMEN'S RESULTS:

Overall - 1st Toni O'Donovan (CORKO) 2nd Una Creagh (3ROC) 3rd Eadaoin Morrish (LEEO)

Event	Course length	Distance climbed	Winner	Club	Time
UNDERAGE					
W10A	1.6km	30m	Erinna Foley-Fisher	MNAV	16:49
W12A	2.2km	60m	Jane Hingerty	GEN	31:06
W14A	2.6km	70m	Niamh O'Boyle	CNOC	20:14
W14B	2.2km	60m	Niamh Lalor	GEN	39:43
W16A	4.2km	155m	Laura Cotter	BOC	56:53
W16B	2.6km	70m	June O'Neill	CNOC	48: 33
W18A	5.3km	200m	Susan Healy	GEN	64:14
COMPETITION					
W20L	6.4km	220m	Aislin Austin	CORKO	66:09
W20S	4.2km	210m	Karen Thompson	DUO	78:51
W21E	7.0km	240m	Toni O'Donovan	CORKO	72:09
W21L	6.8km	230m	Cecilia Eriksson	TABY	81:05
W21S	4.2km	210m	Miriam Feehan	BVOC	49:11
VETERAN					
W35L	6.4km	220m	Clare Heardman	CORKO	71:16
W35S	4.2km	210m	Ruth Blair	NWOC	60:42
W40L	5.9km	220m	Ruth Lynam	CNOC	70:32
W40S	3.6km	140m	Annemarie Lucey	BOC	73:39
W45L	5.3km	200m	Teresa Finlay	FERMO	67:08
W50L	4.2km	210m	Jean O'Neill	FINGAL	44:55
W50S	3.6km	140m	Claire McGrath	3ROC	67:12
W55L	4.2km	210m	Clare Nuttall	LEEO	54:27
W60L	3.6km	140m	Faith White	SET	64:58

E: *elite* **L:** *long course* **S:** *short course*
A: *greater difficulty (underage)* **B:** *lesser difficulty (underage)*

PITCH AND PUTT

The Pitch and Putt Union of Ireland

House of Sport, Long Mile Road, Walkinstown, Dublin 12. (01) 4509299 Fax: (01) 4564399 e-mail: ppui@iol.ie

Founded 1961
President .... Mervyn Cooney
Vice-President .... Myles McMorrow
Honorary Secretary .... Peg Smith
Honorary Treasurer .... Des Flanagan
Registrar .... Ben Lennon
Competition Secretary .... Liam Houlihan
PRO .... John Manning
Development / Coaching Administrator .... Michael Hayes
Number of Clubs 155
Number of Provincial Councils .... 2 *See Below*
Number of County Regional Boards .... 16 *See Below*
Total Number of Members 14,000
Number of Coaches 215

Regional Statistics

LEINSTER COUNCIL ● **President:** Billy Lynch ● **Hon. Secretary:** Rita Martin ● **PRO:** Dick Abraham
MUNSTER COUNCIL ● **President:** Myles McMorrow ● **Hon. Secretary:** Roger Barron ● **PRO:** Phil Allen

COUNTY / REGIONAL BOARDS ● **Carlow/Kilkenny/Wexford** ● **Cavan/Down/Monaghan** ● **Clare** ● **Cork** ● **Dublin** ● **Galway/Sligo** ● **Kerry** ● **Kildare** ● **Limerick** ● **Longford** ● **Louth** ● **Meath** ● **Offaly** ● **Tipperary** ● **Waterford** ● **Westmeath**

1998 NATIONAL RESULTS

1998 Gents Matchplay Champion .... Ray Murphy (Templebreedy)
1998 Gents Strokeplay Champion .... Frank O'Donoghue (Templebready)
1998 Ladies Matchplay Champion .... Marion Byrne (St. Bridget's)
1998 Ladies Strokeplay Champion .... Bernadette Coffey (St. Bridget's)

PAST PRESIDENTS

Year	President *(Club)*
1961-62	Patrick A. Murphy *(Woodvale)*
1963-64	Laurence J. Furlong *(Athgarvan)*
1965-66	William Somers *(Woodvale)*
1967-70	Patrick A Murphy *(Garda)*
1971	Paddy Dalton *(Ardnacrusha)*
1972	Bill Humphries *(Glenville)*
1973	Paddy Harkins *(Rocklodge)*
1974	Mick Geraghty *(Athgarvan)*
1975-76	Chris Twohig *(Douglas)*
1977-79	Eamonn Birchall *(Shandon)*
1980-82	Thomas Murphy *(Seapoint)*
1983-85	Liam Houlihan *(St. Anne's)*
1986-88	John Smith *(Lucan)*
1989-91	Liam Houlihan *(St. Anne's)*
1992-94	Aidan O'Brien *(Skryne)*
1995-97	Terry Hayes *(St. Otteran's)*

RACQUETBALL

The Racquetball Association of Ireland

c/o John Comerford, 5 Edenvale Close, Kilkenny. Web site: http//members.tripod.com/~Haverty/racquetball

Founded 1979
President .... Philip Duignan
Vice-President .... Anthony Butler
General Secretary .... John Comerford
Treasurer .... Pat Traynor
Tournament Secretary .... Michael Haverty
PRO .... Position Vacant
Development Officer .... Michael Murphy
Youth Development Officer .... Christy Slattery
Affiliated Racquetball Clubs in Ireland .... 40 approximately.

RACQUETBALL was introduced to Ireland in the 1970s and is played now in almost all parts of the country. The association sanctions many tournaments, the most popular of these being the Irish Open in Arklow Co Wicklow, Castlebar Open and the Irish Junior Open for underage players, and hosts National Championships (All Irelands) in various skill levels from Novice , D, C, B to Open and also age groups from Under 12 years to over 55 years.

1998 DOMESTIC RESULTS

Date / Category — **Competition / Winners**

14-15.02.98 .... **Moylagh Open - Moylagh ,Co Meath**
Mens Open Singles .... Noel O'Callaghan (Fermoy)
Ladies Singles(Olympic format) .... Karen Grumbridge (Fermoy)
4-5.03.98 .... **Kilkenny Open - Kilkenny City**
Mens Open Singles .... Noel O'Callaghan (Fermoy)
Mens A Singles .... Stephen O'Loan (Queens Belfast)
Ladies Singles (Olympic format) .... Karen Grumbridge (Fermoy)
Mens Open Doubles .... Christy Slattery (Templederry) / Michael Boyce (Fermoy)
Ladies Doubles .... Grainne Shanahan (Templederry) / Elma Gibney (Moylagh)
7-8..03.98 .... **All Ireland Club Championships - Arklow, Co. Wicklow**
Novice Team 1 .... Castlebar (Michael Kelly, Terry O'Hara, Oliver Moran)
20-22.03.98 .... **8th Baxter Healthcare Castlebar Open - Castlebar, Co Mayo**
Mens Open Singles .... Noel O'Callaghan (Fermoy)
Ladies Singles(Olympic format) .... Grainne Shanahan (Templederry).
Mens Open Doubles .... Cristy Slattery (Templederry) / Michael Boyce (Fermoy)
Ladies Doubles .... Grainne Shanahan (Templederry) / Elma Gibney (Moylagh)
Boys U15 .... Pa Boyce (Fermoy).
Girls U15 .... Michelle Haverty (Castlebar)
Boys U12 .... Alan Grimes (Ballinrobe)
Girls U12 .... Karen Kyne (Castlebar)
18-19.04.98 .... **2nd Irish Junior Open - Castlebar, Co. Mayo**
Boys .... U10 J.J. Coffey, U12 Matthew Ryan, U14 Daniel Shanahan, U16 Pa Boyce, U18 Michael Keane
Girls ....U10 Sarah Harkin, U12 Michelle Hogan, U14 Siobhan O`Doherty, U16 Sonya Donnelly, U18 Elma Gibney
1-2.05.98 .... **Irish Open - Arklow Sports & Leisure Centre, Arklow, Co Wicklow**
Mens Open Singles .... Noel O'Callaghan (Fermoy)
Ladies Singles(Olympic) .... Elma Gibney(Moylagh)
Mens Open Doubles .... Stephen O'Loan (Queens,Belfast) / Martin McConnon (Kingscourt)
Ladies Doubles .... Karen Grumbridge / Anee Marie Grumbridge (Fermoy)
9-10.05.98 .... **All Ireland Junior B Championships - Fermoy, Co. Cork**
Boys .... U12 Mike Haverty, U14 Willie Power, U16 Denis Coffey, U18 Fintan Whyte,
Girls .... U12 Deirdre Grall, U14 Aoife Hickey, U16 Anita Grimes, U18 Paula Magnier
16-17.05.98 .... **All-Ireland Singles' Championships - Moylagh & Oldcastle, Co. Meath**
Mens Open Singles .... Noel O'Callaghan
Womens B Singles .... Grainne Shanahan
30.05.98 .... **Men's Open Doubles - Arklow, Co Wicklow**
1st .... Sean O'Hagan / Paul Cloney (Fermoy)

1998-99 TOURNAMENT CALENDAR

3-4.10.98	**JUNIOR INTERPROVINCIALS**	Moylagh, Co. Meath
17-18.10.98	**LEINSTER OPEN**	Arklow, Co. Wicklow
7-8.11.98	**MUNSTER OPEN**	Fermoy, Co. Cork
15.11.98	**U11, U13, U15 & U17 PROVINCIAL CHAMPIONSHIPS**	Provincial Venues
21-22.11.98	**ALL IRELAND DOUBLES CHAMPIONSHIPS**	Moylagh, Co. Meath
5-6.12.98	**ALL IRELAND U11, U13, U15 & U17 CHAMPIONSHIPS**	Castlebar, Co Mayo
17.01.98	**PROVINCIAL CLUB CHAMPIONSHIPS**	Provincial Venues
30-31.01.99	**ALL IRELAND CLUB CHAMPIONSHIPS**	Moylagh, Co. Meath
14.02.99	**U12, U14, U16 & U18 PROVINCIAL CHAMPIONSHIPS**	*tba*
20-21.02.99	**MOYLAGH OPEN**	Moylagh & Oldcastle, Co Meath
6-7.03.99	**ALL IRELAND U12, U14, U16 & U18 CHAMPIONSHIPS**	Moylagh, Co Meath
19-21.03.99	**NINTH BAXTER HEALTHCARE CASTLEBAR OPEN**	Castlebar, Co. Mayo
10-11.04.99	**THIRD IRISH JUNIOR OPEN**	Fermoy, Co Cork
17-18.04.99	**KILKENNY OPEN**	Kilkenny City
25.04.99	**PROVINCIAL U12, U14, U16 & U18 B CHAMPIONSHIPS**	Provincial Venues
1-3.05.99	**ARKLOW OPEN**	Arklow, Co Wicklow
9-10.05.99	**ALL IRELAND B U12, U14, U16 & U18 CHAMPIONSHIPS**	Arklow, Co Wicklow
15-16.05.99	**ALL IRELAND SINGLES CHAMPIONSHIPS**	Ballinrobe, Co Mayo

MAIN CLUBS

● Fermoy, Co. Cork ● Macroom, Co. Cork ● Tralee, Co. Kerry ● Kilkenny City ● Callan, Co. Kilkenny ● Newry, Co. Down ● St Mary's Sligo, Co. Sligo ● Clones, Co. Monaghan ● Ballinrobe, Co. Mayo ● Castlebar, Co. Mayo ● Ballina Co. Mayo ● Aghamullen, Co. Monaghan ● Salthill, Galway City ● University College, Galway ● Athenry, Co. Galway ● Currandulla, Co. Galway ● Loughrea, Co. Galway ● University College Dublin ● Arklow, Co. Wicklow ● Moylagh, Co. Meath ● Oldcastle, Co. Meath ● Kingscourt, Co. Cavan ● Templederry, Co. Tipperary ● Fethard, Co. Tipperary ● Golden, Co. Tipperary ● Oldtown, Co Dublin ● Castledermot, Co Carlow ● Tournaneena, Co Waterford ● Carrickmore, Co. Tyrone ● Queens University Belfast.

1979-98 CHRONOLOGY OF SINGLES WINNERS

Year	Men's Open	Club	Ladies Open	Club
1979	T Hurley	(Sutton)	M Duignan	(Dublin)
1980	T Hurley	(Sutton)	M Duignan	(Dublin)
1981	P McGee	(Newport)	M Duignan	(Dublin)
1982	A Byrne	(Ashbourne)	M Duignan	(Dublin)
1983	P Duignan	(Dublin)	M Duignan	(Dublin)
1984	P Duignan	(Dublin)	M Duignan	(Dublin)
1985	J McDonald	(Kilkenny)	A M Whelan	(UCD)
1986	J McDonald	(Kilkenny)	M Duignan	(Dublin)
1987	B Doyle	(Arklow)	M Duignan	(Dublin)
1988	J Gannon	(Arklow)	A M Whelan	(UCD)
1989	A Butler	(Arklow)	O Ryan	(CNN)
1990	A Butler	(Arklow)	O Ryan	(CNN)
1991	N O'Callaghan	(Fermoy)	A M Whelan	(UCD)
1992	N O'Callaghan	(Fermoy)	B Brennan	(Fethard)
1993	N O'Callaghan	(Fermoy)	M Duignan	(Dublin)
1994	N O'Callaghan	(Fermoy)	B Brennan	(Fethard)
1995	N O'Callaghan	(Fermoy)	*No Event*	-
1996	N O'Callaghan	(Fermoy)	K Curran	(Tralee)
1997	N O'Callaghan	(Fermoy)	*No Event*	-
1998	N O'Callaghan	(Fermoy)	*No Event*	-

ROWING

Irish Amateur Rowing Union

House of Sport, Long Mile Road, Walkinstown, Dublin 12. Tel. (01) 4509831

Founded 1899
Number of Clubs 70
Number of Members 8,290
Number of Provincial Branches .... 4 (Connacht, Leinster, Munster and Ulster)
President .... Thomas Fennessy
Vice-Presidents .... Terry O'Brien (Connaught), Frank Durkin (Leinster), Michael O'Callaghan (Munster), ... Robbie Clarke (Ulster)
Honorary Secretary .... James Bermingham
Administrator .... Peadar Casey
Honorary Treasurer .... John McGeehan
PRO .... Dermot Henihan
International Team Manager .... Dermot Henihan
Best International Result .... Niall O'Toole - Gold Medal, Mens Lightweight Single Scull (Vienna, 1991)

PROVINCIAL BRANCHES

CONNAUGHT ● **Chairman:** Ms Neasa Folan ● **Honorary Secretary:** Terry O'Brien ● **Honorary Treasurer:** Gerry Small ● **Clubs:** (7) Athlunkard BC, Carrick-on-Shannon RC, CR Colaiste Iognaid, Galway RC, St Joseph's College RC, Tribesmen RC, UCG BC.

LEINSTER ● **Chairman:** Frank Durkin ● **Honorary Secretary:** Jimmy O'Neill ● **Honorary Treasurer:** Anthony Dooley **Clubs:** (19) Anna Liffey BC, Athy RC, Athlone BC, The Bluecoat Club, Carlow RC, Commercial RC (Dublin), Defence Forces RA BC, Dublin City University RC, Dublin Municipal Rowing Centre, Dublin University BC, Dublin University Ladies BC, Garda Síochana BC, King's Hospital BC, Neptune RC, New Ross BC, Offaly RC, Old Collegians' BC, UCD BC, UCD Ladies BC.

MUNSTER ● **Chairman:** Michael O'Callaghan ● **Hon. Secretary:** Denis O'Regan ● **Honorary Treasurer:** Paul Kavanagh **Clubs:** (26) Bantry RC, Cappoquin RC, Castleconnell BC, Clonmel RC, Commercial RC (Killarney), Cork BC, Cork IT RC, Fermoy RC, Flesk Valley RC, Fossa RC, Killarney RC, Killorglin RC, Lee RC, Limerick BC, Monkstown and CH RC, Muckross RC, Presentation College RC, St Michael's RC, Shandon BC, Shannon RC, Skibbereen RC, UCC RC, University of Limerick BC, Waterford BC, Waterford IT RC, Workmen's RC.

ULSTER ● **Chairman:** Robbie Clarke ● **Honorary Secretary:** Elaine Russell ● **Honorary Treasurer:** Ryan Price **Clubs:** (18) Bann RC, Belfast BC, Belfast RC, City of Derry BC, Coleraine Academy Institute BC, Enniskillen RC, The Lady Victoria BC, Lagan Scullers' Club, Methodist College RC, Newry RC, Our Lady's Grammar School BC, Portadown BC, Portora BC, Queen's Uni. BC, Queen's Uni. Ladies BC, Royal Belfast Academy Inst. BC, University of Ulster RC (Coleraine), University of Ulster RC (Jordanstown).

1997-98 INTERNATIONAL RESULTS

● **Best International Result** Niall O'Toole Gold Medal, Men's Lightweight Single Scull, Vienna 1991 ● **Team Manager** Dermot Henihan ● **National Director of Coaching** Thor Nilsen ● **Physiotherapist** Fiona Wilson ● **Coaches:** Michael Desmond, John Holland, Dermot Keogh ● **National Squad for World Rowing Championships:** Men's Lightweight Coxless 4: Tony O'Connor, Neville Maxwell, Brendan Dolan, Derek Holland. Men's Lightweight Quadruple Scull: Owen Byrne, Neal Byrne, Niall O'Toole, Gearoid Towey. Women's Lightweight Quadruple Scull: Audrey Phelan, Meadhbh Terry, Helen Dixon, Ailish Houlihan. Men's Lightweight Single Scull: Sam Lynch. Women's Lightweight Single Scull: Ruth Doyle. Men's Lightweight Double Scull: John Armstrong, Eugene Coakley. Men's Single Scull: Albert Maher.

Date	Event	Venue	Winner	Irish Placing
6.7.98	Home counties	-	Scotland (jnr. Women)	3rd (jnr. Women)
	International		England (jnr. Men)	2nd (jnr. Men)
			England (women)	3rd (women)
			Scotland (men)	3rd (men)
1-2.8.98	Coup de la Jeunesse	Candia, Italy	Great Britain	5th (men: 5th, women: 4th)
6-13.9.98	World Rowing C'ships	Cologne, Germany	Men's Lightweight Coxless 4	8th
			Men's Lightweight Quadruple Scull	4th
			Women's Lightweight Quadruple Scull	9th
6-13.9.98	World Rowing C'ships	Cologne, Germany	Men's Lightweight Single Scull	7th
			Women's Lightweight Single Scull	12th
			Men's Lightweight Double Scull	16th
			Men's Single Scull	14th

1998 NATIONAL JUNIOR & SENIOR CHAMPIONSHIPS

Event	Result
Men's 8	Neptune RC
Men's 4+	Neptune RC
Men's 4-	Neptune RC
Men's 4x	Commercial RC
Men's 2-	Neptune RC
Men's 2x	Neptune RC
Men's 1x	Neptune RC (A. Maher)
Men's Lwt 1x	St Michael's RC (S. Lynch)
Men's Intermediate 8	University College Dublin BC
Men's Intermediate 4+	Muckross RC
Men's Intermediate 2-	Commercial RC
Men's Intermediate 1x	Dublin Uni. BC (J. Lupton)
Men's Novice 8	UCC RC
Men's Novice 4	Neptune RC
Men's Novice 1x	UCD BC (C. Collis)
Jnr Men's 8	Skibbereen RC
Jnr Men's 4+	Skibbereen RC
Jnr Men's 4x	Skibbereen RC
Jnr Men's 2-	Galway RC
Jnr Men's 2x	Neptune RC
Jnr Men's 1x	Offaly RC (P. Hussey)
Women's 8	Commercial RC
Women's 4-	Commercial RC
Women's 4x	Commercial RC
Women's 2-	Commercial RC
Women's 2x	Commercial RC
Women's 1x	Commercial RC (M. Hussey)
Women's Intermediate 8	UCD Ladies BC
Women's Intermediate 4x	Fossa RC
Women's Intermediate 1x	Commercial RC (A.Phelan)
Women's Novice 8	Muckross RC
Women's Novice 4+	Muckross RC
Women's Novice 1x	Offaly RC (E. Moran)
Jnr Women's 8	Muckross RC
Jnr Women's 4-	Muckross RC
Jnr Women's 4x	Offaly RC
Jnr Women's 2-	King's Hospital RC
Jnr Women's 2x	Bantry RC
Jnr Women's 1x	Offaly RC (N. Ní Cheilleachair)

IRISH SENIOR ROWING CHAMPIONS 1912-1997

Name	Club	No. Wins
Frank Moore	Garda/Neptune	14
Gerry Murphy	Neptune	14
Eunan Dolan	Neptune	13
Niall O'Toole	Commercial	12
Willie Ryan	Garda	12
Neville Maxwell	Neptune	11
John Armstrong	Queen's/LVBC	10
Lar Collins	Skibbereen/Commercial	10
Brendan Dolan	Neptune	10
Tony O'Connor	Neptune	10
Jim Cassidy	Neptune	9
Christy O'Brien	Garda	9
Phil Browne	Neptune	8
Colm O'Rourke	Neptune	8
Dominic Casey	Skibbereen	7
Jim Muldoon	Garda/Neptune	7
Denis Murphy	Garda	7
Ted Ryan	Garda	7
Barry Currivan	Neptune	6
Derek Holland	Neptune	6
Des McCann	UCD/OC/Neptune	6
Pat McDonagh	Commercial/Neptune	6
Colm Butler	Neptune	5
Tony Corcoran	Carlow/Dungarvan/Cork/Shandon	5
John Fahy	Garda	5
Pat Gannon	Garda	5
Donal Hanrahan	DU BC/St. Michael's	5
Gerry Macken	DU BC/Neptune	5
Gary O'Neill	Neptune	5
Alan Thomas	Neptune	5
Women		
Nicole Ryan	Comm./Anna Liffey/Workmen's	13
Frances Cryan	Carrick-on-Shannon	11
Cathy Buchanan	Queen's Ladies/Belfast RC	10
Mary Hussey	Offaly/Commercial	7
Clare Morrissey	Commercial	6
Vanessa Lawrenson	UCD LBC	6
Grainne O'Donovan	Skibbereen	6
Debbie Stack	Offaly/UCD LBC	6
Angela Hamilton	Belfast RC	5
Coxes		
Liam Williams	Neptune	13
Joe Homan	Commercial/Garda	6
Gerry O'Brien	Neptune	5

RUGBY

the new professionals

by **victor costello**

IRISH RUGBY INTERNATIONAL

THERE is little doubt that the mid-90s advent of professional rugby caught the Irish rugby world, players and officials, in a state of something less than preparedness. The *laissez faire* attitude, prevalent in the higher echelons of the Union, would eventually trickle down to the playing field, with the all too predictable scenario of some of Ireland's finest players departing the home sod for the lucrative contracts being offered by English club sides, who had professional structures in place long before the game itself embraced the ethos.

The problems caused by our failure to anticipate this `professional revolution' are frequently touted as the reasons for a slump at international level in recent times. However, this is something that the Irish authorities have finally begun to address, as the necessity of keeping our best prospects on home soil becomes more of a priority. Club, Provincial and International contracts - while not yet on a par with those on offer in England - are, nonetheless, sufficiently substantial to convince large numbers of our young players that their future does not lie in mass emigration. This philosophy is crucial to the preservation of the game in Ireland, and the return of players like Eric Millar can only add to the profile of the Inter-provincial and All Ireland League competitions.

It's all a far cry from the mid-1990s when English Club contracts were, in a lot of cases, considerably more lucrative than the International alternatives on offer from the Irish Rugby Football Union. It became something of a trend for Irish Internationals to cross the sea to ply their trade, sold on the twin attractions of what was assumed to be a better quality of rugby and a better quality of contract.

So it was that I found myself winging my way to the clubhouse at Sunbury, home of London Irish, for the start of the 1995/96 season. I was in good company; fellow internationals Gabriel Fulcher, Niall Woods and Jeremy Davidson had all taken similar decisions. As Irishmen, a contract with London Irish was certainly more desirable than one with any other club in England. These were exciting times. For guys who had been brought up to play rugby for love of the sport. Suddenly we were being offered the opportunity to play the game as full-time professionals - given cars, money and a chance to be the ground breakers for all future generations of professional Irish rugby players.

Life, as we know, has a nasty way of reminding you who's boss, and the London dream was to quickly develop into something of a nightmare. An early season victory over a highly fancied Northampton side gave little indication of the catastrophes to follow. A bad sequence of results was followed by the added distraction of Clive Woodward's departure and the appointment of Willie Anderson as new

Head Coach. Relationships between the exiles and the IRFU were becoming increasingly strained as the Club threatened that Irish players would not be released to play at home.

My personal situation was compounded by the fact that I had suffered a dip in form and after only five games of the season, I was warming an increasingly familiar spot on the Sunbury bench, consequently being dropped from the Irish squad for the Five Nations Championship.

The sheer enormity of London was also posing problems, as the players found themselves increasingly on their own. In London, we missed the thrill of the big Donnybrook crowd, the post-mortems in Kiely's, and all the familiar faces along the way. Rugby with London Irish was simply business, and if your last game was a nightmare then your whole week was a nightmare. Loyalty to the club was taking a back seat to personal loyalty, and our results at London Irish were a sad reflection of this harsh start.

With a growing sense of disillusionment, I began to regret having turned my back on the IRFU. We had genuinely believed that our defection to the English club scene was a defection to a better quality of rugby. This final fallacy was laid to rest one Saturday afternoon, as we watched Munster methodically mangle a Wasps side who were very much the king pins of English club rugby. My mind was clear; my future lay at home in Ireland. Thankfully mine was only a one-year contract, and before the summer had begun, I was back at St. Mary's in the 'comfort zone' where Ciaran Fitzgerald had suggested I would play my best rugby.

The English experiment certainly proved a valuable lesson. There is no doubt that Irish players playing in England are at a disadvantage to their counterparts on the domestic scene. A heavy schedule of games increases the possibilities of burn out, while it seems that home-based players are finding international favour with less difficulty at the moment.

I believe it is in the interests of Irish Rugby to have our best players based at home. In order to achieve this, we will need not alone better contracts but also a more competitive structure of games for our provincial teams. It would appear from current trends that the importance of the province will be accentuated at the expense of the clubs which, it seems, are going to develop into an effective feeder system.

As we approach 1999, Irish rugby appears to be on the way up. There are a number of exciting young players who will shortly burst onto the international scene with obvious benefits for the Irish game. Leinster outside centre Shane Horgan, scrum half Ciaran Scally and Ballymena and Ulster centre Sheldon Coulter are as good as any young players in the Five Nations.

Warren Gatland's new Irish side are still at the early stage of their development, yet must be confident of a strong performance in the Five Nations, where a Triple Crown victory would not be beyond the realms of possibility. As regards the World Cup, our primary goal will be to qualify for the knock-out stages and after that who knows? Certainly, a much better level of consistency will have to be achieved if the glory days of the mid-1980s are to be re-lived, and Ireland becomes a feared Rugby Nation once again. It is our hope that the teething problems experienced with professionalism in the earlier stages have now been passed and the 'good ship Gatland' is sailing to its destiny of glory for all Irish rugby.

Irish Rubgy Football Union

62 Lansdowne Road, Ballsbridge, Dublin 4. Tel. (01) 6684601

Founded	1874
President	Niall Brophy
Secretary	P.R. Browne
Treasurer	P.R. Browne
Public Relations Officer	John Redmond

DOMESTIC STATISTICS

Number of Clubs		250
Number of members		60,500
Of which:	**Men**	60,000
	Women	500
Oldest Club		Dublin University, founded 1854
Main Stadium		Lansdowne Road, capacity 49,638
Biggest Recorded Attendance		55,000 (Five Nations Championship)

1997/98	**Champions**	**Runners Up**
All-Ireland League Division One	Shannon	Garryowen
All-Ireland League Division Two	Galwegians	Buccaneers
All-Ireland League Division Three	Portadown	Ballynahinch
All-Ireland League Division Four	County Carlow	Richmond
Provincial Series	Leinster	Munster

	Top Try Scorer	**Club**	**Tries**	**Top Points Scorer**	**Club**	**Points**
Division One	Denis Hickie	St Mary's	12	Andrew Thompson	Shannon	155
Division Two	Pat Duignan	Galwegians	9	Jimmy Dempsey	Skerries	126
Division Three	Simon Dogget	UCD	6	Philip Nelson	Ballynahinch	107
Division Four	Andrew Melville	County Carlow	10	Philip Jones	County Carlow	68

INTERNATIONAL STATISTICS

National Manager	Donal Lenihan
National Coach	Warren Gatland
Most Capped International	C.M.H. Gibson, 69 Caps (1964-79)
Top International Points Scorer	M.J. Kiernan, 308 points (43 internationals)
Top International Try Scorer	B.J. Mullin, 17 tries (55 internationals)
First International Game	v. England 1875
Best World Cup performance	Quarter finalists (1987, 1991 and 1995)
Grand Slam Winners	1 (1948)
Triple Crown Winners	6 (1894, 1899, 1948, 1949, 1982 and 1985)
International Championship Winners	18 times (including 10 outright wins)

IRISH RUGBY FOOTBALL UNION, CONNACHT BRANCH

Unit 30, Kilkerrin Park, Liosban Industrial Estate, Tuam Road, Galway. Tel. (091) 770237

Founded	1896
President	J.F. Smith
Honourary Secretary	R.P. McGann
Honourary Treasurer	E.G. Feely
Administrative Officer	P.M. Cawley
Public Relations Officer	R.P. McGann
Number of Senior Clubs	8
Number of Junior Clubs	11
Number of Affiliated Schools	25
Main Stadium	Sportgrounds, Galway (capacity 5,600)

1997/98	**Winners**	**Runners Up**
Connacht Senior Cup	Corinthians	Galwegians
Connacht Senior League	Buccaneers	
Connacht Senior Schools	Garbally College, Ballinasloe	St Saran's, Ferbane

Number of Interprovincial Titles Won ... **Overall:** 2 ... **Outright:** 0 ... **Grand Slams:** 0

IRISH RUGBY FOOTBALL UNION, LEINSTER BRANCH

Donnybrook, Dublin 4. Tel. (01) 6689599

Founded	1879

President	C. Powell
Secretary	A. Heffernan
Honourary Treasurer	P.J. Boyle
Chief Executive	E. Wigglesworth
Public Relations Officer	P. Geraghty
Number of Senior Clubs	17
Number of Junior Clubs	40
Number of Affiliated Schools	76
Number of Members	15,000+
Oldest Club	Dublin University (founded 1854)
Main Stadium	Donnybrook (capacity 8,000)
Biggest recorded attendance	7,000 (Leinster v. Leicester in Heineken European Cup)

	Winners	Runners Up
Leinster Senior Cup	Lansdowne	Skerries
Provincial Towns Cup	Naas	Kilkenny
Metropolitan Cup	St. Mary's College	Blackrock
Leinster Senior Championship	Lansdowne	Terenure College
Leinster Senior Schools	Clongowes	Terenure College
Number of Interprovincial Titles Won	**Overall:** 21	**Outright:** 14 **Grand Slams:** 8

IRISH RUGBY FOOTBALL UNION, MUNSTER BRANCH

Penrose Wharf, Penrose Quay, Cork. Tel. (021) 501533

Founded	1880
President	B. McCarthy
Honourary Secretary	D. B. Kelly
Honourary Treasurer	T.M. Wallace
Administrative Officer	J. C. Coleman
Public Relations Officer	D.B. Kelly
Number of Clubs	60
Oldest Club	UCC (founded 1872)
Main Stadium	Thomond Park (Capacity 16,000)

1997/98	Winners	Runners Up
Munster Senior Cup	Shannon	Young Munster
Munster Junior Cup	Midleton	Cork Constitution
Munster Clubs (League)	Cork Constitution	
Munster Senior Schools	C.B.C.	P.B.C.
Number of Interprovincial Titles Won	**Overall:** 18	**Outright:** 11 **Grand Slams:** 7

IRISH RUGBY FOOTBALL UNION, ULSTER BRANCH

Ravenhill Grounds, 85 Ravenhill Park, Belfast BT6 0DG. Tel. (01) 649141

President	J. Callaghan
Chief Executive and Public Relations Officer	M. Reid
Honourary Secretary	J.S. Gardiner
Honourary Treasurer	J. McComish
Administrator	L. McFadden
Number of Clubs	70
Oldest Club	North of Ireland Football Club, founded 1859
Main Stadium	Ravenhill

	Winners	Runners Up
Ulster Senior Cup	Dungannon	Malone
Ulster Junior Cup	Ballymena IIs	Banbridge
Ulster Senior League	Ballymena	Instonians
Ulster Senior Schools	R.B.A.I.	C.A.I.
Smithwick's Towns Cup	Coleraine	Dromore
Number of Interprovincial Titles Won	**Overall:** 26	**Outright:** 18 **Grand Slams:** 13

I.R.F.U. NUMBER OF AFFILIATED CLUBS

Province	Clubs	Commercial Clubs	Schools
Connacht	19	0	23
Leinster	71	8	75
Munster	59	5	41
Ulster	56	17	107

Continued from previous page

Province	Clubs	Commercial Clubs	Schools
London Irish	1	0	0
Total	206	30	246

INTERNATIONAL RESULTS, 1997/98 SEASON

Senior Internationals

Date	Venue	Irish Scorers	Opponents' Score
15.11.97	Lansdowne Road	**Ireland 15**	**New Zealand 63**
		(Woods 2T; Elwood 2C, 1P)	(7T, 5C, 6P)
30.11.97	Lansdowne Road	**Ireland 33**	**Canada 11**
		(Nowlan 2T; Elwood 2P, 1C; McGuinness 1T; Maggs 1T; Costello 1T)	(1T, 2P)
20.12.97	Bologna	**Ireland 22**	**Italy 37**
		(Humphreys 5P; Elwood 1P, 1C; O'Mahony 1T)	(6P, 3T, 2C)
07.02.98	Lansdowne Road	**Ireland 16**	**Scotland 17**
		(Humphreys 2P, 1DG, 1C; penalty try)	(4P, 1T)
07.03.98	Stade de France	**Ireland 16**	**France 18**
		(Elwood 3P, 1C; Hickie 1T)	(2T,2P,1C)
21.03.98	Lansdowne Road	**Ireland 21**	**Wales 30**
		(Elwood 3P, 1C; Ward 1T; Costello 1T)	(3T, 3P, 3C)
04.04.98	Twickenham	**Ireland 17**	**England 35**
		(Hickie 2T; Elwood 1P, 2C)	(4T, 3P, 3C)
13.06.98	Bloemfontein	**Ireland 13**	**South Africa 37**
		(Elwood 2P, 1C; Bishop 1T)	(5T, 2P, 3C)
20.06.98	Pretoria	**Ireland 0**	**South Africa 33**
			(5T, 4C)

Five Nations Championship, Final Table

	P	W	D	L	F	A	Pts
France	4	4	0	0	144	49	8
England	4	3	0	1	146	87	6
Wales	4	2	0	2	75	145	4
Scotland	4	1	0	3	66	120	2
Ireland	4	0	0	4	70	100	0

Irish tour to South Africa, Representative Matches

Date	Venue	Irish Scorers	Opponents' Score
30.05.98	Wellington	**Ireland 48**	**Boland 35**
		(Elwood 2P, 6C; Topping 2T; O'Cuinneagain 1T; Hickie 1T; O'Shea 1T; McGuinness 1T)	(5T, 5C)
03.06.98	George	**Ireland 20**	**South West District 27**
		(Humphreys 5P, Foley 1T)	(4P, 2T, 1DG, 1C)
06.06.98	Cape Town	**Ireland 6**	**Western Province 12**
		(Humphreys 2P)	(4P)
09.06.98	Kimberley	**Ireland 13**	**Griqualand West 52**
		(Foley 1T; O'shea 1T; Humphreys 1P)	(7T, 7C, 1P)
17.06.98	Pootchefstroom	**Ireland 26**	**North West Districts 18**
		(Humphreys 7P; R. Wallace 1T)	(2T, 2P, 1C)

FIRA World Junior (U19) Championship Results

Date	Venue	Irish Scorers	Opponents' Score
04.04.98	Samatan	**Ireland 47**	**USA 13**
		2T McCarey; Rossi 1T, 2C, 1P; Urquhart, Broughall, Wallace, Kearney, Good 1T each.	2T, 1P
06.04.98	Londez	**Ireland 17**	**South Africa 17**
		O'Driscoll 2C, 1P; Wallace 1T; McCarey 1T	2T, 2C, 1P
09.04.98	Colomiers (Semi Final)	**Ireland 18**	**Argentina 3**
		O'Driscoll 2P, 1C; Campbell 1T; Coughlan 1T	1P
12.04.98	Toulouse (Final)	**Ireland 18**	**France 0**
		Wallace 1T, 1DG; Holt 1T; O'Driscoll 1P, 1C	-

EUROPEAN COMPETITION RESULTS, '97/98 SEASON

European Cup

06.09.97: Leinster 25, Toulouse 34.
07.09.97: Harlequins 48, Munster 40.
08.09.97: Ulster 12, Glasgow 18.
12.09.97: Leinster 16, Leicester 9.
13.09.97: Cardiff 43, Munster 23; Swansea 33, Ulster 16.
20.09.97: Milan 33, Leinster 32; Munster 17, Bourgoin 15.
21.09.97: Wasps 56, Ulster 3.
27.09.97: Ulster 28, Swansea 20; Munster 32, Cardiff 37; Leicester 47 Leinster 22.
03.10.97: Ulster 21, Wasps 38.
04.10.97: Leinster 23, Milan 6; Bourgoin 21, Munster 6.
11.10.97: Toulouse 38, Leinster 19.
12.10.97: Munster 23, Harlequins 16; Glasgow 30, Ulster 15.

European Shield

Pool Matches

09.09.97: Connacht 43, Northampton 13.
14.09.97: Nice 16, Connacht 20.
21.09.97: Begles-Bordeaux 9, Connacht 15.
27.09.97: Connacht 28, Nice 25.
04.10.97: Connacht 22, Begles-Bordeaux 15.
11.10.97: Northampton 15, Connacht 20.

Quarter Final

08.11.97: Agen 40, Connacht 27.

European Competitions 1997/98, Final Tables

European Cup Pool A	P	W	D	L	F	A	Pts
Toulouse	6	5	0	1	200	121	10
Leicester	6	4	0	2	163	117	8
LEINSTER	6	2	0	4	137	167	4
Milan	6	1	0	5	111	206	2

European Cup Pool D	P	W	D	L	F	A	Pts
Harlequins	6	4	0	2	198	141	8
Cardiff	6	4	0	2	184	146	8
MUNSTER	6	2	0	4	141	180	4
Bourgoin	6	2	0	4	93	149	4

European Cup Pool B	P	W	D	L	F	A	Pts
Wasps	6	6	0	0	243	104	12
Glasgow	6	3	0	3	132	167	6
Swansea	6	2	0	4	157	161	4
ULSTER	6	1	0	5	95	195	2

European Conference Pool D	P	W	D	L	F	A	Pts
CONNACHT	6	5	0	1	144	97	10
Northampton	6	3	0	3	161	116	6
Begles	6	3	0	3	112	110	6
Nice	6	1	0	5	94	188	2

DOMESTIC RESULTS, 1997/98 SEASON

All-Ireland League Division One

19.11.97: Lansdowne 35, Old Belvedere 20.
22.11.97: Ballymena 45, Dolphin 16; Clontarf 11, Old Crescent 8; Cork Constitution 15, Terenure College 18; Shannon 20, Dungannon 13; St Mary's College 41, Blackrock College 23.
23.11.97: Garryowen 3, Young Munster 3.
05.12.97: Old Crescent 0, Shannon 50.
06.12.97: Blackrock College 54, Lansdowne 32; Dolphin 25, Garryowen 24; Dungannon 18, Cork Constitution 9; Old Belvedere 12, Ballymena 26; Terenure College 18, St Mary's College 12; Young Munster 25, Clontarf 19.
13.12.97: Ballymena 44, Blackrock College 6; Dolphin 15, Young Munster 31; Garryowen 37, Old Belvedere 22; Shannon 31, Clontarf 6; St Mary's College 70, Dungannon 29.
14.12.97: Lansdowne 9, Terenure College 9; Old Crescent 10, Cork Constitution 17.
03.01.98: Blackrock College 8, Garryowen 29; Clontarf 3, Cork Constitution 11; Dungannon 28, Lansdowne 8; Old Belvedere 15, Dolphin 23; Terenure College 5, Ballymena 25.
10.01.98: Ballymena 27, Dungannon 12; Cork Constitution 11, Shannon 12; Dolphin 13, Blackrock College 13; Lansdowne 51, Old Crescent 6; St Mary's College 12, Clontarf 23; Young Munster 26, Old Belvedere 12.
17.01.98: Blackrock College 44, Old Belvedere 19; Clontarf 42, Lansdowne 10; Cork Constitution 16, Young Munster 9; Dungannon 10, Garryowen 37; Old Crescent 9, Ballymena 6; Shannon 32, St Mary's College 11; Terenure College 23, Dolphin 10.
24.01.98: Ballymena 46, Clontarf 18; Dolphin 18, Dungannon 10; Garryowen 34, Old Crescent 13; Lansdowne 18, Shannon 14; Old Belvedere 12, Terenure College 10; St Mary's College 38, Cork Constitution 23; Young Munster 26, Blackrock College 16.
31.01.98: Clontarf 14, Garryowen 16; Cork Constitution 26, Lansdowne 19; Dungannon 16, Old Belvedere 12; Old Crescent 24, Dolphin 9; Shannon 19, Ballymena 13; St Mary's College 13, Young Munster 7; Terenure College 13, Blackrock College 20.
11.02.98: Lansdowne 10, St Mary's College 42.
14.02.98: Ballymena 6, Cork Constitution 19; Blackrock College 23, Dungannon 9; Dolphin 21, Clontarf 46; Old Belvedere 27, Old Crescent 23; Young Munster 22, Terenure College 16.
15.02.98: Garryowen 14, Shannon 17.

21.02.98: Clontarf 17, Old Belvedere 10; Cork Constitution 15, Garryowen 23; Dungannon 22, Terenure College 28; Lansdowne 9, Young Munster 16; Old Crescent 5, Blackrock College 3; Shannon 30, Dolphin 3; St Mary's College 64, Ballymena 33.

28.02.98: Blackrock College 13, Clontarf 29; Dolphin 29, Cork Constitution 35; Garryowen 13, St Mary's College 12; Old Belvedere 20, Shannon 70; Terenure College 41, Old Crescent 23; Young Munster 29, Dungannon 13.

14.03.98: Ballymena 31, Lansdowne 20; Garryowen 36, Terenure College 26; Old Crescent 16, St Mary's College 17.

15.03.98: Shannon 16, Young Munster 10.

28.03.98: Ballymena 13, Young Munster 21; Clontarf 36, Terenure College 17; Cork Constitution 63, Old Belvedere 12; Lansdowne 30, Garryowen 27; Old Crescent 16, Dungannon 13; Shannon 37, Blackrock College 6; St Mary's College 36, Dolphin 32.

11.04.98: Blackrock College 20, Cork Constitution 29; Dolphin 13, Lansdowne 13; Dungannon 47, Clontarf 12; Garryowen 66, Ballymena 29; Old Belvedere 15, St Mary's College 41; Terenure College 17, Shannon 19; Young Munster 19, Old Crescent 15.

Semi-finals

18.04.98: Shannon 28, St Mary's College 21.

19.04.98 Young Munster 10, Garryowen 24.

Final

25.04.98: Garryowen 9, Shannon 15.

Division 1/2 playoff:

1st leg 18.04.98: Buccaneers 11, Dungannon 17.

2nd leg 25.04.98 Dungannon 10, Buccaneers 27.

Buccaneers promoted to Division One, Dungannon relegated to Division Two.

All-Ireland League Division Two

22.11.97: Bective Rangers 5, Sunday's Well 23; Buccaneers 42, DLSP 3; Galwegians 32, Wanderers 18; Monkstown 11, Greystones 14; Skerries 16, Malone 10; UCC 22, City of Derry 13.

05.12.97: Sunday's Well 10, UCC 10.

06.12.97: City of Derry 7, Buccaneers 30; DLSP 15, Galwegians 22; Greystones 24, Old Wesley 21; Instonians 19, Bective Rangers 9; Malone 26, Monkstown 8; Wanderers 19, Skerries 16.

13.12.97: Buccaneers 21, Sunday's Well 6; Galwegians 50, City of Derry 13; Greystones 25, Instonians 15; Monkstown 22, Wanderers 15; Old Wesley 25, Malone 17; Skerries 19, DLSP 18; UCC 14, Bective Rangers 9.

03.01.98: Bective Rangers 6, Buccaneers 25; City of Derry 13, Skerries 3; UCC 22, Instonians 20.

10.01.98: Buccaneers 38, UCC 0; Galwegians 25, Bective Rangers 13; Greystones 20, Wanderers 22; Instonians 10, Malone 17; Monkstown 15, City of Derry 40; Old Wesley 24, DLSP

17.01.98: Bective Rangers 25, Skerries 16; City of Derry 8, Old Wesley 22; DLSP 23, Greystones 16; Sunday's Well 18, Monkstown 13; Wanderers 28, Malone 14.

18.01.98: UCC 18, Galwegians 25.

24.01.98: Galwegians 15, Buccaneers 10; Greystones 14, City of Derry 25; Instonians 16, Wanderers 14; Malone 18, DLSP 14; Monkstown 14, Bective Rangers 31; Old Wesley 15, Sunday's Well 20.

31.01.98: Bective Rangers 24, Old Wesley 24; Buccaneers 30, Skerries 5; City of Derry 26, Malone 15; DLSP 22, Wanderers 11; Galwegians 49, Instonians 8; Sunday's Well 12, Greystones 12; UCC 13, Monkstown 5.

08.02.98: DLSP 22, Monkstown 23.

14.02.98: Greystones 6, Bective Rangers 13; Instonians 22, DLSP 24; Malone 17, Sunday's Well 34; Monkstown 20, Buccaneers 31; Old Wesley 34, UCC 8; Skerries 11, Galwegians 22; Wanderers 19, City of Derry 18.

21.02.98: Bective Rangers 12, Malone 13; Buccaneers 20, Old Wesley 15; City of Derry 31, DLSP 19; Galwegians 20, Monkstown 16; Skerries 33, Instonians 3; Sunday's Well 34, Wanderers 13; UCC 15, Greystones 26.

28.02.98: DLSP 34, Sunday's Well 10; Greystones 3, Buccaneers 8; Instonians 17, City of Derry 27; Malone 18, UCC 30; Monkstown 15, Skerries 45; Old Wesley 6, Galwegians 18; Wanderers 9, Bective Rangers 30.

08.03.98: Skerries 9, Sunday's Well 14.

14.3.98: Buccaneers 37, Instonians 13; Malone 25, Greystones 14; Skerries 35, UCC 18; Sunday's Well 15, Galwegians 26; Wanderers 24, Old Wesley 6.

28.03.98: Bective Rangers 19, DLSP 18; Buccaneers 19, Malone 9; Galwegians 13, Greystones 10; Monkstown 30, Instonians 27; Skerries 31, Old Wesley 17; Sunday's Well 15, City of Derry 29; UCC 22, Wanderers 8.

11.04.98: City of Derry 27, Bective Rangers 14; DLSP 41, UCC 12; Greystones 20, Skerries 9; Instonians 23, Sunday's Well 41; Malone 11, Galwegians 19; Old Wesley 34, Monkstown 15; Wanderers v Buccaneers postponed.

All-Ireland League Division Three

22.11.97: Ballynahinch 49, Corinthians 8; Dublin University 20, Portadown 21; Highfield 6, Bohemians 3; NIFC 17, Suttonians 10; UCD 43, Collegians 6.

06.12.97: Bohemians 12, Ballynahinch 20; Collegians 11, NIFC 33; Corinthians 21, UCD 15; Portadown 49, Queen's University 11; Suttonians 22, Dublin University 23.

13.12.97: Ballynahinch 16, Highfield 0; Dublin University 20, Collegians 13; NIFC 28, Corinthians 16; Queen's University 12, Suttonians 13; UCD 21, Bohemains 0.

10.01.98 Collegians 41, Queen's University 24; Corinthians 23, Dublin University 6; Highfield 6, UCD 7; Suttonians 7, Portadown 28.

17.01.98: Dublin University 21, Bohemians 26; NIFC 3, Highfield 9; Portadown 28, Collegians 8; Queen's University 8, Corinthians 21; UCD 20, Ballynahinch 19.

24.01.98: Ballynahinch 28, NIFC 18; Bohemians 51, Queen's University 22; Collegians 9, Suttonians 9; Corinthians 21, Portadown 27; Highfield 25, Dublin University 3.

31.01.98: NIFC 11, UCD 34; Portadown 24, Bohemians 14; Queen's University 10, Highfield 35; Suttonians 24, Corinthians 42.

14.02.98: Ballynahinch 49, Suttonians 22; Bohemians 18, Corinthians 13; Highfield 28, Collegians 16; NIFC 35, Queen's University 17; UCD 3, Portadown 9.

21.02.98: Collegians 12, Bohemians 28; Dublin University 16, NIFC 32; Portadown 16, Ballynahinch 11; Queen's University 16, UCD 25; Suttonians 10, Highfield 24.

28.02.98: Bohemians 10, NIFC 7; Collegians 7, Ballynahinch 16; Corinthians 13, Highfield 32; Queen's University 3, Dublin University 16; Suttonians 17, UCD 18.

14.03.98: Bohemians 32, Suttonians 19; Corinthians 0, Collegians 7; Dublin University 17, Ballynahinch 24; Portadown 9, NIFC 6.

27.03.98: UCD 36, Dublin University 21.

28.03.98: Ballynahinch 53, Queen's University 5; Highfield 5, Portadown 6.

Division 3/4 play off:

1st leg 11.04.98 Richmond 15, Collegians 8;
2nd leg 18.04.98 Collegians 10, Richmond 15. Richmond promoted to Division 3, Collegians relegated to Division 4.

All-Ireland League Division Four

22.11.97: Ballina 15, Waterpark 16; CIYMS 0, County Carlow 60; Creggs 3, Omagh Academicals 8; Richmond 20, Bangor 20; Sligo 8, Ards 23.

06.12.97: Ards 16, Ballina 18; Bangor 30, Sligo 17; County Carlow 3, Richmond 7; Omagh Academicals 32, CIYMS 0; Waterpark 19, Creggs 14.

13.12.97: Ballina 23, Sligo 12; CIYMS 16, Bangor 28; County Carlow 26, Waterpark 10; Creggs 11, Richmond 15; Omagh Academicals 19, Ards 3.

17.01.98: Ards 27, Creggs 10; Richmond 14, Omagh Academicals 12; Sligo 6, CIYMS 6; Waterpark 13, Bangor 8. *(Continued on next page)*

All-Ireland League Final Tables

Division One

	P	W	D	L	F	A	Pts
Shannon	13	12	0	1	367	142	24
Garryowen	13	9	1	3	361	224	19
Young Munster	13	9	1	3	244	176	19
St Mary's	13	9	0	4	409	274	18
Cork Constitution	13	8	0	5	289	217	16
Ballymena	13	7	0	6	344	287	14
Clontarf	13	7	0	6	276	266	14
Terenure College	13	5	1	7	241	263	11
Lansdowne	13	4	2	7	264	328	10
Blackrock College	13	4	1	8	249	326	9
•Dungannon	13	4	0	9	239	309	8
***Dolphin**	13	3	2	8	227	345	8
***Old Crescent**	13	4	0	9	168	298	8
***Old Belvedere**	13	2	0	11	208	431	4

* Relegated
• Relegated after a playoff with Buccaneers

Division Two[1]

	P	W	D	L	F	A	Pts
†Galwegians	13	13	0	0	336	164	26
§Buccaneers	12	11	0	1	311	102	22
Sunday's Well	13	7	2	4	252	227	16
City of Derry	13	8	0	5	277	255	16
UCC	13	6	1	6	204	282	13
Skerries	13	6	0	7	248	224	12
DLSP	13	6	0	7	280	269	12
Old Wesley	13	5	1	7	256	246	11
Greystones	13	5	1	7	204	212	11
Bective Rangers	13	5	1	7	210	233	11
Malone	13	5	0	8	210	255	10
Wanderers	12	5	0	7	200	252	10
***Monkstown**	13	3	0	11	207	336	6
***Instonians**	13	2	0	12	205	341	4

§ Promoted after playoff with Dungannon.

Division Three

	P	W	D	L	F	A	Pts
†Portadown	10	10	0	0	217	106	20
†Ballynahinch	10	8	0	2	285	125	16
UCD	10	8	0	2	222	126	16
Highfield	10	7	0	3	170	87	14
Bohemians	10	6	0	4	195	165	12
NIFC	10	5	0	5	190	160	10
Corinthians	10	4	0	6	178	214	8
Dublin University	10	3	0	7	163	225	6
•Collegians	10	2	1	7	130	229	5
***Suttonians**	10	1	1	8	153	255	3
***Queen's University**	10	0	0	10	128	339	0

† Promoted
* Relegated
• Relegated after playoff with Richmond

Division Four

	P	W	D	L	F	A	Pts
†County Carlow	9	8	0	1	284	56	16
§Richmond	9	7	1	1	171	113	15
Bangor	9	5	1	3	175	144	11
Ballina	9	5	0	4	169	128	10
Waterpark	9	5	0	4	131	155	10
Omagh Academicals	9	4	0	5	137	147	8
Ards	9	4	0	5	109	158	8
CIYMS	9	3	1	5	122	202	7
***Sligo**	9	2	1	6	111	147	5
***Creggs**	9	0	0	9	89	248	0

†Promoted
§Promoted after playoff with Collegians
* Relegated

1. The 1998/99 Second Division will have 16 teams. Wanderers were not relegated and the Malone/Ballynahinch play-off was cancelled with both teams due to play in Division Two in 1997/98.

All-Ireland League Division Four *Continued from previous page*

24.01.98: Bangor 23, Ards 0; CIYMS 18, Richmond 30; Creggs 10, Ballina 26; Omagh Academicals 11, County Carlow 37.
31.01.98: Ards 12, CIYMS 16; Ballina 32, Bangor 14; County Carlow 68, Creggs 3; Richmond 14, Sligo 8; Waterpark 31, Omagh Academicals 16.
14.02.98: Ballina 3, Carlow 7; Sligo 9, Waterpark 12.
21.02.98: Ards 12, Richmond 10; Bangor 6, County Carlow 18; CIYMS 13, Waterpark 3; Omagh Academicals 21, Ballina 19; Sligo 13, Creggs 10.
28.02.98: County Carlow 42, Ards 0; Creggs 16, Bangor 28; Waterpark 15, Richmond 38.
14.03.98: Ards 16 Waterpark 12; Bangor 18, Omagh Academicals 12; CIYMS 44, Creggs 12; Richmond 23, Ballina 14; Sligo 16, County Carlow 23.
28.03.98: Ballina 19, CIYMS 9; Omagh Academicals 6, Sligo 22.

Connacht Senior Cup

First round

05.04.98: UCG 31, Westport 21; Ballina 20, Sligo 18.
08.04.98: Creggs 18, Connemara 18.
12.04.98: Connemara 37, Creggs 13 (replay).

Quarter finals

19.04.98: UCG 21, Connemara 27; Ballina 5, Corinthians 14.

Semi finals

03.04.98: Galwegians 59, Connemara 23; Buccaneers 22, Corinthians 41.

Final

10.05.98: Galwegians 15, Corinthians 41.

Leinster Senior Cup

First round

18.04.98: Lansdowne 16, Wanderers 14. Skerries 19, Greystones 10.

Second round

24.04.98: Terenure 29, UCD 19.
25.04.98: Suttonians 18, Dublin University 22.
01.05.98: DLSP 51, Old Belvedere 14
02.05.98: Clontarf 52, Carlow 29; Skerries 21, St Mary's 20; Old Wesley 25, Garda 25 aet (Old Wesley won on try countback); Lansdowne 26, Monkstown 10; Blackrock 20, Bective Rangers 26.

Quarter finals

05.05.98: Lansdowne 32, Old Wesley 6; Skerries 32, Clontarf 20; DLSP 33, Bective Rangers 15; Terenure College 37, Dublin University 13.

Semi Finals

09.05.98: DLSP 33, Lansdowne 30; Skerries 21, Terenure College 7.

Final

19.05.98: Lansdowne 23, Skerries 17.

Munster Senior Cup

First Round

Young Munster 21, Dolphin 13; Highfield 21, Bohemians 12; Bruff 18, Waterpark 15; Sunday's Well 18, Shannon 35; Cork Constitution w/o Garryowen.

Second Round

Cork Constitution 61, Richmond 27; Highfield 14, UCC 17; Old Crescent 24, Shannon 44; Young Munster 30, Bruff 6.

Semi Finals

Shannon 25, Cork Constitution 16; UCC 10, Young Munster 33.

Final

Shannon 19, Young Munster 18.

Ulster Senior Cup

First Round

Ballymena 30, Instonians 14; NIFC 21, City of Derry 22; Malone 17, Banbridge 8; Ballyclare 20, Queen's University 17; Bangor 36, Ards 3; Dungannon 66, CIYMS 0.

Second Round

Dungannon 32, Portadown 16; Malone 28, Ballymena 11; Ballyclare 15, Bangor 16; Ballynahinch 24, City of Derry 15.

Semi Finals

Malone 38, Bangor 5; Dungannon 25, Ballynahinch 10.

Final

Dungannon 19, Malone 16.

Other Results

OLD BELVEDERE FLOODLIT CUP

Semi finals

11.11.97: Clontarf 29, Old Belvedere 14.
12.11.97: Lansdowne 43, Wanderers 17.

Final

27.11.97: Clontarf 15, Lansdowne 10.

LEINSTER SCHOOLS SENIOR CUP

Semi finals

Terenure College 21, Roscrea 14.
Clongowes 41, St Mary's College 17.

Final

Clongowes 37, Terenure College 18.

INTERNATIONAL TEAM STATISTICS

International Team Factfile

Name	Club	Position	D.O.B.	Born	Caps	Points	Debut
BISHOP, Justin	London Irish	Wing	08.11.74	Sussex	2	1T	v South Africa '98
BRENNAN, Trevor	St Mary's College	Lock	22.09.73	Kildare	2	-	v South Africa '98
CLARKE, Ciaran	Terenure College	Full Back	08.03.69	Dublin	5	1 DG	v France '93
CLOHESSY, Peter	Young Munster	Prop	22.03.66	Limerick	20	1T	v France '93
CORKERY, David	Cork Constitution	Flanker	06.11.72	Cork	25	3T	v Australia '94
CORRIGAN, Reggie	Greystones	Prop	10.11.70	Dublin	6	-	v Canada '97
COSTELLO, Victor	St Mary's College	No. 8	23.10.70	Dublin	13	2T	v US '96
DAWSON, Kieron	London Irish	Flanker	29.01.75	Bangor	3	-	v N. Zealand '97
ELWOOD, Eric	Galwegians	Out-half	26.02.69	Galway	27	58PG 2DG, 21C	v Wales '93
ERSKINE, David	Sale	Flanker	14.10.69	London	3	-	v N. Zealand '97
FITZPATRICK, Justin	Dungannon	Prop	21.11.73	Chichester	2	-	v South Africa '98
FULCHER, Gabriel	Lansdowne	Lock	27.11.69	England	21	1T	v Australia '94
GALWEY, Mick	Shannon	Lock	08.10.66	Kerry	23	1T	v France '91
HALVEY, Eddie	Shannon	Flanker	11.07.70	Limerick	8	2T	v France '95
HENDERSON, Rob	Wasps	Centre	27.10.72	New Malden	7	-	v W. Samoa '96
HICKIE, Denis	St Mary's College	Wing	13.02.76	Dublin	12	5T	v Wales '97
HUMPHREYS, David	Dungannon	Out-half	10.09.71	Belfast	10	8PG 2DG, 3C	v France '96
JOHNS, Paddy	Saracens	Lock	19.02.68	Portadown	43	2T	v Argentna '90
KEANE, Killian	Garryowen	Out Half	14.08.71	Drogheda	1		v England '98
MAGGS, Kevin	Bath	Centre	03.06.74	Bristol	9	1T	v N. Zealand '97
McCALL, Mark	Dungannon	Centre	29.11.67	Bangor	13	-	v N. Zealand '92
McGUINNESS, Conor	St Mary's College	Scrum-half	29.03.75	Dublin	7	1T	v N. Zealand '97
McWEENEY, John	St Mary's College	Wing	26.05.76	Dublin	1	-	v N. Zealand '97
MILLER, Eric	Leicester	No. 8	23.09.75	Dublin	8	1T	v Italy '97
NESDALE, Ross	Newcastle	Hooker	30.07.69	N. Zealand	7	-	v Wales '97
NOWLAN, Kevin	St Mary's College	Full Back	26.06.71	Dublin	3	2T	v N. Zealand '97
O CUINNEAGAIN, Dion	Sale	Flanker	24.05.72	South Africa	2	-	v South Africa '98
O'KELLY, Malcolm	London Irish	Lock	19.07.74	Essex	9	-	v N. Zealand '97
O'MEARA, Brian	Cork Constitution	Scrum-half	05.04.76	Cork	4	-	v England '97
O'SHEA, Conor	London Irish	Full Back	21.10.70	Limerick	20	3PG 1DG, 1C	v Romania '93
POPPLEWELL, Nick	Newcastle	Prop	06.04.64	Dublin	48	3T	v N. Zealand '89
WALLACE, Paul	Saracens	Prop	30.12.71	Cork	20	2T	v Japan '95
WALLACE, Richard	Saracens	Wing	16.01.68	Cork	29	5T	v Namibia '91
WARD, Andy	Ballynahinch	Flanker	08.09.70	N. Zealand	5	1T	v France '98
WOOD, Keith	Harlequins	Hooker	27.01.72	Limerick	17	2T	v Australia '94

Caps correct as of print date, September 30, 1998.

Irish teams in the 1997/98 Season

Name	Total Appearances	N.Zealand 15.11.97	Canada 30.11.97	Scotland 07.02.98	France 07.03.98	Wales 21.03.98	England 04.04.98	S. Africa 13.06.98	S. Africa 20.06.98
BISHOP, Justin	2							●	●
BRENNAN, Trevor	2							●(R)	●(R)
CLARKE, Ciaran	2					●	●		
CLOHESSY, Peter	3				●(R)	●(R)			●(R)
CORKERY, David	4			●	●	●	●		
CORRIGAN, Reggie	5		●(R)	●	●	●	●		
COSTELLO, Victor	7		●	●(R)	●	●	●	●	●
DAWSON, Kieron	3	●	●	●					
ELWOOD, Eric	7	●	●		●	●	●	●	●
ERSKINE, David	2	●(R)	●						
FITZPATRICK, Justin	2							●	●
FULCHER, Gabriel	1							●(R)	
GALWEY, Mick	1				●(R)				
HALVEY, Eddie	2	●	●(R)						
HENDERSON, Rob	6	●	●		●	●		●(R)	●(R)

Name	Total Appearances	N.Zealand 15.11.97	Canada 30.11.97	Scotland 07.02.98	France 07.03.98	Wales 21.03.98	England 04.04.98	S. Africa 13.06.98	S. Africa 20.06.98
HICKIE, Denis	8	●	●	●	●	●	●	●	●
HUMPHREYS, David	3			●			●(R)		●(R)
JOHNS, Paddy	8	●	●	●	●	●	●	●	●
KEANE, Killian	1						●(R)		
MAGGS, Kevin	8	●(R)	●	●	●	●	●	●	●
McCALL, Mark	6	●	●	●			●	●	●
McGUINNESS, Conor	7	●	●	●	●	●	●	●	
McWEENEY, John	1	●							
MILLER, Eric	3	●		●		●(R)			
NESDALE, Ross	4	●(R)	●		●(R)	●(R)			
NOWLAN, Kevin	2	●	●						
O CUINNEAGAIN, Dion	2							●	●
O'KELLY, Malcolm	8	●	●	●	●	●	●	●	●
O'MEARA, Brian	2	●(R)		●					
O'SHEA, Conor	4			●	●			●	●
POPPLEWELL, Nick	4	●	●	●(R)	●(R)				
WALLACE, Paul	8	●	●	●	●	●	●	●	●
WALLACE, Richard	4			●	●	●	●		
WARD, Andy	5			●	●	●		●	●
WOOD, Keith	7	●		●	●	●	●	●	●

(R)=replacement

Irish Squad at FIRA World Junior Championships

Name	School/ Club	v. USA 04.04.98	v. South Africa 06.04.98	v. Argentina 09.04.98	v. France 12.04.98
Broughall, D.	UCD	●	●	●	●
Cahill, B.	UCC	●			
Campbell, C.	London Irish	●(R)	●	●	●
Considine, A.	Bective Rangers			●(R)	●(R)
Coughlan, N.	UCD		●	●	●
Cupitt, M.	Instonians	●	●	●	●
Fitzgerald, C.	Garryowen	●(R)		●(R)	●(R)
Flavin, A.	London Irish		●	●	●
Good, C.	RBAI	●(R)			●(R)
Holt, D.	UCC		●	●	●
Kearney, A.	St. Michael's College	●	●	●	●
McCarey, C.	Ballymena	●	●	●	●
McCracken, B.	CIYMS	●			
Mescal, D.	Ballina	●			●(R)
Moore, S. (Captain)	UCD	●	●	●	●
O'Brien, A.	UCD		●	●	●
O'Callaghan, D.	Cork Constitution	●(R)	●	●	●
O'Driscoll, B.	UCD		●	●	●
Reynolds, J.	Watsonians			●(R)	●(R)
Roche, F.	Bohemians	●	●	●	●
Ronan, B.	CBC Cork	●			
Rossi, D.	Clontarf	●	●	●	●
Schofield, C.	Bangor	●	●(R)	●(R)	●(R)
Sheahan, J.	PBC Cork	●			
Urquhart, B.	Methodist College, Belfast	●	●(R)	●(R)	●(R)
Wallace, P.	Campbell College	●	●	●	●

IRISH RECORD HOLDERS

Individual

All Time Top Points Scorer .... 308, Michael Kiernan in 43 matches 1982-91
All Time Top Try Scorer .... 17, Brendan Mullin in 55 matches 1984-95
Longest International Career .... 16 seasons: Tony O'Reilly (1955-70) & Mike Gibson (1964-79)
Most Consecutive Tests .... 52, Willie John McBride 1964-75

Most Internationals as Captain .... 24, Tom Kiernan 1963-73
Most Points Scored in a Single International .... 23, Ralph Keyes against Zimbabwe, Lansdowne Road 1991
Most Tries Scored in a Single International .... 4, Brian Robinson against Zimbabwe, Lansdowne Road 1991
Most Points Scored in an International Championship Season .... 52, Ollie Campbell in 1982/83 season
Most Tries Score in an International Championship Season .... 5, Jack Arigho in 1927/28 season

Twenty Five Most Capped Players

	Name	Caps	Career
1.	Mike Gibson	69	1964-79
2.	Willie John McBride	63	1962-75
3.	Fergus Slattery	61	1970-84
4.	Philip Orr	58	1976-87
5.	Brendan Mullin	55	1984-95
6.	Tom Kiernan	54	1960-73
7.	Donal Lenihan	52	1981-92
8.	Moss Keane	51	1974-84
9.	Nick Popplewell	48	1989-98
10.	Jackie Kyle	46	1947-58
11.	Ken Kennedy	45	1965-75
12.	Michael Kiernan	43	1982-91
13.	Paddy Johns	43	1990-
14.	George Stephenson	42	1920-30
15.	Noel Murphy	41	1958-69
16.	Willie Duggan	41	1975-84
17.	Keith Crossan	41	1982-92
18.	Noel Henderson	40	1949-59
19.	Ray McLoughlin	40	1962-75
20.	Michael Bradley	40	1984-95
21.	Philip Matthews	38	1984-92
22.	Sid Millar	37	1958-70
23.	Hugo MacNeill	37	1981-88
24.	Simon Geoghegan	37	1991-
25.	Neil Francis	36	1987-96

Most Capped Players in Individual Positions

Name	Caps	Position
Tom Kiernan	54	Full-back
Keith Crossan	41	Wing
Brendan Mullin	55	Centre
Jackie Kyle	46	Fly-half
Michael Bradley	40	Scrum-half
Philip Orr	58	Prop
Ken Kennedy	45	Hooker
Willie John McBride	63	Lock
Fergus Slattery	61	Flanker
Willie Duggan	39	No. 8

Team

Biggest Winning Margin .... 60-0 v Romania, Lansdowne Road 1986
Biggest Losing Margin .... 6-59 v New Zealand, Wellington 1992
Longest Winning Sequence .... 6 matches, 1968-69
Longest Losing Sequence .... 11 matches, 1991-93
Most Tries Scored in an International .... 10 tries, v Romania, Lansdowne Road 1986
Most Tries Conceded in an International .... 10 tries, v South Africa, Lansdowne Road 1912
Most Points Scored in an International Championship Season .... 71, in 1982/83 season
Most Tries Scored in an International Championship Season .... 12, in seasons 1927/28 and 1952/53

Irish Records with the Lions

Longest Irish Career for the Lions .... 5 tours (1962-74) Willie John McBride*
Most Consecutive Tests by an Irishman .... 15, Willie John McBride 1966-74*
Most Tests as Captain .... 6, Ronnie Dawson in 1959 tour of New Zealand & Australia*
Most Points Scored by an Irishman in a single International .... 18, Tony Ward v South Africa in 1980§
Most Tries Scored by an Irishman in Internationals .... 6, Tony O'Reilly in 10 appearances*

*= Overall Lions Record
§= Shared Overall Lions Record

Most Capped Irish Lions

Name	Caps	Tours
Willie John McBride	17*	1962 '66 '68 '71 '74
Mike Gibson	12	1966 '68 '71
Tony O'Reilly	10	1955 '59
Sid Millar	9	1959 '62 '68
Noel Murphy	8	1959 '66
Ollie Campbell	7	1980, '83
Ronnie Dawson	6	1959
David Hewitt	6	1959, '62
Jackie Kyle	6	1950
Bill McKay	6	1950
Bill Mulcahy	6	1959 '62
John O'Driscoll	6	1980 '83

** Overall most capped Lions player: Willie John McBride*

IRELAND'S INTERNATIONAL RESULTS

Overall Record

Team	First Match	Most Recent Match	Played	Won	Drawn	Lost
v. Argentina	1990	1990	1	1	0	0
v. Australia	1927	1996	17	6	0	11
v. Canada	1987	1997	2	2	0	0
v. England	1875	1998	111	38	8	65
v. Fiji	1995	1995	1	1	0	0
v. France	1909	1998	72	25	5	42
v. Italy	1988	1997	4	1	0	3
v. Japan	1991	1995	2	2	0	0
v. Namibia	1991	1991	2	0	0	2
v. New Zealand	1905	1997	14	0	1	13
v. Romania	1986	1993	2	2	0	0
v. Scotland	1877	1998	109*	45	5	59
v. South Africa	1906	1981	10	1	1	8
v. Tonga	1987	1987	1	1	0	0
v. United States	1994	1996	2	2	0	0
v. Wales	1882	1998	102	37	6	59
v. Western Samoa	1988	1996	2	1	0	1
v. Zimbabwe	1991	1991	1	1	0	0
Total			**457**	**166**	**26**	**265**

* Excludes abandoned match in 1885.

Results Analysis

Team	Biggest Victory *Year*	*Score*	Biggest Defeat *Year*	*Score*	Longest Run without win	Number of Games	Longest Run without loss	Number of Games
v. Argentina	1990	20-18	--	--	--	--	--	
v. Australia	1979	27-12	1992	17-42	1981-1996	8	1958-68	4
v. Canada	1987	46-19	--	--	--	--	1987-97	2
v. England	1947	22-0	1997	6-46	1875-86	12	1972-76	5
v. Fiji	1995	44-8	--	--	--	--	--	
v. France	1913	24-0	1996	10-45	1984-98	16	1909-14 & 1924-29	6
v. Italy	1988	31-15	1997	37-22	1995-1997	3	--	
v. Japan	1995	50-28	--	--	--	--	1991-95	2
v. Namibia	--	--	1990	15-26	1990	2	--	
v. New Zealand	--	--	1992	6-59	--	--	--	
v. Romania	1986	60-0	--	--	--	--	1986-93	2
v. Scotland*	1950	21-0	1997	10-38	1882-94	13	1939-54	9
v. South Africa	1965	9-6	1912	0-38	1906-1961	6	--	
v. Tonga	1987	32-9	--	--	--	--	--	
v. United States	1994	26-15	--	--	--	--	1994-96	2
v. Wales	1925	19-3	1975	4-32	1971-80	8	1995-97	4
v. Western Samoa	1988	49-22	1996	12-40	--	--	--	
v. Zimbabwe	1991	55-11	n/a		--	--	--	

Detailed Five Nations Results 1947-98

Irish Scores First

Year	France	Wales	England	Scotland
1947	8-12	0-6	22-0	3-0
1948	13-6	6-3	11-10	6-0
1949	9-16	5-0	14-5	13-3
1950	3-3	3-6	0-3	21-0
1951	9-8	3-3	3-0	6-5
1952	11-8	3-14	0-3	12-8
1953	16-3	3-5	9-9	26-8
1954	0-8	9-12	3-14	6-0
1955	3-5	3-21	6-6	3-12
1956	8-14	11-3	0-20	14-10
1957	11-6	5-6	0-6	5-3
1958	6-11	6-9	0-6	12-6
1959	9-5	6-8	0-3	8-3
1960	6-23	9-10	5-8	5-6
1961	3-15	0-9	11-8	8-16
1962	0-11	3-3	0-16	6-20
1963	5-24	14-6	0-0	0-3
1964	6-27	6-15	18-5	3-6
1965	3-3	8-14	5-0	16-6
1966	6-11	9-6	6-6	3-11

Irish Scores First

Year	France	Wales	England	Scotland
1967	6-11	3-0	3-8	5-3
1968	6-16	9-6	9-9	14-6
1969	17-9	11-24	17-15	16-0
1970	0-8	14-0	3-9	16-11
1971	9-9	9-23	6-9	17-5
1972	14-9	-	16-12	-
1973	6-4	12-16	18-9	14-19
1974	6-9	9-9	26-21	9-6
1975	25-6	4-32	12-9	13-20
1976	3-26	9-34	13-12	6-15
1977	6-15	9-25	0-4	18-21
1978	9-10	16-20	9-15	12-9
1979	9-9	21-24	12-7	11-11
1980	18-19	21-7	9-24	22-15
1981	13-19	8-9	6-10	9-10
1982	9-22	20-12	16-15	21-12
1983	22-16	9-23	25-15	15-13
1984	12-25	9-18	9-12	9-32
1985	15-15	21-9	13-10	18-15
1986	9-29	12-19	20-25	9-10
1987	13-19	15-11	17-0	12-16
1988	6-25	9-12	3-35	22-18
1989	21-26	19-13	3-16	21-37
1990	12-31	14-8	0-23	10-13
1991	13-21	21-21	7-16	25-28
1992	12-44	15-16	9-38	10-18
1993	6-21	19-14	17-3	3-15
1994	15-35	15-17	13-12	6-6
1995	7-25	16-12	8-20	13-26
1996	10-45	30-17	15-28	10-16
1997	15-32	26-25	6-46	10-38
1998	16-18	21-30	17-35	16-17

Interprovincial Championship Winners 1946-97

Year	Winner(s)
1946	Ulster*
1947	Munster
1948	Leinster*
1949	Leinster
1950	Ulster*
1951	Ulster*
1952	Ulster & Munster
1953	Ulster
1954	Munster & Leinster
1955	Ulster & Connacht
1956	Ulster, Leinster & Connacht
1957	Munster*
1958	Leinster*
1959	Munster
1960	Leinster
1961	Leinster*
1962	Munster*
1963	Leinster*
1964	Leinster
1965	Munster*
1966	Ulster & Munster
1967	Ulster*
1968	Munster*
1969	Ulster
1970	Ulster*
1971	Leinster*
1972	Leinster, Munster & Ulster
1973	Munster
1974	Ulster
1975	Leinster, Munster & Ulster
1976	Ulster*
1977	Leinster, Munster & Ulster
1978	Munster*
1979	Leinster*
1980	Leinster*
1981	Leinster
1982	Leinster, Munster & Ulster
1983	Leinster
1984	Ulster*
1985	Ulster*
1986	Ulster*
1987	Ulster
1988	Ulster*
1989	Ulster*
1990	Ulster*
1991	Ulster
1992	Ulster*
1993	Leinster, Munster & Ulster
1994	Munster*
1995	Leinster*
1996	Munster*
1997	Leinster

* Denotes Grand Slam winners

All-Ireland League Winners 1991-98

Year	Winners
1991	Cork Constitution
1992	Garryowen
1993	Young Munster
1994	Garryowen
1995	Shannon
1996	Shannon
1997	Shannon
1998	Shannon

CLUB BY CLUB PROFILES

Division One

Club	Ground	Est'd	Colours	President	Honurary Secretary
Ballymena	Eaton Pk	1922	Black	Willie John McBride	Guy McCullough
Blackrock College	Stradbrook	1882	Royal blue & white	Ben Underwood	John Mackey
Buccaneers	Keane Pk		Amber & black	Martin Kiely/	

Continued from previous page

Club	Ground	Est'd	Colours	President	Honurary Secretary
				Michael Fitzpatrick	Michael Kiely
Clontarf	Castle Ave	1876	Royal blue & scarlet	Shay McMonagle	Geoff Blake
Cork Constitution	Temple Hill	1892	White	John Gillane	Michael O'Gorman
Galwegians	Crowley Pk		Sky Blue	Gerard McLoughlin	Shane O'Mahony
Garryowen	Dooradoyle	1884	Light blue & white	Clement McInerney	Ger Clarke
Lansdowne	Lansdowne Rd	1872	Red, yellow & black	Paul Van Cauwelaert	Frank Thompson
Shannon	Thomond Pk	1884	Black & blue	Frank Gallagher	Gerard O'Loughlin
St Mary's College	Templeville Rd	1900	Royal blue & white	John Doddy	John Pyne
Terenure College	Lakelands Pk	1940	Purple, black & white	Brendan Doyle	Maurice Downing
Young Munster	Tom Clifford Pk	1895	Black & amber	Michael Kennedy	Joe Kennedy

Division Two

Club	Ground	Est'd	Colours	President	Honorary Secretary
Ballynahinch	Ballymacarn Pk		Green	David Poole	William Young
Bective Rangers	Donnybrook	1881	Red, green & white	Louis Magee	Terry McCabe
City of Derry	Judge's Rd		Green	Robert Logue	John McBride
DLSP	Kilternan		Black, green & white	Eddie Brennan	Leonard G. Brodie
Dolphin	Musgrave Pk	1902	Navy, yellow & white	Hugh Mullins	Michael A. O'Riordan
Dungannon	Stevenson Pk	1873	Blue & white	Allan Buchanan	Derek Clements
Greystones	Dr Hickey Pk	1937	Green & white	Joey McGettigan	Enda A. Ryan
Malone	Gibson Pk	1892	White	Brian Campbell	Raymond Thomas
Old Belvedere	Anglesea Rd	1930	Black & white	Rory Keogh	Dorothy Collins
Old Crescent	Rosbrien	1947	Navy, blue & white	Bobby Kennedy	Dale Harrow
Old Wesley	Donnybrook	1891	White, red & blue	Les Bredin	Ken Richardson
Portadown	Chamber's Pk		Royal Blue & white	John McQuitty	John Campton
Skerries	Holmpatrick		Gold, blue & cerise	Billy Duff	Terry McDonald
Sunday's Well	Musgrave Pk	1923	Red, green & white	Tadhg Lehane	Ciaran Cashman
UCC	The Mardyke	1872	Red & black	Dr Peter Kenefick	Michael Gillane
Wanderers	Lansdowne Rd	1870	Black, blue & white	Brian Brownlee	Joe McDermott

Division Three

Club	Ground	Est'd	Colours	President	Honurary Secretary
Bohemian	Thomond Pk	1922	Red	John Reidy	David Fitzgerald
County Carlow	Oakpark		Black & amber	Kennedy O'Brien	Harry Southern
Galway Corinthians	Corinthian Pk		Navy, black & white	Declan McDermott	Francis Hennigan
Dublin University	College Pk		White	John Terry	Michael Flahive
Highfield	Woodleigh Pk	1930	Green, red & black	Michael Carroll	Martin McNally
Instonians	Shane Pk	1919	Purple, yellow, black	Bobby Jones	Michael Anderson
Monkstown	Sydney Parade		Royal blue & old gold	Arthur Murphy	Charles O'Shaughnessy
Richmond	Canal Bank	1927	Green	Arthur Sheehy	Tom Cusack
NIFC	Shaftesbury Ave	1859	Red, black & blue	David J. Allardyce	Howard J. Hughes
UCD	Belfield		Blue & saffron	J.A. Kavanagh	Alan Bainbridge

Division Four

Club	Ground	Est'd	Colours	President	Honourary Secretary
Ards	Hamilton Pk		Black	Teddy Sloan	David Herron
Ballina	Heffernan Pk		Green	Walter Rouse	Derek Duffy
Banbridge					
Bangor	Upritchard Pk		Old gold,blue & black	David Edwards	Billy Trimble
C.I.Y.M.S.	Belmont		Black & white	Dermot McKee	Ian Beaumont
Collegians	Deramore		Navy blue	John McQuoid	Shelagh Mateer
Midleton	Town Pk	1967	Red & Black	William Tait	Pierce Young
Omagh	Thomas Mellon Pk		Emerald & white	Jack Reid	James Carberry
Queen's University	Upper Malone		Royal Blue	Prof. Barry Bridges	Nigel McClelland
Suttonians	Station Pk		Blue, white & emerald	Brian Lennon	Jim Dowling
Waterpark	Ballinakill	1925	Red & black	Thomas Nolan	Jim Drohan

TEXACO AWARD WINNERS, RUGBY

Year	Winner	Club
1973	Mike Gibson	North of Ireland, Ireland & The Lions
1974	Willie John McBride	Ballymena, Ireland & The Lions
1975	Tom Grace	St Mary's College & Ireland
1977	Willie Duggan	Blackrock College, Ireland & The Lions
1978	Tony Ward	Garryowen, Ireland & The Lions
1979	Fergus Slattery	Blackrock College, Ireland & The Lions
1980	John O' Driscoll	London Irish, Ireland & The Lions
1982	Ollie Campbell	Old Belvedere, Ireland & The Lions
1983	Ciaran Fitzgerald	St Mary's College, Ireland & The Lions
1985	Mick Doyle	Ireland manager
1986	Keith Crossan	Instonians & Ireland
1987	Hugo McNeill	London Irish, Ireland & The Lions
1990	Pat O' Hara	Cork Constitution & Ireland
1991	Ralph Keyes	Cork Constitution & Ireland
1993	Nick Popplewell	Greystones, Ireland & The Lions
1994	Simon Geoghegan	London Irish & Ireland
1997	Keith Wood	Harlequins, Ireland & The Lions

Past Presidents of the I.R.F.U.

Year	Name
1874-76	Duke of Abercorn
1876-79	Duke of Marlborough
1879-80	W. C. Neville
1880-81	Sir W. Goulding
1881-82	R.B. Wallcington
1882-83	G. Scriven
1883-84	A.R. McMullen
1884-85	R.E. McLean
1885-86	G. Scriven
1886-87	W.L. Stokes
1887-88	J. Chambers
1888-89	R. Biggs
1889-90	Sir F. W. Moore
1890-91	M.H. Turnbull
1891-92	H. Hook
1892-93	J.R. Blood
1893-94	R. Garratt
1994-95	J. Macaulay
1895-96	R.G. Warren
1896-97	J. Dodds
1897-98	J.F. Maguire
1898-99	J.B. Moore
1899-1900	S. Lee
1900-01	J. O'Sullivan
1901-02	T. Thornhill
1902-03	J. Johnston
1903-04	V.J. Murray
1904-05	A.D. Clinch
1905-06	F.M. Hamilton
1906-07	J. Flynn
1907-08	G.H.B. Kennedy
1908-09	A. Barr
1909-10	Prof. C. W.L. Alexander
1910-11	F.C. Purser
1911-12	J.H. O'Conor
1912-13	Major R. Stevenson
1913-16	F.H. Browning
1919-20	A. Tedford
1920-21	W.P. Hinton
1921-22	R.M. Magrath
1922-23	G.G. McCrea
1923-24	H. Thrift
1924-25	J.J. Coffey
1925-26	F. J. Strain
1926-27	G. T. Hamlet
1927-28	Judge Sealy
1928-29	H.J. Millar
1929-30	T. J. Greeves
1930-31	J.G. Musgrave
1931-32	W.A. Clarke
1932-33	C.S. Neill
1933-34	S.E. Polden
1934-35	J. Wallace
1935-36	Sir S.T. Irwin
1936-37	Mr Justice C. Davitt
1937-38	H.E. Emerson
1938-45	J.J. Warren
1945-46	H.J. Anderson
1946-47	W.A.B. Douglas
1947-48	T.M. McGrath
1948-49	G.P.S. Hogan
1949-50	W.G. Fallon
1950-51	Air Vice-Marshall Sir W. Tyrrell
1951-52	D.F. O'Connell
1952-53	V.E. Kirwan
1953-54	J.B. O'Callaghan
1954-55	C.J. Hanrahan
1955-56	H.M. Read
1956-57	Capt. J.R. Ramsey
1957-58	W.E. Crawford
1958-59	J.J. Glynn
1959-60	J.R. Wheeler
1960-61	N.F. Murphy
1961-62	L.B. McMahon
1962-63	J.A.E. Siggins
1963-64	T.A. O'Reilly
1964-65	C.C. Harte
1965-66	P.F. Murray
1966-67	D.G. O'Donovan
1967-68	

Year	Name
1968-69	C.P. Crowley
1969-70	J.W.S. Irwin
1970-71	E. Patterson
1971-72	D.A. Dineen
1972-73	Mr Justice J.C. Conroy
1973-74	I.F. Mahony
1974-75	H.R. McKibbin
1975-76	J.J. Keane
1976-77	J.A.D. Higgins
1977-78	J.F. Coffey
1978-79	K.J. Ouilligan
1979-80	J. Montgomery
1980-81	R. Ganly
1981-82	J.J. Moore
1982-83	J.E. Nelson

Year	Name
1983-84	G.F. Reidy
1984-85	M.H. Carroll
1985-86	D. McKibbin
1986-87	Sir Ewart Bell
1987-88	P.F. Madigan
1988-89	T.J. Kiernan
1989-90	A.R. Dawson
1990-91	N.J. Henderson
1991-92	Dr A.D. Browne
1992-93	C.A. Ouaid
1993-94	M. Cuddy
1994-95	K.E. Reid
1995-96	Dr S. Millar
1996-97	R.M. Deacy
1997-98	N.H. Brophy

SAILING

The Irish Sailing Association

3 Park Road, Dun Laoghaire, Co. Dublin. Tel: (01) 2800239 Fax: (01) 2807558 e-mail: isa@iol.ie

Founded......1946
President......Neil Murphy
Vice-Presidents......John Crebbin (Boating Division-Safety and Cruising Committees)
......Alan McCracken (Training Division-Coaching, Youth Sailing and Yachtmaster Committees)
.Maria Walsh (Racing Division-Race Mngment, Racing Rules, Rating & Handicapping and Olympic Committees)
Honorary Treasurer......Paddy Maguire
Honorary Secretary......Riocard O'Tiarnaigh
Number of Category One Clubs......43
Number of Members (Category One)......16,000
Principle Venues......Dublin Bay, Howth, Cork, Kinsale
ISA International Affiliations: International Sailing Federation, European Boating Association, European Sailing Federation, European Union Sailing Association, Olympic Council of Ireland, International Association for Sea Survival Training.
Number of Branches......4 (North, South, East and West)
East Coast Branch President......Padraig Boyle
Southern Branch President......Clayton Love
Best International Result......Silver Medal, 1980 Olympic Games (David Wilkins & Jamie Wilkinson)
1997 Senior Helmsman Champions......David McHugh and Tom Fitzpatrick
1997 Junior Helmsman Champion......Gerald 'Gerbil' Owens
1998 Senior Helmsman Champions......*tba*
1998 Junior Helmsman Champion......Gerald 'Gerbil' Owens

CLASS ASSOCIATIONS

The boat classes affiliated to the ISA are primarily categorised according to boat types.
These include the International Class Associations:
● 420 ● 470 ● Dragon ● Enterprise ● Europe ● Finn ● Fireball ● Flying 15 ● Ireland International Dart Assoc. ● J24 ● Laser ● Laser II ● Mirror ● Optimist ● Topper
and the National Class Associations:
● 1720 ● Albacore ● Cork Harbour J Class ● Cruisers III ● GP14 ● IDRA 14 ● Mermaid ● Multihull ● National 18 ● Ruffian 23 ● Shipman ● Shannon One Design ● Skiff ● Squib ● Wayfarer ● Windsurfing Association

1998 INTERNATIONAL RESULTS

● **International Judges:** Ron Hutchinson, William Lacy, Norman Long, Tony O'Gorman, Ken Ryan ● **Best Ever International Result:** Silver Medal, 1980 Olympics (David Wilkins & Jamie Wilkinson - Flying Dutchman)

Date	Event	Venue	Class	Results
12 Oct. 97	**ISA Dinghy Team National c'ships**	**Royal St. G YC**	**Dinghy**	Ballyholme YC
July 98	**Cork Dry Gin Round Ireland**	**Wicklow SC**	**Cruisers**	Overall Result
				1st Colin Barrington - Jeep Cherokee
				2nd Tim Little - Keep on Smiling
				3rd M. Slade - Bridgestone
14-18 July.	**Ford Cork Week**	**Royal Cork YC**	**All Classes**	Top Results
			1720	Mark Mansfield - Union Chandlery
			Class 0	Harold Cudmore - Barlo Plastics
			Big Boat	R. Loftus - Desparado
27 July	**1998 Optimist World C'ships**	**Portugal**	**Optimist**	Lorcan Lennon (69th)
22-25 Aug.	**Cutty Sark Tall Ships Race**	**Dublin**	**Tall Ships**	Cuauhtemoc (Cutty Sark Trophy)
23-29 Aug.	**Heineken World Championships**	**Bray SC**	**Enterprise**	**See Below**
1	Ian Fisher and Simon Cook	Hallamshire SC GBR 22821		23 pts
12	Ger Dempsey and Shane McCarthy	Bray SC IRL 22572		88.7 pts
13	Roy Van Maanen & Sally Brightling	Greystones SC IRL 22748		102 pts
20	Marty Cuppage and John Cuppage	Bray SC IRL 22819		136pts
August	**Finn Gold Cup**	**Athens**	**Finn**	D. Burrows (35th)

Date	Event	Venue	Class	Results
1998	**ISAF World Championship**	**Dubai**	**All Classes**	Irish placings as below

Continued from previous page

Date	Event	Venue	Class	Results
J/22 Keelboat-open)	Mark Mansfield/Dan O'Grady/Michael Evans			(13 out of 51)
J/22 Keelboat-women fleet	Maria Coleman/Nuala McGrogan/Melissa Evans/Pauline McKechnie			(8 out of 25)
Multihull (Open)	John Mullan & Ian Wilson			(44 out of 60)
Multihull (Women)	Cathy McAleavy & Julie Maguire			(17 out of 23)
470 (Men)	Tom Fitzpatrick&David McHugh			(38 out of 77)
470 (Women)	Laura Dillon & Karena Knaggs			(29 out of 48)
Laser (Men)	Jon Lasenby			(22 out of 130)
Laser Radial (Women)	Ciara Peelo			(40 out of 52)

1998 DOMESTIC CHAMPIONS

Date	Event	Venue	class	Result
30-31 May	National Championship	Monkstown Bay SC	Albacore	John Wallace
12-14 Jun.	National Championship	Greystones SC	Enterprise	Roy Van Maanen
2-8 Aug.	National Championship	Tralee SC	Mermaid	Percy Boyle
19-23 Aug.	National Championship	National YC	Optimist	Dylan Gannon
19-23 Aug.	National Championship Juniors	-	Optimist	Simon Mitton
22-24 Aug.	National Championship	Waterford Hbr SC	Flying 15	J. Lavery & G. Donleavey
26-31 Aug.	National Championship	Howth YC	Cruiser 3	P. Watson - *Pathfinder*
26-29 Aug.	National Championship	Lough Ree YC	IDRA 14	Terry Harvey
27-30 Aug.	National Championship	Lough Derg YC	Laser	Bill O'Hara
29-30 Aug.	National Championship	Royal St George YC	Multihull	Stephen Duffy
4-6 Sep.	Disabled Sailing Championship	Kinsale	-	John Sullivan
12 Sep.	National Championship	Royal Cork YC	National 18	Tom Dwyer
-	National Championship	-	420	Neil Spain
-	National Championship	-	Dragon	Michael Cotter
-	National Championship	-	GP14	Damian Bracken
-	National Championship	-	Squib	Andrew Sargent
-	National Championship	-	Laser 2	Michael Ennis
-	National Championship	-	Shannon 1 Design	Jonathan Craig
-	National Championship	-	Skiff	Maurice O'Connell
-	National Championship	-	Dart 18	Richard Swanston
-	National Championship	-	1720	Gareth Flanagan
28-30 Aug.	Stentor Challenge Cruisers	Dublin Bay		Max McMullan - *Mustang*
29-31 Aug.	Cork Dry Gin Nationals 1720	-		Alan Espey - *Red-Green*

Royal Yachting Association

Northern Ireland Council, House of Sport, Upper Malone Road, Belfast BT9 5LA.
Tel. (01232) 381222 Fax: (01232) 682757

Founded 1875
Number of Affiliated Clubs 35
President .... HRH Princess Anne, The Princess Royal
Chairman .... Patrick Knatchbull
Honorary Secretary .... Harold Boyle
Number of Coaches .... 250 (approx.)
Principal Venues .... Belfast Lough, Strangford Lough, Lough Neagh and Lough Erne
Vice-Chairman .... Dr. Curly Morris
International Competitors .... John Driscoll and Colin Chapman (Finn Class)
.... aiming to qualify for the Irish team for the Sydney Olympic Games in 2000.

IRISH OLYMPIC PARTICIPANTS, 1948-1996

1948 London *(Torquay)*

Firefly .... Jimmy Mooney
Swallow .... Alf Delaney

1952 Helsinki

Finn .... Alf Delaney

1956 Melbourne

Finn .... J. Somers Payne

1960 Rome

Finn .... J. Somers Payne
Flying Dutchman .... Johnny Hooper, Peter Gray
Dragon .... Jimmy Moony, David Ryder, Robin Benson

1964 Tokyo

Finn .... Johnny Hooper
Dragon ...... Eddie Kelliher, Harry Maguire, Rob Dalton

1968 Mexico *(Acapulco)*

no competitors

1972 Munich *(Kiel)*

Tempest .... David Wilkins, Sean Whitaker
Dragon Robin Hennessy, Harry Byrne, Owen Delaney
Finn .... Kevin McLaverty
Flying Dutchman .. Harold Cudmore, Richard O'Shea

1976 Montreal *(Kingston)*

470 .... Robert Dix, Peter Dix
Flying Dutchman .... Barry O'Neill, Jamie Wilkinson
Tempest .... David Wilkins, Derek Jago

1980 Moscow *(Talinn)*

Flying Dutchman .... David Wilkins, Jamie Wilkinson
Silver Medal Winners

1984 Los Angeles (Long Beach)

Finn .... Bill O'Hara

1988 Seoul *(Pusan)*

Finn .... Bill O'Hara
Flying Dutchman .... David Wilkins, Peter Kennedy
470 (women) .... Cathy MacAleavy, Aisling Byrne

1992 Barcelona

Flying Dutchman .... David Wilkins, Peter Kennedy
Star .... Mark Mansfield, Tom McWilliam

1996 Atlanta *(Savannah)*

Europe .... Aisling Bowman
Finn .... John Driscoll
Laser .... Mark Lyttle
470 (women) .... Denise Lyttle, Louise Ann Cole
Star .... Mark Mansfield, Tom McWilliam
Soling .. Marshall King, Garrett Connolly, Dan O'Grady

AMATEUR SNOOKER

Republic of Ireland Billiards & Snooker Association

House of Sport, Longmile Road, Dublin 12. Tel. (01) 4509850

Founded .... (Modern Association) 1959
President .... Tommy Martin
Secretary .... Eamonn Kearns
Number of Provincial Regions .... 4 (Connacht, Dublin, Leinster, Munster)
Number of Clubs 82
Number of Coaches 6

RESULTS

1998 Riley Irish Snooker Championship. Ivy Rooms, Carlow 29 May-1 June.

Last 32 (7 Frames)

TJ Dowling (1)	bt	Conor O'Dwyer	4-0
John Cronin	bt	Shay Healey	4-1
John Farrell (9)	bt	John Greer	4-3
David Forde (25)	bt	Shane Corr	4-3
Rodney Goggins (5)	bt	Mick Kane	4-2
Carl Murphy (12)	bt	John Connolly (21)	4-1
Dave Kelly (13)	bt	Leo Browne	4-2
Stanley Murphy (4)	bt	Mike Howley	4-1
Robert Murphy (3)	bt	Donal Quigley	4-0
Martin McCrudden (19)	bt	Clinton Franey (14)	4-0
Douglas Hogan (11)	bt	James Bateman	4-1
Tom Gleeson	bt	Eamonn Deane	4-0
Mark Maher (7)	bt	Paul Carbin	4-1
Mark Dooley (23)	bt	Robert Redmond (10)	4-1
Gary Hardiman (18)	bt	John Torpey (15)	4-2
Joe Delaney (3)	bt	Phil Martin (31)	4-2

Last 16 (7 Frames)

TJ Dowling (1)	bt	John Cronin	4-0
John Farrell (9)	bt	David Forde (25)	4-1
Rodney Goggins (5)	bt	Carl Murphy (12)	4-1
Dave Kelly (13)	bt	Stanley Murphy (4)	4-2
Robert Murphy (3)	bt	Martin McCrudden (19)	4-3
Douglas Hogan (11)	bt	Tom Gleeson	4-2
Mark Dooley (23)	bt	Mark Maher (7)	4-0
Joe Delaney (3)	bt	Gary Hardiman (18)	4-2

Quarter Finals (9 Frames)

TJ Dowling (1)	bt	John Farrell (9)	5-3
Rodney Goggins (5)	bt	Dave Kelly (13)	5-0
Douglas Hogan (11)	bt	Robert Murphy (3)	5-2
Joe Delaney (3)	bt	Mark Dooley (23)	5-2

Semi-Finals (11 Frames)

TJ Dowling (1)	bt	Rodney Goggins (5)	6-4
Douglas Hogan (11)	bt	Joe Delaney (3)	6-5

Final (15 Frames)

TJ Dowling (1)	bt	Douglas Hogan (11)	8-4

Ladies Championship

Semi Final (5 Frames)

Julie Kelly	bt	Edel Cosgrave	3-0
Greta Browne	bt	Avril Murphy	3-0

Final (7 Frames)

Julie Kelly	bt	Greta Browne	4-0

Billiards Championship

Semi Final (650 Up)

Phil Martin	bt	Victor O'Gorman	650-583
Dick Brennan	bt	Larry Drennan	650-480

Final (750 Up)

Phil Martin	bt	Dick Brennan	750-668

Leinster Open 147 Club, Wexford March 1998

Quarter Finals

J. Farrell	Dublin	bt	M. Maher	Dublin	4-2
J. Delaney	Wexford	bt	R. Goggins	Wexford	4-1
M. Hayden	Wexford	bt	C. Freaney	Wicklow	4-1
T. J. Dowling	Dublin	bt	C. Murphy	Kildare	4-2

Semi Finals

J. Delaney	Wexford	bt	J. Farrell	Dublin	4-3
T.J. Dowling	Dublin	bt	M. Hayden	Wexford	4-0

Final

J. Delaney	Wexford	bt	T.J. Dowling	Dublin	5-4

Highest Break: J. Farrell, 116.

Munster Open

Quarter Finals (7 Frames)

R. Goggins	Wexford	bt	J. Farrell	Dublin	4-3
B. O'Donoghue	Tipp.	bt	K. Sheldrick	Dublin	4-3
T. Gleeson	Tipperary	bt	M. Hayden	Wexford	4-0
J. Linehan	Cork	bt	E. Hughes	Dublin	4-1

Semi-Finals (7 Frames)

R. Goggins	Wexford	bt	B. O'Donoghue	Tipp.	4-0
T. Gleeson	Tipperary	bt	J. Linehan	Cork	4-0

Final (9 Frames)

T. Gleeson	Tipperary	bt	R. Goggins	Wexford	5-4

National Snooker Championship Past Winners

Year	Winner
1983	J. Long
1984	Paul Ennis

Continued from previous page

Year	Winner
1985	Gay Burns
1986	Gay Burns
1987	Ken Doherty
1988	John Buckley
1989	Ken Doherty
1990	Stephen O'Connor
1991	Jason Watson
1992	Jason Watson
1993	Colm Gilcreest
1994	Mick Kane
1995	Tom Gleeson
1996	Joe Canny
1997	TJ Dowling

PAST PRESIDENTS OF R.I.B. & S.A.

John Shortt; William R. Trulock; Paddy Comerford; Finbarr Ruane; Jack Rogers; Eamonn Kearns; Michael Bodkin; Paul Fidgeon.

PROFESSIONAL SNOOKER

Former Irish World Champions

Year	Winner	Runner Up	Score
1972	Alex Higgins	John Spencer	37-32
1982	Alex Higgins	Ray Reardon	18-15
1985	Denis Taylor	Steve Davis	18-17
1997	Ken Doherty	Stephen Hendry	18-12

1998 World Championship, Irish Results

1st Round

Ken Doherty ....bt ....Lee Walker (Eng)...10-8
Fergal O'Brien ....bt....James Wattana (Thai)...10-9
Terry Murphy.......lost to ....Peter Ebdon (Eng)...10-3
Joe Swail ....lost to Ronnie O'Sullivan (Eng)...10-5
Jason Prince.......lost to .....Darren Morgan (Wal)...10-8

2nd Round

Ken Doherty ....bt ....Stephen Lee (Eng)...13-8
Fergal O'Brien ....lost to ....Peter Ebdon (Eng)...13-5

Quarter Finals

Ken Doherty ....bt..Matthew Stevens (Eng).13-10

Semi-Final

Ken Doherty ....bt ....Mark Williams (Wal).17-14

Final

Ken Doherty........lost to ....John Higgins (Sco).18-12

1998 Benson & Hedges Irish Masters Results

1st Round

Fergal O'Brien ....bt ....Peter Ebdon (Eng).....6-2
John Parrott (Eng) .....bt ....Tony Drago (Malta).....6-2
R. O'Sullivan (Eng) ....bt ....Jimmy White (Eng).....6-2
Steve Davis (Eng) ......bt ....Nigel Bond (Eng)..........

Quarter Finals

John Parrott (Eng) .....bt ....Mark Williams (Wal).....6-3
Ken Doherty ....bt.................Fergal O'Brien.....6-1
R. O'Sullivan (Eng) ....bt ...Stephen Hendry (Sco).....6-3
John Higgins (Sco) ....bt ....Steve Davis (Eng)..........

Semi-Finals

Ken Doherty ....bt ....John Parrott (Eng).....6-1
R. O'Sullivan (Eng) ....bt ....John Higgins (Sco).....6-4

Final

R. O'Sullivan (Eng) ....bt...................Ken Doherty.....9-3
Highest Break: Ken Doherty - 129.

Ronnie O'Sullivan was stripped of his title on July 6th, 1998. Traces of a non performance enhancing drug were found in a urine sample which he gave at Goffs.

the irish leagues . . . in the shadow of the english premiership

by ***steven beacom***

the **BELFAST TELEGRAPH**

TRUE story: I was walking into Windsor Park for an international in October. As I leisurely strolled towards my destination - the packed press box - I found myself listening to a conversation between two 30 somethings who appeared to be friends. One was from Dublin and the other a native of Belfast. In between the two six-footers was a little boy, who I, as it turned out, correctly assumed was the son of the gentleman from the fair city. After talking about how Keith Gillespie was still Northern Ireland's great enigma - the Belfast man in his broad city accent (you know the one) looked down at the well-behaved child and asked him which football team he supported.

Before the lad could reply, the man, we'll call him Davy, answered his own question - and rather irritatingly several times at that.

Davy said with a smile on his face "It's Linfield isn't it? You love the Blues", clearly hoping the answer would be 'yes'.

The boy looked perplexed. "You don't like the Glens do you?" Davy continued.

Still a puzzled gaze from the little lad. "It's Cliftonville then", says Davy, still with that wide grin.

A look at the boy told me obviously not the Reds then. Trying a different approach - a little more southern if you like - Davy says:

"Bohemians, St Patrick's Athletic, Shamrock Rovers? Not Derry City surely not Felix Healy's useless lot!" Still not a flicker or even a murmur come to that from our little hero, displaying admirable manners in the face of this onslaught.

By now a frustrated and agitated Davy was looking at the boy's father: "Well, who the hell is it then?" he bellowed.

By this stage, I was as interested to know the youngster's allegiance as the inquisitive Davy. The little one, showing calm beyond his years, unzipped his oversized grey coat. Positioning myself rather hurriedly, there it was, underneath the boy's big jacket, an item of clothing which left Davy aghast, stunned and silent for a few moments. It was, shock horror, A MANCHESTER UNITED TOP, one of the 85 versions they've had in the last two years. Eventually came Davy's disdainful reaction: "I meant an Irish team, not THEM".

At last the boy spoke: "I don't like Irish teams, just United".

For me, now ready to let the trio go on their merry way to watch a largely uneventful international, I thought 'well there you go then'. For Davy, it was almost too much too take as he proceeded to argue with his friend about teaching his son the value of supporting your local gunfighter. Perhaps the wrong phase to use in conjunction with Ireland but you know what I mean.

If you're from Sligo, you should support the Rovers. If you are from Newry, follow the Town and so and so on. Some will have you believe it used to be that way. I would say there's always been a penchant in Ireland, north and south, to support those clubs an Irish Sea away. Rangers, Celtic, Manchester United, Liverpool, Arsenal. They all have incredible support over here and it is getting bigger and bigger and bigger again.

Media coverage, and in particular television, has so much to do with that. Young boys see Giggs, Owen, Beckham, Bergkamp and Co. on the box and see them as everything they want to be. Successful, rich and famous. Having that three out of three certainly ain't bad at all. Loyalty to your own town or nearest football club is unfortunately becoming a distant fourth. There are ways of bucking the trend, and we'll come to that in a moment - but first this.

Earlier this season I was speaking to a United director about the thousands of people who travel from all over Ireland for an audience with their Old Trafford gods. He told me that in terms of support in the emerald isle 'The Sky was the limit' for United. A few months later, those words came ringing back to me when a certain Rupert Murdoch told the world he was going to buy the Red Devils. Some United fans thought the Sky had indeed fallen in on them with the soul of the club about to fall out. But now it seems the greater majority of Alex Ferguson's followers are quite happy to go along with it - and, let's be frank, there hasn't been that much argument from supporters on this side of the water.

Murdoch brings with him television. United games will be wall to wall. Old Trafford tickets are like gold dust as it is; think what it would be like watching your heroes week in week out from the comfort of your own home. Of course the atmosphere of the Stretford End won't be the same in your living room - most of the noise has already disappeared anyway - but think of the savings in flight and hotel bills.

Thought about it? Now think about the savings you would make by going to your local ground and cheering on home grown talent, who you never know might go on to be mega-stars in England. Didn't the likes of Roy Keane, Steve Staunton, Steve Lomas and Neil Lennon all start here a not-so-long time ago.

One man who would tell you that is St. Patrick's Athletic manager, Irish football enthusiast and general all round good guy, Pat Dolan. He led the fight to keep Wimbledon out of Dublin, and now the Ulster footballing folk are having to do the same to stop the Dons coming to the province. You get the feeling though that the business consortium involved in this idea are actually more interested in Wimbledon coming over here than Wimbledon are.

Every football fan, however, is interested to different degrees in what happens in England. You can watch highlights on *Match of the Day* and live action on Sky. Heck, even RTÉ now have a Saturday night highlights Premiership programme. At least though, that network shows National League games live on some occasions, which is a lot more than can be said for BBC Northern Ireland or Ulster television. A few minutes on the local news programmes is all those stations can muster. Come on folks, you can do better than that. Irish League football can be entertaining - and incredibly atmospheric. Go to a match between Linfield and Glentoran if you don't believe me.

The authorities and clubs can help themselves of course by letting children in free of charge on given days and also by enhancing that old community spirit. A visit or two from players to schools would do no harm at all. And also sort out the stadiums. Make them a place families want to go to - not a rundown hovel which even the rats are escaping from. The governments, British and Irish, can also help by giving football clubs money to upgrade facilities. It would certainly beat some of the rubbish our taxes are used for. The Millennium Dome. I ask you.

And don't forget we have that all important 'dreams can come true scenario' in the National League and the Irish League. It doesn't just happen for Owen and Beckham. If you had said a few years ago that last season, St. Pat's would win the title down south, you would have received a few quizzical looks. And as for Northern Ireland in 1997-98, we are still attempting to recover from the shock of Cliftonville being crowned champions for the first time in 88 years. The Titanic had not even set sail the last time the Reds wore the champion crown. It was an incredible achievement for Marty Quinn's mighty men. A miracle even, and you know where it happened - here in Ireland.

See, there is hope. Well, a little bit anyway despite all those youngsters running around in Manchester United tops.

The Football Association of Ireland

80 Merrion Square, Dublin 2. Tel. (01) 6766864

Founded 1921
President .... Pat Quigley
General Secretary/Chief Executive .... Bernard J. O'Byrne
Press Officer .... Brendan McKenna
Number of Affiliated Clubs 4,139
Number of Coaches .... 4,000 (at various levels)

1997/98 Champions	**Winners**	**Runners Up**
National League Premier Division	St. Patrick's Athletic	Shelbourne
National League First Division	Waterford United	Bray Wanderers
Harp Lager F.A.I. Cup	Cork City	Shelbourne

Top Scorer 1997/98 National League Premier Division .... 17 (Stephen Geoghegan, Shelbourne)
Main Stadium .... Dalymount Park, capacity 18,000 (Lansdowne Road used for International games)

INTERNATIONAL

National Manager .... Mick McCarthy
Top International Goalscorer .... Frank Stapleton (20 Goals)
Biggest Recorded Attendance 47,000
World Ranking 48th
Most Capped Player .... Paul McGrath (83)
1998 Senior Player of the Year .... Kenny Cunningham
Best World Cup Result .... Quarter-final 1990 (beaten by Italy)

INTERNATIONAL RESULTS

Republic of Ireland World Cup Qualifying Results 1996-97

DATE	VENUE	HOME TEAM	SCORE	AWAY TEAM	SCORE
31.08.96	Eschen	Liechtenstein	0	Republic of Ireland Quinn 2, Harte, O'Neill, Townsend	5
09.10.96	Lansdowne Road	Republic of Ireland Cascarino 2, McAteer	3	FYR Macedonia	0
10.11.96	Lansdowne Road	Republic of Ireland	0	Iceland	0
02.04.97	Skjope	FYR Macedonia	3	Republic of Ireland McLoughlin, D. Kelly	2
30.04.97	Bucharest	Romania	1	Republic of Ireland	0
21.05.97	Lansdowne Road	Republic of Ireland Connolly 3, Cascarino 2	5	Liechestein	0
20.08.97	Lansdowne Road	Republic of Ireland	0	Lithuania	0
06.09.97	Reykjavik	Iceland	2	Republic of Ireland Roy Keane 2, Connolly, Kennedy	4
10.09.97	Vilnius	Lithuania	1	Republic of Ireland Cascarino 2	2
11.10.97	Lansdowne Road	Republic of Ireland Cascarino	1	Romania	1

Play-off

DATE	VENUE	HOME TEAM	SCORE	AWAY TEAM	SCORE
29.10.97	Lansdowne Road	Rep. of Ireland Irwin	1	Belgium	1
15.11.97	Brussels	Belgium	2	Republic of Ireland Houghton	1

Belgium qualified for World Cup.

UEFA Group Eight Final Table

	P	W	D	L	F	A	Pts
Romania	10	9	1	0	37	4	28
Republic of Ireland	10	5	3	2	22	8	18
Lithuania	10	5	2	3	11	8	17
FYR Macedonia	10	4	1	5	22	18	13
Iceland	10	2	3	5	11	16	9
Liechtenstein	10	0	0	10	3	52	0

Republic of Ireland Friendly Results

DATE	VENUE	HOME TEAM	SCORE	AWAY TEAM	SCORE
25.03.98	Olomouc	Czech Republic	2	Republic of Ireland Breen	1
22.04.98	Lansdowne Road	Republic of Ireland	0	Argentina	2
23.05.98	Lansdowne Road	Republic of Ireland	0	Mexico	0

Republic of Ireland European Cup Qualifying Results 1998-99

DATE	VENUE	HOME TEAM	SCORE	AWAY TEAM	SCORE
05.09.98	Lansdowne Road	Republic of Ireland Irwin (pen), Roy Keane	2	Croatia	0
14.10.98	Lansdowne Road	Republic of Ireland Robbie Keane (2), Roy Keane, Quinn, Breen	5	Malta	0

Remaining Group Eight Fixtures: 18.11.98: Yugoslavia v Rep. of Ireland; 27.03.99 FYR Macedonia v Rep. of Ireland; 05.06.99: Rep. of Ireland v Yugoslavia; 04.09.99: Croatia v Rep. of Ireland; 08.09.99: Malta v Rep. of Ireland; 10.10.99: Rep. of Ireland v FYR Macedonia.

Republic of Ireland U21 International Results

DATE	VENUE	HOME TEAM	SCORE	AWAY TEAM	SCORE
European Championship Qualifying Round					
10.10.97	Drogheda	Republic of Ireland	0	Romania	2
Friendly					
24.03.98	Drnovice	Czech Republic	3	Republic of Ireland	0
Triangular Tournament					
18.05.98	Ballybofey	Republic of Ireland Connolly, Hawkins, Grant	3	Scotland	0
22.05.98	Castlebar	Republic of Ireland	0	Northern Ireland	1
Euro 2000 U21 Qualifier					
04.09.98	Kilkenny	Republic of Ireland Conlon, Baker.	2	Croatia	2

UEFA U18 Championship Finals, Cyprus 19-26 July '98

Date	Venue	Stage		
19.07.98	Ayia Napa	Group Match	Rep. of Ireland 5 George 2, Keane, McPhail, Partridge	Croatia 2
21.07.98	Derynia	Group Match	Rep. of Ireland 0	England 1
23.07.98	Ayia Napa	Group Match	Rep. of Ireland 3 A. Quinn, Keane 2.	Cyprus 0
26.07.98	Larnaca	Final	Republic of Ireland 1 A. Quinn 71	Germany 1

Ireland won 4-3 on penalties.

Final Group Standings

GROUP A	P	W	D	L	F	A	Pts
Germany	3	2	0	1	11	4	6
Portugal	3	2	0	1	5	2	6
Spain	3	2	0	1	5	6	6
Lithuania	3	0	0	3	2	11	0

GROUP B	P	W	D	L	F	A	Pts
Rep. of Ireland	3	2	0	1	8	3	6
Croatia	3	2	0	1	8	5	6
England	3	2	0	1	3	4	6
Cyprus	3	0	0	3	1	8	0

Final: Winners Group A v Winners Group B

U18 European Championships. Group Four Qualifying Matches

Date	Venue	Home Team	Away Team
05.10.98	Tolka Park	Republic of Ireland 5 Baker 2, Doherty, Healy, O'Grady	Cyprus 1
07.10.98	Richmond Park	Republic of Ireland 2 Healy, Barrett	Poland 2
09.10.98	Tolka Park	Republic of Ireland 1 Healy	Russia 0

Final Qualifying Group Standings

Group 4	P	W	D	L	F	A	Pts
Republic of Ireland	3	2	1	0	8	3	7
Russia	3	2	0	1	3	1	6
Poland	3	0	2	1	3	5	2
Cyprus	3	0	1	2	2	6	1

UEFA U16 Championship, Scotland 26 April-8 May '98

Date	Venue	Stage		
26.04.98	Stirling	Group Match	**Rep. of Ireland 0**	**Scotland 0**
28.04.98	Stirling	Group Match	**Rep. of Ireland 2** A. Reid 4; G. Barret 23	**Finland 0**
30.04.98	Stirling	Group Match	**Rep. of Ireland 1** D. McMahon 63	**Spain 0**
03.05.98	Stirling	Quarter final	**Rep. of Ireland 2** G. Barret 32; S. Byrne 60	**Denmark 0**
05.05.98	Perth	Semi final	**Rep. of Ireland 2** S. Byrne 52, 80	**Portugal 0**
08.05.98	Perth	Final	**Rep. of Ireland 2** K. Foy 35; D. McMahon 57	**Italy 1** Pelanti 52

NORDIC CUP (U16), Iceland 4-8 August '98

Date	Stage		
04.08.98	Group Match	**Republic of Ireland 4** Robinson 2, Melligan, Cawley	**Denmark 0**
05.08.98	Group Match	**Republic of Ireland 1** Doyle	**Iceland 0**
07.08.98	Group Match	**Republic of Ireland 1** Doyle	**Norway 0**
08.08.98	Final	**Republic of Ireland 3** Doyle, Reid, Byrne	**England 2**

DOMESTIC RESULTS

FAI National League

Premier Division Final Table 97/98	P	W	D	L	F	A	Pts
St. Patrick's Athletic	33	19	11	3	46	24	68
Shelbourne	33	20	7	6	58	32	67
Cork City	33	14	11	8	50	40	53
Shamrock Rovers	33	14	10	9	41	32	52
Bohemians	33	13	11	9	50	36	50
Dundalk	33	12	9	12	41	43	45
Sligo Rovers	33	10	14	9	46	49	44
Finn Harps	33	12	7	14	41	43	43
Derry City	33	10	10	13	30	31	40
U.C.D.	33	9	12	12	36	38	39
Kilkenny City	33	4	7	22	27	63	19
Drogheda United	33	2	9	22	20	55	15

Top Scorers:

Stephen Geoghegan	Shelbourne	17
Tony Cousins	Shamrock Rovers	14
G. Lawlor	Bohemians	13

First Division Final Table 97/98	P	W	D	L	F	A	Pts
Waterford United	27	18	6	3	35	17	60
Bray Wanderers	27	17	3	7	51	21	54
Limerick FC	27	14	8	5	41	25	50
Galway United	27	13	4	10	38	29	43
Home Farm/Everton	27	9	11	7	28	22	38
Cobh Ramblers	27	10	5	12	32	41	35
Athlone Town	27	8	7	12	31	37	31
St. Francis	27	7	8	12	29	40	29
Monaghan United	27	6	4	17	26	44	22
Longford Town	27	2	6	19	12	47	12

Top Scorers:

Fergal Coleman	Galway United	13
Kieran O'Brien	Bray Wanderers	11
Richie Parsons	Bray Wanderers	11

UCD beat Limerick 5-2 on aggregate in a Promotion/Relegation play-off to retain Premier Division status.

1997/98 Premier Division Results

	Bohemians	Cork City	Derry City	Drogheda U	Dundalk	Finn Harps	Kilkenny C	St Pats	Shamrock R	Shelbourne	Sligo R	UCD
Bohemians	---- ----	4-2	1-0	1-1 2-1	2-0	4-2 1-0	8-1 4-3	0-0	1-1 0-1	1-0 0-1	1-1	0-0 2-0
Cork City	1-1 2-0	---- ----	2-0 0-1	1-1	3-0 0-0	3-1	1-0	0-1 1-1	2-1	4-4	1-1	1-0 1-2
Derry City	1-0 1-0	1-1	---- ----	4-1 3-0	1-2 0-0	1-0 0-0	1-1	1-1	0-1	2-2 1-2	0-0	1-1 0-3
Drogheda Utd	0-1	1-2 1-2	0-1	---- ----	1-0	0-2	0-0 1-1	1-3 1-2	1-3 0-1	0-1	2-4 1-1	0-0
Dundalk	2-2 3-3	1-0	0-1	1-1 0-2	---- ----	2-0 2-1	3-0 1-0	0-0	0-0	0-1 2-1	5-0	1-1 1-2
Finn Harps	3-2	2-1 1-2	1-0	2-0 1-0	0-1	---- ----	2-1	1-2 0-2	2-1	3-1 0-0	1-1	1-0 1-2
Kilkenny City	1-1	0-2 1-2	0-5 1-0	2-1	1-2	2-3 2-2	---- ----	0-2 1-2	1-2 1-1	1-3	0-1 2-1	1-1
St Patrick's Ath	0-0 0-2	3-3	0-0 1-0	2-0	1-0 4-2	1-0	1-0	---- ----	2-0	2-3 0-0	1-2	1-1 1-0
Shamrock Rovers	2-1	1-3 2-2	1-0 3-1	0-0	1-2 5-2	2-1 2-2	1-0	0-1 0-1	---- ----	0-2	1-1 0-0	2-0
Shelbourne	0-1	3-1 1-1	1-0	5-0 1-0	2-0	3-2	2-1 3-0	0-2	1-1 2-1	---- ----	3-0 2-0	3-1
Sligo Rovers	2-2 2-1	0-2 4-1	3-0 1-1	2-1	3-3 3-0	2-2 0-2	2-0	3-4 1-1	0-1	1-1	---- ----	2-1
UCD	2-1	0-0	1-2	3-0 1-1	1-3	0-0	1-2 1-0	1-1	0-3 0-0	2-1 2-3	1-1 5-1	---- ----

1997/98 First Division Results

	Athlone T	Bray W	Cobh R	Galway Utd	Home Farm	Limerick FC	Longford T	Monaghan	St Francis	Waterford U
Athlone Town	---- ----	1-2	2-0 2-4	2-1 2-0	0-1	1-1	2-0	2-1	1-4 1-1	0-1 0-1
Bray Wanderers	2-1 1-1	---- ----	7-0 0-0	2-1	2-0 0-1	3-2	4-0	4-0 1-0	1-0 2-1	0-1
Cobh Ramblers	2-1	0-1	---- ----	1-0 1-1	1-0	2-1	1-0 2-0	0-1 2-1	2-3 1-3	1-2 0-1
Galway United	2-1	1-4 1-0	4-1	---- ----	2-1	2-2 2-1	1-0	3-1 2-0	5-0 1-0	0-1
H. Farm Everton	1-2 4-1	0-0	2-1 0-1	1-1 0-0	---- ----	1-2 0-0	1-0 0-0	2-1	1-1	3-0
Limerick FC	0-0 1-1	1-0 2-1	1-0 2-2	1-0	1-1	---- ----	1-0 6-0	3-1	2-0	1-2
Longford Town	2-2 1-2	1-0 1-3	2-2	1-2 0-2	0-1	0-2	---- ----	0-2 0-4	1-1	0-0 0-2
Monaghan Utd	0-2 1-1	0-2	2-1	2-1	3-3 0-0	1-2 1-2	1-3	---- ----	1-2	1-2 0-2
St Francis	1-0	4-3	1-3	1-2	1-1 0-2	1-2 0-2	0-0 2-0	0-1 0-0	---- ----	1-4
Waterford Utd	2-0	0-3 1-3	1-1	1-0 2-1	1-0 1-1	3-0 0-0	1-0	2-0	1-1 0-0	---- ----

1998 Harp Lager FAI Cup

First Round

Athlone Town	3	College Corinthians	0
Bohemains	0	Cork City	1
Cobh Ramblers	0	Galway United	2
Derry City	7	Rockmount	0
Drogheda United	1	Shamrock Rovers	1
Dundalk	5	Swilly Rovers	0
Fanad United	0	Whitehall Rangers	3
Finn Harps	2	Bray Wanderers	0
Home Farm Everton	3	Home Farm	1
Kilkenny City	0	UCD	4
Monaghan United	0	Cobh Ramblers	3
St Francis	1	Cherry Orchard	0
Shelbourne	4	Limerick	1
Sligo Rovers	1	Mervue United	1
Waterford United	2	St Patrick's Athletic	2
Wayside Celtic	0	Longford Town	0

First Round Replays

Shamrock Rovers	2	Drogheda United	0
Mervue United	0	Sligo Rovers	2
St Patrick's Athletic	3	Waterford United	0
Longford Town	1	Wayside Celtic	1 aet
Wayside Celtic	0	Longford Town	1 aet

Second Round

Athlone Town	2	Shamrock Rovers	1
Cobh Ramblers	1	St Patrick's Athletic	3
Cork City	1	Derry City	1
Dundalk	0	Shelbourne	0
Galway United	2	Finn Harps	2
Longford Town	1	Whitehall Rangers	0
Sligo Rovers	2	St Francis	0
UCD	1	Home Farm Everton	1

Second Round Replays

Derry City	0	Cork City	1
Shelbourne	2	Dundalk	0
Finn Harps	3	Galway United	1
Home Farm Everton	0	UCD	1

Quarter-Finals

Athlone Town	1	Longford Town	1
Cork City	2	Sligo Rovers	0
St Patrick's Athletic	2	Shelbourne	2
UCD	0	Finn Harps	1

Quarter-Final Replays

Longford Town	1	Athlone Town	2
Shelbourne	1	St Patrick's Athletic	1 aet
Shelbourne	2	St Patrick's Athletic	2 aet

Shelbourne won 5-3 on penalties

Semi-Finals

Athlone Town	1	Cork City	3
Finn Harps	0	Shelbourne	0

Semi-Final Replay

Shelbourne	1	Finn Harps	0

Final

Cork City	0	Shelbourne	0

aet= after extra time.

Harp Lager FAI Cup Final (Replay)

DALYMOUNT PARK, DUBLIN. Saturday 16 May 1998. Att: 6,400; **Half Time Score:** Cork City 0, Shelbourne 0; **Full Time Score:** Cork City 1, Shelbourne 0; **Goal:** Coughlan (Cork City 75 mins) **Man of the Match:** Patsy Freyne (Cork City); **Referee:** Gerard Perry (Dublin); **Assistant Referees:** Paul Moyer and Tony Ryan.

CORK CITY

Mooney

O'Donoghue Coughlan Daly (c) Cronin

Flanagan Freyne Hill Cahill

Caulfield Hartigan

Subs: Glynn for Hartigan (55mins)
Long for O'Donoghue (76 mins)

Manager: Dave Barry
Assistant Manager: Liam Murphy
Trainer: J. Harris

SHELBOURNE

Gough

Smith Scully McCarthy D. Geoghegan

Kelly Fitzgerald Fenlon Rutherford

S. Geoghegan Baker

Subs: Neville for Fitzgerald (84 mins)
Morley for Geoghegan (81 mins)
Sheridan for Rutherford (81 mins)

Manager: Damien Richardson
Trainer: Fred Davis.

REPUBLIC OF IRELAND SENIOR TEAM FACTFILE

Name	Club	Position	D.O.B.	Born	Caps	Goals	Debut
BABB, Phil	Liverpool	Defender	30.11.70	Lambeth	26	0	23.03.94
BRANIGAN, Keith	Bolton Wanderers	Goalkeeper	10.07.66	Fulham	1	0	11.02.97
BREEN, Gary	Coventry City	Defender	12.12.73	London	16	3	29.05.96
CARSLEY, Lee	Derby County	Midfielder	28.02.74	Birmingham	8	0	11.10.97
CASCARINO, Tony	A.S. Nancy	Striker	01.09.62	Kent	77	19	11.09.85
CONNOLLY, David	Wolves	Striker	06.06.77	Willesden	13	6	29.05.96
COYNE, Tommy	Dundee	Striker	14.11.62	Glasgow	22	6	25.03.92
CUNNINGHAM, Kenny	Wimbledon	Defender	28.06.71	Dublin	18	0	24.04.96

Republic of Ireland Senior Team Factfile (Continued)

Name	Club	Position	D.O.B.	Born	Caps	Goals	Debut
DELAP, Rory	Derby County	Striker	06.07.76	Donegal	3	0	25.03.98
DUFF, Damian	Blackburn Rovers	Striker	02.03.79	Dublin	4	0	25.03.98
EVANS, Michael	West Brom	Striker	01.01.73		1	0	11.10.97
FARRELLY, Gareth	Everton	Midfielder	28.08.75	Dublin	5	0	25.05.96
FLEMMING, Curtis	Middlesbrough	Defender	08.10.68	Manchester	10	0	24.04.96
GIVEN, Shay	Newcastle United	Goalkeeper	20.04.76	Lifford	19	0	29.03.96
HARTE, Ian	Leeds United	Defender	31.08.77	Drogheda	18	2	02.06.96
HOUGHTON, Ray	Reading	Midfielder	09.01.62	Glasgow	73	6	26.03.86
IRWIN, Denis	Manchester United	Defender	31.10.65	Cork	49	3	12.09.90
KAVANAGH, Graham	Stoke City	Midfielder	02.12.73	Dublin	1	0	25.03.98
KEANE, Robbie	Wolves	Striker	08.09.80	Dublin	5	2	25.03.98
KEANE, Roy	Manchester United	Midfielder	10.08.71	Cork	40	5	22.05.91
KELLY, Alan	Sheffield United	Goalkeeper	11.08.68	Preston	20	0	17.02.93
KELLY, David	Tranmere Rovers	Striker	25.11.65	Birmingham	26	9	10.11.87
KELLY, Gary	Leeds United	Defender	09.07.74	Louth	28	1	23.03.94
KENNA, Jeff	Blackburn Rovers	Defender	27.08.70	Dublin	26	0	26.04.95
KENNEDY, Mark	Wimbledon	Midfielder	15.05.76	Dublin	19	1	06.09.95
KILBANE, Kevin	West Brom	Striker	01.02.77	Preston	3	0	06.09.97
KINSELLA, Mark	Charlton Athletic	Midfielder	12.08.72	Dublin	4	0	25.03.98
MAYBURY, Alan	Leeds United	defender	08.08.78	Dublin	1	0	25.03.98
McATEER, Jason	Liverpool	Midfielder	18.06.71	Liverpool	27	1	23.03.94
McLOUGHLIN, Alan	Portsmouth	Midfielder	20.04.67	Manchester	34	2	03.06.90
MOORE, Alan	Middlesbrough	Midfielder	25.11.74	Dublin	8	0	24.04.96
O'NEILL, Keith	Norwich City	Striker	16.02.76	Dublin	10	4	29.05.96
PHELAN, Terry	Everton	Defender	16.03.67	Manchester	38	0	11.09.91
QUINN, Niall	Sunderland	Striker	06.10.66	Dublin	64	17	25.05.86
STAUNTON, Steve	Liverpool	Defender	19.01.69	Drogheda	76	6	19.10.88
TOWNSEND, Andy	Middlesbrough	Midfielder	23.07.63	Maidstone	70	7	07.02.89

Caps correct as of 14.10.98

Republic of Ireland teams since October 1997

Name	Total	Romania 11.10.97	Belgium 29.10.97	Belgium 15.11.97	Czech R 25.03.98	Argentina 22.04.98	Mexico 23.05.98	Croatia 05.09.98	Malta 14.10.98
BAAB, Phil	4	●				●(S)	●	●	
BREEN, Gary	4	●			●	●	●		●
CARSLEY, Lee	7	●	●(S)	●	●	●	●	●(S)	●(S)
CASCARINO, Tony	4	●	●	●				●(S)	●(S)
CONNOLLY, David	4		●	●(S)	●		●		
COYNE, Tommy	1		●(S)						
CUNNINGHAM, Kenny	4		●	●	●			●	●
DELAP, Rory	3				●(S)	●(S)	●(S)		
DUFF, Damian	3				●		●	●	●
EVANS, Michael	1	●(S)							
FARRELLY, Gareth	2				●		●		
FLEMING, Curtis	2	●(S)					●		
GIVEN, Shay	6		●	●	●	●	●	●	●
HARTE, Ian	4		●	●		●	●		
HOUGHTON, Ray	3	●	●	●(S)					
IRWIN, Denis	3		●			●(S)		●	
KEANE, Robbie	4				●(S)	●	●	●	●
KEANE, Roy	1							●	●
KAVANAGH, Graham	1				●(S)				
KELLY, Alan	2	●				●(S)			
KELLY, Gary	5		●	●	●	●	●		
KELLY, David	2	●(S)		●(S)					
KENNA, Jeff	6	●	●(S)	●	●	●		●(S)	●
KENNEDY, Mark	4	●	●	●			●(S)		●(S)
KILBAINE, Kevin	2				●(S)	●			
KINSELLA, Mark	3				●	●		●	●

Name	Total	Romania 11.10.97	Belgium 29.10.97	Belgium 15.11.97	Czech R 25.03.98	Argentina 22.04.98	Mexico 23.05.98	Croatia 05.09.98	Malta 14.10.98
MAYBURY, Alan	1				●				
McATEER, Jason	2	●						●	●
McLOUGHLIN, Alan	3	●		●	●(S)				
O'NEILL, Keith	1							●	
PHELAN, Terry	1	●							
QUINN, Niall	1					●			●
STAUNTON, Steve	4		●	●		●		●	●
TOWNSEND, Andy	2		●	●					

S = Substitute

REP. OF IRELAND U18 UEFA FINALS APPEARANCES

Name	Club	v Croatia	v England	v Cyprus	v Germany
CASEY, Ryan	Swansea	● (S)			● (S)
CROSSLEY, Ger	Celtic	●	●	●	●
DELANEY, Dean	Everton				
DOHERTY, Gary	Luton Town	●	●		
DONNELLY, Paul	Leed United			● (S)	● (S)
DOYLE, Keith	St Patrick's Athletic	●	●	●	●
DUNNE, Richard	Everton	●	●	●	●
FREEMAN, David	Nottingham Forest	● (S)		● (S)	
GAVIN, Jason	Middlesbrough		● (S)	●	●
GEORGE, Liam	Luton Town	●	●	●	●
HEARY, Thomas	Huddersfield	●	●	●	●
KEANE, Robbie	Wolverhampton Wanderers	●	●	●	●
McPHAIL, Stephen	Leeds United	●	●		●
O'BRIEN, Ronnie	Middlesbrough		● (S)	●	
O'REILLY, Alex	West Ham	●	●	●	●
PARTRIDGE, Richard	Liverpool	●	●	● (S)	●
QUINN, Alan	Sheffield Wednesday		● (S)	●	● (S)
QUINN, Barry	Coventry City	●	●	●	●

FAI RECORDS

League of Ireland Championship Winners and Runners Up

Season	Winners	Runners Up
1921-22	St. James's Gate	Bohemians
1922-23	Shamrock Rovers	Shelbourne
1923-24	Bohemians	Shelbourne
1924-25	Shamrock Rovers	Bohemians
1925-26	Shelbourne	Shamrock Rovers
1926-27	Shamrock Rovers	Shelbourne
1927-28	Bohemians	Shelbourne
1928-29	Shelbourne	Bohemians
1929-30	Bohemians	Shelbourne
1930-31	Shelbourne	Dundalk
1931-32	Shamrock Rovers	Cork
1932-33	Dundalk	Shamrock Rovers
1933-34	Bohemians	Cork
1934-35	Dolphin	St. James's Gate
1935-36	Bohemians	Dolphin
1936-37	Sligo Rovers	Dundalk
1937-38	Shamrock Rovers	Waterford
1938-39	Shamrock Rovers	Sligo Rovers
1939-40	St. James's Gate	Shamrock Rovers
1940-41	Cork United	Waterford
1941-42	Cork United	Shamrock Rovers
1942-43	Cork United	Dundalk
1943-44	Shelbourne	Limerick
1944-45	Cork United	Limerick
1945-46	Cork United	Drumcondra
1946-47	Shelbourne	Drumcondra
1947-48	Drumcondra	Dundalk
1948-49	Drumcondra	Shelbourne
1949-50	Cork Athletic	Drumcondra
1950-51	Cork Athletic	Sligo Rovers
1951-52	St. Patrick's Athletic	Shelbourne
1952-53	Shelbourne	Drumcondra
1953-54	Shamrock Rovers	Evergreen United
1954-55	St. Patrick's Athletic	Waterford
1955-56	St. Patrick's Athletic	Shamrock Rovers
1956-57	Shamrock Rovers	Drumcondra
1957-58	Drumcondra	Shamrock Rovers
1958-59	Shamrock Rovers	Evergreen United
1959-60	Limerick	Cork Celtic
1960-61	Drumcondra	St. Patrick's Athletic
1961-62	Shelbourne	Cork Celtic
1962-63	Dundalk	Waterford
1963-64	Shamrock Rovers	Dundalk
1964-65	Drumcondra	Shamrock Rovers
1965-66	Waterford	Shamrock Rovers
1966-67	Dundalk	Bohemians
1967-68	Waterford	Dundalk
1968-69	Waterford	Shamrock Rovers

Season	Winners	Runners Up
1969-70	Waterford	Shamrock Rovers
1970-71	Cork Hibernians	Shamrock Rovers
1971-72	Waterford	Cork Hibernians
1972-73	Waterford	Finn Harps
1973-74	Cork Celtic	Bohemians
1974-75	Bohemians	Athlone Town
1975-76	Dundalk	Finn Harps
1976-77	Sligo Rovers	Bohemians
1977-78	Bohemians	Finn Harps
1978-79	Dundalk	Bohemians
1979-80	Limerick United	Dundalk
1980-81	Athlone Town	Dundalk
1981-82	Dundalk	Shamrock Rovers
1982-83	Athlone Town	Drogheda United
1983-84	Shamrock Rovers	Bohemians
1984-85	Shamrock Rovers	Bohemians

Premier Division		
Season	Winners	Runners Up
1985-86	Shamrock Rovers	Galway United
1986-87	Shamrock Rovers	Dundalk
1987-88	Dundalk	St. Patrick's Athletic
1988-89	Derry City	Dundalk
1989-90	St. Patrick's Athletic	Derry City
1990-91	Dundalk	Cork City
1991-92	Shelbourne	Derry City
1992-93	Cork City	Bohemians
1993-94	Shamrock Rovers	Cork City
1994-95	Dundalk	Derry City
1995-96	St. Patrick's Athletic	Bohemians
1996-97	Derry City	Bohemians
1997-98	St. Patrick's Athletic	Shelbourne

1st Division		
Season	Winners	Runners Up
1985-86	Bray Wanderers	Sligo Rovers
1986-87	Derry City	Shelbourne
1987-88	Athlone Town	Cobh Ramblers
1988-89	Drogheda United	U.C.D.
1989-90	Waterford United	Sligo Rovers
1990-91	Drogheda United	Bray Wanderers
1991-92	Limerick City	Waterford United
1992-93	Galway United	Cobh Ramblers
1993-94	Sligo Rovers	Athlone Town
1994-95	U.C.D.	Drogheda United
1995-96	Bray Wanderers	Finn Harps
1996-97	Kilkenny City	Drogheda United
1997-98	Waterford United	Bray Wanderers

F.A.I. Cup Final Results

Year	Venue	Winners	Runners Up	Drawn	Score
1922	Dalymount Park	St. James's Gate	Shamrock Rovers	1-1	1-0
1923	Dalymount Park	Alton United	Shelbourne		1-0
1924	Dalymount Park	Athlone Town	Fordsons		1-0
1925	Dalymount Park	Shamrock Rovers	Shelbourne		2-1
1926	Dalymount Park	Fordsons	Shamrock Rovers		3-2
1927	Shelbourne Park	Drumcondra	Brideville	1-1	1-0
1928	Dalymount Park	Bohemians	Drumcondra		2-1
1929	Shelbourne Park	Shamrock Rovers	Bohemians	0-0	3-0
1930	Dalymount Park	Shamrock Rovers	Brideville		1-0
1931	Dalymount Park	Shamrock Rovers	Dundalk	1-1	1-0
1932	Dalymount Park	Shamrock Rovers	Dolphin		1-0
1933	Dalymount Park	Shamrock Rovers	Dolphin	3-3	3-0
1934	Dalymount Park	Cork	St. James's Gate		2-1
1935	Dalymount Park	Bohemians	Dundalk		4-3
1936	Dalymount Park	Shamrock Rovers	Cork		2-1
1937	Dalymount Park	Waterford	St. James's Gate		2-1
1938	Dalymount Park	St. James's Gate	Dundalk		2-1
1939	Dalymount Park	Shelbourne	Sligo Rovers	1-1	1-0
1940	Dalymount Park	Shamrock Rovers	Sligo Rovers		3-0
1941	Dalymount Park	Cork United	Waterford	2-2	3-1
1942	Dalymount Park	Dundalk	Cork United		3-1
1943	Dalymount Park	Drumcondra	Cork United		2-1
1944	Dalymount Park	Shamrock Rovers	Shelbourne		3-2
1945	Dalymount Park	Shamrock Rovers	Bohemians		1-0
1946	Dalymount Park	Drumcondra	Shamrock Rovers		2-1
1947	Dalymount Park	Cork United	Bohemians	2-2	2-0
1948	Dalymount Park	Shamrock Rovers	Drumcondra		2-1

Continued from previous page

Year	Venue	Winners	Runners Up	Drawn	Score
1949	Dalymount Park	Dundalk	Shelbourne		3-0
1950	Dalymount Park	Transport	Cork Athletic	2-2, 2-2	3-1
1951	Dalymount Park	Cork Athletic	Shelbourne		1-0
1952	Dalymount Park	Dundalk	Cork Athletic	1-1	3-0
1953	Dalymount Park	Cork Athletic	Evergreen United	2-2	2-1
1954	Dalymount Park	Drumcondra	St. Patrick's Athletic		1-0
1955	Dalymount Park	Shamrock Rovers	Drumcondra		1-0
1956	Dalymount Park	Shamrock Rovers	Cork Athletic		3-2
1957	Dalymount Park	Drumcondra	Shamrock Rovers		2-0
1958	Dalymount Park	Dundalk	Shamrock Rovers		1-0
1959	Dalymount Park	St. Patrick's Athletic	Waterford	2-2	2-1
1960	Dalymount Park	Shelbourne	Cork Hibernians		2-0
1961	Dalymount Park	St. Patrick's Athletic	Drumcondra		2-1
1962	Dalymount Park	Shamrock Rovers	Shelbourne		4-1
1963	Dalymount Park	Shelbourne	Cork Hibernians		2-0
1964	Dalymount Park	Shamrock Rovers	Cork Celtic	1-1	2-1
1965	Dalymount Park	Shamrock Rovers	Limerick	1-1	1-0
1966	Dalymount Park	Shamrock Rovers	Limerick		2-0
1967	Dalymount Park	Shamrock Rovers	St. Patrick's Athletic		3-2
1968	Dalymount Park	Shamrock Rovers	Waterford		3-0
1969	Dalymount Park	Shamrock Rovers	Cork Celtic	1-1	4-1
1970	Dalymount Park	Bohemians	Sligo Rovers	0-0, 0-0	2-1
1971	Dalymount Park	Limerick	Drogheda	0-0	3-0
1972	Dalymount Park	Cork Hibernians	Waterford		3-0
1973	Flower Lodge	Cork Hibernians	Shelbourne	0-0	1-0
1974	Dalymount Park	Finn Harps	St. Patrick's Athletic		3-1
1975	Dalymount Park	Home Farm	Shelbourne		1-0
1976	Dalymount Park	Bohemians	Drogheda United		1-0
1977	Dalymount Park	Dundalk	Limerick		2-0
1978	Dalymount Park	Shamrock Rovers	Sligo Rovers		1-0
1979	Dalymount Park	Dundalk	Waterford		2-0
1980	Dalymount Park	Waterford	St. Patrick's Athletic		1-0
1981	Dalymount Park	Dundalk	Sligo Rovers		2-0
1982	Dalymount Park	Limerick United	Bohemians		1-0
1983	Dalymount Park	Sligo Rovers	Bohemians		2-1
1984	Tolka Park	U.C.D.	Shamrock Rovers	0-0	2-1
1985	Dalymount Park	Shamrock Rovers	Galway United		1-0
1986	Dalymount Park	Shamrock Rovers	Waterford United		2-0
1987	Dalymount Park	Shamrock Rovers	Dundalk		3-0
1988	Dalymount Park	Dundalk	Derry City		1-0
1989	Dalymount Park	Derry City	Cork City	0-0	1-0
1990	Lansdowne Road	Bray Wanderers	St Francis		3-0
1991	Lansdowne Road	Galway United	Shamrock Rovers		1-0
1992	Lansdowne Road	Bohemians	Cork City		1-0
1993	Lansdowne Road	Shelbourne	Dundalk		1-0
1994	Lansdowne Road	Sligo Rovers	Derry City		1-0
1995	Dalymount Park	Derry City	Shelbourne		2-1
1996	Dalymount Park	Shelbourne	St Patrick's Athletic	1-1	2-1
1997	Dalymount Park	Shelbourne	Derry City		2-0
1998	Dalymount Park	Cork City	Shelbourne	0-0	1-0

Season-by-Season Leading League of Ireland Goalscorers

Season	Name	Club	Goals
21/22	Jack Kelly	St. James's Gate	11
22/23	Bob Fullam	Shamrock Rovers	27
23/24	Dave Roberts	Bohemians	20
24/25	Billy Farrell	Shamrock Rovers	25
25/26	Billy Farrell	Shamrock Rovers	24
26/27	David Byrne	Shamrock Rovers	17
	John McMillan	Shelbourne	17
27/28	Charlie Heinemann	Fordsons	24
28/29	Eddie Carroll	Dundalk	17
29/30	Johnny Ledwidge	Shelbourne	16
30/31	Alec Hair	Shelbourne	29
31/32	Pearson Ferguson	Cork	21
	Jack Forster	Waterford	21
32/33	George Ebbs	St. James's Gate	20
33/34	Alf Rigby	St. James's Gate	13
34/35	Alf Rigby	St. James's Gate	17

Season	Name	Club	Goals
35/36	Jimmy Turnbull	Cork	37
36/37	Bob Slater	Shelbourne/Waterford	20
37/38	Willie Byrne	St. James's Gate	25
38/39	Paddy Bradshaw	St. James's Gate	22
39/40	Paddy Bradshaw	St. James's Gate	29
40/41	Mick O'Flanagan	Bohemians	19
41/42	Tommy Byrne	Limerick	20
42/43	Sean McCarthy	Cork United	16
43/44	Sean McCarthy	Cork United	16
44/45	Sean McCarthy	Cork United	26
45/46	Paddy O'Leary	Cork United	15
46/47	Paddy Coad	Shamrock Rovers	11
	Alf Hanson	Shelbourne	11
47/48	Sean McCarthy	Cork United	13
48/49	Bernard Lester	Transport	12
	Eugene Noonan	Waterford	12
	Paddy O'Leary	Cork Athletic	12
49/50	Dave McCulloch	Waterford	19
50/51	Dessie Glynn	Drumcondra	20
51/52	Shay Gibbons	St. Patrick's Athletic	26
52/53	Shay Gibbons	St. Patrick's Athletic	22
53/54	Danny Jordan	Bohemians	14
54/55	Jimmy Gauld	Waterford	30
55/56	Shay Gibbons	St. Patrick's Athletic	21
56/57	Tommy Hamilton	Shamrock Rovers	15
	Donal Leahy	Evergreen United	15
57/58	Donal Leahy	Evergreen United	16
58/59	Donal Leahy	Evergreen United	22
59/60	Austin Noonan	Cork Celtic	27
60/61	Dan McCaffrey	Drumcondra	29
61/62	Eddie Bailham	Shamrock Rovers	21
62/63	Mick Lynch	Waterford	12
63/64	Eddie Bailham	Shamrock Rovers	18
	Jimmy Hasty	Dundalk	18
	Johnny Kingston	Cork Hibernians	18
64/65	Jackie Mooney	Shamrock Rovers	16
65/66	Mick Lynch	Waterford	17
66/67	Johnny Brooks	Sligo Rovers	15
	Danny Hale	Dundalk	15
67/68	Carl Davenport	Cork Celtic	15
	Ben Hannigan	Dundalk	15
68/69	Mick Leech	Shamrock Rovers	19
69/70	Brendan Bradley	Finn Harps	18
70/71	Brendan Bradley	Finn Harps	20
71/72	Alfie Hale	Waterford	22
	Tony Marsden	Cork Hibernians	22
72/73	Alfie Hale	Waterford	20
	Terry Harkin	Finn Harps	20
73/74	Terry Flanagan	Bohemians	18
	Turlough O'Connor	Bohemians	18
74/75	Brendan Bradley	Finn Harps	21
75/76	Brendan Bradley	Finn Harps	29
76/77	Syd Wallace	Waterford	16
77/78	Turlough O'Connor	Bohemians	24
78/79	John Delamere	Shelbourne/Sligo Rvr.	17
79/80	Alan Campbell	Shamrock Rovers	22
80/81	Eugene Davis	Athlone Town	23
81/82	Michael O'Connor	Athlone Town	22
82/83	Noel Larkin	AthloneTown	18
83/84	Alan Campbell	Shamrock Rovers	24
84/85	Tommy Gaynor	Limerick City	17
	Michael O'Connor	Athlone Town	17

PREMIER DIVISION

Season	Name	Club	Goals
85/86	Tommy Gaynor	Limerick City	15
86/87	Mick Byrne	Shamrock Rovers	12
87/88	Jonathan Speak	Derry City	24
88/89	Billy Hamilton	Limerick City	21
89/90	Mark Ennis	St. Patrick's Athletic	19
90/91	Peter Hanrahan	Dundalk	18
91/92	John Caulfield	Cork City	16
92/93	Pat Morley	Cork City	20
93/94	Stephen Geoghegan	Shamrock Rovers	23
94/95	John Caulfield	Cork City	16
95/96	Stephen Geoghegan	Shelbourne	19
96/97	Tony Cousins	Shamrock Rovers	16
	Stephen Geoghegan	Shelbourne	16
97/98	Stephen Geoghegan	Shelbourne	17

FIRST DIVISION

Season	Name	Club	Goals
85/86	Con McLaughlin	Finn Harps	11
	Harry McLaughlin	Sligo Rovers	11
86/87	Alex Kristic	Derry City	18
87/88	Con McLaughlin	Finn Harps	19
88/89	Pat O'Connor	Home Farm	14
89/90	John Ryan	Bray Wanderers	16
90/91	Jim Barr	Monaghan United	12
	Con McLaughlin	Finn Harps	12
91/92	Con McLaughlin	Finn Harps	12
	Barry Ryan	Limerick City	12
92/93	Mick Byrne	Monaghan United	15
	Richie Parsons	Longford Town	15
93/94	Karl Gannon	Home Farm	16
94/95	Michael O'Byrne	U.C.D.	14
	Philip Power	Home Farm	14
95/96	Jonathan Speak	Finn Harps	17
96/97	Richie Hale	Kilkenny City	13
	Tony Izzi	Cobh Rambs/Limerick	13
97/98	Fergal Coleman	Galway United	13

Top Republic of Ireland Goal Scorers

Player	No. of Goals
1. Frank Stapleton (1977-90)	20
2. John Aldridge (1986-97)	19
3. Don Givens (1969-81)	19
4. Tony Cascarino (1986-)	19
5. Niall Quinn (1986-)	16
6. Noel Cantwell (1954-67)	14
7. Gerry Daly (1973-86)	13
8. Jimmy Dunne (1930-39)	12
9. Liam Brady (1975-90)	9
10. Kevin Sheedy (1984-93)	9
11. David Kelly (1987-)	9
12. Dermot Curtis (1956-63)	8
13. Tony Grealish (1976-85)	8
14. Paul McGrath (1985-96)	8
14. Andy Townsend (1989-97)	7
15. Arthur Fitzsimons (1949-59)	7
16. Paddy Moore (1931-37)	7
17. Alf Ringstead (1951-59)	7

FAI League Cup Final Results

Year	Winners	Runners Up	Score
1974	Waterford	Finn Harps	2-1
1975	Bohemians	Finn Harps	2-1
1976	Limerick	Sligo Rovers	4-1A
1977	Shamrock Rovers	Sligo Rovers	1-0
1978	Dundalk*	Cork Alberts	4-4
1979	Bohemians	Shamrock Rovers	2-0
1980	Athlone Town	St Patrick's Athletic	4-2
1981	Dundalk*	Galway Rovers	0-0A
1982	Athlone Town	Shamrock Rovers	1-0
1983	Athlone Town	Dundalk	2-1
1984	Drogheda United	Athlone Town	3-1
1985	Waterford United	Finn Harps	2-1
1986	Galway United	Dundalk	2-0
1987	Dundalk	Shamrock Rovers	1-0
1988	Cork City	Shamrock Rovers	1-0
1989	Derry City	Dundalk	4-0
1990	Dundalk*	Derry City	1-1
1991	Derry City	Limerick City	2-0
1992	Derry City	Bohemians	1-0
1993	Limerick	St. Patrick's Athletic	2-0
1994	Derry City	Shelbourne	3-1A
1995	Cork City	Dundalk	2-1A
1996	Shelbourne*	Sligo Rovers	2-2A
1997	Galway United	Cork City	4-2A
1998	Sligo Rovers	Shelbourne	1-0A

A- Denotes aggregate score
* - Denotes won on penalties

AWARDS

FAI/Opel Player of the Year Awards 1998

Award	Player & Club
Player of the Year	Kenny Cunningham (Wimbledon)
Young Player	Robbie Keane (Wolves)
U21 Player	Kevin Kilbane (West Brom)
Youth Player	Barry Quinn (Coventry City)
National League	Colin Hawkins (St Pats)
Junior Player	Philip Long (St Kevin's Boys)
U16 Player	Shaun Byrne (West Ham)
U15 Player	Clifford Byrne (Home Farm/Sunderland)
Schools	Kevin Doherty (St Joseph's Fairview)
Women	Yvonne Lyons (Benfica)
Hall of Fame	Shay Brennan & Tony Dunne
Special Merit	Noel O'Reilly
International Personality	Nobby Stiles

Former FAI/Opel International Player of the Year Recipients

Year	Name
1989	Kevin Moran
1990	Paul McGrath
1991	Paul McGrath
1992	John Aldridge
1993	Steve Staunton
1994	Ray Houghton
1995	Andy Townsend
1996	Alan McLoughlin
1997	Roy Keane

Former FAI/Opel National League Player of the Year Recipients

Year	Name	Club
1993	Pat Morley	Cork City
1994	Stephen Geoghegan	Shamrock Rovers
1995	Liam Coyle	Derry City
1996	Tony Sheridan	Shelbourne
1997	Peter Hutton	Derry City

Texaco Award Winners

Year	Winner	Club and Country
1958	Noel Cantwell	West Ham & Republic of Ireland
1959	Charlie Hurley	Sunderland & Republic of Ireland
1960	Fionan Fagan	Derby County & Republic of Ireland
1961	Ronnie Nolan	Shamrock Rovers & Republic of Ireland
1962	Danny Blanchflower	Tottenham & Northern Ireland
1963	William Browne	Bohemians & Republic of Ireland
1964	Andrew McEvoy	Blackburn Rovers & Republic of Ireland
1965	S. Thomas	
1966	Thomas Dunne	Dundalk & Republic of Ireland
1967	George Best	Manchester United & Northern Ireland
1968	Johnny Giles	Leeds United & Republic of Ireland
1970	Steve Heighway	Liverpool & Republic of Ireland
1971	Frank O' Farrell	Manchester United manager
1972	Johnny Giles	Leeds United & Republic of Ireland
1973	Pat Jennings	Tottenham & Northern Ireland
1974	Johnny Giles	Leeds United & Republic of Ireland
1976	Liam Brady	Arsenal & Republic of Ireland

Continued from previous page

Year	Winner	Club and Country
1978	Pat Jennings	Tottenham & Northern Ireland
1979	Liam Brady	Arsenal & Republic of Ireland
1980	Sammy McIlroy	Manchseter United & Northern Ireland
1981	Billy Bingham	Northern Ireland manager
1982	Gerry Armstrong	Watford & Northern Ireland
1983	Pat Jennings	Arsenal & Northern Ireland
1984	Liam Touhy	Shamrock Rovers & Republic of Ireland
1985	Pat Jennings	Arsenal & Northern Ireland
1986	Jim McLoughlin	Shamrock Rovers Manager
1987	Liam Brady	West Ham & Republic of Ireland
1988	Packie Bonner	Celtic & Republic of Ireland
1989	Ronnie Whelan	Liverpool & Republic of Ireland
1990	Packie Bonner	Celtic & Republic of Ireland
1991	Niall Quinn	Manchester City & Republic of Ireland
1992	Kevin Moran	Blackburn Rovers & Republic of Ireland
1993	Paul Mc Grath	Aston Villa & Republic of Ireland
1994	Roy Keane	Manchester United & Republic of Ireland
1995	Bryan Hamilton	Northern Ireland manager
1996	Denis Irwin	Manchester United & Republic of Ireland
1997	Roy Keane	Manchester United & Republic of Ireland

NATIONAL LEAGUE PREMIER DIVISION CLUB STATISTICS

BOHEMIAN F.C. Founded: 1890. **Ground:** Dalymount Park, Phibsboro, Dublin 7. **Capacity:** 14,700. **Phone Number:** 01 8681022. **Colours:** Red & Black stripes. **Manager:** Roddy Collins. (GM Turlough O'Connor) **President:** Tony O'Connell. **FAI League Titles:** 7. 1924, 1928, 1930, 1934, 1936, 1975, 1978. **FAI Cups:** 5. 1928, 1935, 1970, 1976, 1992. **FAI League Cups:** 2.

BRAY WANDERERS F.C. Founded: 1942 **Ground:** Carlisle Grounds, Bray, Co. Wicklow. **Capacity:** 7,500. **Phone Number:** 01 2828214. **Colours:** Green & White stripes. **Manager:** Pat Devlin. **Chairman:** Philip Hannigan. **FAI League Titles:** 0. **FAI Cups:** 1. 1990. **FAI League Cups:** 0.

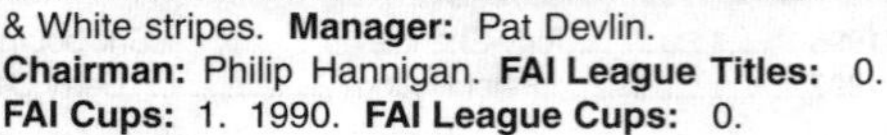

CORK CITY F.C. Founded: 1984. **Ground & Capacity:** Turner's Cross. 7,000. **Address:** Turner's Cross, Cork. **Phone Number:** 021 345588. **Colours:** Green, Red & White. **Manager:** Dave Barry. **Chairman:** Terry Dunne. **FAI League Titles:** 1. 1993. **FAI Cups:** 1. 1998. **FAI League Cups:** 2. 1988 and 1995.

DERRY CITY F.C. Founded: 1928 (affiliated F.A.I. 1985). **Ground:** The Brandywell, Derry. **Capacity:** 7,500. **Phone Number:** 0801504 374542. **Colours:** Red & White stripes. **Manager:** Felix Healy. **Chairman:** Kevin Friel. **FAI League Titles:** 2. 1989, 1997. **FAI Cups:** 2. 1989, 1995. **FAI League Cups:** 4. 1989, 1991, 1992, 1994.

DUNDALK F.C. Founded: 1926. **Ground:** Oriel Park, Carrick Road, Dundalk, Co Louth. **Capacity:** 13,600. **Phone Number:** 042 35894. **Colours:** White & Black. **Manager:** Jim McLaughlin. **Chairman:** Enda McGuill. **FAI League Titles:** 9. 1933, 1963, 1967, 1976, 1979, 1982, 1988, 1991, 1995. **FAI Cups:** 8. 1942, 1949, 1952, 1958, 1977, 1979, 1981, 1988. **FAI League Cups:** 4. 1978, 1981, 1987, 1990

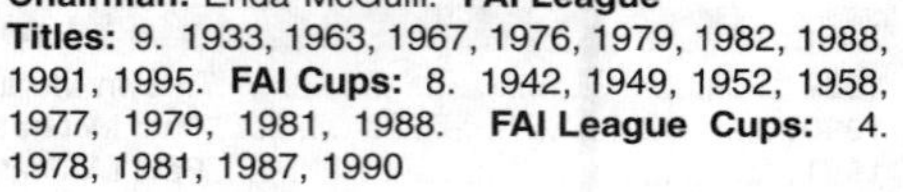

FINN HARPS F.C. Founded: 1954. **Ground:** Finn Park, Ballybofey, Co. Donegal. **Capacity:** 8,000. **Phone Number:** 074 32635. **Colours:** White & Blue. **Manager:** Charlie McGeever. **Chairman:** Derek Wilkinson. **FAI League Titles:** 0. **FAI Cups:** 1. 1974. **FAI League Cups:** 0.

ST. PATRICK'S ATHLETIC F.C. Founded: 1929. **Ground:** Richmond Park, 125 Emmet Road, Inchicore, Dublin 8. **Capacity:** 5,800. **Phone Number:** 01 4546332. **Colours:** Red & White. **Manager:** Liam Buckley. **Chairman:** Pat Dolan. **FAI League Titles:** 6. 1952, 1955, 1956, 1990, 1996, 1998. **FAI Cups:** 2. 1959, 1961. **FAI League Cups:** 0.

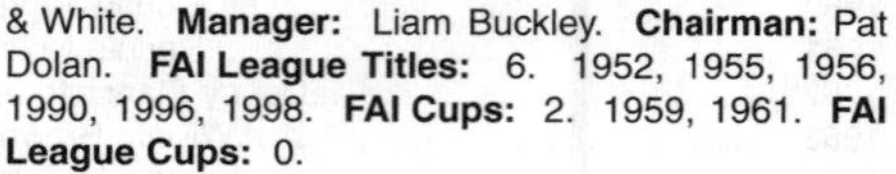

SHAMROCK ROVERS F.C. Founded: 1901. **Ground:** Tolka Park. **Capacity:** 10,000. **Phone Number:** 01 4925660. **Colours:** Green & White hoops. **Manager:** Mick Byrne. **Chairman:** Brian Kearney. **FAI League Titles:** 15. 1923, 1925, 1927, 1932, 1938, 1939, 1954, 1957, 1959, 1964, 1984, 1985, 1986, 1987, 1994. **FAI Cups:** 24. 1925, 1929, 1930, 1931, 1932, 1933, 1936, 1940, 1944, 1945, 1948, 1955, 1956, 1962, 1964, 1965, 1966,

1967, 1968, 1969, 1978, 1985, 1986, 1987. **FAI League Cups:** 1. 1977.

SHELBOURNE F.C. Founded: 1895. **Ground:** Tolka Park, Richmond Road, Dublin 3. **Capacity:** 10,000. **Phone Number:** 01 8368781. **Colours:** Red. **Manager:** Dermot Keely. **Chairman:** Finbarr Flood. **FAI League Titles:** 8. 1926, 1929, 1931, 1944, 1947, 1953, 1962, 1992. **FAI Cups:** 6. 1939, 1960, 1963, 1993, 1996, 1997. **FAI League Cups:** 1. 1996.

SLIGO ROVERS F.C. Founded: 1928. **Ground:** The Showgrounds, Sligo. **Capacity:** 5,900. **Phone Number:** 071 71212. **Colours:** Red & White. **Manager:** Nicky Reid. **Chairman:** Ray Gallagher. **FAI League Titles:** 2. 1937, 1977. **FAI Cups:** 2. 1983, 1994. **FAI League Cups:** 1. 1998.

UCD A.F.C. Founded: 1895. **Ground:** Belfield, Stillorgan, Co. Dublin. **Capacity:** 6,000. **Phone Number:** 01 2698099. **Colours:** Sky blue. **Manager:** Theo Dunne. **Chairman:** Gerald Horkan. **FAI League Titles:** 0. **FAI Cups:** 1. 1984. **FAI League Cups:** 0.

WATERFORD UNITED F.C. Founded: 1930. **Ground:** Regional Sports Centre, Cork Road, Waterford. **Capacity:** 8,250. **Phone Number:** 051 381036. **Colours:** Blue & White stripes. **Manager:** Mike Flanagan. **Chairman:** Bertie Rogers. **FAI League Titles:** 6. 1966, 1968, 1969, 1970, 1972, 1973. **FAI Cups:** 2. 1937, 1980. **FAI League Cups:** 2. 1974 and 1985.

NATIONAL LEAGUE FIRST DIVISION CLUB STATISTICS

ATHLONE TOWN F.C. Founded: 1887. **Ground:** St. Mel's Park, Athlone, Co. Westmeath. **Phone Number:** 0902 78377. **Capacity:** 10,200. **Colours:** Blue & Black stripes. **Manager:** James Coll. **Chairman:** Tony Knight. **FAI League Titles:** 2. 1981, 1983. **FAI Cups:** 1. 1924. **FAI League Cups:** 3. 1980, 1982, 1983.

COBH RAMBLERS F.C. Founded: 1922. **Ground:** St. Colman's Park, Cobh, Co. Cork. **Phone Number:** 021 812371. **Capacity:** 7,000. **Colours:** Claret & Blue. **Manager:** Stewart Ashton. **Chairman:** John O'Rourke. **FAI League Titles:** 0. **FAI Cups:** 0. **FAI League Cups:** 0.

DROGHEDA UNITED F.C. Founded: 1919. **Ground:** United Park, Windmill Road, Drogheda, Co. Louth. **Phone Number:** 041 30190. **Capacity:** 6,400. **Colours:** Claret & Blue. **Manager:** Martin Lawlor. **Chairman:** John Little. **FAI League Titles:** 0. **FAI Cups:** 0. **FAI League Cups:** 1. 1984.

GALWAY UNITED F.C. Founded: 1937. **Ground:** Terryland Park, Dyke Road, Galway. **Capacity:** 6,580. **Phone Number:** 091 561000. **Colours:** Maroon & Blue. **Manager:** Don O'Riordan. **Chairman:** Gerry Gray. **FAI League Titles:** 0. **FAI Cups:** 1. 1991. **FAI League Cups:** 2. 1986 and 1997.

HOME FARM EVERTON F.C. Founded: 1928. **Ground:** Whitehall, 97A Swords Road, Whitehall, Dublin 9. **Capacity:** 3,000. **Phone Number:** 01 8371001. **Colours:** Blue & White. **Manager:** Liam Brien **Chairman:** Willie O'Brien. **FAI League Titles:** 0. **FAI Cups:** 1. 1975. **FAI League Cups:** 0.

KILKENNY CITY F.C. Founded: 1966. **Ground:** Buckley Park, Tennypark, Kilkenny. **Capacity:** 6,900. **Phone Number:** 056 51888. **Colours:** Black & Amber. **Manager:** Alfie Hale. **President:** Patrick Henderson. **FAI League Titles:** 0. **FAI Cups:** 0. **FAI League Cups:** 0.

LIMERICK F.C. Founded: 1937. **Ground:** Hogan Park, Rathbane North, Limerick. **Capacity:** 10,000. **Phone Number:** 087 549124. **Colours:** Blue & White. **Manager:** Dave Connell. **Chairman:** Fr. Joe Young. **FAI League Titles:** 2. 1960, 1980. **FAI Cups:** 2. 1971, 1982. **FAI League Cups:** 2. 1976 and 1993.

LONGFORD TOWN F.C. Founded: 1924. **Ground:** Strokestown Road, Longford. **Capacity:** 8,750. **Phone Number:** 043 41637. **Colours:** Red & Black. **Manager:** Michael O'Connor. **Chairman:** Michael Cox. **FAI League Titles:** 0. **FAI Cups:** 0. **FAI League Cups:** 0.

MONAGHAN UNITED F.C. Founded: 1979. **Ground:** Gortakeegan, Newbliss Road, Monaghan. **Capacity:** 5,600. **Phone Number:** 047 84450. **Colours:** Blue & White. **Manager:** Tom O'Connor. **Chairman:** Eamon White. **FAI League Titles:** 0. **FAI Cups:** 0. **FAI League Cups:** 0.

ST. FRANCIS Founded: 1958. **Ground:** John Hyland Park, Baldonnel, Co. Dublin. **Capacity:** 2,000 **Phone Number:** 01 4594403. **Colours:** Green & White hoops. **Manager:** Pete Mahon. **Chairman:** Christy Maguire. **FAI League Titles:** 0. **FAI Cups:** 0. **FAI League Cups:** 0.

PAST PRESIDENTS

W.H. Ritchie; Sir H. McLaughlin; J. Cunningham; O. Grattan-Esmond; Dr. W.F. Hooper; O. Traynor T.D.; D. O'Malley T.D.; N.T. Blaney T.D.; D. O'Halloran; C.H. Walsh; F. Davis; C. Cahill; Dr. B. Menton; J.J. Farrell; D. Casey; P. O'Brien; F. Fields; M. Hyland; L.D. Kilcoyne; Pat Quigley (current).

Irish Football Association

20 Windsor Avenue, Belfast BT9 6EG. Tel. (01232) 669458

Founded 1880
President .... Jim Boyce

1997/98 Season	Winners	Runners Up
Irish League, Premier Division	Cliftonville	Linfield
Irish League, First Division	Newry Town	Bangor
Bass Irish Cup	Glentoran	Glenavon
Nationwide Gold Cup	Glenavon	Coleraine
Ulster Cup	Ballyclare Comrades	Distillery
Coca Cola Cup	Linfield	Cliftonville
Calor Co. Antrim Shield	Linfield	Crusaders
Irish News Cup	Omagh Town	Ballymena United
Main Stadium and Capacity		Windsor Park (28,500)

INTERNATIONAL

Northern Ireland Manager .... Lawrie McMenemy
Top International Goalscorer .... Colin Clarke (13 goals in 38 apperances)
Most Capped Player .... Pat Jennings (119 caps)
Best World Cup Result .... Quarter finals (1958 World Cup in Sweden)

INTERNATIONAL RESULTS

Northern Ireland World Cup Qualifying Results 1996-97

Date	Venue	Home Team	Score	Away Team	Score
31.08.98	Windsor Park	Northern Ireland	0	Ukraine	1
05.10.96	Windsor Park	Northern Ireland Lennon	1	Armenia	1
09.11.96	Nurnburg	Germany	1	Northern Ireland Taggart	1
14.12.96	Windsor Park	Northern Ireland Dowie (2)	2	Albania	0
29.03.97	Windsor Park	Northern Ireland	0	Portugal	0
02.04.97	Kiev	Ukraine	2	Northern Ireland Dowie (Pen)	1
30.04.97	Yerevan	Armenia	0	Northern Ireland	0
20.08.97	Windsor Park	Northern Ireland Michael Hughes	1	Germany	3
10.09.97	Zurich	Albania	1	Northern Ireland	0
11.10.97	Lisbon	Portugal	1	Northern Ireland	0

UEFA Group Nine Final Table

	P	W	D	L	F	A	Pts
Germany	10	6	4	0	23	9	22
Ukraine	10	6	2	2	10	6	20
Portugal	10	5	4	1	12	4	19
Armenia	10	1	5	4	8	17	8
Northern Ireland	10	1	4	5	6	10	7
Albania	10	1	1	8	7	20	4

Northern Ireland Friendly Results

Date	Venue	Home Team	Score	Away Team	Score
25.03.98	Windsor Park	Northern Ireland Lomas	1	Slovakia	0
22.04.98	Windsor Park	Northern Ireland Patterson	1	Switzerland	0
03.06.98	Santander	Spain	4	Northern Ireland Taggart	1

Northern Ireland European Cup Qualifying Results 1998-99

Date	Venue	Home Team	Score	Away Team	Score
05.09.98	Istanbul	Turkey	3	Northern Ireland	0
10.10.98	Windsor Park	Northern Ireland Rowland	1	Finland	0

Remaining Fixtures: 18.11.98: Northern Ireland v Moldova; 27.03.99: Northern Ireland v Germany; 31.03.99 Moldova v Northern Ireland; 04.09.99: Northern Ireland v Turkey; 08.09.99: Germany v Northern Ireland; 09.10.99 Finlad v Northern Ireland.

Northern Ireland U21 International Results, 1997/98

Date	Venue	Competition	Home Team	Score	Away Team	Score
21.04.98	Lurgan	Friendly	Northern Ireland Mulryne (Pen), Coote	2	Switzerland	1
20.05.98	Sligo	P. Cup	Scotland	1	Northern Ireland Mulryne	1
22.05.98	Castlebar	P. Cup	Republic of Ireland	0	Northern Ireland Coote	1
Northern Ireland win President's Cup						
22.09.98	Coleraine	Friendly	Northern Ireland Convery	1	Germany	2
24.09.98	Ballymena	Friendly	Northern Ireland	0	Germany	0
04.05.98	Cocail (Turkey)	ECQ	Turkey	2	Northern Ireland	0
09.10.98	Windsor Park	ECQ	Northern Ireland Coote	1	Finland	1

ECQ=European Championship Qualifier P. Cup= President's Cup

Northern Ireland U18 International Results, 1997/98

Date	Venue	Competition	Home Team	Score	Away Team	Score
07.10.97	Dublin	Friendly	Republic of Ireland	4	Northern Ireland	0
03.11.97	Bangor	ECQ	Northern Ireland Boyle	1	Croatia	2
07.11.97	Belfast	ECQ	Northern Ireland Harkin, Healey (2), Graham, Hughes	5	Andorra	0
22.08.98	Connah's Quay	ECQ	Northern Ireland Hawe (2), McCann	3	Azerbaijan	0
24.08.98	Bangor	ECQ	Wales	1	Northern Ireland Hamilton, McAreavey	2
26.08.98	Bangor	ECQ	Northern Ireland Hamilton, McAreavey	2	Moldova	0

ECQ=European Championship Qualifier

Northern Ireland U16 International Results, 1997/98

Date	Venue	Competition	Home Team	Score	Away Team	Score
30.01.98	Lurgan	Friendly	Northern Ireland Morrison	1	Scotland	2
23.02.98	Portadown	ECQ	Northern Ireland Simms	1	Belgium	0
27.02.98	Lurgan	ECQ	Northern Ireland	0	Republic of Ireland	0

ECQ=European Championship Qualifier

DOMESTIC RESULTS, 1997/98 SEASON

IFA IRISH LEAGUE: 1997/98 Premier Division Results

	Ards	Ballymena	Cliftonville	Coleraine	Crusaders	Glenavon	Glentoran	Linfield	Omagh	Portadown
Ards	----	2-1	2-3	0-0	1-1	3-4	1-1	0-1	2-2	1-1
	----	0-2	1-1	1-0	0-1	1-1	0-2	1-5	1-2	0-1
Ballymena United	3-1	----	2-0	1-0	2-3	0-0	0-2	1-1	4-2	1-2
	1-1	----	4-0	2-2	1-0	2-1	1-2	0-2	2-1	1-2
Cliftonville	1-0	0-2	----	3-1	2-2	1-1	0-2	2-1	4-0	3-1
	2-2	5-2	----	1-0	0-1	1-0	1-1	0-3	1-0	1-0
Coleraine	2-1	0-1	5-1	----	4-0	1-2	2-1	1-0	4-3	0-1
	2-2	0-0	0-2	----	0-0	0-1	1-5	0-0	1-1	2-0
Crusaders	4-0	4-2	2-2	1-3	----	3-2	0-2	1-0	1-0	1-3
	1-0	3-4	0-2	3-0	----	4-1	0-3	1-2	2-2	2-1
Glenavon	1-2	1-2	0-0	1-1	2-0	----	1-0	2-3	2-2	1-5
	0-0	3-3	0-0	4-0	2-2	----	1-0	2-4	2-4	3-0
Glentoran	3-0	1-2	0-2	1-0	1-1	0-1	----	0-3	1-0	1-1
	2-0	2-2	1-0	3-0	1-1	1-0	----	1-1	2-0	2-1
Linfield	4-0	0-0	0-1	1-1	0-0	1-1	2-0	----	1-1	0-0
	2-0	1-0	0-1	1-0	0-0	2-0	3-0	----	0-0	1-1
Omagh Town	2-4	3-2	0-1	1-3	1-1	2-2	1-1	1-0	----	1-2
	2-1	3-0	0-1	1-3	1-2	2-1	0-5	0-3	----	0-2
Portadown	1-0	1-1	0-2	0-1	1-1	2-1	3-2	0-2	3-1	----
	1-0	4-0	1-2	1-1	3-2	2-0	2-0	0-0	1-1	----

1997/98 First Division Results

	Ballyclare	Bangor	Carrick	Distillery	Dungannon	Larne	Limavady	Newry
Ballyclare Comrades	----	0-1	1-1	0-3	0-1	3-1	3-2	0-2
	----	2-1	2-0	2-4	3-2	2-0	0-1	2-2
Bangor	1-2	----	3-2	3-0	1-2	2-0	0-0	1-0
	2-1	----	2-1	2-2	3-0	1-0	4-0	1-2
Carrick Rangers	0-1	0-2	----	1-2	0-0	0-1	3-1	1-4
	2-3	1-2	----	1-2	1-3	2-1	0-3	0-5
Distillery	2-1	2-1	1-0	----	2-2	0-2	3-0	2-2
	1-5	1-2	1-0	----	1-2	3-0	0-0	1-0
Dungannon Swifts	4-5	3-3	2-1	2-2	----	4-2	9-0	0-4
	3-1	3-4	4-1	0-2	----	4-3	2-1	1-1
Larne	1-1	1-2	1-0	3-2	1-2	----	3-2	0-2
	3-2	0-3	1-2	0-1	2-2	----	1-0	0-6
Limavady United	1-2	0-3	4-0	0-5	1-2	5-1	----	2-0
	0-2	0-1	1-0	0-1	1-3	1-2	----	1-3
Newry Town	3-1	0-0	3-0	2-1	2-1	3-0	4-1	----
	1-0	1-0	3-0	1-1	1-0	1-0	3-1	----

DOMESTIC RESULTS

Premier Division Final Table 1997/98

	P	W	D	L	F	A	Pts
Cliftonville	36	20	8	8	49	37	68
Linfield	36	17	13	6	50	19	64
Portadown	36	17	9	10	50	38	60
Glentoran	36	17	8	11	52	34	59
Crusaders	36	13	12	11	51	51	51
Ballymena United	36	14	9	13	54	55	51
Coleraine	36	11	10	15	41	47	43
Glenavon	36	9	12	15	47	56	39
Omagh Town	36	7	10	19	43	68	31
Ards	36	4	11	21	31	63	23

Top Scorer:
Vinny Arkins ....**Portadown**...................**22**
Ards relegated. Omagh won a two leg playoff with Bangor to retain Premier Division status.

First Division Final Table 1997/98

	P	W	D	L	F	A	Pts
Newry Town	28	20	5	3	61	18	65
Bangor	28	18	4	6	51	26	58
Distillery	28	15	6	7	48	34	51
Dungannon Swifts	28	14	6	8	63	49	48
Ballyclare Comrades	28	13	3	12	47	45	42
Larne	28	8	2	18	30	58	26
Limavady United	28	6	2	20	29	60	20
Carrick Rangers	28	3	2	23	20	59	11

Top Scorer:
Crawford McCrae.............**Ballyclare Comrades**....**23**

Newry Town promoted.

1997/98 Bass Irish Cup

First Round

AFC Craigavon................1....Annagh United............3
Abbey Villa.......................3....Civil Service.................1
Ards Rangers....................2....Donard Hospital...........0
Ballycastle United............0....Islandmagee..................1
Ballymacash Rangers......1....Northern Telecom........4
Barn United.......................0....Rathfriland Rangers.....2
Bessbrook United.............1....Wellington Recreation .3
Bridgend United...............2....Orangefield Old Boys...4
Cullbackey.........................2....Armoy United..............4
Downshire Young Men......3....Portstewart...................1
Dromore Amatuers...........3....Shorts Brothers.............1
Dungiven............................4....Saintfield United...........2
First Bangor Old Boys......3....Ballynahinch United.....1
Glebe Rangers..................5....Laurelvale.....................0
Killyleagh Youth Club.......0....Dromara Village...........0
Malachians........................5....UUC...............................1
Portglenone.......................1....Bangor Amatuers..........0
Queens University............4....Mountnorris...................4
Roe Valley..........................3....Harland & Wolff..............2
Seapatrick..........................1....Albert Foundry...............6
Sirocco Works....................0....Drummond United........5
Tandragee Rovers.............5....East Belfast...................5
UUJ....................................3....Comber Recreation......4
Warrenpoint Town.............2....Larne Tech Old Boys ...1

First Round Replays

Dromara Village..............1....Killyleagh Youth Club ...5
East Belfast.......................9.... Tandragee Rovers.......0
Mountnorris.......................5....Queens University........3

Second Round

Albert Foundry...................2....Abbey Villa.....................0
Annagh United...................2....Downshire Young Men .1
Ards Rangers.....................2....Mountnorris...................1
Armoy United.....................0....Portglenone...................2
Dromore Amateurs............3....East Belfast...................1
Drummond United............1....Comber Recreation.......3
Dungiven............................1....Islandmagee..................0
(match abandoned 44 minutes)
Killyleagh Youth Club........8....Wellington Recreation..0
Malachians.........................3....Glebe Rangers...............1
Rathfriland Rangers.........1....First Bangor Old Boys .1
Roe Valley..........................3....Orangefield Old Boys...1
Warrenpoint Town.............3....Northern Telecom........9
Dungiven............................2....Islandmagee..................0

Second Round Replay

First Bangor Old Boys ....Rathfriland Rangers.......
(First Bangor Old Boys won 4-2 on pens)

Third Round A

Annagh United..................1....Northern Telecom........2
Ards Rangers.....................6....Dungiven........................1
First Bangor Old Boys......4....Portglenone...................4
Killyleagh Youth Club........6....Malachians.....................1

Third Round A, Replay

Portglenone.......................3....First Bangor Old Boys .4

Third Round B

Ards Rangers.....................2....First Bangor Old Boys .0
Albert Foundry...................4....Comber Recreation.......3
Dromore Amateurs............3....Killyleagh Youth Club ...3
Northern Telecom..............7....Roe Valley......................2

Third Round B Replay

Killyleagh Youth Club........6....Dromore Amateurs.......1

Fourth Round

Ballymoney United.............2....Kilmore Recreation 1
Banbridge Town.................1....RUC 3
British Telecom..................1....Armagh City...................7
Chimney Corner.................6....Coagh United.................0
Crumlin United...................3....Crewe United.................0
Donegal Celtic....................1....Killyleagh Youth Club ...1
Drumaness Mills................0....Brantwood.....................0
Dundela..............................7....Moyola Park...................1
Dunmurry Recreation........3....Cookstown United.........1
FC Enkalon........................1....Ballinamallard United...2
Institute.............................5....Northern Telecom 1
Tobermore United.............6....Albert Foundry..............0

Fourth Round Replays

Brantwood.........................4....Drumaness Mills............2
Donegal Celtic....................0....Killyleagh Youth Club ...2

Fifth Round

Ards...................................0....Institute.........................2
Ballyclare Comrades.........5....Ballymoney United.........1
Ballymena United..............1....Glentoran.......................1
Carrick Rangers................2....Armagh City...................3
Cliftonville.........................0....Glenavon........................2
Coleraine...........................3....Chimney Corner.............1
Crusaders..........................1....Bangor...........................0
Distillery............................2....RUC...............................0

Drumaness Mills	0	Killyleagh Youth Club	0
Dungannon Swifts	6	Ballinamallard United	2
Dunmurry Recreation	0	Ards Rangers	4
Larne	1	Portadown	2
Linfield	1	Tobermore United	0
Loughgall	4	Crumlin United	0
Newry Town	1	Dundela	0
Omagh Town	3	Limavady United	0

Fifth Round Replays

Drumaness Mills	0	Killyleagh Youth Club	2
Glentoran	2	Ballymena United	1

Sixth Round

Armagh City	0	Ards Rangers	0
Crusaders	2	Killyleagh Youth Club	1
Dungannon Swifts	0	Institute	1
Glenavon	0	Ballyclare Comrades	0
Glentoran	3	Coleraine	2
Linfield	2	Newry Town	1
Loughgall	1	Distillery	2
Portadown	2	Omagh Town	0

Sixth Round Replays

Armagh City	3	Ards Rangers	1
Ballyclare Comrades	0	Glenavon	4

Quarter-Finals

Crusaders	4	Institute	0
Distillery	0	Glenavon	2
Glentoran	3	Armagh City	1
Linfield	3	Portadown	0

Semi-Finals

Glenavon	3	Crusaders	1
Linfield	1	Glentoran	2

Bass Irish Cup Final

WINDSOR PARK, BELFAST Saturday 2nd May 1998. Attendance: 8,250. **Half Time Score:** Glentoran 0, Glenavon 0. **Full Time Score:** Glentoran 0, Glenavon 0. **Final Score:** Glentoran 1, Glenavon 0 (aet). **Booked:** Mark Glendinning (Glenavon). **Referee:** L. Irvine (Limavady).

Glentoran: Russell, Nixon, Kennedy, Walker, Devine, Leeman, Mitchell, Finlay, Kirk, Batey, Hamill. Subs: Livingstone for Leeman (97 mins): Subs not used; Elliott; Smyth.

Glenavon: O'Neill, Wright, Glendinning, Quigley, Cash, Smyth, McCoy, Byrne, Shepherd, Grant, Caffrey. Subs: Murphy for Cash (80 mins); O'Flaherty for Wright (102 mins); Welch for O'Neill (108 mins).

Nationwide Gold Cup, 1997/98

Section A

Dungannon Swifts	1	Crusaders	2
Larne	1	Glenavon	3
Ballyclare Comrades	1	Ballymena United	0
Ballymena United	0	Larne	2
Crusaders	3	Ballyclare Comrades	1
Glenavon	3	Dungannon Swifts	0
Ballyclare Comrades	2	Glenavon	4
Crusaders	3	Ballymena United	2
Dungannon Swifts	4	Larne	0
Dungannon Swifts	2	Ballymena United	5
Glenavon	1	Crusaders	1
Larne	2	Ballyclare Comrades	1
Ballyclare Comrades	2	Dungannon Swifts	3
Ballymena United	1	Glenavon	1
Larne	1	Crusaders	2

Section B

Distillery	2	Linfield	0
Limavady United	1	Coleraine	4
Bangor	2	Ards	3
Ards	2	Distillery	0
Coleraine	2	Bangor	1
Linfield	7	Limavady United	0
Bangor	1	Linfield	0
Coleraine	5	Ards	2
Limavady United	2	Distillery	4
Distillery	1	Bangor	1
Limavady United	1	Ards	1
Linfield	3	Coleraine	1
Ards	1	Linfield	5
Bangor	2	Limavady United	0
Distillery	3	Coleraine	1

Section C

Carrick Rangers	0	Glentoran	1
Newry Town	2	Portadown	0
Omagh Town	0	Cliftonville	0
Cliftonville	2	Newry Town	0
Glentoran	1	Omagh Town	4
Portadown	6	Carrick Rangers	0
Carrick Rangers	0	Newry Town	1
Glentoran	0	Cliftonville	0
Omagh Town	2	Portadown	0
Carrick Rangers	0	Cliftonville	3
Newry Town	0	Omagh Town	1
Portadown	7	Glentoran	3
Newry Town	2	Glentoran	1
Omagh Town	2	Carrick Rangers	2
Cliftonville	1	Portadown	1

Quarter-Finals

Cliftonville	0	Coleraine	1(aet)
Linfield	0	Glenavon	1
Newry Town	0	Crusaders	1
Omagh Town	3	Distillery	1

Semi-Finals

Glenavon	3	Crusaders	1
Coleraine	3	Omagh Town	1

Final

Glenavon	4	Coleraine	2

NORTHERN IRELAND SENIOR TEAM FACTFILE

Name	Club	Position	D.O.B.	Born	Caps	Goals	Debut
DOWIE, Iain	Queens Park Rangers	Striker	09.01.65	Hatfield	51	11	27.03.90
FETTIS, Alan	Blackburn Rovers	Goalkeeper	01.02.71	Belfast	24	0	13.11.91
GILLESPIE, Keith	Newcastle United	Midfielder	18.02.75	Larne	23	1	07.09.94
HILL, Colin	Northampton Town	Defender	12.11.63	Uxbridge	27	1	27.03.90
HORLOCK, Kevin	Manchester City	Midfielder	01.11.72	Erith	15	0	26.04.95
HUGHES, Aaron	Newcastle United	Defender	08.11.79	Magherafelt	5	0	25.03.98
HUGHES, Michael	Wimbledon	Midfielder	02.08.71	Larne	44	3	13.11.91
JENKINS, Iain	Dundee United	Defender	24.12.72	Whiston	5	0	30.04.97
LENNON, Neil	Leicester City	Midfielder	25.06.71	Lurgan	23	1	11.06.94
LOMAS, Steve	West Ham United	Midfielder	18.01.74	Hanover	26	2	23.03.94
MAGILTON, Jim	Sheffield Wednesday	Midfielder	06.05.69	Belfast	39	5	05.02.91
McCARTHY, Jon	Birmingham City	Midfielder	18.08.70	Mid'brough	8	0	24.04.96
McMAHON, Gerry	St. Johnstone	Striker	29.12.73	Belfast	17	2	22.05.95
MORROW, Steve	Queens Park Rangers	Defender	02.07.70	Bangor	34	1	18.05.90
MULRYNE, Philip	Manchester United	Midfielder	01.01.78	Belfast	7	1	11.02.97
NOLAN, Ian	Sheffield Wednesday	Defender	09.07.70	Liverpool	7	0	05.10.96
O'BOYLE, George	St. Johnstone	Striker	14.12.67	Belfast	13	1	03.06.94
PATTERSON, Darren	Dundee United	Defender	15.10.69	Belfast	12	1	03.06.94
QUINN, James	West Bromwich Albion	Striker	15.12.74	Coventry	14	1	24.04.96
ROWLAND, Keith	Queens Park Rangers	Defender	01.09.71	Portadown	15	1	08.09.93
TAGGART, Gerry	Leicester City	Defender	10.10.70	Belfast	45	7	27.03.90
WHITLEY, Jeff	Manchester City	Midfielder	28.01.79	Zambia	3	0	11.02.97
WHITLEY, Jim	Manchester City	Midfielder	14.04.75	Zambia	2	0	03.06.98

Details correct as of 10.10.98

Northern Ireland teams since October 1997

Name	Total	Portugal 11.10.97	Slovakia 25.03.98	Switzerland 22.04.98	Spain 03.06.98	Turkey 05.09.98	Finland 10.10.98
DOWIE, Iain	6	●	●	●	●	●	●
FETTIS, Alan	6	●	●	●	●	●	●
GILLESPIE, Keith	4		●	●		●	●
HILL, Colin	3	●	●			●	
HORLOCK, Kevin	3	●				●	●
HUGHES, Aaron	5		●	●	●	●	●
HUGHES, Michael	6	●	●	●	●	●	●
JENKINS, Iain	3		●	●	●		
LENNON, Neil	6	●	●	●	●	●	●
LOMAS, Steve	3	●	●	●			
MAGILTON, Jim	2	●			●		
McCARTHY, Jon	4	●(S)	●(S)		●		●(S)
McMAHON, Gerry	1	●(S)					
MORROW, Steve	6	●	●	●	●	●	●
MULRYNE, Philip	3				●(S)	●	●
NOLAN, Ian	1	●					
O'BOYLE, George	3		●(S)	●(S)			●(S)
PATTERSON, Darren	3			●	●(S)		●
QUINN, James	4		●	●		●(S)	●(S)
ROWLAND, Keith	2					●	●
TAGGART, Gerry	2	●			●		
WHITLEY, Jeff	1				●(S)		
WHITLEY, Jim	2				●	●(S)	

(S)=Substitute

IFA RECORDS

Irish Cup Final Results

Year	Winner	Runners Up	Score
1881	Moyola Park	Cliftonville	1-0
1882	Queen's Island	Cliftonville	1-0
1883	Cliftonville	Ulster	5-0
1884	Distillery	Wellington Park	5-0
1885	Distillery	Limavady	2-0
1886	Distillery	Limavady	1-0
1887	Ulster	Cliftonville	3-1
1888	Cliftonville	Distillery	2-1
1889	Distillery	Belfast YMCA	5-4
1890	Gordon Highlanders	Cliftonville	3-0
	Gordon Highlanders	*Cliftonville*	*2-2*
1891	Linfield	Ulster	4-2
1892	Linfield	Black Watch	7-0
1893	Linfield	Cliftonville	5-1
1894	Distillery	Linfield	3-2
	Distillery	*Linfield*	*2-2*
1895	Linfield	Bohemians	10-1
1896	Distillery	Glentoran	3-1
1897	Cliftonville	Sherwood Foresters	3-1
1898	Linfield	St Columb's Hall	2-0
1899	Linfield	Glentoran	1-0
1900	Cliftonville	Bohemians	2-1
1901	Cliftonville	Freebooters	1-0
1902	Linfield	Distillery	5-1
1903	Distillery	Bohemians	3-1
1904	Linfield	Derry City	5-0
1905	Distillery	Shelbourne	3-0
1906	Shelbourne	Belfast Celtic	2-0
1907	Cliftonville	Shelbourne	1-0
	Cliftonville	*Shelbourne*	*0-0*
1908	Bohemians	Shelbourne	3-1
	Bohemians	*Shelbourne*	*1-1*
1909	Cliftonville	Bohemians	2-1
	Cliftonville	*Bohemians*	*0-0*
1910	Distillery	Cliftonville	1-0
1911	Shelbourne	Bohemians	2-1
	Shelbourne	*Bohemians*	*0-0*
1912	Linfield	Awarded Cup	
1913	Linfield	Glentoran	2-0
1914	Glentoran	Linfield	3-1
1915	Linfield	Belfast Celtic	1-0
1916	Linfield	Glentoran	1-0
	Linfield	*Glentoran*	*1-1*
1917	Glentoran	Belfast Celtic	2-0
1918	Belfast Celtic	Linfield	2-0
	Belfast Celtic	*Linfield*	*0-0*
	Belfast Celtic	*Linfield*	*0-0*
1919	Linfield	Glentoran	2-1
	Linfield	*Glentoran*	*1-1*
	Linfield	*Glentoran*	*0-0*
1920	Shelbourne	Awarded cup	
1921	Glentoran	Glenavon	2-0
1922	Linfield	Glenavon	2-1
1923	Linfield	Glentoran	2-0
1924	Queen's Island	Willowfield	1-0
1925	Distillery	Glentoran	2-1
1926	Belfast Celtic	Linfield	3-2
1927	Ards	Cliftonville	3-2
1928	Willowfield	Larne	1-0
	Willowfield	*Larne*	*1-1*
1929	Ballymena	Belfast Celtic	2-1
Year	**Winner**	**Runners Up**	**Score**
1930	Linfield	Ballymena	4-3
1931	Linfield	Ballymena	3-0
1932	Glentoran	Linfield	2-1
1933	Glentoran	Distillery	3-1
	Glentoran	*Distillery*	*1-1*
	Glentoran	*Distillery*	*1-1*
1934	Linfield	Cliftonville	5-0
1935	Glentoran	Larne	1-0
	Glentoran	*Larne*	*0-0*
	Glentoran	*Larne*	*0-0*
1936	Linfield	Derry City	2-1 aet
	Linfield	*Derry City*	*0-0*
1937	Belfast Celtic	Linfield	3-0
1938	Belfast Celtic	Bangor	2-0
	Belfast Celtic	*Bangor*	*0-0*
1939	Linfield	Ballymena United	2-0
1940	Ballymena United	Glenavon	2-0
1941	Belfast Celtic	Linfield	1-0
1942	Linfield	Glentoran	3-1
1943	Belfast Celtic	Glentoran	1-0
1944	Belfast Celtic	Linfield	3-1
1945	Linfield	Glentoran	4-2
1946	Linfield	Distillery	3-0
1947	Belfast Celtic	Glentoran	1-0
1948	Linfield	Coleraine	3-0
1949	Derry City	Glentoran	3-1
1950	Linfield	Distillery	2-1
1951	Glentoran	Ballymena	3-1
1952	Ards	Glentoran	1-0
1953	Linfield	Coleraine	5-0
1954	Derry City	Glentoran	1-0
	Derry City	*Glentoran*	*2-2*
	Derry City	*Glentoran*	*0-0*
1955	Dundela	Glenavon	3-0
1956	Distillery	Glentoran	1-0
	Distillery	*Glentoran*	*2-2*
	Distillery	*Glentoran*	*1-1*
1957	Glenavon	Derry City	2-0
1958	Ballymena United	Linfield	2-0
1959	Glenavon	Ballymena United	2-0
	Glenavon	*Ballymena United*	*1-1*
1960	Linfield	Ards	5-1
1961	Glenavon	Linfield	5-1
1962	Linfield	Portadown	4-0
1963	Linfield	Distillery	2-1
1964	Derry City	Glentoran	2-0
1965	Coleraine	Glenavon	2-1
1966	Glentoran	Linfield	2-0
1967	Crusaders	Glentoran	3-1
1968	Crusaders	Linfield	2-0
1969	Ards	Distillery	4-2 aet
	Ards	*Distillery*	*0-0*
1970	Linfield	Ballymena United	2-1
1971	Distillery	Derry City	3-0
1972	Coleraine	Portadown	2-1
1973	Glentoran	Linfield	3-2
1974	Ards	Ballymena United	2-1

Year	Winner	Runners Up	Score
1975	Coleraine	Linfield	1-0
	Coleraine	*Linfield*	*1-1*
	Coleraine	*Linfield*	*0-0*
1976	Carrick Rangers	Linfield	2-1
1977	Coleraine	Linfield	4-1
1978	Linfield	Ballymena United	3-1
1979	Cliftonville	Portadown	3-2
1980	Linfield	Crusaders	2-0
1981	Ballymena United	Glenavon	1-0
1982	Linfield	Coleraine	2-1
1983	Glentoran	Linfield	2-1
	Glentoran	*Linfield*	*1-1*
1984	Ballymena United	Carrick Rangers	4-1
1985	Glentoran	Linfield	1-0
	Glentoran	*Linfield*	*1-1*
1986	Glentoran	Coleraine	2-1
1987	Glentoran	Larne	1-0
1988	Glentoran	Glenavon	1-0
1989	Ballymena United	Larne	1-0
1990	Glentoran	Portadown	3-0
1991	Portadown	Glenavon	2-1
1992	Glenavon	Linfield	2-1
1993	Bangor	Ards	1-0
	Bangor	*Ards*	*1-1*
	Bangor	*Ards*	*1-1*
1994	Linfield	Bangor	2-0
1995	Linfield	Carrick Rangers	3-1
1996	Glentoran	Glenavon	1-0
1997	Glenavon	Cliftonville	1-0
1998	Glenavon	Glentoran	1-0 aet

aet= after extra time
Results given in italics are from drawn finals.

IRISH LEAGUE PREMIER DIVISION CLUB STATISTICS

BALLYMENA UNITED Founded: 1928 **Ground:** The Showgrounds, Warden Street, Ballymena. **Capacity:** 8,000. **Phone Number:** 01266 659490. **Colours:** Sky Blue & White. **Manager:** Alan Fraser. **Chairman:** Edwin McLaughlin. **Irish League Titles:** 0. **Irish Cup:** 6 1929, 1940, 1958, 1981, 1984, 1989.

CLIFTONVILLE Founded: 1879 **Ground:** Solitude, Cliftonville Street, Belfast BT 14 6LP. **Capacity:** 8,000. **Phone Number:** 01232 754628. **Colours:** Red & White. **Manager:** Marty Quinn. **Chairman:** Harry McCourt **Irish League Titles:** 3. 1906, 1910, 1998. **Irish Cups:** 8. 1883, 1888, 1897, 1900, 1901, 1907, 1909, 1979.

COLERAINE Founded: 1927. **Ground:** The Showgrounds, Ballycastle Road, Coleraine. **Capacity:** 12,500 **Phone Number:** 01265 53655. **Colours:** Blue & White. **Manager:** Kenny Shiels. **Chairman:** Sammy Lyle. **Irish League Titles:** 1. 1974. **Irish Cups:** 4. 1965, 1972, 1975, 1977.

CRUSADERS Founded: 1898. **Ground:** Seaview, Shore Road, Belfast BT 15 3PL. **Capacity:** 9,000. **Phone Number:** 01232 370777. **Colours:** Red & Black. **Player/Manager:** Aaron Callaghan. **Chairman:** Jim Semple. **Irish League Titles:** 4. 1973, 1976, 1995, 1997. **Irish Cups:** 2. 1967, 1968.

GLENAVON Founded: 1889. **Ground:** Mourneview Park, Mourneview Avenue, Lurgan BT 66 8EW. **Capacity:** 10,971. **Phone Number:** 01762 325047. **Colours:** Royal Blue & White. **Manager:** Roy Walker. **Chairman:** Adrian Teer. **Irish League Titles:** 3. 1952, 1957, 1960. **Irish Cups:** 5. 1957, 1959, 1961, 1992, 1997.

GLENTORAN Founded: 1882. **Ground:** The Oval Grounds, Mersey Street, Belfast BT 41FG. **Capacity:** 30,000. **Phone Number:** 01232 457670. **Colours:** Green, Red & Black. **Manager:** Roy Coyle. **Chairman:** Ted Brownlee. **Irish League Titles:** 19. 1894, 1897, 1905, 1912, 1913, 1921, 1925, 1931, 1951, 1953, 1964, 1967, 1968, 1970, 1972, 1977, 1981, 1988, 1992. **Irish Cups:** 17. 1914, 1917, 1921, 1932, 1933, 1935, 1951, 1966, 1973, 1983, 1985, 1986, 1987, 1988, 1990, 1996, 1998.

LINFIELD Founded: 1886. **Ground:** Windsor Park, Donegall Avenue, Belfast BT12 6LW. **Capacity:** 28,500. **Phone Number:** 01232 244198. **Colours:** Royal Blue & White. **Manager:** David Jeffrey. **Chairman:** Billy McCoubrey. **Irish League Titles:** 42. 1891, 1892, 1893, 1895, 1898, 1902, 1904, 1907, 1908, 1909, 1911, 1914, 1922, 1923, 1930, 1932, 1934, 1935, 1949, 1950, 1954, 1955, 1956, 1959, 1961, 1962, 1966, 1969, 1971, 1975, 1978, 1979, 1980, 1982, 1983, 1984, 1985, 1986, 1987, 1989, 1993, 1994. **Irish Cups:** 35. 1891, 1892, 1893, 1895, 1898, 1899, 1902, 1904, 1912, 1913, 1915, 1916, 1919, 1922, 1923, 1930, 1932, 1934, 1936, 1939, 1942, 1945, 1946, 1948, 1950, 1953, 1960, 1962, 1963, 1970, 1978, 1980, 1982, 1994, 1995.

NEWRY TOWN Founded: 1923 **Ground:** The Showgrounds, Newry. **Capacity:** 5,000. **Phone Number:** 01693 252581. **Colours:** Blue & White. **Joint Managers:** Ollie Ralph & Harry Fay. **Chairman:** Joe Rice. **Irish League Titles:** 0 **Irish Cups:** 0.

OMAGH TOWN Founded: 1962. **Ground:** St Julian's Road, Mullaghmore, Omagh. **Capacity:** 8,000. **Phone Number:** 01662 242927. **Colours:** Black & White. **Manager:** Roy McCreadie. **Irish League Titles:** 0. **Irish Cups:** 0.

PORTADOWN Founded: 1924. **Ground:** Shamrock Park, Brownstown Road, Portadown. **Capacity:** 15,000. **Phone Number:** 01762 332726. **Colours:** Red. **Manager:** Ronnie McFall. **Chairman:** Roy McMahon. **Irish League Titles:** 3 1990, 1991, 1996. **Irish Cups:** 1. 1991.

❐

IRISH LEAGUE FIRST DIVISION CLUB STATISTICS

ARDS Founded: 1902. **Ground:** Castlereagh Park, Newtownards. **Capacity:** 10,000. **Phone Number:** 01247 813370. **Colours:** Red & Blue. **Manager:** Tommy Cassidy. **Irish League Titles:** 1. 1958. **Irish Cups:** 4. 1927, 1952, 1969, 1974.

BALLYCLARE COMRADES Founded: 1919. **Ground:** Dixon Park, Ballyclare. **Capacity:** 4,500. **Phone Number:** 019603 52319. **Colours:** Red & White. **Manager:** Alan Campbell. **Chairman:** George Herron. **Irish League Titles:** 0. **Irish Cups:** 0.

BANGOR Founded: 1918. **Ground:** Clandeboye Park, Clandeboye Road, Bangor. **Capacity:** 5,000. **Phone Number:** 01247 457712. **Colours:** Gold & Royal Blue. **Player/Manager:** Stephen McBride. **Chairman:** Hugh Ashe. **Irish League Titles:** 0 **Irish Cups:** 1. 1993.

CARRICK RANGERS Founded: 1939. **Ground:** Taylor's Avenue, Carrickfergus. **Capacity:** 5,000. **Phone Number:** 01960 351009. **Colours:** Amber & Black. **Manager:** Jim O'Rourke. **Chairman:** D. Kelly. **Irish League Titles:** 0. **Irish Cups:** 1. 1976.

DISTILLERY Founded: 1879. **Ground:** New Grosvenor Stadium, Ballyskeagh, Lambeg, Lisburn. **Capacity:** 7,000. **Phone Number:** 01232 301148. **Colours:** White & Dark Blue. **Manager:** Paul Kirk. **Chairman:** T. Allen. **Irish League Titles:** 6. 1896, 1899, 1901, 1903, 1906, 1963. **Irish Cups:** 12. 1884, 1885, 1886, 1889, 1894, 1896, 1903, 1905, 1910, 1925, 1956, 1971.

DUNGANNON SWIFTS Founded: 1949. **Ground:** Stangmore Park, Dungannon. **Capacity:** 5,000. **Phone Number:** 01868 723257. **Colours:** Royal Blue & White. **Manager:** Colm Malone. **Chairman:** David Flack. **Irish League Titles:** 0. **Irish Cups:** 0.

LARNE Founded: 1900. **Ground:** Inver Park, Inver Road, Larne. **Capacity:** 12,000. **Phone Number:** 01574 274292. **Colours:** Red & White. **Manager:** Frankie Parks. **Chairman:** Sam McCready. **Irish League Titles:** 0. **Irish Cups:** 0.

LIMAVADY UNITED Founded: 1876. **Ground:** The Showgrounds, Rathmore Road, Limavady. **Capacity:** 1,000. **Phone Number:** 01504 764351. **Colours:** Royal Blue & White. **Manager:** Jimmy Calvin. **Chairman:** William Dunn. **Irish League Titles:** 0. **Irish Cups:** 0. ❐

PAST PRESIDENTS

1881-1914 .... Lord Moyola
1914-44 .... Captain Sir James Wilton
1944-54 .... Austin Donnelly
1954-57 .... Fred Cochrane
1957-58 .... Joe McBride
1958-93 .... Harry Cavan
1994-95 .... Sammy Walker
1995- .... Jim Boyce

SPECIAL SPORTS

Special Olympics Ireland

Ormond House, Upper Ormond Quay, Dublin 7. Tel. (01) 8720300 Fax. (01) 8720400

Founded 1978
Chairman .... Cyril Freaney
Secretary .... Myra O'Leary
No. of Sports .... 9 Summer Sports (Athletics, Basketball, Tenpin Bowling, Swimming, Table Tennis, Gymnastics, Soccer, Equestrian and Golf); 2 Winter Sports (Polo Hockey and Alpine Skiing) plus two non-competitive motor activities
No. of Clubs .... 100 clubs (*approx.*)
No. of Members .... 12,000 (*approx.*)

DOMESTIC RESULTS

Special Olympics - 20th National Games (June, 1998)

Ten Pin Bowling

Section	Name	Club	Score
Section 1:	J. O'Brien	(MUBW)	1335
Section 2:	M. Hughes	(LEBW)	1331
Section 3:	P. Drugan	(NIBW)	1142
Section 4:	C. Ryan	(COBW)	992
Section 5:	M. McGuane	(COBW)	1020
Section 6:	M. Cahill	(MUBW)	802

Outdoor Soccer

Team	Score	Team	Score
Munster A	3	Munster C	1
Northern Ireland A	1	Munster C	1
Munster A	7	Leinster B	0
Munster B	0	Leinster A	0
Leinster B	0	Northern Ireland A	5
Leinster A	4	Northern Ireland B	1
Munster B	2	Northern Ireland B	0
Munster A	5	Northern Ireland A	0

Rhythmic Gymnastics

Age	Event	Name	Province
8-11 years	Ball	H. Forsythe	N. Ireland
	Ribbon	H. Forsythe	N. Ireland
	Hoop	D. Convery	N. Ireland
	Floor	D. Convery	N. Ireland
	Overall	D. Convery	N. Ireland
12-15 years	Ball	C. Leech	Connacht
	Floor	C. Leech	Connacht
	Ribbon	C. Leech	Connacht
16-21 years	Hoop	J. Williams	Munster
	Ribbon	J. Williams	Munster
	Ball	J. Williams	Munster
	Rope	J. Williams	Munster
	Overall	J. Williams	Munster
16-29 years	Ball	B. Mallon	Leinster
	Ribbon	P. Carrol	Leinster
	Floor	P. Carrol	Leinster
	Hoop	P. Carrol	Leinster
	Overall	P. Carrol	Leinster
Open	Hoop	E. Gormley	Leinster
22-30 years	Hoop	N. Gilton	Leinster
	Hoop	S. Barret	Leinster
	Ribbon	C. Cleary	Leinster
	Ball	N. Gilton	Leinster
	Ball	C. Cleary	Leinster
	Rope	N. Gilton	Leinster
	Rope	C. Cleary	Leinster
	All Round	N. Gilton	Leinster
	All Round	C. Cleary	Leinster
Open	Ribbon	R. Hoffman	Leinster
	Rope	E. Gormley	Leinster
	Ball	E. Gormley	Leinster
	Hoop	E. Gormley	Leinster
	Overall	E. Gormley	Leinster

Northern Ireland Blind Sports

12 Sandford Avenue, Belfast BT5 5NW. Tel. (01232) 657156

Founded 1989
Secretary .... Lisa Royal
Number of Clubs 16
Number of Teams 2
Number of Members (N.I.) 600
Number of Associated Sports .... 9 (athletics, football, indoor mat bowling, tandem cycling, golf, sailing, sea angling, ten pin bowling and water-skiing)

Irish BlindSports

c/o 25 Turvey Close, Donabate, Co. Dublin. Tel. (01) 8436501

Founded 1989
President .... Liam Nolan
Secretary .... Catherine Walsh
Number of Members 300
Number of Associated Sports .... athletics, judo, water-skiing, tenpin bowling, adventure weekends
International Results (1998) .... World Cross Country Championships (Bronze) and World Athletic Championships (Gold, Silver and Bronze)

SQUASH

Irish Squash

House of Sport, Long Mile Road, Dublin 12. Tel. (01) 4501564. Fax: (01) 4502805

Founded ....1993 (amalgamation of Irish Squash Rackets and Irish Women's Squash Rackets Associations)
Number of Clubs 111
Total Number of Members 250
President ....Paddy McIlroy
Vice-President ....Deirbhile O'Byrne
Treasurer ....Michael Hickey
Director ....Myra McNamara
Number of National Coaches 8
Number of Provincial Associations 4

1997-98 INTERNATIONAL STATISTICS

National Senior Men's Coach ....Eoin Ryan
National Senior Women's Coach ....Elvy D'Costa
Number of Irish Team 20
Ireland's European Ranking (women) 9th
Ireland's European Ranking (men) 10th
Most Capped Competitor ....Derek Ryan (1998 European Champion of Champions Winner)
Top Ranked Irish Player (women) ....Aisling McArdle
1997 Irish National Champion (women) ....Madeline Perry
1997 Irish National Champion (men) ....Derek Ryan

Ulster Squash

House of Sport, 2a Upper Malone Road, Belfast, BT9 5LA. Tel. (01232) 381222

Founded ....1995 (amalgamation of Ulster men's and women's associations)
Number of Clubs 49
Total Number of Teams 119
of which: **men** 88
women 33

SURFING

Irish Surfing Association

Easkey House, Easkey, Co. Sligo. Tel: (096) 49020 Fax: (096) 49020. e-mail: isasurf@iol.ie

Founded 1967
President .... Brian Britton
Chairman .... Roci Allan
Treasurer .... Henry Moore
Administrator .... Zoë Lally
Number of Clubs .... 12 *See Below*
Number of Members .... 1,500 approximately (1150 males, 350 females)
Number of Coaches 75

1997-98 INTERNATIONAL RESULTS

● **International Rankings:** 6th (Senior - Europe), 5th (Junior - Europe), 18th (World) ● **Best International Result:** 2nd in the 1998 Reef World Big Wave Challenge (Team), Grant Robinson - '87 and '97 European Masters Champion ● **1998 World Surfing Games, Lisbon, Portugal - Guinness Irish Surf Team: Manager:** Stevie Burns **National Coach:** Peter Cook **Ass. Managers:** Michael Vance, Joe McNulty.

Profiles of 1998 Guinness Irish Surf Team at World Surfing Games

Surfer	Age	From	Competition
BREEN, Ronan	27	Waterford	Longboard
BYRNE, Andrew	22	Tramore	Open
BYRNE, Jamie	14	Tramore	Junior
CONWELL, Stephen	17	Co. Tyrone	Open
FERGUS, Kelli	26	Co. Donegal	Open
GANNON, Brendan	16	Co. Cork	Junior
KELLY, Martin	20	Co. Antrim	Bodyboard
LALLY, Anna	19	Donegal	Open
McAULEY, Bryan	18	Antrim	Bodyboard
MacDERMOTT, Conn	16	Co. Sligo	Junior
MENNIE, Alastair	17	Co. Down	Open
O'BRIEN, Keith	19	Waterford	Open
O'DONNELL, David	19	Sligo	Open
O'HARE, Colin	19	Sligo	Open
SHIELDS, David	22	Portrush	Bodyboard
WARD, Kenny	18	Bundoran	Open
WARD, Tania	24	Antrim	Bodyboard

Date	Event	Venue	Result
Sep. 97	European Championships	Bundoran, Co. Donegal	Ireland: 6th overall
			Grant Robinson - 1st Masters
			Joe McNulty: 3rd Longboard
Feb. 98	Reef Big Wave Championships	Mexico	Irish Team: 2nd
			Terrence McNulty: 2nd
			Joe McNulty: 3rd
-	Europe /African Challenge	-	Bryan McAuley: 1st Bodyboard
Oct. 98	Junior Europeans	-	5th place

1997-98 DOMESTIC RESULTS

Due to bad surfing conditions, many of the competitions this summer had to be postponed, including the National Senior Championships, to the end of November

National Junior Championships (Winners)

U18 .... Stephen Conwell
U18 Girls .... Easkey Britton
U16 .... Conn MacDermott
U14 .... Jamie Byrne

National Junior Championships (Winners)

U12 .... Cain Kilcullen
U18 Bodyboard .... Bryan McAuley
U18 Girl Bodyboard .... Áine O'Doherty
1998 INTERCOUNTY CHAMPIONS .... Sligo

CRITERIA ON WHICH SURFERS ARE JUDGED

1 Radical Controlled Manoeuvres - basically changes of direction of the board on the wave while the surfer is in full control of the board.

2 Most Critical Section - the section on the wave (ie the pocket closest to the curl) where manoeuvres should be performed for optimum scoring.

3 Selection of the Biggest and/or the Best Waves.

4 Longest functional distance - the longest possible distance on a wave that a surfer rides across the judge's field of vision while performing manoeuvres.

NATIONAL COMPETITION CHRONOLOGY

Year	Main Venue	Intercounty Champions	Irish National Champions	International Champions
1967	Tramore	Not Held	Kevin Cavey	Rod Sumpter (Eng)
1968	Tramore	Down	Ted Alexander	Rod Sumpter (Eng)
1969	Rossnowlagh	Waterford	Alan Duke	Rod Sumpter (Eng)
1970	Lahinch	Antrim	Hugh O'Brien Moran	Graham Nile (Eng)
1971	Tramore	Antrim	Hugh O'Brien Moran	Peter Bounds (Wales)
1972	Rossnowlagh	Antrim	Alan Duke	Not Held
1973	Lahinch	Antrim	Derek Musgrave	Graham Nile (Eng)
1974	Dingle	Antrim	Alan Duke	Not Held
1975	Strandhill	Antrim	Alan Duke	Aaron Lloyd (USA)
1976	Rossnowlagh	Fermanagh	Grant Robinson	Not Held
1977	Lahinch	Waterford	William Britton	Peter Bounds (Wales)
1978	Strandhill	Antrim	William Britton	Dave Govern (Ire)
1979	Strandhill	Derry	Grant Robinson	Peter Bounds (Wales)
1980	Portrush	Antrim	William Britton	Not Held
1981	Easkey	Waterford	Grant Robinson	Not Held
1982	Easkey	Donegal	Hugh O'Brien Moran	Peter Lazcelles (Aus)
1983	Tramore	Fermanagh	Hugh O'Brien Moran	Not Held
1984	Easkey	Waterford	Hugh O'Brien Moran	Ian McKay (Scot)
1985	Easkey	Donegal	Michael Vance	Thierrie Fernandez (Fra)
1986	Easkey	Donegal	Kevin Tobin	Mark Foley (NZ)
1987	Easkey	Donegal	Kevin Tobin	Not Held
1988	Ballybunion	Donegal	Hugh O'Brien Moran	Cyril Roberts (Fra)
1989	Ballybunion	Donegal	Andrew Hill	Not Held
1990	Portrush	Antrim	Andrew Hill	Andrew Hill (Ire)
1991	Rossnowlagh	Antrim	Andrew Hill	Not Held
1992	Easkey	Fermanagh	Andrew Hill	Drustan Ward (Eng)
1993	Rossnowlagh	Donegal	Andrew Hill	Andrew Hill (Ire)
1994	Bundoran	Donegal	Andrew Hill	Not Held
1995	Strandhill	Donegal	Darren Twomey	Laurent Pujol (Fra)
1996	Tramore	Leitrim	Darren Twomey	Colin O'Hare (Ire)
1997	Bundoran	Leitrim	Joe McNulty	-
1998	-	Sligo	*tba*	*tba*

CALENDAR OF EVENTS 1999

3-5 Apr.	**Tramore Open**	Tramore, Co. Waterford
May	**Irish National Championships**	-
26 Jun.	**Tiki Junior Championships**	Portrush, Co. Antrim
1-2 August	**Co. Sligo Open**	Strandhill, Co. Sligo
14-15 Aug.	**Tiki Junior Classic**	Rossnowlagh, Co. Donegal
September	**European Cup Bodyboarding C'ships**	-
October	**Europe-Africa Challenge**	-
18-19 Oct	**Intercounty Championships**	-

SURF CLUBS

- **BALLYBUNION SURF CLUB:** Founded: 1995. Contact: Audrey Horan, Kerrylands, Ballybunion, Co. Kerry.
- **BUNDORAN SURF CLUB:** Founded: 1990 Contact: Annemarie Stewart, Fitzgerald's Surf World, Main Street Bundoran, Co. Donegal. Tel: 072 41223.
- **CASTLE WARRIORS SURF CLUB***:* Founded: 1995 Contact: Eithna McShane, Easkey House, Easkey, Co. Sligo. Tel: (096) 49020.
- **CAUSEWAY COAST SURF CLUB:** Founded: 1990 Contact: Ian Hill, Troggs Surf Shop, Portrush, Co. Antrim. Tel: (01265) 823923
- **COUNTY SLIGO SURF CLUB:** Founded: 1992 Contact: Susan McLoughlin, Swan House, Strandhill, Sligo. (071) 68284
- **EAST COAST SURF CLUB** Founded: 1998 Contact: Ciaran Casey, Sarsfield Quay, Dublin 7. (01) 4602497
- **EAST COAST BOARD RIDERS:** Founded: 1992 Contact: Deddie Green, 31 Rossmore Ave., Belfast BT7 3HB (01232) 6432234
- **KERRY SURF CLUB:** Contact: Paude Kenny,

Cahersfee, Tralee, Co. Kerry. (066) 21412

- **NORTH WEST STORM RIDERS:** Founded: 1995 Contact: Hugh McKendrick, 93 Whitehouse Park, Buncrana Road, Derry.
- **ROSSNOWLAGH SURF CLUB:** Founded: 1968 Contact: NC Britton, Durnish, Rossnowlagh, Co. Donegal. Tel: (072) 51974
- **T-BAY SURF CLUB:** Founded: 1978 Michael Kelly 4 Little Market Street, Tramore, Co. Waterford. Tel: (051) 386034
- **WEST COAST SURF CLUB:** Founded: 1971 Contact: Tom Buckley, Lahinch Surf Shop, Lahinch, Co. Clare.

SWIMMING

by ***chalkie white***

FORMER INTERNATIONAL SWIMMER AND IRISH INDEPENDENT COLUMNIST

SWIMMING had plenty of news coverage over the past year but not always for the right reasons. While swimmers like Hugh O'Connor, Nick O'Hare and Colin Lowth were setting new standards at senior level, and Chantal Gibney, Niamh Cawley and Lee Kelleher posting new junior figures during the season, other issues dominated the headlines depriving these swimmers of proper recognition for their achievements.

In December 1997, former Olympic and National Coach, Derry O'Rourke, pleaded guilty in the Dublin Circuit Court to numerous counts of sexually abusing many underage female swimmers whom he had coached. In January, he was sentenced to 12 years behind bars.

O'Rourke was the second National coach in as many years to face these charges. There was general public outrage when it later emerged that the Irish Amateur Swimming Association (IASA), which governs the sport in the country, had many questions to answer with regards to their handling of these and other cases.

As a result, in February 1998 the Minister for Sport, Recreation and Tourism, Dr. Jim McDaid, ordered an enquiry into the situation and appointed Senior Counsel Dr. Roderick Murphy to head the inquiry. Dr. McDaid also cut off all Government funding to the IASA - which amounted to £280,000 during the previous year - until the recommendations of the Murphy Report were implemented.

At the end of September 1998, Government funding had not been restored. However, for all the money that comes from the government, the general body of swimmers sees very little of the Association's £330,000 income (made up of the Government grant plus approximately £50,000 in swimmers licence fees). To be more precise, almost 50% of this money is spent on a small group of about 20 people. This number includes the top 10 to 15 Irish elite swimmers plus the few coaches and officials who travel abroad on international duty with them. The remainder of the money is spent on administering the organisation.

What does the general body of swimmers gain from being in the IASA? Well, the association organises seven national events. Most swimmers are eligible to swim in two, maybe three, of these competitions. The costs of running these events are all covered by what the swimmers pay in entry fees, usually up to £2. So, not only do they pay to be members of the association with few benefits, they also contribute to the costs of running the competitions.

The triple Olympic Champion, Michelle de Bruin, was also in the news during the past year. In October 1997, she was injured in a road traffic accident that caused her to miss the World Championships in Australia the following January. She returned to competition in early 1998 and continued with a few more record-breaking swims the most impressive of which was her 8 mins 40.01 secs for the 800m freestyle in April.

At the same time, she also hit the headlines when she was charged by FINA (the world governing body of swimming) for tampering with an out of competition urine sample. The case progressed, and in August she was given a four-year ban which she appealed to the Sports Arbitration Panel in Switzerland. In late September 1998, the case was still under examination.

While swimming was being publicly scrutinised for non-swimming reasons, swimmers got on with the job of swimming. Although the atmosphere around most competitions during the year was very subdued, there was every reason to feel optimistic about the future as more and more talent continued to emerge through the system.

Most notably was the emergence of Hugh O'Connor as Ireland's top male swimmer. Up to this summer, he was kept in the shadow of his older brother Adrian - previously Ireland's top backstroker and a well-established world class, short course swimmer. The New Ross man threatened that superiority by breaking his brother's national record for the 200m backstroke event with an incredible 1 min 59.33 secs, half a second inside the already impressive record.

Later in the summer, O'Connor went on to establish himself as Ireland's premier backstroker by winning the 50, 100 and 200m backstroke events at the National Championships in July. However, it was his equally impressive swims in the freestyle events which gained him the recognition as Ireland's top male swimmer.

Although he cannot yet claim to be Ireland's premier freestyler - a title which goes to Atlanta Olympian Nick O'Hare - his best times for the 50m (23.44 secs), 100m (50.94secs) and 200m (1:50.99 mins) events, all achieved this year, will be enough to keep O'Hare on his toes over the next year or so in the run up to the Sydney Olympics.

Nick O'Hare himself has also developed enormously over the past year. A relatively late comer to the sport, he has improved immensely, producing more consistent high-quality performances. He has amassed an incredible five sub-23 second 50 metre swims and the same number of sub 51 second 100 metre swims. With his National record standing at 50.02 seconds, there are many who believe that his first sub 50 second swim could come before the end of the year at the European Short Course Championships in December.

Colin Lowth was the other swimmer to set new senior record figures during the year. Swimming at the World Championships in Australia, the 21-year-old Drogheda man stripped almost a full second off his best time in the 200m Fly. However, it was his impressive 2:00.33 mins in the 200m Fly Final at the Nationals that restored confidence in his ability to make the next Olympics in Sydney.

Top junior swimmer, Chantal Gibney, playing second fiddle to Michelle de Bruin for so long, continued to etch her way closer and closer to the triple Olympic Champion's national record in the 50 metre free. With the record standing at 25.85 secs, the young Dubliner is now less that half a second adrift of that time following her National Championship win in 26.19 secs. A clear definite for the Sydney Olympics, she enhanced her chances with two excellent swims, again at the National Championships in Belfast, in the 100m (56.54 secs) and 200m freestyle (2:01.87 mins) events, the latter being within two seconds of Michelle de Bruin's National record.

Cork's Lee Kelleher had a return to form this past year with an excellent Irish Junior record in the girls 100m fly. Although she performed well at the European Junior Championships, her time for the 100m fly at the Nationals (62.78 secs) was by far her best swim in two years.

Claremorris' Niamh Cawley is another very promising talent who looks a real certainty for the Sydney Olympics. The 16-year-old was a finalist at the Junior Europeans in Antwerp this summer, and she stamped a real claim on an Olympic berth with her Irish Junior record in the 200m backstroke record at the Nationals.

Conor Morris (15) and Florry O'Connell (14) are two juniors showing real signs of being future greats. Morris continued to dominate the junior scene by winning five out of a possible six titles at the Irish Age Groups Championships. O'Connell equalled that feat and went on to win the 200m Fly at the British Age Group Championships.

Trojan Swim Team finished the year as top club in the country, following their convincing win at the National Championships in both the Senior and Junior categories. Coached by Carole Walsh who has kept the club in the top spot for the past five years, they continued to produce quality swimmers that will form the basis of future National Teams. ❑

Irish Amateur Swimming Association

House of Sport, Long Mile Road, Dublin 12. Tel. (01) 4501739

Founded 1893
Number of Provincial Branches .... 4 (Connacht, Leinster, Munster and Ulster)
Number of Clubs 149
Number of Members 6,500
Number of Swimming Pools nationwide 219
President .... Mary O'Malley
Honorary Secretary .... Mrs. Pat Donovan
Honorary Treasurer .... Wally Clark
Number of Coaches 50
Number of Teachers 1,500
Biggest Recorded Attendance .... 2,000 (Leisureland International Meeting, Galway March 1997)

DOMESTIC RESULTS

National Championships (Grove Pool, Belfast) July 21-25 1998

WOMEN

Event	Winner	Club	Time	2nd	Club	3rd	Club
50m Freestyle	C. Gibney	Trojan	26.01	J. Douglas	Alliance	E. Sigurdard	Iceland
100m Freestyle	C. Gibney	Trojan	56.54	J. Douglas	Alliance	L. Biagard	Iceland
200m Freestyle	C. Gibney	Trojan	2.01.87	E. Konradsdotter	Iceland	L. Donnelly	Portmarnock
400m Freestyle	N. Pepper	Cormorant	4.30.81	L. Donnelly	Portmarnock	H. Kelly	Templeogue
800m Freestyle	L. Biargard	Iceland	9.03.92	C. Kearney	Portmarnock	A. Mason	Lisburn
50m Backstroke	N. Cawley	Claremorris	30.23	L. Kelleher	City of Cork	E. Konradsdottir	Iceland
100m Backstroke	E. Konradsdottir	Iceland	1.04.18	C. Hogan	St Paul's	S. Doyle	Trojan
200m Backstroke	N. Cawley	Claremorris	2.16.37§	E. Konradsdottir	Iceland	N. Pepper	Cormorant
50m Breaststroke	L. Robinson	Bangor	33.66	K. Marshall	Ards	E. Robinson	Coleraine
100m Breaststroke	L. Robinson	Bangor	1.12.26	K. Marshall	Ards	H. Thorgeirsd	Iceland
200m Breaststroke	M. Corless	Tuam	2.35.50	H. Thorgeirsd	Iceland	K. Marshall	Ards
50m Butterfly	E. Konradsdottir	Iceland	28.83	L. Kelleher	City of Cork	E. Sigurdsdottir	Iceland
100m Butterfly	L. Kelleher	City of Cork	1.02.78§	L. Cardwell	Bangor	S. O'Herlihy	Trojan
200m Butterfly	L. Kelleher	City of Cork	2.17.52	L. Cardwell	Bangor	S. O'Herlihy	Trojan
100m I.M.	L. Kelleher	City of Cork	1.06.12	L. Biargard	Iceland	C. Gibney	Trojan
200m I.M.	L. Kelleher	City of Cork	2.21.26§	L. Biagard	Iceland	J.McGlynn	Portmarnock
400m I.M.	L. Kelleher	City of Cork	5.03.32	M. Corless	Tuam	J.McGlynn	Portmarnock

MEN

Event	Winner	Club	Time	2nd	Club	3rd	Club
50m Freestyle	N. O'Hare	Eastern Bay	22.76*	H. O'Connor	New Ross	W. Carey	Limerick
100m Freestyle	N. O'Hare	Eastern Bay	50.41	H. O'Connor	New Ross	I. Claxton	King's Hospital
200m Freestyle	H. O'Connor	New Ross	1.50.99	C. Lowth	Cormorant	I. Claxton	King's Hospital
400m Freestyle	C. Lowth	Cormorant	4.04.27	N. Cameron	Leander	O. Fridriksson	Iceland
1500m Freestyle	N. Cameron	Leander	16.13.06	O. Fredriksson	Iceland	P. Mulcahy	Limerick
50m Backstroke	H. O'Connor	New Ross	26.20	M. Reidy	Trojan	J. Kealy	Aer Lingus
100m Backstroke	H. O'Connor	New Ross	55.52	M. Reidy	Trojan	A. Reid	Larne
200m Backstroke	H. O'Connor	New Ross	1.59.42	M. Reidy	Trojan	D. Wyatt	Leander
50m Breaststroke	M. Giles	Coolmine	29.44	H. Gudmundsson	Iceland	N. Moraghan	Trojan
100m Breaststroke	H. Gudmundsson	Iceland	1.04.61	M. Craig	Ards	N. Moraghan	Trojan
200m Breaststroke	M. Craig	Ards	2.18.01	M. Williamson	Lisburn	A. Bree	Ards
50m Butterfly	A. Reid	Larne	24.93	C. Osborough	Terenure	J. Kealy	Aer Lingus
100m Butterfly	A. Reid	Larne	55.67	P. McCarthy	New Ross	C. Lowth	Cormorant
200m Butterfly	C. Lowth	Trojan	2.00.33*	P. McCarthy	New Ross	S. McCauley	Otter
100m I.M.	H. O'Connor	New Ross	58.75	J. Kealy	Aer Lingus	G. Beegan	Comorant
200m I.M.	G. Beegan	Cormorant	2.06.30	I. Claxton	King's Hospital	A. Bree	Ards
400m I.M.	A. Bree	Ards	4.33.96	I. Claxton	King's Hospital	P. Mulcahy	Limerick

RELAYS

Event	Winners	Time	2nd	3rd
Men's 4x100m Freestyle Relay	New Ross	3.32.91	Iceland	Ternure
Men's 4x200m Freestyle Relay	Terenure	7.54.53	Leander	Lisburn
Men's 4x100 Medley Team Relay	New Ross	3.48.31*	Trojan	Iceland
Women's 4x100m Freestyle Relay	Iceland	3.55.78	Trojan	Bangor
Women's 4x100 Medley Relay	Iceland	4.23.09	Trojan	Bangor

* Denotes Irish Senior record. § Denotes Irish Junior Record.

Leisureland International Meet (Galway) February 28 - March 1 1998

Event	1st	Club	Time	2nd	Club	3rd	Club
			WOMEN				
50m Freestyle	W. Van Hofwegen	Holland	25.70	C. Gibney	Trojan	N. Cawley	Claremorris
100m Freestyle	W. Van Hofwegen	Holland	55.54	C. Gibney	Trojan	D. Wieldraaijer	Holland
200m Freestyle	W. Van Hofwegen	Holland	2.02.95	C. Gibney	Trojan	D. Simms	Leander
400m Freestyle	M.de Bruin	MS 3Gold	4.14.02*	M. Van Harn	Holland	C. O'Keefe	Dolphin
800m Freestyle	C. O'Keefe	Dolphin	9.18.12	H. Kelly	Templeogue	E. Bergin	Templeogue
50m Backstroke	N. Cawley	Claremorris	30.20	C. Darby	Leander	C. Hogan	St Paul's
100m Backstroke	N. Cawley	Claremorris	1.03.66	C. Hogan	St Paul's	S. McNally	Longford
200m Backstroke	N. Cawley	Claremorris	2.17.42	S. McNally	Longford	L. Donnelly	Portmarnock
50m Breaststroke	H. Broekhuizen	Holland	33.62	L. Robinson	Bangor	K. Marshall	Ards
100m Breaststroke	H. Broekhuizen	Holland	1.12.34	K. Marshall	Ards	L. Robinson	Bangor
200m Breaststroke	M. Corless	Tuam	2.35.31	H. Broekwoizen	Holland	C. Nixon	Ards
50m Butterfly	W. Van Hofwegen	Holland	27.95	L. Kelleher	City of Cork	M. Van Harn	Holland
100m Butterfly	W. Van Hofwegen	Holland	1.01.99	L. Kelleher	City of Cork	S. O'Herlihy	Trojan
200m Butterfly	L. Kelleher	City of Cork	2.18.57	S. O'Herlihy	Trojan	N. Pepper	Cormorant
100m I.M.	W. Van Hofwegen	Holland	1.04.58	L. Kelleher	City of Cork	M. Van Harn	Holland
200m I.M.	M. Van Harn	Holland	2.21.17	C. Hogan	St Paul's	C. Nixon	Ards
400m I.M.	M. de Bruin	MS 3Gold	4.56.04	M. Van Harn	Holland	A. Mason	Lisburn
4x50m Freestyle Relay		Holland A	1.48.62		Trojan		Enniskillen
4x50m Medley Relay		Holland A	2.01.89		Trojan		Bangor

Event	1st	Club	Time	2nd	Club	3rd	Club
			MEN				
50m Freestyle	N. O'Hare	Eastern Bay	22.76	M. Fibbins	Camden	S. Brinn	Univ. of Bath
100m Freestyle	M. Fibbins	Camden	50.12	S. Brinn	Univ. of Bath	Nick O'Hare	E. Bray
200m Freestyle	S. Brinn	Univ. of Bath	1.52.01	D. Rjinbeek	Holland	B. Wennwken	Holland
400m Freestyle	C. Lowth	Cormorant	3.58.23	B. Wennwken	Holland	F. Willemse	Holland
50m Backstroke	H. O'Connor	New Ross	26.79	J. Bunger	Hamburg	M. Reidy	Trojan
100m Backstroke	H. O'Connor	New Ross	56.55	D. Hyde	Limerick	M. Reidy	Trojan
200m Backstroke	H. O'Connor	New Ross	2.01.91	F. Willemse	Holland	M. Reidy	Trojan
50m Breaststroke	D. Dekker	Holland	0.28.47	B. Kiupers	Holland	F. Bailie	Bangor
100m Breaststroke	B. Kuipers	Holland	1.02.61	R. Dekker	Holland	N. Moraghan	Trojan
200m Breaststroke	B. Kuipers	Holland	2.16.52	A. Bree	Ards	N. Moraghan	Trojan
50m Butterfly	M. Fibbins	Camden	24.42	J. Olsen	Phoenix, USA	J. Kealy	Aer Lingus
100m Butterfly	I. Wesseling	Holland	57.34	D. Hyde	Limerick	P. McCarthy	New Ross
200m Butterfly	C. Lowth	Cormorant	2.00.65*	B. Wennwken	Holland	P. McCarthy	New Ross
100m I.M.	D. Rijnbeek	Holland	58.29	S. Brinn	Univ. of Bath	I. Wesseling	Holland
200m I.M.	G. Beegan	Cormorant	2.06.72	F. Willense	Holland	A. Bree	Ards
400m I.M.	F. Willense	Holland	4.31.62	A. Bree	Ards	A. Ferns	Cormorant
4x50m Freestyle Relay		Holland	1.33.90		Aer Lingus		Bangor
4x50m Medley Relay		Holland	1.44.02		New Ross		Trojan

* National Record

INTERNATIONAL RESULTS

World Championships (Perth, Australia) January 12-18 1998

Date	Event	Competitor	Time	Heat Pos.	Overall Pos.
12.01.98	200m Freestyle	Colin Lowth	1.59.37	2nd	45th
	200m Freestyle	Adrian O'Connor	1.58.38	3rd	43rd
14.01.98	100m Freestyle	Nick O'Hare	0.53.35	6th	51st
	100m Freestyle	Hugh O'Connor	0.54.05	6th	55th
	200m Butterfly	Colin Lowth	2.03.25 (NR)	1st	26th
15.01.98	100m Backstroke	Adrian O'Connor	0.58.50	7th	35th
	100m Backstroke	Hugh O'Connor	0.59.50	5th	37th
16.01.98	100m Butterfly	Colin Lowth	0.57.56 (PB)	4th	49th
18.01.98	200m Backstroke	Adrian O'Conor	2.08.10	5th	24th
	200m Backstroke	Hugh O'Connor	2.08.20	6th	26th
	50m Freestyle	Nick O'Hare	0.23.90	6th	38th

NR= National Record, PB= Personal Best

IRISH NATIONAL RECORDS

Men's Records

Event	Short Course Time	Name	Date	Long Course Time	Name	Date
50m Freestyle	22.76	Nick O'Hare	28.02.98	23.36	Nick O'Hare	17.05.96
100m Freestyle	50.02	Nick O'Hare	29.01.97	50.91	Earl McCarthy	24.08.95
200m Freestyle	1.49.38	Ken Turner	15.03.92	1.52.58	Earl McCarthy	22.08.95
400m Freestyle	3.53.82	Ken Turner	24.07.91	4.02.12	Ken Turner	02.07.88
800m Freestyle	8.02.88	Ken Turner	10.02.89	8.32.00	David Teevan	04.03.88
1500m Freestyle	15.33.57	Ken Turner	25.02.89	16.11.76	Kevin Williamson	18.04.76
50m Backstroke	25.76	Adrian O'Connor	23.07.97	26.96	Adrian O'Connor	31.03.94
100m Backstroke	55.23	Adrian O'Connor	15.03.92	57.56	Adrian O'Connor	26.05.96
200m Backstroke	1.59.33	Hugh O'Connor	20.03.98	2.04.73	Adrian O'Connor	28.04.96
50m Breaststroke	28.59	Gary O'Toole	10.02.90	29.30	Michael Giles	31.05.97
100m Breaststroke	1.01.87	Gary O'Toole	02.02.92	1.04.15	Gary O'Toole	03.08.93
200m Breaststroke	2.11.35	Gary O'Toole	10.02.90	2.15.73	Gary O'Toole	18.08.89
50m Butterfly	24.67	Andrew Reid	23.08.97	25.96	William Johnston	02.05.89
100m Butterfly	55.41	Declan Byrne	27.03.93	56.80	Declan Byrne	14.06.92
200m Butterfly	2.00.65	Colin Lowth	28.02.98	2.03.25	Colin Lowth	12.01.98
100m I.M.	57.39	Standard				
200m I.M.	2.02.23	Gary O'Toole	24.02.90	2.05.46	Gary O'Toole	18.08.89
400m I.M.	4.22.97	Gary O'Toole	06.02.93	4.32.06	Gary O'Toole	04.08.93
RELAYS						
4x50 Freestyle, Club	1.32.93	Coolmine	12.03.95			
4x50 Freestyle, Nat	1.32.92	National Team	30.03.91			
4x100 Freestyle, Club	3.25.47	Coolmine	29.07.95	3.37.30	Coolmine	16.07.95
4x100 Freestyle, Nat	3.24.66	National Team	09.12.94	3.30.12	National Team	24.08.97
4x200 Freestyle, Club	7.34.35	Glenalbyn	23.07.91			
4x200 Freestyle, Nat	7.27.78	National Team	15.03.92	7.38.45	National Team	16.08.89
4x50 Medley, Club	1.45.13	Coolmine	06.11.94			
4x50 Medley, Nat	1.43.89	National Team	29.03.91			
4x100 Medley, Club	3.49.06	New Ross	22.07.97	4.06.91	The King's Hospital	30.06.91
4x100 Medley, Nat	3.45.66	National Team	09.12.94	3.50.82	National Team	22.08.97

Women's Records

Event	Short Course Time	Name	Date	Long Course Time	Name	Date
50m Freestyle	25.85	Michelle Smith	11.12.94	26.20	Michelle Smith	28.05.95
100m Freestyle	54.87	Michelle Smith	29.07.95	57.53	Michelle Smith	27.04.97
200m Freestyle	1.59.69	Michelle Smith	03.04.98	1.59.93	Michelle Smith	20.08.97
400m Freestyle	4.14.02	Michelle Smith	01.03.98	4.07.25	Michelle Smith	28.08.96
800m Freestyle	8.44.06	Michelle Smith	03.12.94	8.52.10	Michelle Smith	26.04.97
1500m Freestyle	16.46.75	Michelle Smith	12.12.94	17.46.79	Carol Ann Heavey	27.06.82
50m Backstroke	29.44	Niamh O'Connor	29.03.91	30.84	Michelle Smith	20.01.95
100m Backstroke	1.02.36	Michelle Smith	19.02.94	1.05.54	Michelle Smith	07.01.95
200m Backstroke	2.10.76	Michelle Smith	22.03.94	2.17.95	Michelle Smith	16.03.96
50m Breaststroke	32.47	Gina Galligan	02.02.92	32.96	Gina Galligan	30.11.96
100m Breaststroke	1.10.71	Siobhan Doyle	06.11.93	1.11.80	Gina Galligan	31.05.92
200m Breaststroke	2.32.26	Sharlene Brown	14.03.92	2.36.86	Sharlene Brown	23.05.92
50m Butterfly	28.15	Michelle Smith	03.01.95	28.64	Michelle Smith	25.08.95
100m Butterfly	59.99	Michelle Smith	03.01.95	1.00.59	Michelle Smith	22.08.95
200m Butterfly	2.07.04	Michelle Smith	27.03.94	2.09.91	Michelle Smith	28.08.96
100m I.M.	1.02.70	Michelle Smith	04.01.95			
200m I.M.	2.13.46	Michelle Smith	03.01.95	2.13.93	Michelle Smith	24.08.96
400m I.M.	4.36.84	Michelle Smith	27.03.94	4.39.18	Michelle Smith	20.08.96
RELAYS						
4x50 Freestyle, Club	1.50.91	Trojan	02.03.96			
4x50 Freestyle, Nat.	1.49.03	National Team	26.01.92			
4x100 Freestyle, Club	3.59.60	Trojan	26.07.97	4.16.99	Trojan	04.05.91
4x100 Freestyle, Nat	3.54.72	National Team	18.03.91	4.04.04	National Team	06.04.91
4x200 Freestyle, Nat	8.25.94	National Team	17.03.91	8.38.66	National Team	03.07.88
4x50 Medley, Club	2.01.07	Trojan	19.02.94			

4x50 Medley, Nat	1.58.93	National Team	26.01.92			
4x100 Medley, Club	4.22.99	Glenalbyn	24.07.91	4.39.54	The King's Hospital	26.07.79
4x100 Medley, Nat	4.15.90	National Team	15.03.92	4.29.08	National team	21.04.90

I.M. = Individual Medley All records correct as of April 25, 1998.

Past National Champions 1980-89 (Men)

MEN

Year	50m Freestyle Winner	Club	Time	100m Freestyle Winner	Club	Time
1980	-	-	-	D. Cummins	Cormorant	0.54.74
1981	-	-	-	W.Johnston	Leander	0.53.68
1982	-	-	-	W. Johnston	Leander	0.52.72
1983	W. Johnston	Leander	24.19	W.Johnston	Leander	0.53.33
1984	D. Connaughton	King's Hospital	24.82	D. Connaughton	King's Hospital	0.53.47
1985	D. Connaughton	King's Hospital	24.16	D. Connaughton	King's Hospital	0.52.13
1986	P. Kilmartin	King's Hospital	24.15	D. Connaughton	King's Hospital	0.52.56
1987	D. Connaughton	King's Hospital	24.2	D. Connaughton	King's Hospital	0.52.06
1988	D. Connaughton	King's Hospital	24.53	D. Connaughton	King's Hospital	0.51.80
1989	W. Johnston	Leander	23.61	K. Turner	Aer Lingus	0.52.31

Year	200m Freestyle Winner	Club	Time	400m Freestyle Winner	Club	Time
1980	K. Williamson	Terenure	1.58.85	K. Williamson	Terenure	4.11.14
1981	K. Williamson	Terenure	1.56.31	K. Williamson	Terenure	4.00.95
1982	K. Williamson	Terenure	1.56.13	K. Williamson	Terenure	4.09.21
1983	K. Williamson	Terenure	1.55.16	K. Williamson	Terenure	4.00.63
1984	D. Connaughton	King's Hospital	1.56.57	A. Towey	Terenure	4.03.38
1985	A. Towey	Terenure	1.56.18	S. Walsh	Glenalbyn	4.04.13
1986	P.O'Neill	King's Hospital	1.55.54	A. Towey	Terenure	4.03.95
1987	E. McCarthy	King's Hospital	1.54.87	M. Millar	Leander	3.57.87
1988	D. Connaughton	King's Hospital	1.55.03	G. O'Toole	Trojan	4.05.66
1989	K. Turner	Aer Lingus	1.53.12	P. McGillion	Omagh	4.00.64

Year	1,500m Freestyle Winner	Club	Time	100m Breaststroke Winner	Club	Time
1980	K. Williamson	Terenure	16.54.20	L. Bohan	King's Hospital	1.10.7
1981	K. Williamson	Terenure	16.12.98	E. McCauley	King's Hospital	1.09.19
1982	K.Williamson	Terenure	16.33.21	E. McCauley	King's Hospital	1.09.22
1983	K. Williamson	Terenure	15.59.70	F. Freeman	King's Hospital	1.08.21
1984	A. Towey	Terenure	16.06.06	F. Freeman	King's Hospital	1.08.41
1985	S.Walsh	Glenalbyn	16.10.03	A. Turner	Aer Lingus	1.07.66
1986	S.Walsh	Glenalbyn	15.49.84	J. McGrath	Trojan	1.05.55
1987	M.Millar	Leander	15.52.80	G. O'Toole	Trojan	1.04.62
1988	D. Teevan	Glenalbyn	16.15.43	D. Connaughton	King's Hospital	1.05.87
1989	K. Turner	Aer Lingus	15.54.14	J. Stynes	Kingdom	1.06.41

Year	200m Breaststroke Winner	Club	Time	100m Backstroke Winner	Club	Time
1980	L. Bohan	King's Hospital	2.35.4	D. Cummins	Cormorant	1.00.14
1981	P. McHaffey	Leander	2.28.99	S. Magowan	Bangor	1.02.37
1982	P. McHaffey	Leander	2.30.09	S. Magowan	Bangor	1.01.64
1983	F. Freeman	King's Hospital	2.30.60	P. Reardon	Terenure	1.01.28
1984	F. Freeman	King's Hospital	2.28.22	P. Reardon	Glenalbyn	1.01.26
1985	A. Turner	Aer Lingus	2.23.94	T. Healy	Terenure	1.01.59
1986	G. O'Toole	Trojan	2.20.57	E. McCarthy	King's Hospital	1.00.87
1987	G. O'Toole	Trojan	2.18.61	E. McCarthy	King's Hospital	0.59.17
1988	G. O'Toole	Trojan	2.19.90	R. Gheel	Omagh	1.00.73
1989	D. Connaughton	Trojan	2.21.18	A. O'Connor	New Ross	0.58.06

Year	200m Backstroke Winner	Club	Time	100m Butterfly Winner	Club	Time
1980	D. Cummins	Cormorant	2.13.67	D. Cummins	Cormorant	0.58.91
1981	M. Kral	Trojan	2.19.23	A. Morrison	Leander	1.00.08
1982	P. Reardon	Terenure	2.15.70	A. Morrison	Leander	0.58.69
1983	P. Reardon	Terenure	2.13.19	B. Neylon	Terenure	0.59.83
1984	T. Healy	Terenure	2.12.20	A. Towey	Terenure	0.58.84

Continued from previous page

Year	200m Backstroke Winner	Club	Time	100m Butterfly Winner	Club	Time
1985	T. Healy	Terenure	2.11.81	P. O'Neill	King's Hospital	0.58.28
1986	E. McCarthy	King's Hospital	2.12.12	G. O'Toole	Trojan	0.57.96
1987	E. McCarthy	King's Hospital	2.07.68	P. O'Neill	King's Hospital	0.58.37
1988	R. Gheel	Omagh	2.11.03	A. Towey	Terenure	0.57.72
1989	A. O'Connor	New Ross	2.05.95	A. Towey	Terenure	0.57.87

Year	200m Butterfly Winner	Club	Time	200m Individual Medley Winner	Club	Time
1980	D. Cummins	Cormorant	2.08.83	...		
1981	A. Morrison	Leander	2.11.03	K. Williamson	Terenure	2.14.99
1982	A. Morrison	Leander	2.09.2S	K. Williamson	Terenure	2.13.29
1983	A. Towey	Terenure	2.10.S2	K. Williamson	Terenure	2.13.15
1984	B. Desmond	Shark	2.18.S4	M. Coughlan	King's Hospital	2.14.98
1985	P. O'Neill	King's Hospital	2.06.63	G. O'Toole	Trojan	2.11.25
1986	A. Towey	Terenure	2.0S.38	G. O'Toole	Trojan	2.08.80
1987	A. Towey	Terenure	2.06.0S	G. O'Toole	Trojan	2.07.13
1988	A. Towey	Terenure	2.07.32	G. O'Toole	Trojan	2.09.87
1989	A. Towey	Terenure	2.05.43	D. Byrne	Trojan	2.07.68

Year	400m Individual Medley Winner	Club	Time	4x100m Freestyle Relay Winner	Club	Time
1980	L. Bohan	King's Hospital	4.43.09	Terenure		3.42.27
1981	K. Williamson	Terenure	4.42.99	Terenure		3.40.47
1982	K. Williamson	Terenure	4.48.68	Terenure		3.38.85
1983	M. Coughlan	King's Hospital	4.53.15	Terenure		3.36.93
1984	M. Coughlan	King's Hospital	4.51.43	King's Hospital		3.34.74
1985	G. O'Toole	Trojan	4.40.61	King's Hospital		3.34.72
1986	J. McGrath	Trojan	4.37.54	King's Hospital		3.44.29
1987	G. O'Toole	Trojan	4.32.34	King's Hospital		3.32.26
1988	D. Connaughton	King's Hospital	4.38.73	King'sHospital		3.31.24
1989	P. McGillion	Omagh	4.26.56	Aer Lingus		3.29.04

Year	4x200m Freestyle Relay Winner	Club	Time	4x100m Medley Relay Winner	Club	Time
1980	Terenure		8.12.74	King's Hospital		4.11.14
1981	Terenure		7.57.87	Leander		4.10.55
1982	Terenure		8.04.43	Leander		4.11.11
1983	Terenure		7.49.51	Terenure		4.05.72
1984	Terenure		7.53.99	King's Hospital		4.01.30
1985	Terenure		7.50.31	King's Hospital		4.00.37
1986	King's Hospital		7.50.31	King's Hospital		3.55.64
1987	Terenure		7.46.32	King's Hospital		3.56.07
1988	Trojan		7.49.72	Trojan		3.58.68
1989	Aer Lingus		7.42.06	Aer Lingus		3.56.76

Past National Champions 1980-89 (Women)

WOMEN

Year	50m Freestyle Winner	Club	Time	100m Freestyle Winner	Club	Time
1980	-	-	-	A. Cummins	Cormorant	1.00.91
1981	-	-	-	C.A. Heavey	Trojan	0.59.92
1982	-	-	-	C.A. Heavey	Trojan	0.59.94
1983	C.A Heavey	Trojan	27.16	C.A. Heavey	Trojan	0.59.82
1984	G. O'Connor	King's Hospital	28.31	P. McCahill	Trojan	1.00.09
1985	L. Keogh	Glenalbyn	28.2	A. Convery	Glenalbyn	1.00.13
1986	L. Keogh	Glenalbyn	27.99	A. Convery	Glenalbyn	0.59.78
1987	M. Madine	Leander	27.69	M. Madine	Leander	0.58.62
1988	N.Campbell	Trojan	=28.11*	N. Campbell	Trojan	0.59.61
	S. Dougherty	Omagh	=28.11*			
1989	S. Farrelly	Aer Lingus	27.4	S. Farrelly	Aer Lingus	0.59.45

Year	200m Freestyle Winner	Club	Time	400m Freestyle Winner	Club	Time
1980	A. Cummins	Cormorant	2.11.45	C.A. Heavey	Trojan	4.37.54
1981	C.A. Heavey	Trojan	2.05.75	C.A. Heavey	Trojan	4.28.64
1982	C.A. Heavey	Trojan	2.11.11	C.A. Heavey	Trojan	4.34.50
1983	C.A. Heavey	Trojan	2.07.95	C.A. Heavey	Trojan	4.25.60
1984	A. Mulcair	King's Hospital	2.10.98	A. Mulcair	King's Hospital	4.31.81
1985	A. Mulcair	King's Hospital	2.07.16	A. Mulcair	King's Hospital	4.23.04
1986	D. Ward	Trojan	2.08.45	A. Mulcair	King's Hospital	4.27.47
1987	M. Madine	Leander	2.05.20	M. Madine	Leander	4.21.95
1988	D. Ward	Trojan	2.06.80	M. Smith	King's Hospital	4.21.66
1989	D. Ward	Trojan	2.08.84	M. Madine	Leander	4.27.79

Year	800m Freestyle Winner	Club	Time	100m Breaststroke Winner	Club	Time
1980	A. Donovan	King's Hospital	9.31.28	C. Bohan	King's Hospital	1.16.00
1981	C.A. Heavey	Trojan	9.19.06	J. Parkes	Bangor	1.17.98
1982	C.A. Heavey	Trojan	9.20.18	C. Bohan	King's Hospital	1.15.62
1983	C.A. Heavey	Trojan	9.12.01	C. Bohan	King's Hospital	1.16.58
1984	A. Mulcair	King's Hospital	9.24.14	D. Morris	Aer Lingus	1.15.20
1985	A. Mulcair	King's Hospital	9.02.07	L. Keogh	Glenalbyn	1.15.19
1986	A. Mulcair	King's Hospital	9.14.36	L. Keogh	Glenalbyn	1.14.77
1987	M. Madine	Leander	9.07.41	L. Keogh	Glenalbyn	1.13.71
1988	M. Smith	King's Hospital	8.57.46	N. Byrne	Trojan	1.14.59
1989	C. Redmond	Templeogue	9.19.65	S. Farrelly	Aer Lingus	1.13.21

Year	200m Breaststroke Winner	Club	Time	100m Backstroke Winner	Club	Time
1980	C. Bohan	King's Hospital	2.44.31	A. Donovan	King's Hospital	1.10.28
1981	C. Bohan	King's Hospital	2.42.99	P. Campion	Dolphin	1.09.38
1982	C. Bohan	King's Hospital	2.46.09	P. Campion	Dolphin	1.09.34
1983	C. Bohan	King's Hospital	2.42.30	A. Reddington	Aer Lingus	1.07.86
1984	D. Morris	Aer Lingus	2.41.19	A. Reddington	Aer Lingus	1.08.20
1985	N. Byrne	Trojan	2.41.25	M. Smith	King's Hospital	1.07.56
1986	L. Keogh	Glenalbyn	2.40.30	M. Smith	King's Hospital	1.06.28
1987	L. Keogh	Glenalbyn	2.38.14	A. Convery	Glenalbyn	1.04.85
1988	L. Keogh	Glenalbyn	2.40.41	N. O'Connor	New Ross	1.05.72
1989	S. Farrelly	Aer Lingus	2.35.34	N. O'Connor	New Ross	1.05.25

Year	200m Backstroke Winner	Club	Time	100m Butterfly Winner	Club	Time
1980	A. Donovan	King's Hospital	2.27.78	J. Law	College Square	1.06.15
1981	P. Campion	Dolphin	2.28.96	J. Parkes	Bangor	1.06.69
1982	P. Campion	Dolphin	2.28.69	J. Parkes	Bangor	1.05.39
1983	K. Nolan	Trojan	2.24.95	J. Parkes	Bangor	1.05.71
1984	M. Smith	King's Hospital	2.27.67	A. McElwee	King's Hospital	1.03.96
1985	M. Smith	King's Hospital	2.24.33	A. McElwee	King's Hospital	1.05.20
1986	M. Smith	King's Hospital	2.19.50	M. Smith	King's Hospital	1.05.01
1987	A. Convery	Glenalbyn	2.17.24	M. Madine	Leander	1.05.24
1988	M. Smith	King's Hospital	2.27.72	N. Campbell	Trojan	1.05.27
1989	M. Smith	King's Hospital	2.16.48	S. Farrelly	Aer Lingus	1.04.66

Year	200m Butterfly Winner	Club	Time	200m Individual Medley Winner	Club	Time
1980	J. Law	College Square	2.23.90	-	-	-
1981	P. Campion	Dolphin	2.25.43	P. Campion	Dolphin	2.26.83
1982	J. Parkes	Bangor	2.21.06	J. Parkes	Bangor	2.24.60
1983	J. Parkes	Bangor	2.20.94	J. Parkes	Bangor	2.24.30
1984	P. Campion	Dolphin	2.23.41	P. McCahill	Trojan	2.26.12
1985	A. McElwee	King's Hospital	2.21.41	N. Byrne	Trojan	2.26.04
1986	M. Smith	King's Hospital	2.21.84	M. Smith	King's Hospital	2.24.76
1987	M. Madine	Leander	2.20.10	A. Convery	Glenalbyn	2.23.05

Continued from previous page

Year	200m Butterfly Winner	Club	Time	200m Individual Medley Winner	Club	Time
1988	M. Smith	King's Hospital	2.21.43	M. Smith	King's Hospital	2.24.09
1989	M. Smith	King's Hospital	2.19.42	M. Smith	King's Hospital	2.20.86

Year	400m Individual Medley Winner	Club	Time	4x100m Freestyle Relay Winner	Club	Time
1980	C. Bohan	King's Hospital	5.06.53	College Square		4.15.71
1981	P. Campion	Dolphin	5.04.34	Trojan		4.17.78
1982	P. Campion	Dolphin	5.40.0	Trojan		4.10.19
1983	P. Campion	Dolphin	5.06.96	Trojan		4.06.36
1984	P. Campioll	Dolphin	5.05.16	King's Hospital		4.04.19
1985	M. Smith	King's Hospital	5.04.84	Glenalbyn		4.04.93
1986	M. Smith	King's Hospital	5.07.07	King's Hospital		4.05.48
1987	M. Smith	King's Hospital	5.02.88	Trojan		4.01.65
1988	M. Smith	King's Hospital	4.57.56	Trojan		4.04.19
1989	M. Smith	King's Hospital	5.02.20	Trojan		4.03.69

Year	4x100m Medley Relay Winner	Club	Time
1980	King's Hospital		4.46.06
1981	Trojan		4.43.52
1982	King's Hospital		4.42.60
1983	King's Hospital		4.37.48
1984	King's Hospital		4.35.98
1985	King's Hospital		4.33.59
1986	King's Hospital		4.33.24
1987	Glenalbyn		4.31.23
1988	Trojan		4.29.66
1989	Glenalbyn		4.33.76

* Dead Heat

PAST PRESIDENTS

Year	President	Year	President	Year	President
1894	E. Kirkpatrick	1927	W. Cheater	1954	L. McDonnell
1895	E.H. Andrews	1928	A.J. Cullen	1955	J.E. Rodgers
1896	R.C. Norrie	1929	R. Gamble	1956	J. Browne
1897	W. Findlater	1930	H.F. Brennan	1957	L. Clarke
1898	Major J.H. McCormick	1931	J.P. Goss	1958	S. Lawlor
1899	J.V. Lahiff	1932	D. Murtagh	1959	J.F. Younger
1900	R. Cotter	1933	J.J. Crawford	1960	J. Cranny
1901-03	R.M. Peter	1934	Dr. H.G. Ellerker	1961	J. Crockett
1904	H. Martin	1935	W. McCreedy	1962	K.W. McCullagh
1905	P.J. Stokes	1936	J.S. Brady	1963	J.C. Lavery
1906	J. Carmichael	1937	F. Cunningham	1964	G. Walsh
1907	W.J. Hegarty	1938	J.P. Weldon	1965	Mrs P. O'Brien
1908	W.M. Atkins	1939	C. Fagan	1966	F. Donegan
1909	A. Bowman	1940	J. Allen	1967	J. Kernaghan
1910	W. Burnham	1941	A.A. Healy	1968	Commdt. J.J. Griffin
1911	H.M. Dockrell	1942	W.J. McCormick	1969	D. Desmond
1912	G.H. Leitch	1943	J.P. Bradley	1970	B.T. Barry
1913	R.N. Taggart	1944	R.C. Bogan	1971	J. Stevenson
1914-18	L.F. Daly	1945	T.H. Corrigan	1972	C. Dooley
1919	W.E. Morris	1946	G.B.J. Johnston	1973	E. Campion
1920	N.M. Purcell	1947	H.J. Ormond	1974	H. Kavanagh
1921	F.Bradley	1948	E. Heron	1975	J.H. Kidd
1922	H. Lemon	1949	W. Hamill	1976	Fr. D. Moloney
1923	Dr.J. Beckett	1950	P. Walsh	1977	D. O'Sullivan
1924	M.F. Long	1951	P.J. Lavery	1978	L. Byrne
1925	H. Megarry	1952	J.T. Munroe	1979	Mrs M. Simpson
1926	Major M.A. O'Connor	1953	W. O'Brien	1980	Mrs E. Byrnes

Year	President
1981	M. Bowles
1982	Dr. M. O'Brien
1983	F. Parkes
1984	G. Heskin
1985	D. Mahon
1986	T. Dorgan
1987	W. Moore
1988	M. Walsh
1989	P. Dunford
1990	T. Healy
1991	Mrs D. Budd
1992	Col. P. Begley
1993	M. Mulcair
1994	F. Barron
1995	F. Stevens
1996	P. Brennan
1997	D. Barry
1998	Mrs M. O'Malley

TAEKWONDO

Taekwondo Association of Northern Ireland

c/o 20 Lester Avenue, Lisburn, Co. Antrim BT28 3QD. Tel. (01846) 604293

Founded 1978
Chairman .... Glen Culbert
Honorary Secretary .... Bertie Nicholson
Public Promotion Officer .... Brian Kerr
Number of Clubs 16
Number of Teams 2
Number of Members (N.I.) 600
Number of Coaches 15
All Time Record Attendance at a Taekwondo Tournament 650
International Statistics:
- **National Senior Coach** .... Paul Gibson
- **Most Capped Competitor** .... Jason Creighton
- **Best International Result (individual)** .... 2 off Silver Scottish International

TENNIS

Tennis Ireland

Argyle Square, Morehampton Road, Donnybrook, Dublin 4. Tel. (01) 6681841.

Founded 1908
Provincial Branches ....4 (Connacht, Leinster, Munster and Ulster)
Number of Clubs 220
Total Number of Members 92,500
of which: **Men** 25,500
Women 21,000
U18s 46,000
President ....Ms Olwyn Raftery
Honourary Secretary....Mr Ciaran O'Donovan
Honourary Treasurer....Mr Tony Locke
Chief Executive Officer....Mr Des Allen
Top Ranked Irish Players (men) ....Owen Casey (World Rankng 810); Scott Barron (World Ranking 1011)
Top Ranked Irish Players (women)....Kelly Liggan (World Ranking 432); Gina Niland (World Ranking 1010)
Number of Coaches....191

	MEN'S	WOMEN'S
Irish Close Champions 1998, Senior	Owen Casey	Gina Niland
Irish Open Champions 1998, Senior	Ross Matheson	Julia Lutrova
Irish Indoor Champions 1998, Senior	Owen Casey	Gina Niland

Principal Venue ....Riverview, Donnybrook

PROVINCIAL OFFICERS

Branch	President	Hon Secretary	Hon Treasurer
Connacht	James Ward	Rosaleen Ó Muircheartaigh	John McHugh
Leinster	Dee Jennings	Ann O'Connor	Billy Meehan
Munster	James Foley	Claire McNamara	Peter Scott
Ulster	Seamus McCusker	George Stevenson	Peter Bayliss

DOMESTIC RESULTS

1998 Carlsberg Irish Open

Men's Singles

4th Round

V. Snyman (1)	bt	I. Donkar	6/3 7/6
P. Scullard	bt	M. Tanjeford (16)	6/2 6/3
T. Spinks (4)	bt	J. Green (11)	6/0 6/3
J. Davidson (6)	bt	J. Pringle (10)	6/2 6/4
O. Casey (5)	bt	R. Hanger (14)	6/2 6/1
R. Matheson (3)	bt	E. Collins (12)	7/6 6/2
J. Doran (8)	bt	S. Taylor	6/4 6/4
K. Rudman (2)	bt	F. Ofori (15)	1/6 6/3 7/5

Quarter Finals

V. Snyman (1)	bt	P. Scullard	6/2 7/5
T. Spinks (4)	bt	J. Davidson (6)	6/7 6/4 6/3
R. Matheson (3)	bt	O. Casey (5)	7/6 6/4
J. Doran (8)	bt	K. Rudman (2)	6/3 3/6 7/6

Semi Finals

T. Spinks (4)	bt	V. Snyman (1)	
R. Matheson (3)	bt	J. Doran (8)	3/6 6/2 6/3

Final

R. Matheson (3)	bt	T. Spinks	5/7 6/4 7/6

Women's Singles

M. Joubert (1)	bt	S. Perkins	6/2 6/1
G. Niland (6)	bt	E. Bollard	6/0 6/1
L. Gabai (3)	bt	G. O'Donoghue	6/0 6/1
Y. Flynn (8)	bt	L. Carmody	6/0 6/1
V. Davies (5)	bt	D. Kelly	6/0 6/1
J. Dawson (4)	bt	A. Hogan	6/1 6/4
L. O'Halloran (7)	bt	Z. Wolseley	7/6 6/2
J. Lutrova (2)	bt	A. Napier	6/1 6/2

Quarter Finals

M. Joubert (1)	bt	G. Niland (6)	6/4 6/2
L. Gabai (3)	bt	Y. Flynn (8)	6/1 6/2
J. Dawson (4)	bt	V. Davies (5)	6/4 6/4
J. Lutrova (2)	bt	L. O'Halloran (7)	6/0 6/3

Semi Finals

M. Joubert (1)	bt	L. Gabai (3)	w/o
J. Lutrova (2)	bt	J. Dawson (4)	6/4 6/4

Final

J. Lutrova (2)	bt	M. Joubert (1)	6/3 7/5

Men's Doubles

Quarter Finals

James Davidson/ Vaughan Snyman (1)........................bt.........Julian Foxon/Paul Scullard........................6/3 6/3
Owen Casey/John Doran (3)..bt.........Isaac Donkar/Frank Ofori (7) 6/3 7/5
Joe Green/James Pringle (8) ....bt.........Kyle Rudman/Andrew Turner (4)..........6/7 6/2 6/3
Ross Matheson/Tom Spinks (2) ....bt.........Rhys Hanger/Daniel Sewell (5).................6/3 7/6

Semi Finals

Owen Casey/John Doran (3)..bt.........James Davidson/ Vaughan Snyman (1).....6/4 6/2
Ross Matheson/Tom Spinks (2) ....bt.........Joe Green/James Pringle (8)....................6/3 6/4

Final

Ross Matheson/Tom Spinks (2) ....bt.........Owen Casey/John Doran (3) 6/7 7/6 6/2

Women's Doubles

Quarter Finals

Mareze Joubert/Julie Dawson (1) ....bt.........Rachel Fagan/Elaine Fagan ....w/o
Lesley O'Halloran/Karen Nugent.....................................bt.........Alex Napier/Derbhla Kelly 3/6 7/6 6/1
Gina Niland/Yvonne Flynn ....bt.........Elaine Tritschler/Suzy Perkins...................6/0 6/1
Julia Lutrova/Victoria Davies (2)....................................bt.........Zara Wolseley/Emma Bollard...................6/0 6/0

Semi Finals

Lesley O'Halloran/Karen Nugent.....................................bt.........Mareze Joubert/Julie Dawson (1).......6/3 3/6 6/0
Julia Lutrova/Victoria Davies (2)....................................bt.........Gina Niland/Yvonne Flynn..............................w/o

Final

Julia Lutrova/Victoria Davies (2)....................................bt.........Lesley O'Halloran/Karen Nugent 6/4 7/5

Other Irish Open Champions

45 & Over Mens Doubles Final

Ben Cranwell/Gerry McGrath (2) ....bt.........Johnny Cunningham/Eddie Savage (1) 6/1 7/6

35 & Over Mixed Doubles Final

Ben Cranwell/Catherine Holohan (3) ....bt.........Johnny Cunningham/Marion McVeagh (4) 6/1 6/3

Class 4 Mixed Doubles

David Fox/Jenny O'Hare ....bt.........Shay Dolan/Phyliss Mullen 2/6 6/2 6/3

35 & Over C3 Mens Doubles

Dermot Burke/Noel Murphy (1) ....bt.........David Barber/John Goggin (2) 4/6 6/3 7/6

Class 6 Mens Doubles

Duncan Black/Sean Fitzpatrick ....bt.........Gerry Leckey/Ciaran Roche................7/5 6/7 6/4

Class 6 Womens Doubles

Maeve O'Neill/Roisin Norris ....bt.........Lolo O'Donoghue/Maree Mathews 6/3 6/3

1998 Carlsberg Irish Close Championships

Men's Singles

Owen Casey.............bt....Feargal McDonogh...6/0 6/3
Robert Collins...........bt....Neil Fagan 6/1 6/2
George McGill ....bt....David O'Connell........6/4 7/6
Nicholas Malone........bt....James Pringle.....7/6 4/6 6/4
David Mullins ....bt....Donal Glennon 6/0 6/0
Joe Green..................bt....James Colhoun.........6/1 6/0
Conor Taylor ....bt....Cormac Jennings 6/3 6/1
Peter Wright..............bt....Victor Drummy..........6/2 6/3

Quarter Finals

Owen Casey ....bt....Robert Collins...........6/1 6/2
George McGill ....bt....Nicholas Malone.......6/2 6/4
David Mullins ....bt....Joe Green.................6/2 6/3
Conor Taylor ....bt....Peter Wright........6/2 6/7 6/2

Semi Finals

Owen Casey ....bt....George McGill 6/0 6/2
David Mullins ....bt....Conor Taylor 3/6 7/5 6/3

Final

Owen Casey ....bt....David Mullins 6/0 6/1

Women's Singles

Gina Niland................bt....Kathy Curran 6/0 6/0
Zara Wolseley............bt....Ann Marie Hogan 6/3 6/2
Yvonne Flynn ....bt....Derbhla Kelly 6/3 6/4
Sinead Walsh ....bt ...Catriona Hannigan ...6/1 6/2
Heidi Butler................bt....Kathryn Leonard.......6/1 6/4
Lesley O'Halloran ......bt....Patricia D'Arcy 6/0 6/1
Della Kilduff ....bt ...Lisa O'Shea 6/0 6/1
Claire Curran ....bt....Noelle Dunny ....w/o

Quarter Finals

Gina Niland................bt....Zara Wolseley...........6/1 6/1
Yvonne Flynn ....bt....Sinead Walsh............6/4 6/1
Lesley O'Halloran ......bt....Heidi Butler...............6/0 6/2
Claire Curran ....bt....Della Kilduff 6/0 6/0

Semi Finals

Gina Niland................bt....Yvonne Flynn............6/3 6/4
Claire Curran ....bt....Lesley O'Halloran1/6 6/3 6/3

Final

Gina Niland................bt.... Claire Curran 4/6 6/1 6/1

Men's Doubles

Quarter Finals

O. Casey/P. Wright .... bt .... C. Jennings/C. Watson 6/0 6/1
S. Cooper/D. Mullins .... bt .... N. Malone/S. Taylor 7/6 6/4
J. Green/F. McDonough .... bt .... B. Lawlor/V. Drummy 7/6 7/6
J. Pringle/ C. Óg Molloy .... bt .... G. McGill/R. Collins 6/3 7/5

Semi Finals

O. Casey/P. Wright .... bt .... S. Cooper/D. Mullins 7/6 6/4
J. Pringle/ C. Óg Molloy .... bt .... J. Green/F. McDonough 7/5 3/6 6/4

Final

O. Casey/P. Wright .... bt .... J. Pringle/ C. Óg Molloy 6/2 6/3

Women's Doubles

Quarter Finals

C. Curran/G. Niland .... bt .... P. D'Arcy/E. Moore .... w/o
N. Dunny/A. McKay .... w/o
J. O'Brien/C. O'Sullivan .... bt .... B. Griffith/C. Harrigan 6/2 7/5
Y. Flynn/L. O'Halloran .... bt .... J. Timoney/S. Walsh .... w/o

Semi Finals

C. Curran/G. Niland .... bt .... N. Dunny/A. McKay .... w/o
Y. Flynn/L. O'Halloran .... bt .... J. O'Brien/C. O'Sullivan 6/1 6/3

Final

Y. Flynn/L. O'Halloran .... bt .... C. Curran/G. Niland 3/6 6/3 6/4

Other Irish Close Championship Winners

Mixed 2/3 Final

C. Carroll/D. Dougan .... bt .... G. McGrath/C. Harrigan 4/6 6/3 6/3

Mixed 4/5 Final

J. Doyle/C. Noel .... bt .... B. McGuirk/J. Duignan 4/6 6/1 6/4

Mixed 6 Final

P. Scully/S. Considine .... bt .... J. O'Callaghan/C. O'Callaghan ....

Mens Over 35 Final

Eddie Savage .... bt .... Bryan Smyth 7/6 6/2

Mens Over 35 Doubles Final

Roy Bailey/Tony Connor .... bt .... Harry Henry/John O'Brien ....

Ladies Over 35 Doubles Final

B. Griffith/C. Holohan .... bt .... N. Glynn/G. Wynne ....

Mens Plate Final

Brian Condren .... bt .... Kevin Noble 7/5 6/2

1998 Irish Open Junior Champions

Event	Boys	Girls
Senior Singles	S. Nugent	C. Lynch
Intermed. Singles	M. Finnegan	E. Ó Riain
Junior Singles	S. O'Connor	R. Halligan
Minor Singles	M. Carpenter	L. O'Rourke
Senior Doubles	C. Taylor/ S. Taylor	J. Thompson/ L. Vojnov
Intermed. Doubles	T. Barry/ R. Martin	E. Murphy/ E. Ó Riain
Junior Doubles	R. Kernan/ C. O'Brien	S. Griffith/ C. McMorrow
Minor Boys	R. Green/ D. Rowan	S. Griffith/ A. Wynne

Event	
Senior Mixed Doubles	C Foley/E. Fagan
Intermediate Mixed Doubles	M. Finnegan/C. Lynch
Junior Mixed Doubles	S. O'Connor/R. Halligan
Minor Mixed Doubles	M. Carpenter/S. Griffith

1998 Irish Indoor Junior Champions

Event	Boys	Girls
U14	Stephen O'Connor	Jenny Lawlor
U16	Nelson Boyle	Elsa Ó Riain
U18	Stephen Nugent	Catherine Lynch

INTERNATIONAL RESULTS

Ferderation Cup, Europe/Africa Qualifying Group II. Antalya 5-9 May 1998

5 May. Bosnia & Herzegovina defeated Ireland 2-1

Mervana Jugic (BIH) .... bt .... Lesley O'Halloran (Irl) 7-6 6-1

Asja Tankic (BIH)	bt	Gina Niland (Irl)	6-1 7-6
Yvonne Flynn/Aoife O'Neill (Irl)	bt	Harisa Delic/Adisa Salibasic	4-6 6-4 6-2
6 May. Ireland defeated Estonia 2-1			
Lesley O'Halloran (Irl)	bt	Helen Holter (Est)	7-5 6-1
Gina Niland (Irl)	bt	Liina Suurvarik (Est)	0-6 6-2 6-2
Maret Ani/Helen Laupa (Est)	bt	Yvonne Flynn/Lesley O'Halloran (Irl)	6-2 6-1
7 May. Ireland defeated Moldova 2-1			
Lesley O'Halloran (Irl)	bt	Evghenia Ablovatchi (Mol)	6-1 4-6 7-5
Gina Niland (Irl)	bt	Natalia Volcova (Mol)	7-5 6-2
Elena Petrenco/Natalia Volcova	bt	Yvonne Flynn/Aoife O'Neill (Irl)	6-7 6-4 7-5
8 May. Georgia defeated Ireland 3-0			
Margalita Chakhnashvili (Geo)	bt	Lesley O'Halloran (Irl)	6-4 6-2
Nino Louarsabishvili (Geo)	bt	Gina Niland (Irl)	6-3 6-1
Margalita Chakhnashvili/Nino Louarsabishvili (Geo)	bt	Yvonne Flynn/Aoife O'Neill (Irl)	6-3 6-1

Davis Cup

Ireland v Hungary. Budapest 1-3 May 1998.

Norbet Mazany (Hun)	bt	Scott Barron (Irl)	6-3 0-6 2-6 6-4 9-7
Attila Savolt (Hun)	bt	John Doran (Irl)	6-1 6-3 6-3
C. Bardoczky/Attila Savolt (Hun)	bt	Owen Casey/Tommy Hamilton (Irl)	6-3 6-4 1-6 6-1
John Doran (Irl)	bt	Norbet Mazany (Hun)	6-4 4-6 6-4
Attila Savolt (Hun)	bt	Scott Barron (Irl)	6-4 6-4

Result: Hungary 4 Ireland 1

Ireland v Monaco. Dublin 17-19 July 1998.

John Doran (Irl)	bt	Christophe Bossio (Mon)	6-3 6-3 6-1
Owen Casey (Irl)	bt	Sabastien Graeff (Mon)	6-2 6-3 6-1
Owen Casey/Tommy Hamilton (Irl)	bt	C. Bogetti/Sabastien Graeff (Mon)	7-6 6-4 6-1
George McGill	bt	Christophe Bossio (Mon)	6-3 3-6 7-5
John Doran (Irl)	bt	Sabastien Graeff (Mon)	7-6 7-6 7-6

Result: Ireland 5 Monaco 1

PAST PRESIDENTS

1913-23	Col. A. Courtenay
1924-29	Rt. Hon. Lord Glenavy
1930	R. P. Corry
1931	J.E. McCausland
1932	Dr. W.L. Murphy
1933	T.B. Pedlow
1934	Capt. A.H.C. Home
1935	Hon. Mr. Justice Hannna
1936	De Vere Crossley
1937	K.B. Williams
1938	Capt. C. Campbell
1939	S .F. Scroope
1940	K.B. Williams
1941	F. Egan
1942	E.C. Harrington
1943	H. St. J. Blake K.M.
1944	W. St. G. Perrott
1945	W. St. G. Perrott
1946	N. Colville, De Vere Crossley
1947	C.O. Mansergh
1948	H. St. J. Blake, K.M.
1949	Sen. E.A. McGuire
1950	A.S.C. Burton
1951	J. St. J. Riordan
1952	H. St. J. Blake, K.M.
1953	A. Percy Huet
1954	T.S. Duncan
1955	F. J. Mockler
1956	H. St. J. Blake, K. M.
1957	H.F. Cronin
1958	D.F. Wheeler
1959	H.F. Cronin
1960	M. J. Heverin
1961	R.F. Egan
1962	W.G. Nicholl
1963	A.H. Walsh
1964	E. Harte-Barry
1965	T. McCarthy
1966	L.F. Steen
1967	J.A.D. Magrath
1968	W. O'Regan
1969	I. Claravan
1970	A.H. Walsh
1971	J.A.D. Magrath
1972	F.H. O'Donoghue
1973	D.F. Dempsey
1974	K.W.E. Potterton
1975	D.J.P. Ferguson
1976	J.P. O'Neill
1977	D.F. Dempsey
1978	C.J. Brennan
1979	P.S.F. Bayliss
1980	R. Holland
1981	D.F. Dcmpsey
1982	P.G. Donnellan
1983	M .R. Hogg
1984	P. Daly
1985	P. Daly
1986	C.J. Brennan
1987	P.S.F. Bayliss
1988	H. Clinton
1989	M. McCann
1990	G. More O'Ferrall
1991	A. Taylor
1992	R. McAuliffe
1993	J . Brewster
1994	R. Thompson
1995	G. Stevenson
1996	K. Stanton
1997	C. O'Donovan
1998	O. Raftery

TUG-OF-WAR

Irish Tug-of-War Association

c/o Mrs. Nuala Hubbard, PRO, Longhouse, Ballymore Eustace, Co. Kildare. Tel/Fax: (045) 864222

Founded....1967
President....Eddie Hubbard
Vice-President....James Ward
Chairman....Phil Timoney
Vice-Chairman....Dennis Dunlea
Secretary....Martha Buckley
Treasurer....Sean Foody
PRO....Nuala Hubbard
Number of Clubs....41 *See Below*
Number of Coaches....2 per club
Number of Members....1,400 approx
Affiliated to....Tug-of-War International Federation

PROVINCIAL UNIONS

CONNACHT President: Joe Hughes **Chairman:** Jerry Ferguson **Secretary:** Padraig Rooney **Treasurer:** Michael Brennan **PRO:** Walter Gibbons

LEINSTER President: Kevin Whelan **Vice-President:** Seamus Dowling **Chairman:** Seamus Kilbride **Vice-Chairman:** Eddie Fox **Secretary:** Eddie Hubbard **Treasurer:** Eilish O'Neill **PRO:** Nuala Hubbard

MUNSTER President: Michael Carroll **Vice-President:** P.J. Carey **Chairman:** Dennis Dunlea **Vice-Chairman:** Ted Hurton **Secretary:** Pat Lee **Assistant Secretary:** Teresa Hurton **Treasurer:** Batt McHugh **Assistant Treasurer:** Pat Lee

ULSTER Chairman: James Ward **Secretary:** Bernie Hurson **Treasurer:** Malachy Coyle **PRO:** Colin Higgins

CLUBS

● Ardaghy, Co. Monaghan ● Ballycroy, Co. Mayo ● Bolton Hill, Co. Kildare ● Bremore Farmers, Co. Dublin ● Clohamon, Co. Wexford ● Cloontagh, Co. Donegal ● Coolock, Co. Dublin ● Creewood, Co. Meath ● Dalua Demons, Co. Cork ● Dunderry, Co. Meath ● Drumsna, Co. Leitrim ● Glenade, Co. Leitrim ● Fermoy, Co. Cork ● Hillsiders, Co. Mayo ● Killylough, Co. Monaghan ● Lettercran, Co. Donegal ● Midlanders, Co. Kildare ● Redhills, Co. Cavan ● St. Colman's, Co. Mayo ● Slieve Na Mon, Co. Tipperary ● Two Counties, Co. Galway ● Ard, Co. Offaly ● Boley, Co. Wexford ● Bunclody, Co. Wexford ● Carberry, Co. Cork ● Clonmany, Co. Donegal ● Corcaghan, Co. Monaghan ● Daingean, Co. Offaly ● Donoughmore, Co. Cork ● Drumholme, Co. Donegal ● Erinside, Co. Donegal ● Glen, Co. Donegal ● Glenhill, Co. Cork ● Hughes, Co. Mayo ● Lakesiders, Co. Mayo ● Logg, Co. Offaly ● Rathanna, Co. Carlow ● Rathkeale, Co. Limerick ● Strawbally, Co. Waterford ● St. Mary's, Co. Donegal ● Woodlanders, Co. Carlow

1997-98 INTERNATIONAL STATISTICS

National Senior Coaches Jim Curtis, Padraig Rooney, Brian McLoughlin, Paul Delahan, Martin Egan, Gerry Ferguson, Pat Doherty, Sean Beirne, Sean Foody, Mick Toomey, Finn Delahan, Kevin Whelan, Danny McGonigle, Martin Vaughan, Antony Pender, John Murphy ● **Best International Result:** Youth Team - Silver at 1997 European Championships, Jersey ● **World Rankings:** In Top Six ● **Most Capped Competitor:** Martin Keogh - won 13 gold medals in European and World Championships.

RESULTS

1998 National Championship League Finals

Division	Winning Club	Runners up
Division 1	Killylough, Co. Monaghan (42 pts)	Boley, Co. Wexford (36 pts)
Division 2	Two Counties, Co. Galway (46 pts)	Redhills, Co. Cavan (29 pts)
Division 3	Logg, Co. Offaly (46 pts)	Corcaghan, Co. Monaghan (35 pts)
Division 4	Dunderry, Co. Meath (31 pts)	Drumholme, Co. Donegal
	U21	Corcaghan, Co. Monaghan
Rathanna, Co. Carlow		
Youths	Clohamon, Co. Wexford (26 pts)	Ard, Co. Offaly (25 pts)
Ladies	Bunclody, Co. Wexford	Hughes, Co. Mayo

1997 National Indoor Championships

Division	League Champions	Division	League Champions
Division 1	St. Pats, Co. Louth (42 pts)	U21	Cloontagh, Co. Donegal (28 pts)

Continued from previous page

Division	League Champions	Division	League Champions
Division 2	Redhills, Co. Cavan (36 pts)	Youths	Bremore, Co. Dublin (38 pts)
Division 3	Fermoy, Co. Cork (28 pts)		

1998-99 CALENDAR OF EVENTS

Date	Competition - Venue
15 November, 1998	**National Indoor Competitions, Manorhamilton, Co. Leitrim**
	720 kg in Divisions 1,2,3. U21 640kg. Ladies 540kg
22 November, 1998	**National Indoor Competitions, Youth Centre, Co. Carlow**
	640 kg in Divisions 1,2,3. Youths 580kg.
29 November, 1998	**National Indoor Competitions, Clonmany, Co. Donegal**
	600 kg in Divisions 1,2,3. U21 560kg. Ladies 500kg.
13 December, 1998	**National Indoor Competitions, Clonmany, Co. Donegal**
	560kg in Divisions 1,2,3. U21 600kg. 680kg in Divisions 1,2,3.
24-28 February, 1999	**TWIF World Indoor Tug of War Championships, Carlow**
25th February	TWIF Open Clubs Competition: Men's 560kg, Men's 640kg, Ladies 520 kg, U21 Demonstration
26th February	TWIF Open Clubs Competition: Men's 600kg, Men's 680kg, Ladies 480kg,Youth 560kg
27th February	TWIF World Championships: Men's 560kg, Men's 640kg, Ladies 520kg,Youth 560kg
28th February	TWIF World Championships: Men's 600kg, Men's 680kg, Ladies 480kg
13 June, 1999	**National Outdoor Competitions, Midlands Venue**
	720 kg in Divisions 1,2,3,4. Youths 500kg. Ladies 560kg
27 June, 1999	**National Outdoor Competitions, Glenade, Co. Leitrim**
	680 kg in Divisions 1,2,3,4. U21 640kg. Youths 520kg
11 July, 1999	**National Outdoor Competitions, Creewood, Co. Meath**
	640 kg in Divisions 1,2,3,4. U21 620kg. Youths 480kg
18 July, 1999	**National Outdoor Competitions, Claremorris, Co. Mayo**
	600 kg in Divisions 1,2,3,4. U21 600kg. Ladies 520kg
1 August, 1999	**National Outdoor Competitions, Killylough, Co. Monaghan**
	560 kg in Divisions 1,2,3,4. Youths 560kg, Catch-Weight

PAST PRESIDENTS

Fred Cogley, RTÉ Head of Sport; Dan Ryan, Co. Kildare; Robert Deane, Co. Cork; Kevin Whelan, Co. Wexford.

Irish Windsurfing Association

c/o Boherboy, Dunlavin, Co. Wicklow. Tel: (045) 76187. Web site: http://faraday.ucd.ie/~joseph/iwa/

President.....................Joseph Meehan
Secretary.....................Chris Sparrow
Treasurer.....................John Cullinan

MAIN WINDSURFING SPOTS

THE NORTH COAST: *Donegal:* Port Salon, Magheroaraty (a big wave beach), Marble Hill, Downings Beach, Tramore, Portnoo (nr Ardara), Rosnowlagh. *Northern Ireland:* Portrush and Portstewart (big wave beach with a very strong rip).

THE EAST COAST: Dublin Bay: Dollymount Beach (very popular with Dublin's wavesailers), Poolbeg, Salthill (mainly slalom sailing - behind Dun Laoghaire Harbour), Surf dock (situated in the Canal basin in Dublin city centre - for learners), Sutton (at the North end of Dollymount), Malahide (an estuary to the North of Dublin, best in a westerly wind), Rush (North of Dublin), Skerries, Blessington (inland - the main reservoir for Dublin), Brittas Bay (nice waves but a strong rip current). *Elsewhere:* Cahor (unspoilt spot with long beaches), Rosslare (Co. Wexford - slalom spot but the prevailing wind is cross off-shore), Our Ladies Island (small lake just behind a beach - ideal for speedsailing).

THE SOUTH COAST: *Waterford:* Dunmore East (good for long board sailing up the coast), Tramore (a long open beach facing the swells coming up the Irish sea), Dungarvan (situated in a sheltered inlet - very good for slalom sailing), Clonea Strand (an open beach with potential for some good waves). *Cork:* Cobh (normally from a bay just outside the town), Oysterhaven (a small sheltered bay), Coolmaine (the wave spot near Cork, a southerly facing beach), Garretstown (similar to Coolmaine but with bigger swells).

THE WEST COAST: *Kerry:* The Dingle Peninsula (an ideal windsurfing spot), Brandon Bay (a wide horse-shoe shaped beach that accommodates nearly every wind and swell direction; includes Sandy Bay, Scraganne Bay (good for slalom sailing), North Garrywilliam Point (only for the best and most experienced surfers), Mossies (situated opposite Spillanes Bar), Stoney Gap - dangerous in a big swell, Three Peaks - West of Brandon bay), Inch Strand (beach jutting out to sea for 4 miles with some good quality beach break waves. *Co. Clare:* Lahinch (mostly a surf spot). *Galway:* Oranmore (on Galway bay, opposite to Galway city, good for slalom sailing), Salthill (Galway city - mostly for slalom sailing mainly here), Roundstone (Co. Galway with two different windsurfing spots - Dogs bay and Gorteen bay). *Mayo:* Achill Island, Keel Bay (for experts only), Keel Lake (very good for speed sailing), Belmullet (out on peninsular Co. Mayo, jutting into the Atlantic - one side of the peninsula has good slalom conditions while the other gets the full Atlantic swell). *Sligo:* Easkey (better known as a surfers' break), Strandhill (Co. Sligo - also better known as a surfers' break), Rosses Point (just outside Sligo town).

INLAND: Lurgan (on the shores of Lough Neagh, beside Mullin Marine, a nice conserved recreational park devoted to sports, with windsurfing being included - Ballyronan on the NW shore), Toome Bridge (at the River Bann), Cranfield (near to Randlestown Co. Antrim), Antrim (two sites either side of the river - the swell can be quite steep), Mountshannon (on a lake of the River Shannon), Shannonside, Dromineer.

WRESTLING

Irish Amateur Wrestling Association (IAWA)

c/o 54 Elm Mount Drive, Beaumont, Dublin 9. Tel: (01) 8315522 .

Founded 1947
President .... Michael Whelan
Chairman .... Dan Walsh
Honorary Treasurer/Secretary .... Michael McAuley
Assistant Treasurer .... John Rice
Number of Recognised Free-style Wrestling Coaches 20
Affiliated to .... Federation international de Lutte Amateur *(the world governing body).*
(Free-style wrestling is an Olympic sport)

INTERNATIONAL FIXTURES/RESULTS

● **National Coaches** Michael McAuley, Michael Whelan, Dan Walsh, Brendan Losty, Aidan Rice, John Russell, Ciaron Gogarty, Anthony McLoughlin, Dan McLoughlin, Bill Harmon, Harry Byrne ● **Most Capped Competitor** Joe Feeney (welterweight) won the British title 1957-64 (recorded in the Guinness Book of Records) ● **Best Recent International Result** 1994 Small Nations Championships *(countries with populations under 5 million)* Ireland: won the team event; Individual results - Russell Dunleavy: 1st (82 kg), Danny McLoughlin: 2nd (82 kg)

DATE	EVENT	VENUE	RESULT
Aug. 98	**International Highland Games**	Scotland	Dan McLoughlin: 2nd (13 stone, 7lbs)
	(catch-as-catch can, free style, backhold style)		Elias Salami: 2nd (11 stone, 7lbs)
			Brent Duggan: 3rd (13 stone, 7lbs)
Oct. 98	**Triangular International Competition**	Dublin	Participating: Ireland, Scotland, England
Nov. 98	**Small Nations International C'ships**	Malta	-

1998 DOMESTIC FIXTURES/RESULTS

Event	Winner / Placings
Spartan Cup	Danny McLoughlin: 1st
	Ciaron Gogarty: 2nd
	Elias Salami: 3rd
	Brent Duggan: 4th
Coleman Cup	Daniel Kennedy: 1st
	Aidan Rice: 2nd
Coleman Cup	Nial Rice: 3rd
	Dermot Durack: 4th
Dick Vekins Club Competition	to be held
Irish Close Championships	to be held December
Irish Open Championships	to be held Jan 99

CHRONOLOGY OF IRISH WRESTLING

1947 .... Formation of Eire Amateur Wrestling Assoc.
1948 .... Representatives to Olympic Games, London
1949 .... EAWA changes to title IAWA
1950 .... International: Ireland v. England
1951 .... Second Irish Open Championships
1952 .... Representatives to Olympic Games, Helsinki
.... Triangular International Competition
.... Participating: Ireland-Scotland-England
1954 .... Triangular International Competition
.... Participating: Ireland-Scotland-England
1955 .... Juvenile Division commences
1956 .... Representatives to Olympic Games, Melbourne
1957 .... Triangular International Competition
1960 .... Representatives to Olympic Games, Rome
1963 .... Triangular International Competition
1964 .... Representatives to Olympic Games, Tokyo
1965 .... Schoolboy Division commences
1966 .... Intermediate Division commences
1967 .... Juvenile International
1968 .... Representatives to Highland Games, Scotland
1969 .... Breton wrestlers visit
1970 .... Host Schoolboy International
1971 .... Irish Wrestler wins Australian Title

VOLLEYBALL

Northern Ireland Volleyball Association

House of Sport, Upper Malone, Belfast. Tel. 01232 381222

Founded......1970
President......Patrick Murphy
Secretary......Simon Hunter
Public Relations Officer......Patrick Murphy
Number of Affiliated Clubs......30
Number of Coaches......26

1997/98 Season	CHAMPIONS
Men's Senior League	Larne Old Boys
Womens Senior League	Belfast City Wonmen
Premier 32, All Ireland Men	Belfast City Men
Men's Cup	Portadown Aztecs
Women's Cup	Belfast City Ladies

Previous winners of N.I. senior leagues and senior cup competitions:
MEN: Olympia Belfast; Reebok Lisburn; Larne Old Boys; UUJ;
WOMEN: Belfast City Ladies; Reebok Belfast; CICA Belfast;

OLYMPICS

Olympic Council of Ireland

27 Mespil Road, Dublin 4. Tel. (01) 6680444 Fax. (01) 6680650

President .... Patrick Hickey
Honorary IOC Life President .... Dr. Kevin O'Flanagan
First Vice-President .... Shay McDonald
Second Vice-President .... Dermot J. Sherlock
Honorary Life President .... Louis D. Kilcoyne
Honorary General Secretary .... Peadar Casey

SUMMER OLYMPICS

IRISH OLYMPIANS, 1924-96

PARIS (1924) Athletics: Patrick J. Bermingham, J. P. Clarke, J. Kelly, Sean Lavan, W. J. Lowe, Norman McEacherrn, John O'Connor, John O'Grady, John Ryan, William Shanahan, Larry Stanley. **Boxing:** M. Doyle, Patrick Dwyer, R. Hilliard, J. Kellegher, J. Kidley, M. McDonagh, William Murphy. **Football:** Peter Duncan, John Dykes, Michael Farrell, Peter Ghent, David Hannon, James Kendrick, Harry Kerr, James McCarthy, Edward McKay, Thomas Muldoon, John Murray, Patrick O'Reilly. **Tennis:** William Ireland, Edwin McCrea, Mary Wallis, Rebecca Blair-White. **Water Polo:** C. Barret, J. Beckett, J. Brady, J. Convery, C. Fagan, M. O'Connor, Noel Purcell.

AMSTERDAM (1928) Athletics: Patrick Anglim, Alistair Clarke, G. N. Coughlan, Dan Cullen, Sean Lavan, Norman MacEacherrn, Patrick O'Callaghan, Theodore Phelan. **Cycling:** B. Donnelly, J. Woodcock. **Boxing:** James Chase, Michael Flanagan, G. Kelly, Patrick Lenehan, M. McDonagh, William Murphy, W. O'Shea, Edward Traynor. **Swimming:** W. Broderick, M. Dockrell. **Water Polo:** T. Dockrell, C. Fagan, N. Judd, P. McClure, S. Moore, J. O'Connor, M. O'Connor.

LOS ANGELES (1932) Athletics: Denis Cussen, Eamonn Fitzgerald, Michael Murphy, Patrick O'Callaghan, Robert Tisdall. **Boxing:** R. Barton, J. J. Murphy, James Murphy, Ernest Smith.

BERLIN (1936) *No Irish team travelled.*

LONDON (1948) Athletics: J. J. Barry, Cummin Clancy, D. Coyle, C. Denroche, Paul Dolan, Paddy Fahy, Dave Guiney, F. P. Mulvihill, R. J. Myles, Jimmy Reardon. **Basketball:** H. Boland, P. Crehan, J. Flynn, W. Jackson, T. Keenan, T. Malone, J. McGee, G. McLoughlin, F. O'Connor, D. O'Donovan, D. Reddin, D. Sheriff, P. Sheriff, C. Walsh. **Boxing:** Willie Barnes, Peter Foran, Willie Lenahan, Maxie McCullough, Gearoid O'Colmain. **Fencing:** Dorothy Dermody, P. Duffy, Anthony O'Connor, S. Smith, Owen Toohey. **Football:** W. Barry, D. Cleary, F. Glennon, Patrick Kavanagh, D. Lawler, Patrick McDonald, E. McLoughlin, W. O'Grady, B. O'Kelly, W. Richardson, Robert Smith. **Rowing:** Ray Chantler, Paddy Dooley, Ian Dowdall, Joe Hanley, Denis Sugrue, Morgan McElligot, Wally Stevens, Robin Tamplin, Danny Taylor. **Sailing:** Hugh Allen, Alf Delaney, A.J. Mooney. **Swimming:** Patrick Kavanagh, Stuart Kramm, Ernest McCarthy.

HELSINKI (1952) Boxing: Peter Crotty, Willie Duggan, John Little, John McNally, Terry Mulligan, Anto Reddy, Tommy Reddy. **Equestrian:** Capt. M. Darley, Capt. Harry Freeman-Jackson, Capt. Ian Hume-Dudgeon. **Fencing:** P. J. Duffy, N. Thuillier. **Sailing:** Alf Delaney. **Wrestling:** Jack Vard.

MELBOURNE (1956) Athletics: Ronnie Delany, Eamonn Kinsella, Maeve Kyle. **Boxing:** Tony Byrne, John Caldwell, Freddie Gilroy, Harry Perry, Patrick Sharkey, Martin Smith, Fred Tiedt. **Equestrian:** Capt. Harry Freeman-Jackson, Capt. Ian Hume-Dudgeon, Col. Bill Mullins. **Sailing:** J. Somers Payne. **Wrestling:** Gerald Martina.

ROME (1960) Athletics: Willie Dunne, Michael Hoey, Maeve Kyle, John Lawlor, Paddy Lowry, Gerry McIntyre, Bertie Messit, Frank O'Reilly. **Boxing:** Joe Casey, Patrick Kenny, Adam McClean, Colm McCoy, Eamon McKeon, Bernard Meli, Danny O'Brien, Harry Perry, Ando Reddy, Michael Reid. **Cycling:** Peter Crinion, Anthony Cullen, Seamus Herron, Michael Horgan, Martin McKay. **Equestrian:** Major Boylan, Tony Cameron, Lt. J. P. Daly, Capt. Harry Freeman-Jackson, Capt. C. B. Harty, Eddie Harty, Capt. Ian Hume-Dudgeon, Capt. R. E. Maloney, Lt. E. P. O'Donohoe, Capt. W. A. Ringrose. **Fencing:** Shirley Armstrong Duffy, Chris Bland, George Carpenter, Brian Hamilton, Tom Kearney, Harry Thuillier. **Sailing:** Robin Benson, Peter Gray, Johnny Hooper, Dr A. J. Mooney, Dr D. A. Ryder, J. Somers Payne. **Weightlifting:** Thomas Hayden. **Wrestling:** Dermot Dunne, Joseph Feeney, Gerald Martina, Sean O'Connor.

TOKYO (1964) Athletics: Noel Carroll, Jim Hogan, Maeve Kyle, John Lawlor, Derek McCleane, Tom O'Riordan. **Boxing:** Brian Anderson, Paddy Fitzsimons, Sean McCafferty, Jim McCourt, Chris Rafter. **Equestrian:** Tommy Brennan, Tony Cameron, Capt. Harry Freeman-Jackson, Ms. V. Freeman-Jackson, John Harty. **Fencing:** John Bouchier-Hayes, Michael Ryan. **Sailing:** Rob Dalton, Johnny Hooper, Eddie Kellegher, Harry Maguire. **Wrestling:** Joseph Feeney.

MEXICO (1968) Athletics: Noel Carroll, John Kelly, Pat McMahon, Mick Molloy, Frank Murphy. **Boxing:** Mick Dowling, Brendan McCarthy, Eamon McCusker, Martin Quinn, Eddie Treacy. **Cycling:** Peter Doyle, Morris Foster, Liam Horner. **Equestrian:** Tommy Brennan, Col. Ed Campion, Patrick Connolly Carew, John Fowler, Juliet Jobling Purser, Capt. L. Kiely, Ada Matheson, Penny Moreton, Alan Rillingston, Diane Wilson, Baroness Diana Wrangle. **Fencing:** John Bouchier-Hayes, Fionnbarr Farrell, Colm O'Brien, Michael Ryan. **Shooting (Clay Pigeon):** Gerry Brady, Dermot Kelly, Arthur McMahon. **Swimming:** Liam Ball, Anne O'Connor, Donnacha O'Dea, Vivienne Smith.

MUNICH (1972) Athletics: Phil Conway, Neil Cusack, John Harnett, Mick Keogh, Eddie Leddy, Danny McDaid, Des McGann, Fananan McSweeney, Frank Murphy, Margaret Murphy, Mary Purcell, Clare Walsh, Donie Walsh. **Boxing:** Mick Dowling, Christy Elliot, Neil McLaughlin, Jim Montague, Charlie Nash, John Rodgers. **Canoeing:** Gerry Collins, Ann McQuaid, Brendan O'Connell, Howard Watkins. **Cycling:** Peter Doyle, Liam Horner, Kieron McQuaid, Noel Taggart. **Equestrian:** Billy Buller, Patrick Connolly Carew, Juliet Jobling Purser, Billy McLernon, Commdt. Ronnie McMahon, William Powell-Harris. **Fencing:** John Bouchier-Hayes. **Judo:** Liam Carroll, Anto Clark, Matthew Folan, Paddy Murphy, Terry Watt. **Rowing:** Sean Drea. **Shooting (Clay Pigeon):** Gerry Brady, William Campbell, Dermot Kelly, Arthur McMahon. **Swimming:** Liam Ball, Brian Clifford, Christine Fulcher, Andrew Hunter, Brenda McGrory, Ann O'Connor, Aisling O'Leary. **Sailing:** Harry Byrne, Harold Cudmore, Owen Delaney, Robert Hennessy, Devin McLaverty, Richard O'Shea, David Wilkins, Sean Whitaker. **Weightlifting:** Frank Rothwell.

MONTREAL (1976) Archery: Jim Conroy. **Athletics:** Eamonn Coghlan, Neil Cusack, Eddie Leddy, Danny McDaid, Jim McNamara, Niall O'Shaughnessy, Mary Purcell. **Boxing:** Bryan Byrne, Brendan Dunne, Gerard Hamill, David Larmour, Christy McLaughlin. **Canoeing:** Declan Burns, Michael Keating, Brendan O'Connell, Ian Pringle, Howard Watkins. **Cycling:** Alan McCormack, Oliver McQuaid. **Equestrian:** Eric Horgan, Commdt. Ronnie McMahon, Gerry Synott, Norman Van de Vater. **Rowing:** Sean Drea, Martin Feeley, Iain Kennedy, Andy McDonough, Jim Muldoon, Christy O'Brien, Liam Redmond, Jaye Renehan, Mick Ryan, Willie Ryan. **Sailing:** Peter Dix, Robert Dix, Derek Jago, Barry O'Neill, David Wilkins, Jamie Wilkinson. **Shooting (Clay Pigeon):** Richard Flynn. **Swimming:** Miriam Hopkins, Robert Howard, Deirdre Sheehan, Kevin Williamson.

MOSCOW (1980) Archery: Jim Conroy, Hazel Greene, William Swords. **Athletics:** Eamonn Coghlan, Sean Egan, Ray Flynn, Dick Hooper, Pat Hooper, Mick O'Shea, John Treacy. **Boxing:** Martin Breton, P. J. Davitt, Sean Doyle, Gerard Hawkins, Barry McGuigan, Hugh Russell, Phil Sutcliffe. **Canoeing:** Declan Burns, Ian Pringle. **Cycling:** Billy Kerr, Tony Lally, Stephen Roche. **Judo:** Alonzo Henderson, David McManus. **Modern Pentathlon:** Jerome Hartigan, Mark Hartigan, Sackville Curry. **Rowing:** Frances Cryan, Pat Gannon, Noel Graham, Davey Gray, Iain Kennedy, Pat McDonagh, Christy O'Brien, Denis Rice, Ted Ryan, Willie Ryan, Liam Williams. **Sailing:** David Wilkins, Jamie Wilkinson. **Shooting (Clay Pigeon):** Nicholas Cooney, Thomas Hewitt, Albert Thompson. **Shooting (Target):** Ken Stafford. **Swimming:** Catherine Bohan, David Cummins, Kevin Williamson.

LOS ANGELES (1984) Archery: Hazel Greene, Mary Vaughan. **Athletics:** Paul Donovan, Ray Flynn, Declan Hegarty, Dick Hooper, Monica Joyce, Regina Joyce, Jerry Kiernan, Conor McCullough, Carey May, Liam O'Brien, Frank O'Mara, Caroline O'Shea, Marcus O'Sullivan, Mary Parr, Roisin Smyth, John Treacy, Patricia Walsh. **Boxing:** Tommy Corr, Paul Fitzgerald, Gerard Hawkins, Kieran Joyce, Sam Storey, Phil Sutcliffe. **Canoeing:** Ian Pringle. **Cycling:** Philip Cassidy, Seamus Downey, Martin Early, Paul Kimmage, Gary Thompson. **Equestrian:** Capt. David Foster, Sarah Gordon, Jessica Harrington, Margaret Tolerton, Fiona Wentges. **Judo:** Kieran Foley. **Sailing:** Bill O'Hara. **Shooting (Clay Pigeon):** Roy McGowan, Albert Thompson. **Swimming:** Carol Ann Heavey, June Parkes.

SEOUL (1988) Archery: Hazel Greene, Noel Lynch, Joseph Malone. **Athletics:** Eamonn Coghlan, John Doherty, Dick Hooper, Barbara Johnson, T. J. Kearns, Ann Keenan Buckley, Conor McCullough, Jimmy McDonald, Terry McHugh, Carlos O'Connell, Frank O'Mara, Gerry O'Reilly, Marcus O'Sullivan, Brendan Quinn, Marie Rollins-Murphy, John Treacy, John Woods. **Boxing:** Michael Carruth, Paul Fitzgerald, Kieran Joyce, Joe Lawlor, John Lowey, Wayne McCullough, Billy Walsh. **Canoeing:** Declan Bums, Alan Carey, Peter Connor, Patrick Holmes. **Cycling:** Philip Cassidy, Cormack McCann, Paul McCormack, John McQuaid, Stephen Spratt. **Equestrian:** Paul Darragh, Jack Doyle, Capt. David Foster, Capt. John Ledingham, Comdt. Gerry Mullins, Shea Walsh, John Watson. **Judo:** Eugene McManus. **Rowing:** Frank Moore, Pat McDonagh, Liam Williams. **Sailing:** Aisling Byrne, Peter Kennedy, Cathy McAleavy, Bill O'Hara, David Wilkins. **Swimming:** Aileen Convery, Stephen Cullen, Richard Gheel, Gary O'Toole, Michelle Smith. **Tennis:** Owen Casey, Eoin Collins. **Wrestling:** David Harmon.

BARCELONA (1992) Archery: Noel Lynch. **Athletics:** Noel Berkeley, Victor Costelloe, John Doherty, Sean Dollman, Paul Donovan, Thomas Hughes, T. J. Kearns, James McDonald, Terry McHugh, Catherina McKiernan, Bobby O'Leary, Frank O'Mara, Marcus O'Sullivan, Sonia O'Sullivan, Paul Quirke, Andrew Ronan, Nicholas Sweeney, John Treacy, Perri Williams. **Boxing:** Paul Buttimer, Michael Carruth, Paul Douglas, Paul Griffin, Kevin McBride, Wayne

McCullough. **Canoeing:** Alan Carey, Michael Corcoran, Conor Holmes, Patrick Holmes, Ian Wiley. **Cycling:** Conor Henry, Mark Kane, Kevin Kimmage, Robert Power, Paul Slane. **Equestrian:** Peter Charles, Francis Connors, Mairead Curran, Paul Darragh, Melanie Duff, Sonya Duke, Olivia Holohan, James Kernan, Eddie Macken, Anna Merveldt, Eric Smiley. **Fencing:** Michael O'Brien. **Judo:** Keith Gough, Ciaran Ward. **Rowing:** Niall O'Toole. **Sailing:** Peter Kennedy, Denise Lyttle, Tom McWilliam, Mark Mansfield, Denis O'Sullivan, Conrad Simpson, David Wilkins. **Swimming:** Gary O'Toole, Michelle Smith. **Tennis:** Owen Casey, Eoin Collins.

ATLANTA (1996) Athletics: Niall Bruton, Sean Cahill, Sinead Delahunty, Sean Dollman, Eugene Farrell, Cormac Finnerty, Deirdre Gallagher, Shane Healy, T. J. Kearns, Roman Linscheid, Kathy McCandless, Jimmy McDonald, Tom McGuirk, Terry McHugh, Catherina McKiernan, Marie McMahon, Mark Mandy, David Matthews, Marcus O'Sullivan, Sonia O'Sullivan, Gary Ryan, Neil Ryan, Susan Smith, Nicky Sweeney. **Boxing:** Francis Barrett, Damaen Kelly, Brian Magee, Cathal O'Grady. **Canoeing:** Andrew Boland, Michael Corcoran, Gary Mawer, Conor Moloney, Stephen O'Flaherty, Ian Wiley. **Cycling:** Philip Collins, Martin Earley, Declan Lonergan, David McCann, Alister Martin. **Equestrian:** Mark Barry, Alfie Buller, Peter Charles, Jessica Chesney, David Foster, Heike Holstein, Capt. John Ledingham, Virginia McGrath, Eddie Macken, Eric Smiley. **Gymnastics:** Barry McDonald. **Judo:** Kieran Ward. **Rowing:** Brendan Dolan, Derek Holland, John Holland, Sam Lynch, Neville Maxwell, Tony O'Connor, Niall O'Toole. **Sailing:** Aisling Bowman, David Burrows, Louise Cole, Garrett Connolly, John Driscoll, Marshall King, Denise Lyttle, Mark Lyttle, Mark Mansfield, Dan O'Grady. **Shooting (Clay Pigeon):** Thomas Allen. **Shooting: (Target):** Ronah Barry, Gary Duff. **Swimming:** Earl McCarthy, Marion Madine, Adrian O'Connor, Nick O'Hare, Michelle Smith. **Tennis:** Scott Barron, Owen Casey.

OLYMPIC GAMES (SUMMER)

Year	Venue (Country)	Games
1896	Athens (*Greece*)	I
1900	Paris (*France*)	II
1904	St. Louis (*USA*)	III
1906	Athens (*Greece*)	*
1908	London (*England*)	IV
1912	Stockholm (*Sweden*)	V
1916†	Berlin (*Germany*)	VI
1920	Antwerp (*Belgium*)	VII
1924	Paris (*France*)	VIII
1928	Amsterdam (*Netherlands*)	IX
1932	Los Angeles (*USA*)	X
1936	Berlin (*Germany*)	XI
1940†	Tokyo (*Japan*) and	XII
†	Helsinki (*Finland*)	
1944†	London (*England*)	XIII
1948	London (*England*)	XIV
1952	Helsinki (*Finland*)	XV
1956	Melbourne (*Australia*)	XVI
1960	Rome (*Italy*)	XVII
1964	Tokyo (*Japan*)	XVIII
1968	Mexico (*Mexico*)	XIX
1972	Munich (*Germany*)	XX
1976	Montreal (*Canada*)	XXI
1980	Moscow (*Russia*)	XXII
1984	Los Angeles (*USA*)	XXIII
1988	Seoul (*South Korea*)	XXIV
1992	Barcelona (*Spain*)	XXV
1996	Atlanta (*USA*)	XXVI

** unofficial games; † not held due to war;*

IRISH OLYMPIC MEDAL WINNERS

Games	Name	Event	Result	Medal
Amsterdam (1928)	Dr. Pat O'Callaghan	Hammer	168' 7"	Gold
Los Angeles (1932)	Dr. Pat O'Callaghan	Hammer	176' 11"	Gold
Los Angeles (1932)	Bob Tisdall	400m Hurdles	51.7 seconds	Gold
Helsinki (1952)	John McNally	Boxing (*bantam*)	-	Silver
Melbourne (1956)	Ron Delany	1,500m	3:41.2	Gold
Melbourne (1956)	Fred Tiedt	Boxing (*welter*)	-	Silver
Melbourne (1956)	Freddie Gilroy	Boxing (*bantam*)	-	Bronze
Melbourne (1956)	John Caldwell	Boxing (*fly*)	-	Bronze
Melbourne (1956)	Tony Byrne	Boxing (*light*)	-	Bronze
Tokyo (1964)	Jim McCourt	Boxing (*light*)	-	Bronze
Moscow (1980)	David Wilkins & Jamie Wilkinson	Sailing (*Flying Dutchman*)	30.0 points	Silver
Moscow (1980)	Hugh Russell	Boxing (*fly*)	-	Bronze
Los Angeles (1984)	John Treacy	Marathon	2:09.56	Silver
Barcelona (1992)	Michael Carruth	Boxing (*welter*)	-	Gold
Barcelona (1992)	Wayne McCullagh	Boxing (*bantam*)	-	Silver
Atlanta (1996)	Michelle Smith	Swimming (*400m Ind. Med.*)	4:39.18	Gold
Atlanta (1996)	Michelle Smith	Swimming (*400m Freestyle*)	4:07.25	Gold
Atlanta (1996)	Michelle Smith	Swimming (*200m Ind. Med.*)	2:13.93	Gold
Atlanta (1996)	Michelle Smith	Swimming (*200m Butterfly*)	2:09.81	Bronze

TOTAL: Gold - 8; Silver - 5; Bronze - 6.

NORTHERN IRELAND BORN/BASED OLYMPIC MEDAL WINNERS, REPRESENTING BRITAIN

Games	Name	Event	Result	Medal
Los Angeles (1932)	Sam Ferris (b. Co. Down)	Marathon	2:31.18	Silver
Melbourne (1956)	Thelma Hopkins (b. England*)	High Jump	1.67m	Silver
Innsbruck (1964)†	Robin Dixon, Lord Glentoran (b. Co. Antrim)	Two-man bobsleigh	4:21.90	Gold
Munich (1972)	Mary Peters (b. England)	Pentathlon	4801 points	Gold
Los Angeles (1984)	Billy McConnell (b. Co. Down)	Hockey	-	Bronze
Los Angeles (1984)	Stephen Martin (b. Co. Down)	Hockey	-	Bronze
Seoul (1988)	Stephen Martin (b. Co. Down)	Hockey	-	Gold
Seoul (1988)	Jimmy Kirkwood (b. Co. Antrim)	Hockey	-	Gold
Barcelona (1992)	Jackie Burns-McWilliams (b. Co. Antrim)	Hockey	-	Bronze

** worked / lived in Northern Ireland; † Winter Olympic Games*

IRISH BORN* OLYMPIC MEDALLISTS REPRESENTING IRELAND AND OTHER COUNTRIES, 1896-1936

Games	Name	Country Represented	Event	Medal
Athens (1896)	John Pius Boland	Ireland	Tennis (singles)	Gold
Athens (1896)	John Pius Boland	Ireland	Tennis (doubles)	Gold
Paris (1900)	John Flanagan	USA	Athletics (Hammer)	Gold
Paris (1900)	Denis St. George Daly	UK/Ireland	Polo†	Gold
Paris (1900)	Pat Leahy	Ireland	Athletics (High Jump)	Silver
Paris (1900)	Harold Mahony	UK	Tennis (singles)	Silver
Paris (1900)	Harold Mahony	UK	Tennis (mixed doubles)	Silver
Paris (1900)	John Cregan	USA	Athletics (800m)	Silver
Paris (1900)	Pat Leahy	UK	Athletics (Long Jump)	Bronze
Paris (1900)	Harold Mahony	UK	Tennis (mens doubles)	Bronze
St. Louis (1904)	John Flanagan	USA	Athletics (Hammer)	Gold
St. Louis (1904)	Tom Kiely	Ireland	Athletics (Decathlon)	Gold
St. Louis (1904)	Martin Sheridan	USA	Athletics (Discus)	Gold
St. Louis (1904)	Pat Flanagan	USA	Tug-of-War	Gold
St. Louis (1904)	James Mitchell	USA	Athletics (56lb Weight Throw)	Silver
St. Louis (1904)	John J. Daly	Ireland	Athletics (Steeplechase)	Silver
St. Louis (1904)	Albert Newton	USA	Athletics (Marathon)	Bronze
St. Louis (1904)	Albert Newton	USA	Athletics (Steeplechase)	Bronze
St. Louis (1904)	Martin Sheridan	USA	Athletics (Long Jump)	Bronze
Athens (1906)§	Peter O'Connor	Ireland	Athletics (Triple Jump)	Gold
Athens (1906)§	Con Leahy	UK	Athletics (High Jump)	Gold
Athens (1906)§	Martin Sheridan	USA	Athletics (Discus)	Gold
Athens (1906)§	Martin Sheridan	USA	Athletics (Shot Putt)	Gold
Athens (1906)§	Martin Sheridan	USA	Athletics (Stone Thrower)	Silver
Athens (1906)§	Martin Sheridan	USA	Athletics (Long Jump)	Silver
Athens (1906)§	Peter O'Connor	Ireland	Athletics (Long Jump)	Silver
Athens (1906)§	Con Leahy	UK	Athletics (Triple Jump)	Silver
Athens (1906)§	John McGough	UK	Athletics (1,500m)	Silver
London (1908)	John Flanagan	USA	Athletics (Hammer)	Gold
London (1908)	Martin Sheridan	USA	Athletics (Discus-Freestyle)	Gold
London (1908)	Martin Sheridan	USA	Athletics (Discus-Greek Style)	Gold
London (1908)	Robert Kerr	Canada	Athletics (200m)	Gold
London (1908)	Joe Deakin	UK	Athletics (3 mile)†	Gold
London (1908)	Johnny Hayes	USA	Athletics (Marathon)	Gold
London (1908)	Tim Aherne	UK	Athletics (Triple Jump)	Gold
London (1908)	Con O'Kelly	UK	Wrestling	Gold
London (1908)	Edward Barrett	UK	Tug-of-War	Gold
London (1908)	Matt McGrath	USA	Athletics (Hammer)	Silver
London (1908)	Con Leahy	Ireland	Athletics (High Jump)	Silver
London (1908)	Denis Horgan	UK	Athletics (Shot Putt)	Silver
London (1908)	James Clark	UK	Tug-of-War	Silver
London (1908)	James Cecil Parke	UK	Tennis (mens doubles)	Silver
London (1908)	-	Ireland	Mens Hockey†	Silver

Continued from previous page

Games	Name	Country Represented	Event	Medal
	Eric Allman-Smith	Ireland	Mens Hockey	Silver
	Henry Brown	Ireland	Mens Hockey	Silver
	Walter Campbell	Ireland	Mens Hockey	Silver
	Walter Peterson	Ireland	Mens Hockey	Silver
	C. F. Power	Ireland	Mens Hockey	Silver
	G. S. Gregg	Ireland	Mens Hockey	Silver
	E. P. C. Holmes	Ireland	Mens Hockey	Silver
	Robert Kennedy	Ireland	Mens Hockey	Silver
	Henry Murphy	Ireland	Mens Hockey	Silver
	W. G. McCormack	Ireland	Mens Hockey	Silver
	Frank Robinson	Ireland	Mens Hockey	Silver
London (1908)	Martin Sheridan	USA	Athletics (Long Jump)	Bronze
London (1908)	Robert Kerr	Canada	Athletics (100m)	Bronze
London (1908)	Edward Barrett	UK	Wrestling	Bronze
London (1908)	Con Walsh	Canada	Athletics (Hammer)	Bronze
London (1908)	-	Ireland	Polo†	Bronze
London (1908)	John McCann	UK	Polo	Bronze
Stockholm (1912)	Kennedy McArthur	South Africa	Athletics (Marathon)	Gold
Stockholm (1912)	Pat McDonald	USA	Athletics (Shot Putt)	Gold
Stockholm (1912)	Matt McGrath	USA	Athletics (Hammer)	Gold
Stockholm (1912)	Matt Hynes	UK	Tug-of-War	Silver
Antwerp (1920)	Pat McDonald	USA	Athletics (56lb Weight Throw)	Gold
Antwerp (1920)	Paddy Ryan	USA	Athletics (Hammer)	Gold
Antwerp (1920)	Noel Mary Purcell	UK	Water Polo	Gold
Antwerp (1920)	Capt. Frederick Barrett	UK	Polo†	Gold
Antwerp (1920)	Percy O'Reilly	UK/Ireland	Polo†	Gold
Antwerp (1920)	Frank Heggarty	UK/Ireland	Athletics (8,000m)†	Silver
Paris (1920)	Terence Saunders	UK	Rowing (Coxless Fours)	Gold
Paris (1924)	Matt McGrath	USA	Athletics (Hammer)	Silver
Paris (1924)	Capt. Frederick Barrett	UK	Polo†	Bronze
Los Angeles (1932)	Sam Ferris	UK	Athletics (Marathon)	Silver
Berlin (1936)	B. J. Fowler	UK	Polo	Silver

** Republic of Ireland and Northern Ireland; § Unofficial Olympic Games; † team events*

WINTER OLYMPICS

RESULTS

Winter Olympics - Nagano, Japan (7th - 22nd February, 1998)

Date	Name	Event	Time	Finished
10.2.98	Pauli Patrick Schwarzacher-Joyce	Men's Combined Skiing (Slalom)	1:56:.22	21st
13.2.98	Pauli Patrick Schwarzacher-Joyce	Men's Combined Skiing (Downhill)	1:58.71	27th
14.2.98	Ireland I (T. McHugh and J. Pamplin)	Two Man after 2nd round (Bobsleigh)	1:52.37	27th
14.2.98	Ireland II (S. Linscheid and P. Donohoe)	Two Man after 2nd round (Bobsleigh)	1:54.29	37th
15.2.98	Ireland I (J. Pamplin and T. McHugh)	Two Man after 1st round (Bobsleigh)	3:44.32	27th
15.2.98	Ireland II (P. Donohoe and S. Linscheid)	Two Man after 1st round (Bobsleigh)	3:47.45	35th
20.2.98	Ireland I (Terry McHugh, Gary Power, Simon Linscheid and Jeff Pamplin)	Four Man Heats (Bobsleigh)	55.79	29th
22.2.98*	Ireland (Jeff Pamplin, Simon Linscheid, Gary Power and Terry McHugh)	Four Man (Bobsleigh)	2:47.23	30th

** final placings*

IRISH OLYMPIANS (WINTER OLYMPICS), 1992-98

ALBERTVILLE (1992)

Bobsleigh: John Farrelly, Gerard Macken, Pat McDonagh, Terry McHugh, Gary Power, Malachy Sheridan.

NAGANO (1998)

Bobsleigh: Peter Donohoe, Simon Linscheid, Terry McHugh, Nessan O'Carroll, Jeff Pamplin, Gary Power.
Skiing: Pauli Patrick Schwarzacher-Joyce.

OLYMPIC GAMES (WINTER)

Year	Venue (Country)	Number
1924	Chamonix (*France*)	I
1928	St. Moritz (*Switzerland*)	II
1932	Lake Placid (*USA*)	III
1936	Garmisch-Partenkirchen (*Germany*)	IV
1940	Sapporo (*Japan*) and	†
	St. Moritz (*Switzerland*) and	†
	Garmisch-Partenkirchen (*Germany*)	†
1944	Cortina d'Ampezzo (*Italy*)	†
1948	St. Moritz (*Switzerland*)	V
1952	Oslo (*Norway*)	VI
1956	Cortina d'Ampezzo (*Italy*)	VII
1960	Squaw Valley (*USA*)	VIII
1964	Innsbruck (*Austria*)	IX
1968	Grenoble (*France*)	X
1972	Sapporo (*Japan*)	XI
1976	Innsbruck (*Austria*)	XII
1980	Lake Placid (*USA*)	XIII
1984	Sarajevo (*Yugoslavia*)	XIV
1988	Calgary (*Canada*)	XV
1992	Albertville (*France*)	XVI
1994	Lillehammer (*Norway*)	XVII
1998	Nagano (*Japan*)	XVIII

† not held due to war

LOTTERY FUNDING

NATIONAL LOTTERY SPORTS FUNDING

TOP 30 BENIFICARIES BY NATIONAL SPORTS ORGANISATION 1987-96

	£
1. Olympic Council of Ireland	5,870,000
2. Cumann Lúthchleas Gael	1,273,779
3. Bord Lúthchleas na hÉireann	828,224
4. Association for Adventure Sports	826,100
5. Football Association of Ireland	819,799
6. Irish Amateur Swimming Association	814,699
7. Nat Community Games	760,706
8. Irish Amateur Boxing Association	643,979
9. Irish Amateur Rowing Union	600,078
10. Tennis Ireland	592,372
11. Irish Basketball Association	544,488
12. N.A.C.A.I.	519,637
13. CLLÉ (handball)	457,907
14. Federation of Irish Cyclists	449,335
15. Special Olympics Ireland	431,157
16. Irish Wheelchair Association	383,020
17. CCG (camoige)	376,340
18. Badminton Union of Ireland	346,917
19. Irish Squash	340,392
20. Irish Canoe Union	302,910
21. Equestrian Federation of Ireland	285,215
22. Irish Ladies' Hockey Union	220,808
23. Irish Sailing Association	188,536
24. Irish Amateur Gymnastics Association	188,407
25. Irish Hockey Union	166,956
26. Irish Schools Athletic Association	163,239
27. Volleyball Association of Ireland	163,020
28. Golfing Union of Ireland	135,850
29. Irish Judo Association	135,270
30. Irish Schools Swimming Assoc	121,806

Lottery allocations by Category

Year	Major Facilities £	Elite Athletes[1] £	Sports Organisations[2] £
1996	4,614,807	150,000	2,568,907
1995	3,790,297	150,000	2,947,080
1994	9,660,954	124,989	2,244,934
1993	4,999,991	124,500	2,065,501
1992	4,100,000	68,5000	2,245,586
1991	6,472,175	138,500	2,087,240
1990	2,459,571	143,446	2,146,390
1989	1,870,351	114,000	1,862,379
1988	1,351,294	143,700	2,251,466
1987	-	75,000	1,111,806
Total	39,319,440	1,232,635	21,531,289

1. Excludes 'Atlanta Aid' allocations. 2. Excludes allocations made to individual clubs.

Elite Athlete Allocations By Sport[1]

	1987 £	1988 £	1989 £	1990 £	1991 £	1992 £	1993 £	1994 £	1995 £	1996 £	Total £
Athletics	27,750	34,850	11,000	24,500	29,500	17,000	25,500	36,500	47,500	58,000	312,100
Swimming	7,300	27,350	16,700	25,696	16,000	11,000	15,000	15,000	5,000	8,500	147,546
Rowing	3,500	5,800	5,000	6,000	10,000	5,000	13,500	13,500	19,500	20,500	102,300
Squash	2,500	8,750	9,800	9,500	10,000	8,000	8,000	9,000	8,000	7,000	80,550
Canoeing	5,000	10,200	8,000	12,000	11,000	0	19,000	2,000	4,000	5,000	76,200
Tennis	3,500	9,500	9,000	10,000	7,500	5,500	5,000	7,000	6,000	5,000	68,000
Cycling	4,500	6,500	2,000	4,000	9,500	1,000	6,500	9,000	10,000	9,000	62,000
Boxing	3,400	3,000	3,000	13,000	13,500	0	11,000	3,000	2,000	5,000	56,900
Wheelchair	1,500	2,000	0	4,000	4,500	2,250	6,000	4,200	20,000	10,500	54,950
Golf	1,800	13,800	13,000	8,500	0	0	0	0	0	0	37,100
Snooker	0	4,500	7,500	6,500	3,500	4,000	1,000	1,000	2,000	0	30,000
Handball	1,650	2,750	2,250	1,000	1,000	2,000	2,000	5,000	3,000	2,000	22,650
Table Tennis	1,750	3,100	4,000	3,500	4,000	2,000	0	1,000	1,000	1,000	21,350
Badminton	1,250	3,000	3,750	1,000	2,000	2,000	2,000	3,000	2,500	500	21,000
Judo	1,500	2,000	2,750	2,500	2,000	1,000	4,000	2,000	2,000	1,000	20,750
Other	8,100	6,600	16,250	11,750	14,500	7750	6000	13789	17500	17000	119239
Total	75,000	143,700	114,000	143,446	138,500	68,500	124,500	124,989	150,000	150,000	1,232,635

1. Excludes 'Atlanta Aid'. £150,000 was set aside in '94, '95 and '96 to help athletes qualify for the 1996 Olympic Games in Atlanta.

Elite Athletes Allocations by Number of Beneficiaries

	'87	'88	'89	'90	'91	'92	'93	'94	'95	'96	Total
Athletics	40	29	8	14	14	10	11	13	22	24	185
Swimming	9	12	9	11	7	5	7	7	5	6	78
Wheelchair	2	2	0	4	4	3	6	8	14	13	56
Squash	5	7	5	6	6	4	4	4	5	3	49
Rowing	5	6	1	3	3	3	3	6	7	11	48
Cycling	8	11	1	2	5	1	3	5	6	3	45
Boxing	9	6	3	3	7	0	7	3	2	3	43
Tennis	4	5	5	5	3	3	3	4	4	4	40
Canoeing	6	9	3	4	3	0	4	2	2	4	37
Handball	3	4	2	1	1	2	2	4	3	3	25
Snooker	0	5	4	4	2	2	1	1	2	0	21
Badminton	1	2	4	1	2	2	2	2	2	1	19
Table Tennis	2	4	3	3	2	1	0	1	1	1	18
Judo	1	2	2	1	2	1	2	1	1	1	14
Golf	2	4	3	3	0	0	0	0	0	0	12
Other	16	14	13	11	12	7	6	17	15	21	132
Total	113	122	66	76	73	44	61	78	91	98	822

Grants for Provision of Major Sports Facilities in excess of £250,000

Year	Sports Facility	£
1987	none	-
1988	National Sports Stadium	987,390
	Waterford Regional Sports Centre	300,000
1989	National Sports Stadium	1,140,095
	Portmarnock Community School Sports Hall	298,697
1990	National Coaching & Training Centre, Limerick	657,417
	National Sports Stadium	554,008
1991	National Sports Stadium (site)	4,207,556
	National Sports Stadium (fees)	950,000
1992	National Basketball Arena	899,072
	Synthetic Track adjoining UCG	786,840
	Dublin City University	500,000
	Leisureland Complex, Salthill, Galway	498,143
1993	Sligo Swimming Pool	907,497
	National Basketball Arena, Tallaght	600,928
	Sean Kelly Sports Centre, Co. Tipperary	560,237
	Leisureland Complex, Salthill, Galway	501,857
	Morton Stadium, Santry, Dublin	290,981
1994	Croke Park	4,900,000
	Morton Stadium, Santry, Dublin	1,289,346
	National Hockey Stadium	683,060
	Loughlinstown Leisure Centre	290,000
	Public Service Telecom Sports Club	290,000
	Sligo Swimming Pool	279,814
	Tralee Sports Centre	271,234
1995	Scanlon Park, Kilkenny	450,000
	Parnell Park, Dublin	400,000
	Waterford Regional Sports Complex	336,104
	National Basketball Arena, Tallaght	300,000
1996	Cork Regional Centre	2,267,068
	Schull Sailing Centre	399,926
1997	Knockfree Avenue Pitches, Cork	395,000
	Ridge Project, Cork	350,000
1998	Letterkenny Urban District Council Leisure Centre	285,000
	Salmon Leap Canoe Club, Leixlip, Co. Kildare	285,000
	Naas Sports Group, Co. Kildare	250,000

Allocations to National Sports Governing Bodies, 1998

Organisation	£
Association for Adventure Sports	115,230
Badminton Union of Ireland	79,246
Baton twirling Sport Association of Ireland	1,020
Billiards & Snooker Association	38,155
Bord Lúthchleas na hÉireann	259,556
Ból Chumann na hÉireann	27,180
Bowling League of Ireland	13,250
CCG (camoige)	60,526
Cerebral Palsy Sport Ireland	27,792
CLLÉ (handball)	58,840
Croquet Association of Ireland	1,403
Equestrian Federation of Ireland	201,966
Football Association of Ireland	43,750
Federation of Irish Cyclists	167,304
Golfing Union of Ireland	50,000
Horseshoe Pitchers Association of Ireland	1,530
Irish Rugby Football Union	33,750
Irish Amateur Archery Association	17,590
Irish Amateur Boxing Association	133,806
Irish Amateur Fencing Federation	9,507
Irish Amateur Gymnastics Association	49,259
Irish Amateur Rowing Union	174,351
Irish Amateur Weightlifting Association	4,676
Irish Amateur Wrestling Association	7,210
Irish Baseball & Softball Association	4,040
Irish Basketball Association	167,304
Irish Blind Sports Association	19,225
Irish Canoe Union	165,516
Irish Clay Pigeon Shooting Association	12,754
Irish Cricket Union	34,808
Irish Deaf Sports Association	23,230
IrishFederationof Sea Anglers	4,794
Irish Hang Gliding Association	780
Irish Hockey Union	76,089
Irish Judo Association	52,325
Irish Ladies Golf Union	20,660
Irish Ladies' Hockey Union	85,598
Irish Olympic Handball Association	11,803
Irish Orienteering Association	30,650
Irish Sailing Association	156,519
Irish Schools' Athletic Association	61,938
Irish Schools' Swimming Association	8,500
Irish Sports Acrobatics Federation	11,826
Irish Squash	70,227
Irish Surfing Association	21,700
Irish Table Tennis Association	36,337
Irish Ten Pin Bowling Association	10,250
Irish Triathlon Association	10,504
Irish Tug of War Association	14,553
Irish Underwater Council	11,072
Irish Water Polo Association	13,931
Irish Water Ski Association	5,882
Irish Wheelchair Association	139,133
Irish Wind Surfing Association	4,244
Irish Women's Cricket Union	10,758
Ladies Gaelic Football Association	27,944
Motor Cycle Union of Ireland	22,425
Mountaineering Council of Ireland	24,750
Nat.Athletic & Cultural Association of Ireland	86,093
Nat.Coarse Fishing Federation of Ireland	6,613
Nat.Community Games	131,295
Nat.Rifle & Pistol Association of Ireland	15,536
Parachute Association of Ireland	12,640
Pitch & Putt Union of Ireland	47,830
Racquetball Association of Ireland	6,579
Republic of Ireland Netball Association	2,500
Royal Irish Automobile Club	12,298
Schoolgirl's Basketball Association of Ireland	16,820
Special Olympics Ireland	136,236
Speleogical Union of Ireland	6,942
Tennis Ireland	162,900
Trout Anglers' Federationof Ireland	6,000
Volleyball Association of Ireland	54,876
Total	**3,654,124**

Excluding the Croke Park Project. Irish Amateur Swimming Association allocation to be reviewed in context of the Murphy Report.

Elite Athletes Allocations, 1998

Athlete	Sport	£
Keith Hanlon	Archery	7,900
Sonia O'Sullivan	Athletics	12,000
Susan Smith	Athletics	18,000
Nick Seeeney	Athletics	18,000
Sinead Delahunty	Athletics	12,000
Mark Carroll	Athletics	11,225
Una English	Athletics	12,000
Marie McMahon	Athletics	9,400
David Matthews	Athletics	8,100
Gary Ryan	Athletics	12,000
Niall Bruton	Athletics	12,000
Deirdre Gallagher	Athletics	12,000
Shane Healey	Athletics	12,000
Mark Mandy	Athletics	12,000
Valerie Vaughan	Athletics	12,000
Terry McHugh	Athletics	12,000
Cormac Finnerty	Athletics	7,000
Tom McGuirk	Athletics	7,000
Peter Matthews	Athletics	7,000
James Nolan	Athletics	7,000
Seamus Power	Athletics	7,000
James McIlroy	Athletics	7,000
Antoine Burke	Athletics	3,600
Paul Brizzel	Athletics	3,600
Peter Coghlan	Athletics	3,600
Olivia Kelleher	Athletics	3,600
Gillian O'Sullivan	Athletics	3,600
Gareth Turnbull	Athletics	3,600
Colm McLean	Athletics	1,200
Ciara Sheehy	Athletics	1,200
Thomas Coman	Athletics	1,200
Aoife Hearne	Athletics	1,200
Robert Heffernan	Athletics	1,200
David Keoghan	Athletics	1,200
David Kidd	Athletics	1,200
John Leahy	Athletics	1,200
James Matthews	Athletics	1,200
Grainne Redmond	Athletics	1,200

Athlete	Sport	£
Fiona Norwood	Athletics	1,200
Emily Maher	Athletics	1,200
Sonya McGinn	Badminton	7,000
Keelin Fox	Badminton	1,200
Ciaran Darcy	Badminton	1,200
Bridie Lynch	Blindsports	10,000
Joan Salmon	Blindsports	10,000
Michael Delaney	Blindsports	2,500
Catherine Walsh	Blindsports	3,600
Michael Clarke	Blindsports	1,500
Tim Culhane	Blindsports	1,200
Angela Randall	Blindsports	1,200
Phil Nolan	Bowling	4,300
Stephen Kirk	Boxing	16,000
Brian Magee	Boxing	14,000
Neil Gough	Boxing	18,000
Francis Barrett	Boxing	18,000
Eugene McEneany	Boxing	12,000
Bernard Dunne	Boxing	7,000
Alo Kelly	Boxing	3,600
Aodh Carlyle	Boxing	1,600
Marvin Lee	Boxing	1,200
Paul McDermott	Boxing	1,200
Gary Sheahan	Boxing	1,200
Gavin Brown	Boxing	1,200
Harry Cunningham	Boxing	1,200
James Chislom	Boxing	1,200
Tommy Sheahan	Boxing	1,200
Ian Wiley	Canoeing	24,000
Gary Mawer	Canoeing	18,000
John Mawer	Canoeing	12,000
Conor Maloney	Canoeing	7,000
Brendan Maloney	Canoeing	1,200
Peter Egan	Canoeing	1,200
Eoin Rheinisch	Canoeing	1,200
Neil Caffrey	Canoeing	1,200
Mairead Berry	Cerebral Palsy	5,500
Martin McDonagh	Cerebral Palsy	5,750
Tom Leahy	Cerebral Palsy	5,950
Natasha Phillips	Cerebral Palsy	4,400
Derek Malone	Cerebral Palsy	1,200
Aidan McDuff	Cycling	3,600
Ciaran Power	Cycling	3,600
Michael McNena	Cycling	3,600
Glynn O'Brien	Cycling	3,600
James O'Carroll	Cycling	1,200
John Lawlor	Cycling	1,200
Mark Scanlon	Cycling	1,200
John Kealy	Deaf Sports	4,000
John Twomey	Fencing	7,000
Tony Healy	Handball	1,200
Kenneth Kane	Handball	1,200
Fiona McKenna	Handball	1,200
Paul Brady	Handball	1,200
Julieanne Long	Handball	1,200
Sean O'Sullivan	Judo	10,000
Damien Faulkner	Motor Sports	3,600
Una Creagh	Orienteering	3,000
Toni Maria O'Donovan	Orienteering	1,200
Neville Maxwell	Rowing	15,000
John Armstrong	Rowing	13,500
Emmet O'Brien	Rowing	15,000
Tony O'Connor	Rowing	15,000
Derek Holland	Rowing	15,000
Sam Lynch	Rowing	15,000
Brendan Dolan	Rowing	15,000

Athlete	Sport	£
Neal Byrne	Rowing	15,000
Niall O'Toole	Rowing	13,000
Gearoid Towey	Rowing	7,000
Vanessa Lawrenson	Rowing	7,000
Debbie Stack	Rowing	5,000
Owen Byrne	Rowing	1,200
John Whooley	Rowing	1,200
Eugen Coakley	Rowing	1,200
Jane O'Connell	Rowing	1,200
Niamh Rose	Rowing	1,200
Caroline Rose	Rowing	1,200
Casey O'Gorman	Rowing	1,200
Francis Sheridan	Rowing	1,200
Paul Hickey	Rowing	1,200
Sean Casey	Rowing	1,200
James Lupton	Rowing	1,200
Tim Lohan	Rowing	1,200
Neil Casey	Rowing	1,200
Claire Flanagan	Rowing	1,200
Sive Patrick Geoghegan	Rowing	1,200
Stephen Hurley	Rowing	1,200
Padraic Hussey	Rowing	1,200
Kenneth McCarthy	Rowing	1,200
Niamh NicEileachair	Rowing	1,200
Kevin O'Donovan	Rowing	1,200
Paul O'Sullivan	Rowing	1,200
Pat O'Shaughnessy	Rowing	1,200
Maria Coleman	Sailing	18,000
John Driscoll	Sailing	15,000
David Burrows	Sailing	15,000
Jon Lasenry	Sailing	12,000
Colin Chapman	Sailing	7,000
Karena Knaggs	Sailing	3,600
Laura Dillon	Sailing	3,600
David Crosbie	Sailing	1,200
Richard Honeyford	Sailing	1,200
Clodagh O'Driscoll	Sailing	1,200
Joanna Nelson	Sailing	1,200
Ciara Peelo	Sailing	1,200
Gary Duff	Shooting	5,200
Rhona Barry	Shooting	3,300
Julie Kelly	Snooker	5,000
Robert Murphy	Snooker	3,600
TJ Dowling	Snooker	3,600
Derek Ryan	Squash	15,000
Colin O'Hare	Surfing	3,600
Drioni Lane	Table Tennis	1,200
Alan Monks	Table Tennis	1,200
Eoin M. Byrne	Table Tennis	1,200
Noelle Lennon	Table Tennis	1,200
Scott Barron	Tennis	3,600
Tom Hamilton	Tennis	3,600
Stephe Nugent	Tennis	1,200
Garrett McCarthy	Triathlon	7,000
Wayne Healy	Weightlifting	3,600
Sean O'Grady	Wheelchair Sports	10,000
David Malone	Wheelchair Sports	10,000
John Ahern	Wheelchair Sports	1,200
John Fulham	Wheelchair Sports	5,000
Patrice Dockery	Wheelchair Sports	5,000
Colette O'Reilly	Wheelchair Sports	5,000
Garrett Culliton	Wheelchair Sports	5,000
Roy Patrick Guerin	Wheelchair Sports	5,000
Michael Cunningham	Wheelchair Sports	2,200
Grace Gaughan	Wheelchair Sports	1,700
Tricia Furlong	Wheelchair Sports	1,200

ATHLETICS

BRUTON, Niall (1972-) b. Dublin, athlete. Irish 1,500m Champion 1993, 94, 96, 97. Wannamaker Mile (indoor) winner 1996. World Student Games 1,500m Gold Medallist 1991. 1,500m semi-finalist 1996 Olympic Games and 1997 World Championships. Twelfth in 1,500m at 1998 European Championships.

CARROLL, Mark (1973-) b. Cork, athlete. Irish 1,500m Champion 1995. Gold Medallist 5,000m at 1991 European Junior Championships. Set new Irish records for 3,000m and 5,000m in 1998. Bronze medallist 5,000m at 1998 European Championships. Melrose Games 3,000m Champion (Indoor) 1996, 97, 98.

McGUIRK, Tom (1971-) b. San Francisco, hurdler. Irish 400m Hurdles Champion 1994-98 and national record holder. Semi-finalist 400m Hurdles 1998 European Championship. Competed in 1996 Olympic Games.

McHUGH, Terry (1963-) b. Tipperary, javelin thrower. Irish Javelin Champion 1984-98 and national record holder. Olympian in 1988, 1992, 1996 (team captain in 1996). Seventh in 1994 European Championships, eighth in 1993 World Championships. Represented Ireland in Bobsleigh at 1992 and 1998 Winter Olympic Games.

McKIERNAN, Catherina (1969-) b. Cavan, distance runner. Irish 3,000m Champion 1990-94 and 1996, and national record holder at 10,000m. Silver medallist at World Cross Country Championships 1992-95, Gold Medallist European Cross Country Championships 1994. Competed in 1992 and 1996 Olympic Games. Won Berlin marathon in 1997, setting fastest ever time for a debutant and a new national record. 1998 London marathon winner.

MAHER, Emily (1981-) b. Kilkenny, sprinter. Gold Medallist in the 100m and 200m at the inaugural World Youth Olympics in Moscow in July 1998. Currently studying for the Leaving cert.

MATTHEWS, David (1974-) b. Kildare, athlete. Irish 800m Champion 1994-97 and national record holder at 800m and 1,000m. Represented Ireland at 1996 Olympic Games and 1997 World Championships. Fifth in 800m at 1998 European Indoor championships.

O'SULLIVAN, Marcus (1961-) b. Cork, middle distance runner. Irish 800m Champion 1985, '86 and '92, 1,500m Champion 1984 and national 2,000m record holder (outdoors) and 1,000m and 1,500m (indoors). Gold Medallist in 1,500m in 1987, '89 and' 93 World Indoor Championships, 1,500m silver medallist 1985 European Indoor Championships. Winner of Wannamaker Mile six times. Olympian in 1984, '88, '92, '96. Recorded his 100th sub four-minute mile on February 13th 1998 in the Wannamaker Mile becoming only the third man to do so (prior to 1954 a sub four minute mile was thought to be beyond human capability).

O'SULLIVAN, Sonia (1969-) b. Cork, distance runner. Irish 800m champion 1992, 1,500m Champion 1987, 90, 95, 96 and 98 and national record holder at 800m, 1,000m, 1,500m, mile, 2,000m, 3,000m and 5,000 and indoor 3,000m and 5,000m. Gold Medallist 1,500m 1991 World Student Games; 1994 European Championships 3,000m; 1995 World Championships 5,000m. Silver Medallist 1991 World Student Games 3,000m; 1993 World Championships 1,500m; 1997 World Indoor Championships 3,000m. Bronze Medallist with Irish team in 1997 World Cross Country Championships. Recovered from disappointing performances in 1996 Olympic Games and 1997 World Championships to enjoy her most successful year ever in 1998. Gold Medallist in both the long and short course events at the World Cross Country Championships in Morocco in March 1998. Gold Medallist in 5,000m and 10,000m at European Championships in Budapest in August (an achievement without precedent in women's athletics). Gold Medallist in 5,000m at World Cup in South Africa in September.

SMITH, Susan (1971-) b. Waterford, hurdler. Irish 100m Hurdles Champion 1989, 90, 91, 92, 95 and 98, Irish 400m Hurdles Champion 1992, 96 and 97. Set new Irish records for the 100m and 400m in August 1998 holds Irish 60m hurdles (indoor) record. Finished seventh in 400m hurdles at 1997 World Championships and eighth in 400m hurdles final at 1996 European Championships.

BOXING

BARRETT, Francie (1976-) b. Galway, amateur boxer. Irish light-welterweight champion 1996, he became the first member of the travelling community to represent Ireland in the Olympic Games. Runner-up in Irish welterweight final 1998.

CARRUTH, Michael (1967-) b. Dublin, professional boxer. Irish lightweight champion 1987 and 1988, light welterweight champion 1990 and welterweight champion 1992. 1992 Olympic welterweight Gold Medallist. Defeated on points by Romanian Michael Loewe in WBO welterweight title fight September 1997. Won World Athletic Association welterweight title in September 1998 beating Scott Dixon.

COLLINS, Steve (1964-) b. Dublin, professional boxer. A former WBO super-middleweight champion, Collins retired in October 1997. Won the WBO middleweight world title in 1994, won the super middleweight title in 1995, beating Chris Eubank and then Nigel Benn. Successfully defended his title eight times. His professional record was 35 wins in 38 bouts.

GOGARTY, Deirdre b. Louth, professional boxer. Ireland's first female boxing world champion, she won the WIBF super-featherweight world title in March 1997.

GRIFFIN, Paul (1971-) b. Dublin, professional boxer. Irish Amateur featherweight champion (1991-94), he won the European title in 1991 and a European bronze medal in 1993. Turned professional in 1995.

KELLY, Damean (1973-) b. Belfast, amateur boxer. Irish flyweight champion (1993-1996), Irish bantamweight champion 1997. Flyweight bronze medallist 1993 World Championships and bronze again in the 1995 European Championships. Represented Ireland at the 1996 Olympic Games.

KIRK, Steven b. Belfast, amateur boxer. Irish light heavyweight champion 1995-97. Bronze medallist at 1997 World Championships.

McCULLOUGH, Wayne (1970-) b. Belfast, professional boxer. Irish light flyweight champion 1988, flyweight champion 1990 and bantamweight champion 1992. 1990 Commonwealth Games flyweight champion. Represented Ireland at 1988 Olympics and was 1992 Olympic bantamweight silver medallist. Turned professional 1993. Former WBC super-bantamweight World Champion he lost his title to Mexican Daniel Zaragoza in January 1997, the first defeat of his professional career.

MAGEE, Brian (1975-) b. Belfast, amateur boxer. Irish middleweight Champion since 1995. Represented Ireland at the 1996 Olympics. Silver medallist at 1998 European Championships.

CANOEING

WILEY, Ian (1970-) b. Dublin, canoeist in Men's Slalom K1. Currently ranked No. 2 in the World Cup series, 5th in the Atlanta Olympics, is seen as a medal prospect in the Sydney Olympics. Club: Liffey Valley Canoe Club.

MAWER, Cary (1972-) canoeist in Men's K1 Marathon. Winner in K1 Category 1997 Liffey Descent, 2nd in the 1996 World Marathon Championships in Sweden. Club: Salmon Leap Canoe Club.

O'MEARA, Mick (1969-) canoeist in Men's Wild Water Racing. Winner in Liffey Descent Wildwater Category four years in a row. Club: 180 Kayak Club - Waterford.

NÍ CHALLARAIN, Aodaoin (1973-) canoeist in Women's Freestyle, Women's Slalom. Fifth in the World's Freestyle Championships, first in the Irish Open Slalom Championships. Club: University College Galway.

GAELIC GAMES

BARRY-MURPHY, Jimmy (1954-) b. Cork, dual player, winner of six All-Ireland medals, one in football (1973) and five in hurling (between 1976 and 1986). His other achievements include two All-Ireland Hurling Club Championships, two All-Ireland Football Club Championships, two National Hurling League titles, one National Football League title and four Railway Cup medals in Hurling. An All-Star winner on seven occasions, five in Hurling and two in Football. Retired in 1987. He is the current Cork senior hurling manager.

BOYLE, Tony (1970-) b. Donegal, Gaelic footballer. All-Ireland medallist with Donegal in 1992. All-star award winner 1992.

BOND, Michael b. Galway, hurling manager. Manager of 1983 All-Ireland U21 hurling championship winners, Galway. Took over as Offaly manager in July 1998. Manager of 1998 All-Ireland Senior Hurling champions, Offaly.

BROLLY, Joe (1970-) b. Derry, Gaelic footballer. Holds one All-Ireland SFC medal (1993), two NFL (1995 and 1996) and All-Star awards in 1996 and 1997.

BUCKLEY, Niall (1973-) b. Kildare, gaelic footballer. All-star award winner 1997, midfielder with 1998 All-Ireland finalists Kildare.

CANAVAN, Peter (1971-) b. Tyrone, Gaelic footballer. All-Star award winner 1995 and 1996, Player of the Year 1995. Won two Ulster SFC medals (1995 and 1996).

CAREY, Ciaran (1970) b. Limerick, hurler. Holds two NHL medals (1992 and 1997) twice and All-Ireland SHC runner-up. All-Star award winner 1992, 1996.

CAREY, D.J. (1971-) b. Kilkenny, hurler. Holder of two All-Ireland SHC (1992 and 1993), 2 NHL (1990 and 1995) six All-Star awards (1991-95 and 1997) and 21 All-Ireland handball titles. Announced retirement February 1998 but returned for 1998 Championship. Considered the outstanding player of his generation.

CREGAN, Eamon (1946-) b. Limerick, hurler who won an All-Ireland medal (1973), three Railway Cup medals and a National Hurling League Medal (1971). Won three All-Star awards. He was manager of the Offaly team which defeated his native Limerick in the 1994 All-Ireland hurling final. Appointed Limerick senior hurling manager in 1997.

DALY, Anthony (1970-) b. Clare, hurler. Holder of two All-Ireland SHC (1995 and 1997) when he captained Clare. All-Star award winner three times.

DONNELLAN, Michael (1977-) b. Galway, gaelic footballer. Holder of one All-Ireland SFC (1998), man of the match 1998 All-Ireland football final.

DOOLEY, Joe (1963-) b. Offaly, hurler. Holder of three All-Ireland SHC (1985, 94 and 98) and one NHL (1991). His brothers Billy and Johnny were also members of the 1994 and 1998 All-Ireland SHC and 1991 NHL winning Offaly teams.

DOWD, Tommy (1969-) b. Leicester, Gaelic footballer. Holds one All-Ireland SFC (1996) when he captained Meath, and two NFL (1990 and 1994). Winner of three All-Star awards (1991, 95 and 96).

FALLON, Jarlath *'Ja'* (1973-) b. Galway, Gaelic footballer. Holder of one All-Ireland SFC (1998). All-star award winner 1995. An accomplished rugby player he has represented Connacht.

FENNELLY, Kevin (1954-) b. Kilkenny, hurling manager. Won one All-Ireland SHC medal (1979) and three All-Ireland Club SHC (1981, 84 and 90) with Ballyhale Shamrocks as a player. Manager of the Kilkenny team who were beaten in the 1998 All-Ireland SHC final by Offaly.

FITZGERALD, Maurice (1970-) b. Kerry, Gaelic footballer. Holds one All-Ireland SFC (1997), one NFL (1997), three All-Star awards (1988, 95, 97). Man of the match in the 1997 All-Ireland final and 1997 Player of the Year. In 1989, he won the world long-kicking competition beating professionals from rugby, American football, soccer and Australian Rules.

GILES, Trevor (1976-) b. Meath, Gaelic footballer. Holder of one All-Ireland SFC (1996), two All-Star awards (1996 and 1997). Player of the Year 1996.

KEATING, Babs (1944-) b. Tipperary, dual player who had much success in hurling, winning three All-Ireland medals between 1964 and 1971, two Railway Cup Hurling medals and one Railway Cup Football (1972). Was both an All-Star and Texaco Hurling Sportstar in 1971. Remembered for playing hurling barefoot, he later managed Tipperary to two All-Ireland Senior Hurling Championship titles. Laois hurling manager from 1995-1997. Resigned as Offaly hurling manager in July 1998, following their defeat in the Leinster final.

KIRBY, Gary (1966-) b. Limerick, hurler. Holds two NHL medals (1992 and 1997). All-Star award winner 1991, '94, '95, '96. Twice a beaten All-Ireland finalist (1994 and 1996).

LOUGHNANE, Ger (1954-) b. Clare, hurling manager. Holder of two NHL as a player (1977 and 1978) and two All-Star awards (1974 and 1977) becoming the first Clare man to do so. Manager of the Clare teams which won the All-Ireland SHC in 1995 (their first win since 1914) and 1997. Outspoken and fiercely loyal to his players.

LOHAN, Brian (1971-) b. Clare, hurler. Holder of two All-Ireland SHC 1995 and 1997, three All-Star awards (1995, 96, 97) at full back. Player of the Year 1995.

McCARTHY, **Ger** (1947-) b. Cork, hurling manager. Won four All-Ireland SHC (1970, 76, 77 and 78) and two NHL (1969 and 1972) as a player with Cork. Won two All-Ireland Club SHC (1975 and 1978) with St Finbarr's and was awarded an All-Star in 1975. Managed Cork when they were beaten in the 1982 All-Ireland SHC final. Manager of a resurgent Waterford team which qualified for the NHL final in 1998 and were beaten in the 1998 All-Ireland semi-final.

McDONAGH, Joe (1954-) b. Galway, GAA administrator. President of Cumann Lúthchleas Gael since 1997. Holds one All-Ireland SHC (1980) and an All-Star award (1976). When Galway won their breakthrough All-Ireland in 1980 McDonagh led a rendition of 'The West's Awake' from the Hogan Stand.

MAUGHAN, John (1962-) b. Mayo, Gaelic football manager. Managed Clare to Munster SFC in 1992. Manager of Mayo team beaten in 1996 and 1997 All-Ireland SFC finals.

MULLINS, Brian (1954-) b. Dublin, outstanding Gaelic football midfielder, won four All-Ireland Football medals between 1974 and 1983 (coming back from severe injury to win in 1983). Contested a further five All-Ireland Finals, but Kerry defeated Dublin in each of those. Won two National Football League medals and captained Leinster to Railway Cup success in 1985. Winner of two All-Star Awards, he resigned as Derry manager in 1998 after three years in charge during which Derry won the National football League (1996) and the Ulster Championship (1998).

MULVIHILL, Liam (1946-) b. Longford, GAA administrator. Director General of the GAA since 1979. Presided over the modernisation of the GAA through the ongoing development of Croke Park and various provincial grounds and a better marketing of the games in general.

NALLEN, James (1974-) b. Mayo, Gaelic footballer. All-Star award winner 1996, twice a beaten All-Ireland finalist (1996 and 1997).

O'CONNOR, James (1972-) b. Clare, hurler. Holder of two All-Ireland SHC (1995 and 1997), two All-Star awards (1995 and 1997). Player of the Year 1997, man of the match 1997 All-Ireland final and top scorer 1997 hurling championship.

O'CONNOR, Willie (1967-) b. Kilkenny, hurler. Holder of two All-Ireland SHCs (1992 and 1993), two NHL (1990, 1995), two All-Star awards (1992 and 1997), one All-Ireland Club SHCs (1991) with Glenmore. Corner back with 1998 All-Ireland finalists.

O'DWYER, Mick (1936-) b. Kerry, Gaelic football manager. Won four all-Ireland SFCs (1959, 62, 69 and 70) and eight NFLs (1959, 61, 63, 69, 71, 72, 73, 74) as a player. Managed Kerry to eight All-Ireland SFCs 1975, 78, 79, 80, 81, 84, 85, and 86 and three NFL 1977, 82 and 84. Manager of Kildare 1990-93 and since 1997 in 1998 he guided them to their first All-Ireland final since 1935.

O'MAHONY, John Gaelic football manager. Guided Mayo to 1989 All-Ireland SFC final, Leitrim to 1994 Connacht SFC. Manager of the Galway team which won the 1998 All-Ireland SFC.

O'NEILL, Pat (1971-) b. Kilkenny, hurler. Holder of two All-Ireland SHCs (1992 and 1993), one NHL (1995) and one All-Star award (1992). Man of the match 1992 All-Ireland hurling final.

Ó SÉ, Páidí (1955-) b. Kerry, Gaelic football manager. Holder of eight All-Ireland SFCs (1975, 78, 79, 80, 81, 84, 85, and 86). Captain of Kerry in 1985. Holder of four NHLs (1974, 77, 82 and 84) and five successive All-Star awards (1981-85). Manager of the Kerry team which won the All-Ireland SFC and NHL in 1997.

PILKINGTON, Johnny (1969-) b. Offaly, hurler. Holder of two All-Ireland SHC (1994 and 1998), one NHL (1991), two All-Ireland Club SHCs with Birr (1995 and 1998).

RYAN, Glen (1972-) b. Kildare, Gaelic footballer. Captain of 1998 All-Ireland finalists, Kildare. All-Star award winner 1997.

SHERLOCK, Jason (1975-) b. Dublin, Gaelic footballer, basketballer, soccer player. Holder of one All-Ireland SFC (1995). Has represented Ireland in international basketball and currently plays in the FAI National League with Shamrock Rovers.

SILKE, Ray (1971-) b. Galway, Gaelic footballer. Holder of one All-Ireland SFC (1998), he was the Galway captain. Captained his club, Corofin, to the All-Ireland Club SFC in 1998 (the first Connacht team to win the title).

STOREY, Martin (1964-) b. Wexford, hurler. Holds one All-Ireland SHC (1996) when he captained Wexford to first title since 1968. All-star award winner 1993 and 1996. Player of the Year 1996.

TOHILL, Anthony (1971-) b. Derry, gaelic footballer. Holds one All-Ireland SFC (1993), three NFL (1992, '95 and '96). All-star award winner in 1992, '93 and '95. Played Australian Rules football in Melbourne, and has played soccer for Derry City in the National League.

WHELEHAN, Brian (1971-) b. Offaly, hurler. Holder of two All Ireland SHCs (1994 and 1998), one NHL (1991), two All-Ireland Club SHCs (1995 and 1998) with Birr, All-Star award winner - 1993 and 1995. Man of the match and top scorer in the 1998 All-Ireland hurling final. His younger brother Simon was also a member of the 1998 All-Ireland winning team.

GOLF

CLARKE, Darren (1968-) b. Tyrone, professional golfer. Only Irish member of 1997 winning European Ryder Cup team. Winner of three European PGA tour events, Dunhill Open (1993), German Masters (1996) and Benson & Hedges International Open (1998). Second in 1997 British Open (his best finish in a major). Finished fourth overall in European Order of Merit in 1997. As an amateur he won the 1989 East of Ireland Championship and in 1990 won the Irish Close, North of Ireland and South of Ireland Championships.

D'ARCY, Eamonn (1952-) b. Wicklow, professional golfer. Played in the Ryder Cup four times (1975, 77, 81 and 87) and was member of the 1988 Irish team which won the Dunhill Cup. Winner of eleven European PGA events including the 1983 Spanish Open and the 1990 Desert Open.

HARRINGTON, Padraig (1971-) b. Dublin, professional golfer. Turned professional 1995. Won 1996 Spanish Open. With Paul McGinley, he won the 1997 World Cup for Ireland in South Carolina. As an amateur he won the West of Ireland Championship in 1994 and the Irish Open and Irish Close Championships in 1995. Member of the Walker Cup team in 1991, 93 and 95 (when Britain and Ireland beat the US at Royal Portcawl).

McGIMPSEY, Garth (1955-) b. Co. Down, amateur golfer. North of Ireland Championship winner 1978, 84, 91, 92 and 93; West of Ireland Championship winner 1984, 88, 93 and 96; East of Ireland Championship winner 1988, 94 and 98. He also won the 1988 Irish Close Championship and the 1985 British amateur Championship. Has played on three Walker Cup teams, 1985, 89 (when Britain and Ireland beat the US for the first time in America) and 91.

McGINLEY, Paul (1967-) b. Dublin, professional golfer. Turned professional in 1991 and has won two European PGA Tour events, the Austrian Open (1996) and the Oki Pro-Am (1997). Partnered Padraig Harrington to victory in the 1997 World Cup at Kiawah Island, South Carolina. As an amateur, he won the 1989 Irish Close Championship and the 1991 South of Ireland Championship. He represented Britain and Ireland in the 1991 Walker Cup.

O'CONNOR Jnr, Christy (1948-) b. Galway, professional golfer. Turned professional 1965 and has won eight competitions on the European tour including the 1975 Irish Open, the 1989 Jersey Open and the 1992 British Masters. A member of the 1975 and 1989 Ryder Cup teams.

WALTON, Philip (1962-) b. Dublin, professional golfer. Turned professional 1983 and has four European Tournament wins including the 1990 French Open and the 1995 English Open. A member of the victorious European Ryder Cup team in 1995. As an amateur he won the 1982 Irish Close Championship and was a member of the Walker Cup teams of 1981 and 1983.

HORSE RACING

CROWLEY, Frances (1973-) horse trainer. A former Amateur Champion jockey (1995 and 1996), she was granted her trainer's licence in June 1998.

DUNWOODY, Richard (1960-) b. Co. Down, national hunt jockey. Counts two Aintree Grand Nationals (with West Tipp, 1986 and Minnehoma, 1994), one Cheltenham Gold Cup (with Charter Party, 1988) and one Irish Grand National (with Desert Orchid, 1990) among his many winners. A former champion National Hunt jockey in Britain. Won the 1998 Hennessy Gold Cup with Doran's Pride.

EDDERY, Pat (1952-) b. Dublin, flat jockey. Has had well over 4,000 winners in a career stretching back to 1969. Fourteen English Classic winners include Grundy (1975 Derby), Lomond (1993 2,000 Guineas) and Lady Carla (1996) Oaks. Ten Irish Classic winners include Law Society (1985 Derby), Tirol (1990 2,000 Guineas) and Bolas (1994 Irish Oaks). He has also won the Prix de l'Arc de Triomphe and the French Derby. Eddery is the most successful Irish jockey of all time and one of the most outstanding Irish sportsmen ever.

FALLON, Kieren b. Clare, flat jockey. Champion flat jockey in Britain 1997, he has ridden in excess of 100 winners in each season since 1996. English Classic winners include Reams of Verse (1997 Oaks) and Sleepytime (1997 1,000 Guineas).

KINANE, Mick (1959-) b. Tipperary, flat jockey. Irish Champion Flat Jockey a record ten times between 1983 and 1994 he has had Classics wins in Ireland, England, France, Italy, America and Australia. Perhaps his finest race (certainly his most famous) was in winning the 1993 Melbourne Gold Cup on Vintage Crop. His fifteen year partnership with trainer Dermot Weld has served both well. In 1998 he won the English 2,000 Guineas with King of Kings, the Epsom Oaks on Shahtoush and the Irish National Stakes on Mus-if.

O'BRIEN, Aidan (1969-) b. Wexford, horse trainer. Irish Champion trainer (National Hunt) 1993/94-1997/98. A former champion amateur jockey, he has enjoyed considerable success on the flat training three Irish Classic winners in 1997, Desert King (Derby and 2,000 Guineas) and Classic Park (1,000 Guineas). In 1998, he trained Cheltenham Champion Hurdle winner Istabraq and English Classic winners Shahtoush in the Oaks and King of Kings in the 2,000 Guineas.

ROCHE, Christy (1950-) b. Tipperary, horse trainer. A former champion flat jockey his Classic winners in England include the Derby (1984 with Secreto) and the Oaks (1991 with Jet Ski Lady). In 1997 Roche won both the Irish 2,000 Guineas and the Irish Derby on Desert King. In all Roche has won the 2,000 Guineas four times, the 1,000 Guineas three times, the Derby three times and the St Leger twice. Granted a trainer's license in November 1996, he announced his retirement as a jockey in August 1998.

SWAN, Charlie (1968-) b. Tipperary, national hunt jockey. Has had over 1,000 winners at Listowel in September 1997. Irish National Hunt Champion

Jockey nine times (and the seventh consecutive year). He has won the Irish Grand National and the Galway Plate. He partnered Istabraq to victory in the 1998 Cheltenham Champion Hurdle.

WALSH, Ted (1950-) b. Cork horse trainer. Champion jockey eleven times, he has been a trainer since 1991. He trained his first Cheltenham winner, Commanche Court, in the Triumph Hurdle, in 1997.

RUGBY

CLOHESSY, Peter (1966-) b. Limerick, international rugby player. A member of the Young Munster club in Limerick, he has been capped 20 times by Ireland and has scored one international try.

CORKERY, David (1972-) b. Cork, international rugby player. Plays with Cork Constitution in the All-Ireland league, he has been capped 25 times by Ireland since making his debut in 1994 and has scored 3 tries.

COSTELLO, Victor (1970-) b. Dublin, international rugby player. A member of the All-Ireland League Division One side St Mary's, he has 13 full international caps and has scored two international tries. He has represented Leinster interprovincial level. Irish National Shot Putt champion 1988, 89, 90 and 91, he is a former Irish senior record holder, holds the Irish Junior record and competed in the 1992 Olympic Games.

ELWOOD, Eric (1969-) b. Galway, international rugby player. A member of the Galwegians who compete in the All-Ireland League Division One. He has has won 28 Irish caps and has scored in excess of 200 points. He has been capped by the Barbarians and has represented Connacht at interprovincial level.

GATLAND, Warren (1963-) b. New Zealand, international rugby coach. Appointed Irish coach in February 1998, following resignation of Brian Ashton. As a player, Gatland represented his province Waikato and made 17 representative appearance for the All-Blacks but never won a full cap. Player/coach with Galwegians 1989-93, he managed the Connacht team from 1996-98 guiding them to the 1997 European Shield quarter-final.

HUMPHREYS, David (1971-) b. Belfast, international rugby player. The Dungannon out-half has won 10 international caps since his debut in the Five Nations' Championship in 1998 scoring 36 points.

JOHNS, Paddy (1968-) b. Portadown, international rugby player. A member of the Saracens club in England, he has 43 international caps and scored two tries. He has represented Ulster at interprovincial level. Captain of the Irish team on their 1998 tour of South Africa.

LENIHAN, Donal (1959-) b. Cork, international rugby manager. Won 52 international caps 1981-92, member of the Triple Crown winning sides of 1982, '83 (when Ireland also won the International Championship) and '85. Nominated as a selector during the 1998 Five Nations campaign, he was appointed Irish manager for the 1998 summer tour to South Africa and was appointed to the position for the forthcoming season on his return.

O'KELLY, Malcolm (1974-) b. Essex, international rugby player. Plays with London Irish in the English Premiership One he has won nine caps since his debut against the All-Blacks in 1997.

O'SHEA, Conor (1970-) b. Limerick, international rugby player. A member of the London Irish club, he has won 20 international caps at full back and scored at total of 14 points. He has represented Munster at interprovincial level.

POPPLEWELL, Nick (1964-) b. Dublin, international rugby player. A player with Newcastle in the English Premiership One, he announced his retirement from international rugby at the end of the 1998 Five Nations' championship. In a career stretching back to 1989, he won 48 Irish caps and three caps for the Lions in the 1993 series with New Zealand.

WALLACE, Paul (1971-) b. Cork, international rugby player. A member of the Saracens club, he plays in the English Premiership One. Has won 20 international caps since his debut in the 1995 World Cup and scored two tries. He has represented Munster at interprovincial level and won three caps on the successful 1997 tour by the Lions to South Africa.

WHELAN, Pat (1951-) b. Limerick, former international rugby player and manager. Capped 19 times, he was a member of the Munster team which beat the All-Blacks in 1978. Manager of the Irish international team from September 1995 until he announced his resignation at the end of the 1998 Five Nations' Championship.

WOOD, Keith (1972-) b. Limerick, international rugby player. A member of the Harlequins club which competes in the English Premiership One he has won 17 international caps and has scored two tries (both against New Zealand). Irish captain for the 1997/98 season (excluding South African tour) he has been capped by the Barbarians and won two caps with the Lions on the 1997 tour to South Africa.

SNOOKER

DOHERTY, Ken (1969-) b. Dublin, professional snooker player. Turned professional 1990, World Snooker Champion in 1997 (he beat Stephen Hendry 18-12 in the final) he was beaten 18-12 by John Higgins in the 1998 final. Irish Amateur Champion in 1987 and 1989 he was World Amateur Champion in 1989. Doherty was beaten 9-3 by Ronnie O'Sullivan in the final of the 1998 Irish Masters but was awarded the title when it emerged O'Sullivan had failed a drugs test.

O'BRIEN, Fergal (1972-) b. Dublin, professional snooker player. Ranked number 21 in the world O'Brien has yet to win a major tournament. Reached the second round of the 1998 World Championships.

TAYLOR, Denis (1949-) b. Tyrone, professional snooker player. The 1985 World Snooker Champion, he beat Steve Davis 18-17 on the black ball in the final frame to win what is considered to be the most dramatic final ever. Won the 1984 Rothman's Grand Prix and the 1987 Benson & Hedges Masters. Has announced his intention to retire at the end of the 1998/99 season.

SWIMMING

DE BRUIN, Michelle (1969-) b. Dublin, swimmer. Gold

medallist 200m Butterfly and 200m Individual Medley and silver medallist in 400m Individual Medley at 1995 European Championships. Gold medallist 400m Freestyle, 200m individual medley, 400m individual medley and bronze medallist in the 200m butterfly at 1996 Olympic Games. Gold medallist 400m individual medley and 200m freestyle and silver medallist in the 200m Freestyle and 200m Butterfly at 1997 European Championships. She holds 14 short course and 13 long course Irish records in freestyle, backstroke, butterfly and individual medley events. Banned for four years by the international swimming body, FINA, for allegedly manipulating a urine sample. De Bruin has appealed the ban.

SOCCER

ARKINS, Vinny (1970-) b. Dublin, Irish League soccer player. Plays with Portadown in the Irish League Premier Division he finished the 1997/98 season as the league's top goal scorer with 22 goals. Capped by the Republic of Ireland at 'B', U21 and U18 levels.

BREEN, Gary (1973-) b. London, international soccer player. Plays with Coventry City in the English Premiership he has won 15 caps and scored two international goals for the Republic of Ireland since making his debut in 1996.

CASCARINO, Tony (1962-) b. Kent, international soccer player. Plays with A.S. Nancy in the French League he has been capped 76 times by the Republic of Ireland. With 19 goals he is one goal short of Frank Stapleton's Irish goal scoring record. A member of the Irish squads at the 1998 European Championships and the World Cup finals in 1990 and 1994.

CUNNINGHAM, Kenny (1971-) b. Dublin, international soccer player. Plays with Wimbledon in the English Premiership, he has won 17 caps for the Republic of Ireland.

DONNELLY, Michael (1968-) b. Belfast, Irish League soccer player. Captain of Cliftonville who won the 1997/98 Irish League Premier Division he has been with the club since 1987.

DOWIE, Iain (1965-) b. Hatfield, international soccer player. Plays with Queens Park Rangers in the English First Division he has been capped 50 times by Northern Ireland. With eleven international goals to his credit, he is two goals shy of the Northern Ireland record.

DUFF, Damian (1979-) b. Dublin, international soccer player. Plays with Blackburn Rovers in the English Premiership, he has won three caps for the Republic of Ireland. A member of the Irish team which finished third in the U20 World Cup in 1997.

GEOGHEGAN, Stephen (1971-) National League soccer player. A striker with Shelbourne in the National League Premier Division, he has been the league's top goal scorer in the 1993/94, 95/96, 96/97 and 97/98 seasons. Winner of two FAI Cup winners medals with Shelbourne (1996 and 1997).

GILLESPIE, Keith (1975-) b. Larne, international soccer player. Plays with Newcastle United in the English Premiership he has been capped 22 times and has scored one goal for Northern Ireland.

GIVEN, Shay (1976-) b. Donegal, international soccer player. Goalkeeper with Newcastle United in the English Premiership, he has been capped 18 times by the Republic of Ireland.

HAMILTON, Bryan (1947-) b. Belfast, former international soccer player and Northern Ireland manager. Capped 50 times by Northern Ireland between 1969 and 1980 he scored four international goals. Manager of the Northern Ireland team from February 1994 he was sacked by the IFA in October 1997, when Northern Ireland fared badly in the World Cup qualifiers.

HOUGHTON, Ray (1962-) b. Glasgow, international soccer player. Plays with Reading in the English Second Division. He has won 73 caps and scored six international goals for the Republic of Ireland. A member of the Irish European Championship squad in 1988 (where the goal he scored to beat England assures him sporting immortality), he also played in the 1990 and 1994 World Cup finals (where his goal against Italy gave Ireland a shock victory and revenge for elimination by Italy in 1990). He was FAI Player of the Year in 1994.

HUGHES, Michael (1971-) b. Larne, international soccer player. Plays with Wimbledon in the English Premiership he has won 43 caps and scored three goals for Northern Ireland.

IRWIN, Denis (1965-) b. Cork, international soccer player. Plays with Manchester United in the English Premiership. He has scored three goals in his 49 international appearances for the Republic of Ireland. A member of the Irish World Cup squad at the 1994 World Cup finals.

KEANE, Robbie (1980-) b. Dublin, international soccer player. Plays with Wolverhampton Wanderers in the English First Division, he has won four international caps for the Republic of Ireland. A member of the Irish team which won the U18 European Championship in 1998.

KEANE, Roy (1971-) b. Cork, international soccer player. Captain of Manchester United in the English Premiership Keane is also the current Irish captain and has won 39 caps and scored four goals for the Republic of Ireland. FAI Player of the Year in 1997 he was a member of the Irish squad in the 1994 World Cup.

KELLY, Gary (1974-) b. Louth, international soccer player. Plays with Leeds United in the English Premiership. He has won 28 international caps and scored one goal for the Republic of Ireland since his debut in 1994. A member of the Irish team which qualified for the second round of the 1994 World Cup.

KERR, Brian (1953-) b. Dublin, international soccer manager. Manager of all Republic of Ireland youth teams (i.e. U15, U16, U18 and U20), he has met with unprecedented success. His U20 team finished third in 1997 World Cup in Malaysia, the U16 team won 1998 European Championships and the U18 team won the 1998 European Championships. He is the FAI's Technical Director.

LOMAS, Steve (1974-) b. Hanover, Germany, international soccer player. Plays with West Ham United in the English Premiership. He has won 26 caps and scored two international goals for Northern Ireland.

McCARTHY, Mick (1959-) b. Barnsley, international soccer manager. As a player McCarthy won 57 international caps for the Republic of Ireland and was a member of the Irish squad at the 1988 European Championships and was Irish captain in the 1990 World Cup. Manager of the Republic of Ireland since February 1996 he almost brought them to the 1998 World Cup finals (only losing in a play-off) and has had a promising start to the European 2000 qualifiers.

McGRATH, Paul (1959-) b. Ealing, international soccer player. defender. Now retired, McGrath was capped 82 times by the Republic and scored six international goals. FAI Player of the Year in 1990 and 1991, he was a member of the Republic of Ireland World Cup squads in 1990 and 1994 and the European Championship squad in 1988. Awarded a testimonial by the FAI in May 1998.

McMENEMY, Lawrie (1936-) b.Gateshead, international soccer manager. Manager of Northern Ireland since February 1998, he is assisted by Pat Jennings and Joe Jordan. England assistant manager 1990-93 he has also coached Sheffield Wednesday and managed Southampton and Sunderland.

MULRYNE, Philip (1978-) b. Belfast, international soccer player. Plays with Manchester United in the English Premiership. He has won six international caps and scored one goal for Northern Ireland.

QUINN, Niall (1966-) b. Dublin, international soccer player. Plays with Sunderland in the English First Division. He has won 63 caps with the Republic of Ireland. With 16 goals to his name, he is fifth on the Republic's all-time top scorers list. A member of the Republic of Ireland squad who were quarter-finalists in the 1990 World Cup, injury kept him out of the 1994 World Cup squad. He was a forward on the Dublin team which were beaten in the 1983 All-Ireland Minor Hurling final.

STAUNTON, Steve (1969-) b. Drogheda, international soccer player. Plays with Liverpool in the English Premiership. He has won 75 caps and scored six goals for the Republic of Ireland. The FAI Player of the Year in 1993, he was a member of the Republic of Ireland World Cup squads in 1990 and 1994.

MOTOR SPORT

DUNLOP, Joey (1952-) b. Ballymena, motorcyclist. World TT Formula One championship winner 1982, 83, 84, 85 and 86, he overcame injury to win his 23rd Isle of Man TT race in 1998. His brother Robert won his fifth Isle of Man TT in 1998.

IRVINE, Eddie (1965-) b. Co. Down, Formula 1 driver. A member of the Ferrari team since 1996, Irvine is assured fourth place in the 1998 Formula 1 Drivers' Championship, having scored 41 points and securing two second place and five third place finishes. Made his Formula 1 debut with Jordan in 1993, he has competed in 80 races, 48 of which have been with Ferrari. Prior to Formula 1, he raced Formula 3000 in Europe and Formula Nippon in Japan.

JORDAN, Eddie (1948-) b. Dublin, Formula 1 team owner. Irish Kart Champion in 1971, he won the Irish Formula Atlantic Championship in 1978. Established Eddie Jordan Racing in 1979 - the team competed in British Formula 3 championships throughout the 1980s. Established Jordan Grand Prix in 1991 - the team has finished fifth in the Constructors' championship in 1991, 93 and 96. In 1998, Damon Hill won the team's first Grand Prix at the Belgian Grand Prix.

KAVANAGH, Sarah (1973-) b. Warwickshire, racing driver. A member of the Cerumo Team in Japan's Formula Nippon Championship, she made her name in Britian where she was a support driver for the Supermarketing Racing Team which won the British Championship in 1995. She has also raced in the British Formula Two championship.

OTHER SPORTS

STYNES, Jim (1966-) b. Dublin, professional Australian Rules player. Winner of Brownlow medal (Best and Fairest Player of the Year) in 1991. Played with Melbourne and set an Australian record of 244 consecutive games. Retired from competitive football at end of 1998 season. Represented Ireland (one tour) and Australia (two tours) in the International Rules series.

CYCLING

SCANLON, Mark (1980-) b. Sligo, amateur cyclist. Winner of the 1998 Credit Union Junior Tour, he is Irish Junior cycling champion and in October 1998, he won the World Junior Cycling Championship at Valkenburg in Holland.

BOWLS

JOHNSTON, Margaret (1943-) b. Derry, international bowls player. Commonwealth gold medallist 1986 and 1994, World Singles Champion 1992, World Pairs Champion (with Phylis Nolan) 1988, '92 and '96. Has also won numerous Irish and British Isles titles.

SURFING

BURNS, Stevie (1966-) b. Sligo, manager of Guinness Irish Surf Team at 1998 World Surfing Games and of the Irish Team at Eurosurf 1997, frequently placed at the National Championships. Participated in many European and World Championships.

COOK, Peter (1962-) b. Australia, national coach to the Irish team and technical officer for the French Surfing Federation.

LALLY, Zoë (1971-) b. Donegal, Irish Women's Champion in 1997, team member at Eurosurf 1997. Club: Castle Warriors Surf Club.

McAULEY, Bryan (1980-) b. Antrim, bodyboarder. Member of Guinness Irish Surf Team at 1998 World Surfing Games. U16 National Champion 1996, 5th in U16 Junior Eurosurf 1996, and in the top placings at the in the '98 World Surfing Games in Lisbon, Portugal. Surf Club: Causeway Coast Surf Club.

McNULTY, Joe (1969-) b. California, longboarder, 2nd with brother at Big Wave World Championship 1998 which stunned the surfing world, Assistant Manager of Guinness Irish Surf Team at '98 World Surfing Games, twice WSA West Coast Men's Champion, 4th

Professional Surfing Association of America.

McNULTY, Terence b. California, 2nd with brother Joe in the inaugural Big Wave World Championship 1998 (third in the individual final).

ROBINSON, Grant (1951-) 1997 and 1987 European Masters Champion, as well as being finalist in European Masters on many occasions. Surfing 29 years, club: Rossnowlagh Surf Club.

WARD, Tanya (1974-) f. Antrim, bodyboarder. Has competed at world and European levels, with a bronze medal at Eurosurf '95 and in the top placings at the in the '98 World Surfing Games in Lisbon, Portugal.

TUG-OF-WAR

KEOGH, Martin b. Folksmills, Co. Wexford, most capped competitor in the sport of Tug-of-War. Competed in many European and World championships, winning 13 gold medals and many silver and bronze. Celebrated his 25th year with his club, winning the National Premier League and winning gold and the European Championships in Jersey 1997. Also twice world-ploughing champion.

WEIGHTLIFTING

O'GRADY, Gerry (1961-) power lifter. Irish champion power lifter 13 times, he was a gold medallist at the 1989 World Championships in Canada. Won the 'Ireland's Strongest Man' title in 1995.

❑

ATHLETICS

AHEARNE, Tim (1885-1968) b. Co. Limerick, Representing Britain in the triple jump at the 1908 games in London Ahearne won the gold medal. His jump of 14.91m was a world record. His brother Dan set a new world record two years later.

BULL, Mike (1946-) b. Antrim, Bull was the leading British pole-vaulter for almost ten years, winning no less than thirteen titles while representing Northern Ireland. Winner of eight indoor titles, five outdoors.

CARROLL, Michele (1961) b. Dublin, Dominant in Irish sprinting from the 1970s to the 1990s, winning numerous Irish National titles: fifteen 100m titles (1977-80, 1982-85, 1987-93 and 1995), twelve 200m titles (1977-80, 1983, '85, '87, '89, 1991-93 and 1995), and four 400m titles (1987, '89, '92 and '95). Holder of the Irish women's 100m and 200m records at senior and junior level.

CARROLL, Noel (1941-1998) b. Louth, won a scholarship to Villanova University in the US. A member of the All-American Athletics teams of 1963 and 1965. He and his Villanova team mates set a world record for the 4x880 yards relay. He competed in the Olympics in 1964 and 1968. Won a total of 14 Irish titles, at 440 and 880 yards, three British AAA titles, three European Indoor titles former European 880 yards record holder.

COGHLAN, Eamon (1952-) b. Dublin, 'The Chairman of the Boards', Coghlan was virtually unbeatable on the U.S. Indoor circuit winning 52 out of 70 races including the prestigious Wannamaker Mile seven times. Such was his dominance in the indoor mile that his 15-year-old World Record was not broken until February 1997. Outdoors, Coghlan won gold in the 5,000m at the 1983 World Championships in Helsinki, and has won five national titles at both 800m (1974, 1979-81 and 1983) and 1,500m (1976 and 1978-81) and one 5,000m title (1977). Through bad fortune, he finished fourth in the Olympic Games of 1976 and 1980 and was forced to miss the 1984 Olympics through injury. In 1994 Coghlan ran the mile in 3.58.60 becoming the first man over 40 to run the mile in under four minutes.

DELANEY, Ronnie (1935-) b. Wicklow, the seventh man to break the 4-minute barrier for the mile. Aged just 21, he won the 'Blue Riband' event of the track, the 1,500m, at the Melbourne Olympics in 1956. His scorching 54 second final lap saw him set a new Olympic Record of 3:41.2 (only slightly outside the World Record). An accomplished indoor miler he broke the World Indoor Record on three occasions.

FLANAGAN, John J. (1873-1938) b. Limerick, after emigrating to the US Flanagan became a three time gold medal winner in the hammer event at three different Olympics: Paris 1900, St. Louis 1904, and London 1908. Won an Olympic silver medal in 1904 for throwing the 56lb weight.

FLYNN, Ray (1957-) b. Longford, became the first Irishman to break 3 mins 50 seconds barrier for the mile. Competed in two Olympics (1980 and 1984) he won one National 5,000m title (1982) and the 1,500m twice (1977 and 1985). Flynn still holds the national 1,500m record of 3.33.50 and the national mile record of 3.49.77. Now a sports agent.

HOOPER, Dick (1957-) b. Dublin, Won four national marathon titles. Won the Dublin Marathon three times and competed in the Olympic marathon on three occasions.

HOPKINS, Thelma (1936-) b. Hull, won a silver medal for Britain in the 1956 Melbourne Games in the high jump. Won a total of 33 NI titles from 1951 onwards. Won a European High jump gold medal in 1954 and won the European cup the same year. An all-rounder, she won 45 caps for Ireland at hockey and was later chosen to play squash for Ireland.

KERR, Bobbie (1882) b. Co. Fermanagh, emigrated to Canada at the age of seven, he won gold in the 200m and bronze in the 100m in the 1908 Olympics.

KIELY, Tom (1869-1951) b. Co Tipperary, winner of 53 Irish titles, 18 of them in the hammer, 16 British Crown Gold Medals and 5 British AAA titles. Set a world record in the hammer in 1899 with a throw of 162 feet, the first person ever to throw the hammer over 160 ft. Offered a free trip to the Olympic Games of 1904 if he declared for Britain, Kiely declared for Ireland, paid his own fare, and won the gold medal for the All-Round Championship, the fore-runner to the modern day decathlon.

LEAHY, Con (1876-1921) b. Co. Cork, Leahy, representing Britain, won Olympic gold (high jump) and silver (triple jump) at the 1906 Olympics and, representing Ireland, won silver in the high jump in 1908 Games.

McDONALD, Pat (1878-1954) b. Co. Clare, won a shot putt gold medal for the US in the 1912 Olympic Games, setting an Olympic record, and silver in the two-hand shot event. In 1920 he won gold medal in the 56lb. shot at the Antwerp Games. At 42 years 26 days, he is one of the oldest Olympic gold medal winners in history.

O'CALLAGHAN, Dr. Pat (1905-1991) b. Cork, double Olympic Gold Medallist for the Irish Free State, winning the hammer in Amsterdam (1928) and Los Angeles (1932). In addition to numerous national titles and a European Record of 56.95m (1933) he recorded an unofficial World Record of 59.56m (1937).

O'CONNOR, Peter J. (1874-1957) b. Co. Wicklow, His world long jump record of 24' 11" set in Dublin (1901) stood for more than 20 years and remained an Irish record for a further 89 years. He won a gold medal in the St Loius Olympic Games of 1906 in the triple jump.

O'MARA, Frank (1960-) b. Limerick, won the 5,000m at the World Indoor Championships in both 1987 and 1991, he competed in the Olympic Games in 1984, 1988 and 1992. He won the National 1,500 title four times (1983, '86, '88 and '91) and the 5,000m once (1995).

PETERS, Mary (1939-) b. Lancashire, won gold, when competing for Britain in the Pentathlon at the Munich Olympics in 1972. Setting a new World Record of 4801 points she became Northern Ireland's first Gold medallist. In a long career she won two Commonwealth Pentathlon titles, eight British AAA pentathlons as well an AAA 100m and five AAA shot putt titles.

PURCELL, Mary (1952-) b. Dublin, winner of the Irish National 1,500m title seven times(1972-76, '78), and '80), winner of four British womens AAA titles. In 1982 she won the Irish National Marathon Championship.

RYAN, Paddy (1882-1964) b. Limerick, emigrated to the US in 1910. In 1913, he set a world shot putt record of 189' 6" that was to last for 25 years. It stood as an American record for 40 years. In 1920, representing the US, he won the gold medal at the Antwerp Olympic Games, his victory margin of 15 feet being the biggest ever recorded in the competition. Won a silver medal in the 56lb. shot behind fellow countryman, Pat McDonald.

SHERIDAN, Marty (1881-1918) b. Mayo, set 16 world records in his career and regarded as the finest athlete in the world at his peak. In 1902 he became the first man to throw the discus over 40 metres, holding the world record for ten years, breaking it eight times himself until he reached his all-time best of 43.69 metres. Representing the US, he won a total of nine Olympic medals including five gold, three silver and two bronze. His gold medals came in the discus (St. Louis 1904, Athens 1906 and London 1908), the Shot Putt (Athens 1906) and the Discus Greek Style (London 1908).

TISDALL, Bob (1907-) b. Ceylon, won gold in the 400m hurdles at the Los Angeles Olympics in 1932 but was denied his world-record time, because at that time it was illegal to hit a hurdle (which he did). Immediately after the race he went to support Dr. Pat O'Callaghan who won gold an hour later.

TREACY, John (1957-) b. Waterford, marathon Silver medallist at the Los Angeles Olympics in 1984. He has also won the 1992 Los Angeles and 1993 Dublin Marathons and represented Ireland in four Olympics. An accomplished track and cross-country runner he won the World Cross Country Championship in 1978 and 1979. Also won five national 5,000m titles (1978,'80, '81, '83,and '84) and two national 10,000m titles (1985 and 1987). National record holder at 10,000m, he is the current chairman of the Irish Sports Council.

BOXING

BYRNE, Tony (1929-) b. Louth, Irish Champion three times, he won a bronze medal in the lightweight division in the 1956 Melbourne Olympic Games.

CALDWELL, Johnny (1938-) b. Belfast, won a flyweight bronze medal at the Melbourne Olympics in 1956, when only 18. He turned professional two years later. In 1961 he became World Bantamweight champion by beating Alphonse Halimi of France. He subsequently lost the title to Eder Jofre, of Brazil, in 1962.

DEMPSEY, Jack (1862-1895) b. *John Kelly* Kildare, Dempsey held the World Middleweight title for seven years from 1884. Fighting in America, he defended his title successfully on five occasions.

DOWLING, Mick (1948-) b. Kilkenny, holds a unique record in Irish domestic boxing, winning the National Senior title at bantamweight for eight successive years from 1968. Bronze medalist at the European Championships on four occasions between 1965 and 1971.

GILROY, Freddie (1936-) b. Belfast, bronze medallist (bantamweight) at the 1956 Olympics, he turned professional the following year. Won the European Bantamweight title (1959). In his last fight, he beat Johnny Caldwell for the British and Commonwealth title.

INGLE, Jimmy (1921-) b. Dublin, the first Irish boxer to win a European Amateur title, he won the flyweight title in 1939, aged 17.

McAULEY, Dave (1961) b. Antrim, Dave 'Boy' McAuley made two attempts at winning the world flyweight title, losing to Fidel Bassa both in 1987 and 1988, before finally gaining a world title belt on defeating Britain's Duke McKenzie. Successfully defended his title five times.

McCORMICK, Tom (1890-1916) b. Louth, became World Welterweight Champion in 1914 in Melbourne, Australia. Lost the title later the same year. Killed in France.

McCOURT, Jim (1945-) b. Belfast, winner of seven Irish senior titles at lightweight. In 1964 he won the lightweight bronze medal at the Tokyo Olympic Games. Won a bronze the following year, in the same weight division at the European Championships and boxed in his second Olympics in 1968. Took the gold medal in the Commonwealth Games in Jamaica while fighting at light-welterweight.

McGUIGAN, Barry (1961-) b. Monaghan, won a gold medal at the Commonwealth Games at age 17. Turned professional in 1980, and by 1983, he had both the British and European bantamweight titles under his belt. The highlight of a great career came on 8th June, 1985, when he out-pointed Eusebio Pedrosa, the reigning world champion, to take the WBA world featherweight title in front of a huge outdoor crowd at Loftus Road, London. Defended his title twice before losing it in 1986 to Texan Steve Cruz in the burning heat of a car park in the Nevada Desert. After a brief comeback, McGuigan retired in 1988.

McLARNIN, Jimmy (1906-) b. Down, won 63 of his 77 contests and twice held the World Welterweight title.

McNALLY, John b. Belfast, he took a silver medal in the Bantamweight division at the Helsinki Olympic Games (1952), becoming the first Irish boxer to win an Olympic medal.

McTIGUE, Mike (1892-1966) b. Clare. On St. Patrick's Day 1923 in the La Scala Opera House in Dublin McTigue won the World Light-heavyweight title beating Battling Siki, of Senagal, on points in a 20 round contest. It proved to the last world title fight at any weight to go more than 15 rounds. He held the title for two years.

MONAGHAN, Rinty (1920-1984) b. Belfast, became undisputed flyweight champion of the world in March 1948 when he defeated Scotland's Jackie Patterson in the King's Hall, Belfast. In a great career, Monaghan won Irish, British and European titles. Because of various medical ailments, he was forced to retire in early 1950, ending his career on a high as undefeated World title holder.

NASH, Charlie (1951-) born Derry, after a very successful amateur career during which he won five senior Irish titles, turned professional and earned both British and European titles as a light-weight. Became British champion in 1978 and European Champion in 1979, winning the latter title in his home city. Biggest disappointment was his fourth-round defeat in 1980 by Scotsman Jim Watt in their World title bout.

O'COLMAIN, Gerry (1924-) b. Dublin, won two light-heavyweight titles and seven heavyweight titles in a row (from 1946) in a very successful amateur career. The highlight of his career was winning the European heavyweight gold medal at the European Championships in Dublin in 1947.

O'SULLIVAN, Jim (1959-) b. Wexford, O'Sullivan entered the record books of Irish boxing in 1990 when he became the first and, so far, the only boxer to win ten national senior titles. He won his championships at four different weights, beginning in 1980 at light-middleweight (1), light-heavyweight (1) heavyweight (4) and Super-Heavyweight (4)

RUSSELL, Hugh (1959-) b. Belfast, won a bronze medal in the flyweight division at the 1980 Olympic Games in Moscow. Turned professional in 1981, he became British bantamweight champion in 1984. Successfully defended the title three times.

TIEDT, Fred (1939-) b. Dublin, Silver medallist at Welterweight in the 1956 Olympic Games in Melbourne. Irish Welterweight champion in 1957.

CYCLING

EARLEY, Martin completed the Tour de France on five occasions between 1985 and 1992. He won the 1989 La Bastide d'Armagnac to Pau stage of the Tour. An Olympian in 1984 and 1996.

ELLIOTT, Shay (1934-1971) b. Dublin, professional cyclist. He was the first Irishman to wear the yellow jersey in the Tour de France. Winner the Roubaix stage in the Tour in 1963, he completed three Tours with his best finish (47th place) coming in 1961. Silver medallist in the 1962 World Road Championship.

KELLY, Sean (1956-) b. Tipperary, the most successful cyclist of his generation, Irish or otherwise. The number one ranked cyclist in the world 1984-88, he completed the Tour de France 12 times - winning five stages and winning the points championship on a record four occasions. His best finishes in the Tour were fourth in 1985 and fifth in 1984. In his long prestigious career, Kelly won the Tour of Spain (1988), the Tour of Switzerland (1983 and 1990), the Nissan Classic (1985, '86, '87 and '91), the World Cup (1989) and a number of shorter Classics such as the Paris-Nice, which with seven successive victories he all but made his own.

KIMMAGE, Paul b. Dublin, he joined the select band of Irishmen to complete the Tour de France in 1986 when he finished 131st. An outstanding amateur, he competed for Ireland in the 1984 Olympic Games. Since retirement, he has become one of Ireland's leading sports journalists.

ROCHE, Stephen (1959-) b. Dublin, Roche's achievements in 1987 were breathtaking - he won the Giro d'Italia, the World Championship and, the biggest of them all, the Tour de France. Victory in France sparked off unprecedented national celebration and Roche was conferred with the Freedom of Dublin. As an amateur he won the Paris-Roubaix race in 1980 and won the Paris-Nice as a professional in 1981. The winner of 57 races, he retired in 1993. Roche completed the Tour de France eight times (coming third in 1985 and ninth in 1992) and won three stages. His brother Laurence finished 153rd in the Tour de France in 1991.

McQUAID, Jim (1921-) b. Waterford, winner of Grand Prix of Ireland six times between 1949 and 1960, he competed in four World Championships.

McCORMACK, J.J. (1926-) born Offaly, winner of 26 Irish titles in a long career, represented his country 21 times, including six World C'ships appearances..

O'HANLON, Shay (1942-) b. Dublin, won the Rás Tailteann four times between 1962 and 1967. Winner of 35 national championships and the NCA title in 1979. Retired in 1980.

GAA

BRADY, Phil b. Cavan, winner of three All-Ireland Football medals between 1947 and 1952. He won a National Football League medal in 1948 and a Railway Cup medal in 1950. Known in GAA circles as The Gunner Brady.

CONNOLLY, John (1948-) b. Galway, eldest of the hurling Connolly brothers, won an All-Ireland Hurling medal in 1980 with his brothers Michael, Padraic and Joe. Twice an All-Star Winner, was the the 1980 Texaco Hurler of the Year.

CONNOR, Matt (1959-) b. Offaly, won an All-Ireland Senior Football Championship medal in 1982, when Offaly put an end to Kerry's five-in-a-row attempt. The country's leading scorer for a record five years he won three All-Star awards in the early 80s. A serious car accident in 1984 ended his career.

DORAN, Tony (1946-) b. Wexford, one of Wexford's best known hurlers, played in 20 inter-county campaigns, winning an All-Ireland medal in 1968, two National Hurling League medals and seven Railway Cup medals (two of these as Captain). Won a Hurling All-Star at full forward, was Texaco Hurler of the Year in 1976. Retired from intercounty hurling in 1984 but led his club, Buffer's Alley to an All-Ireland Club Championship in 1989.

DOYLE, Jimmy (1939-) b. Tipperary, hurler, who in his sixteen years senior inter-county career won six All-Ireland medals between 1958 and 1971 (including two as captain). He also won eight Railway Cup medals (a Tipperary record) and six National Hurling League medals. Texaco Hurler of the Year in 1965.

DOYLE, John (1930-) b. Tipperary, holder of eight All-Ireland hurling medals (won between 1949 and 1965) and a record eleven National Hurling League medals (also between 1949 and 1965). The winner of five Railway Cups with Munster, he was the Texaco Hurler of the Year in 1964.

EARLEY, Dermot (1948-) b. Mayo, an All-Star Winner in 1974 and 1979, won two Railway Cup medals. Despite winning five Connacht Senior Football Championship titles between 1972 and 1980 he and Roscommon never won an All-Ireland title. He does, however, hold a National Football League medal from 1979.

FOX, Pat (1961-) b. Tipperary, predatory forward on the All-Ireland hurling winning Tipperary teams of 1989 and 1991. He has been the recipient of three All-Star awards.

HEFFERNAN, Kevin (1938-) b. Dublin, captained Dublin to their 1958 All-Ireland Football win. Winner of three National Football League titles between 1953 and 1958 and seven Railway Cup medals (captaining Leinster in 1959). Manager of the great Dublin team of the 1970s, leading them to three All-Ireland Senior Football titles (1974, '76 and '77).

KEAVENEY, Jimmy (1945) b. Dublin, magnificent rotund Dublin full-forward who won All-Ireland football medals in 1974, 1976 and 1977. Winner of two National Football League medals, three All-Star Awards and two Texaco Gaelic Footballer of the Year Awards (1976 and 1977).

KEHER, Eddie (1941-) b. Kilkenny, renowned Kilkenny hurling marksman, made his senior championship debut aged seventeen in the 1959 All-Ireland Final Replay. In a career that stretched to 1977, he won six All-Ireland Senior Hurling Championship medals, nine Railway Cup medals and three National Hurling League medals. Texaco Hurler of the Year in 1972 and an All-Star Winner on five successive occasions between 1971 and 1975.

LYNCH, Jack (1917-) b. Cork, dual player who won a record six consecutive All-Ireland medals between 1941 and 1946, five in hurling and one in football. Made his debut in 1935 (he retired in 1951) winning three National Hurling League medals and three Railway Cup medals. Entered the Dáil in 1948 and went on to become Taoiseach (1966-1973 and 1977-1979).

McCARTAN Snr, James b. Down, midfielder for Down who won All-Ireland Football medals in 1960 1961, and 1968 and won three Railway Cup medals (1964, 1965 and 1969). His brother Dan won three All-Ireland medals and his son James is the holder of two All-Ireland medals.

McCARTHY, Liam (1853-1928) b. London of Irish parents, McCarthy was the first treasurer of the London GAA County Board. The cup which All-Ireland Hurling winning captains now receive bears his name. The cup was first presented in 1923 and a new Liam McCarthy cup was presented for the first time in 1992.

McDONAGH, Mattie (1935-) b. Galway, footballer for Galway who was one of the outstanding figures of Gaelic Games in the 1960s. Winner of four All-Ireland Football medals between 1956 and 1966 (was part of famous Galway three-in-a-row team of the mid-1960s). He won a Railway Cup medal in 1958 and was Texaco Footballer of the Year in 1966.

McENIFF, Brian (1943-) b. Donegal, footballer for Donegal who won a National Football League medal with New York in 1964. An All-Star in 1972, won two Railway Cup medals with Ulster. As manager of Donegal, he guided the team to its first All-Ireland Senior Football Championship in 1992. Has managed the Ulster Railway Cup side since 1982.

McNALLY, Joe (1964-) b. Dublin, won an All-Ireland football medal and All-Star award with Dublin (1983) in his first Championship season. Played with Dublin in 1995 after a long self imposed absence.

MACKEY, Mick (1912-1982) b. Limerick, a legendary name in the annals of hurling. Won three All-Ireland Hurling medals with Limerick (1934, 1936 and 1940) captaining the team on two occasions. He also won eight Railway Cup medals between 1934 and 1945 and five National Hurling League medals. Managed the Limerick hurling team in the 1950s.

MAGUIRE, Sam (1879-1927) b. Cork, Gaelic footballer who played championship football for London in the early 1900s. Maguire had the distinction of swearing Michael Collins into the IRB, and the cup which All-Ireland Football winning captains now receive bears his name. It was presented for the first time in 1928. The new Sam Maguire cup was first presented in 1988 to Meath's Mick Lyons.

O'CONNELL, Mick (1937-) b. Kerry, one of Gaelic football's most famous names, won four All-Ireland Football medals with Kerry between 1959 (when he captained the team) and 1970, six National Football League medals and one Railway Cup medal. Won an All-Star award (1972) and was Texaco Footballer of the Year in 1962. O'Connell's high fielding was renowned, and he is generally regarded as Gaelic Football's best ever midfielder.

O'HEHIR, Michael (1920-1996) b. Dublin, broadcaster. Worked with *Irish Independent* until 1960. Began his commentary on gaelic football and hurling in 1938 and commentated on 99 All-Ireland finals. Also covered horse racing for RTÉ and BBC. First RTÉ Head of Sport (1960-72). Penned a weekly column with the *Irish Press.* Was most widely known and celebrated voice in Ireland up until his retirement, due to a stroke.

O'ROURKE, Colm (1957-) born Meath, inspiring Meath Gaelic football full forward who won two All-Ireland medals in 1987 and 1988 and two National Football League medals. Holds two All-Stars and in 1991 was the Texaco Footballer of the Year. Retired from inter-county football in 1995. He was manager of the Irish team in the 1998 International Rules series with Australia.

O'SHEA, Jack (1957-) b. Kerry, finest Gaelic footballer of his era. Won seven All-Ireland Football medals from 1978 to 1986. Winner of six consecutive midfield All-Star Awards (1980-1985) and a record four Texaco Awards. 'Jacko' captained the Irish compromise rules teams against Australia in 1984 and 1986. Was manager of the Mayo team for a time and guided them to Connacht success in 1993.

RACKARD, Nicky, Bobby & Billy (1922, 1929 & 1930, respectively) b. Wexford, brothers who formed a formidable backbone in the Wexford Senior Hurling team of the 1950s. All three played in Wexford's All-Ireland Hurling Final successes of 1955 and 1956, while Billy also won an All-Ireland medal in 1960. Between them they also won six Railway Cup medals and three National Hurling medals. In 1992, both Billy and Bobby became All-Time All-Stars.

RING, Christy (1920-1979) b. Cork, recognised as one of the all time greats in hurling. Won eight All-Ireland Hurling medals (three as captain) between 1941 and 1954, 18 Railway Cup medals between 1942 and 1963, and four National Hurling League medals. Ring played with Cork from 1939 until 1962.

SHEEHY, Mikey (1954-) b. Kerry, Gaelic footballer who won eight All-Ireland Football medals between 1975 and 1986. Won seven All-Star awards in an illustrious career.

SKEHAN, Noel (1946-) b. Kilkenny, former Kilkenny Hurling goalkeeper holds a record nine All-Ireland Senior Hurling Championship medals won between 1963 and 1983. Holds four Railway Cup medals. All-Star goalkeeper on seven occasions and Texaco Award Winner in 1982. Retiring from inter-county hurling at the age of 39, he went on to become an accomplished squash player.

GOLF

BRADSHAW, Harry (1913) born Wicklow, winner of the Irish Professional ten times he also won the Irish Open twice (1947 and 1949) and the Dunlop Masters twice (1953 and 1955). A member of three British and Irish Ryder Cup teams (1953, 1955 and 1957). He and Christy O'Connor Senior won the Canada Cup (now the World Cup) in 1958. He died in 1990.

BRUEN, Jimmy (born Antrim 1920). An outstanding amateur golfer he won the Irish Close Championship twice (1937 and 1938) and the British Amateur Championship in 1946. He played in three Walker Cup tournaments including the inaugural British and Irish win in 1938. He died in 1972.

CARR, Joe (born Dublin 1922). Four time Irish Amateur Open winner (between 1946 and 1956), three time British Amateur Championship winner (1953-60), six time Irish Close Championship winner (1954-67) in addition to twelve East of Ireland, twelve West of Ireland and three South of Ireland Championships. He played on a record ten Walker Cup teams between 1947 and 1967.

FEHERTY, David (born Co. Down 1958). Winner of six events on the European tour including the Italian and Scottish Opens in 1986 and the 1989 BMW International. Captain of the victorious Irish team in the 1990 Dunhill Cup. He played in the 1991 Ryder Cup in the United States. Feherty moved to the American circuit in 1994 but retired to take up a position as a golf commentator.

O'CONNOR Snr, Christy (born Galway 1924). Won 24 titles on the European PGA tour (1955-1972) including four Carroll's International events. A member of ten Ryder Cup teams, he played in 36 matches. With Harry Bradshaw he won World Cup in 1958. Ireland's most successful golfer ever he went on to enjoy further success on the Senior Tour.

RUGBY

CAMPBELL, Ollie (1954-) b. Dublin, an out-half, he won 22 caps (1976-84) with Ireland and seven caps with the Lions. An outstanding place kicker, he holds many Irish international scoring records, including most points in an international season - 52 (1982-83); most international dropped goals - 7 (including two in a single international); most penalty goals in an international season - 14 (1982-83); and most points on an Irish international tour - 60 (Australia 1979). In all, scored 217 points for Ireland and 184 points for the Lions.

DAWSON, Ronnie (1932-) b. Dublin, hooker, capped 27 times by Ireland and 6 times by the Lions. He captained the British and Irish Lions tour to Australia and New Zealand. Also captained the Barbarians in 1960 when they defeated South Africa.

FITZGERALD, Ciarán (1952-) b. Galway, hooker, capped 25 times by Ireland (20 times as captain) between 1979 and 1986 and four times (all as captain) by the Lions on their 1983 tour of New Zealand. Under his captaincy, Ireland won the Triple Crown in 1982 and the International Championship in 1983.

GALLAHER, Dave (1873-1917) b. Donegal, emigrated to New Zealand and captained his adopted country in their first ever international against Australia in 1903. Capped six times, he was killed in battle at Passchendale.

GIBSON, Mike (1942-) b. Belfast, Ireland's most capped international, he won 69 caps between 1964 and 1979. In addition, he was capped 12 times by the Lions. In his 16 season international career he scored 115 points.

KEANE, Moss (1948-) b. Kerry, winner of 51 Irish caps (1974-84), he won the Five Nations Championship twice (1974 and 1983) and the Triple Crown in 1982. Capped once on the Lions 1977 tour of New Zealand he was a member of the Munster side who famously defeated the touring New Zealand All-Blacks in 1978.

KIERNAN, Michael (1961-) b. Cork, capped 43 times between 1982 and 1991 his 308 points is an Irish international record. He also holds the Irish record for most penalty goals scored (62) and most international conversions (40 - including a record seven in a single international). His last minute drop goal against England in the 1985 Triple Crown decider handed Ireland victory. Prior to devoting himself entirely to rugby, he won the Irish 200m title (1981).

KIERNAN, Tom (1939-) b. Cork, Ireland's most capped full-back with 54 caps won between 1960 and 1973. He captained Ireland a record 24 times and has scored 158 points. He has been capped five times (four as captain) by the British and Irish Lions, top Irish points scorer Michael Kiernan is his nephew.

KYLE, Jackie (1926-) b. Belfast, Capped 46 times by Ireland (1947-58) and six times by the Lions (1950). He won the Grand Slam (1948), the Triple Crown (1949) and the Five Nations Championship (1951). He is Ireland's most capped outhalf.

Mc BRIDE, Willie John (1940-) b. Antrim, His 63 caps for Ireland between 1962 and 1975 (including a record 52 consecutively) is an international record for a lock. With 17 caps he is the most capped Lions player ever. He won the Five Nations Championship in 1974. He managed the Lions on their 1983 tour to New Zealand and coached the Irish team (1983-84). He was Texaco Sportstar of the Year in 1974.

McLOUGHLIN, Ray (1939-) b. Galway, as a prop forward he won 40 caps (eight as captain) between 1962 and 1975. An integral member of the International Championship winning side in 1974. He was capped three times by the Lions on their 1966 southern hemisphere tour. Captained Ireland to their first ever victory over South Africa in 1965.

MILLAR, Syd (1934-) b. Antrim, capped 37 times as a prop forward between 1958 and 1970, he won nine caps with the British Lions. Irish team coach (1972-75), he managed the Lions on their 1980 tour of South Africa. He is a former President of the IRFU.

O'REILLY, Tony (1936-) b. Dublin, winner of 29 international caps (1955-70) at wing three-quarter in a career which spanned 16 seasons. Capped by the Lions ten times he scored a record six tries. Worldwide President of H.J. Heinz and Chairman of Independent Newspapers.

ORR, Philip (1950-) b. Dublin, Ireland's most capped prop forward with 58 appearances (1976-87), capped by the Lions in 1977. Member of the Triple Crown winning teams of 1982 and 1985.

RINGLAND, Trevor (1959-) b. Belfast, scored seven tries for Ireland in his 34 international appearances between 1981 and 1988. He was a member of the Triple Crown winning sides of 1982 and 1985 and the Championship winning side of 1983. Capped by the Lions in 1983.

WARD, Tony (1954-) b. Dublin, he won 19 Irish caps between 1978 and 1987, scoring 113 points. In his only full Lions appearance, against South Africa in 1980, he scored a record 18 points. Member of the Munster team which defeated the All-Blacks in 1978.

SOCCER

ARMSTRONG, Gerry (1954-) born Belfast, capped 63 times between 1977 and 1986, he scored 12 international goals of which the most memorable was his winner against host nation Spain in the 1982 World Cup finals. Also played in the 1986 World Cup finals. He played club football with Bangor, Watford, Tottenham Hotspur, Real Mallorca, West Bromwich Albion and Chesterfield.

BAMBRICK, Joe (1905-1983) b. Belfast, played with Linfield (winning the Irish Cup in 1930) and with Chelsea in England. With 12 goals in eleven appearances, he held the Northern Ireland scoring record from 1938 until 1992 and remains number two in the Northern Ireland scoring charts.

BEST, George (1946-) b. Belfast, European Player of the Year - 1968 (the only Irishman to win that award). Winner of two League Championships (1965/65 and 1967/68) and the European Cup (1968). Capped 37 times by Northern Ireland he scored nine international goals. Pele once described him as the greatest living footballer.

BINGHAM, Billy (1931-) b. Belfast, Bingham won the League Championship with Everton (1962/63) he counts Glentoran, Sunderland and Luton amongst his former clubs. Capped 56 times between 1951 and 1964 he scored ten international goals. As Northern Ireland manager he guided the team to the World Cup finals in 1982 and 1986 where they rocked some of the more recognised footballing nations. Retired from the manager's job in 1995.

BLANCHFLOWER, Danny (1925-) b. Belfast, Capped 56 times by Northern Ireland he scored two international goals and captained them in the World Cup finals in Sweden in 1958 where they reached the quarter-finals. Captain of Tottenham Hotspur in their FA Cup/League Championship winning year 1960/61. With Spurs he also won the 1962 FA Cup and the 1963 Cup Winners' Cup.

BRADLEY, Brendan (1949-) b. Derry, the League of Ireland's all-time top scorer with 235 goals.

BRADY, Liam (1956-) b. Dublin, midfielder. The only Irishman ever to play in Italy's Serie A, he won two Championships with Juventus (1981 and 1982). Capped 72 times (12 times as captain) by the Republic of Ireland, scoring nine goals. An FA Cup winner with Arsenal in 1979 he managed Celtic (1991-93) and Brighton (1994-95). Currently works with Arsenal's youth teams.

BONNER, Packie (1960-) b. Donegal, has won 80 caps with the Republic of Ireland. Winner of four Scottish League and two Scottish Cup medals with his beloved Celtic, he will be forever remembered for the string of spectacular saves in the 1-0 victory over England in 1988, and his penalty save against Romania in Genoa in 1990, helping the Republic to the World Cup quarter finals.

CANTWELL, Noel (1932-) b. Cork, captained Manchester United to FA Cup (1963) and League Championship (1967) success. Capped 36 times by the Republic between 1954 and 1967 he scored 10 international goals. Capped five times by the Irish cricket team.

CAREY, Jackie (1919-) b. Dublin, won the FA Cup (1948) and the League Championship (1951/52) with Manchester United. Capped 29 times between 1938 and 1953 by the Republic of Ireland, he was capped seven times by Northern Ireland between 1947 and 1949.

CHARLTON, Jack (1935-) b. Newcastle, manager of Republic of Ireland (1986-95). His tenure as manager was the Republic's most successful ever. Led Ireland to the 1988 European Championship and the World Cup finals Italia '90 and US '94. Winner of World Cup medal with England in 1966. Conferred with honorary Irish citizenship in 1996.

CLARKE, Colin (1962-) b. Newry, Holds the Northern Ireland international scoring record with 13 goals in 38 appearances. A member of the Northern Ireland 1986 World Cup squad, he has played club football with Southampton, Bournemouth and Portsmouth.

DOHERTY, Peter (1913-) b. Derry, capped by Northern Ireland 16 times between 1935 and 1951 Doherty won an English League Championship with Manchester City in 1936/37 and the FA Cup with Derby in 1946. Manager of the Northern Ireland team (1951-1962). In 1958, he guided them to their first ever World Cup finals in Sweden where they finished in the top eight.

DUNNE, Jimmy (1905-1949) b. Dublin, scored 170 League goals with English clubs (including Sheffield United, Arsenal and Southampton). Returned to Shamrock Rovers where he won two League Championships (1937/38 and 1938/39) and the 1940 FAI Cup. Scorer of 12 goals in his 15 international appearances for the Free State and Éire.

FARRELL, Peter (1922) b. Dublin, capped 28 times by the Republic between 1946 and 1957. Scorer on the winning Republic side which beat England 2-0 in 1949, the first team to ever beat England at home. Also capped seven times by Northern Ireland.

GALLAGHER, Patsy (1894-1954) b. Donegal, scorer of 184 goals in his 436-game, 15-year career with Celtic. Winner of four Scottish Cups and six League Championships with Celtic. Capped eleven times by Northern Ireland between 1920 and 1927 he also won one international cap with the Free State.

GILES, Johnny (1940-) b. Dublin, capped 59 times (with 30 as captain) by the Republic, he was player-manager from 1973-80. The holder of two Championship and one FA Cup medal with Leeds United he also won an FA cup medal with Manchester United in 1963.

HEIGHWAY, Steve (1947-) b. Dublin, capped by the Republic 34 times. Had an immensely successful career with Liverpool winning two European Cups (1977 and 1978), two UEFA Cups, four League Championships and an F.A. Cup medal.

HURLEY, Charlie (1936-) b. Cork, played with Millwall, Sunderland and Bolton Wanderers. He captained the Republic 21 times (from a total of 40 appearances) and scored two international goals.

JENNINGS, Pat (1945-) b. Newry, Northern Ireland's most capped player. Made his debut in 1964 and won his 119th cap on his 41st birthday against Brazil in the 1986 World Cup finals. With Tottenham Hotspur he won two League Cups (1971 and 1973), a Cup Winners' Cup (1968) and the U.E.F.A. Cup (1972). In addition he won two FA Cup medals (one with Spurs in 1967 and one with Arsenal in 1979). PFA Player of the Year in 1976.

KINNEAR, Joe (1946-) b. Dublin, winner of one FA Cup and two UEFA Cup medals with Tottenham Hotspur in the 1960s and 1970s he was capped 26 times by the Republic. Manager of Wimbledon since 1992 where despite limited resources he has enjoyed some success. Voted Manager of the Year in the English Premiership in 1996/97.

LAWRENSON, Mark (1957-) b. Preston, capped 39 times by the Republic between 1977 and 1987. Winner of five League Championships, one FA Cup and one European Cup with Liverpool in the 1980s. He retired at the age of 30 due to a serious foot injury.

McELHINNEY, Gerry (1956-) b. Derry, capped six times by Northern Ireland in 1984 and 1985. He was a member of the Derry Gaelic football team which won the Ulster title in 1976 and 1977, winning an All-Star award in 1976. He was also an Irish international boxer.

McGEE, Paul (1954-) b. Sligo, a much travelled player he played in Ireland, Canada, England and Holland in a career spanning 25 years and 27 changes of club. Scored four goals in his 15 appearances for the Republic.

MORAN, Kevin (1956-) b. Dublin, winner of All-Ireland football medals with Dublin in 1976 and 1977, Moran went on to have a distinguished career with Manchester United winning two FA Cup medals, but gaining an unwanted place in history as the first player to be sent off in an FA Cup final. Capped 70 times by the Republic scoring six goals, he captained the team during the 1988 European Championship finals.

NEILL, Terry (1942-) b. Belfast, winner of 59 caps with Northern Ireland between 1961 and 1973. Northern Ireland manager in 1973, he managed Arsenal - the club with whom he had spent most of his playing career - when they won the FA Cup in 1979.

O'LEARY, David (1958-) b. London, capped 67 times, O'Leary will forever remembered for scoring the penalty against Romania which sent the Republic into the World Cup quarter finals in 1990. In his 20-year career with Arsenal he won two FA Cups (1979 & 1993), and two League Championships (1988/89 and 1990/91). Differences with Jack Charlton saw him miss out on the European Championships of 1988 and the 1994 World Cup. David's brother Pierce was capped seven times in 1980 and 1981.

RICE, Pat (born Belfast, 1949) Member of the Arsenal F.A. Cup/League double winning side of 1971, he captained Arsenal to F.A. Cup success in 1979. Capped by Northern Ireland 49 times between 1969 and 1980.

ROBERTS, Fred his 96 goals scored for Glentoran in the 1930/31 season is an Irish and British record. Not surprisingly, he ended that season with a League Winners medal. Won the Irish Cup in 1932 and 1933. Capped once by Northern Ireland.

SCOTT, Elisha 'Lee' (1894-1959) b. Belfast, played 429 games in a 22-year career with Liverpool winning two League Championships. Hugely successful manager with Belfast Celtic (1936-49), he led them to six League titles and six Irish Cups. Capped 31 times for Northern Ireland (1920-36).

STAPLETON, Frank (1956-) b. Dublin, holder of the Republic's international scoring record with 20 goals in 70 appearances between 1976 and 1990. A striker of tremendous strength he won three FA Cup medals (one with Arsenal and two with Manchester Utd). His other clubs included Ajax, Le Harve and Blackburn Rovers. Had a short but unsuccessful stint as a manager in the US.

WHELAN, Ronnie (1961-) b. Dublin, with Liverpool he won six League Championships between 1981 and 1990, two FA Cups (1986 & 1989) and a European Cup in 1984. Capped 53 times by the Republic he scored three international goals including a spectacular volley against Russia in Euro '88. Whelan's career was ended by injury in 1995. Currently a club manager in Greece.

WHELAN, Liam (1935-1958) b. Dublin, winner of two League Championships with Manchester United in 1955/56 and 1956/57. He was capped only four times by the Republic before he tragically lost his life in February 1958 in the Munich plane crash which killed eight Manchester United players.

WHITESIDE, Norman (1965-) b. Belfast, at the tender age of 17, he became the youngest player to play in the World Cup finals when he lined out against Yugoslavia in June 1982. Capped by Northern Ireland 38 times (scoring nine goals) he also played in the 1986 World Cup finals. An FA Cup winner with Manchester United in 1983. Serious injury forced his premature retirement in 1990.

OTHER SPORTS

ARMSTRONG, Reg (1930-) b. Dublin, in the four year period 1952-56 Armstrong recorded seven World Championship Grand Prix victories in motor cycling. He finished runner-up in the world championships on five occasions.

BARNVILLE, Geraldine (1942-) b. Offaly, one of Ireland's most successful squash players ever, Barnville was also an international tennis player. At squash, she was capped more than 70 times, making her one of the most capped players in the world.

BARRINGTON, Jonah (1944-) b. Cornwall, world-class squash player Barrington played 18 times for Ireland. Between 1967 and 1973, he won the British Open on six occasions, this being ranked as the premier tournament in world squash.

BRYANS, Ralph (1941-) b. Antrim, he won the World Championship 50 c.c. motor-cycling title in 1965 - the first Irish man to do so. In all he recorded ten Grand Prix victories.

DeLACY, Stan (1915-) b. Limerick, successful Irish hockey player. Won five triple crowns in a career that spanned 17 years (1937-54). Also had the unusual distinction for an Irish international sportsman, of any code, of being on the winning side in each of his first 20 games for his country.

DOYLE, Matt (1955) b. California, tennis player who brought a degree of credibility to Ireland's standing in world tennis in the 1980s when he was the driving force behind the climb to Division One of the Davis Cup competition. The highlight of his individual career was a win in a Grand Prix in 1983 in Cologne. Also won the Irish Open six times.

DREA, Sean won numerous international class sculling races. The highlight of his great career was a silver medal placing in the 1975 World Championships held in England.

FEENEY, Joe welterweight wrestler. Won the British title 1957-64, an achievement recorded in the Guinness Book of Records - he won the title eight times in a row and 14 times overall - and was an olympic representative in 1960.

GILMARTIN, John Joe (1916-) b. Kilkenny, His record of 24 All-Ireland senior titles in handball was only surpassed in the mid-1990s. His status in this widely played Irish sport was such that when he retired in 1947 he had not lost a singles match in more than ten years.

GREGG, Terry (1950-) b. Antrim, one of the greats of Irish hockey, Gregg played a record 103 times for Ireland and 42 times for the Great Britain team. A prolific goal-getter, he brilliantly led Ireland to the final of the Inter-Continental Cup in Rome 1977 - their best ever performance at international level.

HERRON, Tommy (1950-1980) b. Down, regarded as one of the top motorcycle riders in the world in the 1970s. Won three Isle of Man TTs. At the North-West 200 in 1978, he averaged 127.6 m.p.h. to record the fastest time for any racer in either Britain or Ireland.

HIGGINS, Alex (1949-) b. Belfast, professional snooker player. Known as the 'Hurricane", Higgins turned professional in 1971. Won the 1972 World Championship beating John Spencer 37-32 in the final. In 1982, he again won the World Championship beating Ray Reardon 18-15. The 1983 UK Championship, the 1978 and 1981 Benson & Hedges Masters and the 1989 Irish Masters are among the most prominent of his many wins. Has retired from the sport and is poor health.

HOPKIRK, Paddy (1933-) b. Antrim, rally-driver. The highlight of a great international rally-driving career came in 1964 when he won the Monte-Carlo rally. Five years later, when rallying was at its most popular, he came second in the London-to-Sydney race. Hopkirk also won the Circuit of Ireland five times.

JUDGE, David (1936-) b. Dublin, In a twenty one year international career (1957- 1978) Judge played a then record 124 times for Ireland, and a further 15 times for Britain. His career was leaden with both representative and domestic honours.

KIRBY, Pat (1936-) b. Clare, handballer. The highlight of a spectacular career was achieved when he was crowned World Champion in 1970. Won two further world titles in 1971 and 1972. In addition to his world title victories, Kirby, who had emigrated to the US in the late 1950s, won national titles there as well as in Canada and in Ireland. He also won ten Irish singles titles.

KYLE, Maeve (1928-) b. Kilkenny, Kyle concentrated her interests on hockey in her early sporting career winning 58 caps for Ireland, the highlight of which was the 1950 winning of the Triple Crown. She then switched to athletics and represented Ireland on three occasions at the Olympic Games (Melbourne, Rome and Tokyo).

LANGAN, Jimmy (1951-) b. Dublin, an outstanding table tennis player from early childhood, he became the youngest player to represent Ireland in senior sport when, at 12 years of age, he was called for international duty. Went on to play in excess of 200 matches for his country and was Irish senior champion ten times.

LANGRISHE, May b. Dublin, tennis player. When she won the Irish Ladies Singles tennis title in 1879, she became the world's first national women's singles title holder (Ireland being the first to hold a women's national competition). She went on to win the title on two further occasions.

MAHER, Joey (1934-) b. Louth, after winning numerous Irish handball titles at both junior and senior level, Maher emigrated to Canada in 1965 and during his three years there won the Canadian title three times. Highlight of his career was winning the World Handball title in 1967, representing Canada.

McCONNELL, Billy (1956-) b. Down, one of Ireland's most capped hockey player with 135 caps. McConnell won a further 51 caps for Britain. At the Olympic Games of 1984, in Los Angeles, was a member of the British squad which won the Bronze medal.

MILLER, Sammy (1933-) b. Antrim, as a motor cycle trialist, Miller's record will probably stand forever - more than 900 victories in 20 years (1950-1970), British champion for eleven years in a row, five gold medals in team trialing with the British international team, and European champion twice.

MONTEITH, Dermott (1943-) b. Antrim, probably

Ireland's most successful cricketer. He took 326 international wickets, for an average of just over 17 runs per wicket. On 27 occasions in test cricket he took five or more wickets, while his score total of 1,712 runs with the bat places him in the top 20 Irish batsmen of all time.

O'DEA, Donnacha (1945-) b. Dublin, O'Dea smashed all kinds of swimming records when he won more than 90 Irish titles. His greatest achievement was recorded in 1965 when he became the first Irishman to break the 60-second barrier for the 100 metres freestyle.

O'KELLY, Con (1886-) b. Gloun, Co. Cork, wrestler. The only Irishman to win an Olympic gold medal in wrestling. Stood 6'3" and weighed 16 stone with a chest measurement of 50". Left Cork to join the Hull Fire Brigade, England, and became interested in the sport, becoming British Heavyweight Champion within two years. Won his Olympic medal while representing Britain at the 1908 Olympics in London.

O'TOOLE, Gary (1968-) b. Wicklow, swimmer. Ireland's first medallist at a major swimming championships when, in 1989, he won silver in the 200m breaststroke at the European Championships. Gold medallist in the 200m breaststroke at the 1991 World Student Games. A double Olympian, he travelled to Seoul in 1988 and Barcelona in 1994. Holds five national records for breaststroke and medley events.

PIM, Joshua (1869-) b. Wicklow, tennis player. In 1893 he created history by becoming the first Irish man, and the only, to win the Wimbledon Singles tennis title. He retained it the following year.

POTTER, Jacqui (1963-) Held the world record for most capped woman hockey player when she retired in the early 1990s with 83 caps.

PRATT, Don (1935) b. Dublin, squash player. Between 1956 and 1972 Pratt was capped 52 times for Ireland at squash, a then world record for a squash player. Won the Irish title for a record ten times and lost out on four other occasions. Also a cricket international.

ROBB, Tommy (1934-) b. Antrim, won the Irish 500 c.c. championship in 1961, he won the 250 c.c. road racing Grand Prix championship two years later. He had two other Grand Prix victories. Despite many victories Robb won only one TT, with that win coming in 1973.

SLOAN, Marty b. Tyrone, Ireland's most capped hockey player of all time with 149 caps. He captained Ireland 1987-93. Also won a number of caps with the Great Britain team.

THOMPSON, Syd (1912-) b. Antrim, bowls player. In a career spanning more than a quarter of a century (1947-73), he set a then world record for an outdoor bowls player when he represented Ireland 78 times.

TYRELL-SMITH, Harry (1907-) b. Dublin, Motor cyclist par excellence, he was European Champion twice - in 1931 and 1936. Took part in numerous Isle of Man TTs but only won one.

WHITE, Francis *'Chalkie'* (1955-) b. Dublin, swimmer. won the 1,500m freestyle in the 1975 European Cup. Dominated the Irish national swimming championships in the 1970s, winning over 40 national titles. Now frequently contributes to the *Irish Independent* on swimming matters.

WOODS, Stanley (1903-) b. Dublin, until the advent of Dunlop brothers, Woods was the most successful motor-cyclist Ireland had produced. Won five 500cc TT titles, five junior TT titles, 22 Continental Grand Prix victories, and more than forty international titles in all.

❑

INDEX